THE NATIONAL HISTORY OF FRANCE

EDITED BY

FR. FUNCK-BRENTANO

WITH AN INTRODUCTION BY J. E. C. BODLEY

THE
FRENCH REVOLUTION

THE NATIONAL HISTORY OF FRANCE

EDITED BY FR. FUNCK-BRENTANO

WITH AN INTRODUCTION BY J. E. C. BODLEY

Each volume Demy 8vo. Price 12s. 6d. net

LONDON: WILLIAM HEINEMANN LTD.

THE NATIONAL HISTORY OF FRANCE

THE
FRENCH REVOLUTION

[CROWNED BY THE FRENCH ACADEMY]
[GOBERT PRIZE]

BY

LOUIS MADELIN

TRANSLATED FROM THE FRENCH

LONDON
WILLIAM HEINEMANN LTD.
1936

First published, September 1916.
New Impressions, January 1918,
February 1922, *September* 1923,
April 1925, *January, July* 1926,
August 1928, *May* 1930, *March* 1933.
September 1936.

PRINTED IN GREAT BRITAIN BY THE WHITEFRIARS PRESS LTD.
LONDON AND TONBRIDGE

PREFACE

THE idea of publishing a History of the Revolution in this year of grace (1911) will appear the most pretentious undertaking that can well be conceived : of that fact I am well aware. But let me set forth the limits of my pretensions.

There is no question, here, of a school text-book, nor, strictly speaking, of a learned work. I should have found it impossible to bind myself to any educational programme, and I never dreamt, on the other hand, of plunging into that ocean of State Archives the depths of which I had already sounded in the course of labours of quite another nature, and of a narrower scope.

My present task has taught me what an enormous quantity of books and documents connected with the Revolution have been presented to the public within the last half-century.

Reviews and societies have been founded for the sole purpose of this special study; but there is hardly a review in existence which has not largely contributed to the subject. Histories, monographs, biographies, ranging from bulky volumes to modest booklets, constitute a magnificent "revolutionary library." There have been quantities of Memoirs, too, private Journals, Letters, Notes, which reproduce the words used by eye-witnesses—eye-witnesses belonging to every class and every party, from foreign ambassadors to humble village peasants, from the " pro-consuls " of the Terror to the " aristocrats " doomed to the knife, whose voices Pierre de Vaissière has lately evoked for us. Great official works are at this moment in course of publication, or nearing their completion, such as the huge and most valuable collection of the *Actes du Comité du Salut Public*, edited by M. Aulard, the *Cahiers* of the year 1789, which are appearing in all quarters, the *Procès-Verbaux du Directoire*, in the course of which M. Debidour will bring us down to the year 1799, and many other works which enable us to compare official documents with private depositions. I must confess my own personal preference for Letters, type-documents, if I may so term them, which I have always preferred to Memoirs for my own use.

I know many will say that in spite of all these publications we are still only on the brink of the investigation; that I do not deny. In proportion to what remains to be explored, we are indeed at the beginning, but a consideration of what has already been laid before the inquirer leads me to the conviction that I am justified in setting forth, as a temporary measure, the points of which we are already in possession.

I do not claim to do more. There are many readers who will not venture to embark on this labyrinth of works and documents; my desire is to offer to these as far as possible, a summary of all that has been published, in the course of years, on the subject of the Revolution, and to make them acquainted with the conclusions at which my masters and my fellow-workers have arrived. In the Introduction to his Roman History, the worthy Rollin wrote the following words: " I have not concealed the fact that I have made much use of other men's labours. . . ." My work is made up of other men's labours, and if its readers find it interesting, I will beg them to consult the bibliographies, all too scanty, placed at the end of each of my chapters, and in justice, to ascribe the merit of the book to the excellent collaborators therein named.

A great deal of profound synthesis has been accomplished in the course of the last twenty years. My beloved and gifted master, Albert Sorel, has written the diplomatic history of the Revolution, and M. Arthur Chuquet, in a series of lively and well-informed volumes, has given us its military history. M. Pierre de la Gorce is now engaged in tracing its religious history. M. Alphonse Aulard has devoted an important work to its political history, or, to be more exact, to the history of opinion under the Revolution. These works,

PREFACE

so widely different, are all most valuable and encourage synthesis.

My readers will observe that my own attention has been more especially turned to political history. Yet I have not found it possible to limit myself to that alone, according to the suggestion offered me. It is always a dangerous thing in history to separate facts which have inevitably reacted one upon the other. Diplomatic history, military history, political history, financial history, religious history, economic history, social history, literary history, cannot safely be treated *ab abstracto*. Less than any other can the writer on the Revolution escape the necessity of studying concurrently all the facts, every one of which casts its light on others. To cite only one instance, Taine, for whom, however, my admiration is unabated, would have escaped falling into more than one exaggerated statement, if he had read Albert Sorel. This last writer shows us the beleaguered city ; Taine has very often depicted only the demented gestures of the besieged citizens, demoralized or exasperated, profoundly depressed, or excited to the point of madness. Who can doubt that the historian's duty is to take his stand upon the wall of the threatened city, and watch both besiegers and besieged ? Sorel understood this, and so he has attained an atmosphere of the serenest equity.

The prescribed limits of this volume have not allowed of my entering—beyond what was necessary for its preparation—into the details of negotiations and campaigns, nor into those of the various crises, financial, economic, and social. To ensure a clear comprehension of certain facts in our political history, and a final impression in conformity with justice, it was sufficient never to lose sight of them altogether.

I have striven, indeed, to be just. No man quite attains that end. But honestly, I can assert in all sincerity and truth as I put forth this work for the use of the public, that I myself am unable to detect any instance in which I have unfairly apportioned praise or blame.

I have approached this thorny subject without any preconceived views of my own ; in nine cases out of ten, my opinions on the Revolution have altered, in the course of my study of it, in a very remarkable manner. True it is that I have never denied myself the right to reveal my own feeling as to certain persons and certain events: indignation, pity, admiration, are sometimes indispensable components of justice. But it seems to me that I have been just to everybody, even in the case of individuals, scrupulous study of whose lives revealed them, on the final analysis, to be deliberate or unconscious malefactors.

And indeed I have not found it difficult to preserve my freedom of observation and appreciation. I had never felt myself endowed with an authority which would have warranted the pronouncement of any categoric judgment, even in my own mind, as to so complex an event as the French Revolution. I should find it yet more difficult to formulate any, even the briefest, at the present moment: facts, causes, effects, strike me as being still exceedingly open to question: a series of problems lie before us, such as can only be solved, one way or another, in swift and decisive words by minds far superior to my own.

To err is the property of mankind, and the various parties, made up of men, all erred. I have pointed out follies, I have also pointed out crimes. At a moment of such appalling crisis all that is foulest in a nation rises to the surface—" white scum, red scum," as Albert Vandal has put it—and with it all the bestial ferocity and hideous passion that have lain unsuspected in the depths of men's hearts. Hence the atrocities that were committed.

And further, at such periods, when over-excitement is in the air, acts of noble heroism are performed, and to these, too, I have referred. I will not deny that worshipping my country as I do whatever may be the flag under which she conquers or succumbs, I would far rather have dwelt on her military glories than on the massacres of her civil strife. But the plan of this work has not permitted me to obey this desire altogether, and I have been fain, though unwillingly, to submit. On the whole it is more than likely that, like our famous Montaigne, I shall be " flayed by every hand, a Ghibelline to the Guelphs, a Guelph to the Ghibellines." I have made up my mind to that.

PREFACE

In January 1910, my eminent friend Albert Vandal inaugurated a series of lectures on the French Revolution, in which I had the honour of taking a share. He then said (the length of the quotation will be excused, since nobody could have spoken on the subject with greater authority) :

" Our lecturers will, I feel sure, contrive to keep equally between the two extremes : they are not here to deliver a course of instruction in Revolution, nor yet a course of instruction against Revolution. They are simply about to consider as historians events which belong to history. They will avoid, I am quite certain, any sort of preconceived and foregone conclusion, and any systematic process of generalization.

" The Revolution has been compared to a *block*. Apart from the fact that the word is not a particularly agreeable one to my ears, and that I may have a certain personal objection to *blocks* in general, I think I may venture to assert, without fear of error, that to compare the Revolution to a single *block* is to fall into one of the worst errors any Minister or man of parts could possibly commit. The Revolution, far from having been a *block*, was probably the most complex phenomenon that has ever existed, a phenomenon of which the causes, the elements, the movements and the consequences, were essentially multiple. Its aspects are simply innumerable, and to the recent happy expression ' the illimitable heart ' might well be added that of ' the illimitable Revolution.'

" Our lecturers will certainly reveal this excessive complication and astounding complexity of aspects to their audiences, and impress it on them. They will set forth the noble impulses and the fruitful enthusiasms, the gain to progress, the increase of justice and of general advancement, which the mighty throes of the great Revolution have undoubtedly won for France and for the world at large. They will draw attention to the evil doctrines, the destructive ideas, the excesses, the abominations, the crimes, as well as the lofty deeds, and sometimes, too, I doubt not, turning away from the strife within, they will look to the frontier—so fiercely attacked, and so heroically defended —to the camps, the armies, the battlefields, there to glean some of the grandest memories of that harvest of glory which is the proud patrimony of France ! "

PREFACE

I applauded such words then, and shall always applaud them. Under no better auspices could I have placed this work than under those of the great historian whose loss we now mourn, and who so cordially encouraged me to write it. I have done my best to follow his counsels, and the spirit in which he gave them.

LOUIS MADELIN

x

CONTENTS

xi

CONTENTS

CONTENTS

INTRODUCTION

THE FRANCE OF 1789

CHAPTER I

PRODIGAL ANARCHY

" A NEW Year's gift to France ! " These were Necker's words. On January 1, 1789, the news spread abroad that four days previously—on December 27, 1788—Louis XVI, having received M. de Necker's report, had decided in Council on the convocation of the States-General, **Convocation of** and had granted the Third Estate double the **the States-** number of representatives allowed to the two **General.** privileged orders. This was the famous *Result of the Council* which, printed by the thousand copies, was to evoke passionate applause from one end of the country to the other.

For a hundred and seventy-five years, the country had never once been invited to deliberate on its own affairs. And further, general opinion, confirmed by this abnormal concession of a double representation to the Third Estate, was convinced that this time the country was about to deliberate as it had never done before. Had not the Marquis d'Argenson foreseen, even in the year 1750, that "the States-General (if they were called together) would not deliberate in vain," and would be " very serious indeed " ? An indescribable emotion shook the whole country. Necker was dubbed "the delight of the nation," "the divine rescript " was " bathed in the tears " of various functionaries, and a certain parish priest read it from his pulpit to an audience of faithful hearers who were filled " with an ecstasy of admiration and gratitude." I quote actual letters. In Paris, the *Result* soon graced every dressing-table, and waiting-woman and Marquise alike held forth concerning its contents with " emotion," or rejoiced over it with " frenzied joy."

Wherefore this universal rejoicing ?

8

Because in a country where everybody—even the most favoured—thought themselves oppressed, every one fancied this was a glimpse of liberty : because in a country whose worn-out institutions could no longer do their work without galling those they worked on, every one thought this meant the beginnings of reform : and, in a more general sense, because a society nurtured in philosophy, and cramped by the despotic anarchy amidst which it struggled, concluded with delight that now " *the Kingdom would be given a Constitution !* " This word, anything but precise in its meaning, opened the door to every kind of hypothesis, and thus afforded a temporary satisfaction to every aspiration.

*   *   *   *   *

France possessed no " Constitution." Some few persons asserted that she had at one time done so, but it had long The since disappeared. To tell the truth, the word Constitution. Constitution was not understood then as we understand it now : nobody, in those days, thought that a Constitution implied the granting of what we call Parliamentary institutions : it was never suggested that King Clovis had been assisted in his governing functions by two legislative chambers. But this society, governed by philosophers for three-quarters of a century, and insisting that God himself should prove his title to rule the souls of men, was naturally disposed to inquire in virtue of what statute a man was to live at Versailles and reign as it seemed fit to him. Rousseau had brought " contracts " into fashion, and it was regarded as an evident fact that the monarchy, on some bygone day, must have made one with the nation. This contract had been mislaid : another had to be produced.

The populace, in its simpler fashion, felt that it was living not so much under despotism as in anarchy, and that an *organization*—which it called a *Constitution*—could not be anything but a gain.

Fundamentally, a true instinct underlay the theories of the poor classes and the aspirations of the humble: this feeling that institutions which had been justified in the old days were little suited to the present conditions, and that the organs of the national body were unfitted to perform their functions.

A contract there had been, most certainly ;—several, indeed —tacit or written.

A contract between the Capetian King and France, or rather *the Frances*, which had ranged themselves under his sceptre. These sons of Capet—an incomparable line—had not only been redoubtable warriors for centuries. Their swords had brought liberty, freed the Communes from the petty nobles, freed the provinces from the great lords. And when these swords had done their work for freedom, they were used to execute justice. The Capets were "Chief Lords," but they were also "Chief Judges." The Vincennes oak had cast its shade over France, because, said tradition, the King, St. Louis, sitting beneath that tree, had dispensed justice to the widow and the orphan. And when France had grown into a nation, her kings, who had been deliverers and just judges, had also been her defenders against the foreign foe. Now for many years, no king had shown himself on any battlefield, and if the King, who no longer led in time of war, was further, neither the judge of Vincennes nor the protector of the Communes, what was he ? The contract was a dead letter !

> Rois qui de France porte corone d'or
> Preudens doit estre et vaillant de son cors.
>
> S'ainsi nel fet dont pert France son los
> Ce dist l'estoire, coronez est a tort.*

So ran the song in very ancient days.

Dead letters, too, were two other contracts, more or less tacit : those between the country and the great nobles and between the country and the priests. The first were to defend it with their swords, the second were to help it by their prayers. This double service was to be repaid by privileges and immunities. Since the nobles had become mediocre leaders in wartime, since a Chevert, a man of plebeian blood, had done better service than a Clermont-Tonnerre, the privileges of the nobility had no further justification. And since important prelates were seen to neglect the duty of intercession for which

* The King who wears the golden crown of France must be prudent and a man of valour. If he is not, France loses her honour, and history says : he has been wrongly crowned.

they were so richly paid, the third contract too was cancelled.

It was in this sense that the old " constitution," which had never been put into writing, had become effete.

* * * * *

The King was supposed to be absolute. Nothing more easily provokes the smile of the student of the Old Régime than **The King's** declamations against " the despotism of the **absolute power.** King." The King was really the chief slave of a system which he might disapprove, but which he was powerless to modify.

He was an official Chief, indeed, but a slave Chief as well ; the slave of his Court, of his Ministry, of tradition, and his longing for liberty was sometimes even greater than that of his subjects. If a reformer in intention, nothing was more difficult for him than to make any reform. If economical by nature, tradition forced him to scatter gold in all directions, and (the picture of his Court, with its extravagance and its hungry greed, will be in all my readers' minds) he cast it lavishly into outstretched hands—or into silken skirts !

What made the chaos worse, was that under him who governed tolerably ill at Versailles, the Provinces were worse governed still. My readers will not expect me to enter into the labyrinth the superimposition of various authorities had created in France. That would involve the writing of a whole volume, the conclusion of which would be summed up in one word, spoken as early as the year 1750, a *prodigal anarchy.* The King's privilege, ill justified, was working ill.

* * * * *

The peasantry, perhaps, would have endured this anarchy, save for two things which they would no longer suffer : the **Privileges and** existence of privileges, and the financial situation, **taxation.** which, in a certain measure was the result of these.

About two hundred and seventy thousand Frenchmen were supposed to possess privileges.

Most of these held feudal rights, either in money or in kind. These nobles, who, in bygone generations, had been exempted from taxation as a reward for service to the public, had arrogated to themselves, as heads of great agricultural enterprises, all the advantages accruing from these operations : rights of *banvin, banalité, péage,* the monopoly of the dove-cote, and so on, and they had imposed tolls : *cens, censives, carpot, champage, terrage,* etc.* Now these great lords had ceased to direct agricultural undertakings, they no longer lived on their properties, and left them to be managed in such a way that their rights " bring more harm to those who suffer from them than profit to those who enjoy them." Some understanding might perhaps have been reached with the " lords," but they were never at home : the Court had taken the cream of the provincial nobility. Their absenteeism has certainly been exaggerated, but nevertheless, a good three-quarters of the great landowners never appeared in their own domains. Humane, even humanitarian, as these nobles were, they were more odious than their ancestors, for being more needy, the expenses Versailles entailed upon them forced them to be more exacting : so the steward down in the country, who was neither humane nor humanitarian, squeezed—and the squeezed creatures groaned.

* **Banvin.** The right enjoyed by the lord of the manor to sell his own wine in the parish, to the exclusion of any other persons, for a definite period in each year, which varied according to local custom.

Banalité. The feudal owner's right to impose the use of certain things within the radius of his own property, and to charge a certain sum for this use. Thus there were ovens in which everybody was obliged to bake bread, and pay for doing so.

Péage. A toll on all cattle or merchandise taken across a feudal owner's lands, and applied to the upkeep of roads and bridges. Also a toll paid for the right of crossing fords and bridges.

Redevances. The expression used to describe all sums of money, all contributions in kind, all labour, or service, military or otherwise, due to the feudal owner from his vassals.

Cens. The special sum paid by every man who held land within the boundaries of a feudal estate to the owner of that estate. *Cens,* in those days, expressed much what our word " rent " now conveys.

Censives. For the purposes of this chapter, the *censive* may be said to mean the special payments with which any particular farm or country property might be burdened.

Carpot. A claim on the fruits produced by the orchards on a feudal property.

Champage. Dues paid on the delimitation of the boundaries of a farm.

Terrage. Dues levied on various harvests. When a field of corn was reaped, the feudal lord had a right to one out of every ten sheaves.

7

And further, another thing which was beginning to rouse the common folk was *the very principle of these rights*, and that inequality as regards taxation which was even more sensibly odious in their sight than the existence of rights. So deeply was this inequality hated that one *Cahier**—that of La Rochelle—asks for equality in capital punishment, complaining bitterly that one man is hanged, when another is beheaded !

The clergy, whose position was somewhat different, excited almost equal wrath. We will here consider their material Wealth of position only (leaving their mentality to be the Church. examined later). There were something between 120,000 and 140,000 ecclesiastics : about 20,000 to 25,000 monks, 60,000 to 70,000 secular priests, and some 37,000 nuns.

A hundred and thirty bishops ruled the Church of France ; their dioceses were of most unequal sizes (1388 parishes in that of Rouen, nineteen in that of Agde), their revenues more unequal still. One diocese brought its holder 400,000 *livres* a year, and certain others were not worth more than 7000 *livres* to their bishops, known as the " muddy bishops " (*évêques crottés*).

The same inequality marked the revenues of the various abbeys. St. Waast d'Arras, for instance, enjoyed an income of 500,000 *livres* a year, while numbers of small monastic houses had hard work to make up 6000 *livres*.

There has been exaggeration as to the wealth of the Church : M. de la Gorce, in the remarkable study he has lately published on the Church in 1789, gives us the sum of 2,992,538,140 *livres*. After an examination of divers testimonies, I feel bound to agree with him. The annual income was 85,000,000, but this was nearly doubled by the dues levied on the faithful, which came to about 80,000,000 more.

These possessions were made up of gifts and legacies, hundreds of years old, nearly all of which had been bestowed for a definite purpose—prayers for the dead, assistance for the living. Even in her decadent condition, the Church was carrying out this work in part : the expenses of public worship, of instruction, and of almsgiving, did absorb a great proportion

---

* The *Cahiers* were documents setting forth grievances drawn up by the various parishes at the invitation of the king, and confided to the deputies elected to the States-General in 1789. See Chap. v.

8

of her revenue. But too often, and for too long a period now, the higher clergy had seemed to forget, or to scorn, the duties connected with their benefices. " The decay " of this church, according to M. de la Gorce, whom no one can suspect of anti-clerical views, was summed up in "the separation of two things—the wealth accumulated through the liberality of the faithful, from the pious obligations with which such gifts were charged." How many beneficiaries lost sight of the nature of the fortune " confided to their care," and ended by looking on it as their personal property !

Such a condition of things rendered the very possession of the fortune unjustifiable, and the immunities enjoyed by its possessors more unjustifiable still.

And the tithe was detested : the Memorials (*Cahiers*) sent out by the " parishes " which, as we shall see, were to prove them-
Hatred of selves so bravely true to the Church, in the days of
the Tithe. her proscription, furnish us with scores of proofs of the hatred aroused by that particular toll. For a long time the rebellion against it had been taking the shape of lawsuits : when a prelate in the Assembly of Notables, in 1788, defined the tithe as " the voluntary offering of the faithful," the Duc de la Rochefoucauld sharply replied : "A voluntary offering against which 400,000 lawsuits are now going on in France ! "

Further, this wealthy body paid no taxes—having indeed bought itself out, in 1710. From time to time it offered the King a " free gift " (but with the power, which it did not fail to use, of refusing it). And finally, the division of the revenues of the Church within her own borders was a subject of offence and indignation. A bishop, such as a Rohan at Strasburg, scattered gold in all directions, but a whole body of humble parish priests, 60,000 of them, were starving, more or less. The scandal was deepened by the fact that these country priests were the most deserving men in the church (my readers should see what Cardinal Mathieu says on this subject in his book on the *Ancien Régime en Lorraine*) ; a parish priest had 700 *livres* a year, a curate 350, while a prelate, greatly their inferior in piety and morals, drew his 100,000, 200,000, or perhaps 400,000 *livres* a year. The members of this ecclesiastical proletariat were by no means behind the others with their complaints :

9

the most devoted Catholics occasionally shared their discontent, and the " Libertines " and Protestants, naturally incensed by comparatively recent persecutions, denounced with some exaggeration the whole Church as a Babylon, where the corruption of wealth had turned the successors of the Apostles of the Christ into great lords with millions at their command.

*　　*　　*　　*　　*

Nobles and priests alike suffered, in the eyes of the sorely taxed people, the consequences of their immunity. The unfair distribution of the taxes had exasperated the taxed : if every man has to pay, all pay more willingly. Though the nobles now paid the poll-tax, and the tax known as the *vingtième* (that is when they really did pay them !) all privileged persons were exempt from paying the *taille*, and the *taille* was the most unendurable of all the direct taxes. The first two flayed the taxpayer, this last smothered him outright. On an income of 100 *livres*, this direct tax took fifty-three, and it was a tax that might grow heavier and heavier, for with a government which had never since the days of Colbert been capable of economy, the nation, on this first day of the year 1789, was still liable to be taxed as its rulers chose. To make it worse, this exorbitant tax was unfairly distributed and arbitrarily raised ; this made it seem all the more cruel. " A delirium of fiscality ! " writes a foreigner, to sum up his impressions after a journey through France. And the thing that most strikes him is the crying injustice which makes a common man pay fourteen *livres* on his four acres of land, while the noble pays nine on his twelve acres !

The " Taille."

The indirect taxes completed the process of crushing His Majesty's subjects. My readers are aware of the weight of the salt monopoly, that *gabelle* which even more than the *taille*, contributed to the Revolution of 1789 : hateful too were those *aides* or subsidies, which, as in the case of the salt tax, permitted the King's agents to exercise a perpetual inquisition, the most odious form of tyranny in the peasants' eyes—an inquisition that extended from their bread bins to their cellars, and drove them to fury.

The " Gabelle."

PRODIGAL ANARCHY

Beneath the weight of this double, triple, quintuple burden, the peasant's back was bowed : feudal rights, church tithes, royal taxes, he bore well-nigh the whole brunt of them all. In appearance he was poverty-stricken indeed. But we must not allow this to deceive us completely. By what prodigy of thrift did these poor creatures contrive to conceal from their extortioners the means of buying their land ? For it is a fact that *ever since the beginning of the eighteenth century the peasant had been buying the land :* almost one-third of the soil of France was already held by French peasants, who certainly combined a genius for economy with their fierce desire to possess land of their own. Recent works have cast a remarkable light on this unsuspected state of things. But this situation, far from satisfying the peasant, only excited his aspirations. What might he not hope to attain, once freed from the crushing burden laid on him by the State and the privileged classes ? In his case the demand for equality was a legitimate demand for means to acquire a larger amount of landed property.

In the towns, the poor were starving : very naturally they held the King and the Court responsible for this, just as they were to blame the Constituent Assembly in 1791, and the Convention in 1795.

In town and country alike, the populace muttered curses against the government. When the day came, and it was invited to speak out, there were yells of rage and misery.

" All the trouble," writes Turgot to Louis XVI, " is caused by the fact that France has no constitution." He too (he probably had no desire for a constitution on the English model), meant a *rational organization.* For in 1789 there was no question of a bad system ; there was *no system* at all.

One of the last Ministers under the Monarchy, when on the brink of his fall, addressed a report to the King which would be worth quoting here in its entirety.

" France," thus runs its chief passage, " is a kingdom composed of separate states and countries, with mixed administrations, the provinces of which know nothing of each other, where certain districts are completely free from burdens the whole weight of which is borne by others, where the richest class is the most lightly taxed, where privilege has upset all

11

equilibrium, where it is impossible to have any constant rule or common will : necessarily it is a most imperfect kingdom, very full of abuses, and in its present condition, *impossible to govern.*"

Who writes these words ? A middle-class minister ? a reformer ? Turgot ? Necker ? No ! One of the privileged class, the Comte de Calonne—enlightened by the two years he had just spent in office !

And this " prodigal anarchy " appears all the more intolerable, because, thanks to the " progress of knowledge," men's minds were casting off the yoke of tradition more and more.

CHAPTER II

THE PROGRESS OF KNOWLEDGE

TRADITION was the very soul of the system, its sole justification and support : there was no possibility of the one surviving the other. The peasant was in a state of misery, not greater (perhaps even less), than that of a century earlier. The artisan often went hungry—no oftener **Tradition** than he had a hundred years before. Privileges **discredited.** were exorbitant—but no more exorbitant than then. And in certain ways the governing power seemed to be stronger than it had been. But tradition had ceased to uphold the edifice. The philosophers had mined its walls, and were soon to overthrow them. The system, as we have just seen, was an ill-constructed body, but above all, it was, and had been for years, a body out of which the soul was passing. How then could it have continued to live on ?

" It was Rousseau's fault ! It was Voltaire's fault ! " People have laughed this formula to scorn. But its one weakness is that it is too exclusive. " It was the fault " of many other men and many other things, but none the less is it true that when the Revolution conferred *quasi* divine honours, first on Voltaire and then on Rousseau, it recognized its collaborators.

Amidst all the many *Confessions* of the time, let us open those of Mme. Roland. Why is this daughter of a sceptical *bourgeois* **Mme. Roland.** and his pious wife a votary of that Revolution, all the greatness and all the errors of which, to my thinking, she incarnates in her own person ? She was born in 1754. Montesquieu was nearing his end. Voltaire was setting up his " royalty," destined to remain unquestioned thenceforward, at Ferney, and concluding his alliance with d'Alembert against " the infamous one." Duclos, who was elected

18

permanent secretary within a few weeks of her birth, was to instal "philosophy" in the house of Richelieu, where d'Alembert was ultimately to take his place: 1754, too, was the year in which Diderot, in his *Interpretation of Nature*, gave his final adhesion to atheism, the year of the publication of the third volume of the *Encyclopædia*, the existence of which was now ensured by the friendly offices of M. de Malesherbes, Director of the Library : the year in the course of which Jean Jacques Rousseau wrote his *Discourse on Inequality*. Every one of the next ten years was to record some success for "philosophy," and during those ten years (if we except Sieyès and Mirabeau, born in 1748 and 1749) the men who were to be the makers of the Revolution were all to come into the world : Brissot in 1754, Lafayette in 1757, Mounier in 1758, Robespierre, Vergniaud, and Danton in 1759, Desmoulins in 1760, Barnave in 1761—to mention the most important only. I have specially singled out this little Manon Phlipon, destined to become the Citizeness Roland, because, born on that prophetic date, she dwells at length on the authors who formed her mind : after Corneille, who made her a Roman, and Plutarch, who made her a Spartan, came Voltaire, Holbach, Helvétius, Diderot, d'Alembert, Raynal, and last and above all, Rousseau. " I read him too late, and a good thing it was for me ; *he would have made me mad, I should never have read anything else !* "

And the books this young girl read are the books read by all her generation, from Robespierre to Desmoulins, but also from the Abbé Gregoire to the Marquis de Lafayette. Sons and daughters of great nobles, or of petty *bourgeois*, they all drank of the same cup.

It would be interesting, in this place, to make a fresh attempt at the consideration of this fascinating question, Influence of the and once more note its bearing on the theory Encyclopædists. of the "Disciple." When teachers are called Montesquieu, Voltaire, and Rousseau, and their disciples Robespierre, Danton, and Brissot, the study is most attractive. Distrusting formulæ, I determined to make it afresh. I have traced the destruction of ideals right through the century, and for my own personal satisfaction, I have reconstituted each of the score of men who were the protagonists of the great drama

14

that lasted from 1789 to 1799, in the moral and intellectual surroundings amidst which they grew up. Every one of them bears the impress of the same philosophy—a purely destructive philosophy, be it said.

*   *   *   *   *

Such an influence involves more than one consequence. The Revolution, prepared and brought about by men of intellect, and writers who believed themselves to be thinkers, was impregnated with the ideas that had ruled the " republic of letters " for the past fifty years ; ideological dogmatism, classicism, cosmopolitanism, humanitarianism, anti-Christianism, and a philosophism destructive of all authority.

The Revolution, therefore, was to be ideologic and dogmatic. Let us hear the words of the last of the philosophers, destined to sit in two revolutionary assemblies, who, long before 1789 pronounced as follows : " A good law should be good for all men, even as a proposition is true for all men." The capital error of the whole Revolution lies in the dogma thus proclaimed by Condorcet : this mathematician is completely at sea. He and his co-religionists, who knew nothing of true sociology, which has its foundations in psychology, here prove themselves still more ignorant of history.

It would have been useless to tell them so ! They would have served you up Athens, Sparta, and Rome. For centuries Plutarch with his sham Greeks and sham Romans had been be-musing us, and all these men—philosophers and their disciples—were so intoxicated with classicism that the Revolution was to be accomplished in the names, repeated and acclaimed a thousand times, of Harmodius, Leonidas, Gracchus, Brutus, and Cato !

It was to be accomplished, too, in the name of foreign laws. Mme. Roland discovered that she had a " cosmopolitan soul." From Berlin and St. Petersburg, from Geneva and The Hague, still more from Westminster, and above all from Philadelphia, the philosophers had brought back a taste for novelty. Washington and Franklin had been called Brutus and Cato. That was more than enough. They stirred up men's minds, and sowed a ferment within them. The eighteenth century had paved the way by acclaiming all that, in the innovators' eyes, had one sovereign quality : it was not French.

15

This cosmopolitanism fed on humanitarianism. " Man " appeared upon the scene : the " Good Man " who touched all **Cult of** these hearts, " intoxicated with philanthropy " **Humanity.** as one writer puts it. And " Man," on this first appearance, was a fraternal being ; this movement, which might have been one of purely local reform, became revolutionary to excess, in the effort to liberate " Humanity." As far as its formulæ went, it was always to remain impregnated with " tenderness." And hence the inclination, a general one in 1789, indicated by the following incident : when, in the January of that year, Bouillé pointed out the approaching danger to Necker, the minister, who did not deny the fact, remarked that " we must reckon on the virtue of humanity." A whole school of politicians lived on this doctrine, destined to lead them from the benches of the Constituent Assembly to the steps of the scaffold.

If Man be good, it cannot be a bad thing that he should govern himself : the word " Republic " taken in its widest sense, sounded pleasantly in sensitive ears in which, furthermore, the praise of the virtues of the " ancient republics " were ringing. Though nobody, or hardly anybody, thought, in 1789, of setting up the Republic as an *institution*, Danton was right when he exclaimed : " The Republic was in men's minds at least twenty years before it was proclaimed ! " A definite anti-monarchical sentiment had come into being, grown, and spread itself abroad, in the course of the century : M. Rocquain has devoted an authoritative work (which should be consulted by my readers), to *The Revolutionary Spirit previous to the Revolution*. " An anti-monarchical wind," wrote d'Argenson as early as 1751.

An anti-Catholic wind, too ! What use to recall in this place the campaign for sixty years against " the infamous one " ? It had progressed from the elegant indifference of Montesquieu to the hatred of Christianity which neither Helvetius nor Holbach concealed. A threatening conjuncture, when we remember that the Church had always been the strongest buttress of the French monarchy. The Most Christian King's throne—even when the Most Christian King had been but a very poor Christian—had ever depended on the altar for support. If the altar trembled, would the throne stand? Throne, altar, authority of every kind, were as a fact completely undermined in the year 1789.

Was this state of things exclusively the work of the philosophers and men of letters of the century ? Any such assertion would be absurd. These men did not create the classical spirit : it was in existence before their time ; but they carried it to a greater extreme than any others had done. They did not invent the British Constitution, and (though this point may be less incontestable) they did not incite the American colonists to revolt : but they did import the spirit of the Westminster Parliament, and they did laud the Philadelphia Declaration. They were not the creators of humanitarian " sensibility," but they did over-excite that " sensibility." They were not the first to conceive the spirit of criticism and rebellion—since d'Argenson, even in 1751, perceived the possibility of a revolution—but the idea of such a revolution had widened, and spread from a small group to a whole generation, because philosophy had shaken the old-fashioned respect for tradition and authority. Neither were they the inventors of atheism, seeing that a small knot of people professed it even in 1715, but they won over the ruling classes, and even the lower middle class, to the doctrine.

The populace had not read Rousseau, nor Voltaire, nor the *Encyclopædia*, and yet the populace murmured, and sometimes (there were serious riots in the days of Louis XV) it even rose in revolt. But riot was still met by a sovereign power which had not been undermined : and these insurrections, again, were not led by such tribunes and chiefs as the new generation of *bourgeois* was soon to supply, men without whose aid no rebellion could have become a general revolution. Who but the philosophers stultified authority, disarmed the privileged classes, and filled the young *bourgeoisie* with the revolutionary spirit ? Whether they are cursed by the foes of the Revolution, or glorified by its supporters, their responsibility is incontestable.

The Revolution, as we have seen, was the outcome of realities : but it cannot be denied that without the help of " enlightenment," it could not have arisen.

CHAPTER III

THE CLASSES AND THE CRISIS

THE Revolution was to be much more than a political movement : all classes of the nation were to feel the impact : nobles, citizens, priests, peasants, artisans, were to be set face to face. Why were some to be vanquished, and others victors, some to be deceived, and others enslaved ? In 1789, the secret of the future lay in the situation and mental attitude of each one of these classes—and in those of the nation as a whole.

The nobility, which the King of France, by an historical paradox, strove to support at the moment of its fall, gave The ineffectual him neither an army nor a staff ; its following was Nobility. *nil,* and itself incapable.

This would be a harsh saying if it were taken in its most unfavourable sense. The aristocracy was not lacking in intelligence ; some of its members were to make a brilliant figure in the Constituent Assembly, and the hundreds of " *Letters from Aristocrats* " which Vaissière has contributed to this inquiry, to our great good fortune, prove the majority, great and small, to have been gifted with a delightful wit, manifested in a most elegant epistolary style.

But incompetent it was—I mean unfit to defend itself as a body, and unable to come to a reasonable settlement at the right moment. Richelieu—completing a work the Kings of France had been carrying on for centuries—had deliberately lowered the characters of the descendants of the mediæval warriors : Louis XIV had followed on the same lines. These men had been broken of the habit of energy, and care had been taken not to train them in politics : they had been so bowed down that some of them had preserved—and could not rid themselves of—the physical attitude of obeisance.

18

THE CLASSES AND THE CRISIS

Bent as they were by hereditary practice, they were incapable of standing up against the storm.

And further, Louis XIV, after the Valois Kings of St. Germain, had dragged them from the soil, and literally uprooted them : the tree that has no roots cannot withstand the hurricane. The French aristocracy had drawn its strength from the soil of France, from which it had sprung : these leaders of pastoral operations, these masters of great agricultural families, had forsaken their rural undertakings and their bucolic surroundings : sons of the soil, they had thereby lost their strength—as the giant Antæus was unconquerable till Hercules parted him from his mother, Earth. This was what Louis XIV did when he imperiously insisted that his nobles should live at Versailles. Then the members of the agricultural family had lost sight of its chief, and consequently they had lost their affection for him, too. And when, in his hour of peril, he sought the army of his former " clients," he was to find them all ranged against him. The only possible excuse for his incredible apathy, or unspeakable bewilderment, must be found in his sense of his own impotence.

Bent and uprooted, these courtiers, like so many others, were also affected by the malady of their century. I have elsewhere said that philosophy had caused the weapons to drop from hands already over-refined : the descendants of hardy barons, such as Bouchard de Montmorency, Foucauld de la Rochefoucauld, were readers, friends, admirers, disciples, of Voltaire, Diderot, d'Alembert, and Rousseau.

The new teaching had imprinted itself on the minds of these men of noble birth more deeply than on any others. Some had lost all religious belief, and admitted the fact : others, unconsciously, had lost all faith in monarchy : almost all had lost their faith in their own rights. In a delightful book entitled *Gentilshommes libéraux et démocrates*, M. de Castellane has grouped together the most striking figures among the nobles of that time—Liancourt, Larochefoucauld, Virieu, Castellane, Lally-Tollendal, Clermont-Tonnerre. This little work should in itself suffice to enlighten us both as to the generosity and the vanity of their mental attitude. The Revolution, to them, meant a rebellion against the " despotism "

19

of Kings, and the "fanaticism" of priests. When in 1791, the Revolution turned against themselves, they lifted astonished hands to Heaven : Clermont-Tonnerre wept, Virieu swore, Liancourt tried to raise troops for the King—all much too late in the day.

Cleft into two groups, one ready to yield too much, and the other unwilling to give enough, its faith shaken by the spirit of the times, shorn of all following by the policy of its kings, and debased by the necessities of Court life, the generous and polished aristocracy of France could only die nobly—if indeed the death it died was noblest.

*   *   *   *   ●

In default of this enervated nobility, was any reliance to be placed on the clergy ? Even less perhaps ! For here the The mediocre enemy was within the fort, and the fort itself Clergy. in ruins.

"The Church stands in need not of great names, but of great virtues ! " Thus did Massillon, at the beginning of the century, exhort the ruling power. It did not hearken : only too often, in the notices of preferment, we find the " great virtues " sacrificed to the " great names."

There were indeed some most excellent prelates in 1789, and I am only sorry I cannot, like M. de la Gorce and the Abbé Sicard, name them here, and ensure them the esteem they deserve. The drawback of such summaries as this is that their very conciseness makes them sometimes unjust. And though there were some very scandalous instances of Churchmen in high places, the majority was simply mediocre in soul and intellect. Frequently, indeed, soul and intellect were widely divided. When Louis XVI had appointed Bonnal to the diocese of Clermont, and Boutteville to that of St.-Flour, he said, with a smile :

"Je viens d'envoyer le Saint-Esprit en Auvergne ; le Saint à Clermont, et l'Esprit à St.-Flour." *

The majority was mediocre, as I have said. It is humiliating

* "I have just sent the Holy Spirit into Auvergne ; the Holy [*Saint*] to Clermont, the Spirit [*Esprit i.e.* wit] to St. Flour." The witticism is untranslatable.—[Tr.]

20

for the Church of 1789 that in the Abbé Sicard's interesting picture of her condition at that period, he is able to name only fifteen really virtuous prelates among the 130 then holding office. And he is forced—for his impartiality is remarkable—to brand Rohan, Loménie de Brienne, Jarente, Talleyrand and their like, with the infamy they deserve. The majority of the *hauts abbés* were no better, though they had the excuse that being for the most part *commandataires*, they were not priests, at all events.*

The inferior clergy viewed their disreputable superiors with anger, jealousy, and shame. For years these parish priests, **Democratic** sons of the people, and profound believers, save **ideas of the** in a very small minority of cases, had been **lower Clergy.** imbibing the democratic spirit, because they too had become imbued to some extent with the spirit of philosophy.

This inferior clergy was all in favour of innovations. This point is of capital importance, for the tendency was to direct the final issue, and bring about the triumph of the Third Estate by breaking up the opposition of the privileged classes.

No assertion is so valuable as one small fact : let me quote this following one from M. de la Gorce : the discovery in Périgord of two lists of subscribers to the *Encyclopædia*, in which twenty-four out of the forty names are those of parish priests. Why should the priests in Périgord subscribe to the *Encyclopædia* more generally than those of a score of other provinces ? In this case generalization would appear quite permissible, and we shall not be surprised to learn that the worthy Abbé Barbotin, whose letters have lately been published, was in the habit of reading his Mably.† Even Rousseau himself did not offend them all : some of these priests would gladly have accepted the *Vicaire Savoyard* as his curate.

The *régime* was not at all to their liking. Bishops and

* *Hauts Abbés.* The King had power to grant a proportion, great or small, of the incomes of certain ecclesiastical benefices to men of his own choosing, whether churchmen or not. These men were known as *hauts abbés* or *commandataires.* In each of these establishments a genuine abbot ruled the community and managed its business.—[Tr.]

† The Abbé Gabriel de Mably, born at Grenoble 1709, died 1780, author of the *Droit public de l'Europe,* and well known as a student of French history.—[Tr.]

monks who were far too rich, and parish priests who had barely enough to live on : and as these prelates (Cardinal Mathieu quotes more than one instance of this sort in Lorraine), often so courtly and generous in the great world, occasionally treated their diocesan clergy with great severity, the humbler priests were extremely ready in 1789, to throw in their lot with a movement for which their origin, their course of reading, and their own grievances, had all prepared the way.

At the elections in 1789, we shall see them very much inflamed against their bishops. " It is those —— of priests who will be our ruin ! " writes d'Antraigues in May of that year. And as a matter of fact it was " those —— of priests " who made the Revolution a possibility. While their bishops, uncertain, like so many members of the privileged classes, as to the validity of their rights, and hampered by their violet mantles, could make but a poor fight for their own cause, these " —— of priests " were to tuck up their coarse cloth cassocks, and march more fiercely, sometimes, than the *bourgeois* themselves, to the assault of " privilege." The priests it was, who were to ensure the triumph of the Third Estate, and in their company we now approach the camp of the victors of the morrow, the *bourgeois*.

" What made the Revolution ? " said Napoleon one day, " Vanity ! Liberty was nothing but a pretext ! " The words

The revolt against inequality. are too brutal, and so far, unjust, but not altogether so. M. Faguet has demonstrated in some striking pages, that the Revolution of 1789 was much less a rebellion against despotism than a rebellion against inequality. In this respect its nature was far more social than political. Evidently some noble minds in the *bourgeois* class were spurred onward simply by their worship of liberty, as, for instance, Mounier, a most perfect example of the splendid French middle classes ; but he was one of the first to discover that he had been deceived by this " pretext." Liberal *bourgeois* were few and far between : exasperated *bourgeois* were legion. The ambitious *bourgeois* marched at the head of their fellows. They shouted " Long live Liberty ! " but they were Frenchmen —no Frenchman believes himself free unless he has power. At bottom nearly everybody wanted equality for his own benefit: Rivarol and Chamfort, belonging to two opposing camps, each contribute an unexpected justification of Napoleon's scathing sally: "It was not despotism that irritated the nation," says one, "but the prejudice of the nobility." And the other uses almost the same expressions.

Then again, the younger generation of the *bourgeois* class had read the best authors as much, and even more, than the aristocracy. I have already mentioned the books read by Marie-Jeanne Phlipon, and stated that the same works were studied by Robespierre, Brissot, Danton, Barnave, and Desmoulins. They worshipped these writers, who served the cause of their own resentments, and who, clamouring like Rousseau for equality, fed their legitimate pride. The facts that Marie Phlipon, invited to the house of a lady of rank, should have been entertained with her mother in the steward's room, and that Barnave should have seen his mother roughly pushed aside at a theatre by some insolent noble, were decisive incidents that left an unappeasable rage within their hearts. Many of those whose fury was the most terrible had lived too close to the aristocracy, had suffered from its scorn, and that condescension which, to an embittered soul, was more insulting still. Carrier had been steward to the Miramon family in Auvergne. In 1789, these men were in a state of exasperation: Sieyès calls the nobles "Cartouches." And indeed the men of 1789 with few exceptions, full as they were of their "good citizenship," *were only longing for equality so that they might attain to power:* for—and this is the second feature of importance in the period between 1789 and 1799—*they were as undemocratic at bottom as men well could be,* and their feeling for the masses was nothing but a mixture of scorn and fear. "*The perfect type of the bourgeois of '89,*" writes M. Meynier de la Revellière, "*combining hatred of the nobles with distrust of the mob!*" We shall see these men at work, so I need not insist.

*　　　*　　　*　　　*　　　*

But these *bourgeois* had of necessity (during the historic months of the winter of 1789, and the weeks of the electoral Discontent of campaign) to court the humble classes, and the the Peasantry. peasants, above all. So they set out to stir up their discontent and induce them to express it.

This discontent was, in fact, very great. I have spoken—when I described their material condition—of the peasants' grievances. They cared little for liberty ; they had no dreams of Westminster and its two Chambers, nor of a "republican" constitution like that of Philadelphia. Their desire was to *free themselves from feudal rights and crushing taxation,* and also, as I have already shown, to see the kingdom *constituted* in a better way. What restraining power was there on them ? The fidelity of vassals to their lords ? the absence of the lords had killed that. Religion ? They were Catholics, no doubt, and were to prove it later, but the tithe was an unbearable burden. And in two cases out of every three, as we know, the parish priest was not very much inclined to stay the upraised arms that, even in January 1789, began to threaten the Château.

" *To free the land !* " that was the rustic's sole aspiration. If the King helped them to that he would be their " good King," and the land once freed, in August 1789, they asked for nothing more. When the Revolution disgraced itself in their eyes, by the excesses of the " Terror," the triumph of the good-for-nothing fellows in each village, the emission of bad paper money, and the proscription of their parish priests, the peasants turned their faces towards any strong authority that seemed likely to give peace to the nation, and ensure the social and civil benefits won by the Revolution ; as for political liberties, they were very ready to sacrifice them.

For the moment, the *bourgeoisie,* between January and April 1789, put aside its secret pride, and contrived to rouse Coalition of the peasants' interest in its own triumph. The Middle Classes programme of 1789, as we shall see, was the and Peasantry. outcome of a coalition, agreed on by the two classes, between the aspirations of one, and the ambitions of the other.

But still more skilfully did the *bourgeois* use the wretchedness (of which, indeed, an over-exaggerated view must not be taken) of the town-dwellers for his own ends. Most of these townsmen were honest artisans who, like La Fontaine's cobbler, would have been content with very little : " Grégoire " sings, puts nothing by, and would be happy enough if he were not ruined by festivities. But in 1789, " Grégoire " was very hungry (I mean in the lowest class), and for this he blamed the system of government : when some bourgeois—a lawyer, such as Danton, or a doctor, like Marat, or a journalist like Desmoulins—stirred up his bitterness, it was easy to lead him against Bastilles or palaces. If necessity arose, it was as easy to reinforce the workmen of the Faubourgs with low rascals, remnants of bands once led by Mandrin and his like, and so to create the army but for which the eloquence of Barnave, in 1789, or of Vergniaud, in 1792, could never have prevailed. Time and time again they had tried to rise (consult M. Rocquain as to this), always they had been put down. They had gone hungry for a century. Then came that terrible winter of 1788–1789, which killed the poor creatures with hunger and cold. And then, above all, as a writer in the year 1789 put it, "the sword having slipped out of the King's grasp," the populace found itself facing disarmed power, which allowed fortresses and castles to fall into its hands.

The *bourgeoisie*, which had triumphed thanks to the support given it by the peasants at the elections in April 1789, was to use the workmen to break down the doors of the King's Bastilles.

* * * * *

The nobility and the superior clergy, unable to defend themselves, expected the King to do it for them.
Impotence of
the Crown.
Could the King do it ? For more than a century past the throne had professed no doctrine, and consequently no policy. Though the French Monarchy claimed to be absolute, it had given way, from time to time, to its own Parliaments, without ever having known the exact extent of their " rights " as they affected itself, and without any better information, indeed, as to the " rights " enjoyed by the "Estates" of the kingdom, in case of their convocation.

Since its refusal of " Colbert's offer " of which so remarkable a definition has been given by M. Ernest Lavisse, the monarchy had possessed no administrative and financial doctrine, nor any political doctrine either. And if material anarchy was raging in the country, moral anarchy reigned in the governmental doctrine.

Nor had the throne any social doctrine. On what class did it depend ? For a long period, as I have shown, it had leant upon the Communes. And in 1789, the Communes hoped this alliance might be formed afresh. Clearly, since the days of Louis XIV, the King, " the first nobleman in his kingdom," had depended on his nobles : yet all his policy, inherited from his ancestors, tended to the confinement of this nobility within the borders of a mediocrity which had enfeebled it. Ministerial functions were bestowed by preference, from Colbert's time down to Necker's, on members of the middle classes, though a discreet scorn for them was always shown. So that the King leant on an aristocracy that had been deliberately weakened, and governed through a *bourgeoisie* which he despised.

In 1789, no solution for the social and political problems of the day had been considered by the Versailles Government, even hypothetically. It was marching on the abyss, " with the crown over its eyes," as Rivarol expresses it.

The King had convoked the Estates, and granted the Third Estate a double share of representatives. What did that mean ? If the Orders were to vote collectively, what was the use of the innovation ? Were they then to vote as individuals ? Louis XVI did not know, nor his minister. What were the States-General to be allowed to do ? What was to be forbidden them ? Nobody knew. Were the privileges to be defended ? Were they to be relinquished ? Nobody could tell. Were repressive measures to be taken in case of necessity ? Nobody knew—and, I will add, the taking of such measures had become impossible.

For as always happens under a rudderless government, the weapon that trembled in its uncertain grasp played it false at last. This government without a theory of government found itself bereft, at this crucial hour, of that supreme resource of improvident and imperilled authority : armed force.

*   *   *   *   *

" The King has no strength of mind, and lacks the strength of bayonets," wrote a deputy of the Third Estate on July 8,
Disaffection of 1789.
the Troops. The bayonets had been wavering in the soldiers' hands, and the swords in those of their officers, ever

since the beginning of the century. When, towards the close of the year 1788, the King had thought for a moment—before he congratulated Mounier—of repressing him and his friends in Dauphiné, Marshal de Vaux wrote to his Majesty that it was "impossible to rely on the troops." Six months later, on the eve of the opening of the States-General, Necker said, "We are not sure of the troops." And therein lies almost the whole secret of the Government's failures.

The officers had ceased to hold their men. The reason is well known. Most of these officers were of inferior quality, and many had no claim to command, save that of being born into the world colonels in their cradles. The non-commissioned officers, whose promotion had been stopped by the edict of 1781, hated those who reaped the benefit of this new order of things. Some of them, like Oudinot and Massena, left the service ; a few like Murat, spoke out boldly when they went : the rest stayed on, and grumbled.

Under them, there was an army, brave, but dangerous, too often recklessly recruited—ruffians of all kinds, troublesome sons, moral derelicts, " *brigands*," as one of their former leaders, Dubois-Crancé, a democrat of the Constituent Assembly, was to call them, perhaps with a touch of exaggeration.

Such an army would have needed a yoke of iron, and the yoke, as a matter of fact, had been made lighter. Vaublanc depicts the aristocratic officers, influenced, like everybody else, by the spirit of the age, sentimental, humanitarian, but little inclined to use the rod which the minister Saint-Germain had so lately put, paradoxically enough, into their hands.

And more. The army, which had been the cradle, in France, of freemasonry imported by the Irish regiments from England, continued to be its favourite haunt. In 1789, there were five-and-twenty military lodges : the *Parfaite Union* in the Vivarais, the *Saint-Alexandre* in the Musketeers, the *Pureté* in the Sarre regiment and the *Concorde* in the Auvergne—it would be useless to enumerate all the names. We will not ask whether the revolutionary spirit was already alight in these lodges : the spirit of equality certainly reigned in them, in any case. Nothing can be more destructive to discipline than that a colonel should sit down, not only beside, but below, a non-commissioned officer

And that is just what happened. In the *Union* Lodge of the Toul-Artillerie, the senior mason was Sergeant Compagnon, whereas the Marquis d'Havrincourt, a Field-Marshal, was merely the delegate of the Grand Orient. It is not easy to imagine Havrincourt ordering Sergeant Compagnon to fire on a population which, like themselves, was clamouring for " perfect equality."

All this had led up to that disintegration of the army, the stages of which we are about to witness, from the mutiny of the Gardes Françaises in 1789 to that of the garrison of Nancy in August 1790. And this it was, as much as his incoherent policy, which left the King defenceless.

Privileged classes incapable of defending their privileges, a divided and weakened aristocracy, a clergy cleft in twain and uncertain as to its rights, and facing these, a *bourgeoisie* filled with a fierce longing for the power which the conquest of liberty and equality would bring it—an energetic, intelligent, ambitious and greedy class—supported by a rural population determined to attack privileges, and, if the King should defend them, to break his " despotism " to pieces, and a town populace maddened by suffering and easily inflamed into sedition : between these two parties, a government which had no policy, which knew not how to play the part of arbiter, and, being shorn of its strength, could no longer play the part of master.

The situation justified every apprehension. Other elements, of course, were added to the all-important ones just specified— **Various elements of the Revolution.** the elements of every violent revolution, turbid elements from above, turbid elements from below. Above, the leaders, directing all the ambitions, spites, hatreds, of their followers, embittering every disappointment, stirring up all greedy desires. " Those who write the history of the Revolution," asserts a deputy, as early as the year 1789, " will do so in ignorance of a mass of very transient circumstances, of slight apparent importance, which have really had a prodigious influence on events." We are not ignorant of all these circumstances. Nothing would be more interesting than to draw up a list of the leaders, from Lafayette to Santerre, from Mirabeau to Desmoulins, from Barnave to Collot d'Herbois (and I might easily mention fifty more), who were swept into

28

this movement by personal mortifications or personal cupidity. Below, among those who were led, there were other elements of disturbance—all the terrible sediment that hides in the lowest depths of society in our cities, and even in our villages, and rises to the surface at the slightest movement. " A set of men ruined by debt and crime," who " will have no means of subsistence unless everything is overthrown." And to make this inquiry complete, we must refer to the action—undeniable, in these days, though indisputably secondary—of secret societies, foreign cabinets, and mysterious agents of whose hand we have a glimpse here and there, without ever being able to lay hold upon it. By the light of such a study (too wide for the limits of this work) we should learn that the Revolution, which had been an inevitable thing for fifty years, was sometimes, even in its most generous hours, served by ? variety of factors not always avowable.

In reality this Revolution had to be : we shall see it degenerate, and lose its primitive character : but none the less was it **Enervation of** inevitable and indispensable. It was the explo-
the Upper sion and the revenge of the noblest feeling, to
Classes. my mind, of humanity—I mean Energy.

On February 17, 1798, Mallet du Pan wrote his conviction that in France, at that date, " by dint of life in cities, epicureanism, and indolence, all the rich, all the high-born, all the landowners, all the men of breeding, were absolutely enervated." In 1789, the *ancien régime*—and this is the last feature we shall have to note—shows us, in fact, a picture of what may be described as the collapse of energy : it was " enervated." In the old days, energy had been both general and splendid : that of the kings had built up France, that of the feudal lords had battled for her, that of her apostles had evangelized her. But these descendants and successors of great men were, as a whole, utterly devoid of energy, and further, seeing the right to all good things was reserved for birth and privilege, they barred the way to other men's energy and kept it down. Walpole, who saw these people at Versailles, considered them incurably " anæmic."

But Versailles was not France. French energy lived on, it was bubbling in the souls of five hundred thousand of her citizens. Far from having waned, its very repression had given it added strength. Commanded by superior officers of noble birth, soldiers were waiting on wearily—soldiers fiery hearted, and stern as steel, thrilling with youth and military genius : these men, by their mighty labours, were first to cover the young Republic with glory, and then to form the Military Staff of Bonaparte. 1768 saw the births of Murat, Mortier, Bessières ; 1769 those of Hoche, Marceau, Ney, Soult, Lannes, Joubert—and Bonaparte. Under those well-born and mediocre prelates from whom Massillon had vainly striven to save the country, and whose only idea was to join the emigration, we shall note an indomitable clergy, which, having fought for liberty first, will fight again in attics and in caverns, for its proscribed faith. Under this incapable government, a legion of young men was rising up, who lived on Plutarch, " that Bible of the strong," and who, whether they were lawyers, publicists, professors or medical men, all felt their souls ablaze in bodies of bronze.

" The spring that moves me was in my heart : it was held down : the Revolution sets it free, and I shall die a patriot ! " Thus wrote Dugommier, when he had passed his fiftieth year. How then must it have been with this younger generation, whose " souls," as one of them, Saint-Just, so proudly writes, " were not yet weaned " ? All this energy, individual and collective, compressed, as it were, by a worn-out machine, was to blow it into pieces, and overflow for the space of ten years in such a fashion that the world had never beheld such a sight before. To this flood everything that was young and strong was to join itself. " When a man is eighteen," writes Thiébault who was one of the recruits of 1789, " he belongs to any party that will attack."

CHAPTER IV

THE GOVERNMENT OF 1789

THE King's Government had been forced into convoking the States-General : the series of errors, miscalculations, and failures of which this was the result have been explained elsewhere. M. Pierre de Ségur has shown us the *Sunset of the Monarchy*, M. Casimir Stryienski has made my **The Twilight** readers acquainted with the *Dawn of the Revolu-* **of the Kings.** *tion.* These years, 1787 and 1788, is to me the Twilight of the Kings. Everybody was feeling his way : the sun of Louis XIV had set ; the rulers were indeed walking " with the crown over their eyes."

And yet it was the Government that let the country loose in January 1789 ! Having defined the general characteristics of the *régime*, the country and the Government, we must now consider the personages destined to preside over the opening events of the drama. France was rushing towards a revolution. Was it to be long or short, peaceful or violent ? Was there to be drastic reform, or total subversion ? Everything at this moment depended on the persons who governed, and their capacities.

These persons were the King, the Queen, the Princes, and the Ministers.

Louis XVI was not a true scion of his race. Pious to the point of bigotry, and chaste to the extent of neglect- **Protagonists in** ing his own wife, he was the grandson, **the opening** not of the Bourbons—the Verts-Galants—but **drama.** of poor Maria-Leczinska ! Look at the statue of Stanislas at Nancy : and remember that the stout man it represents spent his life in abdications ! It was the blood of Stanislas, far more than the blood of Henri IV, that flowed in the veins of Louis XVI. Labour, love, war, politics, had no charms for him : he had one passion only, the chase, and between two hunting excursions, he worked as a locksmith. We have his journal: "a huntsman's journal," says Taine: lists of splendid holocausts of game. These expeditions gave him a huge appetite, almost the only Bourbon characteristic he had. His appetite fed his optimism, even in the flood-tide of crisis: Gouverneur Morris was shocked, in 1790: "What is to be expected of a man in his position, who eats and drinks heartily, sleeps well, laughs, and is the cheeriest fellow on the face of the earth?"

And merry he was—with a rather rough merriment, if we may rely on various witnesses. It was to hold out for many a day, in the face of overwhelming calamities.

Heavy and vulgar in appearance, he was no fool: there has been much exaggeration on this point; sometimes his sharpness astonished his ministers: several of them **Louis XVI.** were outwitted by him in a trice. He was clear-sighted enough at times, but his good-nature paralyzed his hand, and hampered his action. He was liberal and generous-minded: a sincere Christian, he made a practice of forgiving those who injured him with a calmness much to be deplored. He, too, had undergone the influence of his century; had read Rousseau like other people, and believed that "man was good." He was known to be kindly disposed. On the day of the old sovereign's death, France had hoped everything from the young one. Somebody had written the word *Resurrexit* on the statue of Henri IV on the Pont Neuf. Alas!

His own heart and the action of his times inclined him to reforms both liberal and humanitarian: before 1789 he had already made some very good ones—let not this be forgotten—and that without any external pressure at all. The Protestants owed their liberty to this devout Catholic, who, realizing the sufferings of his "good people," had been striving, for the last fifteen years, to apply some remedy. He called many physicians and even some charlatans to the sick man's bedside: he had reformed himself; he allowed other people to squander money, but he was personally economical, from a sense of right and for example's sake: was it his fault that others followed that example as little as they could? His desire was that it should be followed.

He had no will : this was the most striking point about his character. Easily influenced, he occasionally did, indeed, like all very kind-hearted men, rebel in a sudden and incomprehensible fashion, and would intrench himself behind an obstinate and bewildering determination. As a general rule, he would listen and smile, but seldom took any decision, " his first word always being No ! " as one of his counsellors tells us. He never acted except under some strong pressure—a scene made by distracted courtiers, lively objurgations from the Queen or a minister, some violent incident that stirred him. But such influences as these, coming first from one side and then from another, were always to toss him hither and thither. Thus neither his wife, his brothers, his ministers, nor his subjects ever felt any absolute confidence in him, because, as a certain deputy wrote in June 1789 : " he is known to have no will of his own." On the other hand, Court intrigues, the enterprises of the Assemblies, the popular movement, were never discouraged by him, because nobody took any decision of his to be irrevocable. One and the same watchword ran from the Salon de l'Œil-de-Bœuf to the populous quarters of Paris : " Force the King's hand ! " His hand might be forced, but nobody was ever sure of holding it afterwards ! " Imagine," said his brother Provence, " a handful of oiled ivory balls that you are trying to keep together ! "

At bottom—and this was the worst of his proclivities—his duties bored him. Read the story of that captivity in the Temple, during which he retrieved his past errors so touchingly in the eyes of the whole world—that simple, regular, homely existence, the lessons given to his little son, the meals shared by the whole family—all this made him very happy : it may be fairly said that this unfortunate prince never found true happiness till he was in prison. He was born for private life : the day the crown was set on his head at Reims, he said, " It hurts me." It was always to hurt him. When M. de Malesherbes brought him his resignation in 1776, he exclaimed, " How lucky you are ! Why cannot I resign too ? " Poor man ! the words came from his heart ! " He is a good, kind-hearted man," wrote Morris to Washington in 1790, " who would make an excellent pacific Minister in quiet times." But " his ancestors,"

c

as Mignet puts it, " had bequeathed him a Revolution." Under such an overwhelming impetus, even a Louis XIV might have flinched. To be just in our judgment of the King's weakness, we must allow for the relentless pressure of fate upon him. And we must remember, too, that he refused to shed the blood of Frenchmen, preferring to give his own, and performed this act of self-immolation with great simplicity. We shall see him die, admirable in his sacrifice. Pity has its rights here, though truth has hers also, and always.

A king, in fact, is not a king that he may die nobly, but that he may reign. The Queen used to call him "the poor man!" In 1789, everybody was saying, "He is kind!" Napoleon wrote to King Joseph: "When men call a king a kind man, his reign has been a failure!"

In 1789, the reign was a failure. The King did not know what he wanted. "He asked advice of everybody," writes Malouet, "and seemed to be saying to every soul who approached him, What should be done? What can I do?" He did indeed ask Rivarol that question, through Malesherbes. "Play the King!" was the reply. That was the very last thing Louis XVI could have done, *for he was not born a king*.

At the worst, and failing him, Marie-Antoinette could have "played the King." "The King has only one man about him, Marie-Antoinette. his wife," wrote Mirabeau. A proud and beautiful Queen, who might have been great in other times, and who nevertheless finished the work of ruin! Many things have been said of her, much good and much evil—too much good and too much evil. Incapable of prudence, she was —and this is far more serious—still more incapable of forgetting. Now the sovereign who does not know how to forget certain offences does not know how to reign : there must be no indulgent forgiveness, like that of Louis XVI, but a systematic forgetting. And she, while unable to forgive her enemies, could not renounce her friendships : a fine trait, this, in a woman, a dangerous trait in a queen—especially when her friends abuse her friendship.

Cruelly attacked, slandered and wounded by the Court and the Royal Family, her character, naturally proud, but originally trustful, impulsive, and gay, had grown gloomy and rebellious. She had shut herself up behind a wall of haughty dignity, which was to complete her destruction. "More anxious to meet danger bravely than to avert it," writes La Fayette, whose words are true on this occasion ; she was never able to avert it. Her influence over her "poor man," as she called him, was intermittent, and all she could do was to urge him to actions which she thought vigorous, but which, as they were never followed up, looked more like impulses of defiance.

The King's brothers gave no help : the Comte de Provence, "Monsieur,"—one day to be a somewhat remarkable king—The Comte de was then nothing but a man of wit, who professed Provence. philosophic opinions, believed in the divine right much more than he believed in God Himself, had appeared imbued with all the current ideas of the century till Necker had tried to cut down his pensions, and had been disposed since that time to counsel resistance—but a cautious and underhand resistance at that. Inferior to his brother as far as his heart went, he was very much his superior in intelligence. The King was not very fond of him, distrusted him, and felt, besides, that his brother despised him.

The other brother, the Comte d'Artois, was far more attractive. Very good-looking, active, elegant, always ready to lay The Comte his hand on the hilt of his sword, he was considered d'Artois. a sort of Knight of the Round Table, and "the sword of the Monarchy." Being, unlike his two brothers, an indefatigable "Vert-Galant," he was ready to fancy he had won the battle of Ivry in person. Yet his white plume had never waved elsewhere than in the gardens of Versailles : all through the Revolution he was to talk incessantly about drawing "the sword of his fathers," which was never to leave its scabbard. His character, nevertheless, led him to declaim loudly against the revolutionary idea, but he, too, was to do more harm than good to its opponents' cause. His swagger had some effect upon the King, from time to time, but disgusted all the sensible people about him. With his small brain and his violent attitude, he was a dangerous counsellor, when he obtained a hearing, and a compromising babb'eiwhen he was made to keep his distance.

The King listened to "the family" in intermittent fashion :

85

he took counsel with his ministers in the same way. They never, in 1789, advised the action suggested by his family. But here was the great weakness : the King never could settle the matter between his family and his ministers by his own casting vote.

" M. Necker is the Ministry," wrote a deputy on May 22, 1789. " Everything hangs on M. Necker."

This Genevan financier, whose family had originally come from Brandenburg, had risen, thanks to his own remarkable moral and financial uprightness, and the success he had made of his own business. Because he had managed the Thelusson-Necker Bank well, people came to the conclusion that he alone would be able to save the kingdom from bankruptcy.

Necker.

Public opinion had raised him to power, had regretted his departure in 1781, and acclaimed his return in 1788. This was because, at a very early period, he had opened, in the rooms over his banking offices, that *salon*, the story and the features of which his grandson, M. d'Haussonville, has related to us in such a piquant and independent fashion. The Neckers entertained the philosophers, and the philosophers, grateful to their entertainers occasionally at all events, thought very highly of their Mæcenas, brought him into power in 1781, and again in 1788.

He was no statesman. " I think," wrote Mounier, a year later, " that his knowledge, his zeal for humanity, his spirit of order and economy, would have made him an excellent administrator in times of peace, but that he lacked all the qualities necessary for struggling with factions." What he really lacked, like Louis XVI, was a resolute spirit. " He neither knows what he can do, what he wants to do, nor what he ought to do," wrote Mirabeau harshly. Mirabeau was his enemy, and he was unjust. Necker did want one thing, but that was not enough. He wanted to put the finances on a good basis, and for this purpose to call on the country, and the Third Estate in the country, to abolish immunities, and once the bad condition of the Treasury had been remedied by useful reforms, to be content with that. " His ideal," writes M. de Laborie, " was a kind of paternal government, in which the income of

36

the State would be managed by a first-class financier, under the best of Kings."

" A clock that is too slow," said Mirabeau. Even in 1788 the clock was losing time.

He weighed things too much—a banker's habit : even Mme. de Staël, whose touching worship of her father has evoked occasional jeers, acknowledged his " irresolution." He gave good advice : but he was quite unable to deal with events when they took him unawares or outflanked him. King and Assembly alike were to become acquainted with this temper of his, which Malouet has thus described : " When he was put out, he was unable to govern." He suffered from indigestion into the bargain, and that is a bad complaint for a man who has to lead others.

Recalled in 1788, he continued to believe he was face to face with a financial crisis, when he was really face to face with Revolution. He asked the King to convoke the States-General just as he would have had a body of shareholders called together on any special occasion.

On December 27, 1788, his report, which had been hotly discussed in the Council, had been finally approved : Barentin, Keeper of the Seals, and Villedeuil were the only members who had voted agains tit : Puységur and Nivernais had abstained, Necker, Montmorin, Fourqueux, La Luzerne, and Saint-Priest had voted for it. Louis XVI threw his sceptre into the heaviest side of the scales.

The die was cast. But it was only the die. No distinct plan had been formulated. Neither the King nor Necker was qualified to cope with the events that were to overwhelm them from the very outset of the campaign.

The Government—the most honest, perhaps, that France had ever possessed—was everything, save a government fit to meet a crisis.

CHAPTER V

THE ELECTIONS AND THE MEMORIALS

NOTHING more liberal, nothing more loyal, than the attitude of this Government, can be conceived. On January 24, it issued a set of regulations to the King's agents, attached to which was a preamble that proved the sovereign to be the " good king " his subjects desired to see in

The King as friend of his people.

him. "His Majesty . . . has determined to assemble the States-General of the Kingdom about his own dwelling, not in any way to fetter their deliberations, but to preserve in regard to them the character which lies nearest his heart—that of counsellor and *friend*." This word touched the country deeply ; many of the memorials contain allusions to it.

From the mass of documents collected by M. Brette into one most valuable volume, we may glean the *royal programme* to which M. Aulard has devoted one of his earliest studies— an excellent programme if only it had been followed : the power of consent to taxation to be restored to the nation, the States to meet at settled periods, a budget to be drawn up, the arbitrary power of Ministers with regard to expenditure to be abolished, individual liberty to be guaranteed by the suppression of *lettres de cachet*, freedom for the Press to be instituted by the States, the creation of permanent provincial States, and—the double cry that rose louder than any other from every lip— *a settled Constitution and equal taxation for all.*

There was no mention, indeed, of the manner in which the voting in the States-General was to be done, but Necker's report invited the privileged classes to consent to the system of counting of heads. The King expected this resolution " from their common love for the welfare of the State." The meaning was clear.

Further, the King called on all his subjects to formulate their complaints. In this respect they were not to fail him.

Subjects to formulate complaints. Each order was to vote separately : the Nobility according to its usual practice : the Clergy in increased numbers (this innovation had appeared indispensable), taking in all the parish priests, " good and useful servants," says the *Result of the Council,* " who, applying their minds daily and closely to the poverty of the people and to its relief, have a closer acquaintance with its sufferings."

The Third Estate had been given something that nearly approached universal suffrage. Every man who had reached the age of twenty-five, and was on the tax-collector's list, had a right to vote. " Machiavellism," says M. Aulard : the idea was to swamp the enlightened middle classes with the ignorant masses, who were thought to be faithful and easily led. But at Versailles the favourite reading was not Machiavelli, but Rousseau : if Louis XVI and Necker bestowed universal suffrage on the country, they did it, we know, because man, and especially the man who had not been spoilt by civilization, was virtuous ! One thing is certain, this enlargement of the electorate was very displeasing to certain of the middle classes : Mounier had not asked for so much.

The story of this huge movement would fill a volume. It was not only huge, it was full of an inevitable confusion, for **Elections for the States-General.** this first attempt at elections betrayed none of the pleasing uniformity that marks the elections of our day. Over the greater part of the kingdom, the final vote was taken at the bailiwick—a vote by two and sometimes by three stages.

Then the extraordinary extent of the prevalent anarchy became evident. Bailiwicks fought over parishes, and agents fought for the presidency of the assemblies.

As a matter of fact, it mattered little which agent presided, for Barentin, Keeper of the Seals, had severely cautioned them all in the King's name, " not to endeavour to influence the voters' choice, nor to take any step that might hamper the suffrage." This astonishing Keeper of the Seals was never 'to have a successor of like tendencies—the adventure proved too disastrous to the Government that embarked on it in 1789.

No instance of pressure is discoverable : if there was any at all, it was exercised by seneschals and lieutenants-general (many of whom were candidates) in favour of the ideas which, since the month of January had seemed to be in favour—ideas of reform. " Though very prudent in all social matters," writes M. Onou, " the presidents of assemblies were partisans of the new political ideas, hostile to absolute power, and to ministerial despotism."

The ruling power then—if the term may be used with regard to a government which had so little—made no campaign on its own account. But on the other hand (and until within the last few years nobody seems to have realized this) other people did. To read our old historians (the sort of historical mysticism common to de Maistre and to Michelet) one would fancy all these millions of electors went to the poll guided solely by some supernatural spirit (demoniac, de Maistre would tell us, divine, Michelet would declare) unaffected by any political influence whatsoever. By some miraculous chance, peasants, middle classes and parish priests all express the same unanimous desire, and that frequently in exactly similar terms !

Since critics have turned their attention to the study of the memorials,* there is not an historian who does not recognize the fact that even if no central organization existed, there were certainly local organizations. In their remarkable *Introduction aux Cahiers de Rennes*, MM. Lesort and Sée show us glimpses of a semi-official organization in Brittany, signs of which may be detected in other provinces. " Models " were disseminated all over the country : M. Bloch mentions ten principal ones in the Generality of Orleans : the celebrated *Instructions* of the Duc d'Orléans were utilized over a great part of the Loire valley.

The Memorials.

The dissemination of these " models " was an expensive business. Who paid for the propaganda, after having drawn up the documents ? Here we find ourselves in twilight ; we may even say darkness. M. Dard, the biographer of Laclos, who is well versed in the part the Duc d'Orléans played at this period, tells us : " The Government did not control the elections, but it allowed other people to do so." The Palais-Royal ? Perhaps so.

* Memorials or *Cahiers*, see p. 8.

ELECTIONS AND MEMORIALS

From the beginning of January 1789, the excitement was extreme. It would be interesting to trace, in this place, a picture of these parish assemblies, held in sacristies, in churches, even in cemeteries—where the dead seemed called on to speak, and did sometimes influence the living. These assemblies formulated complaints that were very reasonable sometimes, sometimes very artless, some of them a little grotesque, but oftenest of all tragic : and these were conveyed to the assembly of the bailiwick, where the final Memorial was drawn up.

These assemblies of the bailiwicks, too, were picturesque enough : I should have liked to reproduce here the description of that held at Rennes on April 7, 1789, given by the publishers of the Memorials of that jurisdiction. The 800 delegates from the Breton parishes were seemingly deeply attached to Louis XVI, but they drank so many bowls of cider to their The Breton " good king's " health, that they ended by filling deputies. the minds of all reasonable men with serious alarm. The bowls of cider, no less than the behaviour of the Breton nobility, were responsible for the violence of the Breton deputies, who, when they reached Versailles, were to found that famous " Breton Club " of which the " Jacobins " was the legitimate offspring.

The three foremost of these deputies, Lanjuinais, Defermon, and Le Chapelier, departed from Rennes with hearts full of " hatred of privilege " : an attitude of mind which was to carry the first to the House of Peers under Louis XVIII, and the second to the Ministry under Napoleon I, both of them with the title of Count—while poor Le Chapelier was snatched all too soon from a destiny that might have been brilliant, by the knife of the guillotine, which he himself had sharpened.

The language at the assemblies of the Clergy was exceedingly stormy as a rule, and big with threats. At Le Mans, where they would not let their bishop speak ; at Agen, where they drove the canons out ; at Poitiers, where the Abbé Jallet pointed exultingly at his sorely mortified bishop, perched on the end of a bench ; at Angers, where the offended prelate retired altogether, the same feeling may be noted. From these assemblies were to issue the 208 parish priest deputies who, as one lieutenant-general wrote to Necker were to "take all the tricks."

The most important election of all was that of Comte Honoré de Mirabeau. Ardent and impetuous and like all his race **Election of** ("Shall we never hear people talk of anything **Mirabeau.** but those wild Mirabeaus?"), blazing with passion, he had appealed to the "secret good offices" of the Ministry to get himself accepted as a member of the Order of Nobility. These good offices had been curtly refused by Necker, and the Nobility of Provence had expelled its dangerous kinsman. Then, with great oaths, he had fallen back on the Third Estate. Discourse of this kind inflamed the Provençal mind : Aix and Marseilles fought to possess him. His practice was to give himself out as persecuted by the Ministers and the privileged classes. "A mad dog ? That may be ! But elect me, and despotism and privilege will die of my bite ! "

After a campaign that was literally one long triumph, he was elected by both towns, and took his way to Versailles, in April 1789, intoxicated with popularity, overflowing with bitterness against Necker and the aristocracy, terrible, deservedly dreaded, and convinced that he was destined to triumph over everything, jealousies, hatreds, and the ruling power.

The election of such men as Mounier, Barnave, Lanjuinais, Lafayette, Rabaut, Sieyès, and Mirabeau, some full of faith, some of ambition, some of talent, some of mere pretension, was an important fact in itself, but far more so because they had the masses at their backs. And these masses were to make their entry with them into Versailles—the Nation, bearing the Memorials in her hands.

To conclude a preamble which though necessary, has been far too long, we must say a word or two about these " Memorials."

The *Cahiers*, or Memorials sent in by the three Orders, amounted to some thousands, fifty or sixty, it is said, on the **The " Cahiers "** study of which a posse of hard-working men of **or Memorials.** letters are now engaged. Of these Memorials only a few hundred have as yet been published. Our reference to them must not be taken, therefore, to embody any absolutely final opinion concerning them.

ELECTIONS AND MEMORIALS

Malouet, a wise man, describes them as "the public and unanswerable depository of the opinions and desires of France." Certain historians have treated them with less respect. Babeau, who looked on the Revolution with an unfriendly eye, Loutchisky, and Wahl, regard them as mere "noisy clamour."

This theory is indefensible : one only of its elements we must remember : man, whatever may be the government under which he lives, is always discontented : if any government, even the best in the world, should call on several millions of men to formulate their complaints, they would certainly complain, and complain loudly. If at the present moment, we were to suggest the making of complaints of the same nature, our modern *régime* would more than probably find itself painted in anything but the rosiest colours.

But let us see what the elected members were deputed to demand, and observe the result of the collaboration of the peasants—full of their pigeons and their salt-tax, their rabbits and their *taille* and their tithes—and the petty tradesman or the priests—who had disseminated the models, or used their own pens, and added a representative assembly and a political constitution to the programme. Though some peasants, indeed drew up their own Memorials, the perfect spontaneity of which is evidenced by the picturesqueness of their style, I do not suppose that it was the villagers of Vers (near Nîmes) themselves who placed a quotation from Cicero's *De Officiis* at the head of their written sheets.

But there were certain points, indeed, as to which not only the whole of the Third Estate, but all the Orders of the nation were in full agreement. These were embodied in certain general aspirations of which I shall now give a rapid summary.

The Estates were faithful servants of the King, but they desired a King *of the French*. "May all your subjects, Sire, become as truly French by your government as they are by their love for their King ! "

They desired a *Constitution*, though they did not exactly and invariably define its nature : it must give guarantees for individual liberty : there must be no more *lettres de cachet* nor State prisons (observe that these were things from which the lower orders had never had to suffer) : as regards the liberty

43

of the press, the feeling was less unanimous. There was no definite indication of any desire for parliamentary institutions.

But on the other hand there was a loud cry for *equal taxation :* " equality of the provinces," wrote the clergy of the Upper Limousin, " equality of individuals," cried the whole of the Third Estate and many of the privileged classes as well. Some means must be found of removing the " enormous debt " which " destroyed all credit," wrote the nobility of the Bauvaisis : the " vile salt-tax " must be abolished, the system of levying subsidies must be modified : the " odious *taille* " must be done away with, and if the *vingtième* were allowed to remain in existence, it must be paid by everybody alike.

The abuses in the administration of justice must be abolished. "So enormous were they, according to one of the Memorials from the Clergy, " that every citizen dreaded being called on to defend even the best established of his own rights." And to begin with, the judicial districts must be recast, and the mercenary selling of office " a source of ruin to the people, an opportunity offered to a thousand men of no instruction . . . to attain to offices on which the goods, the honour, and the life of citizens depend," must cease.

In some cases we see the Orders, Clergy included, rise up, " after two centuries and a half of a trial which has been disastrous " against the Concordat : some Memorials even clamour for the election of bishops : in any case there is a strong feeling, amongst the Clergy more particularly, against interference from Rome. The Nobility does not hesitate to assert that : " the Estates are competent to secure discipline in the Church," and finally, the Nobles and the Third Estate agree (though with this the Clergy cannot comply), in a proposal for applying Church property to the furtherance of the public weal : "to establish free justice," say the Nobles of Gien. Those of Montargis ask for the "total and absolute " suppression of the monastic orders. Nothing could give us a clearer conception of the effect produced on the aristocracy, even that of the most remote provinces, by the philosophers of the eighteenth century.

But each Order had its own grievances, and not infrequently its agreement with its fellows soon came to an end. Touching the matter of the casting of all the votes together, the opinion amongst the Nobility was not so unanimous as might have been expected : out of 200 memorials examined by M. Champion, he found that only thirty-nine formally recommended that each Order should vote separately ; nineteen recognized exceptional cases, and twenty-four demanded that all three Orders should vote together.

The lower Clergy laid great stress on the necessity for restricting the powers of the Bishops : let us remember that this question had been debated in the Bishops' presence, and we shall once more realize the strength of the anti-episcopal feeling manifested at this moment.

The Memorials of the Third Estate are the most important, and naturally the most varied, of all, for rich and poor, whether *bourgeois*, rural landowners, or farmers, humble peasants, shop-keepers, craftsmen, or artisans, could all have their say in these pages. I can do no more than sketch the chief features. Some Memorials, as we have seen, quote Cicero and treat of high political questions, and others merely complain that " the fees the parish priests charge for marriages and burials are too high " : some clamour for liberty of conscience, while others, as those from Auvergne, beseech " a virtuous king " to revoke the edict of 1787, which shows too much favour to non-Catholics. Some—the immense majority—boldly demand manhood suffrage : others, as that of Ambert, would only permit it if the action of the States-General be not paralyzed thereby, and others, again, like that of Étampes, reject it altogether. The chief anxiety of some is to found a constitutional monarchy, while others are bent on getting the " roads, which are detestably bad," properly repaired. Some would reform the Church, root and branch ; others humbly request that as teachers are so scarce, " the midwives should know how to read, so as to teach the young people."

Yet touching the great questions there is unanimity, or something very near it : abolition of the immunities, reform of taxation, suppression of feudal rights, liberation of the soil, disappearance of the tithe . . . the Étampes memorial sums up in one appeal the opinion of all the rest : " How happy should we be if the feudal system were destroyed ! "

45

As to industrial matters, opinion in the towns was divided ; out of sixty Memorials, M. Levasseur finds forty-four in favour of industrial freedom, seven in favour of reform, and sixteen in favour of the maintenance of the corporations. All the great industrial cities were in favour of this last. " Nevertheless," as André Lichtemberger observes, " not a hint at any socialistic claim." Property was still regarded as sacred, save that privileged wealth which was considered to have been " usurped."

From all these claims one cry goes up, " *Reform !* "—a radical reform of the whole scheme of government. But the
General demand for Reform.
system was growing old and those who honestly desired reform ran a sore risk of opening the flood-gates to revolution. This would not have been displeasing to all : but the majority was disposed to view it with dread. Once rid of the feudal rights and the crushing weight of the taxes, a good three-quarters of them would have been content. " You will never get rid of them," said the *bourgeois,* honest liberals or ambitious politicians, "unless you have a Constitution ! " So a Constitution they must have.

And thus the programme of 1789 was put together.

When, in the closing days of that month of April, the deputies took coach for Versailles, they carried this formidable programme with them. Along all the highroads in France the travellers rolled, 1600 deputies, an incongruous army, all converging on Versailles—great lords who had got themselves elected by the Nobles, and shabby-looking country gentlemen, prelates such as Talleyrand who had shown their faces in their dioceses at last, and were hurrying back with their electors' mandate in their pockets, parish priests with set faces, strong in their resolve not to be cajoled by " Our Lords the Bishops," lawyers and physicians from little towns and great, prepared, with a mixture of arrogance and fear, to reform the State, and humble rustics in their fustian coats, who had set forth to free the soil.

By the close of April they had all reached Versailles. Even before they were in the town, the Court was laughing at their
The Estates assembled at Versailles.
pretentious airs.

Yet the avalanche thus descending from every corner of the kingdom on the home of the " Great King " was formidable indeed.

ELECTIONS AND MEMORIALS

And there were some who did not laugh at it ! Necker was uneasy : this tremendous political and social movement disturbed the financier's mind. He betrayed his alarm in Malouet's presence. Troops were summoned : on April 15, Morris saw 10,000 soldiers marching towards Paris : and this was necessary enough, for on the 27th the dragoons were needed to put down a bloody riot in the Faubourg Saint-Antoine, which had already risen in revolt, to the alarm of certain of the *bourgeois* deputies, who walked up and down the streets of Versailles and took counsel together.

The behaviour of the " low wretches " who had cut a worthy shopkeeper's throat, filled them with indignation. " Far from having resulted in any loss of favour for M. Necker," one of them hastens to add, " this has only made him yet dearer to the nation ! "

But all did not share this opinion. Louis XVI, shaken and alarmed already by the tempest let loose, and impressed by the reproaches of his nobles, sent, we are told, for the aged Machault, and offered to make him Prime Minister. Machault thought it was too late, and advised the King to keep Necker.

In that crucial hour, when the nation was demanding what might well be a Revolution, the miserable Versailles Government, lacking alike a programme and the resolution to enforce one, was once more to shrink from the suggestion of Reform.

And this meant ruin.

PART I

THE CONSTITUENT ASSEMBLY

CHAPTER I

THE STATES-GENERAL

May–June 1789

The Deputies at Versailles. The procession of May 4. The first
sitting in the Hall of the Menus Plaisirs. The Third Estate refuses
to constitute itself a political body. Negotiations with the other
Chambers. " Those —— of parish priests ". The National
Assembly. The Clergy decides to join the Third Estate. The
incident in the Tennis Court. The Royal sitting of June 24. The
Commons refuse to obey. The King gives way. The Estates form
one Assembly. " The Revolution is over ! "

AT noon on Friday, May 1, all Versailles was astir.
Crowds were hurrying to watch the " king-at-arms "
and his four heralds, as they moved from one square
to another, riding richly caparisoned chargers, and escorted by
mounted hussars. At each open space they halted, the long
The Deputies trumpets rang out three calls, then one of the
at Versailles. heralds shouted " In the King's name ! " and
proceeded to read his Majesty's proclamation of the meeting
of the States-General on May 4.

Many deputies were present, idle, and already discontented.
They had been summoned for April 26, and were waiting
wearily, going about in groups to pay their respects to princes
and ministers, who did not always welcome them graciously.

On May 2, Louis XVI received the representatives of the
Nation at the Palace : the Third Estate, pent between two
barriers in one of the saloons, waited " three mortal hours,"
under the courtiers' somewhat scornful eyes. (We rely upon
a score of letters written that very evening.) Following each
other in seemingly endless file, they reached the royal presence
at last. The King, standing between his two brothers, said not
a word to any of them, and each deputy, having made his

51

obeisance, " made a half-turn to the right." To one alone, old " Father Gérard," in his Breton peasant's dress, did Louis XVI address a syllable. " Good morning, good man ! " said he ; a condescension on which the old man was warmly congratulated. The deputies left the palace " with nerves rather on edge." Their feelings were considerably chilled.

The ceremony on May 4 produced a better impression. It consisted in a procession of the Blessed Sacrament, to be The Procession attended by the Court and all the three Orders. of May 4. This had attracted the whole of Paris to Versailles, where people let their windows for three louis each. The Court made a splendid show : the King wore the full robes of the Order of the Holy Ghost, the Queen was blazing with jewels, their suite was also resplendent. The Nobles of the States-General wore coats made of cloth of gold, and white-plumed hats " *à la* Henri IV," the superior Clergy were robed in red and violet mantles : the parish priests and the Third Estate alone appeared as a dark mass, in which one body was hardly distinguishable from the other, for the priests wore their black cassocks and cloaks, and the Third Order had been obliged, not without some feelings of bitterness, to don garments of a uniformly sable hue, which looked, as one deputy declares, " like the dress worn by the Oratorians ! "

For three mortal hours the assembly waited in the Cathedral of Saint Louis for the King. One deputy began to grumble : " No single individual should keep a whole nation waiting ! " The general company avenged itself by acclaiming the Duc d'Orléans, who, in accordance with a scenario deliberately planned at the Palais-Royal, did not make his entry with the Court, but came as a deputy. On the other hand, when some voices raised cheers for the Queen, others called out " Shame ! " When the princes made their entry, there was an icy silence. For a moment, the tapers carried by the deputies might have suggested the lighted candles round a bier !

The procession set out : at the corners of the canopy, walked four young princes : their names, as we read them, stir our hearts with memories of sixty years of civil strife ; Berry and Enghien, one doomed to die by the assassin's knife, the other by Napoleon's bullets, Angoulême, to be known for a short hour as Louis XIX, and Chartres, one day to reign as Louis Philippe.

La Fare, Bishop of Nancy, who preached the sermon, read the Court a lecture. The deputies applauded; once the Queen bit her lip; the King went to sleep—he did better perhaps than if he had listened. But Louis XIV would never have dozed, and would, no doubt, have packed La Fare off to Nancy that very evening, there to meditate on the dangers of reading lectures.

Louis XVI, having gone to sleep, was in a position to declare himself well pleased: he showed a smiling face, and this did as well as a formal approval of the bishop's words. The deputies were delighted: the " good king " was retrieving his position. There could be no doubt that he realized his people's sufferings, as denounced by the sacred orator. At the morrow's sitting, no doubt, he would point out the remedy, and, as a first step, would invite the three Orders to combine and thus work out the common good of the kingdom. On that evening of May 4, Versailles was illuminated, and confidence reigned everywhere.

At eight o'clock the next morning the deputies passed into the *Salle des Menus Plaisirs :* this hall in which the Revolution First sitting in was to be made bore the name of the monarch's the Menus *Menus Plaisirs* (diversions)! The calling of the Plaisirs. roll by the heralds lasted till one o'clock in the afternoon: for 1700 deputies were crowded together in front of the platform hung with violet velvet studded with fleur-de-lis on which the throne was set, under a splendid canopy.

At one o'clock, the King made his entry: everybody rose, every head was uncovered: the Queen followed, and took the armchair prepared for her at her husband's side: behind them stood the ministers, among them the Keeper of the Seals in violet silk. Louis XVI took his seat and read a speech of no great length, keeping his plumed hat on his head the while. In his loud rough voice he set forth his rights, for the most part: though he had not hesitated to restore the custom of holding the States-General, he alone must decide as to the subjects of their deliberations: it was absolutely indispensable that the

53

finances of the country should be put in order. That done, were the States to sit periodically ? Was the voting of the Orders to be by individual, as the granting of the double representation gave grounds for hoping ? Nobody knew ! The King gave an assurance that his subjects might hope everything from his " sentiments." All this was very vague. Our thoughts fly back, as we read his speech, to those vigorous and familiar words spoken by Henri IV to the States in 1593 : " I have called you together to receive your counsel, to believe it and follow it . . . : the strong love I bear my subjécts, my great desire to add to my name two noble titles, those of the liberator and restorer of this State, will make things easy and honour-able. . . ." Had Louis XVI simply re-edited his ancestor's discourse, the thunders of applause would have shaken the very walls of the Salle des Menus Plaisirs !

But some applause there was, and the Keeper of the Seals, Barentin, seemed to give a promise of good things : " all titles were to be merged in that of citizen " : all should be equal in the matter of taxation. This was good : but his voice was so low, and so monkish (*si capucine*) that a full quarter of his audience failed to catch what he said.

Next came Necker, whose speech, which lasted two hours, fell very far below the general expectation. Applauded, when he began, by an audience which trusted him, the minister grew first emphatic, and then tired, and the close of his address was read for him by a clerk. His long-winded sermon satisfied nobody : " He said nothing at all about a Constitution, and seems to accept the division of the three Orders," writes one discontented deputy, and another says : " After having led the Third Estate into exaggerated opinions by his ' *Result*,' . he now seems to be contradicting himself."

At half-past four in the afternoon, the sitting closed : and in spite of the general disappointment, the feeling of loyalty was still so strong that the gathering sent up a universal shout of " *Vive le Roy !* " Even the Queen, who had not been cheered for months, was acclaimed again and again, so gracious was her curtsey of acknowledgment. After all, this was no more than a moment of uncertainty. The majority of the Third Estate hoped for a peaceful settlement of the difficulty the

King had not ventured to decide. Others took a darker view. "The battle has begun," wrote a deputy from Lorraine.

On that May 5, Louis XVI had been neither Louis XIV, the imperious arbiter, nor Henri IV, the conciliator.

*   *   *   *   *

And the authorities had shown as little foresight in small matters as in great. One of their most imprudent actions was that by allotting separate apartments to the first two Orders for their deliberations, they left the Third Estate in the common Hall of the States-General, where, just as it most desired, it took on the appearance of a National Assembly.

By nine o'clock on May 6 it had promptly taken up its quarters. Once gathered, there was a moment of perplexity Session of amongst the members: they were not all so May 6. resolute as most people imagine—many, as they themselves were to acknowledge, were afraid of the "hot-heads." But the majority—and they were very loyal to the King—thought that as he had not ventured on any open pronouncement against the cumulative vote, his private opinion was favourable to it, and he was only waiting for them to force his hand. Wherefore that must be done. Only in this horde of five hundred deputies, who possessed neither leaders nor orators, there was as yet no mutual understanding. Yet one idea was evolved by the whole gathering: every member of it desired to see the three Orders formed into one single Assembly, and accordingly they would not constitute themselves a "Third Estate." The two other Orders might possibly, without any pressure from the Third, decide on a common examination into the powers of all three. It would be better to wait.

Within a few moments news was brought that the motion in favour of this step brought forward by the liberal members of the two other "Chambers," had been lost in both. But the numbers were not disheartening. Though only 47 out of 188 nobles had voted for the proposal, 144 of the clergy had been for it, out of 247. In this case ten more votes would have won the battle.

But Malouet desired to adhere to the ancient practice. Distracted by the difficulty of the situation, the assembled deputies knew not what course to adopt. Suddenly a strange figure appeared on the rostrum, gesticulating fiercely, a figure with a powerful flushed face ravaged by passion, fiery bloodshot eyes, and a bull neck ; a name ran round the crowd, " Riquetti de Mirabeau " ! The *bourgeois* distrusted this fallen noble ; " he was in disgrace," says Dumont : they had hissed when he took his place amongst the deputies of the Third Estate on May 5. And at this solemn moment when, for the first time, he mounted the steps of the rostrum he had resolved to make his spring-board, and meanwhile his pedestal, he was frigidly received. A tribune after the manner of the Gracchi, whose praises he had sung, he would have no agreement with the Order that had cast him out : no official nor semi-official suggestion to the privileged Chambers : by sheer inertia they would end by overcoming the two higher Orders, already divided amongst themselves !

Mounier had no particular affection for this tribune, in whom he scented a despot. Was the Third Estate to be made the instrument of the hatreds of this renegade ? He induced the Assembly to decide that its members were " authorized " to wait on the two other Chambers, and plead for amalgamation with them. He himself headed this semi-official deputation.

The Clergy received it with friendliness : for several hours the cause Mounier had come to defend had been pleaded by the democrats among the parish priests, and by six prelates— among them the venerable Lefranc de Pompignan, the great respect enjoyed by whom was founded on a blameless episcopate of sixty years. Commissaries were appointed, who were shortly to convey the reply of the " Chamber."

The Nobles, meanwhile, were courteous : they listened politely to the request. Some of their number accompanied Mounier and his friends to the door of the apartment, and told him " Our hearts go with you ! " They were indeed the smiling patricians we see in the old pastel portraits !

The Third Estate waited, and appointed no president, being resolved that above all things there should be no formal constitution of their Chamber till the " dissidents " (the two privileged Orders) came " to take their places " in the general

Hall. When a deputation consisting of the commissaries or the Clergy brought their answer, which was in the negative,

The Third Estate refuses to constitute itself. an attempt was made to instal them in the places intended for their Order : " Your seats are empty ! " was the cry. The Third Estate followed these tactics with a perseverance and an intelligence which throw a yet clearer light on the embarrassment of the other Orders, and the mediocre policy pursued by the Government.

The Government, in fact, kept in the background. It may be that in its alarm at the tendencies manifested by the deputies, **Negotiations with the other Chambers.** it was already thinking of making the disagreement between the three Orders a pretext for dissolving the States-General. For ten days there was a perpetual interchange of embassies between one " Chamber " and another. Men may well have wondered whether such things as King, Ministry, or Executive, existed in Versailles !

Those ten days were critical ; the Third Estate grew bitter and angry. When, at the end of them, the Ministry proposed a compromise—the verification of the powers of the States by commissaries deputed by the three Orders—the Third Order refused what it would very probably have accepted at first.

The King's circle found in this refusal a pretext for a cry against " sedition." Louis, uncertain and vacillating, had fallen into the hands of the princes (to be understood here as the Queen and the Comte d'Artois, then in momentary agreement). The little Dauphin had died on June 9, and the King, in very great grief, had retired with " the family," to Marly. The opportunity for lecturing him was not neglected : the Third Estate, he was told, had revolted " against the Constitution of the kingdom " : it must be reduced " to obedience." On June 14, when the senior member of the Commons, Bailly, waited on the King, to present an explanatory memorandum from the Third Estate, he had a harsh reception. " I will read the memorandum of the Third Estate," said the King, in the rough tone he always used when he was moved, " I will inform it of my intentions." This deliberate ungraciousness was very much felt by " the Commons."

They believed they would win, if the executive power was not brought into play. And indeed the disunion among the privileged Orders was increasing. The "forty-seven" were gaining recruits among the nobles: and as a consequence, a lively feeling of irritation had sprung up amongst the majority who were perpetually talking, now, of "drawing the sword." This idea was encouraged by the conservative section of the Clergy. When the president of this Order, Cardinal de Larochefoucauld, received the delegates of the Nobles on May 30, he addressed them as follows: "Your forefathers founded our churches and defended them. . . . You will now be the defenders of your country!" But already certain prelates who had at first been hostile to "union" were looking about for a compromise. And as for the parish priests, they were raging. When an Abbé abused the Third Estate, one priest called out, "Hold your tongue!" and another, looking straight at the Abbé Maury, one of the forty members of the Academy, declared "The village priests may not have the talents of Academicians, but they have at least the good sense of villagers!" Jallet, who was one of the leaders, snubbed the bishops, "In this place, my lords, we are all equal!" The rugged Grégoire gathered some sixty democrat priests about him every evening, and was busily paving the way to a "rupture between the two Clergies." The Third Estate was aware that all these divisions existed: they justified its boldness, and increased it.

It had been strengthened and confirmed, on May 25, by the tardy arrival of the deputies of Paris, all of them determined Liberals. At their head was the aged Bailly, "a member of three Academies," an astronomer who was about to cast himself into a well. But he aroused less curiosity than the Abbé Joseph Sieyès. This Abbé, a deserter, like Mirabeau, from his own order, arrived at Versailles with an aureole about his head: many deputies regarded him as a prophet. "What must the Third Estate be? . . . Everything!" Even a slighter tribute would have been well received. He made his entry with all the assurance of a pontiff who was also a philosopher. From the first chapter of this history to its last, he will perpetually reappear, and always

Arrival of Bailly and Sieyès.

in this dual character, full of himself, with a touch of mystery about him, encircled by prestige. On that first occasion, it seemed as though he were preparing to open at once the tabernacle of his own thoughts and the cave of the tempest.

It was Mirabeau who informed the Assembly that " a deputy from Paris " would bring forward an important motion on June 12. Sieyès made his appearance, cold and imposing, and read his proposal for an address to the privileged Orders, " summoning them," for the last time, to come and join the Third. As no member of the " dissident " Chambers put in his appearance, the Commons decided to proceed without their assistance to the verification of the powers of all deputies.

The Nobility having received the address, decided once more against it, by a majority of 173 votes : 79 were cast in its favour. The Clergy delayed their answer. And thus, when the Third Estate met on the morning of June 13, it perceived, with a sense of real anxiety, that the benches reserved for the " privileged " Orders were still empty. This anxiety was well justified. Since not a single adhesion had been given in, the Third Estate remained that day, as it had been on the previous one, a " Chamber " in revolt against its two fellows.

Suddenly, a noise was heard at the entrance of the hall— shouts and plaudits : three parish priests, all from Poitou, **The Clergy** Lecesve, Ballard, and Jallet, had made their **joins the Third** appearance. Jallet spoke : " Preceded by the **Estate.** torch of reason, led by our love for the public weal, and by the cry of our consciences, we come to join our fellow-citizens and our brothers ! " There was a tempest of rejoicing. " I clapped my hands," wrote Biauzat that evening, " with a violence which showed me that the heart imparts a healthy vivacity to our movements." Tears were shed, embraces exchanged. These three country priests were no great thing, yet they were everything. Others were certain to follow in their wake. A breach had been made in the fort of privilege ! A new fact had been demonstrated : " The representatives of the Nation were here ! " The very next day, nine more ecclesiastics came, and were cordially embraced. This was the first step of the Revolution, thus did it sally forth from the presbyteries it was destined to lay waste !

From that moment the Third Estate was ripe for the boldest undertakings. When the roll was called on the 15th, twelve priests answered to their names. Thenceforward the Assembly looked on itself as the sole body representing the Nation. This had to be solemnly affirmed. A stirring debate ensued. On the 17th, one of the deputies for Lorraine suggested the title of *National Assembly*, and supported his proposal by an argument the brutality of which reveals the rapid progress of the " sedition " : it was quite unnecessary to wait for the King's sanction, he said : *" had the United States waited for the sanction of the King of England ? "* This was a rebel cry ! Individualist though he was, Sieyès knew how to take what he found ; he pounced on the formula, and the title *National Assembly* was applauded and carried by acclamation. " The great step has been taken at last ! " writes one of the deputies : as a matter of precaution, the cry of " Long live the King " was duly raised But if the King were allowed to " live," would he let the " National Assembly " " live " too ? Talleyrand, who even at this period, was playing a double game, asserts that he advised Louis XVI, that very evening, to punish this " insolent usurpation." But the King thought that if he were to dissolve it, " the Assembly would not obey " : and " there was no means of forcing it." Yet many deputies expected a dissolution, and prepared to depart. " We shall soon be back in our provinces ! " wrote one.

To their great surprise, nothing happened. They grew bolder, and on the 17th they proclaimed that the " taxes, though they had been illegally levied and exacted, should continue to be levied in the same manner until the day on which the Assembly should break up," but that " once that day had passed, the Assembly ordered and decreed that any levy of taxes that had not been specifically, formally, and freely voted by the Assembly, should at once cease in every province in the Kingdom." Four committees were appointed to deal with food supply, verifications, drafting of decrees, and standing orders. The country was on the high-road to Revolution.

The Nobles were in a state of violent excitement : " in an incredible condition of ferment," relates a member of that body, " expecting to have to fight, believing there was a plan to massacre them." Challenges were exchanged between Liberals and those who would not hear of compromise: when the minority deputed Clermont-Tonnerre to make a fresh proposal for union with the Third Estate, Cazalès said something about "deserters;" Caylus sprang to the floor of the apartment, sword in hand, every man of the minority prepared to draw his weapon, and the president broke up the sitting.

That same day, while the Clergy were sitting in debate, the Bishop of Chartres made a vehement speech in favour of union. On the 19th, the "Chamber" met again, resolved to reach some definite decision. A huge crowd was besieging the "Hotel des Menus," when the window of the apartment on the first storey, in which the Clergy held their sittings, was suddenly thrown open—it was six o'clock in the evening—and a priest appeared, shouting, "*Won! Won!*" There was a "noise like thunder" that reached the Palace itself. Wild with excitement, the crowd of spectators fell on each other's necks. By a majority of 149, the "Chamber" of the Clergy had at last voted the "union." The departure of the members was a tumultuous business: the "fusionist" prelates were seized and borne along in triumph : there were six of them, the Bishops and Archbishops of Vienne, Bordeaux, Chartres, Coutances and Rodez, and the Abbot of Prémontré. Behind them, shouting, laughing, crying, all at once, marched 143 priests and monks. "Long live the good bishops!" yelled the mob: Lefranc de Pompignan, "that patriarch whom we would all have gladly embraced," proceeded to the Hall of the Third Estate : he was greeted with wild acclamations. "We were all weeping . . . the spectators' handkerchiefs were wet with their tears." Nobody dreamt of the future, of the Clergy, first to be stripped, and then forced to choose between schism and proscription—and the Carmelite Convent, to be bespattered, only three years later, with the blood of those very priests! Meanwhile, the "anti-revolutionary" prelates, hooted and insulted, hurried to Marly, and there besought the King to protect "his" Clergy and "his" Nobles.

"Everybody about the Queen and the King is on the side of the Nobles and the Clergy," wrote one of the foreign ambassadors, on June 18. Rigorous measures were decided on: there should be a Royal Sitting, which all the three Orders should attend, and the King would command them to sit apart! The King might (perhaps) have done so on May 5, but on June 20, the attempt came too late. Men had lived a year in those six weeks.

The date of the Royal Sitting was fixed for the 23rd: but as there were to be no more " scandalous " scenes before that day, the assembly hall should be closed till then. So on the morning of the 20th, when the deputies arrived, they found the doors locked in their faces. The upholsterers, they were told, were preparing things for the sitting on the 23rd: this puerile pretext transformed a tardy display of firmness into a dubious and timorous demonstration.

For a moment there was considerable dismay: then a cry was raised, " To the Tennis Court! " This building, in which The sitting in the princes sometimes played, was close by. the Tennis Into it the assembled deputies poured, and in an Court. instant the huge bare space was filled. Bailly was lifted on to a table, and presided over the meeting: round the astronomer's feet, the crowd of deputies surged, ready, as it seemed, for action of the extremest nature: Sieyès was anxious the whole body should proceed to Paris. Mounier was later to plead the anxiety into which this excessive excitement had thrown him, as an explanation of the celebrated motion he then brought forward. The deputy for Grenoble, who was to be driven, some three months later, into the ranks of the reactionary party, deceived himself as to his own attitude. A liberal by conviction, he found himself, on that morning of June 20, face to face with the threat of a *coup d'état*, and the instincts of the man of Vizille * woke within him. The Assembly must be called on to take an oath " never to separate, and to meet wherever circumstances might make it necessary for it to meet, *until the Constitution had been established and set on a firm foundation.*" A great shout of assent greeted the

---

* On July 21, 1788, in the local Assembly of Vizille, Mounier and Barnave brought forward and passed their famous motion to the effect that " the Provinces refused to pay taxes until these had been discussed by their representatives in the States-General of the kingdom of France."

drawing up of this motion, and it was soon covered with signatures. Seven (the only ones present) out of the nineteen priests who had been sharing the deliberations for the past week, signed their names. Not a single noble was there, whatever some persons may have asserted, and not a single monk either, though for the sake of picturesqueness, David (whose famous picture, indeed, is exceedingly inaccurate in various other details) has placed the white-robed figure of Gerle, a Carthusian, in the foreground of his canvas. Every member of the Third Estate save one signed, " carried away " (as Guilhermy afterwards said, beating his breast), " by a wave of unspeakable enthusiasm." A few hours later, the deputies, wild with excitement, were busily spreading the news of their oath all over Versailles. Every man of them thought himself a " Brutus."

The Comte d'Artois thought he was making a very clever stroke when he ordered the Tennis Court to be reserved for his match, the next day. The blow was soon parried. The parish priest of Saint-Louis opened his church " to the Nation." Here, on the 21st, the Third Estate assembled, and for the first time two nobles, Virieu and Blacons, appeared in its ranks. While the plaudits of the Assembly filled the nave of the great church, the choir gates opened, and the aged Archbishop of Vienne, with his 148 colleagues of the Clergy in his train, issued from them. Thus, on the very eve of the Royal Session, the cause of the Court was hopelessly compromised.

" A Bed of Justice," the coming sitting was called : the King's mind was said to be very firmly made up, and Necker was supposed to have bowed to his will : the minister was not present at the session. The princes felt sure of victory : troops were drawn up all round the place of meeting, when the deputies, summoned by Orders, entered the building. After feverish discussion at the Breton Club, then in its infancy, on the preceding night, a policy of passive resistance had been resolved on.

The King entered. The Comte d'Artois seemed " full of pride," but Louis " appeared sad and gloomy." He spoke, and The Royal here and there his voice, which " shook and Session on trembled," grew very rough. His declaration June 24. agreed in every particular with the wishes of the privileged classes. The " anti-historic " alliance, as it has been very justly called, between the Monarchy and the Nobility was formulated in the presence of the "dismayed Nation." The Estates were to deliberate in their separate Chambers : they were to deliberate on questions of taxation, but they were to have nothing to do with "any business connected with the ancient and constitutional rights of the three Orders, the form of the Constitution to be given at the next States-General, feudal and seignorial property, and the just rights and titular prerogatives of the first two Orders." Thus, at the very hour when a Revolution against the aristocracy was in process of preparation, this scion of Kings who, from the first of the Capets to the last of the Bourbons, had always fought against the feudal system, compromised himself with that system, and doomed himself to sink with it. In the hearts of some members of the Third Estate, "grief and indignation struggled for mastery."

The King had said "This is my will." The Assembly had to break up. Only the night before, the saying had been current : "Cy veult le roy, cy veult la loi" (The King's will is law). Here was one of those solemn junctures which make men feel that times have changed.

Louis XVI had said all were to depart. He himself had risen from his seat and left the hall, and the trumpets had sounded as he got into his coach. The Nobility, triumphant, but somewhat uneasy, had followed him in a body : since the King had spoken, even the dissidents had gone out with the rest of their Order. The Clergy, too, had departed in a body.

But in the centre of the hall the Third Estate, "in gloomy silence," still held its ground.

Suddenly Dreux-Brézé, Grand Master of the King's Household, in full Court dress, appeared upon the scene : "His The Third Majesty requested the deputies of the Third Estate refuses Estate to retire." Deadly pale, Bailly replied to withdraw. that "the Assembly would consider the question." Behind the Grand Master soldiers were drawn up beside the door—a picket of the Gardes Françaises, and another of the Swiss Guard. Then Mirabeau saw his chance. He threw himself forward, his shoulders heaving, his bloodshot eyes blazing : "Sir," he cried, "go tell your master that nothing but bayonets will drive us out from here ! " Some declare his words were more violent still, others, again, quote but one brief phrase.

Dreux-Brèzé carried back the answer, which smelt of gunpowder. All eyes were turned upon the King. He made a **The King gives** weary gesture : " They mean to stay ! . . . Well **way.** then, . . . let them stay ! " Fear was at the bottom of it all : " The King and Queen are in mortal terror," wrote Morris on the preceding evening, " and the conclusion I draw is that there will be more concessions." As a matter of fact, they dreaded that the troops might refuse to use their bayonets.

Meanwhile Sieyès had not lost this splendid opportunity for pompous rhetoric. " To-day," he said to the Third Estate," you are what you were yesterday : let us deliberate ! " Eighty of the priests had come back. The deliberations proceeded : it was decided that the enactments already made should be maintained, and the deputies' persons declared sacred. The King had no thought of violating them. Necker had threatened to retire, and a pretext for retreat was thus provided.

On the evening of the 23rd Necker was still minister, and the next day the Third Estate was sitting again, and the majority **Amalgamation** of the Clergy had joined it once more. On the **of the Three** 25th, forty-seven nobles came too, greeted by **Estates.** shouts and tears of joy. When the Duc d'Orléans' name was called, and he answered " Here," the excitement became delirium.

The Court continued irresolute. There was disobedience everywhere : some talk of calling out the troops was heard, but, as a letter written that day assures us, " the defection of the troops is a certain thing : the Gardes Françaises have given out that they belong to the Third Estate, and that they will only fire on nobles and ecclesiastics : the officers cannot control their men : one of them has had his ears boxed by a soldier." Disheartened, Louis XVI now wrote that he desired the amalgamation of the Three Estates. On June 27, the whole of the Clergy, and—acting upon the King's letter—the Nobility, joined the Third Estate. There was a general sense of relief : the recalcitrant nobles were received with courteous deference :

" Proofs after letters ! " these belated members were called.
" The Revolu- There was a universal feeling of emotion. " The
tion is over ! " Revolution is over ! " wrote one Frenchman.
" It will not have cost one drop of blood ! "

Louis XVI believed himself still a King. But he was King
no longer. Neither the law nor the power were in the King's
hand, now Both had " slipped " into the hands of the
nation !

SOURCES. Brette, *Recueil des actes relatif à la convocation des États
Généraux*, 1894–1904 ; Aulard, *Société des Jacobins*, I, 1889 ; The Deputies :
Duquesnoy, *Journal*, 1894 ; Gaultier de Biauzat, *Correspondance*, 1890 ;
Abbé Jallet, *Journal*, 1871 ; Silléry (in Vaissière's *Lettres d'Aristocrates*) ;
Maupetit, *Lettres* (*Rev. Rev.*, IX) ; Rabaut, *Correspondance* (*Rev. Fr.*,
1898) ; anonymous noble deputy, *Lettres* (*Rev. Rev.*, II) ; Virieu, *Lettres*
(in Castellane's *Gentilhommes democrates*) ; Bouillé, *Lettres* (*Rev. Rev.*,
XVI) ; Bouchette, *Lettres*, 1909 ; Abbé Barbolin, *Lettres*, 1911 ; Lofficial,
Lettres (*Nouv. Rev. Retr.*, 1897) ; P. de Vaissière, *Lettres d'Aristocrates*,
1907 ; Gouverneur Morris *Journal* (Pariset ed., 1901) ; *idem.*, *Lettres*
(in Esmein, *Gouverneur Morris*), 1906 ; Morellet, *Correspondance*, 1898 ;
Baron de Staël-Holstein, *Correspondance*, 1881. Mounier, *Recherche sur
les Causes*, etc., 1792 ; Ferrières, *Mémoires*, 1799 ; Malouet, *Mémoires*, I,
1868 ; Talleyrand, *Mémoires*, 1894 ; Lameth, *Appendice de l'Histoire
de la Constituante*, 1828 ; Guilhermy, *Papiers*, 1895 ; Bailly, *Mémoires*,
1821 ; Mallet du Pan, *Mémoires*, I, 1895 ; Mme. de Chastenay, *Mémoires*,
1896 ; Dumont, *Souvenirs*, 1832 ; Abbé Vallet, *Souvenirs* (*Nouv. Rev.
Retr.* XVIII) ; Mme. de Staël, *Considérations*, 1823 ; Esmein, *Gouverneur Morris*, 1906.

WORKS. De Lanzac de Laborie, *Mounier*, 1887 ; Néton, *Sieyès*,
1900 ; Charavay, *La Fayette*, 1898 ; Cahen, *Condorcet*, 1904 ; Sicard,
L'ancien Clergé de France, 1900 ; Dejean, *Un projet de discours de Louis
XVI par Necker* (*Rev. Rétr.*, 1909) ; Aulard, *La Serment du Jeu de Paume*
(*Etudes*, I) ; Castellane, *Gentilshommes démocrates*, 1875

CHAPTER II

THE FOURTEENTH OF JULY

Troops pour in. The dismissal of Necker. Paris during the summer of 1789. The Coming of the Bandits. Famine and insurrection. Desmoulins and the Palais-Royal. Attitude of the Garde Française. The " electors " assemble. The *Bourgeoisie* arms itself against the Populace. July 12 at the Palais-Royal. The charges on the Place Louis XV. The exploits of the 13th. The night of July 13–14. The taking of the Bastille. The lust for blood. July 14 and 15 at Versailles. The Assembly approves the rioters. The King at the Assembly. The Deputies and the King at the Hôtel-de-Ville. " Has the King signed his capitulation ? "

" **D**IEU des Juifs, tu l'emportes ! " (God of the Jews, thou hast conquered) cried the Abbé de Montesquiou, when, at the King's command, he took his way to the general Hall of Assembly. The words betray the luke-warm nature of his enthusiasm. The majority of the nobles longed for revenge, but the King was apparently delighted : he received the deputation from the National Assembly in the Palace, and this time every door was set wide open. " He had an air of joy : he looked like a child that had been taken out of its swaddling clothes ! " In reality he felt he was stripped of his weapons. " The sword has slipped out of the monarch's hands and he does not realize it,"—these words were written on July 1. He was doing his best to recover it ; all round Paris troops were being massed. Lameth has described Versailles, with the soldiers marching across the Place d'Armes amidst the dubious silence of the crowd.

.The deputies thought their safety was threatened : they compared themselves, with a certain exaggeration, to the Roman senators in their curule chairs. They were engaged in voting the preliminary clauses of the Constitution, but the

The King's acquiescence.

Troops brought into Versailles.

question that demanded their attention most urgently was that of food supply. This matter, alarming for everybody, was especially so for them. For famine was increasing every day, and soon the cry in the streets would be that " when there was one King, there had been bread, at all events, but now that there were 1300 kings, there was none ! " Report said that the Parisian populace was beginning to grow restless : the members of the Assembly, who were anything but democrats, dreaded this exceedingly, but they were set between two terrors, for the troops which the Court, in view of possible disturbances, had been collecting ever since July 1 filled them with a constantly growing alarm. A heavy atmosphere seemed to brood over Versailles, a condition well described by a contemporary writer as a " period of disturbance and gloom," interspersed with " false alarms which fostered suspicion and irritability." Yet the troops were intended for Paris rather than for Versailles. This did not prevent the Assembly from requesting their withdrawal on the 8th.

One fact alone did somewhat reassure these anxious minds; as long as Necker was there, nobody would dare to lay a finger
Dismissal of on the representatives of the nation : for Necker
Necker. had completely recovered the popularity he had so nearly lost. Now on July 11, the Assembly was informed that the Genevan Minister, " that —— foreigner," as the Comte d'Artois called him, had just received his dismissal from the King. His fall had been brought about by the Comte d'Artois and his cabal—" and by the Queen as well," so wrote the Baron de Staël, the disgraced Minister's own son-in-law. The new ministers were believed,—incorrectly, as it happened—to be resolute opponents of the Revolution : they were Broglie, a man of very enlightened mind, Breteuil, a great noble whose antecedents should have sufficed to ensure his popularity, and Foulon, abominably slandered by those who ascribed to him the horrible remark: "If they have no bread, let them eat hay ! " But too many people found it to their interest to slander the King's ministers; " Odious fellows," wrote that excellent son-in-law the Baron de Staël. The dismissal of Necker came on the Assembly like a thunderclap. " The King's abominable counsellors have at last obtained his dismissal ! " writes Sillery,

one of the leaders of the Orléans group, on the 13th. That was the general view. The 12th being a Sunday, there was no session of the Assembly, but as soon as that of the 13th opened, a protest was raised. Grégoire spoke with great violence : the Assembly, he said, " must proceed to chastise the authors of the dismissal." A deputation waited on the King, and the Archbishop of Vienne, in the presence of the new ministers, ventured to tell his Majesty in the name of the Assembly " that it would never cease to regret the former minister, and would never feel any confidence in the new ones." Louis XVI made a curt reply. There was a fresh debate in the hall of the Menus Plaisirs ; the responsibility of the King's counsellors, "whatever their rank might be," was affirmed— this was a threat against the Comte d'Artois—and it was decided that the Assembly should sit permanently, listening to the reports from Paris. At that moment, indeed, Paris was in a state of convulsion, and all interest had been diverted from the debates of an Assembly which was, after all, powerless, and was riveted on the popular drama in course of enactment from the Palais-Royal to the Bastille.

*   *   *   *   *

The dismissal of Necker had come at a moment when the minds of Parisians were already in a state of violent excitement. **Paris during the summer of 1789.** A band of men within the walls of the city were watching the opportunity to serve their own ends by turning the terrified citizens against the regular government.

Ever since the beginning of April, Paris and its immediate neighbourhood had been living in a state of terror, all the more poignant because it was undefined. It was certainly not the " enterprises of the Court " that filled these hearts with alarm. The whole country was in the grip of that mysterious fear, a sort of national hysteria, which historians will never be able to explain.

In Paris this mighty fear dated not from June, but from the month of April. In that month it had become known that the **The Bandits.** Ile-de-France was full of robbers. These bands had flowed in the direction of Paris during the spring of 1789. From all the suburbs of the great city there came reports of pillage and incendiarism : supplies were cut off. Sometimes the bandits would force their way through the city gates and join the rough element in uneasy Paris, whence the Lieutenancy of Police, itself suffering from the general unrest, failed to dislodge them. The terrified *bourgeois* found themselves left defenceless just at the critical moment when the old order was crumbling away, and the new had not yet come into existence.

Though the population of Paris loathed these ruffians, yet it was likely to become their easy prey. The general misery was terrible, and the prevalent anarchy had increased it. Hunger is apt to go to the head : and the excessive heat to which letters written in the course of July 1789 refer, had fired men's brains rather than cowed their courage. In the gardens of the Palais-Royal, " as full as an egg," a young tribune, Camille Desmoulins by name, his face distorted by hate, was endeavouring to stir up the people with his outcry for a war upon society. " The beast has fallen into the snare, let us strike it down ! Never have victors been offered a richer prey ! Forty thousand palaces, town houses and country mansions will be the reward of valour ! "

Camille Desmoulins.

This same " valour " caused the *bourgeois* great alarm. As the central authority was apparently defenceless, they had set up a kind of illegal committee, the " Committee of Electors," to which—a fresh proof of anarchy—the Communal authorities, in their weakness, had allotted an office in the Hôtel-de-Ville. This " Committee," which had no legitimate powers, held sittings every night, —a fact in itself indicating a state of chaos, but which was almost legitimized by the anarchy existing in all quarters, from the highest to the lowest. For it was to ensure the safety of Paris against the successors of Mandrin and the friends of Desmoulins that the electors of Bailly and Sieyès slipped, almost with its connivance, into the place of the civic authority. And these *bourgeois*, true liberals though they were, were more disturbed by the meetings in the Palais-Royal than by the enterprises of the Comte d'Artois.

" Committee of Electors."

One great cause of alarm at this moment was the extra-

ordinary attitude of the Gardes Françaises. They were assiduous
Attitude of the attendants at the Palais-Royal gatherings, where
Gardes Fran- like the Invalides, they were regularly entertained.
çaisse. "The people," said these old warriors, "had no
reason to fear the soldiers : the troops belonged to the nation
which gave them their pay, and not to the King, who claimed
to command them." As they left the Palais-Royal, the troops
would shout "All's well ! Do what you like ! " to the delighted
populace.

It is not surprising that these men should soon have passed
all bounds. On June 24, two companies refused to obey orders.
Their colonel, du Châtelet—the true type of the high-born
officer whose mind had been warped by " philosophy "—failed
seriously in the performance of his duty. Not daring to treat
the rebels with severity, he simply confined them to barracks ;
then, when the taint of insubordination began to spread to the
other companies, he applied the same treatment to the whole
regiment. Meanwhile, on June 28, in view of probable and
imminent popular disturbances, ammunition was most imprudently served out to these dangerous men, and they were
warned that they would most likely be called on to restore
order. They threw down their muskets, broke out of barracks,
and rushed away to warn the Palais-Royal, shouting, " We are
the soldiers of the nation ! Long live the Third Estate ! " They
returned to their barracks that evening, drunk with popularity
and liquor : they were arrested and conveyed to the Abbaye.
But on the next day but one, the mob, urged on by another great
popular leader, Loustalot, rose, attacked the Abbaye, released
the prisoners, and kept them inside the Palais-Royal, guarded by
" good citizens," until the day when, the Assembly having intervened, the King was weak enough to pardon the " heroes," who
from that moment believed they might do as they chose.

* * * * *

It will be readily understood that the government in such
circumstances as these, thought it well to march other troops
Formation of on Paris. The least reactionary authority in
the Garde the world would have been forced to do so. At
Nationale. Versailles, on the 4th, a deputy whose views were
of the most advanced kind, made no attempt to deny the bad

behaviour of the Garde Française. The Parisians felt that
this extraordinary garrison ensured their safety so insufficiently,
that on the 25th, the "Electors," sitting at the Hôtel-de-Ville,
decided to raise a citizen militia, the future National Guard, not
at all, as historians and their readers have believed for the last
hundred years, as a protection against the Court, but as a shield
against the robbers, whom they dreaded—as the "Electors'"
records prove—far more than any other danger. The robbers
were, in fact, to force their way into Paris, to the general
terror, in the night of the 12th–13th of July.

They came at a moment when political effervescence, now
at the boiling-point, was easily made to serve their ends.

On the 12th the dismissal of Necker had become generally
known. This dismissal did really impart a new significance to
July 12 at the the massing of troops on the outskirts of the city
Palais-Royal. and on the Champ-de-Mars. Even in the *salons*,
the conviction was universal, if we may believe Morris, that " the
States-General were to be dissolved and bankruptcy declared."

On that day the Palais-Royal surged like an angry sea.
The alarm that swept over it was more justified than that
felt at Versailles. If the Maréchal de Broglie really intended
to purge the city of the impure elements, the gardens of the
Palais-Royal were likely to become empty! All of a sudden
a name was spoken, a name that was then the most popular
of all : Desmoulins ! Camille bounded on to a chair, a tall,
bilious-looking, sinewy fellow, wildly excited. " To arms!"
he cried. " Not a moment must be lost ! I have just come
back from Versailles. M. Necker has been dismissed! His
dismissal sounds the tocsin of the Saint-Bartholomew of
patriots ! To-night all the Swiss and German battalions in
the Champ-de-Mars will come out and slaughter us ! We
have but one chance left—to fly to arms ! " The answer was
a thunderous roar. Ten thousand men, a threatening army,
every element of disorder within its ranks, hemmed the palace
in. Some badge of recognition they must have : each man
stuck a leaf from the chestnut-trees in his hat-band or his
buttonhole; for four-and-twenty hours the green cockade was
to be the rallying sign. Then the huge human waterspout
burst on the terrified town.

Some of the rioters had laid hands on busts of Necker and of the Duc d'Orléans, in Curtius' gallery of portraits in wax. Conflict in the Behind these trophies the procession formed. On Place Louis XV.the Place Vendôme the mob stoned a detachment of the Royal Allemand regiment : on the Place Louis XV (now the Place de la Concorde) they met a regiment of dragoons : at its head rode the Prince de Lambesc, of the House of Lorraine— " vile Lambesc," as one of the rioters, Fournier " the American," calls him.

The Pont de la Concorde was in process of construction, and part of the square was covered with heavy building stones. The crowd, to escape the expected charge, took refuge behind them. Others got away on to the Terrace of the Tuileries. " The sanguinary Lambesc and his blindly ferocious troops " were remarkably gentle—to this fact we have the testimony of half a score of witnesses. Though they were stoned by the rioters who had taken refuge in the work-sheds, they rode slowly forward without attempting to charge. But soon the men, thus attacked, put their horses to the gallop. One trooper was knocked off his charger, seized, and very roughly treated to begin with. On the Tuileries side, the garden chairs were hurled at the dragoons ; they tried to drive back their assailants, and appear to have knocked over an old man, " who either could not or would not get out of the way." He was only wounded, but for the purposes of the popular cause, he was given out to be dead. The fact that only one old man was knocked down, and that so much clamour was made over it in the rebel camp is a better proof than any contemporary account we have of the extreme gentleness of the " repression." We find Esterhazy, in his memoirs, shrugging his shoulders at such weakness. But Bezenval, who had 5000 men under his command on the Champ-de-Mars, did not support Lambesc. He feared a horrible conflict For the Gardes Françaises had come to the fore again. Swarming in a frenzy out of their barracks, they had first of all come into collision with the dragoons. " Are you for the Third Estate ? " they shouted. " We are for those who give us our orders ! " was the reply—the only sensible thing said during the whole of that day. It was rewarded by a volley that killed some dragoons and drove the others back. A moment later the frantic mutineers had reached the Place Louis XV, and thrown themselves between the crowd and the dragoons, on whom they fired shot after shot. At this first symptom of civil war Lambesc took fright. He withdrew his men towards the Champs Elysées, and soon the dragoons were retreating on the Champ-de-Mars, with the mob at their heels, howling and throwing stones. This retreat handed Paris over to insurrection.

Night was falling—a July night, swelteringly hot. From the streets a great noise rose up: " The people have crossed the Rubicon " was the terrified cry. " Victory or the hangman's rope—that must be our motto now." And here and there, in the wild mob, hideous faces looked out.

Suddenly, in the night, the tocsin began to clang from the belfry of the Hôtel-de-Ville. Until lately the sound of that
Arrival of the bell, in the minds of the historians of the Revolu-
Bandits. tion, has meant a very definite thing—a summons to the great city to rise up against the rulers at Versailles. But modern research (and that of a kind that cannot be suspected of any anti-revolutionary feeling) has given us a very different impression. The city was sending out a wild cry for help, because the bandits so dreaded for the past three months had come at last, and were pouring through the streets, sacking the shops and stripping the passers-by. Far from desiring to overthrow the Bastille, these citizens, who had been staunch liberals only the night before, would fain have raised up twenty more and filled them with the beasts of prey who were invading the terrified town. That was the true message of the tocsin whose gloomy note rang out from the Faubourg Saint-Antoine to the Chaillot Gate.

* * * * *

On the 13th, from dawn onwards, the greatest agitation reigned in the city. The Hôtel de-Ville was surrounded by a
The exploits of seething mob, in the ranks of which the most
July 13. sinister figures moved : a priest, the Abbé Rudemare, deeply imbued with the new ideas, has left us an account of this multitude, some members of which, he tells us, were " wild beasts." There were country folk, too, armed with ironshod staves, who had fled from bandits, more or less imagi-

74

nary, and little dreamt they were now strengthening the hands of others of the most genuine description. The green cockade was still worn and forced on those who desired to avoid insult. The disbanded men of the Garde Française moved hither and thither arm-in-arm with the " victors " of the Place Louis XV. Their presence, indeed, imparted a certain appearance of order to the general anarchy.

There was another evident proof that the plunderers had made their way into the town : they had pillaged the bakers' shops, sacked the Garde-Meuble, the Lazarist Convent, and (here the sons of Cartouche gratified a grudge of long standing) the house of the Lieutenant of Police. One band had broken into the prison of La Force, and delivered some very uninteresting captives, who straightway swelled the ranks of this threatening army.

This last exploit made a particularly deep impression on the citizens : it was the characteristic expression, in fact, of a movement in which politics, as one of the ambassadors of the time puts it, " were a mere pretext." The Provost of the Merchants, chief magistrate of the city, was sorely perplexed. He was an upright, if somewhat timorous man, named Flesselles. He had been desired to distribute arms to the militia, but fearing the weapons might fall into dangerous hands, he asked for instructions from the Court. No answer was given him till the 13th : then he was authorized to organize an armed force of 12,000 men. It is a stupefying fact that on the morrow this correspondence between the Court and Flesselles was taken, even by temperate men, to be an " unfortunate connivance," which almost justified the subsequent massacre of the magistrate by the populace. The incomprehensible indignation roused by this very natural proceeding is an evidence of the moral upheaval of the moment.

Even before the answer from Versailles had been made known, the " Electors " had begun to organize their forces. The presence of all " these vagabonds and people who had been imprisoned for their crimes " inspired the citizens with downright terror. Etienne Charavay has summed up in a sentence the measures they took on the very eve of the destruction of the Bastille : " Less terrified by the plans of the Court than by the men on whom the name of bandits had already been bestowed, they formed themselves into a militia to resist them : that was their only thought. The movement that carried the gates of the Bastille on the following day might perhaps have been suppressed by the National Guard, if its organization had been more solid."

As a matter of fact it was too late. The militia was still without arms on the morning of the 14th. And Bezenval, who had no orders from the Court, was keeping his troops, **July 14.** described by an eyewitness as " sad, gloomy, and depressed "—as troops who have been exposed to insult and left to humiliation quickly become—within the limits of the Champ-de-Mars.

The populace, on the other hand, was taking up arms : from the Garde-Meuble strange weapons, even " Saracen pikes," had been snatched. On the morning of the 14th the mob attacked the Invalides and seized twenty-seven guns, a mortar, and 32,000 muskets. The Gardes Françaises, who had been persuaded that their officers had intended to blow them up in their barracks, were thirsting for revenge. Every sort of story gained credence : the legends of July 14 were current before the Bastille had actually fallen. In its wild excitement the mob looked hither and thither for some exploit it might perform. And further, the people were determined to have arms, and the answer at the Arsenal, as one Pitra tells us, had been that all the gunpowder had been taken to the Bastille. " To the Bastille ! " shouted some ruffian.

The Bastille ! It was nothing but a bogey fortress ! The muzzles of a few guns appeared between its battle-**Taking of the** ments, but that was because salutes were fired **Bastille.** from them, according to the old tradition, on festivals : since the distant days of the Fronde never a ball had issued from those muzzles. The people living in the Faubourg had seen those guns every morning, but such was the general frenzy that on this particular morning they fancied they looked dangerous. A deputation went to the Hôtel-de-Ville and requested that the threatening artillery might be removed. Then the " Electors," too, sent their delegates to the Governor of the Bastille, de Launcy—a kindly man who smiled at the complaint, and demonstrated its absurdity, but had the guns withdrawn from the embrasures, and kept the " Electors," quite reassured, to breakfast with him.

This did not suit the agitators at all. A pretext was what they wanted. At their request, Thuriot, a barrister, paid another visit to the fortress : Launey received him with the same civility, and (the best answer to all this alarm) paraded all his little garrison before him—ninety-five pensioners and thirty Swiss Guards. Finally, as his last concession, the Governor had the empty embrasures blocked up with wooden boards. Quite satisfied, Thuriot, too, went his way. But the mob, which was already surging round the walls, did not depart with him. The longing to destroy was hot within it.

Launey left the entrance of the outer courtyard unguarded : and having gathered his little garrison within the outer enclosure, simply had the drawbridge that gave access to the " government court " raised. The assailants pretended to believe this to be a deliberate preparation for action ; there must be some counter-demonstration : two men, one of them a Garde Française, rushed forward and severed the chains of the bridge with axes. Suddenly it dropped, and in an instant the courtyard was full of men. A witness of the scene who was in the crowd, and not inclined to criticize it too severely, asserts that most of those he saw there were " plunderers " : after a moment the assailants caught sight of a few of the defenders, and fired on them.

The Governor was really bound to order his men to fire in reply. He was face to face with a mob, a large proportion of which were disciples of the famous Cartouche; it had made an irruption into the interior of a fortress committed to his care. He ordered his men to fire. And that very evening, in order to glorify the contemptible business, the story was put about that the Governor had caused a message of peace to be carried to the crowd, that it had moved forward, relying on his word, and had been mowed down by his men's musketry fire. Not a single historian now accepts this tale.

Terrified at first, the mob took to its heels, but it soon returned to the charge. Yet the business made no progress :

highway robbers can sack a farm, but the taking of a fortress is soldiers' work.

The soldiers were coming in, though—the mutineers of the Garde Française. The sight of them was enough to demoralize **Murder of** the garrison. It forced the broken-hearted de **de Launey.** Launey to capitulate. One of the subordinate officers of the rebel Garde, Élie by name, testifies that the Bastille surrendered " on the faith of the word he himself gave, as a French officer, that no harm should be done to any person." In spite of which (and in spite, indeed, of Élie's own efforts) within a few minutes de Launey was murdered. He was a brave man : when they fell on him he fought till he dropped riddled with wounds. They tore him to pieces. Desnot, a " cook's apprentice," who " knew how to cut up meat," struck off his head. He made a boast of it for ten years and got a medal for it. Major de Losne-Salbray was cut down too, then an adjutant, the lieutenant of the pensioners, and one of the pensioners as well. Two others were hanged.

Enough has been said of the scenes of cannibalism that ensued. Knowing, as we do, the nature of the elements of this **The lust** so-called crowd of Parisians, we cannot feel **for blood.** surprised. But the Paris mob had been seized by this time with that horribly contagious disease—the lust for blood. While the few prisoners the assailants had released (four coiners, two madmen, and a sadic debauchee) were borne out in triumph, the defenders were dragged into the street and hailed with savage yells. And Paris, sick with terror, beheld the howling mob as it poured back, while blood-stained heads with half-closed eyes, set upon pikes, nodded above its ranks. The mob acclaimed the bandits, gave them civic rights that were to last for years—and the right to rule from that moment.

* * * * *

The " Electors," meanwhile, had but little idea of what had happened. Flesselles was sitting in council with them, **Murder of** when, towards seven o'clock, a great eddy made **Flesselles.** itself apparent in the crowd on the Place de Grève. Shouts of " Victory ! Victory ! " were heard, and the " victors " appeared with their spoils, the flags of the Bastille.

with other and more sanguinary trophies. Nothing could stand against these " victors." They poured into the room, taxed Flesselles fiercely with being " a traitor," an accomplice of de Launey, unworthy to sit at the Hôtel-de-Ville, and told him they would turn him out if he did not go quietly ! He went out, deadly pale, and before he had gone three steps he was cut down and torn to pieces. A few moments more and another head was brandished on a pike. " Cruelties worthy of another century," wrote one man on the following day, and Thiébault, who had joined the mutineers by chance, talks of " assassinations." The heads were set up at last in the garden of the Palais-Royal. " Women and children," we are told, " danced round them, shouting their regret that there were not a thousand of them ! " Here we note the rising tide of the lust for blood. Meanwhile the mob was carrying the Garde Française who had been the first man inside the Bastille, shoulder high. On his coat glistened the Cross of Saint-Louis torn from de Launey's breast.

And already the most extravagant stories were current all over the town : the soldier and the magistrate who had been faithful to their trust were dubbed traitors, for all time : the wretches who had done the deed were called " heroes " ; " the people of Paris " had set interesting sufferers free ; skeletons had been discovered in the dungeons ; instruments of torture in the prison chambers, and " hideous mysteries " in the archives. " The perfidious stratagem of the infamous governor who had hailed bullets on a generous and confiding populace " excited general indignation !

At the bottom of their hearts the inhabitants of Paris were " dismayed " (so we learn from the Baron de Staël, though it was his father-in-law, Necker, who had been thus " avenged "). They knew the real truth about these " victors "—the " greatest ruffians in Paris," as Mirabeau himself was to write them down before long.

But when the *bourgeois* heard, next morning, that the deputies at Versailles considered the day had been a " glorious " one, they began to think they had better get some glory out of it themselves. The very men who had been banding themselves together on the evening of the 13th to resist disorder, and had looked on the taking of the Bastille on the 14th as an act of " brigandage," would have had the whole enterprise hailed on the 15th as one undertaken by the City of Paris against despotism. They gloried in that which had been their own defeat. And to give themselves a right to glory in it they, too, transformed what had been the act of ruffians into the performance of heroes. The National Guard, organized to put down the rising, was given the credit of having wrought the Revolution of Freedom. Thus, out of a mighty lie, a new era sprang into life. Liberty was smirched from the first moment of her birth, and the misunderstanding thus created was destined never to be cleared up.

* * * * *

The Assembly was the first to invent the legend.

Ever since the 13th it had been living in dread of the steps the Court might take. On the evening of the 14th, a deputation **July 14 and 15** of " Electors " waited on it and reported, as one **at Versailles.** of the members tells us, " the gloomy story of the terrible catastrophe they had just witnessed ; " this deputy goes on to describe the huge hall, dimly lit by a few glimmering candles and filled with a tumultuous assemblage. These " Electors " were in terror lest Paris should be held responsible for the "catastrophe." But instead of exonerating the well-conducted part of the population from all responsibility, they cast the blame on de Launey, who, they declared—and perhaps, having heard the thing so constantly repeated in the course of the past few hours they really believed it—had attracted the concourse of people and then fired on the " unfortunate creatures." The Assembly, full of bitterness against the Court, accepted this statement, not as an extenuation, but as a **The Assembly** very legitimate justification, of what had happened **approves the** in Paris. The report was greeted with an out- **Rioters.** burst of indignation, not against those who had cut the Governor to pieces (although two deputies, d'Ormesson and Wimpfen, both testified that they had seen heads carried on pikes), but against the hapless Governor himself. Letters written on June 15 by half a score of deputies are all accessible to the student, and it will be found that the most moderate express admiration of the " ¬rder " and " wisdom " shown by the " populace in the taking of the Bastille." " M. de Launey," adds one of these letters, " was sentenced to lose his head." The expression would lead one to fancy he had been condemned by some august tribunal. " The people did justice " is the expression that occurs in all; " with calmness, though without any formalities," adds one deputy, whose words have almost the ring of an ill-timed jest.

There was a feeling of relief in reality in the Hall of the Menus Plaisirs. Since the fortress was in the hands of the people, there could be no Bastille for any of the deputies. " A lucky error," writes one deputy, " which has saved us from the most horrid outrages." He voiced the general sentiment.

The Assembly having sat all through the night of July 14, one of the liberal noblemen, the Duc de Liancourt, thought it well to wake up the King, who, as usual, had been out hunting all day. The King appeared greatly astonished. " This is a revolt !" he said. " No, Sire ! it is a revolution !" Louis XVI seemed distressed by de Launcy's " felony," and promised to have the troops withdrawn. As soon as it was daylight he would himself go to the Assembly. Meanwhile excitement was rising higher and higher. " Yes, truly," wrote a deputy on the morning of the 15th, " we shall be free ! Our hands will never wear shackles again ! " This worthy man —Duquesnoy—had never worn any at all, save of the most metaphorical description, but he was destined to make acquaintance with others, of a far more genuine kind, at Nancy in Year II of the Republic.

The King was shaken ; it would be well to send him a deputation to induce him to grant concessions. Mirabeau thought it well to provide its members with grandiloquent instructions, embodied in one of those tremendous tirades which nowadays merely provoke a smile, but which a hundred and twenty years ago would inflame a whole assembly : " hordes of foreigners," courtiers who " mingled their dances with the sounds of savage music," " ferocious counsellors who drove back the supplies of flour," and so forth.

Louis XVI arrived, " with no escort save his own virtues," and so little was there about what he said of the " bloody tyrant," and so much good-nature, that the Assembly, whose nerves were strained to breaking-point, gave him an ovation. He had said, among other things, that he pur-posed to proceed to Paris on the morrow. The Assembly resolved to send its own deputation thither that very day. The delegates found the city in a state of confusion that touched their hearts. A " pink and blue " cockade had been adopted on the 14th, and this was noticed in the square cap of a surpliced priest in command of a patrol. A deputy who reported this detail felt tears of emotion fill his eyes as he related it. When they reached the Hôtel-de-Ville, he and his colleagues were really seized with a sort of delirium. The Arch-bishop of Paris, who only a week before had made a protest against the union of the three Orders, proposed going to Notre-Dame and there singing a *Te Deum* (the deputies had just looked on the blood-stained limbs of Flesselles and de Launey). And there, amidst the tears of his audience, Lally-Tollendal pronounced a discourse of a nature so " sublime " that he was requested to repeat it word for word from the rostrum the next day. Whereupon Liancourt having referred to the " pardon " that ought to be granted to the mutinous deserters from the Garde Française, Clermont-Tonnerre exclaimed against the humiliating nature of the expression, and lauded the behaviour of the worthy fellows, who, as another deputy writes, " had not forsaken their colours—seeing they had taken them with them."

The King at the Assembly.

The *bourgeois* militia, which had completed its organization, forthwith laid hands on Lafayette and made him Commandant, while the " Electors " acclaimed Bailly " Mayor of Paris." There was a procession to Notre-Dame, where a *Te Deum* was duly sung in presence of 2000 persons, all wearing " blue and red cockades." " On my honour," writes one gentleman, " they all seem stark mad ! '

The King was invited to come and set his seal on the " recon-ciliation." So on the 17th he took his way to Paris in his coach, attended by three-fourths of the members of the Assembly, marching two-and-two, " a duke beside a parish priest, a bishop next to a labourer," while before them " fish-wives waving branches adorned with ribbons pranced like so many Bacchantes."

At the city gates Louis XVI was met by the " Mayor "—
a person who had no legal status, and whom the King should
not have recognized—who presented the keys of the city to
him. " These same keys were presented to Henri IV : he had
reconquered his people : now the people has reconquered its
King ! " The phrase was extraordinarily daring. Louis XVI,
leaning over to the Prince de Beauvau, said in an undertone :
" I do not know if I ought to hear ! "

Yet he had made up his mind to hear and see every imaginable thing. For the grandson of Louis XIV, when he reached
The King and the Hôtel-de-Ville, passed unmoved before the
the deputies at flag of the Bastille, which had been torn from
the Hôtel-de- his own royal fortress. He had to put on the
Ville. tricoloured cockade—the white had been slipped,
as a matter of civility, between the red and the blue that day.
The populace was delighted. " Well done ! He belongs to the
Third Estate ! " The Comte d'Estaing, in a state of wild
excitement, began to prophesy : " Sire, with that cockade and
the Third Estate you will conquer Europe ! "

At the Hôtel-de-Ville Bailly had arranged the whole scene
beforehand. He it was who conferred the cockade on the King,
seated him on the throne, and called on the various orators
who, under colour of paying homage to the Sovereign, read
him lectures. He listened to them all, and never flinched.
Several times over in his speech, Lally used the expression
" Behold him, this King who " . . . " Ecce Homo ! " said somebody at last. Louis XVI was in a hideously false position.
" I felt humiliated myself," wrote the Curé Lindet, himself a
great opponent of the Court. "His dull and foolish face was
pitiable." He sat very still, an uncertain smile upon his lips.
His departure was the signal, nevertheless, for a great ovation.
The King was praised for his labours in the cause of " concilia-
tion." But the common people, who never trouble themselves
much with the hypocrisies of formula, yelled to the deputies :
" Has the King signed his capitulation ? "

SOURCES. Works, quoted above, of Duquesnoy, Jallet, Morris,
Biauzat, Baron de Staël, Malouet, Vaissière, Lameth, Dumont, Mme. de
Chastenay.—Comte de Salmour, the Marquis de Cordon, Berkemoode,
Simolin, Chestrel, Capello (foreign diplomatists) ; *Lettres de juillet,*

1789 (*Nouv. Rev. Retr.*, July, 1898) ; Thibaudeau, *Correspondance*, 1898 ; Mirabeau, *Correspondance avec le Comte de la Marck*, 1851 ; Abbé Rudemare, *Journal* (*Rev. Rev.*, I) ; *Lettre de Gudin de la Ferlière* ; *Lettre d'un officier aux Gardes Françaises* (*Rev. Retr.*, XI) ; *Relation* of Guyot de Fléville (*Rev. Retr.*, 1885) ; *Relation* of Pitra, 1892 ; Fournier l'Américain, *Mémoires*, 1903 ; Desmoulins, *Œuvres* (Claretie ed.), 1874 ; Mathieu Dumas, *Mémoires*, I ; Thiébault, *Mémoires*, 1894 ; Esterhazy, *Mémoires*, 1903.

WORKS. Works already quoted by Esmein, Laborie, Castellane, Charavay—Taine, *La Révolution*, I, 1896 ; Claretie, *Desmoulins*, 1908 ; Funck-Brentano, *Le 14 juillet* (in *Légendes et Archives de la Bastille*, 1904) ; Flammermont, *Le 14 juillet*, 1892, *id.* ; *Les Gardes Françaises en juillet*, 1789 (*Rev. Fr.*, 1889) ; Bournon, *La Bastille*, 1902 ; Dard, *Hérault de Séchelles*, 1907 ; Arnaud, *Fréron*, 1909 ; Fournel, *Les Hommes du 14 juillet*, 1890 ; Comte d'Haussonville, *Le Salon de Madame Necker*, 1882.

CHAPTER III

A COUNTRY IN DISSOLUTION

Anarchy. Paris a centre of anarchy; the murders of Foulon and Bertier. "After all, was that blood so pure?" Anarchy in the provinces. The *Great Fear*. General devastation. Massacred officials. Spontaneous birth of the "Communes;" their weakness in the face of insurrection.

"SPONTANEOUS anarchy," wrote Taine. The expression has had the most extraordinary success, but as applied to the state of France just after July 14, it is not correct. That great anarchy was let loose under the action of two separate events—the capture of the Bas-"Spontaneous tille, and the night of August 4; it was an Anarchy." anarchy that was encouraged, and occasionally even instigated.

The taking of the Bastille was in itself, in the highest degree, a factious proceeding; yet, if it had preserved its true character, it might have been devoid of consequences. But, approved and lauded as it was, it ended by growing big with anarchy. The so-called "ruling classes" were overtaken for a moment by a fit of the most inconceivable folly. A deputy belonging to the nobility, who had hitherto held the most uncompromising views, writes on the 16th: "This is a fine and useful lesson for Ministers." A Royalist whose earlier letters prove him to have been most hostile to the revolutionary movement, writes, on the 18th, his formal approval of the city "which had broken all political bonds so as to recover its natural rights." And Gouverneur Morris, so unfriendly to the Revolution both before and after the event, tells us that he considers the taking of the Bastille on the 14th to have been a "great example of intrepidity," and drinks "to the liberty of the French nation" in the best claret. That was on the 15th, and on the 18th,

85

having had time to think the matter over, he rejoiced at the overthrow of " that devilish castle."

It was Louis XVI who led the American, remarkable for his steady common sense, to accept the legend of the " devilish castle," for the King consented to the erection of a statue of himself on the site of the Bastille, which had been completely demolished immediately after the 15th. And fashion taking a hand in the game, not fierce democrats only, but fair ladies, bought up the stones of the fortress by the pound, " paying as much for them as for a pound of good meat," to have them set as ornaments afterwards.

At Versailles there was a tremendous reaction against the " Artois faction," for the " factious persons " of July 14th were the dwellers within the Palace ! When the Comte d'Artois departed on the 17th, " the Augean stable was cleansed ! " Who wrote those words ? A member of the revolutionary party ? No. They were penned by one of the contemporary writers on whose assertions historians hostile to the Revolution most willingly rely.

Paris having thus been completely exonerated, the provinces began to draw the moral from these strange happenings, and concluded that, seeing what was permitted inside the walls of Paris was permissible outside them as well, it could not be a bad thing for soldiers to desert and mutiny, for the magistrates of the old order to be driven out and killed if they offered any resistance, and for the populace to attack the châteaux, the " forty thousand *Bastilles*," set fire to them, and if necessity arose, burn their owners as well. What a rich treasure of simplicity is revealed to us by the deputy who writes, on July 18, after a glorification of the doings on the 14th : " Excitement will die down, everything will fall back into its place, military discipline will be restored ; the national spirit is the remedy for all things ! "

*   *   *   *   *

" There is no more King, no more parliament, no more army, no more police ! " moaned a deputy of the Left that day. Mounier was soon to describe the terrible anarchy that followed in France after July 14, and Taine, a hundred years later, was to underline Mounier's words with facts and figures.

A COUNTRY IN DISSOLUTION

Paris the centre of Anarchy.

The great centre of it all was Paris. " Everybody," Bailly admits, " knew how to command, and nobody knew how to obey." Every district of the city, and there were sixty of them, thought it possessed sovereign authority. One took upon itself to open all ministerial despatches, to " see that they do not contain anything against the nation ! " Another, soon after, was to stop a wagon laden with silver for the Limoges mint, " because the coinage should be struck in Paris and not at Limoges." The National Guard, which was no more by this time than " terror under arms," was incapable of keeping any kind of order. It was only at La Fayette's disposal on days that suited it. " What is the use of the *bourgeois* militia of Paris," writes a deputy, and one of advanced opinions, Biauzat, " if murders are planned and executed in the public squares of the town ? " He refers here to the murders of Foulon and Bertier. The various poignant accounts of these murders are worth quoting.

Murder of Foulon and Bertier.

Foulon, who had been arrested at Viry, was brought to Paris on July 22. " M. de La Fayette did everything that was possible to save him, but *the people were determined to have blood ;* they have grown greedy for the sight of it ! " The doors of the Hôtel-de-Ville were broken in, and the victim seized and tortured with a " ferocity which revolted the hearts of the most hardened spectators." Then came the turn of Foulon's son-in-law, Bertier, Intendant of Paris, who was accused of having done his simple duty—he had served out gunpowder to the King's troops on the eve of the 14th—and was hacked to pieces " with sixty sword-thrusts." " All his limbs were borne in triumph ; his heart was presented to M. le Maire on the point of a pike." Meanwhile the head of Foulon—the mouth stuffed with hay—was being carried about on another pike, and when the bearers of the two met, the heads were made to touch each other : " Kiss papa ! Kiss papa ! "

La Fayette sent in his resignation, and then took it back again ; the deputies deplored the incident. Barnave was to reassure them ; blood had been shed, indeed, but " *was it such very pure blood ?* " The Abbé Jallet vowed the words were " those of a true Roman." The country hearkened, alas !

it learned, from the lips of this "generous" deputy, that there was some blood in the nation's veins that was not pure, and that it might be justly shed. Unfortunately, Barnave's own blood was in its turn to seem so far from pure that within three years the "Roman" was to tread the Calvary along which Foulon had passed.

*   *   *   *   *

The terrible example was soon followed in the provinces. Taine, who sometimes exaggerates, speaks sober truth when he asserts that though during the sultry summer of 1789 the provinces of the West, the Centre, and the South were comparatively free from disturbance, " in the Eastern provinces, over an area from thirty to fifty leagues wide, and right down to the borders of Provence, there was a general conflagration." Among the men who burned down the châteaux many were Mandrin's followers. They had got their hands in in Paris, and then come back into the provinces. One dweller in these provinces foresaw this with alarm when, on July 14, he expressed a hope that " the great town would not get rid of its bandits too quickly ! " What could the armed force do against them ? If it continued faithful, it was scorned. " Three months ago the sight of a soldier inspired fear ; now we hear talk of attacking whole regiments." The agents of the ruling powers effaced themselves ; the murders of Flesselle, Launey, Bertier, and Foulon had struck terror into the hearts of the official class. The King was known to be incapable, on account of his " great weakness " (the words quoted were written on July 25), " of protecting those who zealously support his authority." The dread of being left to their fate made cowards of these men.

Yet never had the need for some vigorous authority been more keenly felt. The poor were starving ; famine always lies at the bottom of insurrection. Emile Levasseur has explained in the most masterly manner, that economic causes prevailed in this case over political. He has entitled one chapter of his work " Corn and Insurrction." To a large extent this scarcity was the result of anarchy. The producers of grain were hiding it, simply because they were afraid of being plundered ; the market at Étampes, where 1500 and 1600 sacks of corn often changed hands, could not boast more than 160 after the insurrection.

The populace was not only starving, it was distraught; the bandits, according to the common rumour, were appearing in every quarter. *"The Brigands!"* The word **The Great Fear.** flew from the outskirts of Paris to the most remote villages, sowing wild panic as they went. Here again, was that mysterious *"Great Fear"* which sends a chill to our own hearts, a hundred and twenty years after the event, as we study the scores of descriptions, all full of the same story. We will only glance at one here, the journal of a vine-grower in the Franche-Comté: " Towards the end of July a story got about that brigands were coming, foreigners most of them, who made havoc in the countryside and burned the corn, being paid by great nobles, so it was said, to destroy everything, whereas it has been seen since that it was all done by the Assembly—that is to say by factious persons—to try the people and find out how much use might be made of them." Here we see the hovering shadow of all the legends that distorted public opinion. Brigands there were, indeed, as we well know; the scum of the boiling population was rising to the surface. But the brigands were not in every place. This nightmare, terrifying the nation, was an inevitable thing. The wild terror was really the instinctive dizziness of a population that found itself standing on the edge of a half-suspected abyss. A frightful presentiment clutched all hearts; they were moving on towards huge hecatombs, and civil strife and war with foreigners, proscriptions, massacres; such things were inconceivable to them; they were giddy and bewildered. Here they were, without guides or protectors, the tutelary powers that had ruled them for centuries crumbling at their feet; they were terrified! In every village the men flew to arms; if the brigands had come, they would have cut them down and thus made themselves champions of order; but many, in their excitement, became themselves the instruments of a vast disorder. Once armed, they gathered themselves together; then the scoundrels among them, real brigands these, would egg them on to attack the neighbouring country-houses. There was a rumour current that if the papers belonging to the nobles were destroyed, nobody would have to go on paying rents and dues. No description from the pen of the historian is so illuminating as the fifty letters from small provincial nobles who suffered these attacks, published by Vaissière. " Set fire to the cupboards ! If there are papers in them, they will be burnt ! " shouted the crowd assembled in front of the Château de La Touche. So the house was burnt, and the cupboards, and now and then their owners as well.

Woods were devastated, the hunting and shooting destroyed. After that night of August 4, on which the Assembly **General** with such extraordinary imprudence, overthrew **devastation.** every institution, the country was convinced it might do just as it chose. The poaching instinct became stronger than any other. " Everybody has a right to kill game ! " " The right to kill game, even under the walls of the Palace of Versailles," write two deputies from Alsace. One native of that province relates that not only was the game all destroyed, but the very forests were devastated. The population which had taken up arms against the brigands, ended by taking to brigandage itself.

In the towns there were sanguinary riots. " At Metz, at Strasburg, at Nancy," on August 1 we hear of " excitement and **Massacre of** disturbances." At Agde, far away at the other **officials.** end of the country, the Bishop was dragged along the streets and forced to sign a paper relinquishing all claim to his own mill. He would have been slaughtered if he had refused. At the very gates of Paris the " Mayor of Saint-Denis has had his throat cut by the cruelty of the women of the people, who wanted to insist on his fixing the price of bread at two *sols* and six *deniers*," writes Vergennes on August 5. At Troyes, again, the Mayor was murdered in the most horrible fashion, and at Caen (I select the four cardinal points of the country) Belzunce, Major of the Swiss Guard, was torn to pieces. In some cases the " brigands " really were at the head of the disturbance, as at Besançon, where several of the leaders were known to be released felons. Even at Versailles the populace, so utter was its demoralization, rescued a parricide from the executioner's hands. The revolutionary deputy who reports the fact is himself indignant at it. Every human law was subverted.

90

A COUNTRY IN DISSOLUTION

People who were engaged in devastating woods, stealing corn, and carrying off salt, naturally refused to pay taxes. Officers, officials, financial agents were all living in a state of terror and keeping out of sight.

     *   *   *   *   *

It was not unnatural that when the ruling power failed, an effort was made to organize some sort of new authority, **Birth of the** to work either beside it, or instead of it. The **" Communes."** *bourgeoisie* might favour reform, but it dreaded insurrection. Faced by insurrection, it sought to ensure its own safety. And then, just as in Paris in July 1789, certain " Electors " who had no special mandate, now the elections were over, formed themselves into committees, or " Communes." This was the communal movement of the summer of 1789. Here we have irregular illegal powers, the outcome again of anarchy, but powers which have really been instituted for the purpose of making a stand against the anarchy below. The majority of the members of these " Communes " were conservative, but the origin of their functions was revolutionary all the same. This weakened their authority. " Who made thee a duke ? " they might say to the leader of some riot. " Who made thee a king ? " might be his answer. What was the source of their power ? The King ? He had not appointed them. The people ? The people had not elected them for this purpose. Thus insurrection easily swept them away. " Hardly ever," runs a contemporary document, " does a municipality call anyone to order. It will permit the greatest excesses rather than bring an accusation for which its fellow citizens might endeavour, sooner or later, to make it responsible. The municipalities are now quite unable to refuse to authorize anything."

On the whole, these municipalities were in favour of revolution, and this was also the tendency of the National Guard, **Their inability** a moderate revolution, such as was now an **to keep order.** almost established fact, but which, they feared, might be repealed. This feeling induced a persistent distrust of the Court and the nobles and, before long, of the clergy as well. And in their fear that any repression might bring about a reaction, these municipalities and National Guards, into whose hands the power had slipped, left the second gang of revolutionaries a free hand.

From that moment the general anarchy denounced by Mounier began. Country houses were burnt down, woods were devastated, magistrates dismissed, and, worse still, there was a general acceptance of the theory that within the nation there existed a class of *pariahs*—that class which had lately possessed privileges, and which was now its persecutors' lawful prey. "There is not a man in the country," wrote a contemporary on July 27, "who will not take upon himself to arrest all whom he regards with suspicion."

The anxiety at Versailles in view of this state of things was very great, both on Necker's part—he was back in office, but deeply distressed—and on that of the Assembly. "If a Constitution is not quickly put together," wrote a deputy on August 5, "this kindly nation, this tender-hearted and loyal population, will be transformed into a horde of cannibals, until it becomes a miserable drove of slaves!" The liberal politician who penned these words had caught a glimpse of the Cæsar of the year XII beyond the Brutii of the year 1793.

The sword, then, had "slipped out of the King's hands," but was the Assembly about to pick it up?

SOURCES. *Works* of Duquesnoy, the Député Noble, Morris, Jallet, Thiébault, Mounier, Vaissière, already quoted.—Madame Roland, *Correspondance* (Perroud ed.), 1900; Barnave, *Lettres* (Beylie ed.), 1906; *Notes* by the vinegrower Laviron (*Rev. Rev.*, XVI); *Documents sur l'approvisionnement de Paris*, 1789–1790 (*Rev. Fr.*, II).

WORKS. Works by Laborie, Taine, Dard, Cahen, and Charavay, already quoted.—Cosnard, *La Grande Peur dans le Dauphiné*, 1904; Levasseur, *Histoire des Classes ouvrières*, I (ed. of 1903–4); Meynier, *La Revellière-Lepeaux*, 1905; Goncourt, *La Société sous la Révolution*, 1854; Costa de Beauregard, *Le Roman d'un Royaliste* (Virieu), 1892

CHAPTER IV

THE NIGHT OF AUGUST 4 AND THE DECLARATION
July–October 1789

The twofold terror of the Assembly. "Jean sans Terre" at the rostrum. The night of August 4. The general emotion. The *Te Deum* of the privileged classes. The Declaration. The contradiction between the Declaration and the Constitution The Promised Land. It is refused. Fears inspired by the Court. The Queen's attitude. The "traitorous" Assembly votes the "*Veto*." Paris decides to "go to Versailles."

TWO terrors hung over the Assembly : terror of the Court and terror of the populace. The first, seemed for a moment to be dying down. The King was surrounding himself with ministers professing the tenets of 1789. These ministers of a King, who but a day before had been an Twofold terror absolute monarch, passing from one extreme to of the the other, had informed the Assembly, "that Assembly. they would not exercise any public function that the Assembly had not authorized," and, on the faith of their declaration, this docile executive had ceased to govern altogether, leaving the deputies to settle matters with the nation.

The Nation, we know, had been giving itself over to the *canaille* for a month past. The word occurs in the notes of the democrat deputies themselves, and denotes the horror with which the exploits of the bands of plunderers filled the ancient Third Estate. But this *canaille*, if it was not pleased, would destroy every one and everything ! There was indeed the possibility of getting beforehand with it by destroying anything that remained for it to demolish, but these middle-class men felt a certain scruple as to this ; many of them were jurists : they did not quite see how they were to set about stripping the nobles and the clergy of rights that were centuries old. Yet how, if they were not stripped, was the

93

populace to be satisfied ? They were a sorely perturbed body of men.

Then, all of a sudden, at eight o'clock on the evening of August 4, just as the sitting was about to close, the Vicomte de Noailles stood up in his place. A decree intended to " calm the provinces " had just been read. The Vicomte began to speak : the one thing that drove the populace to sack the country houses, he said, was the heavy burden of the seignorial rights and dues—an odious remnant of the feudal system ; they must be swept away ! The Third Estate, struck dumb with astonishment at first, broke into wild applause. Noailles stood for the whole nobility of the country, voluntarily holding out its neck to the axe ; here was the solution. Nobody cared to remember that this Louis de Noailles, the son of a younger branch of his family, and a ruined man, had no authority whatever for what he said. In his own circle he was nicknamed " Jean sans Terre " (John Lackland). Then the Duc d'Aiguillon, vexed at seeing a revolutionary nobleman like himself outstripped by " Jean sans Terre," supported the resolution. A fresh storm of acclamation greeted him, and there was another when the Duc du Châtelet held forth against the feudal system.

Jean sans Terre.

Upon this a hurricane of wild generosity was unloosed ; never was the French character to be proved more unsuited for calm deliberation, more subject to fits of irresistible impulse. Honestly, it may have been, Noailles thought he had the right to sacrifice the fortunes of his whole Order. On the morrow a nobly born deputy noted in his *Journal* (secretly of course): " The deputies did not possess any of the powers they assumed." No matter ! " Every man," writes a witness of the scene, " generously gave away that which he did not own." As a matter of fact, the men who had elected Noailles had never given him any authority to ruin them, neither had the Lorraine clergy sent the Bishop of Nancy to Versailles to renounce the rights of his Order to all its benefices ; this La Fare did, amidst universal applause. The 1700 deputies were " like so many madmen " ; they wept and embraced each other. And each man vied with his fellows in the race for applause. The Bishop of Chartres and the Arch-

Resignation of privileges.

bishop of Aix came to approve La Fare, " in the name of the Clergy." The Bishop of Chartres resigned sporting rights ; that was the only moment at which the nobles felt a certain misgiving. Du Châtelet was heard to mutter: " Ah ! the Bishop is taking away my game ; I'll take something from him ! " And he took his tithes. But the nobility of the magistracy, represented by Lepelletier de Saint-Fargeau, President of one of the Courts of Justice, was already at the rostrum, demanding the abolition of financial privileges. There was a roar of delight. Whereupon certain parish priests offered to give up their occasional dues. The hall rang with shouts of admiration; it was not till the 8th that it was discovered that one was relinquishing twenty livres, and the other fifteen. The warrens were put down, so were the vintage dues.

" It was a delirium, an intoxication ! " The Marquis de Blacons suggested that the provinces, too, should resign their privileges : Brittany, Languedoc, Artois, Burgundy, Lorraine, obeyed the call.

And when everything had been completely overthrown, the Archbishop of Paris proposed that a *Te Deum* should be sung in the Palace Chapel, while two noblemen, Liancourt and Lally, had Louis XVI proclaimed " the restorer of French liberty."

I have before me the notes of some half-dozen *bourgeois* deputies ; all are full of bewilderment and emotion. " We felt ourselves in a transport of joy and delirium," writes one, " as the scene changed from good to better, and we beheld all the great obstacles sinking down and disappearing ! " Another stammers delightedly : " I invoke the help of the Divinity to inspire me with suitable expressions ! " And a third says, " We wept, we embraced each other. What a nation ! What glory ! What an honour to be a Frenchman ! "

By eight o'clock next morning, some thirty decrees had legalised the most extraordinary social upheaval any nation has ever known. " In ten hours," wrote a deputy that day, " we have done what might have gone on for months." But the very same man was to acknowledge, a few weeks later, that the work of that unfortunate night had created an impossible situation for the Assembly itself, for my readers will readily imagine that months had to elapse before anything even tolerably coherent could be evolved out of these legislative effusions.

However that might be, the middle-class deputies, quite reassured, proceeded to the chapel to sing their *Te Deum*, The Te Deum filled with a comfortable conviction that "the popu- of the lace, touched by so much generosity, would forth- privileged with settle down quietly." They were somewhat classes. mistaken. The " populace " was to claim more than it had been given. When the deputies began to look closely into matters, they were forced to establish certain distinctions. Certain rights, such as those of the local lord and master, might be abolished without indemnity, but others, those of the proprietary over-lord, could only be bought out. Now, as these rights were very much intermingled, the populace, being simple in its ideas, could not distinguish one from the other. Surely it had been informed on August 5, in letters blurred with the Assembly's tears, that " the feudal *régime* had been totally abolished ? " " The people," we are told, are deeply sensible of the benefits promised them," and as Reubell, the Alsacian deputy, informs us, " refused to lose this sense." Nothing could induce them to accept the restrictions the Com- mittee of Feudal Rights desired to impose. They regarded all such restrictions as a deliberate failure to keep the " great promise." Woe to the prudent deputies of this Committee who attempted to minimize the inflammatory declarations of Jean de Noailles and the Bishop of Nancy ! The Third Estate itself was not to sing *Te Deum* for long.

As for the nobles and the clergy, they sang it that August morning at the top of their voices, their hearts full of emotion at their own action : *"Te Martyrum candidatus laudat exercitus."*

*　　*　　*　　*　　*

So the feudal system had been abolished, and all French citizens were now equal. It appeared necessary to make some The Declara- proclamation of their rights : it might indeed, tion of Rights. as Mirabeau said, ha e been more opportune, considering the events then convulsing the provinces—the pillage and the murders ; the incendiarism, the refusal to pay taxes, and the mutinies among the troops—to proclaim " not the rights but rather the duties of citizens," but there was a great eagerness to " declare the rights."

The Assembly had been at work on this Declaration ever since the end of July. Its principles had been brought over from Philadelphia by La Fayette, and those principles once accepted, the ideas it was to embody had been supplied by the Genevan philosopher.

Yet logically speaking, the Declaration ought to have sprung from the substance of the Memorials. And Clermont-Tonnerre did evolve eleven very obvious clauses from this source. Their origin was neither Philadelphian nor Genevan; they were purely national. Shame upon him ! Was the Assembly to work for one nation only ? " We desire to make a Declaration for all men, for all times, for every country, that will be an example to the whole world ! " cried one deputy. This pretension brought a smile to the lips of Morris, who came from Philadelphia, and Dumont, who hailed from Geneva. " A childish fiction," this last dubbed it. Jean-Jacques himself would have been startled by it.

A Declaration founded on his ideas had necessarily to be exceedingly democratic. The *bourgeoisie* would have perhaps preferred it otherwise ; but they were outnumbered by the liberal nobles and the democratic clergy. On August 1, Montmorency, supported by the Comte de Castellane, had proclaimed the necessity for voting the Declaration in its integrity. Some of the *bourgeois*, a M. Crinière, and a M. Grandin, showed signs of alarm. Mirabeau, too, thought it "imprudent " to lift " the curtain " too suddenly. The populace, he said, would soon " abuse " its power ; the Rights of Man "were a secret which should be concealed until a good Constitution had placed the people in a position to hear it without danger." And Malouet very wisely asserts : " Why should we carry men up to the top of a mountain and thence show them the full extent of their rights, since we are forced to make them descend again, and assign them limits, and cast them back into the world as it is, in which they will come on boundary-marks at every step ? " But following on Montmorency and Castellane, Virieu, Lameth, Lally, Talleyrand, Rochefoucauld, not to mention the Archbishop of Bordeaux. Champion de Cicé, a most

G

enthusiastic reporter, brought in clauses very democratic in character, which were hailed with loud applause. They were all of them sincere ; there may have been a sort of unconscious spite against the Third Estate at the bottom of their hearts, which led them to force it into going to the extreme limit of democracy at once. Mounier was certainly one of the chief inspirers of the motion, but he was greatly influenced by the democratic nobles.

The Declaration was drawn up in public session. Two foreigners who were present at these sittings—Campe, a German, and Dumont, a Genevan—thought them incoherent to the last degree. "Empty disputes over words, a farrago of metaphysics . . . the Assembly turned into the school of the Sorbonne," says Dumont. "Such a confusion," writes Campe, on August 12, "that you would take it for a witches' sabbath."

The Declaration thus built up out of one amendment upon another was, as M. Aulard remarks, almost republican in character. It was not a rationalist effusion. Rousseau would have forbidden that. The Vicaire Savoyard helped the Comte de Virieu to ensure the recognition of the Supreme Being, and to have the Declaration marked, as he put it on August 20, with "the seal of God."

One of M. Aulard's most interesting pages demonstrates the absurd contradiction between this Declaration and the Constitution of which it was to be the foreword.

Contradiction between the Declaration and the Constitution. The middle class was, in fact, laying the foundations of its ultimate compensation. "The Catechism of the Nation," was the cry, once the vote had been taken ; but this same catechism was to be shut up in a tabernacle, the curtain of which was to be carefully dropped ; "there was a curtain-policy." The men of 1789 lowered this curtain after they had raised it ; the men of 1793 strove to rend it ; those of 1795 stitched it together again ; it has not been altogether lifted yet. The Constitution dropped the curtain. "All men, being born equal, should have equal rights," says the Declaration—but according to the Constitution, they cannot have them. It would have been wiser, after all, to listen to Malouet, and not lead men up to the top of the mountain and show them a Promised Land which was to be refused them afterwards.

* * * * *

One factor which had swept the Assembly along the road to revolution in August and September was the fresh alarm **Fears inspired** inspired by the Court. The Queen had thrown **by the Court.** herself into the arms of the friends of the Comte d'Artois. Offended by the abominable attacks made on her, and alarmed by the disorganization in the royal camp, she was looking about her for support. Unhappily she was quite unable to stem the tide by the adoption of any skilful policy. The Revolution had already reached a stage at which only those who had unloosed it might have been able to check its impetus. La Fayette, greatly dismayed, had offered to try : Mirabeau had been sounding the Court for a month past. The right course would have been to summon one of these two men to the Ministry. But the Queen had no talent for forgetting ; she would have none of them. Mirabeau, furious at being kept at a distance, was going back to his old policy of violence. " The King and Queen will both perish, and the populace will batter their corpses ! "

The Assembly had become unpopular ; this led Marie-Antoinette to believe the hour of reaction had come, and to **The Queen's** reckon on a counter-revolution. The populace **attitude.** was certainly discontented ; it was angry. " The fire is burning under the ashes, or rather under the flour," wrote some one on August 17, and responsibility for the scarcity was being cast on the Assembly, against which, " the current of opinion daily increases," adds the same correspondent on the 18th.

The Queen was seriously thinking of a dissolution. All that would be necessary would be to ensure the fidelity of a few of the troops. Her programme was divined in the Assembly, where suspicion of her intentions drove a certain number of moderate Liberals towards the Left. The Declaration once voted, the debate on the Constitution began. Mounier, the reporter of the Committee, desired to see it conservative in tendency. In August, 1789, he said to Virieu, " We thought we must arm ourselves with the club of Hercules to crush abuses, and now we need the shoulders of Atlas to hold up the monarchy." He would have liked a Constitution after the English model :—two Chambers, and a strong executive. But he failed. His fellow deputies desired neither an Upper Chamber nor a strong government. The party of the Bi-Camerists was beaten—nay, crushed. It retired from the committee, Mounier at its head, and thus on September 15, the Left obtained a majority of votes. When the proposal to give the King a *Veto* was brought forward, there was a passionate discussion.

The Parisian populace laid hold of this question. Agitators were on the look-out for a pretext. The scarcity of food might, **The Veto.** it had been written, " help on and hasten a second revolution." But nothing so thoroughly excites the passions of the mob as words that it does not understand The demagogues of the street-corners fell upon the *Veto*. " Do you know what the *Veto* means ? Listen ! You go home, and your wife has cooked your dinner. The King says *Veto*—No more dinner for you ! " When the Assembly voted a *suspensory veto*, the populace was indignant. Early in October, a street orator was heard to shout : " We have no bread, and here's the reason why : only three days ago the King was given this *suspensory veto*, and now all the aristocrats have bought *suspensory vetoes*, and they are sending all the corn out of the country." His audience applauded— " Faith, he's quite right ! That's how it is ! "

"The Assembly is packed with traitors," they cry. " We must go and tear them off their benches ! " shouts Loustalot. Marat writes that the Assembly must be dissolved. Crowning infamy of all, that wretched Assembly had elected Mounier, a traitor, a Bi-Camerist, an aristocrat, to be its President ! But the Assembly was not the only object of attack. The King had just refused to sanction the Decrees of August 4, the Declaration and the clauses of the Constitution, so far as they had been voted, saying, very wisely, that " all these things need to be put in order." Was the Revolution to " stagnate " ? " We must have a second fit of Revolution," writes Loustalot, on October 4. Little Mme. Roland, quivering with impatience down at Lyons, hoped that " France would wake up." It

100

THE DECLARATION

was a moment of strong pressure—the Palais-Royal abusing
the Court, the Assembly charging La Fayette and Bailly with
lukewarmness, the prevailing want helping on the agitators'
Paris decides plans. Hunger was the predominant factor.
to go to "Let us go to Versailles," was the cry, "and
Versailles. bring back the baker and his wife and the baker's
boy ! " And at the same time the Archbishop of Paris, who had
evidently "paid the millers to stop making flour," might be killed
in the presence of the whole Assembly. The agents of the Duc
d'Orléans certainly fed the flame—for the moment, "Philippe
le Rouge " fancied the hour was ripe. The Breton Club, too,
the most violent of them all, was sending emissaries to Paris,
and practising, so Sieyès asserts, an "underground policy,"
while Mirabeau was inciting the people to a course which might
possibly result in his own appearance as a "saviour." We
need not seek very obscure causes; the revolutionaries of the
lower stratum—Loustalot and his fellows—were determined
there should be a "second fit of revolution." On October 4,
Loustalot and Desmoulins, who had quarrelled, made it up
again. Thenceforward all that remained to be done was to
draw up a list of grievances and throw the bands of ruffians
into Versailles. The *Veto*, the election of Mounier, the
King's refusal of his sanction, were already sufficient for this
purpose; certain hesitating attempts on the part of the Court
to bring about a counter-revolution were to supply a further
pretext. And beneath all these lay the hunger of the
people.

The Queen was dreaming of the dissolution of the "unpopular"
Assembly. The Assembly was thirsting to reduce the Queen's
coterie to impotence. The People—by this we mean the pseudo-
people of the " days "—was to take its way to Versailles, to
sweep away both Court and Assembly, cast Mounier from his
chair, and " Antoinette " from her throne.

SOURCES. Works of Biauzat, Duquesnoy, Maupetit, Mounier,
Lameth, Dumont, the Baron de Staël, Morris, Morellet, Madame Roland,
and the Deputé Noble, already quoted. Aulard, *Société des Jacobins*,
I, 1889; Vaissière, *Lettres d'Aristocrates*, 1907.—Campe, *Journal (Rev.
fr.*, 1910).

WORKS already quoted by Levasseur, Taine, Lanzac de Laborie,
Costa de Beauregard, Haussonville, Goncourt.—Sagnac, *Le Comité des*

Droits féodaux (Rev. fr., 1905) ; L. de Chilly, La Tour du Pin, 1907 ; Mathiez, Les Journées d'Octobre (Rev. Hist., 1898–9) ; Bergasse, La Déclaration (Réforme Sociale, 1908) ; Boutmy, La Déclaration (Annales des Sciences politiques, 1902) ; De la Gorce, Histoire religieuse de la Révolution, I, 1909 ; Duvergier de Hauranne, Histoire du Gouvernement parlementaire, Introduction, 1857.

CHAPTER V

THE DAYS OF OCTOBER

The Regiment of Flanders at Versailles. The scenes of October 1.
The women of Paris at Versailles. Disorderly scenes in the
Assembly. Mounier at the Palace. The Palace besieged.
Soldiers without cartridges. La Fayette at Versailles. "He
slept against his King!" The surprise of October 6. The
Queen threatened. The King goes to Paris.

THE arrival of the Regiment of Flanders at Versailles,
towards the end of September, had already roused
suspicion in the Assembly. It was said to be faithful
to the King. Was it to be used for a *coup d'état*? This,
despite the obstinate endurance of the legend, is absolutely
The Regiment unproved. M. Mathiez points out that the colonel
of Flanders at of the regiment, M. de Lusignan, sat in the
Versailles. Assembly among the deputies of the Left. The
idea was more probably to protect the Assembly itself against
a sudden attack, and it was the municipality of Versailles, in its
terror of the danger threatening from Paris, which requested
the executive to reinforce the troops in the town.

None the less is it true that on October 1 a scene took place
so evidently anti-revolutionary in its character that the friends
Scene of of the Revolution may well have taken alarm.
October 1. For several weeks past, so Paroy, a strong Royalist,
informs us, the ladies about the Court had been indulging in a
foolish practice of wearing lilies and white gowns ; innocent
enough, indeed, but most imprudent. Still more so was the
scene on the 1st. After a dinner given by the Gardes du Corps
to the Regiment of Flanders and some other troops in the hall
of the Palace theatre, the company, "their hearts warmed and
satisfied, toasted the Royal family." The King, just back
from hunting, made a sudden appearance in one of the boxes,
accompanied by the Queen and the Dauphin. "Five or six

men of the Regiment of Flanders, heated with wine, tore off their red and blue cockades "—I take these details from the most reliable authority available, the Marquis de Vergennes—crying, "The Assembly may go to the deuce ! We belong to the King only, and we are ready to die for him. Let us go back to his uniform and our white cockades ! " By the time the royal family had departed, the soldiers were in a state of the wildest excitement ; they swarmed out into the courtyards, and two of them climbed up to the balcony on which the King was standing, shouting, "Sire ! it is thus we make the assault; we devote ourselves to your service only ! "

That was all, but it was too much. If there had been any intention of attempting a *coup d'état*, it was revealed ; if there had been no such idea, the report had been provided with a foundation. It was the useless bravado of swashbucklers, a highly dangerous antic.

On the 2nd all Paris knew of it. The agitators were delighted ; here was the pretext they had been seeking for the past month! The day's proceedings were organized in the most artful manner. As the screams of the women of the people over the scarcity of food were shriller than those of the men, it was to be a woman's revolt. Who would dare to fire on starving women ? And behind the women the men would slip in. By five o'clock in the morning, 10,000 women were running riot. They were by no means irreproachable either as to virtue or manners. Mlle. Therwagne de Marcourt (such was her real name), who made her first appearance on this occasion, was no Lucretia, and little Madeleine Chabry, who was to address the King, sold bouquets (and kisses) in the Palais Royal. The strongest contingent, however, came from the Halles ; terrible women, these, sometimes in favour of the King, sometimes against him, always violent in the extreme. To swell the ranks of the " female " populace, there were numbers of men, shaved and painted and petticoated, soldiers of the Garde Française, dressed in women's jackets—a grotesque masquerade.

March of Women to Versailles.

An obscure bailiff of the name of Maillard took a drum and beat the charge. Within an hour 7000 or 8000 women— or so-called women—were marching wildly on Versailles.

104

Thiébault, with some half-score other witnesses, has left us a terrifying description of this mob.

The wretches had hardly started before the National Guard declared it must follow them. La Fayette, "that sycophant," writes Fournier l'Américain, refused at first. "S'death! General." shouted his men, "you'll stay with us!" "To Versailles or to the lamp-post!" they yelled to the hesitating Marquis. He declared later that they would have gone without him. And, indeed, Fournier was quite prepared to suborn his men. "We must bring the whole cursed lot to Paris!" he cried, and was answered by thunders of applause. La Fayette made the Commune give him formal orders to march, "seeing it was impossible to refuse"—a pitiful consideration. And at four o'clock the National Guard started noisily, led, to all appearance, by La Fayette.

*　　　*　　　*　　　*　　　*

At five that morning the Assembly was feeling nervous. Since Mounier's election (by secret ballot) the Extreme Left, **Disorderly** greatly irritated, had been preparing its revenge; **scenes in the** the most advanced of the deputies—the Breton **Assembly.** Club, which, according to Sieyès' expression, "proposed outrages as expedients"—were in constant communication with the Palais Royal, where the Orléans party and Mirabeau's emissaries were hard at work. For the past few weeks Mirabeau had been paying great court to Desmoulins.

The House was waiting on October 5 for the King's reply as to his sanction of the Decrees. It came; Louis XVI deferred his sanction of the Declaration, and only gave his temporary approval to the clauses of the Constitution which had been voted. There was an outcry from the Left. The "orgies of the Gardes du Corps" were indignantly denounced. Mirabeau used language of the most unprecedented kind. He would brand the real culprits, he declared, on condition that the King's person *only* was declared sacred! And that there might be no mistake as to what he meant, he added in a distinct voice, as he left the rostrum, that if necessary he would denounce the Queen. The whole hall was instantly in an uproar, and Mounier, in great distress, was about to close the sitting and so try to avoid the impending scandal, when the women

105

arrived from Paris. They were surging like a flood round the walls of the Menus Plaisirs. Twenty of them, led by Maillard, were admitted to the Hall. He poured forth a fierce denunciation of the persons who had bought up all the corn. The women yelled that the Archbishop had paid the millers to cease grinding ; this idiotic grievance was perpetually cropping up. Meanwhile certain deputies had the "indecent imprudence," so one of their colleagues writes, "to leave their seats and go and talk to the women," whose numbers were visibly increasing. They kept going back to the question of bread. "Your fine talk won't give us bread ! Talk to us about bread ! " they shouted, when the deputies promised them they would go to the King and force him to grant his "sanction." Mounier was weak enough, so says one deputy, to have a decree (quite useless) as to the food-supply voted and read aloud. "The corn decree has been put together," writes Lindet on October 6—"botched" would have been a better word. As to the "sanction," the President, coerced by the Assembly, consented, much against his will, to go and demand it from the King. Giving up his presidential chair to the Bishop of Langres, his predecessor, he proceeded to the Palace.

After his departure the tumult grew worse than ever. All the women had got in by this time. The worthy Bishop made **Mounier at** artless appeals for order. "We don't care a **the Palace.** snap (the expressions were far stronger) for order ! We want bread ! " the fishwives bawled. They were coming in from every quarter. The Vicomte de Mirabeau, thinking this a fine opportunity to shock his colleagues, took the best-looking of them on his knee. They had invaded the President's platform, and capered about yelling and screaming. "Put thy thumbs on the table, old shaveling ! " When, amidst bursts of hideous laughter, the Bishop had obeyed, writes Virieu, they ordered : "Now kiss me ! " And sighing heavily, he kissed them. They insisted that their "little mother Mirabeau " should mount the rostrum, and now and then they talked about "playing bowls with the head of that d——d Abbé Maury." The poor Bishop of Langres waited helplessly till ten o'clock at night for Mounier to come back.

* * * * *

THE DAYS OF OCTOBER

Mounier had found the Palace in a state of siege. About four o'clock in the afternoon the women had entered the Avenue de Paris and shouted to one of the Gardes du Corps who happened to be there, " Go up to the Château and tell them we shall soon be there to cut off the Queen's head ! " The Ministers, in a fever of alarm, were sitting in council, and could not get any precise directions from the King. " But something must be done ! " said Marie-Antoinette. " Gently, gently," replied Louis, and added that there could be no firing upon women.

The Palace besieged by the mob, October 5.

Meanwhile, in the mist of the autumn evening, troops were marshalled in front of the Palace, the famous Regiment of Flanders, the Bercheny Regiment, and the Regiment of the Three Bishoprics. The women came up to them. " Let us pass, Monsieur le Garde," said one to Lieutenant d'Albignac. " Impossible," he replied ; " and besides, what do you want to pass for ? " " To speak to the King ! " " What do you want him to do for you ? " " Let him resign, and all the trouble will be over ! " Their language about the Queen was not so moderate ; every one of them meant to " take back a bit of Marie-Antoinette." " I'll have her thighs ! I'll have her entrails ! " and they danced a saraband, holding out their aprons the while.

Meanwhile the majority in the Council was much in favour of driving the mob back. But the Minister of War, La Tour du Pin, shook with terror at the very thought of giving the mildest order. D'Estaing refused to serve out cartridges (of which there were plenty) to the Regiment of Flanders, and soldiers who were on the side of " the nation " put their ramrods down the barrels of their muskets to show the women they were empty.

At last the King sent word that a few of the women were to be allowed to pass, and he thus received two deputations and assured them he was about to give orders for the distribution of the corn in the grain stores of Corbeil and Etampes. At this moment Mounier made his appearance.

All these things had made a breach in the wall—a weak wall already—of the military force, as against the rioters. The mob was growing terribly bold. Though a bullet had laid

107

one of their officers low, the soldiers maintained their impassive attitude. The National Guard of Versailles hurried up, much more disposed to support the riot than to put it down. The Gardes du Corps, assailed with insults, made no reply. At last the King sent out an order : the troops were to retire, and the National Guard was to take over the duty of protecting the Château. Within a few minutes the Gardes du Corps, who had retired within the Palace gates, found it very difficult to defend them.

Louis XVI could not make up his mind to do anything. When Mounier besought him to grant his " sanction " he at first refused, thought he would escape through the Trianon and so to Rouen ; then he gave in—he would grant his sanction after all. Mounier started on his way back to the Menus Plaisirs distributing the news as he went. " Aha ! " cried the viragoes, " we have forced the blackguard to give the sanction ! " They did not know to what.

Now came a fresh complication—the National Guard of Paris was close at hand. After a moment of hesitation La **Arrival of La** Fayette had crossed the Rubicon by the Sèvres **Fayette at** bridge. At ten o'clock at night he appeared, **Versailles.** hung with tricolor ribbons.

He went to the hall of the Assembly, and found hideous disorder there. Mounier had returned, and read the King's declaration. One clamour had risen from the crowd : " Will that give us bread ? " Again and again the piteous cry went up, " Bread ! " Much affected, the President sent for bread, wine was brought, too, and within an hour the whole mob was drunk with wine as well as with its own yells. It was horrible.

In the midst of this vile orgy La Fayette appeared. Sharply Mounier addressed him. " What had he come to do there ? " " To protect the King," answered the Marquis. And, drawing nearer the President's chair, he added that he wanted to induce the King to withdraw the Regiment of Flanders. Thereupon he betook himself to the Château. He was coldly received. " Here comes Cromwell ! " said somebody. " Cromwell would not have come alone ! " was his reply. Once he had reached the King's presence, he protested his loyalty to the sovereign

" in a tearful voice." And indeed he got what he wanted. The King was to retire to his own apartments—it was two o'clock in the morning—the old Gardes Françaises, whom the general had brought down from Paris with the National Guard, were to replace the Gardes du Corps within the Palace. The Royal Family went to bed, and " General Morpheus," that inducer of sleep, hurried to the Assembly and persuaded the exhausted Mounier (who was spitting blood) to close the sitting. The mob stayed on alone ; when the deputies had departed, the women were seen taking off their muddy skirts to dry them. " The scenes that took place amongst those people," writes an officer, " were anything but decent ! " We may well believe it.

For the moment, however, the noise in Versailles seemed to have died down ; the mob bivouacked in the great avenues. Save at one gate, the Gardes Françaises had taken over the duties of the Gardes du Corps. At five o'clock La Fayette lay down and slept.

*   *   *   *   *

" He slept against his King ! " The scathing words were written the next day by Rivarol. But the accusation is not just. He slept because he believed it possible, in spite of the experience of two months, to stop a riot by giving way to the rioters. How can we wonder at this, when, after the experience of three and forty years, we see that the same thing was done in 1832 !

The Château had been almost denuded of defenders. At three o'clock in the morning de Guiche had marched all the Gardes du Corps, save a few who kept one post, through the Trianon to Rambouillet.

Now towards six o'clock groups of rioters began to prowl round the gates ; by some misunderstanding the gates into the courtyard had been left unlocked and un-
The surprise of October 5. guarded. Ruffians, armed with axes and muskets, passed through it.

The men of the Gardes du Corps hurried up, and their officer des Huttes, parleyed with the intruders. He was surrounded and driven back to the lowest step of the Marble Staircase. His comrades, overpowered by numbers, retired slowly, shouting to him, "Get to the King's rooms! Run!" It was too late. He was knocked down, his head struck off, and in a moment the rioters were crowding up the staircase. One Garde du Corps called out to the invaders, asking what they wanted. "The hearts of the King and Queen and their entrails, to make into cockades!" yelled one of the wretches. And up the stairs they came; the Gardes du Corps threw themselves into the King's saloon, then into the Queen's, and finally into the Œil de Bœuf, inside which they threw up a barricade. Before they reached this apartment Varicourt had been knocked down and torn to pieces, and his head set on the end of a pike. The royal apartments were bespattered with blood. Some of the Gardes Françaises rushed up to support their comrades. "Put on our cockades!" they cried. For everybody was still supposed to be fighting for one cockade or the other!

The Queen, warned of her peril by the Gardes du Corps, fled, half naked, to the King's apartments. The assailants **Peril of the** were howling that they meant to make "her **Queen.** liver into a fricassee!"

Utter confusion reigned within the palace walls. At last La Fayette woke up. He entered the King's apartment. His Majesty must now give his formal promise to start for Paris and take up his residence in the Louvre. The " good people " wanted their King! So be it. The news spread, and was hailed with shouts of joy. By this time the mob had crowded into the Cour de Marbre. The King's name was received with wild acclamation, but the Queen was still to be " torn to pieces." She was forced to show herself at the window, with La Fayette at her side, and was hailed with yells of " Bravo." Over the crowd the heads of des Huttes and Varicourt swayed, dripping with blood. The mob swept them away with it in its progress to the Avenue, whence it was to conduct the Sovereigns in procession to Paris. The coaches were made ready. No question this time of going to Rouen to recover possession of the crown! They were going to Paris, there to lose it altogether.

*   *   *   *   *

The sitting of the Assembly began at 11 o'clock that morning. Mounier, white with emotion, was in the chair.

In spite of his protests, motion after motion of the most

THE DAYS OF OCTOBER

revolutionary kind was brought forward. The most memorable
of all was proposed by Barnave : " The Assembly will follow
the King to Paris." The hideous invasion of the preceding day,
the decrees imposed on the Assembly by the popular will, the
sight of the Legislative Chamber polluted by the indecencies of
drunken women, none of these lessons had been taken to heart.
At Versailles the deputies fancied themselves too far away
from their tyrants.

A few hours more and the procession was formed. The
mob, mad with the joy of its triumph, moved on towards Paris,
dancing, singing, howling curses on the priests
and the nobles who were to be "strung up on
the lamp-post " when the city was reached, waving
poplar-branches, and a less idyllic trophy, the severed heads
of the two murdered soldiers. Those two blood-stained pikes
were the cross and banner of this strange procession. There were
men in it of the National Guard, of the Gardes Françaises, and
men of the Gardes du Corps, too, who were dragged along by
their conquerors, and subjected to perpetual insults. They had
tried to march with drawn swords on each side of the King's
coach. They had been forced to put their swords back into their
scabbards, and they looked like cattle on their way to the
slaughter-house. Lost in the crowd, the coaches moved along
bearing the King, the Queen, the Dauphin, Madame, and La
Fayette. "Here come the baker and his wife and the little
baker's boy ! " screamed the women. " Versailles to let ! "
shouted some sorry joker. The mob laughed and yelled, and
pushed on every side.

At half-past seven in the evening Paris was reached. Bailly
the inevitable harangued the King. " He was set down at the
Hôtel-de-Ville," writes a deputy. In every street the Queen
had been insulted ; "the lamp-posts were waiting for her,"
she was told ; obscene abuse was hurled at her. When the
Ministers who were Bishops made their appearance (it will be
remembered that one of these had been the real promoter of
the Declaration of Rights) the populace yelled : " To the
lamp-posts with every bishop ! "

At half past nine, by torch-light, the sovereigns arrived
at the Tuileries. " The King looked radiant. The Queen was

111

The King and Queen go to Paris.

dressed in a black mantle and a cap, and wore no rouge. She had lost that fixed look and haughty air peculiar to her. Supper was served at ten o'clock." Louis XVI, so another eye-witness informs us, astonished those about him by his huge appetite.

Then the gates of the Palace, the ante-room of the prison in the Temple, closed on the Royal family.

" Six Gardes du Corps have been killed," wrote some one that evening, "not a single citizen has perished."

SOURCES. *Works* of Vaissière, Duquesnoy, Virieu, Fournier l'Américain, Malouet, Ferrières, Mathieu Dumas, Lameth, Barnave, Mirabeau, Madame Roland, Madame de Chastenay, already quoted.—Aulard, *Société des Jacobins*, I ; Legrain, *Souvenirs sur Mirabeau (Nouv. Rev. Retr.*, XV) ; La Fayette, *Mémoire et Correspondance*, 1837–8 ; Cubières and Faydel, *Relations* (in Maricourt's *En Marge de l'Histoire*, 1895) ; Kowalewsky, *Relazioni degli ambasciatori veneziani*, 1895 ; Paroy, *Souvenirs*, 1895.

WORKS. Those already quoted by Mathieu Laborie, Taine, Charavay, Castellane.—D'Aussy, *Loustalot (Rev. Rev.*, XI).

CHAPTER VI

THE ASSEMBLY, THE CLUBS, AND THE CONSTITUTION

"The Deputies will be in the Riding-school, but the horsemen will be at the Palais-Royal." The Constituent Assembly. Parties and orators. The Society of the Jacobins. Intrigues of Mirabeau. The debates on the Constitution. The Constitution of 1789–1791. A middle-class and anarchical Constitution. The Communes and the Departments. The partition of the provinces. The destruction of the Parlements. A tottering edifice.

"THERE can be no question as to the liberty of the rostrum in a place so remarkable for its order and decency," wrote Gouverneur Morris on October 7. He was one of those wise Americans who were shortly to transfer the seat of their Congress far from populous cities, to Washington, a **The Deputies** town where the representatives would be their **to sit in the** own masters.

Riding-school. Our representatives cast themselves headlong into the abyss. They decided to sit in the Archiepiscopal Palace until the Hall of the Riding-school in the Tuileries could be made ready for them. "They will be in the Riding-school," quoth the ill-natured, "but the horsemen will be at the Palais Royal." Mounier, who could not believe in the possibility of free deliberation under such circumstances, endeavoured to induce the more moderate members to resign in a body. He failed, resigned his own seat, made a vain attempt to raise a revolt in his native Dauphiné, and ended by emigrating. The Revolution was already beginning to eliminate the real men of 1789, preparatory to "devouring" them. The eager deputy for Vizille was its first victim.

H

THE FRENCH REVOLUTION

The Assembly now appeared in its definite form. The
Right and the Left stood out on either side, and fought for the
The Constitu- five or six hundred uncertain votes which were
ent Assembly. cast one way or the other, according to the
preoccupations of the hour.

There were many capable men in the Right, the Centre,
and the Left. They must not be judged by their work, which
was frequently very mediocre. But ten years later Bonaparte,
that great constructor, was to find excellent elements for government among them, from Lebrun the Consul, to Mounier the
Prefect ; from Treilhard the Councillor of State, to Talleyrand
the Minister. Malouet (who might well have been bitter)
acknowledges that he saw a great many " competent men "
on those benches.

On the Right we see the Abbé Maury, a violent man, vulgar,
sometimes familiar, sometimes terrible, often very clear-sighted,
unfortunately greatly discredited ; this son of an artisan, a
true plebeian by nature, remained the champion of the counter-
Revolution to the very end ; he had no principles, and narrowly
escaped destruction at the hands of his own " side." The
Abbé de Montesquiou, keen-witted, exceedingly aristocratic,
but gifted with remarkable good sense, was an attractive
personality : " a little snake " Mirabeau called him. Cazalès
was an excellent speaker ; " he spoke like a God," exclaimed one
of his colleagues ; he was an officer, full of religious faith, and
an unswerving Royalist, but his thrilling and polished oratory
was applauded even by the Left, which, indeed, respected him
for his noble qualities. Malouet was perhaps the only fervent
and prominent Royalist of the Third Estate. Before his election
he had been employed in the administration, and, no common
thing at that period, he was of a practical turn of mind, and
preached loyalty to the Assembly, liberalism to the Court,
and moderation to all.

These were the most prominent figures on the Right. The
rest were curiously mediocre ; the Vicomte de Mirabeau,
" Mirabeau the Barrel," though a very intelligent man, had
taken the line of being as eccentric in his motions as in his
appearance ; his violence, whether intentional or mere banter,
seemed to go to his head, and nobody could take him seriously.

114

The Right, in short, with its angry nobles, its exasperated country gentlemen and agreeable prelates, none of them capable of figuring at the rostrum, backed by a handful of terrified *bourgeois*, carried but little weight on the whole, and was soon to crumble away. Even during the summer of 1789 Mounier perceived that its attendance at the sittings was very perfunctory. Lindet rejoiced to see its benches empty from five in the afternoon onwards, thus permitting the passing of revolutionary motions between six and seven. "It was impossible for them," says Mounier, "to put off their meal till a later hour." Thus, thanks to the desertion of the Right, the Revolution was largely carried through by candle-light. Many of the members of the party were careless, others were frightened. The Left would shout to them, "We'll notify you to your departments!"—a terrible threat to hear in those days of burning country houses.

On the Left and in the Centre (it is not easy, at this period, to define the limits of parties) we see another aristocracy, the liberal nobility, great lords who were very sincerely liberal or democratic, blindly generous, some of them—like Lally-Tollendal, "the angel of eloquence"—crowned too with the glory of his parent's woes; Clermont-Tonnerre, "an eager spirit on fire with philosophic motions," Larochefoucauld-Liancourt, a convinced philanthropist and worthy of all admiration, who, to his last hour, clung imperturbably to his belief that "Man is good." Amongst the democratic clergy the only remarkable orator was the harsh parish priest of Embermesnil, Grégoire, a fervent Christian, a yet more fervent Jansenist, all made up of hatreds, hatred of impiety, hatred of the Papist, hatred of Royalty. He thought himself "evangelical," but it was in a gloomy fashion. Yet he was sincere, upright, and often showed great nobility of character. Maurice de Talleyrand, Bishop of Autun, was his very opposite; even then he was "mud in a silken stocking." On the very eve of the Days of October he was still seeking his road with his nose to the wind. On the morrow his mind was made up; the Revolution had triumphed, and he, seated with the Left, was to betray his Order, his Church, his King, his own soul, and smiling as he did so, to cast away his gown. Without ever stirring

115

anger in the breasts of those he sold, he was to sell all men—seductive, persuasive, corrupt, dishonest, he carried the spirit of treachery to the point of genius. Another priest, Sieyès, is already known to us ; later, we shall once more find him to the fore, and he shall be fully described ; already he was an oracle, supposed to carry the regeneration of all humanity within his mighty brain.

Another deserter to the Left attracts attention—Honoré-Gabriel de Riquetti de Mirabeau. Hideous, his face seamed by small-pox, deep furrows on his forehead, heavy **Mirabeau.** and round-shouldered, thick-set in figure, slow in his movements, but with eyes that flamed, and lips that worked with the fierceness of his passion, and gestures that were terrifying, he turned his repulsive physical appearance to deliberate account. "My ugliness is a power," he said. His almost irresistible eloquence made him the most renowned orator in the Assembly, which he could subdue, on occasions, to his will, leading it on, holding it in check, or even urging it forward for an hour ; his past record, which was very nearly infamous, his habits, which were cynically dissolute, a reputation, partially deserved, for venality, and the scorn he was instinctively felt to nurse for all with whom he came in contact, deprived him, once he had left the rostrum, of any durable influence. He was generous now and then, lazy, sensual, taking a passionate interest in everything, but never going to the bottom of anything. An actor formed by Lekain and Mlle. Clairon, he would make speeches that had been written for him, and yet seemed to come from the very bottom of his heart. But he had admirable ideas on matters of State ; he was, indeed, the only great man in the whole Assembly, though in the chaos of that nebulous parliamentary world he was a useless or a harmful force, which was broken, indeed, at an early stage.

" M. de Mirabeau is the torch of Provence ; M. de Robespierre is the candle of Arras ! " The dismal lawyer from Artois was there. The former *protégé* of the Bishop of Arras went to extremes at once. We shall come upon him one day with the full light beating on him, the proud, bitter, sincere, honest, pompous jurist, whose eloquence, stinking of oil and distilling vinegar, so wrung the nerves of the Assembly at this particular juncture that it was greeted with bursts of scornful laughter. He, bitterly humiliated, sullen, and sore, nursed his hidden hatreds. With Roederer, a supple politician destined to serve more than one *régime*, who at that moment held very advanced opinions ; with Buzot, a hero of romance set on the rostrum, formed and demented by Rousseau and Plutarch, and with Pétion, a good-looking fellow of mediocre powers, whom circumstance was to serve, and one day serve very ill in the most curious fashion, Robespierre was the " purest " of the " pure." This quartette was to constitute an Extreme Left in the Assembly, and in this group we may also place, even at this period, the terrible Barnave, of whose soul of fire in a body of ice we shall later speak, Barnave, who, with Duport and Lameth, formed the famous Jacobin " Triumvirate."

These, with La Fayette and Bailly, were the most noticeable figures, but they were not the leaders. The Assembly, oppressed by its tribunes, trembling before the Clubs, overawed by the mob, and led by events, was always to slip through its leaders' fingers. Infatuated with itself, though, as a whole, incapable of anything, priding itself on being neither disciplined nor led, the Assembly was simply swept along by a confused body of legists, whose eyes were fixed on an ideal Mount Sinaï, and who sought the Law amidst its clouds, whereas it was to rise out of their ancestral soil. Under the leadership of these real, though anonymous and dangerous conductors, were massed what Mme. Roland was scornfully to describe as " the heap of logs at eighteen *livres* a day ! "

Alongside of this confused and over-numerous Assembly which might be influenced, but could not be disciplined, and was at the mercy of any violent impulse from without, the real assembly, that which was to guide all coming events, was taking shape—the Society of the Jacobins.

The nucleus of this had been the Breton Club, a mere gathering of certain deputies. Its founders were three Rennes Society of the lawyers, Lanjuinais, Defermon, and Le Chapelier, Jacobins. with a few democrat *rectors* of Breton parishes. In time, Mirabeau, Sieyès, Barnave, Pétion, Volney, Grégoire, Robespierre, the two de Lameth brothers, and the Duc d'Aiguillon, were admitted to its meetings.

When the Assembly moved to Paris, the Club moved too, and took up its quarters at 7 Place de la Victoire. But a larger body was even then about to absorb it, the "Society of the Friends of the Constitution," which was beginning to meet in the Convent of the Jacobins Saint-Honoré. Hither the whole of the "Breton" staff betook itself, and forthwith found itself surrounded by its soldiers and its masters, small Parisian tradesmen and artisans who composed the *Society*, and who, while seeming to follow in the deputies' wake, practically led them. Before the end of 1790 the Jacobin Society was to be the great fountain of opinion. Soon these eleven hundred clubmen of the Rue Saint-Honoré (*see* the official list for 1790) were not content to lead Paris only; they laid the foundations of that huge organization which was to forward the consumma-tion of the "second Revolution." By the beginning of 1791 the Society had 227 daughter societies in the provinces; three months later it had 345, and when the Constituent Assembly came to an end, 406. Through these provincial societies it ruled the whole country. First it swept it along with it, and then it quelled it. Thus the deputies naturally fell into the habit of ceasing to turn their eyes towards their own constituencies, and looking rather towards that former chapel of the Jacobin monks wherein public opinion was elaborated.

Thus, from 1790 onwards the Club became the master of the Assembly.

*   *   *   *   *

The Assembly, thus held in bondage by the Club, fancied it had the King entirely in its power. Louis XVI seemed to have resigned himself to his part as King Log. Greatly discouraged, he hoped to "put an end to the Revolution" by giving way to it. Even the people about him seemed paralyzed; the Comte de Provence had ceased plotting against the Revolution, save in the most underhand way. And, besides, order was re-established. La Fayette had guaranteed this. Mirabeau was the one person who continued to advise the Court not to trust to the seeming lull.

He was not in the Ministry, and that made him furious. While in the Assembly, where he courted popularity, he

118

would support motions of the most demagogic nature, he was sending letter after letter to the Court, sometimes going so far as to flatter the Queen, "the only man the King has about him," sometimes full of the boldest threats, and a clear-sightedness as to the future that astounds us nowadays, for he foretold everything that would ultimately happen if nothing were done to stem the tide. He thirsted to come into power. But neither the King nor the Assembly could make up their minds to place such a tyrant over them. And the Assembly finally destroyed all his hopes, voting, in spite of him, a motion brought in by Lanjuinais, which forbade any deputy to hold ministerial office. The Right voted for the motion out of sheer hatred of Mirabeau, and the Duc de Levis has acknowledged the enormity of its mistake. Mirabeau felt the blow cruelly. "Let the House simply vote that M. de Mirabeau is to be excluded from the ministry !" he said. In his rage against the Right he resolved that his "stupid" opponents should pay dearly for their blind hatred, and though he still continued his offers of help to the Court, he struck at the Government more fiercely than ever. Talleyrand, who had been put aside by the same measure, was more moderate in his attitude ; but he, too, was embittered, and became more and more of a demagogue in his utterances. These three men, Mirabeau, La Fayette, and Talleyrand, thus cut off from ministerial functions in which, perhaps, they might have been able to stem the tide of Revolution, were driven out of their course, and hurried on the movement they were no longer in a position to arrest.

Intrigues of Mirabeau.

❋   ❋   ❋   ❋   ❋

Amidst all these intrigues the debates pursued their course. The discussion of the Constitution was apparently ended in February 1790. Administrative and judicial reform grafted on to political reform was to develop into the Constitution known as that of 1791, because, though it was reconsidered and recast in the course of 1790 and 1791, it was not until September in that year that it was finally approved by the King, and thus became law.

Debates on the Constitution.

THE FRENCH REVOLUTION

When the Assembly moved to Paris the work was already far on the way to completion. The ground had been cleared of the proposals as to a second Chamber, and very unwillingly the King had been allowed a suspensory veto.

The royal Veto decreed.

This last concession was almost regretted. More and more every day, and in spite of the King's submissive behaviour, the Executive was looked on as the enemy. The Assembly was soon to enfeeble it beyond all reason. The mistake is susceptible of explanations ; these deputies of 1789 were unacquainted as yet with the excesses of a popular despotism, neither did they know anything of the abuses of a parliamentary *régime*. None of them, with the exception of Mirabeau and Mounier, were clear-sighted enough to foresee them. All they realized was the excess of the sovereign's absolute power. Louis XVI was not a threatening figure, indeed, but we must remember that the Revolution was directed against Louis XIV. The Constitution of 1791 being the outcome of a feeling which may thus be explained was necessarily the outcome of a reaction against absolutism, far more than that of a democratic revolution. "They were more anxious to rule the King than to rule through him," wrote Mirabeau.

We will not go back to the Veto ; Mirabeau, who believed himself at that moment to be just about to come into power, had carried the motion with great difficulty, crying out, that if it were rejected he would "rather live in Constantinople than in France." "I could imagine nothing more terrible," he had added, "than a sovereign authority made up of 600 persons ! " He did not share the opinion of that other deputy who held that the King could not stand out, even for a day, against the Assembly's will, for "it is a glory for a King to share the errors of his people."

The suspensory Veto authorised Louis XVI to refrain during the existence of three legislatures (six years) from "sharing the errors of his people." This was a prerogative ; we shall see to what circumstances reduced it.

When the discussion was over what was the new sovereign ? Yes, the new sovereign ! for he was to be crowned again forthwith. The King was to be kept because, as Rabaut Saint-Étienne had pointed out, in Sparta, which was a Republic, there were two Kings (the argument is racy of the times); but the King's title must be changed, he was to be *King of the French*. Some people proposed a still more radical change, *Louis the First, Emperor of the French*. These were men in a hurry, who were fated to wait fifteen years before they heard the title of their dreams, borne by a man very different from " Louis the First ! "

The King was nothing more now than the supreme agent of the nation, the first servant of the law. The heading of all public documents established the order of this hierarchy; the Nation—the Law—the King.

The King the "Chief Officer" of the Nation.

The King was the supreme head of the army and the administration, he had power to nominate the highest functionaries. All the rest—that is, all matters of administration, of justice, of the army—were taken out of his hands.

He was to coin money, to direct the military forces, to sign treaties, and—when expressly authorized by the Assembly— he might declare war. He was free to choose his ministers and to dismiss them, and, finally, as we know, he might oppose for the space of three Legislative Assemblies the passing of any law that had been voted.

In appearance he had a certain power ; in reality he was impotent. This grandson of Louis XIV was not granted a fourth part of the powers possessed by our present President at the Elysée.

The Veto was to be annulled ; his right to dismiss his ministers was to be openly contested. Every time the King attempted to use the rights left him, the Nation was to hold that he was abusing them.

And even could he have enjoyed them unmolested, he must always have been in a position of marked inferiority as regards the Assembly, for he could not dissolve it; the appeal to the people was denied him. In every case of conflict the Assembly was to have the upper hand ; if it was annoyed by the King's veto, it could strike at the Ministry by refusing to vote the budget. But the King could never touch the Assembly.

And, therefore, from that moment, he necessarily became its slave, its " chief officer," as Rivarol put it.

" Chief Officer," well and good ! if only he could have performed his duties ! But for this, two things would have been indispensable, that he should have been able to keep up constant relations with the Assembly through a Parliamentary Ministry, and, secondly, that he should have been allowed to keep a real hold over the functionaries charged under him with the duty of ensuring respect for the law.

One of the Assembly's capital errors was the voting, on November 7, 1789, the motion which excluded its own members from any ministry. The constitutional *régime* which these men fancied they were installing was thus radically warped from the very outset by their own act. The law was specially levelled at certain ambitious men, but the exclusion, before long, attained the dignity of an intangible dogma. It made a watertight compartment between the two branches of power and organized misunderstanding. That decree of September 7, 1789—one of the capital clauses of the Constitution —was in itself enough to make the whole of the new political order impracticable.

The paralysis of the Sovereign was completed by the organization of the administration. He was the head of the administration ; this is set forth in the constituting document. But how was the King to rule functionaries the huge majority of whom were elected by the nation, and whom he consequently could neither dismiss nor even suspend from their functions ? The question had come up before the Constitution had been completely voted. " What is to be done." La Fayette asks Gouverneur Morris, " in the case of disobedience on the part of the provincial administrators ? They are under the King's orders, but their functions being elective, they may refuse to respect him." The Assembly, which had disarmed the Sovereign, as far as it was itself concerned, by refusing him the power of dissolution, and which had paralyzed his good intentions by depriving him of the right to choose his ministers among its own members, forbade him the exercise of any serious action on public functionaries. "The Assembly," writes Mirabeau, " has not created any executive power. . . . I maintain that no

122

such power can exist without agents and without organs." The Assembly, having turned the King into its chief servant, did not even grant this servant the possibility of serving it well.

* * * * *

What was this sovereign legislative power ? It was to be vested in a single Chamber, the Legislative Assembly. It A middle-class and anarchical Constitution. was a suspicious power, fearful alike of an appeal to the people, and an appeal to the soldiers ; the King might not send the members of the Assembly to face their electors, and the army was forbidden to approach within 60,000 yards of the spot on which the sittings were held.

The deputies, indeed, were only elected for two years. This was a sacrifice to the sovereignty of the people, a sacrifice which, if the Constitution were to be applied, would singularly fetter the work of Parliament ; every two years proposals already considered were to be reconsidered, and newly voted laws interpreted in a different spirit by men who had not voted them in the first place. And in 1791 the difficulty was aggravated by the crowning arrangement (and crowning folly), whereby members of one Constituent Assembly were declared ineligible for the next. To this we shall refer later.

Every two years, then, the country was to elect its representatives. What was this country ? It is at this point that the *bourgeois* of the Assembly *drew back the curtain.* " All men are born equal " ; universal suffrage would seem the inevitable outcome of this Declaration ; Condorcet would even have given votes to women.

The Constituent Assembly does not appear to have been much inclined to do this ; even amongst men, a certain difference was to be made.

" All men are born equal " ; the clause was voted in an outburst of enthusiasm ; the phrase was dictated by Rousseau, and perhaps M. de la Palisse had a hand in it ! But this memorable sitting once closed, the members of the Assembly opened their Montesquieu, and read the following words : " It was only through the corruption of certain democracies that the artisans contrived to attain citizenship." In reality the bulk of these men—those who survived the Terror—reached their

Promised Land under the *régime* that began in July 1830. What a pity it is that Duquesnoy died before the days of Guizot's Ministry! "There are certainly no true citizens but property-owners," writes that liberal member of the Constituent Assembly! This suffices to explain the *marc d'argent*.

This *marc d'argent* was the formula which embodied the whole system. All men are citizens, but there are *passive* citizens—the poor—and *active* citizens ; the passive citizens have no votes, the active citizens have votes. And even among the active citizens a special hierarchy is created by the law of December 29, 1789. The man who paid taxes equivalent to the value of three days' work was an elector in the first degree ; that made up an electorate of 4,298,360 ; this was "the country," according to the law. But were these men to elect the deputies ? No ! they were simply to elect the delegates who were to choose the deputies, and these delegates were to be chosen amongst taxpayers of the value of ten days' work. Were these men—these fairly well-off men—to be eligible as members of the Assembly ? Not at all ! No man who did not pay taxes to the amount of a *marc d'argent* (fifty *livres*), and was a landed proprietor as well, could be a deputy.

In this form the proposal was voted ; but the opposition to it, which had been extremely violent, did not die down, and for two years the *marc d'argent* was the *Delenda Carthago* of the Extreme Left. A deputy belonging to the Centre notes with extreme annoyance that on January 25, 1790, one month after the passing of the measure, the *marc d'argent* had been rediscussed for the eighth time. And this was to go on until it was finally suppressed. But would it be more democratic to decree that the Assembly was to be elected solely by absolute owners, or life-owners of property valued locally at 150 to 200 days' labour, by tenants of houses rated at the value of 100 to 150 days, and by *métayers* and farmers of property reckoned at 400 days ?

Artisans, in accordance with Montesquieu's views, were to be excluded from citizenship. In a bitter letter written on April 28, 1791, Mme. Roland expresses her indignation on this subject. As a democrat she was right ; as a revolutionary she was wrong. A particular class attaches itself strongly

124

to a form of government only if that form of government confers benefits upon it. The huge middle class, which now included not only the bankers of the Chaussée d'Antin, but all the new and very small rural landowners, was to be the real rampart of the Revolution ; for it was grateful to the Revolution which had inscribed the legend of " Equality " on the pediment of the edifice, at the expense of the aristocracy, and had done it, in fact, for the sole benefit of the *bourgeois*, great and small. The words of our friend the deputy were realized : " There are no real citizens save property-owners."

It was this privileged body, then, which was to elect the 750 deputies, who, by a strange contradiction, might be chosen (as we shall see in September 1791) from the ranks of the class least well provided with capital or landed property.

*   *   *   *   *

But the face of the earth must be changed, and the face of France to begin with. At one fell swoop all the old organizations, the old officials, the old administrative and judicial districts, were swept away. The new spirit required new forms from top to bottom. A system had sprung up spontaneously out of the Revolution—the new Commune. This was organized and confirmed, and, as the Revolution already owed it a great deal, it was deliberately strengthened. In this particular the Constituent Assembly did a work of decentralization. Each Commune was a little republic in itself. It elected its own magistrates, executive, and legislative, its mayor and municipality, its general council, and procurator ; it directed the armed force, the National Guard ; it assigned and collected the taxes. To this we must add—but freed from the central control, now so despotic—all those police and other powers confided to the municipalities of the present day. The Procurator of a Commune soon became a petty despot.

The Communes.

These Communes were to remain very " advanced " in their opinions. From the revolutionary point of view the course pursued in giving them such large powers was therefore an intelligent one.

On the other hand, thanks to the suspicion with which
The Provinces provincial opinion was regarded, even after the
cut up into provinces had been cut up, very little power was
Departments. conferred on the departments.

This institution of the departments, by decrees passed on
November 11 and 12, 1789, and February 15 and 26, 1790,
was, from the standpoint of the Assembly, that of the triumph
of the Revolution, a stroke of genius. By this dismemberment of the country all resistance on the part of the provinces
to the law imposed on them by Paris was rendered impossible.
The process weakened France, indeed, in every bone. The
country was to suffer, and certain of its limbs were to be permanently crippled ; the consequent anæmia was to become
chronic ; the head was to grow out of all proportion. Let us
bid farewell, this winter of 1789-1790, to the old " country,"
which the Revolution was about to break up.

Eighty-five departments were definitely organized by the
decree of February 15, 1790, with their sub-divisions, their
districts and cantons, and that of the 26th baptized them, if
we may use the expression, with names that had been hastily
chosen and were in some cases absurd. Over the selection
of the chief town or village of each department and district
there were great bickerings, as revealed in the correspondence
of half a score of deputies.

Departments and districts had elected Administrations,
Directories, Councils, all with collective powers. In every department, as in every district, these bodies were set in motion by a
Procurator Syndic, who was the chief power, though his power
was not so great as that of the Procurator of the tiniest Commune.
For the Department, compared with the Commune, was weak,
a fresh element of anarchy in this strange administration.

* * * * *

Judicial reorganization was modelled on that of the Administration.

Judges of every degree were elected. To the Constituents
this was a return to primitive rights. Had not their colleague
Bouche informed them that " until the year 697 the people
had chosen their own judges, and that at this period (at which
the clergy were admitted to the States-General) the people
126

began to lose its rights?" What could be said in answer
an erudition so self-confident? An intelligent man, Thoma
Lindet, writes that the people "is about to take back th
rights usurped by its kings."

One great advantage was that of being able to suppress
the Parlements, which the deputies loathed. These "Courts"
The Parle- had been opposing the Assembly, sometimes
ments openly, sometimes stealthily, for the last six
abolished. months. The deputies, less patient than the
Bourbons, held no "bed of justice," they simply hunted the
members out of their *fleur-de-lysed* seats.

Their places were to be taken by other magistrates, men
chosen by "the country." For here again the King might
say nothing; this was a cruel indignity, seeing the Sovereign,
as "chief lord," was likewise "chief judge"; but everything
was to be uprooted, including the Vincennes oak! Justices
in the cantons, judges of civil courts in the districts, judges of
criminal courts in the departments, with juries accusatory and
judicial, all were to be elective. The public Ministry connected
with these tribunals was not entirely in the King's hands, for
though the Commissary who reported to the court was his
nominee, the Public Prosecutor was an elected official. The
Judges of the Court of Appeal were elected too—one for each
department—and so were those of the High Court at Orleans,
which sat to try persons accused of treason against the King,
and, much oftener, against the Revolution.

*　　　*　　　*　　　*　　　*

This huge work of reform—unique in history—was a monument indeed, but very poor and fragile in construction. I
A tottering have already referred to the unparalleled weak-
Edifice. ness of the central government; power existed
in high quarters, but it never came from above. The Government issued orders to people who could disobey them with
impunity, because it had no hold on them. And on the other
hand these same people were at the mercy of citizens whom
it was their duty to rule, and between whom they had to judge.
It was a scandalous situation.

If all these citizens had even voted, good government might
perhaps have resulted in the end. But the busy men. and

therefore the best citizens, worn out by this abuse of elections, were soon to cease voting altogether. Local politicians, or rather political organizations, *Societies*, took advantage of this to job the elections. And when these *Societies*, urged forward by the Jacobins, formed a federation, an unacknowledged government speedily took the place of the nominal one. That huge organization of the *Popular Societies* would never have taken possession of the country, if it had been confronted by a strong administration.

The Administration constructed by the Constituent Assembly during the winter of 1789-1790 was weak and infirm. France, as I have said, had been robbed of her bones; when an attempt to build up a new body was made, the bones were brought together in what looked like a fine arrangement, but muscles there were none. When the Convention, still under the nominal *régime* of the Constitution of 1791, took the King's place, the mistake made by the Constituent Assembly became so evident that the Assembly, to get soldiers and money, and obtain obedience to the laws of the country, was fain to appoint those Commissaries and " Representatives delegated by the Government " who were to find it so easy, in a country every muscle of which had been severed, to usurp pro-consular powers. The unconstitutional missions of the year II are the completest possible criticism of the work of the years 1789 and 1790. The introduction into that ill-balanced body of the extraordinary supporting frame, which kept it, as by a miracle, upon its feet, had become an inevitable necessity.

From 1791, when the edifice was set up, onwards, we shall see it rocking on its weak foundations. " The Constitution is of such a nature," wrote Gouverneur Morris on November 20, 1790, " that the Almighty Himself could not make it work unless He created a new species of man." La Fayette himself was assailed by doubts. Mirabeau was to declare, after a more brutal fashion, that "*the disorganization of the kingdom could not have been better planned.*" Even in 1792 the cracks were showing in the walls. Until the great reconstruction of the year 1800 the Convention was constrained to stop the gaps in the monument of 1791 with its own hideous mortar.

ASSEMBLY, CLUBS, CONSTITUTION

SOURCES. Works by Morris, Vaissière, Duquesnoy, Thibaudeau, Aulard (*Jacobins*), Baron de Staël, Morellet, Mirabeau, Virieu, Talleyrand, Rabaut, Mme. de Chastenay, Guilhermy, Lameth, Legrain, already quoted.—Thomas Lindet, *Correspondance*, 1899 ; Frenilly, *Souvenirs*, 1908 ; Lacretelle, *Dix ans d'Epreuves*, 1842 ; Schmidt, *Tableaux de la Révolution*, 1867–1871 ; Louise Fusil, *Souvenirs*, 1841.

WORKS already quoted by Goncourt, Levasseur, Cahen, Laborie, Castellane, Neton, Esmein, Sicard.—Aulard, *Les Orateurs de la Constituante* (ed. of 1905) ; Hamel, *Robespierre*, I, 1865 ; Hérissay, *Buzot* ; Plan, *Un collaborateur de Mirabeau*, 1874 ; Sorel, *Montesquieu*, 1895 ; Frédéric Masson, *L'Organisation de l'Administration par la Constituante* (*Jadis*, III, 1909) ; Simonnet, *Le Gouvernement parlementaire et l'Assemblée Constituante*, 1899.

CHAPTER VII

THE NATIONALIZATION OF CHURCH PROPERTY

General discontent. The Clergy, hitherto friendly to the Revolution, rise up against it. Church property. The financial crisis. Talleyrand's proposal. The debates. The vote of November 1789. The *Assignats*. Consequences of the event. The Clergy embittered. Discussions in the Assembly. Increasing anarchy in the country.

ON February 4, 1790, the Assembly, informed by its President that his Majesty was about to appear in the Chamber, broke into loud applause. And when the King, having duly arrived, affirmed his perfect agreement with the Assembly, and his consequent approval of the measures The King for- already voted, and "clearly expressed his dis- mally sanctions pleasure against those who might attempt to the Revolution. stop or delay the Revolution," the House, write Lindet, Thibaudeau, Duquesnoy, and various other deputies, broke into "transports of affection and emotion." "The best of kings" was passionately thanked.

All this emotion sprang out of a genuine anxiety. For the more complete the Revolution became, the more evident were the dissatisfactions it evoked. The movement, hailed with acclamation by the country all through the spring and summer of 1789, had changed its direction, and in the course of its deviations too many people had been crushed by it.

It is a curious fact that those who had apparently suffered the most cruel injury at the hands of the Revolution, the nobles, Apathy of the seemed to feel it least of all. These charming nobility. beings possessed a fund of the most admirable apathy. Ruined by the abolition of the feudal rights, persecuted in the provinces, reviled in Paris, threatened everywhere, the greater number, as we see them in the hundreds of

130

letters from aristocrats published by Vaissière, went on their way with a smile. When a deputy of the Left writes: "A few weathercocks have been pulled down, and even a few country-houses set alight," we have a pretty clear idea of the indifference of the Assembly. But what is far more astonishing is the calm fatalism with which the victims themselves allowed their persecutors to smoke them out. Their resignation did them no service, nor did the attitude of patriotic zeal assumed by some of their number. They were considered enemies, and all the more so because they were oppressed. It was not credible that men so cruelly ill-treated would not conspire. If they were hunted into emigration, they went abroad to plot. If they stayed in France, it was to plot again. Treated more and more rigorously, still they smiled.

The hymn *À la lanterne* was yelled beneath the windows of the Faubourg Saint-Germain, that lamp-post,

> "Des vengeances du peuple et de la liberté
> Monument à la fois glorieux et funèbre." [1]

Litanies to the lamp-post were chanted under these windows too :

> " Epouvantail des scélerats, vengez-nous,
> Effroi des aristocrates, vengez-nous : "

Nothing seemed to move the threatened caste. The winter of 1789–1790 was particularly gay. "We have had some delightful tea-parties the last few days. We are all amusing ourselves," writes one doomed aristocrat. On December 31 they bade the old year a joyous farewell; as midnight struck, the gentlemen gaily kissed the ladies of the company. And not a head there but was shaking on its owner's shoulders! They made fun of the Revolution. When Mme. de Simiane was struck by an apple thrown from the upper gallery of the Théâtre Français, crowded with people of the humbler class, she sent it to her brother-in-law, La Fayette, and wrote, "Here,

> - " Glorious and awful monument
>   Of the vengeance of people and liberty."

> : " Scarecrow of rascals, avenge us,
>   Terror of aristocrats, avenge us ! "

my dear General, is the first fruit of the Revolution that has reached my hands!" And what amusement was caused by the expression used by the market-women of the Halles, when they went to wish the Assembly a Happy New Year: "Our children, when they see you, will call you their fathers!" There was much joking, too, over La Fayette and his National Guard. But that was the only vengeance taken. One lady laughed at her shoemaker, who said to her just after the famous sitting of February 4: "I very much hope my son will some day be what a Marshal of France is now. Am I not myself the Major of my battalion?" She thought this very farcical, but she was wrong. The shoemaker had revealed to the high-born lady one of the forces destined to ensure the triumph of the Revolution. "My son will some day be what a Marshal of France is now!"

All this was beyond the comprehension of aristocratic society. Was it ever to understand? When it did not treat the Revolution as a subject for scornful mirth, it turned it into a fashionable toy. There were patriotic trinkets, trinkets "à la Constitution," tricolour snuff-boxes, dresses "à la Constitution," hats "à la Révolution." How was anybody to complain of events that had brought in the taste for the antique and driven out the late fashions, thus enabling "the dealers in frivolities" to change the wares they showed? Those dealers in frivolities! They were ubiquitous all through that winter of 1789-1790, while the picks of the Assembly were tearing down the old kingdom of France, her Parlements, her Provinces, her Corporations, her Clergy, and her Army!

But if the aristocrats seemed resigned to their fate, others were far from being so. The parlementaires were much less Protests of the quickly subjugated. Those "crowns that were Parlements. shaved in four and twenty hours," as Seneffe puts it, rebelled for one, at all events. Some Parlements entered protests; haughty from Rennes, lachrymose from Rouen, wheedling from Metz. But the Rennes men were forced to come up to Paris and apologize; the old Fronde was fain to humble itself at the feet of the new Revolution on January 7. This wrought secret bitterness in the hearts of the bourgeois, whose lives gravitated round the old Courts.

132

Some of the Provincial Estates lodged protests also. Certain provinces betrayed an intention of separating since their individuality was to be suppressed. Nancy desired to remain the capital of its own duchy; Corsica threatened to sever itself entirely from France; the Assembly was obliged to place Paoli, who led this opposition, at the head of the new department. In every direction there were evident signs of the jealousy with which the provinces regarded Paris, " which is absorbing everything," writes a Lorrain deputy tartly, and, within the provinces, of the anger of the towns deposed from their former pre-eminence in favour of the new departmental centres.

And everywhere, too, the artisans were in a state of the most lively discontent. The suppression of the corporations Dissatisfaction met with vehement opposition; Marat protested of the artisans. against it fiercely. The Assembly was to forbid and prosecute with the greatest severity all " working men's coalitions "—syndicates and strikes, as we should call them nowadays. And, further, the general poverty was extreme; on this point every witness is agreed. Corn was growing more and more scarce; there was very little bread to be had, and that little was very dear. At Lyons 28,000 people were living on public charity. At Louviers Young saw the spinning factories standing empty. The fortunes of the privileged classes had been attacked, but industry and commerce, as an inevitable result, had suffered too, and the workman, consequently, was likewise suffering. The Constituent Assembly was forced to open *charity-workshops*. In May 1790 these workshops were supporting 11,800 artisans, in October there were 18,800 in them. Fifteen millions *livres* were spent on keeping them going in the course of the year 1790. But workmen fed by the nation never think they receive enough.

Meanwhile the manufacturing and commercial classes saw their businesses going to rack and ruin, and their hostility was unconcealed. They had favoured the movement of 1789, but they thought they were paying too dearly for it now.

And then the Clergy, which had also supported the Revolution during the closing months of 1789, was suddenly attacked and driven into opposition by the merciless measure for the sale of all Church property. This event, one of capital **Revolt of the** importance in the history of the Revolution, was **Clergy.** to earn it the bitter enmity of the victims of the sales, and the interested support of those who made their profit out of them. For this reason we must devote a little space to the consideration of the matter.

*　　*　　*　　*　　*

The motive of the measure would appear to have been of a financial nature.

" You sit discussing things," once more we hear Mirabeau's voice of thunder, " and bankruptcy is at your doors ! " He was right. Bankruptcy was at the doors. Necker had exhausted every expedient ; two attempted loans—one of 30 and the other of 80 millions—had fallen through ; it was impossible to collect the new taxes ; patriotic offerings, encouraged by the deputies, who nobly snatched off and gave the silver buckles on their shoes, brought "tears to the eyes," but barely produced 7 millions. The Banque d'Escompte, to which 155 millions were already owing, hesitated to increase the loan, and when Necker tried to establish a National Bank, the undertaking failed for lack of security. Every day saw some fresh proposal and some fresh disappointment. Certain deputies were seized with visionary ideas. " Gentlemen ! " cried Wimpfen, " give me your attention for twenty minutes and I'll give you 600 millions ! " But his twenty minutes never brought a farthing.

The Assembly was at bay. What was to be done ? Spoliation had to be accepted perforce ; the money must be taken wherever it was to be found, and that was in the coffers of the Church.

*　　*　　*　　*　　*

" Kings," we read in the Memoirs of Louis XIV, " are the absolute masters of all property, whether secular or ecclesiastical, to use it with a wise economy, that is to say, according to the necessities of the State." Circumstances had led the Constituent Assembly to an opinion identical with that of Louis XIV.

CHURCH PROPERTY

The wealth of the Church was considerable, and for more than a century needy statesmen had looked on it with longing eyes.

The confiscation of Church property. Obliging theorists, ready to calm their scruples, had not been wanting. This wealth, they said, accumulated by the will of dying persons, was no more than a deposit in the hands of the Church. "The Church," one orator declared, "is the agglomeration of all faithful believers, not the priests alone!" Now the faithful were the citizens. All this smacks of sophistry. The real fact was that the money was wanted.

And one group, whose concern was not so closely connected with the empty coffers of the State, was pushing forward the measure. This was the anti-Catholic party. The members of this party were not sorry to make bad blood between the Clergy and the Revolution, and thus ruin the Church and the ecclesiastical body at one fell blow. Rabaut Saint-Etienne, the Protestant pastor, makes a remarkable display of his delight the day after that on which the measure was passed. "It (the Clergy) has ceased to be an Order! It has ceased to be a constituted body! It has ceased to be a republic within an empire! The priests will have to keep in step with the State now. The only thing left for us to do is to marry them!" This small knot of men who exercised, as we shall see, a powerful action in the matter of the civil Constitution, made tools of deputies who, like Duquesnoy, returned the same simple answer to every objection: "With what do they expect us to pay the debts?"

The tithe had been suppressed, and this by agreement with the Clergy. This compliant attitude, it was hoped, would continue. It might have been a clever move on the Clergy's part to come forward and win over those whose sole anxiety was the existing deficit, by making a certain sacrifice, and undertaking to guarantee a loan. Two months later, Boisgelin, the most intelligent of all the prelates who sat in the Assembly, openly regretted that this timely offer had not been made. "But," he said, "my worthy colleagues never went beyond the Hall of the Augustines" (where the gatherings of the Clergy were formerly held). An advance of 400 millions might have saved everything. But, as we have already remarked, the privileged classes knew nothing of defence or of strategy.

And, further, the Clergy was blinded by its own very genuine sympathy with the Revolution. It did not foresee any hostile proceeding because it did not believe in the existence of any hostility. Its ears were deafened by its own *Te Deums*, and it could not make up its mind to the idea that it was to be stripped as a reward for singing them.

A member of its own body put the match to the train long since laid. On October 10, Talleyrand, Bishop of Autun, Talleyrand's crept into the rostrum. He was not clamorous. proposal. His proposal was gently slipped in towards the close of a sitting; he moved that the property of the Church be placed at the disposal of the State. The very next day Mirabeau gave his support to the motion. The debate was of the most passionate nature. An analysis of the discussion would be deeply interesting.

The Clergy made a lively defence. It had given up the tithe, which was worth eighty millions a year; it refused to give up the Church property, which brought in a smaller sum, because this would amount to accepting its own downfall and lapsing into servitude, and would be an abuse of confidence into the bargain. The Bishop of Autun could, if he chose, give up his own property left by the dead. Maury fought the measure fiercely, Sieyès opposed it firmly; Boisgelin pointed out, very truly, that the Church properties had not been given to the *Church*, but to divers institutions, abbeys, parishes, hospitals, colleges, and so forth, to be applied to specified objects. On the 31st he threw parts of his cargo overboard, and offered a loan of 400 millions. It would have been well to have accepted his proposal. The Nation was about to do a sorry piece of business. La Fare pointed out that the country would have to undertake very heavy responsibilities, all the educational and charitable work now fed by the wealth it threatened. Le Chapelier replied that the Clergy merely exercised "a barren and dangerous charity, calculated to encourage idleness and fanaticism," "whereas in those houses of prayer and repose, the Nation will set up workrooms which will be useful to the State, and in which the poor man will find a subsistence, thanks to his own labour. *There will be no more poverty-stricken people save those who choose to remain so.*" Let us recollect that these words were spoken a hundred and twenty years ago !

This Le Chapelier gives us a glimpse of the idea that guided a whole group of deputies ; the deficit was in their minds, of course, but beside this, "*it was not politic to allow large bodies of men to hold property.*" It was Mirabeau, however, who really forced the measure through.

Grégoire and some twenty other priests voted for the motion. But, in spite of this, " there was such distress," says one of those who voted, " at the idea that the ownership of property was vested in the State," that the measure placing the wealth of the Church at the disposal of the Nation was only passed by 868 votes as against 346 ; forty deputies having abstained from voting, while three hundred, almost all belonging to the Right and the Centre, were absent.

*　　*　　*　　*　　*

This transaction put something like three billions into the hands of the State. To Necker it was almost a difficulty. The Necker's em- measure was repugnant to him on conscientious barrassment. grounds, and, further, the liquidation of the properties in question, most of which were in land, appeared to him likely to prove a very difficult matter. The market was to be flooded quite unexpectedly, and at a moment of great insecurity, with an enormous amount of real estate. Was not the probable consequence an extreme depreciation in the value of the said property ? To gain time the Genevan financier took to his bed.

The Clergy had not lost all hope. The ownership of the property might perhaps be left to them after the sums needed by the Treasury had been raised.

On April 10, 1790, this hope was to be swept away. Prieur of the Marne presented a request that all ecclesiastical property might be declared the property of the Nation. Boisgelin made a final effort at conciliation in the course of the debate. He proposed that the property of the Church should simply be used to guarantee a loan. But the hostility of the majority in the Assembly to the Clergy themselves had already deepened,

137

and the Clergy, under the influence of the threatened danger, appeared less favourable to the Revolution than in 1789; a rupture was in sight. When Dom Guerle, a democratic monk who had voted for the confiscation, artlessly proposed his celebrated motion to proclaim Catholicism the State religion, an indignant outcry rose from the benches around him. It was on this occasion that Mirabeau made a first allusion to the balcony from which Charles IX had fired on the Huguenots. The motion was lost by 495 votes to 400, and on April 16 the Assembly voted the nationalization of all Church property. To counterbalance this a *Budget of Public Worship* was established. " The final blow struck at the Clergy," wrote a deputy of the Left very truly. The measure involved, indeed, a terrible downfall from the moral point of view, for the successors of Bossuet and Fénelon. It made them dependent on the State, which was soon to feel itself justified in meting out punishment to any " bad bishop " or " bad parish priest," in other words, any ecclesiastic who declined to render unto Cæsar more than that which was Cæsar's due.

One important question remained unsettled. How was this Church property to be realized ? Sales would not be easy ; they would be hampered by the general insecurity and by religious scruples. The municipalities seemed fitted to serve a useful purpose in this connection. The Paris municipality was the first to come to the rescue. Bailly offered to buy the properties of twenty-seven religious houses for 200 millions. His offer was accepted, and the arrangement extended to other Communes. The payments were made in municipal bills guaranteed on the purchased properties. But, as these bills were imposed on the creditors of the State, it would be better on the whole to issue paper money, the payment of which should be guaranteed by the three billions represented by the Church property. These paper bills were the famous *assignats*. Originally each *assignat* represented its own value in national property ; it was a forced currency, and any man who held *assignats* could get himself paid in property. Thus was the enormous operation represented by this unprecedented displacement of ownership facilitated. As early as January 10 the moral result of the measure had been clearly realized. " The *assignats*," writes Thomas Lindet,

" will soon be dispersed over the country, and, in spite of himself, every man who holds them will become a defender of the Revolution." This operation, said the chairman of the committee in charge of the law in April, " will bind all citizens to the public weal."

The debate took place on April 10, 15, 16, and 17. The Right fought against the establishment of a theory which was to sanction and complete the sale of Church property. Maury's anger endued him with prophetic powers, for he foretold that the *assignat* would have a stormy career and end in bankruptcy. But Pétion prophesied not less truly when he declared that " the benefits of the *assignats* will be that they will ensure the Revolution." Neither spoke the other's language, but both spoke truth. The *assignat* did almost ruin France, but it " ensured the existence of the Revolution."

On April 17 the law giving the new bills a money value was duly voted.

*　　　　*　　　　　*　　　*

There was strong opposition all over the country. The Clergy thundered from their pulpits against any man who The Clergy should dare to acquire the " goods of the Church." embittered. And thus the *assignat*, from the very outset, was sorely discredited.

The sale of the national property certainly did create, as we shall see, a body of men who steadily defended the Revolution which had enriched them. But the necessity for paying the priests a salary was to lay bonds of a most irksome kind on the Legislature, removing, for many years to come, all possibility of a separation between Church and State, otherwise than by the committal of an act of gross injustice. And as we shall shortly see, this consequence led up to the absurd system of the Civil Constitution.

Another immediate consequence of the measure was the severance of the great mass of the Clergy from the Revolution, which it had hitherto rather favoured than opposed, and which, almost everywhere, it had welcomed with acclamation. Those of the parish priests who had been most devoted to the new form of government (even Grégoire himself for several days) were now quite put out of countenance. The reply to their enthusiastic adhesion had been an act of spoliation, accompanied by words of the most insulting kind. One lady connected with the triumphant party had written: " Sell all the ecclesiastical property! We shall never get rid of the wild beasts till we have destroyed their lairs!" Condorcet, who can hardly be accused of any tender feeling towards the Catholic clergy, was to assert a year later that the operation had been performed " without equity and without prudence," and that the Revolution, by " making victims " of the priests had deprived itself of a source of strength.

Within a few weeks the dissolution of the Religious Orders was to increase the bitterness. Can we wonder that the Clergy, thus injured and wounded in every kind of way, lifted up its voice in bitter protest ; that certain episcopal charges should have made acrimonious references to " perverted men " and their " monstrous excesses," and that some bishops, such as the Bishop of Tréguier, even went so far (nothing of the sort had happened before) as to anathematize the whole Revolution, and express a hope that France would " wake up," and a general cry be raised " to claim our ancient laws and the re-establishment of public order."

Many citizens, as we have seen, were ready to lend an ear to such an appeal. The Assembly, which, moreover betrayed the utmost scorn for the " wretched Memorials "— now looked on as " real fairy tales," and so completely outstripped that they were quite unappreciated—had evoked so much discontent that by February 1790, it found itself forced to publish a proclamation justifying itself in the eyes of the country. " Wake up, Louis! It is time, it is more than time, to prove yourself a Bourbon!" was the appeal shouted to the King. And, therefore it was that the revolutionary party insisted on the King's appearance at the Assembly on February 4, and that his presence was greeted with genuine enthusiasm ; for the King, as Mme. de Beauplan's shoemaker triumphantly remarked to her, seemed, when he declared himself " Chief of the Revolution," to endorse the work of that Revolution and impose it unreservedly upon the country.

    *   *   *   *   *

CHURCH PROPERTY

So the Assembly went its way. "Each day," wrote one of its members, " it makes some steps towards reason." They Futile discus- were the steps of an ataxic patient! For the sions in the last six months a confused labour had absorbed Assembly. it; discussion of the Constitution, reform of the Administration, organization of the Municipalities, debates on the deficit, ecclesiastical property, Corsica, the Army, the Colonies, the emancipation of the negro races, the management of the press, the re-organization of taxation, food supply, not to mention the hundred and fifty sittings taken up by unforeseen incidents. It had worked, as Lindet says, "groping its way," piling one discussion on the other, breaking off a deliberation connected with the Army to debate the subject of the Religious Orders or of slavery. The members were still struggling, in February 1790, with the difficulties arising out of the hasty action of the night of August 4, "ruinous in so many respects," as a deputy of the Left wrote. Sometimes, worn out or intoxicated, this Assembly would stumble amidst the ruins it had made!

The Ministers now sent all business back to the Assembly for decision, thus forcing it into a labyrinth from which, as Lameth tells us, " it could not escape." It dreaded this " business," yet it challenged it; its treatment of it all was most confused. " The cards are all in such confusion in this gambling hell," wrote Mirabeau, " it is so difficult to play any systematic game, that after a waste of intelligence and activity that wears one out by the end of every day, one finds oneself back at the same point, that is to say, in the midst of chaos!" Meanwhile "anarchy," writes a foreign minister, "is apparently increasing all over the kingdom." It came from above.

Summer opened, and still the Assembly lived in a whirlwind. "The heat is extreme," we read in a letter written in June, "yet the Assembly really needs ice to cool its effervescence!" Occasionally it made itself ridiculous, as when it gravely received at the bar of the House "a deputation from all the nations of the earth, Indians, Arabs, Armenians, Egyptians, and so forth." "Ambassadors who had no credentials," writes another deputy belonging to the Left; among these envoys the Baron de Crussol recognized a negro

141

servant employed by one of his friends, " playing the African "
in return for a certain remuneration. Having laid down
laws for the Universe, the deputies found it pleasant to receive
congratulations from the Universe, even a Universe of this
adulterated type!

The Court was doing nothing to stem the tide that swept
the Assembly along. The Comte de Provence had first of all
Inertia of the Court. incited Favras to plot, then suddenly forsaken
him, and left him to be hanged. Such incidents
damped the most ardent courage. But, indeed, the King would
do nothing to encourage the " politicians " who would have so
gladly have checked the movement. He paid Mirabeau to
advise him, but he did not follow his advice. The Court
remained inert, inactive, undirected, disavowing those who
revolted, but refusing all assistance ; it got rid of Necker, who
departed secretly ; it kept the puzzled La Fayette at a distance ;
it dreaded Mirabeau, who was ready to serve it ; it seemed willing
to submit to all things, great sacrifices or petty mortifications.
One vengeance only it took, that of forcing the Assembly
every day to face the Revolution it served ; the *tête-à-tête*
was anything but pleasant.

The country—while the Constitution was being evolved—
paid no attention to the laws. " Mandrin," we read, " might
Increasing anarchy in the country. make himself king to-day, in one or even in several
provinces ! "
Again we must make a general survey of France.
In Paris the Districts kept the Commune in check, and the
Commune served the Assembly after the same fashion. The
whole of the South was in a state of violent excitement ; from
Lyons to Toulouse the worst elements of the population were
seething in a revolutionary ferment ; at Toulon, in December
1789, the populace had risen against the authority of the
Naval Commandant, d'Albert de Rions, and had forced the
municipality to cast him into a dungeon ; at Marseilles, in
March 1790, the *Nervi* * rebelled, carried the National Guard
with them in their attack on the regular troops, and murdered

* The dockers of Marseilles, generally full-blooded, or at all events
half-blooded, Italians.

CHURCH PROPERTY

an officer, M. de Bausset. On this occasion La Fayette drew attention to the anarchy existing in the kingdom "from Strasburg to Nîmes." It would be well if his speech could be reproduced here.

The Assembly, not daring to resort to measures of repression itself, would not permit the King to use them either. And by this time repression was beginning to appear impossible, for the army, which for some months had been wavering, now rose in revolt, and a fresh convulsion began.

SOURCES. Works by Aulard (*Jacobins*), Morris, Dumont, Duquesnoy, Lameth, Vaissière, Rabaut, Mounier, Thomas Lindet, Mirabeau, Biauzat, Abbé Rudemare, Mallet de Pan, Mme. Roland, Esterhazy, already quoted.— *Impressions d'un Garde national normand* (*Rev. Fr.*, 1908); *Journal d'une Bourgeoise* (Mme. Jullien, published by Lockroy, 1891); Bouillé, *Mémoires*, 1797.

WORKS already quoted by Sicard, I, Levasseur, Néton, Esmein, Cahen, Charavay, de Chilly.—Jaurès, *Histoire Socialiste. La Constituante*, 1904; Marion, *Vente des biens nationaux*, 1908; Vialay, *Vente des biens nationaux*, 1908; Stourm, *Les Finances de l'ancien Régime et de la Révolution*, 1885; Gomel, *Histoire financière de la Constituante*, 1896; Lichtemberger, *Le Socialisme et la Révolution*, in *L'Œuvre Sociale de la Révolution*, 1901; Sagnac, *La propriété et les paysans* (*ibidem*); Seiout, *Histoire de la Constitution civile*, 1872.

CHAPTER VIII

THE REVOLT OF THE TROOPS AND THE FEDERATION

Ferment in the Army. The officers overpowered. The Federation.
The Festival of Love : its dissolvent effect upon the Army. The
rebellion at Nancy. The alarm caused by the Army brings about
a wish for war.

ON February 20, 1790, the Assembly set itself a question which has preserved its tragic and ever-vital interest throughout a stormy century. " When and under what circumstances ought a soldier to fire on citizens ? " The soldier of that moment solved the problem in the simplest **Ferment in** fashion by replying : " Never ! " He was far **the Army.** more disposed to come to terms with the rioters than to put down riot.

The aged Kellermann was to say : " The Revolution was due to the regiments of the line." He meant that the Army might perhaps have stifled the Revolution and did not choose to do so.

I have already referred to the composition of this Army ; men of ill-fame, many of them ex-convicts, ruffians whom Dubois-Grancé, himself an officer sitting with the extreme Left, described at the rostrum as " brigands " ; non-commissioned officers, whose promotion had been brutally checked, and whose legitimate jealousy had been fanned to a flame ; officers sorely divided among themselves, some eager to hasten their own advancement by practising demagogic tactics, or favouring them at all events, others disgusted by the Revolution, but completely disarmed by their own weakness, or that of the men in the highest commands—the King first of all. Vaissière's *Letters from Aristocrats*, many of which bear the signatures of officers, give us little reason to regard these as

144

Pretorians. The ruling feeling in these letters is a bitter melancholy, largely caused by their writers' very reasonable sense of their own impotence. " They have struggled," writes Captain Désiles on June 21, 1790, " as hard as they could." But they were baffled not so much by the insolent insubordination of their men as by the treacherous delation rife in their own body.

And, further, they knew, as I have already said, that they ran a perpetual risk of being abandoned to their fate. The Minister of War, La Tour du Pin, who had fought bravely in the Seven Years War, was a straightforward, honest, kindly man, but, as Esterhazy tells us, he was " weak and ruled by his son, a fierce democrat " ; the sort of man who would try to put out a fire with a wet sponge ! A sponge had already been used to wipe out the exploits of the Gardes Françaises, and on August 13, Noailles, who can hardly be accused of any tendency to reaction, had ventured, though in somewhat timid terms, to point out the increasing insubordination in every quarter. The Assembly had responded by appointing a Committee charged with the duty of forming " a new army." The old army had taken this as a fresh encouragement to dissolve.

From October 1789 onward, the leaven worked, and by June 1790, its ravages had become so great as to be self-evident in certain quarters. Here and there a mutiny broke out, was settled by concessions, broke out again, of course, and ended, being unpunished, by generating fresh incidents of the same nature.

One of the most characteristic of these occurred at Hesdin, in the Royal Champagne Regiment, when a young officer of Perpetual nineteen, whose name was later to become mutinies famous, Nicolas Davout (then written d'Avoust), against officers. led the non-commissioned officers and men of his regiment into the presence of his Colonel, ordered him to " hand in his accounts," and caused him, or allowed him, to be insulted ; the regiment had been ordered to leave Hesdin, where the National Guard was supporting it in its opposition to its commanding officers, on May 15, 1790 ; the men objected, refused to move, and were actually brazen enough to make a complaint to the Assembly. The Assembly did, indeed,

K 145

express its " pained surprise." But, as the regiment obstinately refused to obey its Colonel and march out of Hesdin, the deputies gave in. From that moment, and for many months to come, the garrison of Hesdin was in a state of anarchy, the officers were scoffed at, the men would obey nobody save young Lieutenant d'Avoust, and the bad example was followed all over the country.

We may, in fact, from January to July, 1790, follow the progress right across France of a movement that showed how completely all discipline had been destroyed. We shall see the Dragoons of Lorraine plundering the regimental coffers and driving out their officers at Tarascon, " Auvergne " rising in mutiny at Le Quesnoy, " Colonel-Général " doing the same thing at Lille, " Penthièvre " at Rennes, " Guyenne " at Nîmes, " Vivarais " revolting on the road between Béthune and Verdun to get back to the garrison from which the authorities desired to remove it, " Vexin " forcing its officers, who had been accused of a plot to poison their men, to share the men's meals with them, " Royal-Marine " ordering its officers to depart, " Beaune " demanding as a rightful claim 11,000 *livres*, " Forez " claiming 39,000, "Poitou" 40,000, "Salm-Salm" 44,000, "Châteauvieux" 201,000, " Beauce " 240,000 and snatching the officers' gold coins and money bills out of their hands, "Touraine " rising at Perpignan, refusing to obey the non-commissioned officers who had remained faithful, besieging the house of their Colonel, the Vicomte de Mirabeau, who hurried to the spot, and when his rough good-natured attempts to reason with his men had failed, was forced to make his way out sword in hand. In the course of the spring of 1790 a score of regiments ill-treated, insulted, threatened, and robbed their officers. And very soon three regiments at Nancy were to throw certain superior officers into prison—a downright insurrection, only saved from becoming civil war by the unaided energy of General de Bouillé.

What was the Assembly doing ? It was greatly disturbed and " painfully surprised " by the news of each succeeding Supineness of mutiny. This surprise is a surprise to us. Letter the Assembly after letter from La Tour du Pin (who, by the in dealing with way, could do nothing but write letters) had remutineers. ported the anarchy in the army, quoted the most revolting cases of insubordination, and on June 4 (let our readers note his words) pointed out as a most threatening event "the formation of this *military democracy, a sort of political monster which has always ended by devouring the empires that have produced it.*" The Assembly greeted his warning with applause, but took no action, for we cannot call it taking action to "beseech the King to mete out severe punishment to every act of disobedience to the military laws." The Constituent Assembly would have been most happy to leave the unpopular duty of repression to the hated Executive Power, and to lay the blame on it the next day. This is proved by the fact that when a definite case was submitted to the deputies they flinched and passed it over.

Was it "the officers' fault?" The soldiers at Valence gave over their commanding officer to the populace, who murdered him, as Belzunce had already been murdered at Caén, because, so a certain well-known writer assures us, "by the fault of the Executive Power, officers who were the enemies of the Revolution had been left in their regiments." On June 4, Robespierre cast all the blame of the disorder on the officers who were opposed to the Revolution; the idea was to force them to resign. "It will be difficult," wrote Lindet on June 14, "to keep up discipline as long as the old body of officers remain in command. Their best course would be to resign in a body.

This, if the Assembly was to maintain its dubious attitude, was a self-evident proposition. A far better plan, as Mirabeau wrote, would have been "simply to disband the King's army and enrol another on revolutionary principles." This would at all events have deprived the mutinous soldiers of their pretext. Meanwhile the Assembly dared not put down "the monster" described by La Tour du Pin, and was quite unable to tame it. Yet it did make an effort. The troops were invited to send their deputies to the Federation on the Champ de Mars; there, amidst the tender outpourings of fraternal sentiment, they would, it was hoped, understand that they did wrong when they treated chiefs, who were stretching out affectionate arms to them, as enemies, and grieved the Assembly which had so maternally summoned them to Paris.

* * * * *

THE FRENCH REVOLUTION

The Federation ! In June 1790 the word was in every mouth !
The National Federation was to set the seal on the voluntary
The Federation. unions that were being formed in every direction, the smaller federations of villages and public
bodies, and towns and provinces. In the threatening gloom which
anarchy was casting over the unhappy country, men were stretching out groping hands to each other. The King had been the
bond that held the nation together ; that bond was weakening,
it seemed dangerously near the breaking-point ; the instinct
of national self-preservation drove these poor people to band
themselves together. There was a breath of generous fraternal
feeling about it, too. The expression has been so cruelly
abused that it provokes a smile ; but in the France of 1789
the feeling was sincere ; the hands that were stretched out in
fear were really clasped in love. The movement started in the
West. On October 26, 1789, fifteen Breton Communes formed
themselves into a federation ; on November 29, fourteen towns
in Dauphiné, at the other end of the country, made a similar
union ; and all over France, in the course of that winter, the
big villages made friendly advances one to the other. The
destruction of the public bodies and the provinces by the Constituent Assembly had threatened to crumble France to nothing,
and, spontaneously, this admirable country built up its own
unity once more. When the Communes had bound themselves
together by the hundred, the Provinces, in their turn, began
to "federate" ; on February 15, 1790 (the date should be
remembered, for it marks the beginning of a most important
movement) the delegates of Anjou and Brittany met at Pontivy,
"solemnly declaring that they were neither Bretons nor An-
gevins, but citizens of one and the same empire." The Assembly,
filled with a vague dread of the movement, endeavoured to
direct its course. Delegates from the National Guards, representing the various federations, were bidden to a grand ceremony in Paris. These delegates began to arrive in the early
days of July. The strength of the loyal feeling of the provinces, obscured by the revolutionary clubs, then became
apparent.

The delegates arrived, in fact, overflowing with artless
affection for their King. When those from Touraine were

148

received by Louis XVI they offered a ring that had been worn by Henri IV for his acceptance. The Bretons, who had been described as fervent revolutionaries, threw themselves weeping at their Sovereign's feet. Their leader offered his sword to the King, with the words : " It will never be stained with any blood but that of your enemies, Sire ! " Louis embraced him; " I have never doubted the affection and fidelity of my dear Bretons," he said. " Tell them all that I am their father, their brother, and their friend."

The Monarch was carried away by the flood of generous feeling (sometimes a little foolish) which the preparations for the coming festival had evoked in every quarter.

Before tiers of grassy seats, into which the whole of Paris had crowded (seats built up with their own hands by great The Festival of ladies, monks, fish-wives, and citizens, opposite Federation. the Altar of the Fatherland), the ceremony was performed. Many are the descriptions of it. The Bishop of Autun in his sacerdotal robes mounted the steps of the altar, said Mass, assisted by 400 priests, their white albs girt with tricolour sashes, and then, mitre on head and staff in hand, blessed the oriflamme of the National Guard and the banners of the eighty-three departments.

La Fayette on the preceding evening had taken command of the business ; it was *his* festival. He advanced to the altar, laid his sword upon it, and took the oath of fidelity to the Nation, the Laws, and the King. Excitement rose to madness ; the Commandant of the National Guard was hoisted up and carried round in triumph on men's shoulders.

Then the President of the Assembly, de Bonnay, took the oath, and all the deputies repeated it after him, but the public gave its representatives a cold reception. There was some quizzing ; they had appeared between a body of children and a body of old men. *Royal Pituite and Royal Bamboche,* laughed the crowd. But Louis XVI was cheered. The shouts of " Long live the King " were louder than those of " Long live The King and the Nation." Yet he did not go up to the Queen altar, but stood in front of his armchair, and acclaimed. said, " I swear to use all the power delegated to me by the constitutional act of the State to maintain the

149

Constitution decreed by the National Assembly and accepted by me." There was more shouting then; the Queen, carried away by the applause, lifted up the future Louis XVII in her arms: "Here is my son! he and I both share these sentiments!" Then ecstasy reached the point of frenzy; the banners were dipped, the guns roared. Everybody "sailed in the blue"; one delegate vowed he had heard the King say "that if necessary he would shed his own blood in the defence of the Revolution!"

In the evening there were great illuminations, and while 600 musicians performed the *Taking of the Bastille, a hierodrama, with words by King David*, in the Cathedral of Notre-Dame, the populace danced on the site of the ruined fortress. "Generally speaking, everybody is drunk with love for the King and the Royal Family!" The words were written on July 16.

As a matter of fact the day gave food for reflection. Mirabeau, who was furious at that moment with La Fayette, was very sorry it had turned into an apotheosis for "Clown (Gilles) Cæsar"; he would have had the King arrive on horseback, as "General of the Federation," and seen him pass from his throne to the altar, whither he should have been borne by the "arms of the men whom some would use to threaten him, but to whom monarchism really is the breath of life."

Nevertheless, the day on the whole had been favourable to the King. On this point every witness is agreed. The "mud-stained" Assembly had been laughed at; Mirabeau deplored this. The next day people were singing:

> "Fallait voir nos deputés
> Dont quelques uns faisaient la moue,
> C'étaient de vrais culs crottés
> Qui se trainaient dans la boue!" *

* * * * *

It was only logical that as the Court had not turned the Federation to account, the Federation should turn against the Court. Its effect on the military delegates was particularly

* "You should have seen our deputies.
  Some of them very sulky.
  They were real draggle-tails
  Wallowing in the mud."

disastrous. The Club had made a great deal of them, and in the course of the process had carefully instructed them **Disastrous** in their new duties ; they must mistrust their **effect of the** officers, all of them declared " aristocrats," and **Festival on the** even at the risk of disobeying the King, they **Army.** must not imbrue their hands in the blood of any Frenchman, save that of their own chiefs ! " This festival," writes Bouillé, " has poisoned the troops." The very next morning the Queen's Regiment mutinied at Stenay on the plea that the officers intended to hand the town over to the Austrians. But this was a slight matter compared with events at Nancy.

The Assembly, to which La Tour du Pin had reported on August 6, " a torrent of military insurrections," did at **Mutiny at** last, on the 16th, vote a decree ordering repressive **Nancy.** measures. The King despatched M. de Malseigne to Nancy to inspect the accounts. He was at once assaulted and seized by the Swiss, and obliged to draw his sword before he could make his way out of the barracks. The soldiers followed him, and besieged the house of the Commandant of the troops, yelling threats the while. M. de Malseigne, driven out in another direction, sought refuge at Lunéville. De la Noue, the Commandant, was seized in his own house, and dragged, wounded, to a dungeon, with several other superior officers. Finally, Malseigne was handed over by the Lunéville troops to the Nancy mutineers, and brought back to that place on the 30th, an execrated captive, amid shouts of " *À la lanterne !* "

La Fayette, in face of this " general outbreak," had induced the Assembly to pass from threats to genuine repressive measures, and Bouillé, Commandant of the fortress of Metz, was deputed to put down the " military revolution." He collected 90 battalions and 104 squadrons of men, and forthwith marched on Nancy. His swift action was wise ; the Assembly, moved by the outcry raised by Robespierre, weakened, and voted an Order of the Day of the most indefinite description, formulated by Barnave, and intended to delay Bouillé's march.

But he had reached Nancy already, after a pretty hot engagement at the Stainville Gate, during which he lost 56

151

of his men, and the gallant Desîles. He forced his way into the heart of the town, under a heavy fire, which cost him 400 of his rank and file, and some 40 officers. The insurrection was quelled.

The matter of punishment had now to be considered. The Swiss were made over, in virtue of special statutes, to the judgment of their own officers ; 33 were executed, and 44 condemned to the galleys. These latter were carried round the streets of Paris in triumph before two years were out ! The men of the other corps did not wait so long for their absolution. The Commissaries sent down by the Assembly insisted on overlooking their offences, " and did a great deal of harm by their extreme indulgence." But the deputies were already nursing a spite against Bouillé, for having executed the rebels too promptly, and within three months poor La Tour du Pin himself was to be dismissed.

This faltering behaviour destroyed the effect the repressive measures should have produced. In every quarter the soldier delegates who had returned from the Federation Festival had sowed seed that was ripening apace. From Besançon to Cahors, from Rennes to Huningue, all through these months of August and September, there were constant and violent collisions between the troops and their officers. So manifestly was the military force "falling to pieces" that certain deputies, both of the Right and Left, began to nurse a secret hope of war, believing this would force the troops to turn passion which really seemed beyond repression against the enemies of their country. It is true that others—and these were the majority— less optimistic, trembled at the very thought of war with Europe at a moment when the army appeared to be in utter disintegration. But the question was arising, during that autumn of the year 1790. Europe and the Revolution, though neither had as yet resolved on attack, were standing face to face, each seeking to measure the other's strength. The morrow of the Festival of the Federation, celebrated in such a frenzy of universal love, threatened to be terrible indeed.

Insubordination of the Army produces a wish for war.

SOURCES. Works by Aulard (*Jacobins*), Vassière, Thomas Lindet, Mirabeau, Biauzat, Lameth, Bouillé, Frénilly, Louise Fusil, Paroy,

THE REVOLT OF THE TROOPS

Thiébault, Esterhazy, already quoted.—*Rapport de l'attaché saxon* (*Rev. Rev.*, IV) ; *Lettre d'un délégué de Bordeaux* (*Rev. Retr.*, XIII) ; *Impressions d'un Garde national normand* (*Rev. Fr.*, 1908) ; Girardin, *Souvenirs*, 1828 ; Mme. de Tourzel, *Mémoires*, 1893.

WORKS already quoted by Chilly, Charavay, Meynier.—Claretie, *Desmoulins*, 1908 ; Tiersot, *Les Fêtes et les Chants de la Révolution*, 1908.

CHAPTER IX

PEACE OR WAR ?

Europe and the Revolution. Europe in the year 1789. Its mistake as to France in general and the Revolution in particular. The divisions of Europe. The Eastern Question. The Polish Question. Poland our salvation for six years. Catherine II. The Emperor Leopold. Alsace. " France renounces all ideas of conquest." The Avignon business. Europe gathers itself together in 1790, but still hesitates. Leopold waits for an appeal from Louis XVI.

"CORN we have, and we shall soon have a Constitution," wrote a deputy on July 5, " but my opinion is that a war will sweep away our corn, our Constitution, and our *assignats.*" This idea, as some of their letters prove, was haunting many deputies at the time. An hour had struck Europe and which forced them to look far beyond the walls of the Revolution. the Manège, and even beyond the frontiers of France. Hitherto, in spite of many difficulties, they had been building up their monument, at least in its chimerical sections. But here was a fresh factor—the external one. There was a rumour, which people were beginning to believe, that Europe intended to interfere in French affairs ; this was an alarming report, a serious anxiety in every way. For every intelligent mind at once perceived that war would force the Revolution either into retreat or into exaggeration—a twofold danger particularly alarming to the men of 1789.

For many years past three questions have been debated. Why did not the monarchies of Europe crush in the egg the Revolution that was about to menace them ? . . . How was it that the coalition tardily formed by all these Powers was held in check by France, single-handed, torn by anarchy, abandoned by her military commanders, and led by a government in many respects so new and untried ? By what miracle did it
154

come to pass that Europe, scarcely beaten, fell into disunion before the barely victorious Revolution, and actually came to terms with it, only to be dismembered by its own hand for the benefit of modern France?

Albert Sorel discovered the solution of this triple problem in that comprehensive view of the continent, just before and just after the Revolution, which he presents to his readers, and in which we will now, for a moment, follow him.

* * * * *

Why was the intervention of Europe tardy, ill-judged, and eventually unsuccessful? *Simply because "Europe," as a whole, did not exist.*

The ancient Christian republic of the Middle Ages had passed away. For four centuries everything—the common religion, Europe in family bonds, monarchic solidarity, and the most 1789. solemn oaths of alliance and friendship, had been sacrificed to a selfish and ferocious policy of self-aggrandizement.

Right had ceased to exist; might ruled everything; successful blows had broken every bond between the "Christian" princes. Quite lately—to take this one example among many—two "philosopher" Sovereigns, Frederick II and Catherine II, and an "apostolic" Princess, Maria-Theresa, had dismembered Poland. Europe no longer possessed what Metternich was to describe, in later days, as "the bowels of a State." And when Europe decided on marching "against the Revolution," as she said, it was not in obedience to a feeling for the solidarity of monarchs, but in the hope that another Poland might be discovered and dismembered west of the Rhine. That "good brother," Louis XVI, was only to be succoured when his helpers believed him at their mercy, and when he was ready to repay the "good brothers" who came to his rescue by the cession of a province or two.

"The cause of kings! The cause of dynasties!" was to be the hypocritical cry of 1792, but in 1789 and 1790 Europe was neither alarmed nor scandalized, but rather the reverse, by the Revolution. Her rulers, and here they were wrong, regarded it as a revolt, likely to weaken France, a country they feared and hated. Now the policy of Europe had always been to give open encouragement to people who rebelled against their sovereigns. The Revolution was taken for a rebellion, like any against the Emperor, in Hungary or Belgium. The expansive force of the French movement was not foreseen; it was not till fifty years later that Metternich was to say jestingly : "When France catches cold, Europe sneezes."

Europe, indeed, was neither shocked nor alarmed. Attacks on sovereigns had lost their effect. Candide saw half a score of dethroned monarchs in Venice. Even the regicide of January 21 had plenty of precedents; Catherine II only reigned because she had caused her own husband, Peter III, to be murdered ; the first Queen led to the scaffold was not Marie-Antoinette, but Mary Stuart, and she was sent there by Elizabeth, whom every prince in Europe, including James of Scotland, her victim's own son, had tried to marry ; Cromwell, who cut off his king's head, had seen a King of France sue for his friendship. The blood of kings had ceased to be sacred in the eyes of their fellow kings.

And, further, since kings had used the vilest instruments, and tolerated the most merciless proceedings in carrying out their plans, Europe, morally speaking, was powerless to withstand the Revolution. She could not intervene on the score of principle, for Europe had no principle save one—reasons of State. This tendency sowed in all these rulers' minds that ineradicable feeling of distrust which, for a considerable time, was to prevent any coalition at all, and after thoroughly weakening that ultimately formed, was swiftly to destroy it.

* * * * *

This mutual distrust would not have sufficed, however, to delay European intervention, if her sovereigns had not been entertaining the same idea for some years past. They were convinced that France, that nation once so dangerous and so heartily feared, was on the brink of dissolution.

Europe's misconception as to the Revolution.

That France was "the insolent nation" there was no doubt. But Europe identified the nation with its kings. And to some extent, Europe was right. The really admirable policy of the Capetian kings throughout nine centuries, had certainly been the making of France. The desire and dream of these kings had always been a France that should grow great and ever

156

greater. Europe took this *imperialism* to be the dream of an insatiably ambitious dynasty; once the dynasty was bound hand and foot or cast out, France would evidently be content to accept a humbler fate.

A gross mistake! If the Capetian kings led the country to such heights, it was because France—from the humbler classes to the patriotic *bourgeoisie* which had given ambitious legists to Philippe le Bel, and imperialist counsellors to Louis XIV—carried her princes along with her.

The great majority of the men of 1789 were legists too, sprung from the same stock as those who advised Philippe le Bel and the Bourbon kings. The humanitarian spirit of 1789 was certainly opposed to conquest of any kind, but the spirit of 1789 was not long to prevail against the instinct that was always to urge the nation on towards its natural borders. Even in 1748 d'Argenson acknowledged that "the populace" was dreaming of great conquests. Now it was the populace that was rising. And it was very ready to be led into the immediate application of the old policy of its kings, because the kings, as a matter of fact, had never done anything but apply the policy of the nation.

But Europe, being ill-informed, saw none of these things. So long and so perseveringly had the greatness of France been served by its sovereigns, that the two seemed bound up together. Since the King was weakened, France would be weakened too. As a factor in the complex European problem she was about to disappear; thus the Revolution, far from calming the bitter quarrels that parted the various countries of Europe in 1789, encouraged their continuance by imbuing those concerned in them with a feeling of false security regarding the Rhine. No clearer proof of the decrepitude of ancient Europe could be offered than this idiotic theory.

* * * * *

"It was in the North and East of Europe," writes Albert Sorel, "that the crisis occurred which stirred up the great The divisions Powers of Europe against each other from 1789 in Europe. till 1795, revealed the antagonism of their pretensions, called forth their rivalries, demonstrated the vices of their public governments, distracted their attention till the close of 1791 from the affairs of France, delayed their coalition for a considerable time, paralyzed it once it had been formed, and eventually broke it up."

For a century past Russia had been forcing her way into the European Concert and helping to unsettle it. This Asiatic and Continental power was bent on becoming European and maritime. Two seas gleamed before her eyes, the Black Sea and the Baltic ; the roads to these were closed to her by Turkey and Sweden, and Poland barred her way into civilized Europe. The successors of Peter the Great looked forward to the destruction of these three barriers, and Catherine II, who ruled in the year 1789, was fiercely resolved about the matter. In 1789 she had despoiled Poland, half of which country was now dismembered, and her eye was upon the paladin King at Stockholm and the " sick man " as he already was, at Constantinople. This merciless sovereign had been fain to admit Prussia and Austria to a share in the first partition of Poland ; her dream was to devour the rest of the unhappy country alone ; but above The Polish all she was determined, when Sweden and Turkey, Question. in their turn, should appear ripe for absorption, to exclude her late allies from any share in that plunder. To this end she sought to occupy her former partners' sharp teeth elsewhere. She did not, at first, perceive the use to which the Revolution might be put in this connection ; but in 1791 the advisability of creating a diversion became apparent to her ; the thought of putting down the Revolution, and collaterally annexing a few French provinces, would surely tempt the two great German Powers to march on the Rhine ; and that being so, the Vistula, the Baltic, the Danube, and the Balkans would be left to her. This wily plan was always half-suspected by the Germans, who hesitated, consequently, to move all their troops towards the Rhine.

In 1789 Catherine was at war with Turkey ; Austria was her ally, but there was an extremely strong suspicion at St. The Eastern Petersburg that Prussia and England were secretly Question. supporting the successful resistance of the Osmanlis. Reckoning on the French dislike of England the Czarina had suggested an alliance against that country between herself and Louis XVI. This had been declined, and Catherine

was very bitter against the Bourbons, all the more so because
the Turkish campaign was going badly for her troops. Meanwhile, Prussia, delighted to hamper the progress of the Russians
whom she feared, and to be disagreeable to the Austrians,
whom she hated, went so far as to stir up disorder in Poland.

The game on the European chess-board, in the year 1789,
was thus of a most complicated nature. If the Revolutionary
party, in the first instance, had betrayed any inclination to
interfere, and throw the chessmen into confusion, and still
more, if it had shown any desire to take possession of the board,
the whole problem might have been given up, until the dis-
turbers had been crushed. But though the Revolution had
paralyzed the French game, it had solemnly disclaimed any
intention of ever taking part in any other. This caused,
among the other players, a scorn which was to ensure the safety
of the movement for two whole years. The Powers once more
bent threatening brows on their own game, and scarcely gave
a thought to the events that were convulsing Paris and Versailles in July and October, 1789.

The disturbances in France then gave satisfaction in
Europe. When the populace greeted the fall of the Bastille
with delight, the kings only saw the weakening of "their good
brother at Versailles "; "France," wrote Mercy, "is being reduced
to nothing " ; "France," said Catherine II, "is hopelessly lost."
As for Frederick William of Prussia, who had long been alarmed
and harassed by the Austro-French alliance, all he perceived
in "the Austrian's " downfall was an excellent opportunity
for undermining Choiseul's handiwork, and he forthwith entered
into formal relations with the leaders of the Assembly. In
England, George III and his Minister, Pitt, simply argued
that a king who was not able to defend his fortress in the
Faubourg Saint-Antoine need not inspire much alarm, even if he
deserved some pity ! It would be a long time before the French
got to Antwerp !

European indifference was more disturbed by the Belgian
Revolution, which set Brabant and Liége in revolt against
Austrian domination on October 20, 1789 ; here too, indeed,
the hand of Prussia was far more clearly seen than that of
France. The "Belgian Republic " sent its ambassadors to

the French Assembly, but the deputies, strongly advised by Mirabeau, who was all for peace at that moment, refused their support, and the ambassadors were not received by Louis XVI. Joseph II, who clearly perceived the finger of Prussia, Holland, and England in the events in the Low Countries, was bent on chastising the rebels and their perfidious allies, when on July 20, 1790, he died.

His successor, Leopold, was of a less irritable temperament. He had been Grand Duke of Tuscany, and had studied his **The Emperor** Machiavelli in the Palazzo Pitti. He was a **Leopold.** diplomatic Prince. He promised the Belgians their pardon, and then craftily caused the English Ministry to be informed that he would rather hand Belgium over to France than recognize it as an independent state. Pitt was horrified ; he put pressure on Prussia, and that country withdrew the support it had been giving the Belgians. On June 26, 1790, Frederick William received the Austrian, Dutch, and British envoys at Reichenbach. They begged him to cease his efforts in connection with the Low Countries, and he was given a hint that a united campaign against France might very well provide him with an opportunity of enlarging his own borders. As at this same moment Catherine was making overtures to the King of Sweden, the friend of Marie-Antoinette, at Verela, it seemed as if during the summer of 1790, Europe, so long torn by divisions, had begun concentrating her forces. The Revolution did not inspire actual fear as yet, but the Powers had realized that intervention was likely to provide them with a diversion or a solution of their own quarrels. Russia believed this to be a way of keeping the Germans busy, the Germans saw in it a method of satisfying their own greed, and further, of settling all the matters in debate at the expense of a nation divided against itself.

*   *   *   *   *

Pretexts for this intervention were not lacking. Though the correctness of the Assembly's behaviour with regard to the **German rights** Belgian business had removed one of these, two **in Alsace.** separate questions were forcing the new government to enter into contact, and forthwith into conflict, with two of the Powers—the Empire and the Pope. The question in the first instance was that of Alsace ; in the second, that of Avignon.

The overthrow of the feudal rights had affected a number of German princelings, who held domains in Alsace. They had refused to submit to the law that dispossessed them, and had appealed to the German Powers who had guaranteed the Treaty of Westphalia. This was in September 1789. The Powers, all of them busy elsewhere, and divided among themselves, had reserved the question, at the same time sending a formal memorandum on the subject to the Cabinet at Versailles. Montmorin, Minister for Foreign Affairs, had transmitted a protest to the Assembly. It was not till April 28, 1790, that the Constituent Assembly decided that the complainants were to receive indemnities. But the complainants asked for more than this : they demanded, and based their claim on the words spoken by Louis XIV at the meeting in Alsace, that the decrees of August 4 should make an exception in their favour. The Assembly refused this claim, and declared it was not bound by Louis XIV's word.

It went further, indeed, asserting that in the new era now opening, no king's word could be binding on it. This was clearly proved, when, a quarrel having broken out just at this juncture between England and Spain, the latter appealed to the Cabinet at the Tuileries for its support on the basis of the "Family Compact." The Assembly refused to accept the consequences of this alliance ; it did try indeed to discover some principle (we know how it dealt in principles), on which it might found its refusal. Robespierre, who, despite his eternal snubbings, was always on the look-out for some opportunity of getting himself into prominence, supplied the need.

"France renounces all idea of conquest." *"We must declare that France renounces all thoughts of conquest, that she considers her limits to be fixed by an eternal destiny."* Pacific as Mirabeau was, he was too intelligent not to betray the deep alarm with which this huge piece of folly inspired him. He saw the impossibility of living without a foreign policy, of ceasing to keep up the country's position, and to prepare for war, so long as the rest of Europe remained under arms. "Till that moment," exclaimed the deputy for Aix on May 20, *"perpetual peace remains a dream, and a dangerous dream, if it is to lead France to disarm in the face of a Europe under arms !"* But Rollet, a parish priest, had answered him promptly : "when every nation is free, like ours, there will be no more war !" And forthwith the theorists of universal peace fell into the rut of anti-militarism. Cazalès, who had uttered a magnificent profession of patriotism, was forced to make his excuses afterwards, and was hooted as he made them? No more diplomats! No more soldiers! No more immoral alliances with kings! And the celebrated motion of May 22 : *"The French Nation renounces the thought of undertaking any war with the object of conquest,"* which, to ensure its eternal presence on the pediment of the monument raised by the Constituent Assembly, was to form Article VI of the Constitution, was carried by acclamation.

In a subsequent speech, Mirabeau, whose prophetic utterances prove his foresight, demonstrated the absurdity and inanity of the declaration. But prophet though he was, did he perceive, as in a blazing blood-stained vision, Jemmapes, and Belgium conquered within two years; Fleurus, and Holland occupied before two more were out ; Millesimo, and Piedmont stripped ; Rivoli, and Austria forced back to her own ground ; the Pyramids, and Egypt subdued ; Marengo and Hohenlinden ; Italy overrun by the invaders ; Austerlitz, Jena, Sommo-Sierra, Wagram and Moskowa, Brussels, Amsterdam, Mayence, Milan, Venice, Rome, Naples, Vienna, Berlin, Madrid, Warsaw, Moscow—the whole of Europe trampled underfoot for the glory of soldiers who wore the tricolour cockade, and marched under the standard of July 14 ?

" The Nation renounces the thought of undertaking any war with the object of conquest ! "

*   *   *   *   *

" The Assembly," writes Sorel, " believed itself to be setting an example that was disinterested in the extreme, and was sincerely proud of it. Europe considered that France was giving a proof of extraordinary weakness, and rejoiced." From London the French Ambassador wrote that the following words were ringing all over the city : " England has nothing more to fear from France, and may claim supremacy in both hemispheres, without fear and without scruple." For once England's credulity was even more artless than the sincerity of France. All Europe took the country thus proceeding to disarm to be an easy prey. And this first fit of pacifism, stirring the greed of all its neighbours, and stilling their fears, was to hasten the coming of war.

Now the matter of the Alsatian possessions of the German Princes was still to the fore, and supplied a possible pretext The occupation for intervention by the Empire. That of the of Avignon. Comtat Venaissin was to create another. The Comtat belonged to the Pope, who ruled at Rome, and on June 11, 1790, the people of Avignon, infected with the revolutionary spirit of their neighbours, drove out the Pope's Legate, formed themselves into a Commune, and offered themselves to France. The real men of 1789 opposed the enemies of the Pope, who, of course, favoured this annexation, and pleaded the motion of May 20, which forbade all conquest. And the inanity and hypocrisy of the formula in question at once became apparent. The cry was raised by the Extreme Left, "there would be no conquest." Avignon was offering itself, and the offer ought to be accepted ; Robespierre himself put forward this distinction, and a formidable breach it made in the original principle. On November 20, 1790, the King was requested to send troops to occupy Avignon.

From that moment the motion passed in May became a dead letter. Paris was swarming with a cosmopolitan host, Europe refugees from Germany, Switzerland, and Italy, alarmed. who proceeded to " offer " their various countries ; they were "the ambassadors of the human species." Further, encouraged by such men as Desmoulins, for instance, they fomented disturbances beyond the frontiers, any of which might end in a revolt or an insurrection, enabling one canton or another to " offer " itself at one and the same time to Liberty and France. So it came about that by the autumn of 1790, Europe, which had been scornful at first, and simply watchful afterwards, began to take alarm.

First it looked towards the Emperor, who, as Marie-Antoinette's brother, and as the protector to whom the princes had made their appeal, had two pretexts for action in his hand. But the Emperor, a cool and calculating man, replied that nothing could be done without a direct appeal from the Tuileries ; the King of France had accepted the Revolution, and it was not possible for other people to be more royalist than the King himself.

Leopold waits for an appeal from Louis XVI

But the appeal from the Tuileries was soon to come. For the first time Louis XVI, who had honestly accepted the Revolution, was rebelling against it. It was not his kingly dignity that was in question now, it was his conscience as a Christian man. The Constituent Assembly had just committed an enormous blunder, destined to produce quite incalculable consequences ; it had voted the Civil Constitution of the Clergy. Out of this Pandora's box every sort of evil was to issue ; the final divorce between the Clergy (even its most liberal section) and the Revolution, the religious persecution, big with civil strife, and the King's sudden revulsion, with its encouragement to foreign intervention. For the war so dreaded in October 1790 by every enlightened supporter of the Revolution was far more the outcome of that fatal measure than of the affairs of Alsace and Avignon.

Sources. Works by Thomas Lindet, Mirabeau, Desmoulins, Campe, Baron de Staël, Dumont, La Fayette, and Mallet du Pan already quoted. *Papiers Rostopchine (Archives Woronzoff, VIII)*, 1876 ; *Letters of Catherine II to Grimm*, 1878 ; *Mémoires* of the Comte de Bray ; *La Révolution et la Politique des Puissances Européennes*, 1911.

Works. Sorel, *L'Europe et la Révolution*, vols. I and II, 1897, 1901 ; Sybel, *Geschichte der Revolution*, vol. I, 1877 ; Stanhope, *William Pitt*, 1862 ; Geffroy, *Gustave III*, 1867 ; D'Arneth, *Joseph II und Leopold*, 1896 ; Ferrand, *Histoire des trois démembrements de Pologne*, 1820 ; Frédéric Masson, *Bernis*.

CHAPTER X

THE CIVIL CONSTITUTION

" We have power to change our religion." The Assembly and the
Catholic Church. *The Dead speak.* Rome and the Revolution.
" An evangelical Reform." The Martineau Report. Why the
Church was not separated from the State. Voltaire's theory.
The new Church. Exchange of views with Rome refused.
Anguish of Louis XVI. He promulgates the Law. The Church
of France offers a passive resistance. The idea sprang from the
Oath. Vote of November 27, 1790. The administration of the
Oath. The failure of the Civil Constitution. The consecration
of the bishops who had taken the Oath. Louis XVI driven into
conflict with the Revolution.

"THE Church is part of the State ; we are a Convention ;
we have power to change our religion." Camus was the
man who affirmed this theory at the sitting of June 1,
1790, Camus who had once been the Clergy's own lawyer.
A bitter Jansenist, his longing to avenge the destruction of
" We have Port-Royal carried him to the utmost limits of
power to alter the doctrine of the power of the State in religious
religion." matters. A certain deputy was to assert that
" three Latin words, *Veto, Deficit,* and *Unigenitus,* have been
the ruin of France." Camus was bent on forcing the Pope to
repent of his *Unigenitus* Bull. And the hour of reckoning did
seem to have struck. Gallicans and Jansenists alike were
resolved to mortify Rome, which had mortified them. The
dead of Port-Royal spoke by their mouths. And other dead
stirred the hearts of such men as Rabaut Saint-Étienne—those
who, from the days of Luther and Calvin, had denounced the
" great harlot " and her ways. Simple indeed are those who
wonder why the Assembly, in its desire to reform the Church
of France, did not turn for help to Rome ! In the eyes of Camus,
that embittered Jansenist (Mathieu Dumas mentions the " ill-

considered zeal of certain Jansenists "); of Grégoire, a fierce
Gallican; of Rabaut, a pastor driven out into the wilderness,
in whom dwelt the spirit of eight generations of persecuted
men, the great object was to banish Rome from every matter
that affected France. A " patriot " was to write in later days :
" The Civil Constitution was snatched from the patriot party
by sectarian feeling." The Assembly, which fancied itself so
modern, was led into its worst mistake by a coalition of hatreds
centuries old. The dead did truly speak in this Assembly,
causing it to stumble.

* * * * *

It troubled itself very little about the Clergy now. True,
the enthusiasm of the priests in the lower ranks was abating.
Yet it was not till October 1790 that the Bishop of Embrun
was to write to Bernis : " The parish priests . . . are beginning
to find out that they have been duped." Certain Bishops
such as Boisgelin, still clung to the principles of 1789, and
that in spite of the nationalization of Church property. We
could quote many proofs of this fact. Even when they were
threatened with the Civil Constitution, many ecclesiastics, and
even the Bishop of Arras, Conzié, shortly to be driven by persecution into the councils of the *émigré* princes, officiated at
the Festival of the Federation.

Pius VI, a pontiff whose many defeats had taught him pru-
dence, had confined his protests every time the Assembly had
Rome and the   infringed Church rights to lamentations. He had
Revolution.   never thundered.

Thus the Revolution had been singularly favoured. The
priests it had stripped were still singing *Te Deums*, and the
Papacy, often so prone to take offence, held its peace. The
nobility, which received no support from the Catholic nations,
seemed prepared to endure all things ; and Europe, though
certainly in a watchful mood, had not as yet induced the Emperor to move. To conclude, Louis XVI, a most invaluable
Sovereign, bowed his head before the Law and the will of the
Nation.

The right course, in June 1790, would have been to stop
short, to be content with the results already acquired, to restore authority, hold the conquered liberties fast, and rally the

whole nation to the standard of the principles that had triumphed. But such an attitude would by no means have suited men whose minds were set on fishing in troubled waters, any more than those others, merciless sectarians, who thought the moment to avenge a series of victims, from Coligny to the Nuns of Port-Royal, had arrived. For these last the Civil Constitution was the weapon of their long desired revenge; for the others it was the whirlwind that would stir up the depths.

*   *   *   *   *

To all appearances the reform was evangelical in character; it was time, according to some of its promoters, to get back Evangelical to the apostolic days, when the faithful elected reform. their own pastors. Little, it is true, was known of those times, or of the manner in which the elections were conducted. In any case, the primitive Christian body had disappeared; how was it to be reconstituted? In the first place the Protestants and Jews, on whom citizenship had just been conferred, would have to be driven out, and the whole body of free-thinkers as well! But such an argument would seem despicable to a man animated by the "true spirit of the Gospel."

It was to be an administrative reform, too, and one worthy of but little blame, if it had been moderate. "We find," reports the Chairman of the Committee on the Law, "dioceses containing no more than 80, 60, 50, 40, 20, and even 17 parishes; while others contain 500, 600, 800, and even 1400." The geometric sense of the Constituent Assembly was offended. Ought not all this to be brought within the rigid (and artificial) framework of the departments? Any thinking person, it must be acknowledged, will see the comic side of this admixture with an "evangelic reform," of a consideration so thoroughly Cæsarian as this of forcing a diocese into the limits of a civil district. The Church was to be brought back to the Catacombs, but the Catacombs were to be ruled out and squared by Diocletian!

It was a political reform likewise. The Concordat was to be abolished—"the profane and scandalous Concordat!"—as the virtuous Mirabeau declared it, concluded "between an immoral

Pope and a despot, without the knowledge of Church or Empire," for the purpose of dividing "the rights and the gold of Frenchmen between two usurpers !" A great deal might be said about this verdict, a summary one at least, on the arrangement made in 1515. As a matter of fact it had become generally odious.

On May 29, 1790, the discussion of the Civil Constitution as suggested by Martineau began. It lasted for six weeks, constantly interrupted by other debates. It was closed on July 12 by the passing of the law.

Interest is concentrated on the general debate which lasted three days. Martineau had summed up the details of the reform ; the old districts were to be abolished : there was to be a Bishop in each department ; ten departments were to form a district under a Metropolitan : there were to be "episcopal Vicars," without whose consent no Bishop was to exercise jurisdiction : the Chapters were altogether suppressed ; the parish boundaries were all to be settled afresh. Bishops, episcopal Vicars, and priests were all to be chosen by the electoral body of each Department or Commune : the parish priests were to be instituted by their Bishops, the Bishops by the Metropolitans. Not one word about Rome from beginning to end. Such was the conception, evangelical, geometrical, and canonical, evolved by the deliberations of the Ecclesiastical Committee of the Assembly, and presented to the deputies by Martineau.

Martineau's report.

Reform of some kind had become essential—this was evident even to the most unyielding Catholics ; the Assembly might very well have defined certain of its points. The dioceses were absurdly unequal in area : the Bishops lived too much away from them : certain Chapters did no useful work : and the re-delimitation of parishes was a step in the right direction. It would not have been a bad thing to give the faithful a certain share in the choice of their pastors, and for that purpose to revise the Concordat. On such a basis it would have been possible for the King to enter into negotiations with the Pope. The Assembly had frequently given this Catholic Church, which it now desired to remodel, its further qualifying title of Roman. What strange fancy was this, to reform the Roman Church without consulting Rome itself !

THE CIVIL CONSTITUTION

There was, indeed, another possible solution—that of separating Church from State. In this case the State would have Why the had nothing to do with the Church, which would Church was not have governed itself according to the statutes separated from given by Rome, and constituted a sort of private the State. corporation, quite distinct from the State, as the Church does in America in the present day. But just that word corporation (the safeguard of the Catholic Church beyond the Atlantic Ocean in our time), was odious to the ears of the Constituent Assembly. These liberals of the year 1789 were Cæsarians at bottom, though they did not know it. They drew their inspiration from Voltaire, who had written as follows to Shuwalof in 1768 : " Your illustrious Sovereign is the only one who knows how to reign. She pays the priests : she opens their mouths and shuts them up : they obey her orders, and everywhere there is peace." Martineau, with his desire to break up the Concordat was really the precursor of Bonâparte, who was to reconstruct it, partly for the sake of having a hold upon the priests. Further,—and here we come back to the nationalization of Church property—there had been a solemn undertaking that the expenses of public worship should be paid : if the Church and the State were sundered, would not the Assembly be forced to return the money that undertaking had brought into its hands ?

No ! Far better create a State Church that would be quite independent of Rome—and to that end have no dealings with Rome at all.

Treilhard and Camus proclaimed, above all things, the right of the nation to reform religion. I have already quoted Camus' words. Here are Treilhard's : " When a sovereign judges any reform to be necessary no opposition can be made. A State may accept or refuse to accept a religion." Napoleon was never to travel as far as his future Councillor of State.

The part played by the Clergy in this controversy was far from brilliant. On the one hand there had been too many Debates on the abuses, and the Concordat really was a moth-constitution of eaten affair : it is true, indeed, that a Church the Church. which had produced such men as Bossuet and Massillon could not be thoroughly bad : but the Dubois of the

169

Church had outnumbered its Bossuets. And on the other hand the Clergy, as we know, were not above reproach : some of its Bishops (and certain of them belonged to the Assembly) were living abuses in themselves Finally, the Clergy was Gallican in the best sense of the term : it had no affection for the Curia : it was the Clergy of the Declaration of 1682 : to the very last, the Committee of Bishops, led by Boisgelin, was to devote its best attention—to the great annoyance of Salamon the Papal agent—to preserving the liberties of the Gallican Church. This disarmed it to some extent when it was called upon to protect the rights of Rome. All it could say to the reformers was : "You are going too far !" This argument, in the face of the trenchant speeches of Camus and Treilhard, was a weak one.

Boisgelin made concessions in every direction : but he objected, and very reasonably, that these new elections by the people would not be comparable in any sense with the old canonical elections. And, above all, he could not admit the propriety of making such numerous reforms in the Church without the intervention of the Church herself. His mind leant, if not to the Curia, at all events to some assembly of the French clergy which should oblige the " Head of the Church " to accept certain new arrangements.

But Camus would not even admit the primacy of the Pope. " What is the Pope ? A Bishop, the minister of Jesus Christ, The Pope's just like any other, whose functions are circumprimacy scribed within the limits of the diocese of Rome. rejected. It is high time that the Church of France, which has always been jealous of her liberties, should be freed from this servitude ! " Lanjuinais never spoke of Pius VI otherwise than as the " Bishop of Rome."

In a very remarkable analysis of the debate M. Mathiez admits that all this was loose talk ; the Committee, and possibly the Assembly too, would really have preferred an understanding with Rome. " The King shall be besought to take all the measures considered necessary to the full and complete execution of the decree." This, says M. Mathiez, expresses the feeling of the Ecclesiastical Committee, and would appear to authorize a negotiation between the King and the Holy See. But the clause was thrown out by the Assembly, and the formula, to say the least of it, was certainly obscure.

The law was passed on July 12, and brought up to the King for his sanction that very day.

*   *   *   *   *

Louis XVI was in terrible anguish of mind : Vicq d'Azyr, his physician, found him in a high fever, the cause of which Anguish of he easily determined. The King foresaw that the Louis XVI. law would be passed : he had warned the Nuncio, Dugnani, of the fact, and had besought the Curia to be prudent. Once the measure was voted, Louis XVI wrote to the Pope to the same effect. Pius VI replied that he would look into the matter.

But, meanwhile, the Ecclesiastical Committee was imperiously demanding the Royal sanction. The Ministers, and among them two Bishops, were dissuading the King from applying his veto. Suddenly he promulgated the law : Montmorin wrote to Rome that " His Majesty has done what his religion inspired him to do." Deeply offended, the Vatican held its peace ; but on October 22, Pius VI plainly told Bernis that he certainly could not accept the decrees "as they were." Meanwhile the King, tortured by remorse, remained in a burning fever.

The Civil Constitution was proclaimed in the provinces, and the Bishops opposed it by a system of passive resistance. Passive resist- It became necessary to dissolve the Chapters ; ance of the this proceeding gave rise to regrettable scenes ; Clergy. everywhere the Bishops were found to be standing in the way. The administrators of the law, who were being driven forward by the " Societies," found themselves powerless. Then the Ecclesiastical Committee made up its mind to "muzzle the Clergy," as Mirabeau put it. "These rebellious functionaries " must be reduced to obedience. The Jacobin press advised a little summary punishment : "if two or three of these gentlemen were haled before the tribunal of the people," the others would soon become " more circumspect."

The idea of forcing prelates and priests alike into a formal acceptance of the law was gaining ground. On November 26, Voidel read the Assembly a report from the Committee

171

declaring itself in favour of an oath. " When the public will has been expressed, individuals are bound to obey." A refusal was to be equivalent to resignation ; any violent opposition was to be punished by prosecution. Thus was the road opened to disaster.

Passions had reached the boiling point. When the Bishop of Clermont, a very moderate man, made a speech claiming the right of the Church of France to assemble in council and hold consultations, he was interrupted repeatedly. The whole debate, indeed, was marked by violence and confusion. The King, grieved to the heart, followed it from the Tuileries. If the decree imposing the oath was voted, a religious struggle was inevitable. And must he, a prince whose whole heart was full of piety and faith, give his sanction to this new law, so much more terrible than its predecessor ? Mirabeau thought he had saved him from this horror by proposing to get the law thrown out by dint of outbidding it ; but he became so exasperated by the stupid opposition of the Right that he worked himself and others into a paroxysm of fury, and provoked the dangerous intervention of Maury, who tore the Civil Constitution to ribbons with fierce words, and foretold a hideous religious war. The decree was passed on November 27, and, as Montlosier said, "the bridges were destroyed."

On December 3 the King besought the Pope to give his consent to both laws. Pius VI, relying this time on the " refutations " of ninety-three French Bishops, replied to Bernis on the 14th that if he did such a thing he would incur the disapprobation, not of the Universal Church only, but of " the Gallican Church " as well. All he could do was to defer his decision.

But in France events were hurrying on. The Civil Constitution had created several new dioceses, and these had to be filled. The electors were called together. On The decree November 23 a Bishop of the Ardennes was sanctioned by the King. chosen, and another for Mayenne on December 12. It was currently believed, indeed, that the huge majority of the priests would take the oath, and on December 20 Louis XVI was called on to sanction the decree.

He spent hours of great misery ; in his despair he applied

172

to Boisgelin, and this prelate, who was himself to refuse to take the oath, advised the unhappy King to sanction the law "provided his acceptance bore the appearance of having been forced upon him"; the King's old friend Saint-Priest, who had but lately been an uncompromising member of his Ministry, also counselled submission. On the 26th the heart-broken monarch sanctioned the law. That very evening the President, amidst a scene of intense emotion, read the Assembly the King's letter announcing his acceptance of the decree. The Left was full of exultation. "Here's an Octave of Saint Stephen," wrote Lindet, who was shortly to cast off the cassock, "which may well bring down a shower of stones." The stones were to fall on every head.

* * * * *

"It is believed that the great majority of the Clergy will obey," wrote la Marck to Mercy on December 30. This was The best of the the general opinion. But it was erroneous. The Clergy refuse to Clergy sitting in the Assembly set the first example. take the Oath. On January 4, forty-seven bishops out of forty-nine, and two-thirds of the priests who had been elected deputies, all of them sincere in their devotion to the Revolution hitherto, and even now inclined to accept the Civil Constitution, had refused to take the oath to this very Revolution; they had sacrificed their material advantages on its altar, but they could not, till Rome had spoken, sacrifice their religious fidelity.

This example made a great impression on the country. When, after mass had been said on January 9, the Bishops and priests who were not members of the Assembly were called on to take the oath, revolutionary opinion was bitterly disappointed. About half consented, but many of them retracted as soon as Pius VI's condemnation of the Civil Constitution became known. Even before its promulgation fifty-five out of every hundred refused to swear. The body of the Clergy was severed into two halves, and the struggle was soon to begin.

All the Bishops refused the oath save four: Talleyrand, Bishop of Autun, whom we already know too well; Jarente, Bishop of Orléans, "a ruffian" one of his contemporaries calls him: Savine, a madman; and Cardinal Loménie de Brienne, the ex-Prime Minister, a born courtier of whatever party was in power; an atheist-archbishop, who presided over the meetings of the Club at Sens in a cap of liberty fashioned out of his Cardinal's hat; all of them the worst products of the *List of Benefices*. For a "return to apostolic times," this was a bad beginning! Two other prelates gave in their adhesion—Bishops *in partibus infidelium*—Gobel of Lydda and Miroudot of Babylon.

Meanwhile the recalcitrant Bishops had been formally deposed. Between February and May their successors were Consecration of elected; nineteen of these were both priests and new Bishops. deputies, Grégoire the chief among them. These Bishops had to be consecrated: and Talleyrand, by a strange paradox, agreed to act as the father of this "regenerated" Church. Lydda and Babylon supported Autun. On February 20, 1791, they laid their hands on the heads of three new Bishops in the Church of the Oratory. These in their turn, consecrated their fellow-Bishops: for Talleyrand, after having endued the regenerated church with life, was just about to leave it himself, with a final "right about," and return to "the century." Gobel was to receive the thirty pieces of silver in the shape of the mitre of the Archbishopric of Paris, and to wear it till his final apostasy, and the hour of his bloody expiation. On May 14, 1791, Lindet, who was to become Bishop of the Eure, wrote these strange words: "At last those who had been sitting at table have risen from their places, and those who had been standing and fasting have taken their seats, and are now to be fed." This priestly deputy seems to have been strangely haunted by his interest in alimentary details. He may have found the board too poorly supplied, for ere three years were out he too had cast off mitre and cassock.

A sorry banquet it was, and bitter to the taste. These sham prelates were fed upon affronts. Not all, it should be said, were men like Talleyrand and Lindet. Some of them, such as Grégoire and Le Coz, did honestly believe themselves to be purifying a polluted Church; in 1793 and 1794 certain among their number were to face the persecutions of their former friends with extraordinary courage. But, taken as a whole, they were but a poor staff for an army whose ranks were soon

174

to lack even soldiers. This was the most signal failure of the factitious work performed by the Constituent Assembly.

By the end of January it was clear that the Pope's voice would be raised in condemnation only; a deputy of the Left writes that "the Cardinals could not accept the Civil Constitution without making a revolution at Rome of which they themselves would be the first victims." Nobody could entertain a doubt as to the Pope's refusal. His Briefs of March and April 1791 confirmed the general expectation. They solemnly condemned the Civil Constitution as schismatic.

The Pope condemns the Civil Constitution.

From that day forward Louis XVI, a most sincere and logical Catholic, considered himself a sinner. His sanction had been dragged from him against his will. As the course of events led him to recall his "fault" with ever increasing bitterness, or forced him into aggravations of it, his longing to cast off the yoke which had first abased his dignity as a king, and then his conscience as a Christian, grew deeper. Now, for the first time, the Revolution was really threatened from above; and, simultaneously, it came into collision with one of the most deeply rooted sentiments of the population below—its Catholic feeling.

Louis XVI driven into conflict with the Revolution.

Sources. Works already quoted by Thomas Lindet, Mirabeau, Talleyrand, Biauzat, Paroy, Mathieu Dumas, Aulard (*Jacobins*, I), Morellet.—Theiner, *Documents relatifs aux affaires religieuses*, 1857; Robinet, *Le mouvement religieux à Paris pendant la Révolution* (Documents), 1898, vol. I; Salamon, *Correspondance*, 1897, and *Mémoires*, 1899; Grégoire, *Mémoires*, 1823.

Works. Those already quoted by Sorel (II), Pierre de la Gorce, Frédéric Masson, Sicard Sciout.—Mathiez, *La France et Rome sous la Constituante* (*Rev. Fr.*, 1908); Sagnac, *L'Eglise de France et le Serment* (*Revue d'histoire moderne*, VIII), and *Clergé constitutionnel et Clergé réfractaire* (*Rev. Fr.*, 1907); Lafont, *La Politique religieuse de la Révolution*, 1909; Gazier, *Etudes sur l'histoire religieuse de la Révolution*, 1887; Delarc, *L'Eglise de France de 1789 à 1801*; Cretineau Joly, *L'Eglise de France et la Révolution*; Bourgouing, *Pie VI*, 1824; Louis Madelin, *Pie VI et la Première Coalition* (*Rev. Hist.*, 1902).

CHAPTER XI

THE CRISIS OF THE REVOLUTION

December 1790—May 1791

The King, the Queen, and Europe. The *émigrés*. The Assembly gives pretexts to Europe. The annexation of Avignon a fatal move. Austria still hesitates. Internal convulsions. The desire of the country to stop short. Reaction within the Assembly. A split in the Revolutionary party. Mirabeau and La Fayette. Their disagreements prevent the formation of a moderate party. Death of Mirabeau. Oppression of the Royal Family Its illusions. Plans for departure.

" I WOULD rather be King of Metz than continue to be King of France in such a position as the present," said Louis XVI, when he signed the decree imposing the oath on the Clergy, " but it will soon be over ! " At that moment, indeed, he had cast away all the scruples of 1789 and 1790, and was thinking of calling Europe to his aid.

The King and Queen entertain the idea of foreign intervention.

The Queen had thought of it already. Let us not pass too hasty a judgment upon them. That appeal to the foreigner, which now strikes us as such an odious thing, was a traditional method. Coligny and the Huguenots had summoned English and German troops to France in their time, and the League had appealed to the House of Austria. The great Condé, a Prince of the Royal House, would have brought the Spaniards into Paris, after the Fronde. And, further, there was nothing abnormal about the fact that Louis XVI was keeping up relations with foreign cabinets quite different and apart from those governing his official diplomacy : there had always been a " secret of the King " at Versailles. In the case of Louis XVI—when we consider the traditions and the habits of his day—the

176

only thing that should astonish us is the duration of his scruples.

For a considerable time Marie-Antoinette, "Austrian" though she was, seems to have nursed them herself. She does not seem to have dreamt of appealing to Europe before the summer of 1790. And, indeed, the world in general knows little about her conception of the meaning of this appeal; it was feminine and thoroughly childish. She never thought of a counter-revolution carried to Paris in the transports of the foreigner : her idea was that there should be a mere frontier demonstration, whereby the Powers would prove that they "disapproved of the fashion in which the King was being treated." The Emperor would mass his troops and create an impression that he was about to advance; Louis XVI would put himself at the head of the French Army, and Leopold would then gracefully retreat before his brother-in-law, who would march back to Paris, glorified by his victory, and girt about with the love of his people, who would have had a good "warning" into the bargain. This scenario, which cast Leopold for a tolerably silly part, was a mere foolish fancy. Yet the Queen had her brother sounded. The reply that he was to make, unwaveringly, till June 1791, was : he would not come to any decision till the King had left Paris, where he would be exposed, in case of invasion, to the worst dangers. This was fairly sensible, as the events of August 1792 were to prove.

But Louis XVI had hitherto given no sign of his approbation of this appeal to the Emperor's kindness. It was on the day

Leopold invoked.

    he signed the Decree of the Oath that he made the Queen's plan his own. Breteuil, whom he appointed his plenipotentiary in Europe, was desired to beg the Emperor, in the King's name, to turn his attention to what was happening in Paris.

Leopold, who had just brought Belgium into submission, had drawn nearer to Prussia ; and Catherine II, who had won a final victory over the Turks in December 1790, had fixed her greedy eyes on Poland, half of which country still remained to be devoured. To keep her accomplices in the first dismemberment out of the way, she was urging them on towards the Rhine.

THE FRENCH REVOLUTION

On February 20, 1791, the Emperor received an envoy from Prussia at Vienna, and lent a friendly ear to his proposals.

The *émigrés* were playing the part of the fly on the coach-wheel. Their numbers had rapidly increased. The first emi-
The "Emigrés." gration—that of 1789— had been, as a deputy of the Right phrased it, "the emigration of pride." But there had been a second, more excusable, caused by the burning of the *châteaux*, and the creation, as far as the nobles were concerned, of a pariah class. Fashion, indeed, had played its part in the emigration, and self-respect as well. Let us lend an ear to some of the friends of the nobility, rather than to its enemies. Frénilly says that "it was the emigration alone, and not the decrees, that destroyed the nobility." "It was," he says, "a deplorable epidemic." It deprived the King of useful friends within the country. "A difficult game may be won," wrote a clever woman forty years before this period, "but there is no such thing as winning a game that has been given up!" The worst of it was that these "loyal and unfortunate victims of ambitious intrigues," as Frénilly calls them, forsook the game in France only to ruin it outside.

Europe had received the first *émigrés* with astonishment, gradually transformed into a feeling of exasperation. Their reception had been tolerably cordial in the first instance : they were believed to be both wealthy and charming. But from Brussels to Turin they carried that terrible smile of the Frenchman travelling abroad, and princes and populations alike ended by taking offence. Besides, they had less money than had been expected, and this, too, was a disappointment. Finally, their "thoroughly French frivolity" scandalized the middle class, whether in Germany, Switzerland, or Brabant. Before long they were hated.

Exile had ended by inflaming as well as unsettling their minds. The Comte d'Artois had said, "We shall be back in
Mischievous influence of the Comte d'Artois. three months;" he did not return for twenty-five years: the mistake was no trifling one. "We shall be back" with bag and baggage, he meant, and with absolute power in our portmanteaux! This prince, "the only free" member of his family, had forthwith constituted himself the sole representative
178

of the throne and dynasty, whose " business " he laboured to " re-establish." At Turin, the capital of his brother-in-law of Sardinia, he soon gained the name of a dangerous busybody. And the daily increasing crowd of *émigrés* at Mayence, Coblentz, Treves, and Brussels, shared his regrettable reputation. These noisy conspirators, with their dreams of stirring up Europe against France, were really stirring up the continent against themselves. The very idea of being used as the instrument of these particular Frenchmen against the others would have sufficed, for a moment, to stay the foreigner's arm.

They amused themselves : the letters published by Vaissière shed a depressing light on these poor people : they played cards and supped and danced, they made fun of the dull Germans and Belgians, the " beer-drinkers," the " devils of bigots " ; " frivolities " were still bought and sold : fashions were set : the men made love to the ladies. " A life of this sort," writes an *émigrée* herself, " will strike you as being but little suited to people who aspire to be the reformers of a State."

What they desired above all things was a counter-reform. They panted to destroy the work of 1789 and punish its authors : the most moderate of these were considered the most guilty, as, for instance, the Comte de Lally (" *la lie* (the dregs) of the populace," as a wit called him) : and, to get rid of these moderate men, excesses must be encouraged : " The greater the evil, the more prompt will be the remedy."

True Frenchmen they still remained—good Frenchmen, too, after their own fashion. They called on Europe to intervene, but they did it proudly : they would have flown at the throat of the first man who dared to talk of paying for foreign intervention by the cession of a single fortress belonging to the kingdom. It was as a matter of monarchical solidarity that Europe, in their eyes, " owed it to herself," to interfere.

*   *   *   *   *

The Comte d'Artois was all for a regular invasion. Breteuil, the King's plenipotentiary, considered the brilliant prince more troublesome than any other man in the world. He warned Leopold against him, and in January 1791 that monarch showed the King's brother the door. Marie-Antoinette was resolved to keep things in her own hands, and clung, besides, to her idea of a mere demonstration.

Meanwhile, the Assembly was furnishing Europe with pretext after pretext. It had not dared to strike at the *émigrés*, **The Assembly** but it showed great bitterness against the petty **gives pretexts** princes who had welcomed them. Still, the **to Europe.** chief danger of an explosion was connected with the Avignon business. The deputies were beginning to lose their heads about that. The Pope having condemned the Civil Constitution on April 13, the populace had burned him in effigy in the Palais-Royal on May 4, and the Nuncio had taken flight. When the affair of the Comtat Venaissin came up again in the Assembly, on April 30, the progress made by the party in favour of annexation became very evident. This party secured the acceptance of the principle that Avignon rightfully belonged to France, and that the inclusion of the cantons in question would involve no conquest at all. Clermont-Tonnerre objected that to annex them would involve a threat to the whole of Europe : might it not be proclaimed, one of these days, that Brussels rightfully belonged to France, because Charles the Bold had reigned there, and Aix-la-Chapelle, too, because Charlemagne was buried there ? The orator fancied he was indulging in a humorous sally : but his words were a true prophecy. Meanwhile, the proposal for annexation was only lost by six votes—it had become inevitable. And so that Europe might have no doubt as to the meaning involved in the measure, Barère had declared that " I consider that France, to ensure her own safety, might use the same rights as those used by Louis XIV and Louis XV for less important interests."

Austria, fortunately, was more than ever uncertain as to whether she should intervene or not. Catherine II was causing **Austria** anxiety. The Czarina was quite determined to **hesitates.** make an end of Poland. That country had been " audacious " enough on May 31, 1791, to attempt to reform its own Constitution, with the object of safeguarding the last remnant of its independence. On this attempt Catherine had seized as pretext for her own final intervention. But more than ever was she resolved that this time she would sit down to the feast alone. "I am racking my brains," she wrote, "to find means of inducing the courts of Vienna and Berlin to interfere in French affairs, so as to get elbow-room for myself." If she had said "a free and hearty meal" she would have been nearer the mark.

Then a downright comedy began. Catherine, pretending to confuse the "revolution in Poland" with that in France, **Intrigues of** poured forth violent vituperations on "the **Catherine II.** Jacobins of the two countries." "Each one of us," she wrote, "must carry out our counter-revolution, the Germans in Paris, the Russians at Warsaw." From that moment she became the self-made protagonist of a coalition she had no intention of joining, inflating the Comte d'Artois' conceit by her "divine messages," thrusting Gustavus III forward, urging on the Emperor Leopold.

The Emperor had a very fair idea of the real game of this Machiavelli in petticoats. So when he met the Comte d'Artois at Mantua on May 11, his face was set like a flint. And when the King of Prussia begged an interview with him at Pilnitz, in the course of the summer, at which the affairs of France should be discussed, he consented, indeed, but added that he intended to "leave events to ripen and wait till the French Nation itself felt the need of change."

The Nation felt no "need of change." But more than ever it was feeling the necessity for a halt in the wild course along **Internal** which some would fain have dragged it. Already **convulsions.** the protagonists of 1789 had been shouldered out by those of 1790, and in this year, 1701, a whole section of the revolutionary leaders would have stopped short : but the new gangs were pushing them on, treading on their heels, driving them forward, and threatening to pass over their bodies.

The country was sick of politics : many electors had already ceased to cast their votes, and the elections were left in the hands of the popular "Societies." And France, being sick of politics, would gladly have seen "the resumption of business." Starvation threatened half a score of trades. Marat himself reckoned that a sum equal to forty millions of pounds sterling had disappeared since the beginning of the Revolution : half the shops had been shut up, and a third of the workshops. Letters written during the winter of 1790–1791 prove the general discontent to have been extreme.

Discontent was rife in every quarter, from the workmen who could get no work, and only had harsh treatment from the Assembly, to the tradesmen whose customers had disappeared : some turned to the preachers of a second Revolution ; the enthusiasm of others for the first was singularly chilled.

   *   *   *   *   *

Thus the unanimous current of opinion which had carried away the Nation in 1789 had died out. There were two opposing currents now : some desired to stop short and even to go back, others sought to proceed further yet.

These two currents forced the leaders of the Revolution into mutual opposition. The party which hitherto had either directed the course of events, or tamely followed it, was cut in half.

On the Extreme Left a definitely republican group was beginning to take shape. This party had come into the world, **A split in the revolutionary party.** so M. Aulard tells us, "on the sofa of Mme. Robert-Keralio," "a clever, witty, shrewd little woman," says Mme. Roland, who was married to a heavy, thick-headed Belgian journalist, Robert by name, and prompted the violently anti-royalist pamphlets he was in the habit of publishing. On the other hand, as the majority in the Assembly seemed inclined to a more anti-democratic policy, the Extreme Left, spurred by its desire to raise another army of rioters, grew more and more demagogic. On April 20, 1791, Robespierre, generally so conservative in all social matters, actually read a violent diatribe against the rich at the Cordeliers Club, the influence of which was then outstripping that of the Jacobins. This "production of a wise mind and a pure spirit" earned its author the congratulations of the "Society of the Indigent ! "

Many deputies thought this a deplorable state of things. Two men, Mirabeau and La Fayette, might have marshalled **Mirabeau and La Fayette.** them into a party that would have offered a most serious resistance.

Mirabeau had made up his mind to resistance—not to

reaction. Necker had quitted the ministry : and Mirabeau, in spite of the opposition of every sort with which he was meeting, hoped to take his place, to direct the course of events, and make himself their master. He was furious with the revolutionary movement, which had carried him high enough, but had not, as yet, brought him into any port. He was very ill already, fretted and worried, his brain on fire, his blood soured, his whole constitution ravaged by his wild life, and he raged perpetually, now against the Assembly, that " wild ass," and then against the Royal Family, "royal cattle " as he called it. The King paid him but did not employ him. There can be no doubt that he did sell himself : "but he did it," so La Fayette declared, as a corrective, "in accordance with his own opinions." And, as a matter of fact, he sincerely desired both the maintenance of the benefits gained by the Revolution and the restoration of the King's authority. His letters to the Court reveal his possession of a remarkably powerful brain, but his passions kept it in a perpetual fever.

La Fayette, too, would fain have organized some kind of resistance to the demagogues. If we may take Esterhazy's word for it, he had already submitted a plan of this nature to the King : and this testimony finds its corroboration in his own correspondence. He had stood by Bouillé when he marched on Nancy, and on September 2, 1790, he broke up, with a vigorous hand, the mobs collected in Paris, and roused the fury of Marat by his action. From that time forth he booame the object of frantic attacks on the part of the Jacobin press. His popularity had not seemed, so far, to have seriously suffered. He was very powerful, and with Mirabeau as his ally, he could have done anything.

The Court distrusted the two men equally : Mirabeau took this as a reason for forcing its confidence, but La Fayette, as splenetic as the other was violent, piled grievance on grievance. The thing he feared most in the world was the entrance of Mirabeau into the Ministry. An impenitent liberal, he looked on the Provençal tribune as a tyrant-minister in embryo. With considerable slyness, he sought his rival's fall. But Mirabeau continued to make way. In March 1791 the electors made him Director of the Department of Paris. " We hope," an " aristocrat " writes, " he will re-establish order and have the laws enforced. This man, who has done us so much harm, may now do us some good. Every hope and every eye is fixed upon him."

La Fayette took fright : to prevent the fiery tribune's threatened election to the presidential chair, he himself drew nearer to the Extreme Left. He secured his rival's defeat on the first occasion. "I don't care a fig!" wrote Mirabeau ; but when he was finally elected President, thanks to the support of the Right, he was wild with delight. As President of the Assembly and deputy for an important department, he seemed to have reached the pinnacle : he had obtained an audience with Marie-Antoinette, and had left the Queen half won over to his side. Perhaps, even without La Fayette's support, he might have succeeded in driving back the flood of democracy! But Death had laid his finger on him. On March 27 he made a **Death of** speech in the Assembly, his features so wrung by **Mirabeau.** the agony of a frightful attack of nephritic pain that his hearers were terrified. On the 30th he took to his bed : his state was hopeless. Paris was overwhelmed. The King's and the Jacobins' messenger met on his doorstep. The crowd surged round his house in the Chaussée d'Antin. He lay dying within its walls, and dying with a courage touched, as always, with an element of cynicism, and also, from time to time, with bitter regret for his failure. " I see so clearly," he had written, "that we are in the midst of anarchy, and sinking deeper into it every day : I am overwhelmed by the thought that all I have done has been to help on a huge destruction. . . ."

His death was an event. He was borne to the Pantheon with extraordinary pomp. The people mourned him : but the Court had far more reason to regret him. He alone—perhaps —might have saved the King !

" I carry the last rags of the Monarchy away with me ! " he said to Talleyrand. The very night before he died he advised against the King's flight. He had felt—with his usual power of divination—that it was being prepared. It was a settled thing.

The populace, too, suspected it. The Royal Family was closely and tyrannically watched, and this had exasperated all its members. The very desire to keep the King where he was, was driving him into flight.

A succession of incidents occurred. One day a report got about that Monsieur (the Comte de Provence) was about to

Coercion of the Royal Family. depart. The crowd besieged the Luxembourg; the prince was obliged to show himself and drive round Paris in his coach, crammed with market-women who half-stifled him with their kisses. When the King's aunts, daughters of Louis XV, made an attempt to get out of Paris they were stopped, and the mob gathered in front of the Tuileries and forced Louis XVI to make the " old ladies " go back. Then there was another adventure : a story spread that a subterranean passage connecting the Tuileries with Vincennes had been discovered : the populace took alarm, and flew first to Vincennes and then to the Tuileries : La Fayette had to dismiss the rioters with all sorts of promises and oaths : he betook himself to the palace, but finding that several noblemen had hurried thither to defend the King, he made a scene, very nearly took the Duc de Villequier by the throat, and loudly denounced "these knights of the dagger " to the King. The expression was a popular success : the people were obstinately persuaded there had been a plot to carry off the Royal Family. So indignant was Louis XVI at the two-fold intrusion of La Fayette and the mob that he fell ill.

And, indeed, the approach of Easter was filling him with terror. He had felt himself a sinner ever since he had given his sanction to the decrees, and now he ought to go to confession ! But, in his despair of obtaining absolution, he made up his mind to abstain. The rage of the people who had imposed the decrees upon him was extreme. These freethinkers, curiously enough, were loud in their demand that the King should perform his Easter duties. When Louis XVI, in his desire to escape notice, would have betaken himself to St.-Cloud, the mob forthwith besieged the Palace and guarded every outlet. When the Sovereign tried to issue forth the National Guard itself objected. A score of ruffians began to shout " He shall not go out ! " La Fayette hurried to the spot and tried to parley with them : he was scoffed at for his pains. The Royal Family was forced to give up the idea of going to St.-Cloud.

White with anger, the Queen said to La Fayette : "At least you will acknowledge, now, that we are not free ! " La Fayette handed in his resignation and took it back again. "He should have broken his sword on the spot," writes the Baron de Staël on April 21, "the very instant his troops refused to obey his orders ! "

That same day the *Department* addressed a "dictatorial" letter—thus Morris describes it—a regular reprimand on the subject of this incident, to the King. Louis was on fire with impatience to get away. He was exasperated, determined to depart whatever it might cost him. He dissembled, submitted to everything : an authoritative demand was made for a circular letter affirming his perfect freedom, to be sent to all the Courts : he wrote it on the 20th : another demand insisted on his making his confession to a priest who had taken the Oath : he made it ; that he should receive the Holy Communion : he received it. Many worthy people felt themselves humiliated in the King's person : his state appeared lower than one of tutelage, it was almost childishness. Since April 18, when La Fayette had proved himself powerless, Louis XVI had been left at the mercy of any sudden blow.

Within the Tuileries the propitious moment was thought to have arrived. Europe was gathering herself together behind Illusions of Leopold to force intervention upon him. The the Royal country, meanwhile, seemed bewildered, and the Family. revolutionary party divided. The Assembly was unpopular. Once the King was gone, would it find it possible to rule ? And would not the dictatorship be too heavy a burden for "that Clown-Cæsar," La Fayette ? Moreover, and here was the crux of the whole matter, Paris had become unendurable to the King. His liberty, his dignity, his very conscience was violated there. He would go to the Metz army, of which Bouillé held the command—the last troops, it was said, that remained faithful to him. When his presence there was known, the Nation, whose illusions had now been destroyed for over a year, would cast itself at his feet, and in Paris the Assembly would either dissolve or submit. Thus there would be no need of the white-coated Austrians, nor even of Condé's "red heels," to bring the King back to his capital. He would

186

come back with Bouillé, and himself grant pardon, give peace, and restore all things.

What Louis did not know was that Bouillé's troops were as disaffected as the rest, and would only afford him the most **Plans for** unwilling help in his operations; and that the **flight.** Nation, which clung both to the Revolution and to what it had won for it, would regard his own flight as an attempt on the very existence of Liberty. That it would easily guess that the King, once he was on the frontier, would become the ally and perhaps the tool of the German troops fast mustering there; that the whole population, whether violent or moderate, citizens and artisans, peasants led by good priests, and peasants led by bad, would forget their disagreements and think of nothing but the safety of the Revolution and the Nation, and that the Assembly, backed by public opinion, would make itself the Dictatorship of Public Safety. Mirabeau would have warned him. But he would not have gained a hearing. In the eyes of the Royal Family the cup was full to the very brim.

SOURCES. Works already quoted by Vaissière, Madame Roland, Mirabeau, Morris, Mallet, Esterhazy, Virien (in *Castellane*), Dumont, Thibaudeau, Legrain, Malouet, Thomas Lindet, Morellet, Biauzat, Baron de Staël, Esterhazy, Madame Jullien, Schmidt I; *Correspondance des deputés de l'Aude* (published by M. Bloch, *Rev. Fr.*, 1895). Aulard (*Société des Jacobins*, II, 1801.

WORKS. Those already quoted by Meynier, Goncourt, Charavay, Esmein, Néton, Levasseur, Claretie (*Desmoulins*); Tarlé, *La classe ouvrièr et le parti contre-révolutionnaire sous la Constituante* (*Rev. Retr.*, 1909).

CHAPTER XII

VARENNES

The flight. Drouet's gallop. Varennes. The Royal Family is
stopped. Paris distracted. La Fayette undertakes to direct
matters. Romeuf at Varennes. Death-agony of the monarchy
in the house of " Père Sauce." The hideous return journey.
The King re-enters Paris.

A T seven o'clock in the morning of June 21, Lemoine, a
valet de chambre, entering Louis XVI's bedchamber,
found the bed empty. He gave the alarm, and a
hurried search was made in the Queen's rooms and those of her
The Flight. children. They were all deserted. Within an hour
the tocsin was ringing out over a distracted Paris.

Eluding the close attention of the watchers set about his
person, the King, who had just held a long conversation with
La Fayette, had slipped out of the Palace, disguised as a servant,
climbed into a huge travelling coach, and quitted Paris with
the whole of his family. He had taken his way to the Argonne,
and hoped to be able to reach Montmédy. The moment he was
through the Argonne, Bouillé, with his Army Corps from Metz,
was to join the Royal Family.

All day on the 21st, the Baronne de Korff (the Queen), with
her family and house-steward (the King), travelled unmolested
under a burning sun along the white roads of Champagne.
Once Châlons lay behind, the Royal Family believed safety
had been attained ; at Sainte-Menehould they expected to
meet Damas' dragoons, sent forward by Bouillé.

Damas' dragoons did indeed reach Sainte-Menehould, but
their disposition was as insubordinate as that of the rest of the
army. Their presence was more harmful than useful, for it
attracted attention to the coach, already noticeable on account
of its monumental proportions. Yet the post-master, Drouet,

did not feel himself obliged to do more than enjoin the postilions "not to founder their horses." But when the *berline* had rolled away, Drouet's son, and a certain Guillaume, surnamed La Hure, offered to go on to Clermont and stop the suspicious-looking travellers there: a few moments later they had plunged into cross-roads through the Argonne woods which would take them to Varennes before the King could reach it.

At Clermont, where the King arrived at nightfall, he found the Comte de Damas waiting for him, but no dragoons. Their *Drouet's ride.* commanding officers had felt so little confidence in them that they had not dared to let them ride on. Thus the coach was unescorted; it started forth again within a very few minutes, on its way to Montmédy, by the road that runs through Varennes. Soon after its departure the population of Clermont rose, disarmed the dragoons (easily enough), and sounded the tocsin.

Meanwhile Drouet and Guillaume were galloping hard. How often wandering through those well-known woods, have I fancied I heard their horses yet! Fate hung on that young Drouet's crupper as he rode! No wonder he reached his goal! And while the ex-trooper was doing his best to kill his mount, the heavy coach rolled slowly along through the hot night.

It had half an hour's start of the riders; this advantage was lost in the lower part of the town of Varennes; Drouet *Varennes.* made straight for the point the travellers must pass on their way to Montmédy. He raised an alarm, took a cart, had it drawn across the bridge over the Aire, which the coach would have to cross, and sent to the Procurator of the Commune, "Father Sauce," who hurried to the spot.

My readers know the rest of the story: how the coach was stopped by the barricade, and the feverish parleying of its occupants, and the hesitation of Sauce, who recognized the validity of the travellers' passports, and only gave in under pressure from Drouet. The King lost patience and shouted: "Come, postilions, get on!" But muskets were cocked in the crowd: "Not a step, or we'll fire!" Discouraged, Louis, who hoped Bouillé's soldiers would very soon be on the spot, consented to accept the hospitality offered him by Sauce. The hussars arrived, but were straightway debauched by the people;

their fidelity once shaken, they became more a danger than a help.

At last Louis XVI, recognized by one of the Varennes men, acknowledged his identity, and with an impulse which reveals The Royal the strangeness of his nature, he opened his arms Family stopped. wide and embraced the man who had just identified him, embraced Sauce, embraced all the members of the Council of the Commune. He would have been ready to embrace Drouet too ! Had he any hope that he might appease these people ? Even if Sauce had given in, the mob gathered by this time round his grocery shop would not have permitted the coach to depart. The King was to set forth again, indeed, but on his way to Paris, and barricades were thrown up against the approach of Bouillé, who became, at this moment, a sort of bugbear to the Revolution. " To Paris ! " was the cry, " To Paris ! Or we will shoot him in his coach ! " Louis tried to gain time : Sauce found himself in a difficulty : he sent off an express messenger to Paris. The messenger met those the Assembly had despatched on the King's track.

Paris, as we know, had become aware of the flight at seven o'clock on the morning of the 21st. At eight o'clock the whole city Paris in a fer- was surging round the walls of the Tuileries like ment at the a mighty flood. In the course of a few hours— flight. General Thiébault lays great stress on this feature —the crowd travelled through a whole gamut of feeling, stupor, terror, indignation, furious rage : and, finally, the Paris street-boy gained the upper hand, and jeering irony prevailed.

La Fayette's position was compromised : he was considered either the dupe of the attempt or its accomplice. He faced La Fayette the position with great coolness, sallied forth takes the helm. into the midst of the gathering mob, reached the Palace, joined on his way by Bailly, the Mayor, who was shaking with fear, and Alexandre de Beauharnais, the President of the Assembly. Which of them was to sign the order to bring the King back, alive or dead ? La Fayette took up a pen, signed the paper, and half a score of aides-de-camp rushed off in different directions.

Meanwhile the mob invaded the Tuileries : a cherry-hawker with her flat basket throned it on the Queen's bed : when a distracted postman looked about for somebody to whom he might deliver his letters, the *titis* bawled " Gone away, and left no address ! " Already Paris had begun to laugh. " House to let " was the inscription on a card hung on the Palace door. At bottom, the people were laughing to keep themselves from weeping : there was an extraordinary feeling of nervousness ; nobody would have been very much surprised if the Austrians had made their appearance at the city gates.

The Assembly was far from finding the situation entertaining. The members had come together at nine o'clock, under **Beauharnais** the presidency of Beauharnais : the " handsome **President of** dancer " carved out a part for himself that day. **the Assembly.** La Fayette had seized the rudder at the Hôtel-de-Ville ; Beauharnais followed his example at the Salle du Manège. For a moment this man of mediocre parts, an aristocrat sitting on the Extreme Left, took on the appearances of a leader. The populace jokingly dubbed little Eugène, the "handsome dancer's " son by the Creole Joséphine de la Pagerie, " the Dauphin."

" I imagine," said Beauharnais, "that in a conjuncture so unforeseen and so important as this, the National Assembly will think it well, for the tranquillity of the Kingdom and the maintenance of the Constitution, to give prompt orders that the country shall be informed as quickly as possible, in every quarter, of this fresh alarm." The Assembly decided to sit without rising ; and the sitting did not close till the evening of the 25th. No order of the day was issued.

It was settled, at last, that the Minister of the Interior was to despatch couriers into every department, with orders that any person who endeavoured to leave the kingdom should be arrested. This decree was passed without a dissentient vote. Even the Right, struck with dismay, or terrified into submission, voted for it. For the rest, all the quarrels in the Left had ceased ; the Assembly formed one compact block.

Romeuf, aide-de-camp to La Fayette, whose order for the King's arrest had been confirmed by the Assembly, was speeding **Romeuf at** along the highroads of Champagne. By midnight **Varennes.** he and his comrade Bayon, with whom he had fallen in, had reached the foot of the Argonne. They climbed its slopes, passing through excited villages brigh̊t with torches and ringing with the sound of ·the tocsin, rode down the pass of Les Islettes to Clermont, reached that place, filled with a seething crowd at five o'clock in the morning, learnt what had happened at Varennes, hurried thither, and found the King in the house of " Father Sauce." Sadly and respectfully they presented the Monarch with the decree of the Assembly. " There is no longer a King in France ! " was Louis XVI's bitter reply. Little did he think how true his words were : the Monarchy had died at Varennes ; all that Paris was to do, a year later, was to bury it.

*   *   *   *   *

In good truth those closing scenes at Varennes were the death-throes of the Monarchy. Then came the return to Paris— *The return to Paris.* a real Calvary—the coach literally carried along, so close was the pressure round it, by the crowd which, swelled as it was at every stage by the dregs of the populace in the various towns, grew more and more abusive ; the travellers seated in the vehicle vilely insulted and greeted with howls of derision : the King's monotonous protest, " I did not intend to leave the kingdom " ; the Queen overwhelmed with the most filthy epithets : a journey that knew no rest and scarcely a halt amidst the most sweltering heat, the clouds of white dust of the Champagne highroads, and the jeering hatred of the six or seven thousand peasants who formed the escort. At Châlons the reception was of a piece with the rest : the most cruel insults were heaped upon the Bourbons ; " Capet is quite fat enough for what we want to do with him ! " shouted the wretches, amidst shrieks of laughter. They vowed they would " make cockades out of the bowels of Louis and Antoinette and belts out of their skins." There were calls for " their hearts and livers " to be cooked and eaten. From Châlons to Epernay the coach moved along through a tempest of abuse : at Chouilly the horrified peasants saw some of the ruffians spit in the King's face. The Sovereign sat unmoved, while the Queen and Madame Elisabeth shed tears of indignation. When the mob was not abusing the travellers some pedant would read them a lecture. The coach reached Épernay, and Louis, surrounded by the local magistrates, wiped the sweat

192

from his face, whereupon one of them sententiously remarked : " That's what you get by travelling ! " In every way, the royal prestige was falling to pieces.

Between Épernay and Château-Thierry the King met three deputies sent down by the Assembly, La Tour-Maubourg, Barnave, and Pétion. The King's arrest had not become known in Paris till the 24th. During those two anxious days the excitement had been constantly on the increase. The mob hid or allayed its anxiety by a mask of raillery. To all appearances it was making up its mind to do without a king. " Lost ! a king and queen ! " they cried through the streets, " A good reward will be given to him who fails to find them." Desmoulins made merciless jokes about the " *decampativos* of the Capets, male and female." The Assembly, still at its permanent sitting, sought to play the part of the Roman Senate, *impavidum ferient ruinæ*, and pretended to discuss the clauses of the new penal code.

Barnave, Pétion, and La Tour-Maubourg sent to meet the King.

But the letters of such of its members as Roger, Biauzat, and Lindet betray their mortal anxiety. " May God help us ! " writes Biauzat on the 21st. " God will help us ! " he writes again on the 22nd. The agreement instantly re-established amongst the supporters of the Revolution " whether they were men of '89 or Jacobins," as one of them writes, rejoiced the deputies' hearts. But during the daylight hours of the 20th, which dragged by without news, the tide of anxiety rose higher and higher.

At half past nine o'clock that evening the " lethargy " of the deputies was disturbed by shouts from outside their place of meeting : " The King is taken." A moment later Beauharnais was reading the letter two couriers white with dust had just brought in from Varennes. Three deputies were forthwith appointed to go and meet the King, bring him back, and, possibly, protect him. At four o'clock in the morning Pétion, Barnave and Latour-Maubourg were already well on their way.

They met the King at the hamlet of La Cave, and turned back towards Paris in his company, the three deputies and the Royal Family all crowded, in offensive familiarity, into the same coach.

N   193

THE FRENCH REVOLUTION

At three o'clock in the afternoon, under a burning sun and a temperature of over 89 degrees, the procession was at Pantin. **The entry into Paris.** Once the gate of Paris was passed the abuse ceased, but the silence of the mighty crowd was yet more ominous. The order had gone forth. Not a hat was raised. The King never flinched. " Our poor Queen," wrote one of her friends, " hung her head down almost to her knees." The National Guard, with arms reversed as for a funeral, lined the streets. A letter written by Roger, a deputy, on the 26th, gives us a striking picture of this unprecedented scene.

When Louis got out of the coach at the Tuileries, he mounted the entrance steps without a word. The Queen's appearance elicited a murmur from the crowd. At seven o'clock the gate of the Palace had closed on the royal pair.

The sitting of the Assembly, which had lasted four days, now ended. La Fayette proceeded to the Tuileries and asked for the King's orders. " It seems to me," said Louis XVI, with a laugh, "that I am much more at your orders than you at mine." The King had learnt that the Assembly had decided, that afternoon, that he was to be suspended from his functions and kept a safe prisoner in the Tuileries. His laughter sounds painfully in our ears. He continued to smile when certain deputies appeared on the morrow (the 26th) and cross-questioned him like any accused prisoner. He treated them with great good humour. But the Queen's reception of them was frigidly polite ; she made them take armchairs, and herself, **The Queen's hair blanched in one night.** in the most pointed manner, sat on an upright seat. She seemed to have aged by twenty years ; when she had taken off her nightcap that morning her waiting-woman had perceived that her hair had turned quite white, " like the hair of a woman of seventy."

For weeks now the doors of the Tuileries, closely kept by the National Guard, were to be shut. The king was safe, but the throne was lost.

Sources. Works already quoted by Biauzat, Malouet, Lindet, Morris, Vaissière, Bouillé, Madame Roland, Madame Campan, Madame de Tourzel ; *Lettres du Constituant Roger* (*Rev. Fr.*, 1902) ; Bimbeuet, *Relation*, 1884 ; *Mémoires du Général Radet*, 1892.

Works. Lenôtre, *Le Drame de Varennes*, 1905 ; Charavay, *La Fayette*, 1898 ; Klinckowstrom *Le Comte de Fersen et la Cour de France*, 1878.

CHAPTER XIII

THE VOLLEYS ON THE CHAMP-DE-MARS

The King suspended. The Clubs bent on his overthrow. Neither
the Provinces nor the Assembly desire it. Barnave. Rupture
within the Jacobin Club. The Feuillants. The Champ-de-Mars
on July 17. The demonstration. Martial law. La Fayette
and Bailly give the order to fire. The Assembly too weary to
attempt reactionary measures.

"THE wise measures taken by the Assembly have convinced even the humbler folk *that they can do without a king*, and in every square I hear the same cry *' we no longer need a king.'*" Thus writes a correspondent of the Prince of Salm, on June 24.

A wave of Republicanism seemed about to carry off at one fell swoop the Constitution and the Bourbon throne.
The King suspended. There was no necessity for dethroning the King. "He is dethroned," wrote a Constitutional Bishop, Suzor, on the 22nd ; and this ecclesiastic believed the flight to have been an abduction.

Whether fugitive or kidnapped, Louis XVI had become an object of the deepest scorn. "A royal lay-figure to be kept under lock and key," writes Mme. Roland. "Louis the False," "Fat Pig," shouted the Faubourgs. The most serious feature of all was that this contempt was visible even in the speeches of those deputies who defended the monarchical system in the Assembly. Even in the journal of Gouverneur Morris, himself so hostile to the Revolution, we find an echo of these degrading terms : "A despicable and cruel nature," he writes, "brutal and peevish," and winds up : "It is not surprising that *such an animal* should have been dethroned." These were the words of a man who was friendly to the Court.

As a fugitive the King had been obnoxious : as an abducted

person he would have been contemptible, as a prisoner he was ridiculous : the Sovereign who had been brought back to Paris with the saliva of the provinces on his face was degraded in all eyes.

The Nation, on the other hand, had grown greater in its own estimation, and the Revolution, thanks to the general effect of "the electric shock" (as one deputy described it), which had drawn every man to his feet from the Hôtel-de-Ville in Paris to the tiniest Communes in the Argonne, felt more secure. And, further, there had been no disturbance of public order. Hence the conclusion : "A nation may exist without a king, but no king can exist without a nation."

* * * * *

This appeared for a moment, to be the opinion of the Constituent Assembly. Louis XVI was suspended : the Assembly The Fiction of held the Seals of State. Even the Right found the Abduction. it difficult to make any protest. A certain section of the Left did not seem disposed to push its advantage any further. By a fiction, which deceived nobody at all, it was agreed that the King had been abducted. Bouillé, indeed, had written a letter to the public declaring he had planned the abduction, and then proceeded to emigrate. The Assembly poured out anathemas upon his head. Not a move was made in the direction of the dethronement of Louis XVI.

But a proposal of this nature was rife in the Clubs. The Cordeliers embodied it in their order of the day on the 21st, The Clubs bent and requested the Jacobins to give it their con- on the King's sideration. Brissot and Condorcet began a cam- dethronement. paign against the "royal automaton." Pétion was somewhat inclined to follow in their wake, though his determination was shaken by the flattering and absurd conviction that during the return journey from Varennes he had inspired a tender feeling in the heart of the King's sister, Mme. Elisabeth. But Robespierre, with his usual circumspection, pronounced against any attempt at a "second revolution." We shall later have occasion to show how invariably this rhetorician shrank from any direct action. He was always terrified of men with a strong grip, daring spirits like Danton, who was leading the Cordeliers at that particular moment. Marat would have put the King aside and appointed a " military tribune " in his place. (The " Friend of the People " was always a Cæsarian at heart.) Mme. Roland soon perceived that " the happiest moment for Liberty was slipping by, and nobody was taking advantage of it."

The provinces, indeed, which had just proved their " patriotism," were still thoroughly royalist. An obscure The Republic tribune of the name of Cordier had, it is true, suggested. attacked the inviolability of the Sovereign— " as ridiculous as the infallibility of the Pope "—at a club meeting in the town of Angers, and foreseeing (curiously enough) " a war between giants " had suggested the selection of " an Emperor." A club at Montpellier, prompted by Cambon, drew up an appeal to the Assembly for its sister societies. " Make France a Republic ! " But it found no following.

In Paris, however, the republicans did not despair of creating a movement. Anti-royalist pamphlets rained upon the city. The Assembly Still the Assembly stood out. And even Gorsas, upholds the a Jacobin journalist who knew nought of the Monarchy. ideas of the humble Cordier of Amgers, wrote " It is better to have a King Log than a Republican Stork." Already Marat's " military tribune " was viewed with apprehension. Condorcet had extolled the Republic, but another pontiff pronounced against it ; Sieyès dropped an oracular statement, he favoured the Monarchy " which ends in a point," whereas the republican government " ends in a platform." " The triangle of the monarchy is far better adapted than the republican platform," he declared, " to that division of power which is the true bulwark of liberty." In the face of so decisive a pronouncement could there be any room for doubt ?

Barnave finished the work. He was now entirely devoted to the Royal Family. Mirabeau had recognized in this nature so full of exaggeration and passion, at once generous Barnave. and vain, the tribune who might " be won over." The misfortunes of the Royal Family, of which he had had so close a view between Paris and Meaux, had filled him with pity ; his heart now swelled with loyal emotion. Though he never paraded his sentiments, he made a vigorous stand

197

against the idea of proclaiming a Republic. He carried the decrees of July 15 and 16, which affirmed the King's innocence, and re-established his rights, in principle only, for the suspension was to continue in force till the Constitution was proclaimed. As a sop to the republicans there was some talk of forcing a tutor (in the person of Condorcet) on the "royal urchin."

But the great majority of the Jacobins seemed determined to go forward. The petition had been presented to the Club, Split in the and the immediate result had been a split. Lameth, Jacobin Club. Sieyès, Barnave, and others, had protested loudly, left the Club, and founded a rival society at the Convent of the Feuillants, shaking the dust of the "low resort" from their feet, says Rabaut, who adds that its frequenters were talking of setting up, "I know not what sort of a republic." Once rid of the moderate party, the Jacobins decided to support the objects of the petition, and resolved it should be solemnly laid on the altar of the Fatherland on the day after the next—that is, on July 17.

La Fayette, for his part, was quite determined to stop this demonstration by force. The members of the new Feuillants Club were not likely to restrain him. "That infer-
Les Feuillants. nal department of Paris," as Fournier l'Américain called it, was on their side, and ready to take steps, with "the two conspirators Bailly and La Fayette" to carry out "a nationi-cidal machination." In less grandiose language, the National Guard was called out : and Bailly prepared to go to the length of proclaiming martial law.

On the morning of the 17th, groups of people proceeded to the altar, underneath which two men were found, and forth-
The Champ-de- with accused of being there "with the intention
Mars on July of blowing it up." Horrible thought! The
17. mob was on the verge of hysterics : it fell on the poor wretches, and hanged them! The story, altered to suit either party, soon spread all over Paris. To one section the two vagabonds became enemies of the Fatherland, who had meant to blow the petitioners into the air : to the other, they were simply peaceful citizens who had been cruelly massacred. One thing was quite certain, the poor wretches had been done to death after a most revolutionary fashion. The mob

thickened, and La Fayette marched a few of his battalions on to the Champ-de-Mars. The crowd snapped its fingers at them; within the past two years it had grown used to seeing musket barrels drop before it. But this time the *bourgeoisie* was thoroughly frightened, and with good cause. The National Guard, anything but pleased at being kept under arms all through a long hot Sunday, was sick of the whole thing; La Fayette had urged on Bailly, whose presence was also indispensable. Bailly had the red flag, the symbol of martial law,

La Fayette and Bailly give orders to fire on the mob. unfurled. Guard, General, Mayor, and flag, were all greeted with a volley of stones. Even then the Guard fired its first volley into the air; a zealot replied to this comparatively pacific action by aiming straight at La Fayette, and the troops, completely out of patience, instantly fired into the crowd, and made great gaps in it.

There was a wild stampede : the cavalry charged : the mob, which had first been led into boldness by a long period of impunity, and then cruelly undeceived, dispersed in great confusion : the onlookers fled in deadly fear. If Lambesc had only done on July 13, 1789, what "that democrat" La Fayette did on July 17, 1791, there would have been no fall of the Bastille. Yet Mme. Roland exaggerates greatly when she talks of a "massacre." The small amount of carnage that really did take place sufficed to set a great abyss between La Fayette, the *bourgeoisie*, the Municipality, and the Assembly, on the one hand, and the riotous populace, the advanced party, and the Clubs of the Extreme Left, on the other. For a few days, if we may rely on Lindet's letters, the Left itself was full of admiration for the generous moderation evinced by La Fayette, and rejoiced over the "check inflicted on such men as Brissot, Danton, Laclos, and Condorcet."

The Extreme Left foresaw "the proscriptions of Sylla." Here was a great compliment to the consistency of the Assembly and to the energy of La Fayette. This particular Sylla, with his powdered head, had an objection to seeing his lace cuffs stained with blood. Robespierre, with a timorousness by no means foreign to his nature, had dropped out of sight for several days past : he now emerged from his hiding-place. Danton alone was forced, like Bouillé, to emigrate. An inquiry into his conduct was opened, dragged along, and closed without reaching any clear result. And back from England Danton came, bearing the martyr's palm.

The weariness of the Assembly was too great to permit of its inaugurating any system of repression. For that it would have had to begin everything over again, restore its powers to the governing authority, dissolve the Clubs, re-establish the strength of the Army, and look seriously into the anarchy existing in the new Constitution. For all this it had no longer the strength.

The Assembly too weary to attempt reactionary measures.

And, further, the Assembly felt that in spite of the volleys of musketry fire, the denunciations and the prosecutions, the men it had vanquished on July 17 were its own heirs presumptive. Robespierre had just been chosen Public Prosecutor for the Department of Paris by several thousands of Parisian voters, and his friend Pétion had been elected a President of the Law Court. Condorcet, who was to be the oracle of the republican party, was shortly to be made deputy for Paris.

Worn out and disheartened, the Assembly let its arms drop to its sides. It was hurrying with failing breath towards its end.

Sources. Works already quoted by Aulard (*Jacobins*, II), Thomas Lindet, Roger, Biauzat, Morris, Dumont, Madame Roland (*Lettres*), Malouet, Mounier, Vaissière, Rabaut, Maupetit, Fournier l'Américain.— *Lettre de l'Evêque Suzor* (*Annales Rev.*, III) ; Madame Roland, *Mémoires* (ed. Perroud, 1905) ; *Révolution de France*, No. 102 ; Sergent Marceau, *Relation* (*Rev. Retr.*, Series II. 2).

Works. Those already quoted by Cahen, Meynier, Arnaud.—Dard, *Choderlos de Laclos*, 1905 ; Robinet, *Danton*, 1885.

CHAPTER XIV

THE END OF THE CONSTITUENT ASSEMBLY

The Assembly desires, but fails, to revise the Constitution.
Barnave learns the truth too late. The Assembly abandons all
effort. The Decree of non-re-electability. Avignon absorbed
into France. The Pillnitz Meeting. What the German princes
intend as a dilatory measure is taken by the *émigrés* to be a threat.
The Coblentz Manifesto. The King accepts and promulgates
the Constitution. The Festival of the Constitution. The Constituent Assembly imagines it has brought the Revolution to a
conclusion, but leaves the way open before it.

" **F**ROM the eighty-three corners of France," writes the
Jacobin Citizeness Jullien on August 11, "the cry
goes up for a new legislature " !

France was weary of the Assembly; it could not have
been more weary of it than the Assembly was of itself. All
The Assembly its members were longing to be set free; some
fails to revise of them actually worn out by physical fatigue,
the Constitu- others because the last of their illusions had
tion. been destroyed.

" The change in the democratic leaders' manner," writes
a certain ambassador on September 4, " is prodigious; they
now appear convinced of the impossibility of making the Constitution work."

They did indeed endeavour to bolster it up by revising it.
Mirabeau, when he was *in extremis*, had snatched a decision
to this effect from the Assembly. And now Barnave, who
Barnave sees had opposed the measure, was using it as his
the truth too own weapon. I have referred to the frame of mind
late. in which he returned from that terrible journey
across Champagne. This feeling was still at work; the young
deputy was passing through an inevitable process of evolution;
Mirabeau had foretold it. Barnave said to Malouet one day,

201

"I have grown much older in the course of a few months!"
Like Mounier in 1789, like Mirabeau in 1790, Barnave was
perceiving in 1791 that he had worked nothing but "destruction" and beginning to long for restoration. Thus shall we
see Vergniaud and Brissot in 1792, Danton and Desmoulins
in 1794, "grow older" in the course of a few months—all
too late!

This Barnave hid a hot heart beneath an icy exterior.
"He had," a contemporary declares, "all the charm of
youth without its warmth, or rather without its flame, for
within the man was on fire." He was on fire now to repair
the evil done. The Queen was reckoning on his help; the
Clubs were crying out upon his treason. Barnave was edging
towards the Right, "going over to Maury."

He hoped to carry his friends along with him: Lameth,
Le Chapelier, Du Port, the former Jacobin triumvirate,
which had just forsaken the famous Club. They were ready
enough to support a certain reaction, but what they feared
was that the reaction, once begun, would be too strong for
them to control it. "How," said Le Chapelier to Malouet,
"can we restore the energy it now lacks to the Royal authority,
when we must fear it will be turned against ourselves?" They
dreaded being "devoured" by the Clubs for the benefit of
their "enemies" at the Tuileries. In the Assembly itself
the Right refused to welcome their advances. Wimpfen, who
had been the bearer of the proposals of the new Left to the
"Blacks" (the Right), said, as he went off, "You wish to
ruin everything, and unhappily you are ruining everything."

The members of the Right made a mock of these men who,
as Rivarol put it, "had been incendiaries first of all, and now
wanted to be firemen." But it would have been wiser to accept
the offer the "incendiaries" had made; no better firemen
could have been found, for they knew just where the building
had been fired.

The result of this disagreement was that the Left did not
venture on any thorough revision at all. Only hatred such as
that of Mme. Jullien against the new "anti-revolutionary"
party could have ventured to affirm that "every ornament
on the crown had been picked up and artistically fastened on

it once more " by these " revisers " who, as Barbaroux fiercely asserts, were a " dishonour to the Constituent Assembly ! "

And, indeed, when Malouet brought forward a proposal to strengthen the hands of the governing authority, Biauzat, **The Decree of** who sat beside Le Chapelier, called out, " This **ineligibility.** is nothing less than a counter-revolution ! " And Le Chapelier, who had urged Malouet to mount the rostrum, was so alarmed that he actually proposed that the speaker should be silenced by the chairman. The Assembly confined itself to a revision of the electoral law, which gives us no clear idea of how it expected to prevent violent politicians from procuring their own election. On the other hand, to close the mouths of the republicans, whose attitude was most threatening, the House decided that the Constitution was not to be revised on any pretext whatever till ten years had elapsed— in 1801, therefore, and even then by a Convention. Looking back, this decision evokes a smile. Where was the Constitution of 1791 in the year 1801 ? Three other Constitutions, one following on the other, had taken its place, and by that time many of those deputies, more fortunate than Barnave and Le Chapelier, having escaped the guillotine, were officials under the Consulate.

*   *   *   *   *

The weary Assembly still carried on its labours in weather that was tropically hot. It was unpopular and it knew it. **Exhaustion of** The harvest had been a failure ; " fewer sheaves **the discredited** by one fourth than in 1790," writes a dweller **Assembly.** in the country in July 1791. The workmen who had been discharged from the national workshops, were wishing the deputies at the devil. Jests and epigrams rained down upon these men engaged in spoiling their own work. They jeered at themselves. " Faith," said one to his colleague, " that's as foolish as the decree we passed yesterday ! " " Why mention a date, sir ? " quoth his friend. The public agreed with them. We have endless proof of the crushing disfavour under which the dying Assembly had fallen.

It was probably its sense of this unpopularity, unjust in certain respects, which led the Constituent Assembly to commit its crowning folly. Many of the members fancied they were doing a noble thing when they decided that none of them should be eligible for re-election. But this, we say it again, was their crowning folly. The men guilty of it completed the ruin of their own work. A certain contact with business matters was beginning—as the attempts at revision prove—to turn these ideologists into parliamentarians with some knowledge of their work. If they had come back to the Legislative Chamber they might perhaps have . put some balance into the laws they made, and, at any rate, they might have applied the provisions of the Constitution in the sense in which they had ended by voting it. The Right once more failed in comprehension. In its puerile desire to destroy every vestige of an Assembly which had mortified its pride, it forced on the measure. We have Malouet's own confession : " Only one great mistake was left for us to make, and we did not fail to make it."

But Malouet acknowledges that his brain " was exhausted." Rabaut, Biauzat, and a score of letters and newspapers, make the same confession ; the decree was the work of lassitude and abdication.

All difficult discussions were avoided. The Civil Constitution was a failure all over the country ; any debate concerning it was adjourned. The *émigrés*, as we shall see, were raging at Coblentz ; all attempts at taking measures against them were dropped ; "impossible to discover any settled opinion," writes a deputy. The Emperor and the King of The Conference Prussia had a meeting at Pillnitz ; the Con-at Pillnitz. stituent Assembly, so susceptible only a short time since, ignored the Pillnitz interview. It was an ostrich policy. The Army was now in full mutiny ; the Assembly, as a spectator at the debate on August 29 writes, only took "some ridiculous measures." The question of Avignon came up again for the fourth and last time, and to get rid of it, the Assembly settled it after a most radical fashion. In vain did Salamon, the Pope's secret agent, hurry to see Barnave ("I in Barnave's house ! " he writes) ; the decree for the annexa-Avignon tion of the Comtat was voted on September 12. absorbed. Maury made a protest, but its halting style proves even that doughty champion to have exhausted his strength.

* * * * *

Yet this last decree was a serious matter. It furnished Europe with a pretext.

True, the Emperor seemed but little inclined to lay hold of it. He was drawing nearer to Berlin, indeed, and it seemed as if Prussia and Austria were resolved at last to act together. Kaunitz, at Vienna,. had suggested an agreement as to some united action by the various governments. But Leopold's real object in all this was simply to make difficulties for the other Cabinets. Most of these, as he had expected, sent dilatory answers for diverse reasons. Catherine, though she praised the suggested action on the part of Germany, made the "lateness of the season" an excuse for holding back her own troops—in view of her intended enterprise against Warsaw. Prussia herself—always practical—was resolved that before any troops of hers were lent to Austria, that country, vehemently suspected of an intention of enlarging her own borders on the French side, should give solid "guarantees"; she must have compensation promised beforehand, and even handed over at once. All this saved France for another six months.

Meanwhile the *émigrés* were in a state of disappointment and fury. The Comte de Provence, who had escaped from
Ferment among the "Emigrés." France on June 21, was holding his "Court" at Brussels; for he had proclaimed himself "Regent." The King of Sweden's presence at Aix-la-Chapelle had turned the heads of all these poor people. Plans of invasion were drawn up without the smallest reference to the real intentions of the Powers, and the invasion over, everybody was to be hanged, from La Fayette to Barnave. Bouillé, a brave soldier, whose wrath had blinded his eyes, offered to "lead the armies to Paris," and wrote a mad letter to the Assembly, which, but for the reaction among the members, would have sufficed to overturn the throne.

In spite of Louis XVI's prayers the Comte d'Artois went on agitating and muddling. By a process of sheer exhaustion he obtained the Emperor's leave, which he turned into an "invitation," to be present at the Castle of Pillnitz, where the German Sovereigns were to meet.

The Sovereigns intended—so far were they from desiring to make war—to seek some means of delaying any contest. And

when their conversations began, on August 25, they agreed as to the necessity of "putting off" the business. Where-
The German Sovereigns temporize. upon, on the 26th, all the *émigré* leaders—Bouillé, Calonne, Polignac, Condé, and Artois, put in an appearance. They demanded a Declaration in ten clauses, one of them providing for "extermination" in Paris, and "capital punishment" for the supporters of the Revolution. The Sovereigns—just because they had made up their minds to defer any decision—did not like to let these tiresome *émigrés* depart quite empty handed. They drew up a Declaration which they deliberately made exceedingly ambiguous, by which all intervention became dependent on a general European agreement. "Then, and in that case . . ." it ran, and Leopold, as a letter proves, asserted that this dilatory expression rendered the whole action perfectly inoffensive.

But the *émigrés* proceeded to turn this partial check into a brilliant success. While Leopold and Frederick William **The Manifesto of Coblentz.** were advising Louis XVI to accept the Constitution loyally, the Emigration despatched the Pillnitz Declaration, coupled with a commentary of the most revolting nature, to Paris. The commentary in question was the Coblentz Manifesto. Rivarol, though a strong royalist, wrote to Louis XVI that such a manifesto was sufficient "to rally the hearts and minds of all men to the Legislative Body." This document condemned Louis XVI to the fate that now, indeed, did await him ; the King's brothers, in spite of warnings from all sides, seemed bent on his destruction. "Cain !" cried the Queen, when her eyes fell on the signatures of Provence and Artois.

From the rostrum in the Salle du Manège, no sound came. The Assembly was about to depart. The weapon was laid aside, to be used when the time should come. One thing, indeed, these incidents had clearly proved. To sum it all up, there was no attack as yet, there was only a threat. "If all these people let another month go by without attacking us," wrote Mme. Jullien in August, "there will be no war before the spring ! "

* * * * *

THE CONSTITUENT ASSEMBLY

On September 25, the King, having duly accepted and promulgated the Constitution, the Assembly broke up.

The King accepts and promulgates the Constitution. The Constitution had been presented to the King by Thouret on September 4. On the 13th a dignified letter announced that the Sovereign accepted it; he added, "I should, however, fail in truthfulness if I said that I perceive, in the means of execution and administration provided, all that energy which would be necessary to impart activity, and preserve unity, in so huge an empire; but as opinions are divided at the present time on these heads, I am willing that experience alone should be the judge." And then he agreed to come to the Assembly and read his declaration of acceptance on the 14th.

If the Assembly's reception of the King on this occasion was mortifying in certain of its details, the populace did not become aware of it. Louis had accepted the Constitution; there would be peace and quietness now; he was a worthy man. Even Marie-Antoinette, who had smiled in friendly fashion to the deputies, had a moment of popularity, which proved, as her friend the Comte de la Marck wrote to her on the 16th, "the power the Queen might wield if she could overcome her private feelings and cajole this frivolous and fickle people."

There was universal rejoicing; the Assembly had voted an amnesty, both for the *émigrés* who would undertake to come back, and for the persons under punishment for their share in the recent disturbances.

On the 17th all Paris was making holiday. The friends of the Revolution and its enemies, from Biauzat to Morris, draw **The Festival of the Constitution.** glowing pictures of this unique festival. The King moved about in the Tuileries gardens amidst the illuminations, and then went beyond them, and as far as Chaillot, greeted by "constant applause," so writes a deputy of the Left on the 20th. Couplets written in his honour were sung; the Opéra Comique gave *Richard Cœur de Lion*, and Clairval, the singer, thought it opportune to sing:—

> "O Louis, ô mon roi,
> Tes amis t'environment,
> Notre amour t'environne !"

THE FRENCH REVOLUTION

On the evening of the 18th royalist pieces were played and loudly applauded in every theatre : *Gaston et Bayard, Le Siège de Calais, Henri IV à Paris, La Partie de Chasse de Henri IV.* Not a Brutus nor a Scævola was to be seen ! In the streets there was singing :—

> "Not' bon Roi
> A tout fait
> Et not' bonne Reine
> Qu'elle eut de la peine !
> Enfin les v'la
> Hors d'embarras !"

Thus ran the lines heard all over Paris on the 25th. There were more rejoicings that day, and lamps in every window when night fell. Paris, hung with tricolour flags, was celebrating "the end of the Revolution." "At five o'clock," writes an eye-witness, "a balloon was sent up from the middle of the Champs Elysées. It was surmounted by an eagle with outstretched wings, whose rapid flight seemed to bear away the spherical globe, emblem of our Constitution, and raise it up to the clouds. . . . Beneath it was a little car, in which two intrepid voyagers flew up to visit the ethereal spaces where thunderstorms are formed." The simile was exact indeed. The Constitution was in the clouds, and the poor globe, once it reached the "ethereal spaces where thunderstorms are formed," was to be torn to pieces. The eagle alone was to hover on over storm-ravaged France and bide his time !

On that day the Legislative Body was to be dissolved ; Louis XVI repaired to the Hall of the Assembly, and this Dissolution of time he was really greeted as a King. Loud the Assembly. and long was the cheering. Then, the King having departed, the President declared the sittings closed. "Applause from the whole of France !" wrote an impatient member of the new Legislature, not over graciously.

The deputies, as we know, were departing in a state of utter weariness. "We are free at last ! The harness is off our backs !" writes Lindet. Yet they granted themselves some reasons for satisfaction. (The reader should consult the letters of Roger, Rabaut, and Biauzat.) They believed the Revolution to be over. The King had written it down : "The end of the

208

Revolution has arrived; let the Nation revert to its own cheerful nature ! " Thirty letters written by thirty different people, between August 1 and October 1, prove this to have been the general opinion. Worthy owners of country-houses, who had been living in terror ever since July 1789, began to breathe anew ; Fougeret made up his mind to have his " mattresses beaten," and the Princesse de Lamballe, who had emigrated, came joyfully back to France, just one year, to the day, before her head was to be brandished on a pike before Marie-Antoinette's prison window.

And yet, optimistic as the letters of Roger and Rabaut sound, there is a carking doubt about them : " If our successors maintain the Constitution, they will be our saviours ! But if they choose to make another, we are lost ! "

These successors were the newly elected deputies, too young, all of them, and too lately arrived not to desire to do some new thing themselves. In fact, as one of these new men himself wrote, " the workman having deserted his handiwork, the Constitution was left to the mercy of men who were to shake the edifice violently, and be themselves crushed beneath its ruins." Other men were to follow these, Conventionnels, destined to complete the work of destruction. The members of the Constituent Assembly were to be indignant, but the member of the Convention, who proved to one of their number that the Convention, far from destroying the work of the Constituent Assembly, had really carried it to its completion, spoke the truth : " You gave us a corpse, we have buried it ! " Out of the ruins of the ancient edifice of the Monarchy, the Assembly, full of good intentions, generous, patriotic, loving liberty, devoted to the monarchical principle, had raised another, so unsteady, as we have said, that destruction threatened it from the first day of its existence, and it was inevitably doomed to crush both liberty and monarchy in its fall. The storm was beginning to growl : " From the distant horizon "—the words were written on August 31, 1791— " the wildest of children was beginning his furious advance." No very fierce whirlwind was needed to overthrow the political monument erected between 1789 and 1791. Some great principles had been laid down, indeed, and these were to serve

The gathering Storm.

THE FRENCH REVOLUTION

on occasion as the basis for the work of construction successfully performed from 1799 to 1801 by the Consul Bonaparte, and his Council of State. But on these foundations, not all of which indeed were solid, the Assembly had built nothing save fragile walls hidden by a sumptuous façade, which was hardly roughcast when it began to crumble away.

SOURCES. Works already quoted by Roger, Morris, Rabaut, Biauzat, Barnave, Madame Roland (*Lettres, Mémoires*), Lameth, Malouet, Salamon, (*Lettres, Mémoires*), Esterhazy, Thomas Lindet, Mallet du Pan, Mirabeau, Madame Jullien, Guilhermy, Lacretelle, Baron de Staël.—Hua, *Souvenirs*, 1871 ; Brissot, *Mémoires*, 1830 ; Barbaroux, *Mémoires* (ed. Dauban, 1886).

WORKS. Those already quoted by Charavay, Esmein, Meynier, Tiersot.—Du Bled, *Les Causeurs de la Révolution*, 1885.

PART II
THE LEGISLATIVE ASSEMBLY

CHAPTER XV

AN ASSEMBLY OF "ROMANS"

The new members. The Right. The Romans of Bordeaux.
The "Bordeaux group." Its leaders. The Extreme Left. The
Centre. The first skirmish. Brissot against Europe. The
Emigration. Laws against the *émigrés* and the priests. The
deplorable fate of the priests who had taken the oath. They are
avenged. The King refuses to give his approval to the proscriptive laws. The menace of war a pretext for the extremists.

"EVERYBODY is expecting to see men like Aristides,
Fabricius, Cato, and Cincinnatus, arriving from the
depths of the provinces," wrote Citizeness Jullien
on August 14. But Thomas Lindet mentions the existence

The new Members. of "dangerously extravagant persons" among
his colleagues. The Constitutional Bishop was
right.

They were "new to glory," as Necker ironically put it, and
they were every whit as new to business. Ten constitutional Bishops, four brigadier-generals, three colonels, and a
few learned men belonging to the Academies, out of a total of
750 deputies, represented those who had worked their way
to the front ; besides these, there were fifteen priests of inferior
rank, thirty officers, eight and twenty physicians, and a noisy
phalanx of lawyers and literary men. These last, who had
only just found their way into public life, and had all the pretensions peculiar to men who have handled ideas without ever
coming into contact with realities, imparted a very special
character to the Assembly : " Blue stockings," writes Morris :
dangerous tribunes, if we are to believe, with Figaro, that "the
republic of letters is the republic of the wolves." Very few
landowners, or shopkeepers, or agriculturists. Almost all
were needy men : " It has been calculated," we quote from a
letter written in October 1791, "that they have not a settled

213

income of 300,000 *livres* between them." Choudieu used to see some of them borrow three *livres* from their next neighbour to pay for their dinner. This gave a foundation to the report, echoed by Necker, that the eighteen *livres* paid daily to each deputy had not been a matter of indifference to them. Besides all this they were eager to distinguish themselves by the striking of great blows : a terrible inclination this, when we consider, with Frénilly, "that there was nothing great left for them to overthrow, but the throne itself."

A law stronger than their own will assigned places on the benches of the Right to the Constitutionalists, to those **The Right.** "Feuillants" who had sat with the Left in the Constituent Assembly. In that pillory which a seat on the Right had now become, the friends of La Fayette and Barnave, good liberals all of them, were dubbed "the deputies for Coblentz" by those who shrieked at them from the rostrum : Couthon contented himself with dubbing them "soporifics" (*endormeurs*) : Soubrany scornfully denominated the Right "the blind alley " : everyone called them " anti-revolutionaries."

But there was little of this quality about them. General Mathieu Dumas was a fanatical admirer of La Fayette, saluted by his next neighbour, Ramond, as "the eldest son of Liberty." Jaucourt was the true type of the gentleman of 1789 : in 1790, at a crowded gathering of the Jacobin Club he had pronounced an enthusiastic eulogy of the Revolution, " on which the philosopher delights to fix his eyes in tender contemplation." Girardin boasted loudly of his intercourse in bygone days with "his virtuous friend, Jean-Jacques Rousseau." The forty-four deputies of the Right were all men of the same kidney. But it was called "the Right," and before long the Feuillants, detested though they were at Coblentz, were firmly believed to belong "to the Austrian faction." This sufficed to cover them with odium. The Court, nevertheless, both suspected and deceived them. They were not strong in the art of political manœuvre, and they soon appeared doomed to utter eclipse. Thus no surprise can have been felt when a young deputy, the elegant and sceptical Hérault de Séchelles, was perceived, a few weeks later, creeping away on tip-toe from those dangerous benches and joining the cluster of deputies from Bordeaux.

214

AN ASSEMBLY OF "ROMANS"

These Bordeaux deputies were the nucleus of the Left. They were the future Girondins. Against the background formed **The Bordeaux** by this restless party of the Left two men stand **Group.** out: Brissot and Vergniaud, one a man of letters, the other a lawyer; the fact is characteristic, for the party was never fit for anything but talking and writing. Action was the domain of the Extreme Left.

Whenever we hear talk of these fascinating Girondins we must beware of the old tradition of our forefathers' childish days. Lamartine and Michelet, not to mention Alexandre Dumas, have forced us into a position of apparent iconoclasm, if ever we lift a hand, even the gentlest, against that sacred Gironde! Biré, on the other hand, has passed a more than severe sentence upon it. But we must judge these Girondins equitably, and, seeing we find them in October 1791, on the benches of the Left, we must forget the disgrace that was to overtake them in 1793: in 1791 they were fervent Jacobins, and as Jacobins Brissot, Vergniaud, Grangeneuve, Guadet, Gensonné, and Isnard, who took the most prominent part in the debates then just opening, and the hundred deputies who formed their following, would desire to be judged. Between October 1791 and July 1792 they furnished eleven out of the twenty presidents of the famous Club. In certain respects they went further than Robespierre himself: like him they were fanatical disciples of Rousseau, but they did not bow their heads, like Jean-Jacques and his prophet, before the Supreme Being: the greater proportion of them were atheists, not deists. Guadet reproached Robespierre bitterly in January 1792 with having referred to "Providence."

They were pagans indeed, and that because of their artless worship of the ancient times. They were Romans, partisans **The** of Brutus, Gracchus, Cato. They were repub- **"Romans"** licans because they had fed upon Plutarch, and **of Bordeaux.** philosophers because they had fed npon Marcus-Aurelius. When they attacked Louis XVI they called him Tarquin or Caligula. Never was it to be said that they represented the Gironde! They were deputies for the Peloponnesus, or for Latium! Vergniaud's mania in this connection made him intolerable. The Aventine was their

Mount; they would have nothing to do with Robespierre's Sinaï!

Above all things they were lawyers or men of letters. The fine phrase which they loved,—dearly when they heard it spoken, more dearly yet when they uttered it themselves—intoxicated them: Vergniaud and Guadet might mount the rostrum convinced they did not intend to attack the King; they demolished him: they might not mean to excite the populace; they stirred it up. One of their colleagues, Vaublanc, has dwelt on the "intoxication" that overcame them the moment they heard themselves applauded: "They frequently went far beyond the limits of their own feelings, and often, as they left the Assembly they would blush for what they had said." Their temperament, that of the true tribune, led them quite astray: applause was what they hungered for. So they ended by saying terrible things. The whole of the terror was voiced in one sentence spoken by Isnard: "We must cut off the gangrened limb to save the rest of the body!" Not one of them really desired to shed blood: yet everything they said opened a lock through which blood, even their own, was to flow in streams, and that because their rhetoric was fine and resonant, and evoked loud applause.

They loved grandiloquent words, and they loved fine gesture too, and stage effects. In that respect these passionate classicists were terribly romantic. They would have committed suicide, to make a sensation. Their Memoirs—and they all wrote these on the brink of the tomb—prove their persistent ambition to figure as heroes.

Nearly all of them were striking personalities: Guadet (of Bordeaux), very dark and lean, with flashing eyes and a yellowish complexion, much dreaded for his bitter sarcasms, a sedate and tragic humorist: Gensonné (also of Bordeaux), cold and keen-witted, his head crammed with systems and general ideas: Ducos (a Bordeaux man again), enthusiastic and full of literary information, a young hero with a nimbus about his head already; Grangeneuve (again from Bordeaux), audacious, passionate, and violent: Isnard (from Marseilles), "whose words," so his colleague Couthon wrote, "were traced in characters of fire," tragic in style and almost frantic in expression, the words of one beside himself.

Vergniaud (because they were all lawyers) was their master. He was an adept in the art of accusation; his classic eloquence was unequal to the production of anything save a *Philippic* or a Ciceronian invective; his logic was occasionally most persuasive, but his speeches for the most part were made up of imposing sophisms, beautiful expressions, and intense fervour, all handled with so admirable an art as to sound almost like an extemporization : to sum it up, "Vergniaud," so Lamothe, himself a deputy, writes, "created a sensation at once, but he was indolent, voluptuous, with much more of the Byzantine than the Roman about him, depending on Mlle. Candeille, a charming actress, and on her harp, to soothe his dreams and, at a later date, to assuage his bitterness.

Brissot was not so sentimental. He was a good husband, with a Quaker-like appearance, which had increased since his visit to Philadelphia : this affectation of Puritanism impressed the minds of simple folk. Because he had written a great deal he fancied himself omniscient. He was also one of the most susceptible of men, cherishing eternal grudges, from which the Court and Robespierre suffered in turn. "A clever speaker," says Mathieu Dumas, "but possessing," writes another of his fellow-deputies, Beugnot, "want of foresight and intelligence in equal proportions, and thus doomed to lead any party to ruin."

Taking them all together, these men made up a brilliant political staff, though there was not a single statesman among them.

Condorcet. The fact accounts for their artless devotion, proud as they all were, to Condorcet. This "professor of special morality" was to be the Sieyès of the second Assembly, and was therefore shortly to become odious in the eyes of the high priests of the first—Sieyès and Robespierre. As a thinker, the Permanent Secretary of the Academy of Sciences was far superior to the reckless Girondins ; unfortunately, he was nevertheless a terrible bore. His intelligence, so Mme. Roland wrote, was a "delicate liqueur absorbed in cotton wool." Rivarol declared, more brutally, that "he wrote with opium on sheets of lead." He was considered an oracle. When he "made his appearance *at last* " (that *at last* is significant!) there was a strong feeling of curiosity. He was a bore but he was Condorcet. His colleagues soon made up their minds to endure and even to admire him. Every Assembly must have its oracle.

He sat on the edge of the Extreme Left. Here he fell in with some awkward companions. These were the Cordeliers. The Extreme For a considerable time the most prominent figures Left. in this little group were Chabot, Bazire, and Merlin. " We are assured they are zealous patriots, but what men ! " writes Citizeness Jullien herself, in June 1792. These were "the levellers," as Dumas christened them. Thomas Lindet thought the ex-monk Chabot was bound for Charenton : Bazire (of Dijon) and Merlin (of Thionville) were a little superior to this Capuchin who had forsaken his Order and was on the way to become a thief ; but they, too, seemed mad. Yet, of the three, the "horrible Capuchin," as his fellow deputy Dorizy calls him, inspired the deepest dislike and alarm.

On the Left, too, Robert Lindet, an upright citizen of mediocre intelligence, and Lazare Carnot, who said of himself that " being a soldier he spoke but little," " hid themselves in the obscurity of committees," as Lindet himself acknowledges. Bishop Fauchet—a poor enthusiastic priest—represented *Socialism* of the most sentimental kind : he was a sort of Vicaire Savoyard, who had blundered into politics, and was to pay dearly for his divagations.

The Centre was destined to weigh down the scale on every occasion. Here we find Pastoret, an ex-Councillor of the Court of Aids and member of the Academy of Inscriptions ; The Centre. Bigot de Préameneu, a cool and upright administrator ; Cérutti, and Lacépede, who seem to have borne more resemblance to Ramond and Beugnot than to Chabot, or even Brissot. But they were men of prudence. " An immovable phalanx, when good was to be done, and one that never stirred except from fear," wrote their colleague Hua. They considered themselves " impartial." " This M. Pastoret is half one and half the other," runs a reference to him written on September 4. " The brain of a fox in a calf's head," said Mirabeau of this prototype of " impartiality." These capable men were to thread their way through the Revolution ; some died Marquises like Pastoret, or Counts like Bigot : they became

218

Senators under Napoleon, and Peers under Louis XVIII; and even under Louis-Philippe. Yet they proclaimed themselves "Independents." First of all they supported the Right: then they broke up, and joined the Left. Hérault de Séchelles, more resolute than they, did not condescend to tarry in their ranks in his passage from Right to Left.

Constituted as it was, the Assembly was inevitably fated to be led by the Left. The Left alone was possessed of a certain homogeneity. The 130 deputies whose names were on the roll of the Jacobin Club received their orders from that body: they ended by drawing another 400 of their fellow deputies into the Club. Further, the attendance of the members of the Centre and the Right was far from regular: the benches of the Left were the only benches that were always full: Chabot writes to his mother in December 1791, that he sits from morning till evening and occasionally at night as well. The Left was a permanent presence in the Assembly. Its violence intimidated the other parties, its eloquence carried them away. Further, it was supported by the menacing audience in the galleries, and it reckoned on the terror they inspired. Thus it was perpetually demanding that the names should be called over: "If you ask me how we win the day," writes Soubrany, a deputy of the Mountain, "I will answer you thus: by the publicity of the proceedings. You may be quite certain that if the decrees were passed by ballot, the *émigrés* and the King's ministers would do as they liked." Thenceforward the Right was lost. The Left held all the trumps, and a few marked cards as well.

*　　*　　*　　*　　*

The first skirmish was over a matter of formalities. It took place at the opening sitting. Our good deputies had arrived
The first　in somewhat homely garb, "with goloshes and
Skirmish.　umbrellas." This explains the storm raised by a proposal shortly to be made for lowering the pay of members from eighteen *livres* a day to fourteen. But the deputies were quite resolved to bring the throne down to the level of their "goloshes and umbrellas." "What a joy for these gentlemen," writes Necker, "to be able to give orders to their head clerk, the King of France!" The clerk must be put in his clerk's place. Grange-

neuve had proposed that the words *Sire* and *Majesty* should be struck out of the vocabulary, Couthon went further, and suggested that the throne should be done away with. The King could sit in an armchair alongside of the President. This double proposal was duly voted.

But Louis XVI seemed determined not to accept further indignities. He had already given a somewhat sharp reception to a deputation from the Assembly ; he now sent word that if the decree were maintained, he would not come to the Manège. And the Assembly, which was long to waver, had to yield, and repealed it

So the King came. His little victory had melted his temporary stiffness ; he talked about harmony : " May the love of our country draw us together, and may the public interest be an inseparable bond between us ! " He was loudly applauded.

He was applauded, too, when he affirmed the necessity for restoring order in the Army, putting the country into a state of defence, and, at the same time re-establishing a good understanding with Europe.

Europe ! There lay the great anxiety of the moment, and Louis XVI had good reasons for making an effort to put himself The Mani- right in this connection. Brissot, who was ac-
festoes. quainted with both hemispheres, was pronouncing oracles of a most threatening nature. The Declaration of Pilnitz and the Coblentz Manifesto, had roused legitimate anger in the country. That the King's brothers should have signed their names to these threats against the new France was justly regarded as a piece of wicked madness. And the Comte de Provence, the so-called " Regent," had likewise made a protest against the Constitution : the Emigration, directed by the Court of the Exiles, was breaking out at last.

It had become a public danger. The nobles, treated like pariahs in their various provinces, were departing in greater The Emigra- numbers every day. We cannot blame these
tion. *émigrés* of 1791 as we must blame those of 1789 : to remain in the country meant real peril for them. At any rate, before we condemn them, we should read the many letters which reveal not only their fears but also their hesita-

tions. And there was, indeed, a deliberate attempt to force them out of France. Did not some member of the Left say: "All the better! France is being purged!" and one deputy called the emigration "the natural perspiration of the land of freedom!"

The unhappy *émigrés* crowded the banks of the Rhine, and there waited on events. Many of them were already beginning to see the real nature of "the chimeras with which they had been lulled," as the Duchesse de Tavannes writes (all this lady's "disconsolate" letters are worth quoting). It is clear that many of them would have liked to return: some did: "fashion," writes Le Coz, "rather leans to coming back." The Assembly and the Departmental Directories ought to have pursued a very resolute policy towards the burners of country houses, and the petty tyrants in rural localities: if this had been done many *émigrés* would have returned.

But, unhappily, another section of the *émigrés* was stirring up indignation rather than pity. "Feather-heads," one of their comrades called them: they gathered round the princes and fed on idle fancies: they spun perpetual intrigues and disgusted their hosts, whether Belgian, German, Swiss, or Piedmontese, by the wildness of their extravagances and the laxity of their morals. Every one of these pretentious personages preached convulsion in Europe and destruction to France, whether they waited on the Comte d'Artois at his "Court" or sat in the café of the *Three Crowns* at Coblentz, where the old Chevaliers of Saint-Louis carried every fortress in Lorraine, after the manner of the old men in *Lysistrata*, except that the *émigrés* played tric-trac the while, and all of them were more than ever resolved to hang La Fayette, Barnave, Lameth, and Bailly, even before they laid hands on Robespierre or Marat.

A more serious matter was that some of these gentlemen had formed a legion, *the Army of Condé*. At first this business seemed to smack of comic opera: everybody insisted on being an officer, though royal pay was promised to all who would condescend to serve in the ranks. To put a stop to these rivalries, Calonne, the "Regent's" minister, put the various ranks up to auction. The army thus "organized" was now waiting in idleness for the "entry" of the Germans, and pouring forth hideous threats meanwhile. Exile had distracted the wisest among them. "I know the road to Paris," exclaimed the Maréchal de Broglie (whose son was still serving in the ranks of the Nation); "I'll guide the foreign armies thither, and not one stone of that proud capital shall be left upon another!" Words such as these were reported in all the Paris Clubs, filling moderate men, and even the dwellers in the Tuileries, with despair, but causing joy in the party of violence, and arming the Left with poisoned weapons.

This Assembly, less scrupulous than its predecessor, intended to treat these misguided, but generally very unfortunate people, as factious persons. The King had hoped he might be beforehand with it. On October 14 he published a proclamation beseeching the *émigrés* to return. This platonic appeal could not satisfy the Assembly. On the 20th the debate on the emigration opened. It became very heated, as soon as the religious question, which occupied men's minds even more than that of the *émigrés*, was brought into it. The Left, to whose ingrained anti-clericalism we have already referred, reckoned eagerly on including the "refractory" priests in the coming chastisement.

Pius VI, as we know, had pronounced his solemn condemnation of the Civil Constitution : retractations had followed at **Deplorable** once in every quarter, and these had certainly **Position of the** transformed the official church into a schismatic **Juror-Clergy.** minority, which figured on the index of every parish. Nogaret, Bishop of La Lozère, writes : "I am publicly hooted and insulted," and Arbogast, Bishop of the Haut-Rhin, calls on the dying Constituent Assembly for help in his extremity : "Help me, I cannot go on!"

This was an appeal from the new Church to the secular arm. The Legislature, which, as Sorel has clearly shown, was about to have recourse to the laws of Louis XIV in its struggle with the emigration, was fain to adopt the same King's doctrine to protect its ridiculous State Church.

"The hostility of the priests" was the pretext. The existence of this hostility was undeniable. The parish priests, driven out of their churches and their presbyteries, after having

222

been stripped of their worldly goods by the Revolution they had hailed in 1789, were saying hard things about their new masters. From Alsace to the South, in the Central Plateau, and the West, these hard words were approved by the faithful : the agitation had taken shape, here and there, in a hostility directed against the new arrangements as to religion, and in no sense against the new civil laws. This had been noticed in Calvados, and, in a still more threatening form, in the Gévaudan, in Poitou, and in Anjou. Gensonné, who was desired to report on the subject, declared these local movements (in reality spontaneous and quite devoid of any general cohesion) to be the outcome of a vast plot among the priests. The ten embittered juror-prelates who had seats in the Assembly were not much disposed to turn aside the arm to which they had appealed for help only three months previously. All were convinced of the necessity of treating these priests, " accomplices of the *émigrés*," just as they were about to treat the *émigrés* themselves, and the princes, " accomplices of the foreigner."

The *émigrés* were dealt with first ; the debate lasted over eleven sittings ; it revealed the Girondin leaders, who nearly all **Laws** spoke : Brissot, Isnard, Gensonné, Guadet, Ver- **against the** gniaud—and also Condorcet. Brissot proposed **" Émigrés."** measures of the most extreme severity against the *émigrés*—especially those who had been officers or government officials ; they must come back or be condemned to death by default. Isnard supported this view : as usual he spoke with frantic passion : " Your enemies must either be vanquished or victorious : that is what it really comes to, and any man who does not realize this great truth is, in my opinion, a blind politician." A few days later he was to speak against the priests : " If any complaint is brought against a priest who has not taken the oath, he must be forced to leave the country. *No proofs are necessary.*" Vergniaud's speech was the most important of all ; it was Ciceronian ; his forensic eloquence (" Legal proofs ! . . . legal proofs ! . . . legal proofs ! ") led to the same, or very nearly the same conclusion, as Isnard's brutal formula. It was admired and frantically applauded : the Marcus Tullius Cicero of all their dreams had come to life again, and the " Catilines of Coblentz " should be smitten

As to the Princes, everybody was soon agreed : " Tarquins ! " said De Bry. The Right shared the opinion of the

The Princes summoned to return to France. Left that they must be called on to return. Louis XVI himself, offended by the pretensions of the arrogant " Regent," desired he should come back : the Feuillants, who deafened him with their advice, thought (and rightly) that " nobody would believe the King so long as his brothers were to be seen at the head of the Emigration." The Assembly, by a unanimous vote, called on the Prince to return to France within two months, on pain of losing all his rights, both to the regency and to the throne.

The fate of the *émigrés* in general was settled on November 9. Vergniaud's motion, as amended by Isnard, was duly carried. In vain had the Right argued (and Lamothe's letters prove its good faith, while those of the *émigrés* show that its contention was true), that it would be better to leave the plotters to discredit themselves at Coblentz, where nobody took them seriously, and facilitate the return of those other *émigrés* whose eyes had been temporarily " blinded," a return for which many of them already longed. The Left carried the day : the decree declared every *émigré* who was not back in France by January 1, 1792, to be under suspicion as a conspirator : after that date all those who were out of the country were to incur the penalty of death, and their goods were to be confiscated. Condorcet, to his honour be it said, raised his voice against this abominable measure. " The Nation," Vergniaud had exclaimed on October 26, " holds out her arms in kindness to the *émigrés* " ! But for the last two years, unhappily, the hand of the Nation had been very heavy in its dealings with the afflicted.

On November 29 the priests' turn came. The debate had raged most fiercely during ten whole sittings. It was at one **Laws against the Clergy.** of these that Isnard put forward the proposition " *No proofs are necessary,*" which Fouquier-Tinville was to reproduce, in order to bring Isnard's own friends to the scaffold.

The decree was voted : the priests were ordered to take the oath on pain of being treated as suspected rebels : a repetition

224

of his refusal exposed the "refractory" priest to surveillance by the authorities, and, in case of any disturbance in the Commune, he was liable to arrest and then to imprisonment. The scruples of the Constituent Assembly had been left far behind, and matters had grown serious indeed.

*   *   *   *   *

The decrees were submitted to the King. This marked the beginning of a crisis. Louis XVI sanctioned that affecting his brother : this surely should have satisfied the Left. (Vergniaud, of course, had compared the King to Brutus sentencing his own sons.) But he could not accept the two others.

The King refuses to sanction the proscriptive Laws.

At that moment—as three months previously —Louis XVI was strong in his resolution to apply the Constitution : members of the constitutional party were welcomed by him : Barnave found a ready hearing at the Tuileries, and all the ministers were Feuillants. But the November decrees seemed to the King contrary to the Declaration of Rights and to the Constitution.

The misfortune was that when he spared the *émigrés*, he seemed to be acting in obedience to the suggestions of the Court, which was continuing, more or less secretly, to carry on a policy absolutely hostile to Revolution of any description.

But this was a mistaken idea. The Directory of the Department (very constitutional in its opinions) was pressing the King, almost as strongly as the Court was pressing him, not to sanction these decrees. Be this as it may, Louis informed the Assembly on December 11 that as far as the decrees touching the *émigrés* and the priests were concerned, he would "look into the matter"; this was the formula in which the veto was to be couched.

Thus the crisis began : the Constitutionalists seemed ready to support the King, and they might perhaps have succeeded in finally driving back the wave of violence, if, at that very hour, the sudden and hostile change in the attitude of Europe, which had been encouraged by the *émigrés*, had not placed the King, his Ministers, the Right, and all moderate men, in the most difficult of all possible positions,

The Menace of War.

P

by providing the party of violence with the very pretext for
re-opening the campaign for which it had been hungrily searching. The menace of war was to hurry on events, and bring
every plan for opposing the second Revolution to nought.

SOURCES. Works already quoted by Thomas Lindet, Madame Roland
(*Mémoires, Lettres*), Morellet, Vaissière, Esterhazy, Malouet Mallet
du Pan, Morris, Frénilly, Madame Jullien, Schmidt, M. Dumas, Aulard
(*Jacobins*, III, 1892).—Rabusson-Lamothe (deputy), *Lettres*, 1870 ;
Soubrany (deputy), *Lettres*, 1867 ; Pinet (deputy), *Mémorandum* (*Rev.
Fr.*, 1906) ; Chabot (deputy), *Lettres* (*Rev. Retr.*, 2nd series, VII) ; Couthon
(deputy), *Correspondance*, I, 1900 ; Le Coz (deputy), *Correspondance*,
I, 1900 ; Dorizy (deputy), *Souvenirs* (*Rev. Fr.*, 1904) ; Vaublanc (deputy),
Mémoires, 1833 ; Hua (deputy), *Mémoires*, 1871 ; Choudieu (deputy),
Mémoires, 1889 ; Girardin (deputy), *Souvenirs*, 1875 ; Beugnot (deputy),
Mémoires, 1866 ; Brissot (deputy), *Mémoires* (ed. Perroud, 1911) ; Ponte-
coulant (deputy), *Mémoires*, I, 1882 ; Carnot (deputy), *Mémoires*, I, 1860 ;
Moore, *Journal* (*Rev. Rev.*, IV) ; B. de Molleville, *Mémoires*, 1897 ;
Correspondance de Mirabeau avec le Comte de le Marck (letters of de
la Marck, Pellenc, etc., after the death of Mirabeau), II, 1850 ; Louvet,
Mémoirs (ed. Aulard), 1898.

WORKS. Those already quoted by Cahen, du Bled, Dard (*Hérault
de Séchelles, Choderlos de Laclos*), Charavay, Esmein, Goncourt.—Colfavru,
La Législative, 1885 ; Daudet, *Histoire de l'Emigration*, I, 1905 ; Montier,
Robert Lindet, 1899 ; Biré, *La Légende des Girondins*, 1881 ; Guadet,
Les Girondins (ed. of 1889) ; Aulard, *Les Orateurs de la Législative*, 1885 ;
Cornillon, *Fauchet*, 1908 ; Bonald, *Chabot*, 1908 ; Pingaud, *De Bry*,
1909 ; Stéfane Pol, *Autour de Robespierre, Le Bas*, 1901.

CHAPTER XVI

NARBONNE AND THE WAR

" *The Circle of Popilius.*" The Left and the war. The country desires war. Attitude of Robespierre. Narbonne in the Ministry. His reason for promoting war. The Court and the Ministry undermine his position. Dislocation of the Ministry.

THE Girondins were now anxious to come into power. The election of " that dear Pétion," as Robespierre still called him, to be Mayor of Paris, had whetted his friends' appetites. They were bent on driving out the Feuillant ministers : the threatening attitude of the European Powers, " The Circle of which was likely to impart a feverish heat to Popilius." the debates, would enable them to overthrow Lessart (Minister for Foreign Affairs), Duportail (War Minister), and Molleville (Naval Minister), who should all be accused of weakness, and of being dupes, if not accomplices, of the *émigrés*.

As a matter of fact the condition of foreign relations was growing somewhat serious, but the Girondins were making it worse. Immediately after October 20 Brissot, thinking an " imposing attitude " would force the Powers into retreat, had addressed an imperious speech to Europe. The " Senate " of the Manège was still haunted by memories of Rome : " *the Circle of Popilius* " figured in all the speeches delivered during the course of that autumn ; it must, they declared, be drawn round the Electors of the Rhine, who, so the speakers asserted, were concentrating their troops. A deputation proceeded to the Tuileries and requested Louis XVI to play the part of Popilius.

But even at the very moment when the German princes were being called on to retire, and more especially to drive out the *émigrés*, the Paris Clubs were deliberately welcoming,

227

with outstretched arms, other *émigrés* of every kind, Belgian, Dutch, and German "patriots," and spurring them on to raise their various countries in revolt against "the tyrants." The inevitable result of this daily increasing tension was war.

On the benches of the Left, indeed, war was popular. Hérault de Séchelles, who now belonged to this party, hailed **The Left and** it as a means of creating a state of siege, indis- **war.** pensable, in his mind, to the creation of a Dictator- ship of the Public Safety. "The moment has come," he cried, "when a veil must be cast over the statue of Liberty !" Couthon had written, on December 17 : "Perhaps the Revolution needs a war to ensure its consolidation." The " Bordeaux men " did not go so far as this, yet the thought of war was agreeable to them : it would place the King in their hands, for it would be *their* war. They would direct it, prolong it, and terminate it according to their own ideas, and the needs of their domestic policy : it would enable them to confiscate the King's person or to overthrow him, to unmask "the royalist intrigue with Europe," or dash it to pieces. In any case it would be well to put an end to the equivocal situation of the moment.

And they really were following the trend of public opinion. The country, moved by a mysterious impulse, which was to **The Country** foil or sweep away all paltry personal calculations, **eager for War.** was beginning to *desire war ;* this was the real France, stirred by its own warrior blood, and tired of its long slumber. "War ! War ! " says a most pacific member of the Assembly, Bishop Le Coz, on January 9, "War ! This is the cry that smites my ears from every corner of the Empire ! " Brissot's friends, who shouted with the country, won loud applause.

This was very displeasing to Robespierre. Ever since September he had been turning a most unfriendly eye upon the **Attitude of** new party—"troublesome fellows ! " Their suc- **Robespierre.** cess embittered him greatly. He thought their war-like policy imprudent to the last degree. This Maximilian did not hail from Bordeaux ; he came from Arras. His blood never ran riot, and we must fairly acknowledge that at this particular juncture those little green eyes of his under

228

the blue spectacles were clear and farsighted. The war would be the ruin of the Revolution : the country would be beaten, because she would be betrayed ; and if by chance she won the victory, the next move would be either the restoration of the King, or the Dictatorship of a military chief. Even if the sole result was to be a " Bordelais " Ministry, that prospect was quite enough to set Robespierre against the plan.

He cut all the tirades and outbursts of eloquence short. " We shall be betrayed." " All the better," Brissot answered, " . . . We need a few great treasons." His inmost thought was that the consequence of the King's overthrow, or his annihilation, would be the setting up of a " Brissot " dictatorship in the Tuileries, but his talk was all of peoples to be delivered. Condorcet's dream was to set up the United States of Europe.

The Court had not arrived yet at wishing for war, but it appointed the Comte de Narbonne Minister of War, and so made **Narbonne** a concession to bellicose opinion.
Minister of He was a man of great charm, very superior
War. to the Feuillant Ministers among whom he was to sit. His origin was supposed to be illustrious (though mysterious) ; the blood of Henri IV ran, so it was asserted, in his veins ; in spite of a certain licentiousness, there was a great deal of nobility in his nature ; he loved his country, his mind was open to the new ideas, he was very confident of the possibility of an agreement with the Revolution, and deeply interested in all matters connected with the Army. He was ultimately to figure, and very honourably, amongst the aides-de-camp of Napoleon.

He delighted in politics ; he believed the Sovereign, who had not been able to defend himself by energy, might yet save himself by diplomacy. Feuillant though he was, he did not hesitate to give his support to Brissot.

For he desired war. A generous soldier, he realized that the Army was falling to pieces. He believed that once the **Narbonne's** French soldier found himself face to face with the
Reasons for enemy his sense of duty would return. Brissot
desiring War. desired war to unmask the traitor generals :
Narbonne desired it to keep the men from deserting.

And he reckoned on war, too, for the restoration of the King's prestige ; this lethargic Bourbon would recover the characteristics of his race once he was at the head of his own army. ꞉ A war against the German Electors, waged within restricted limits and brought to a swift conclusion, would crown Louis with laurels—easily won but precious indeed.

Returning from a visit to Lorraine, Narbonne declared everything, troops and fortresses alike, to be ready, and in admirable order. He was loudly acclaimed, and for one short hour he was the most popular man in France. This alarmed the Extreme Left. "If he is not sincere he is the most dangerous man imaginable for the Constitution," said a Jacobin to the Baron de Staël.

For the feeling in favour of war had become general. Robespierre, and he alone, held Narbonne to be a traitor, as great, and greater than La Fayette himself. At the Jacobin Club on the 11th, he bitterly opposed the idea of war : Brissot's adherents howled him down. He never was to forgive them for that evening.

In the Assembly Narbonne was supported by Condorcet : this was much. It is a curious fact that this pacifist, for reasons diligently set forth by his latest biographer, had ended by desiring war himself. He thought it would pave the way for the Republic. Though far from sharing Narbonne's views, as my readers see, he now backed up the martial minister, and urged on the Assembly to extreme decisions.

But the flood of Narbonne's allies was too much for him. His plans for a restricted campaign were swamped, and from that moment his departure was looked on as inevitable.

This delighted the Court. Marie-Antoinette, whose exasperation had now reached fever pitch (and who hated Narbonne into the bargain, because of his friendship with Mme. de Staël), favoured solutions of the most extravagant kind. "Every possible danger," she had said to the Russian Minister, "rather than live any longer in my present state of humiliation and misery ! " Her present dream was that the Powers should make a sudden irruption into France, and she was pressing Prussia and Austria to undertake it. At her prayer, Leopold did take one step forward : on February 7 he concluded a definite alliance with Frederick William : on the 28th, Goltz, the Prussian Minister, notified the French authorities that any invasion of Germany would be regarded at Berlin as a *casus belli*. Leopold would no doubt have associated himself with this notification but for his sudden death on March 1.

His successor, Francis II, a strong opponent of the Revolution, was not likely to handle the matter very gently. When **Austria and** Prussia, still as practical as ever, demanded **Prussia decide** solid promises before she dispatched any troops **to attack** to the Rhine, he made them : she then marched **France.** briskly forward : the French party at Berlin appeared quite annihilated; one member of it, Brunswick, actually accepted the chief command. One thing only held the Germans back, the affair of Poland. Catherine II made up her mind, at last, to offer to share the country with Frederick William. From that moment the invasion of France became imminent.

The situation was all in favour of the partisans of violence. Violence, in fact, was the order of the day ; the " *Brissotins* " **Violence of the** encouraged it in the wildest fashion. The Revo- **Brissotins.** lution, on which a lull had fallen all over the country (François de Neufchâteau acknowledged on November 26 that " public spirit was almost extinguished "), was raising its head once more. The newspapers of the Left were fulminating against the King. Placards were posted calling on " the free and sovereign people " to cease to permit its " head clerk to abuse the power confided to him," and accused " Monsieur *Veto* " of being ready to " have the throats of the citizens, their wives and children, cut by all the ministers from beyond the Rhine." Famine, as always, aggravated the public rage : the winter had been cruel. All letters, whether from friends or enemies of the Revolution, agree as to the general misery. On January 30 the *assignat* had fallen 40 per cent. below its face value. The starving city looked on with indifference sometimes, and sometimes again broke into wild fury. The electors had ceased to vote. Pétion had been chosen Mayor by 6600 votes out of an electorate of 80,000. Discontent was universal. The Right gathered courage to take the offensive : it attacked the popular Societies in the

Assembly, and proposed that no deputy should be allowed to belong to any of them. All this betokened the approach of a change in public opinion. War was necessary to bring the country back to the Revolution. But the Feuillants—traitors that they were—would never declare war! There must be "patriot" ministers in power! The Bordeaux men were determined to hurl the Constitutional Ministry from office.

The Court itself weakened the Ministry with incredible folly : Narbonne, accused of "handing over the monarchy to the demagogues," was sharply attacked : the Catholics even went so far as to charge him with carrying on "Protestant intrigues" with Mme. de Staël. His colleague Lessart thwarted his plans. On March 9 Narbonne retired, and his place at the Ministry of War was taken by "the young Chevalier de Grave."

Resignation of Narbonne.

There was great excitement : on the 10th the Left passed a resolution to the effect that the late minister "carried away the regrets of the Assembly with him." Then Brissot proceeded to denounce fresh plots abroad; his melodramatic discourse sent a shudder through his hearers; he moved the members to wild applause when he demanded the impeachment of Lessart, whose weakness, "proved" by the correspondence with Vienna, almost amounted, he averred, to treachery : the Military Committee had already asked for a declaration that "Molleville, Naval Minister, had forfeited the confidence of the Nation." Once Lessart was overthrown, all his fellow ministers would follow him perforce. The Left put down its last stake : it sent Vergniaud to the rostrum. His speech was the most famous, and certainly one of the finest, he ever made. His great object was to terrify the Tuileries, and force the King to accept a Bordelais ministry. "From this rostrum," cried the orator, "we see the Palace within whose walls perfidious counsels are leading the King astray. . . . Terror and dismay have often issued from those Palace doors. Let them re-enter it this day in the name of the Law. Let all its inhabitants learn that *the King's person alone is sacred, that the law will reach all guilty persons within its walls without distinction, and that not a head that is convicted of guilt shall escape its sword!*" The Left and the

NARBONNE AND THE WAR

Mountain yelled their applause, and under that wild blast, as a member of the Right afterwards wrote, "the Centre bent." The Minister's impeachment was duly voted. The Right seemed utterly crushed. "I had never yet seen so dreadful a sitting," one deputy was to declare, "I was ill when I left it!" The Ministry was dead!

Within a week all the ministers, "warned by this terrible blow," had sent in their resignations, with the exception of **Fall of the** de Grave, who, Barbaroux tells us, was con-**Ministry.** sidered "a good Jacobin."

The Bordeaux men were masters of the field; power was within their grasp, and before long they were to render war inevitable.

SOURCES. Works already quoted by Couthon, Hua, Dumas, Carnot, Morris, Vaublanc, Mallet, Salamon, Rabusson-Lamothe, Frénilly, Vaissière, Aulard (*Jacobins*, III).

WORKS. Those already quoted by Montier, Biré, Guadet, Colfavru, Cahen, Esmein.—Chuquet, *L'invasion prussienne*, 1907.

CHAPTER XVII

THE ROLAND MINISTRY AND THE DECLARATION OF WAR

The " Brissotin " Ministry. Dumouriez. The Rolands, husband and wife. Madame Roland and the Ministry. The programme of the " Great Ministry." The patriotic fervour of the country. The sitting of April 20, 1792. War declared. " War against Kings." " So much the better ! " say the Tuileries.

THE ministerial crisis had begun ; everyone felt it must be settled in Vergniaud's lodgings. And there, at 5 Place Vendôme, seated round his breakfast table, he and his feverishly excited guests spent three days drawing up, destroying, and remaking lists of ministers. Brissot carried **The Brissotin** the most weight in these debates. He it was, **Ministry.** who, to please his friend Gensonné, had General Dumouriez included in the list. Even before the ministry had been constituted, Dumouriez had laid a nimble hand on Lessart's portfolio : Foreign Affairs, " external relations."

He was not so young as the men who were putting him forward : a tolerably adventurous career, in fact, already lay behind him. The grandson of Molière's lackey, **Dumouriez.** he had played as many parts as one of Lesage's heroes, and resembled one of Beaumarchais' valets in character. A second-rate soldier, a would-be diplomatist, he had been mixed up before the year 1789 in endless intrigues, had failed to make his fortune by any of them, and was now seeking it in the Revolution. He had no political creed, and looked on the whole of the great tragedy as a splendid *imbroglio*, in which he might find his own account ; a hard liver and a braggart, but with agreeable manners ; he must indeed have had some considerable power of seduction, for he made himself acceptable to the solemn Girondins.

234

He was intelligent, too. He had not been surprised to see the successive shipwrecks of the *Ancien Régime*, of Mounier's *Monarchiens* and of Barnave's *Feuillants*. All, to his mind, were fools hampered by convictions. To him, the Revolution was a fact : wise men must accept it, make the best of it, howl louder than any of the other wolves, put on the red cap, " pull it right down over their ears," and so contrive to cheat the tempest. Appointed Minister on the 11th, he urged the King to accept the presence of " Jacobins " in the Tuileries, where he himself felt he was exposed to the hatred of the Court, and regarded as a " plague-stricken " person.

He had obtained the temporary maintenance of the Chevalier de Grave in his post at the War Ministry, and the promotion of Lacoste, also considered a " good Jacobin," to the Naval Ministry. These three pseudo-Jacobins were soon to form a cabal of their own. The rest was left entirely to Vergniaud and Brissot. At the sittings in the former's house, all who laboured under any suspicion of *Robespierrism*, such as Collot d'Herbois and Danton, who had been thought certain of office, were struck off the list. Brissot insisted on the inclusion of his own kinsman Clavières, a half-bred Genevan who, ever since 1789, had believed himself called by Providence to manage the finances of the country, and was now appointed to do so. " One of the first financiers in Europe," Couthon assured everybody on March 1. Vergniaud's friends were determined the seals should go to a native of Bordeaux : they had them bestowed on the Procurator Syndic of the Gironde, Duranton, an excellent man, considered a " mere cypher," whom everybody expected to lead with ease, and who was destined to astonish those who had put him forward. As de Grave was to be left at the Ministry of War (till Colonel Servan, a close friend of Roland and his wife, was given that office), the list was complete when Roland himself accepted the Home Office (Ministry of the Interior).

The appointment of this M. Roland de la Platière was approved by everybody : an inspector of manufactures, and a former collaborator in the *Encyclopædia*, he was no longer young; he was sixty, but vigorous for his age. He was an upright man, but so narrow, so pedantic, so

The Rolands.

overbearing, that he made uprightness itself seem odious. He combined ideology and hauteur with the face and the soul of a Quaker; his Puritanism was aggressive and ostentatious —he was "Cato"! Thus everybody called him, and more especially his wife. She gives a lively picture of him : severe, austere, with his "weakness for talking too much about himself" and "the ruggedness of his virtue"; he was a bore. "That papa of mine is always scolding me, it is so tiresome!" said his little daughter Eudora : Mme. Roland repeats the remark as if she understood it : he was to weary the King as he had wearied Eudora, scolding him instead of governing the country. To sum him up, he was like the pedagogue in the fable, preaching a sermon to a drowning man.

This Cato had only one thing in his favour—his wife, the fair Marie-Jeanne, known to her intimates as "Manon."

More than most men of her generation did this young woman influence the destinies of France between 1791 and **Madame** 1793. Different as she was from the Cato-**Roland and** Inspector of Manufactures, she was a strangely **the Ministry.** individual creature. When such a woman sets herself to inspire a knot of eager public men, welds them into a party, rules a whole ministry, hurls it down when the time comes, works after its fall to build it up again, *per fas et nefas*, and fills the soul of a Buzot and a Barbaroux, and, further, of a Brissot and a Pétion, with her own enthusiasms and hatreds and prejudices, the historian is constrained to give her his attention. Her rancour against Marie-Antoinette, and later against Danton and Robespierre, were to generate more than one crisis : she was one of the human elements in the Revolutionary drama : she inspired it, led it, diverted its course, till she herself lay crushed beneath the ruins.

A strange mixture of laxity and enthusiasm, of Spartan virtue and romantic passion, of ardent generosity and cold calculation, clear-sighted when all others went astray, and blind, at some moments, to the point of madness, Manon Roland always remained the woman who, in the first months of her married life, had read Shakespeare and Plutarch while she prepared her Cato's dinner—a process apt to result in very poor cooking.

THE ROLAND MINISTRY

Still charming, though she had reached her thirty-eighth year, with a pretty delicate face, like a Greuze picture, and her hair cut short "*à la* Titus," she fancied herself a Greek or Roman heroine—or hero, she would have preferred to say, for she considered herself most masculine ; yet she was womanly to her finger-tips, fanciful, passionate, exaggerated. Her most outstanding characteristic seems to have been her incapacity for sound judgment of any man ; her view was always obscured by her affections or her dislikes.

From the very first she was the soul of the Ministry : this little middle-class woman was the first person to conceive the idea of a homogeneous Cabinet supported by a " parliamentary " group, and closely bound to it. The six Ministers agreed to breakfast in turn in each other's houses, so as to be in full agreement before they attended the King's Council : to these breakfasts the leaders of the Left were to be bidden. Very soon Mme. Roland, too, joined the party ; but from the first she was the real Minister of the Interior, received callers, and sent out circulars : " My wife is not unfamiliar with the business of my office," said Roland to Barras, when the latter showed his surprise at seeing "Manon" seated at her husband's writing-table. The "worthy friend," indeed, was less familiar with it than his mate. But, above all, she was the life and soul of her *salon*, where Ministers and deputies were wont to meet. Brissot, especially, would hold forth there : Gensonné, Isnard, Grangeneuve, and half a score of others carried on discussions ; Pétion, Mayor of Paris, came in to get the password, and young Barbaroux too, " Antinoüs," with an " eagle glance," agent of the Marseilles Jacobins, who poured out all the passionate ardour of the Cannebière at " Manon's " feet. But her great friend, the trusted agent in all her undertakings, was Léonard Buzot, the man of " feeling," the platonic " well-beloved " : the virtuous Saint-Preux of a sublime Héloïse, the faithful lieutenant, the constant lover, who espoused all her quarrels, served all her animosities, and tinged the adventure with romance *à la* Rousseau in the midst of national tragedy.

*   *   *   *   *

The presence of this passionate and eager personality ensured, as my readers will imagine, the vigour of the programme of Ministers and party alike. "Manon" was a republican after the manner of Plutarch. It may very well be that till March 23 she had really aspired to see the formation, after the throne had been overthrown, of "the Republic of virtue." When once the King "called" Roland to his council board, that "tyrant" became endurable. If "Antoinette" would cease trying to pervert "her fool of a husband," all far-reaching projects in that direction might very well be put aside. This feeling was shared by the Left. After March 23 the Bordeaux leaders were inclined to check the republican movement. They had got ministerial office, and this seemed to them a very considerable advance. Politically, the case was normal enough.

But apart from this constitutional question, the Ministry of March 23 was, and continued to be, a Ministry of the Left, The Programme and a "Great Ministry" besides. It had quite of the Great determined to "disaristocratize" France; "sweep Ministry. away," writes Mme. Roland, "the detestable underlings," and cleanse the "Augean stables." Dumouriez was purifying the diplomatic corps. Clavières was doing the same to the "Direction of the Posts," which was particularly "aristocratic," and as "all military men were considered enemies of the Constitution," the Rolands promptly caused Colonel Servan, "about whose principles there could be no doubt, seeing he had set them forth previously to the Revolution in a valued work" (*Le Soldat Citoyen*) to be appointed Minister of War. To such a point did Servan carry his "disaristocratizing" of the Staff that before six months were out Mme. Roland was to think there were too many Cordeliers in it. As for the Rolands themselves, they had a special work of their own—the struggle against the Papacy, which they never forgot for an instant. France was to be forced into yet another step along that revolutionary path on which she still hesitated to advance. The pretext for this was to be the war, now one of the most essential items of the ministerial programme.

       *   *   *   *   *

Immediately after March 27, Dumouriez had dispatched an exceedingly arrogant ultimatum to Vienna and, reckoning on a refusal, had sent Maret into Belgium with orders to stir that country up at once against the House of Austria. On March 29 the Minister for Foreign Affairs, who had a taste for demonstrations, made his appearance in the Assembly in his general's uniform.

Vienna, sure of the support of Prussia, sent a very stiff reply to the ultimatum. This reached Paris on April 18. The War against Ministers decided to call on the Assembly to Austria declare war on the "tyrant of Vienna." There demanded. could be no doubt that the Assembly would welcome the proposal. Yet certain Feuillants pointed out that a great risk was being rashly undertaken : the upper ranks of the army were dwindling steadily. A deputy of the Left had certainly written that this process was "purging" the Army : the fact remained that the departure of 6000 officers, out of 9000, was rather a drastic purge. They were dropping off by degrees, and were to do so until the very eve of the first engagements ; and this, as Rochambeau put it, forced a labour like that of Penelope on the generals in command. La Fayette, very rightly, called on the royalist officers in the name of honour to emigrate at once, so that the situation might at all events be clear. But among the rank and file the lack of discipline was notorious. As to this we must refer our readers to the well-informed pages of M. Arthur Chuquet : the details he gives are stupefying ; the men looked on their officers as traitors and wanted to kill them : the insubordination of the volunteers, who were now coming in, caused absolute consternation. At Phalsbourg, at Lunéville, at Neubrisach, at Strasbourg, there were regular mutinies. Even with the volunteer reinforcements the army was very weak numerically : 150,000 men in all : 110,000 infantry, 30,000 cavalry, 10,000 artillery : Rochambeau was in command of the troops from Dunkirk to Philippeville : La Fayette commanded from Philippeville to the Wissembourg lines : Lückner had the third division—the army of the Rhine—from Wissembourg to Basle. Lückner, whose "manner and good countenance" inspired Couthon with the "greatest confidence" on February 28, was in reality nothing but an elderly German soldier of fortune ; "semi-brutalized," says Mme. Roland, somewhat grotesque, a good second-rate soldier, quite incapable of leadership. La

Fayette, though not the "traitor" Brissot and Robespierre so constantly accused him of being, was more of a politician than a soldier, and was far too much engrossed with the happenings in Paris. Rochambeau, though growing old, was a really good military chief, but he could not get on with Dumouriez, who insisted on managing everything over Servan's head : Dillon and Biron, the men who commanded under Rochambeau, were exceedingly independent. There was no cohesion in the command : the leaders had no confidence in their men, the men had none in their leaders. There had been no preparations of any kind : no rations, no war material, and the fortresses, in spite of Narbonne's assertion, were in very bad repair. Nothing was ready for war.

But what matter ! A fever of patriotism was at work in every corner of the kingdom. This land of warriors had **The patriotic** rusted too long in peace. Some vile passions **Fervour of the** had been roused by the civic fever which had **Country.** lately raged, exciting every brain and swelling every heart : but it had stirred noble aspirations, too : a Frenchman whose heart glows with patriotic fire lays his hand instinctively on his sword-hilt. And, since the Declaration of Pilnitz, a proud feeling of revolt had sprung into existence. France had wrought a Revolution. Was she right or was she wrong ? Had she gone too far or not far enough ? That mattered little ! She had made her Revolution, and now came the foreigner, who threatened to throw obstacles in its way, intervene in her affairs, and impose his will upon her ! At the very thought a shiver of noble indignation shook the country. What does this mean ? May not Frenchmen settle French affairs among themselves ? And with a bound the country sprang to its feet. Threats ? The word went out instantly. "Let us attack first !" "The despots" were raising their arms ? Then France would go out to meet them, even in their own "lairs" ! The timid folk, the politicians, the calculators on Right and Left, had all blundered ; their scruples looked like cowardice, they very nearly cost Robespierre his popularity. "We shall see discipline re-established under the breath of battle : hidden treason will be forced to cast away its mask ! *Ça ira !*" Such was the nation's cry of hope. For six months past volunteers had been pouring in : humble peasants, lawyers' clerks, artisans, and even nobles in whom the military spirit of their race had stirred again—these were the volunteers of 1791. "Scum," said Morris. Some of it, perhaps, but that burning scum was to flow all over Europe and submerge an ancient world !

＊　　＊　　＊　　＊　　＊

Still, the heart of the nation was tense with anxiety. The leap into the gulf must be taken once for all. On April 20 The Sitting of feverish excitement reigned in the Assembly : April 20, 1792. the Council's decision in favour of war had become known. The Ministers were expected, and possibly the King as well. Condorcet was reading a report on the organization of schools in his thin voice, but nobody was thinking much about schools : little Bara did not want to learn his rudiments, he longed to rattle his drum at the head of a battalion on the march.

At noon Louis XVI made his appearance : his eyes were dim and he moved as in a dream ; he had ceased to share his people's fervour ; to him the war was nothing but the outcome of the intrigues of two equally detested factions—the *émigrés* and the Jacobins. He read the document the Ministers had prepared for him, which asserted the necessity for declaring war against Francis II, "in the same tone of voice," writes Mme. de Staël, "as that in which he might have proposed the most unimportant decree in the world." And then, in the midst of a heavy and respectful silence he took his departure.

Outside the streets were in a violent turmoil. It produced its effect upon the deputies. Mailhe, a Girondin, proposed that there should be no Committee report, nor any other preliminary which might delay the decree ; let the debate begin at once ! Mathieu Dumas, a good soldier, but full of common sense, tried to make a stand against this suggestion : he was hooted, and obliged to resume his seat. Pastoret of the Centre, who had been doubtful only the day before, now advocated war. "Victory," he said, "would be faithful to Liberty !" Hua and Becquey of the Right, were brutally shouted down when they tried to advocate a pause for reflection. The Bordeaux group seemed under the influence of some delirium : when Bazire, a faithful follower of Robespierre, begged that at least discussion should be permitted, Mailhe once more opposed the idea : "*The people desires war ;* make haste to give way to its just and generous impatience. You are, perhaps (and here we see the mind of the Girondin), about to decree the liberty of the whole world. I ask the Assembly not to quit this hall till war has been decreed!" The atmosphere in the Manège was that of which Vergniaud was shortly to complain—the heavy and exciting atmosphere of a night sitting, for some special and dramatic intoxication seems to descend from the lighted chandeliers. The moderate party now failed to obtain any hearing at all. At last the decree was proposed, and the debate was declared closed. The voting was just about to begin when a deputy was seen to rush up the steps of the rostrum. It was Merlin of Thionville. As the closure had been voted he was debarred from speaking, but he shouted : "*What I wanted to say was, that we must declare war against kings, and peace with all peoples.*"

A war against kings! All Dumouriez's deep-laid plans to make this war against the house of Austria a war of the old *régime* ; those other plans of certain politicians of the Left, who flattered themselves they held the war in the hollow of their hands, to lead and end it as they chose ; and those ideas of a struggle that should be short and circumscribed, were shattered by that cry. All kings were to hear it : the statesmen of the new *régime* had thought to divide them ; they had forced them into union. France stood alone against the world.

On that basis was this war declared, by a practically unanimous decision—there were seven votes against it— amidst frantic transports of enthusiasm.

War declared. "So much the better!" writes Marie-Antoinette. The Queen had been driven to the extreme of exasperation. Her dream had been an intervention by the European Powers, which would have intimidated France and brought her back to the Sovereign's feet : and this was still the King's idea. The Queen's wish now—an unpardonable wish, born of a thousand feelings all too violent—was that the French army might be defeated and crushed. ‘ On the 30th she revealed the negotiations with Europe which Dumouriez had attempted (and which had failed) to the Austrian Court. England had taken up an attitude of watchful hostility; the King of Prussia had left Berlin on April 26 to march on Paris.

What with the Coalition now an accomplished fact, an ill-guarded frontier, an army stripped of its officers, unreliable **Desperate** military chiefs, a Ministry new to affairs, a **position of** traitorous Court, undisciplined troops, an As-**France.** sembly ruled by the streets, and streets in which licence stalked unchecked, it would be a miracle indeed if France escaped the fate to which Europe destined her. It is a strange fact that two great parties in Paris were reckoning on French defeat : the anti-revolutionists, to stifle the Revolution; the revolutionists, to let it loose once more. Never was a war prepared and desired with so many scarcely concealed ulterior motives.

But the first part of the Girondin programme had been carried out.

SOURCES. Works already quoted by Carnot, Brissot. Dumont, Mallet du Pan, Salamon, Molleville, Couthon, Dumas, Thomas Lindet, Hua, Vaissière, Aulard (*Jacobins*, III).—Dumouriez, *Mémoires*, 1794 ; Sophie Grandchamps, *Souvenirs*, 401–7 (*Appendices aux Mémoires de Madame Roland*, Perroud edition, II, 1905).

WORKS. Those already quoted by Biré, Guadet, Colfavru, Cahen, Albert Sorel (III), Charavay, Meynier, Montier, Esmein, Chuquet.— Welschinger, *Le Roman de Dumouriez*, 1898 ; Raynaud, *Merlin de Thionville*, 1860.

CHAPTER XVIII

THE FALL OF THE "GREAT MINISTRY," JUNE 20

The rout on the 28th of April. Agitation in Paris. The disbandment of the Constitutional Guard. Servan summons the Federates. Rupture between Dumouriez and the Rolands. Dismissal of the Ministers. "Manon" prepares her revenge in her *salon*. The 20th of June. The populace at the Salle du Manège and the Palace. "The King drinks!" General reactionary movement. La Fayette wishes to close the Jacobin Club. He is betrayed by the Court. The Left regains courage.

ON April 30 rumours of a defeat reached Paris. The reality was far worse : the "defeat" had been the most humiliating of routs. Every well-informed or cautious person had foreseen it, and with good reason, but it was worse than anything that had been expected. On the 28th, part of Rochambeau's army, under the command of the Marshal's subordinates, Generals Dillon and Biron, had attacked two separate points on the Belgian frontier. Dillon's column had marched upon Tournai from Lille, but when the Austrian Hussars made their appearance there was the most extraordinary panic : the French cavalry turned, with shouts of *Sauve qui peut!* and when Dillon threw himself in front of the fugitives they cut him down ; finally the troops, not having shed a drop of blood, save that of their own leader, made their shameful way back to Lille. That same day Biron had moved on Mons from Quiéyrain, and then had suddenly abandoned the attack : he found the heights of Jemmapes white with Austrian uniforms, and beat a retreat, thereupon his panic-stricken dragoons turned their horses round, yelling "We are betrayed !" La Tour-Foissac has described the hideous disorder in his memoirs—Biron swept along, arms cast away on the high roads, men falling

The Rout of April 28.

244

down in sheer terror, and the return to Valenciennes, more disgraceful even than the flight of Dillon's troops to Lille.

The Austrians were astounded : they entered French territory, chuckling to themselves and sneeringly declaring that the Frenchmen's motto was "Conquer or run ! " It was clear now that the necessary weapons for putting these Frenchmen to flight were not swords, but whips ! "The whole thing will be over in a few weeks," said one of the ambassadors in Paris to Morris. But this check was the salvation of France : the Austrians, unprepared for so rapid a success, halted, believing they might choose their own time, and gave La Fayette and Lückner (Rochambeau had resigned), the chance of making an attempt to raise to some extent the *moral* of the troops under their command.

In Paris yells of "treason" were raised. The Assembly laid the blame, in the most unexpected fashion, upon the clergy. Agitation in During the last few weeks, indeed, the anti-Paris. clerical fever had been rising steadily. On May 27 the Assembly had voted the decree condemning priests who were "abettors of disturbance " to be deported ; a most peculiar detail was quoted with horror—that among the dead bodies of the enemy (none had been killed by the French troops), those of various non-juror priests had been found disguised as Austrian soldiers. This absurd story was accepted even by the worthy Le Coz.

The distracted Assembly plunged into violent and useless discussion. It had put a premium on military sedition by receiving the rebel soldiers of Châteauvieux, just returned from the hulks, with the most flattering attentions ; and having done so, was artlessly wondering what course it had best pursue to restore discipline in the ranks of the army. It seethed tumultuously, "stunned," writes one authority, "with the noise of cannon " : certain deputies boxed their colleagues' ears : the Right, which had been grossly insulted, proposed that the Clubs which hung over the Assembly should be closed forthwith, but the deputies did not dare to do this. There was fighting everywhere. Fighting, too, in the Clubs, where Robespierre, who had foreseen events, was triumphant over the defeat : he was instructing his supporters to say that the *Brissotins* were drunk with power. They were suspected of sparing the King because their friends were in the Ministry : they handed him over to his enemies to prove they were as incorruptible as Robespierre himself.

There was a story that the Court was " hatching a Saint-Bartholomew of the patriots." " How ? " inquired the Feuil-

The Constitutional Guard disbanded. lants. " The King has disbanded his Gardes du Corps and has no power over the army." But he had a new " Pretorian Guard "—the so-called Constitutional Guard. That must be disbanded, cried voices from the Mountain. On May 29 Gensonné, resolved not to seem less " pure " than Chabot, carried a decree for disbanding the Guard : this measure really left Louis XVI at the mercy of the first riot that might occur.

Yet he sanctioned the decree. The universal opinion from that moment was that the King was lost : contemporary letters describe the Royal Family, living in the midst of threats and insults : the National Guard, terrified at the very idea of a rising, was certainly not sufficient protection for the Sovereign. A rising was being plotted, indeed, and all appearances pointed to the fact that recruits were being made ready to join it.

On June 4, in fact, Servan, now Minister of War, who carried out all Roland's behests in that department, came

Servan enrols the Federates. to the Assembly with a most dangerous proposal. A second Festival of the Federation was to be celebrated on July 14. The Minister now proposed that each canton should send up five Federates, clothed and equipped, and that these, after figuring on the Champ-de-Mars on the festal day, should be formed into a camp numbering 20,000 men on the banks of the Seine below Paris, or somewhere close to the capital. The proposal caused great surprise : Servan had acted without, or rather contrary to, the advice of the Council, where Dumouriez had clearly set forth the danger to public order involved in such a gathering. The debate, quite unexpected by the Right, was very short : Servan put forward his suggestion as a purely military measure : it was passed on June 6.

This put the crowning touch to the anxieties, not only of

FALL OF THE "GREAT MINISTRY"

the King's friends, but of all the partisans of order and of the Constitution. These Federates, who were to play a far more important part in the Paris streets on August 10 than they did at a later date on the frontier, would, it was feared, give active assistance to the populace, which agitators were already stirring up. Barbaroux's correspondence with the municipality of Marseilles proves how well founded these anxieties were. In the Feuillants' opinion the King had made too many concessions already : the Directory of Paris, which was in their hands, requested him not to sanction the decree against the refractory priests, which the Council of Ministers hoped to force upon him. But by this time even the Council itself was divided ; a violent scene between Dumouriez and Servan (they very nearly came to blows) on the subject of the Federates, had made the monarch aware that the ministerial team had ceased to pull together. One section of the Ministers threatened to resign if the King applied his *Veto* to the decrees ; the Sovereign thought this an excellent opportunity to rid himself of men whose presence had become unbearable to him.

On June 10 Roland fancied he would frighten him : he drew from his pocket a " Letter to the King " written from beginning Dismissal of to end by " Manon " : we need hardly say it the Ministers. was anything but complimentary ; it recalled Louis XVI sharply to his duties as head clerk. The King quietly took the letter from the Minister's hand, folded it up, and put it in his pocket But on the 13th, just as Roland was getting ready to go to the Council, he received a note from the King, containing a laconic request that he would " hand back the Portfolio of the Interior " ; Clavières was dismissed at the same moment, and was quickly followed into private life by Servan, whose place at the Ministry for War was taken by Dumouriez.

There was a great uproar. " This boldness stuns me," writes Mme. Jullien, on the 16th. It overwhelmed the Assembly. Retirement of " A lively and painful sensation," says one Dumouriez. deputy. At ten o'clock on the morning of the 14th the Assembly, quite illegally, received the fallen Ministers and greeted them as " martyrs." Orders were given that Roland's letter to the King should be printed, and a motion

247

was passed which declared the Ministers were "taking the regrets of the nation" with them. Just at this moment "that traitor" Dumouriez made his appearance in the Manège : he was fiercely assailed. "Dictator !" cried Guadet, and Lacueé dubbed him "slanderer." He called them all "madmen." He might possibly have been able to stand out against them, but though the King found him more attractive than Roland, he had no more confidence in "that inconsistent feather-head, with whom no honest people could ever associate themselves," than in the rest of his fellows—so wrote Montmorin, the King's chief confidant. The General found himself in a cleft stick between the rage of the Assembly and the distrust of the Court and, being an intelligent man, he took himself out of the way before he had come to any open quarrel with either side. Louis summoned more Feuillants of the second rank to his Council, and these, indeed, Le Coz admits, were not ill received by the Assembly : the deputies, no doubt, had had a fright.

But the Left was in a fury. The Assembly, "pusillanimous and corrupt," as Mme. Jullien writes, had forsaken the Revolution ! The King was casting off the yoke ! There must be a "day !" It should be June 20.

*   *   *   *   *

One of the agitators asserts that "it was really conceived and arranged in Mme. Roland's *salon*." It is true that **Vengeance prepared in "Manon's" Salon.** "Manon" was more furious than anybody, and Roland was mortally offended ; Clavières, too, was sighing for "his finances." Sergent was to notice him, on June 20, urging the populace on the Place du Carrousel to demand, above all things, "the recall of the good Ministers." (One always does one's own work better than another can do it for one !) The frequenters of Mme. Roland's *salon* favoured the "day." The professional agitators—Santerre the brewer, Legendre the butcher, Fournier the American, Lazowski, Chabot, Saint-Huruge—all that band of secret organizers who were to upset the throne on August 10, conducted its proceedings.

On June 20 the avowed intention was only to have the " good Ministers " brought back, and force the King to accept the decrees. If, in the course of the undertaking, the throne did chance to topple over, it would certainly not be set up again.

The pretext was the celebration of the fourth anniversary of the scene in the Salle du Jeu de Paume at Versailles, by planting a Tree of Liberty on the Terrasse des Feuillants at the Tuileries. By dawn 8000 men had set out from the Faubourgs. The day before several correspondents had written that "the people was to march to the Assembly and demand the passing of great measures."

The Assembly was warned by Roederer, the Procurator Syndic; a sitting was in progress when the petitioners arrived and requested admittance. A violent discussion ensued. Once more the Left saluted "the rising of the People." "The People!" cried somebody on the Right, "those persons who are bringing us a petition with cannon and pikes?" But that very evening Soubrany wrote that "in the agreeable variety of weapons and clothing he had recognized with pleasure the essential portion of the people." Guadet, and more especially Vergniaud, insisted that the petitioners should be allowed to enter. ("Every heart was with him!" writes Mme. Jullien.) These people, after all, were the avengers of Roland and Clavières. The corridors were crowded already. A deputation was introduced to begin with: its leader, "a new Cicero," set forth "sublime ideas"; he used fierce language: "the People is on its feet. . . . Blood will flow, or else the Tree of Liberty we are about to plant will blossom in peace! Do the enemies of the Fatherland imagine that the men of July 14 have fallen asleep? . . . Their waking will be terrible!" Thoroughly frightened, the Assembly gave the People leave to "file past." The People may have been "upon its feet," but it certainly had considerable difficulty in maintaining its position. Michelet himself, moved as he is by the situation, is fain to deplore and excuse the fact. "Forced to sustain themselves by seeking some strength in the doctored wine of Paris, they reached the Assembly in a condition hardly worthy of their surroundings." The majority of the deputies who witnessed the scene expressed their disgust: others laughed at it. In the "moving forest of pikes," described by

June 20, 1792.

249

Hua, "burlesque," says M. Aulard, "was the ruling quality."
Yet the *Révolutions de Paris* was to shed a feeling tear over
"all those charcoal-sellers, those sturdy market porters,"
and (this detail touches the miraculous) "more than 200
centenarian Invalides pensioners!" "An open-hearted joy,"
continues the journalist, "enlivened the spectacle," but "the
doctored wine of Paris" must surely have deprived it of the
smallest touch of poetry! Yet for three hours the Assembly
was forced to put up with it.

The President, his hand on his heart, had assured his
"worthy fellow-countrymen" that the Assembly would know
how to deal with "the crimes of the conspirators." They had
no great confidence in his promises, for they suddenly forsook
the Manège and betook themselves to the Palace.

There was no Guard now to defend it : all the mob had to
do was to push open the unlocked doors. In a few moments it
The Mob at had overrun the Royal apartments : the King
the Tuileries. had the doors, on which the rioters were beginning
to batter with their axes, thrown wide open, and appeared
himself. He was very calm : this coolness in the face of the
most hideous danger was his peculiar form of courage. He
was pushed hither and thither, and cursed. "A great deal of
abusive language was used to him," wrote Azéma, the Jacobin
deputy, that very evening; "amongst others a young National
Guard . . . said every imaginable kind of horror to him."
Above the abuse shouts rang out: "Sanction the decrees!
Recall the patriot Ministers! Drive out your priests! Make
your choice between Coblentz and Paris!" Calmly and quietly
Louis replied that this was neither the hour nor the place for
looking into the matter of the decrees : he declared himself "a
patriot," and seeing a red cap on the head of a man near
him, he snatched it off and put it on his own. The gesture
was exaggerated: it caused a sort of stupefaction, and even
—this is very evident—a certain embarrassment among the
"patriots." Yet the mob wanted to see how far it could
make "Veto" go; it was horribly hot, there was drinking
going on : a glass of wine was passed over to the King—he
drank it.

The National Guard appeared on the scene. It cleared a

little space round Louis XVI. There he stood, perspiring under the thick red cap set askew on his powdered head, with " The King the glass of sour wine in his hand : the mob drinks ! " shouted : " The King drinks ! " And he smiled back to it. Vergniaud hurried over from the Assembly; he had fancied his eloquence would suffice to disperse the mob : nobody listened to him. He was hoisted, at last, on to the shoulders of a huge porter from the Halles, and from that strange rostrum he harangued the patriots. They only jeered at him.

At last the Mayor of Paris, Pétion, arrived. This " tall, fair man, with his insipid good looks and his bland air, at heart a knave and coward,"—so Frénilly describes him—was really one of the most sinister figures of his epoch. It was now six o'clock in the evening, the mob had been on the move since four in the morning ; the Mayor, like Pilate, vowed he " had only just been informed." Louis received the traitor coldly. Yet he it was who put a stop to the scandalous scene : the rioters, unable to extort any promise from " Capet," were growing weary : Pétion told them it would never do for the King's reply to have the air of having been forced from him by violent measures—which must have sounded like a joke. And the populace drifted away. Pétion then proceeded to excuse himself, or rather to boast of what he had done, to the Assembly, which admitted this sorry personage to the honours of the sitting.

* * * * *

This had been a lawless outburst : the Left realized the fact, and strove to remove the deplorable effect produced. The word went out that the people " had been to pay a visit to the King." We find this expression in all the letters from deputies of the Left and in the Jacobin newspapers. " The most magnificent things were said to him," writes Mme. Jullien. " The people had proved," writes Soubrany, " by the way they had used their liberty, that they were worthy of it." Condorcet was in ecstasies ; there had been no harm done, he said, beyond " the breaking of a few panes of glass."

Yet the revolutionary party seemed likely to have to pay a heavy price for those panes of glass.

251

The feeling of indignation, in fact, was extremely strong : a very lively reaction in favour of the throne set in, as is General reac-   proved by the letters written in the course of the tionary feeling. following week.

Thoroughly alarmed, La Fayette hurried to the scene of action. He expected to have been joined by everybody who had been disgusted by the events of the 20th, and hoped to take advantage of this to close the Jacobin Club, where he himself was daily dragged through the mud.

On the 28th, in the midst of the greatest excitement, he made his appearance in the Assembly and, " in the name of the La Fayette   indignant Army," poured forth so vehement a denounces the denunciation of the real supporters of the mob Jacobin Club.   —the members of the Club—that for a moment the Left was put out of countenance. The Right applauded him vehemently, and even the Centre acclaimed him, believing his army was close upon his heels. If he had brought it with him there can be no doubt that he could, as M. Mathiez rightly asserts, have made a successful *pronunciamiento*. Guadet dared not attempt any direct attack upon him ; he treated the matter in a tone of bitter irony. But the Assembly was still full of the disgust caused by the incidents of June 20, and, further, La Fayette was still "the eldest son of Liberty " in the eyes of the majority of these *bourgeois*. The Assembly supported him, and threw out the motion for sending him back to the army by 339 votes against 234. The " poor Jacobins " seemed in a bad way. " One hears nothing but anathemas against them."

This check stirred the Left to fury. That very night, at the Jacobins, Robespierre denounced La Fayette, " that enemy of the Fatherland "; " the vilest of wretches," writes Couthon; " a villain and an idiot," said Desmoulins. All this rage would have been quite impotent if the Court and the Court party had supported the General's plans. But at the Tuileries he was still considered the worst of all the King's enemies. The reactionary movement, then evident in the country, was quite incorrectly interpreted by the Court as a counter-revolutionary movement. In its opinion there was no need for La Fayette : " an intriguer, a rascal," writes an " aristocrat " on June 29,

" who is trying, now he sees that luck is turning, to provide an excuse for himself by throwing himself into the other party." While the Jacobins were holding forth against La Fayette's "Monkeries,"the Court was making fun of his "Don Quixotisms." "And, indeed, it would be better to perish," said the Queen, "than to be saved by M. de La Fayette and the Constitutionals ! "

So La Fayette was rejected, and what was worse, he was betrayed. Hearing the King was to review the National Guard

The Court repudiates La Fayette.

on the 29th, the General desired to seize this opportunity of showing himself to the troops he had once commanded, and inducing them to follow him against the Jacobins. The Court, incredible as this may seem, warned Pétion, who countermanded the review. Discouraged, La Fayette left Paris. That very evening " that villain, that knave, Mottié ! "—this was the name now invariably given to the General, who really was called Mottié de La Fayette —was burnt in effigy in the Palais Royal. Once again the Court had ruined its own chance. Disappointment reigned in the Assembly : the Centre, much cast down, was seeking recon-

The Left takes heart again.

ciliation with the Left, when, on July 3, Vergniaud, without venturing to condemn La Fayette, pro- posed, in a crafty speech, that a report should be made on his conduct, and the suggestion was applauded even on the benches of the Right, where alarm was rife. Thus the Constitutionals sanctioned their own final defeat. And this checked the reactionary movement that had followed on the incidents of June 20. The emboldened Left and the enraged Club were both bent on vengeance for their momentary terror.

August 10 was to be their reply to the " seditious " attempt of " that villain Mottié."

SOURCES. Works already quoted by Madame Roland (*Mémoires, Lettres*), Carnot, Hua, Salamon, Morris, Malouet (II), Le Coz, Thomas Lindet, Dumouriez, Dumas, Sophie Grandchamp, Mirabeau, Couthon, Frénilly, Baron de Staël-Holstein, Mallet du Pan, Rabusson-Lamothe, Soubrany, Madame Jullien, Vaissière, Aulard (*Jacobins*, III).—Azema (deputy), *Lettres* (published by C. Bloch, *Rev. Fr.*, 1894) ; Vaudreuil, *Correspondance avec le Comte d'Artois*, 1892 ; Sergent Marceau, *Notice sur le 20 juin* (*Rev. Retr.*, series 2, III).

WORKS. Those already quoted by Colfavru, Biré, Guadet, Cahen, Aulard (*Orateurs*), Castellane, Charavay ; Sagnac, *La chute de la royauté*, 1910 ; Dreyfus, *Liancourt et le projet de départ du Roi* (*Rev. Fr.*, 1903).

CHAPTER XIX

THE QUESTION OF DEPOSITION

The Left threatens the King to force him to recall the Ministers.
Pétion is suspended. The "Lamourette kiss." July 14, 1792.
The coming of the Federates. "The Fatherland in danger!"

THE Left had been terrified : let our readers consult the letters written by Couthon, Mme. Roland, Mme. Jullien, the deputies of the Mountain, between June 20 and July 3; they all betray the same feeling ; and then on the 3rd a great cry of relief rose up. The check of La Fayette, engineered by the Court, had put an end to all these fears.

The leaders of the Left, such men as Brissot and Robespierre, drawn together by a common alarm, were now to all appearance reconciled. And all were waiting the arrival of the Federates to begin another June 20. They reckoned especially on the deputations from Brest and Marseilles, which had started for Paris on the 19th and 22nd. On July 2 the Assembly passed a decree that the Federates should come into the city of Paris, and this was sanctioned by the King. Neither the Marseilles nor the Brest Federates could be at the Champ-de-Mars for the festival on July 14. The one object of their march on Paris was to overthrow the King, for, as *Le Patriote* averred, the great city stood in need of "a reinforcement of patriotism."

Till they came everything possible was done to increase the popular excitement. In all the open spaces songs against the King were being sung.

> "Nous le traiterons, gros Louis, biribi,
> A la façon de Barbarie, mon ami,
> Gros Louis, biribi."

A different lay was making itself heard at the Assembly.

254

THE QUESTION OF DEPOSITION

On July 3 Vergniaud's voice was raised in tragic accents. The deputies must proclaim "the country in danger": this would be a powerful means of rousing the public mind. The "Cicero of Bordeaux" spoke, in very truth, like a Cicero of the Clubs : "the gloomy genius of the Medici," the "bloody hypocrisy of the Jesuits, La Chaise and Le Tellier. . . ." the massacre of Saint-Bartholomew, the *dragonnades*, all the well-worn commonplaces of history, shabby but valuable even yet, were dragged forth : and reference was made likewise to the "insolent smile of our internal enemies, announcing the approach of the troops of the Coalition." As to this last the speaker was right : the Court was rejoicing, and even if Vergniaud himself did not wish to depose the King, such words, passing from the Manège to the crowd in the street outside it, were a preparation for the event. "We are marching on to the catastrophe with long strides," wrote Morris on July 10.

* * * * *

Thereupon it became known that the "infamous Directory" had suspended Pétion and Manuel, the Mayor and Procurator Suspension of of Paris, from their functions. In this case, Pétion. also, punishment had been delayed too long : immediately after June 20, even Pétion's friends had believed such a measure inevitable. A fortnight later, it seemed, or was represented, as the first step of a *coup d'état*.

At that moment the Mayor was the most popular man of his party : all the Left swore by him : "the virgin Pétion" Couthon called him in his excitement on November 19 : by July 7 he had become both virgin and martyr ! Mme. Jullien talked about his "delicious private life" ("There virtue dwells, my son !") ; "Virtue in breeches," she writes on another occasion : the Bordeaux men considered him one of themselves. The mob allowed him to impose his will on it. The first child baptized by Bishop Gobel had been given the names of Pétion Aristide Pique ! This individual, the shallowest personality of his time, was literally deified : to be "Aristides or Socrates," as Mme. Jullien described him, was not enough. A "Life of Pétion" was published, the author of which compared his hero to Jesus Christ, and pointed out that Christ should have been

Mayor of Jerusalem, as Pétion, that second Messiah, had been Mayor of Paris ! At bottom this " Messiah " was a fool and a poltroon. " The coward Pétion," his friends of the year 1792 were to call him. M. Sagnac paints him in alarming colours.

However, that may be, the fact remains that on July 12, when Louis XVI confirmed this sorry fellow's suspension, there was an outburst of fury. The Girondins, whose company the Mayor frequented, were determined to keep their man in, if only as a matter of principle : as for the party which was paving the way to insurrection, it could not reckon on success unless Pétion, wilfully blind, remained in office. And the populace, in its simpler fashion, adoring its " Messiah," yelled " Pétion or death ! "—one of those stupid and declamatory expressions which make a man's fortune. The suspension, justified by the Mayor's behaviour on June 20, and legal in any case, was considered, writes Dumas, " an evident violation of the Constitution." And the deputies, by an equally evident abuse of their power, repealed the order. The King might have seized on this action as his warrant for striking at the Assembly : but, as always, he was baffled : his cause was lost.

* * * * *

Proposals for his dethronement were constantly put forward ; though after July 3 Vergniaud had confined himself to aggres-
The King's sive allusions, Cambon had roundly demanded
Deposition that the King, who was manifestly conniving
suggested. with the foreigner, should be deposed. During the early sittings of July the astonished Girondins beheld their place taken by the Extreme Left. The Girondins were not really sure of what they wanted : the idea of the deposition alarmed them : they had got no further, as yet, than their desire to see the Ministers recalled to office. But though the Girondins still wrapped themselves in clouds and sibylline utterances, such men as Chabot, Merlin, or Cambon, were definite enough. Condorcet himself was content to demand that the King should be rendered " powerless." Torn by conflicting sentiments, and incapable of any decision, the whole Assembly was in a state of hysteria. This fact alone can account for the extraordinary scene known as that of the " Lamourette kiss."

THE QUESTION OF DEPOSITION

Lamourette, Bishop of Lyons, had just made a pathetic appeal for universal union in face of the country's danger when suddenly those deputies, who had been slapping each other's faces only the night before, cast themselves into each other's arms, shedding "torrents of tears." "An incomprehensible miracle of electricity . . ." writes an eye-witness, "the whole Assembly on its feet, with arms upraised. . . . the deputies pulled off their hats and waved them in the air : the people in the galleries stamped with excitement : the vaulted roof rang with the sounds of joy and applause The intoxication was general." The Bishop's formula, "Hatred of the Republic ! " had been applauded to the echo. It had seemed a " cry of reunion," and as such, had filled "the heart" of a certain faithful female adherent of the Jacobins " with fury." The King, who had been notified, hastened to the Hall of Assembly : the good-hearted Louis XVI was the very man for such moments as these. He smiled, he wept, he gave them all his blessing. The Assembly dispersed in tears. And within the space of a few short hours they were all "tearing out each other's eyes again," as Montmorin puts it. This scene reveals a state of nerves which explains everything, the heroisms and the follies, the weakness and the daring, the crimes and the splendid actions, of the period. From the Tuileries to the Faubourg Saint-Antoine all had lost their heads.

On that very evening of the " Lamourette kiss," Le Coz, still intoxicated with tender emotion, was very nearly killed by three citizens drunk with something of a very different description. In reality the Clubs were pushing on their cam paign for the King's deposition, and were set against reconciliation in any form. Yet the Assembly did make one final effort to stand out against the street : on July 10 La Fayette was absolved from all blame by 446 votes against 224 : nothing misled the Court more completely than this vote : when the King took refuge in the Salle du Manège on August 10 it was because he believed the Assembly was still able on occasion to make a firm stand.

But the thought of the danger in which the country stood was raising the fever of the public mind to the point of delirium. On the 11th, the Assembly declared "the Fatherland in danger." This proclamation, on the eve of July 14, was to invest the new Federation with a tragic character.

Pétion, who had been re-established in his functions on the 13th, was the hero of the festival. Like La Fayette two years previously, he was acclaimed on the Champ-de-Mars at the Sovereign's expense. The King and Queen were in great danger : Danton had publicly asserted that the country would rid itself of them on the 14th. They faced the hooting bravely. Mme. de Staël has left us a description of the unhappy pair : the Queen with her eyes full of tears, the King so hustled by the crowd that when he went up to the altar to take the oath, it was thought for a moment that he must be trampled on. " When he mounted the steps of the altar one could fancy one saw a holy victim offering himself a voluntary sacrifice ! "

July 14, 1792.

The Federates had been coming in for a week past ; they were all carried off to the Club, where Robespierre invited them to "save the State." Billaud-Varenne supplied the explanation of this expression : " the Tarquins must be driven out." The Federates undertook to do it ; they refused to leave Paris and go to the frontier. " Not a man of us will go to the frontier if the King is not suspended." The phrase, " the King's suspension," was current all over Paris now, and was even buzzing in the corridors of the Salle du Manège, where, says Lamothe, certain deputies talked of deposing the King " with less ceremony than they would have shown in discharging an ordinary clerk."

Arrival of the "Federates."

The Federates demanded more than suspension ; they insisted on deposition. They kept pouring in ; there were 2690 of them on the 18th : on the 30th they numbered 5314. They were managed by a " *Central Committee*," aided by an " *Executive Directory of Five*," which was assisted by the Paris agitators, Gorsas, Fournier (who refused to go another step " unless he had resistance to oppression in his pocket "), Carra, Santerre, Chabot, Lazowski, etc. On the 17th, urged on by this committee, the Federates presented a petition to the Assembly, denouncing the King as a traitor. The President returned a vaguely worded reply : " the means of saving the nation would be found in the Constitution."

*   *   *   *   *

THE QUESTION OF DEPOSITION

But at that very hour a dramatic demonstration was fanning popular excitement and favouring the plans of the "The Father- conspirators. Our readers are aware that Hérault land in had secured the passing of a proclamation that danger." "*the Fatherland was in danger.*" (He had "aped Mirabeau," wrote Mme. Jullien.) It was during July 22 and 23 that this ominous decree was proclaimed on the public squares by municipal officials. While the alarm gun boomed from the Pont Neuf, and the cannon at the Arsenal boomed a reply, these functionaries, with their tricolour sashes over their shoulders, and attended by a cavalry escort, shouted aloud at every cross-road, "The Fatherland is in danger!" And, meanwhile, on platforms hung with tricolour flags, on which stood a plank laid on a row of drums, volunteers were signing their engagements. Higher and higher the wave of patriotism was swelling, but there was as much rage as enthusiasm in its composition. The rage was justified. "The Austrians," wrote Morris on the 25th, "talk in the most confident way about spending the winter in Paris." The populace was aware of all these boasts : it had a reasonable fear that they might be realized : it distrusted the military commanders, the deputies even, and the Royal Family most of all. And as far as Marie-Antoinette, at all events, was concerned, we know the populace was right. In the Queen's immediate circle the coming of the foreigner was desired and eagerly pressed forward. "Our illness is making good progress!" writes an "aristocrat" joyfully on the 10th.

The people divined these sentiments. The volunteers demanded that if there was to be fighting on the frontier, the "soldiers of the Nation" should not be cut down from behind by "the treason of the Tuileries."

The Assembly was overborne : even the Left felt itself outrun. The "Bordelais" hesitated : if only the King would The Committee recall Roland, Clavières and Servan they would of Twelve. keep him on his throne. Vergniaud, Gensonné, and Guadet sent Louis a secret ultimatum. And then, to frighten him by a public demonstration, they had a summons transmitted to him by the "Committee of Twelve," a legislative committee which, as M. Aulard tells us, was already setting itself up to be a Committee of Public Safety. The "Twelve" presented

259

to the Assembly an address drawn up by Condorcet: " The Nation will no doubt be able to defend and preserve its liberties alone, but it calls on you, Sire, *for the last time,* to join it in the defence of the Constitution and the throne ! "

Brissot secretly offered to save the throne if the King would attach himself to the Girondins. The Left was already be-
Manœuvres of
the Girondins. ginning to suspect him of treachery. " Barnave !"
they would shout at him : Vergniaud, who was also inclined to save the King, if he would make his submission, shared Brissot's disgrace, " *Barnave the Second,*" he was called. At bottom, what these Girondist politicians hoped to do was to forestall a revolution prepared by Chabot in the Assembly, and by Danton in the Clubs. But they were too late. The Court was resolved not to be saved by Brissot any more than by La Fayette, and the conspirators, on their side, were determined that none of these wind-bags should baulk them of their prey.

" Barnave the Second," like Barnave the First the year before, had come too late.

SOURCES. Works already quoted by Dumas, Hua, Couthon, Morris, Malouet (II), Girardin, John Moore, Le Coz Frénilly, Beuguot, Brissot, Rabusson-Lamothe, Fournier l'Américain, Madame Jullien, Madame Roland (*Mémoires, Lettres*), Vaissière.—Aulard (*Jacobins,* IV), 1892 ; Dubreuil (deputy) (*Rev. Rev.,* XIII) ; Barbaroux, *Mémoires,* 1840 ; Roederer, *Chronique de Cinquante Jours,* 1832 ; Pétion, *Lettre du 6 août,* 1792 (*Revue des Autographes,* September 1905).

WORKS. Those already quoted by Albert Sorel (III), Colfavru, Biré, Guadet, Charavay, Cahen, [Sagnac.—Aulard, *Danton et la Révolution du 10 août, Études,* IV ; Mortimer-Terneaux, *Histoire de la Terreur,* 1820.

CHAPTER XX

THE FALL OF THE THRONE

The Marseilles men come in. *The Marseillaise.* The *émigrés* and Europe. Brunswick's Manifesto. The evening of August 9. Danton's stroke at the Hôtel-de-Ville. The insurrectionary Commune. The death of Mandat. Resistance fails. The King at the Assembly. The conflict between the rioters and the Swiss Guard. The massacre of August 10. The Assembly suspends the King, and hands him over to the Commune.

ON July 29 Robespierre made a formal demand in the Assembly for the suspension of the King and the summoning of a National Convention. This was the word of command to all the Paris sections.

These, which had been allowing the lowest of the populace **The Men of** to invade them for the past few weeks in the **Marseilles and** most illegal manner, were most of them led **"The Marseil-** by the conspirators : that of the Théatre-Français **laise."** (the present Odéon) was, in fact, the very hotbed of the conspiracy : Danton, Desmoulins, Fabre d'Eglantine, Chaumette, Marat, Manuel, Fournier l'Américain, and Fréron all worked there. Yet it was the Section of the Fontaine de Grenelle which on July 20 suggested the King's deposition to its fellows. The majority had seemed to welcome the suggestion, but their meetings were mere public gatherings, with no legal status whatever. And, further, there was no certainty that these men, who were making so much noise, would be ready to face the chance of getting their heads broken. Thus the leaders were waiting for the arrival of reinforcements from Marseilles.

These came on July 29. Barbaroux had asked old Mouraille, the Jacobin Mayor of Marseilles, to send up " 600 men who would know how to die." And a hundred of them did in fact die at the Tuileries. But, meanwhile, all along their road from

261

Marseilles to Paris, they had proved that they knew how to sing. For weeks they had marched through France, with burning cheeks and blazing eyes, shouting that *Hymn to the Army of the Rhine*, composed but a few weeks previously by a young officer called Rouget de Lisle quartered at Strasburg, which now seemed so thoroughly identified with themselves that it had been christened *The Marseillaise*. The South has always had a talent for appropriating the products of the North.

On the 29th, then, they were at Charenton, where some of their contemporaries would gladly have shut them up. Barbaroux flew to meet them : " So many Scævolas ! " On the 30th they entered Paris, and that very evening they killed an officer of the National Guard, wounded several soldiers, and created disturbance in every direction.

This alarming invasion produced a reaction. On the 31st, when the Mauconseil section, which was beginning to talk with the accent of Marseilles, made a declaration to the effect that the " King was deposed "—neither more nor less—it found no imitators. But on August 4 there was a change, for early on the 3rd Paris was made acquainted with Brunswick's mad manifesto.

* * ✿ * *

Since the shameful stampedes of the spring, Europe, as we know, had looked on France as her certain prey. The " trip to Paris " would be a very easy matter. Already the spoil was being divided up. Europe had even grown quite cynical. " The re-establishment of order," wrote Cobenzel, the Austrian Minister, " is no longer to be considered the most important object of our military operations. The continuance of disorder and of civil war must even be regarded as favourable to our cause, and the return of peace, consequent on the arrangement of a French Constitution of some kind, will be a benefit which France will have to purchase by the sacrifice of the provinces we shall have conquered." France was to be left to tear herself to pieces for a while : that was the pretext for delay. But in reality neither Prussia nor Austria could bear to leave a free hand to Russia and, indeed, the deepest distrust reigned

The " Émigrés " and Europe.

between these two allies ; one cast suspicious glances on the other as they marched upon Lorraine. This explains the "miraculous" event at Valmy. The Coalition that menaced France was incomplete, unsteady, disturbed by ineradicable suspicions, and a prey moreover, to a dangerous infatuation.

The infatuation of the *émigrés* was worse still : they were the fly on the coach-wheel, and the coach, as they thought, **Brunswick's** was stuck in a rut. They cherished a most **Manifesto.** chimerical plan : France, they said, was terror-stricken by a mob of ruffians : terror must be met by terror. A manifesto that would terrify the whole country would drive it straight back to the King's feet. And that done, Condé's legion would march in, the white flag would be unfurled, and everything would be over at once. Even in these plans for invading France there was a remnant of patriotic feeling : if the country turned and repented in this fashion the ground would be cut from under the foreign invaders' feet : they would have no pretext for taking payment, since submission would have come without their intervention. So these madmen besieged Brunswick, the generalissimo, an undecided, timorous person, who ended by signing, with a shrug of his shoulders, a manifesto drawn up by a certain M. de Lenon. The terms of this production are well known. It addressed France as a rebel, who must cast herself at the King's feet if she desired to escape punishment by arms. Paris was threatened with "total subversion" if a finger were laid on the Royal Family ; the Assembly and the administrators were held responsible, and the inhabitants who might "*dare to defend themselves*" were promised the most terrible chastisement. Nor was any distinction drawn between the "rebels" ; all those who had "rebelled" since May 5, 1789, were threatened equally. Morris gives us an ironical summary of the spirit and consequences of the manifesto : "*Be against me, all of you, for I am against you all, and make a good resistance, for there is no hope left you !*" This "deplorable gasconade," as Frénilly describes it, is more severely but most exactly judged by Mathieu Dumas : "A real fratricide on the part of the French Princes against the King and his family."

*   *   *   *   *

" We are saved ! " cried Condorcet the Republican. This meant the destruction of the throne. On the 3rd, Pétion **The Deposition** appeared at the Assembly bearing, so he affirmed, **demanded.** an address from the Sections, demanding the deposition of the King. Alarmed by the situation, Vergniaud had the discussion adjourned (the worst solution he could have attempted), and when the Mauconseil Section once more proclaimed, on the 4th, that " it had ceased to consider Louis XVI as King of France," the Assembly did indeed quash the whole debate, "considering that the Sovereignty belonged to the People and not to one Section," but the majority buried this decree beneath so much flattery addressed to the Section, that we realize the state of terror into which the deputies had been thrown. An Englishman of the name of John Moore (whose notes on those August days are most interesting reading) saw the Assembly in a state of hopeless confusion : on the 6th, at one and the same sitting, it was to bestow an honourable mention on the Section of the Meuse, which had requested that all petitioners for the King's deposition should be punished, and confer the honours of the sitting on the very petitioners who had come to demand his dethronement. Moore saw the occupants of the galleries insult and jeer, and even threaten the members of the Assembly : " I could not but feel convinced that the people in the galleries were more ready to throw the deputies out than were the deputies to expel them." Meanwhile the Assembly was forsaking the King : it decided that the few battalions of Swiss troops quartered in the outskirts of Paris, the only protection left to the monarch should any rising occur, were to join the Army of the North.

"The National Assembly," writes Mme. Jullien nevertheless on the 8th, " seems to me too weak to back up the People's will, and the People seems to me too strong to allow the Assembly to put it down." " Blood will rain," she goes on. To this end, in fact, the Marseillais had extorted 5000 cartridges from the municipal authorities on the 4th, and as the Commandant of the National Guard, Galliot de Mandat, was a Loyalist, Santerre had undertaken to debauch his troops.

The deputies were well aware that a rising was imminent : fond as they were of permanent sittings, they had no intention

THE FALL OF THE THRONE

of being present in the hour of peril. By seven o'clock on the evening of the 9th they had all dispersed. Brissot had come to the conclusion that, as Louis XVI so obstinately refused to take back his "good ministers," "necessity demanded that the law should be allowed to slumber."

The evening of August 9.

*   *   *   *   *

It was a stiflingly hot night. All Paris was out of doors. The rumour: "It is to be to-night!" was rife everywhere. Suddenly, at a quarter to twelve, the great bell of the Cordeliers began to toll drearily, and was answered, in a very few minutes, by the bells of six other churches. The tocsin! Paris felt a breath of fever pass. "*Ça y est; ça ira!*" ("Here it is! Now we shall get on!")

It was Danton, representing the Procurator-General, who had personally conveyed the signal to the ringers at the Cordeliers. From eight to nine o'clock the Sections had sat in tumultuous meetings; their object was to elect the Commissaries who were to intimidate and, if necessary, replace the Council-General of the Commune at the Hôtel-de-Ville, which was composed of Constitutional Royalists. This *coup d'état* at the Hôtel-de-Ville must of necessity precede the attack on the Tuileries : once the Hôtel-de-Ville was in the conspirators' hands they would suppress Mandat, take possession of the National Guard, and then proceed to throw the men of the Faubourgs and the Marseillais into the defenceless Palace. By eleven o'clock the newly elected Commissaries were all hurrying to the Hôtel-de-Ville.

Danton's Coup d'état at the Hôtel-de-Ville.

The Council-General was in session ; it had sent for Pétion, and, as he failed to appear, it ordered Mandat to beat to arms. Mandat had at once taken the necessary measures, and had then proceeded to the Palace, whither Pétion, with a very ill grace, made up his mind to follow him. Meanwhile Danton entered the Hôtel-de-Ville, where he found the eighty-two leaders of the Sections fuming and raging. These individuals called themselves the "New Commune." The Council-General, which was still sitting, had allowed them to take possession of a room near the Council Chamber, and by so doing had worked its own destruction.

The insurrectionary Commune.

265

Before another hour had gone by the insurrectionary Commune was to have wiped out its legal predecessor.

*   *   *   *   *

At the Tuileries, resistance was being organized. Mandat was not very sure of his National Guard, but the tone of his orders was so resolute that it seemed to steady the troops. He had also sent for all the remaining Swiss troops quartered at Rueil and Courbevoie, and the gendarmerie as well. This brought the total of the regular troops to nearly 1800 men. The presence of these " assassins of the tyrant " was not, it must be confessed, very well received by the gunners of the National Guard, good " men of '89," every one of them.

Mandat organizes the Defence of the Tuileries.

A good man of '89, too, was Roederer, the Procurator-Syndic of the Department, who put in an appearance towards eleven o'clock. This ex-member of the Constituent Assembly was to play a very dubious part : a Jacobin yesterday, a moderate of a kind to-day, a Senator of the Empire on the morrow, and a Peer under Louis-Philippe at last; this Lorrainer, courteous, capable, insinuating, averse to all extreme solutions, was the man of all the world most likely to foil energetic action of any sort. Pétion came too, at last, with his never-failing smile, but, though civilly received by Louis XVI himself, he put forward certain rude remarks made to him by the soldiers as an excuse for allowing himself to be tempted into the Salle du Manège, where a few of the deputies had gathered, and thence he betook himself, not to the Hôtel-de-Ville, as he ought to have done, but to his own rooms in the Mairie ; there, as Barbaroux had foreseen, the riot was to keep him " chained with ribbons."

Roederer.

The sun was just about to rise : Madame Elisabeth lifted a blind : " Sister," she said to the Queen, " come and look at the dawn ! " And Marie-Antoinette watched the last sun of the French Monarchy rise in the rose-coloured sky of a lovely summer morning. Louis XVI announced his intention of going to rest. At that very moment Danton was taking possession of the Hôtel-de-Ville.

He was making a great disturbance there : Pétion's absence had left him a free hand. The Council-General was beginning to take alarm at last : Mandat, its members were assured, was a traitor : he had stationed some troops on the Pont Neuf **Mandat** so as to prevent a junction between the insurgents **massacred.** on the two sides of the river, and this precaution, which prevented any combined movement on their part, was driving the agitators to fury : they were shouting that the " traitor " had arranged a massacre of the people, and that the Court was in league with him.. Hardly knowing what it really wanted, the Council-General sent an order to Mandat at the Tuileries to come down to the Hôtel-de-Ville. He hesitated to obey : the Ministers advised him to stay where he was : Roederer counselled obedience : what need he fear from the Council-General, composed as it was of loyal and honest men ? Mandat knew nothing of the formation of the insurrectionary Commune : he departed without any escort : when he reached the Maison Commune,* he was surrounded, insulted, told that he was deprived of his command, and finally cut down as he went out.

When the new Commune deprived Mandat of his command, it crossed the Rubicon : it proceeded to inform the Council-**" The People** General that, as the " sole representative of the **takes all powers** People," it had decreed that " the Council-**to itself."** General was to be suspended." The step was one of inconceivable boldness : the Council made a protest : it declared the Commissaries had no legal status. " *When the People puts itself into a state of insurrection,*" was the reply, " *it withdraws all powers and takes them to itself.*" The words should be remembered and written on the front page of this history : thus may a handful of agitators give the law to a nation numbering thirty millions of men. But what shall we say of the cowardice of the Council-General which, still protesting, closed its sitting and capitulated ? The Commune took its place, mistress of Paris.

* * * * *

The plan was carried out with wonderful precision. When Mandat had been struck down all defence was disorganized, and bands of rebels began to invest the Tuileries. One of these

* Under the Republic the building answering to the " Town Hall " in England was known as the " Maison Commune."

levelled cannon on the Palace from the Pont Neuf and the Terrace of the Feuillants. Louis XVI was roused from his **Dislocation of** slumbers. The behaviour of the National Guard **the Defence.** was causing alarm. The King went down to review it on the Place du Carrousel: his eyes were red, "his curls all flattened," and all the powder had fallen from one side of his hair. He moved heavily along, incapable of finding one inspiring word : in front of each company he repeated the same phrase: " I love the National Guard ! " Frénilly writes, " I see him yet, as he passed along our front, silent, careworn, with his swaying walk, seeming to say to us ' All is lost ! ' And disbanded gunners began striding in his wake, shouting ' Down with the King ! Down with the fat . . .!' Louis made no reply : at half-past seven he was back in the Tuileries, gasping for breath."

Behind him quarrels were breaking out in the ranks. The gunners loudly declared they would not fire on their brethren, and just at this moment the rioters, beating on the gates and scaling the walls, began to incite them to mutiny.

Roederer, too, had gone down among them. When he came back he preached capitulation. A number of deputies (almost **The King takes** all of them members of the Left) had gathered in **refuge in the** the Manège : why should not the King take **Assembly.** refuge with them ? " Do you think so ? " said the King. " Yes, Sire. There is nothing else for your Majesty to do." The Queen did not wish it. " But we have some troops ! " said she. " What ! are we alone ? Can nobody act ? " " Yes, Madame, quite alone : action is useless, resistance is impossible. All Paris is on foot." (Roederer exaggerated a good deal.) He returned to the charge : " Sire, time presses ! " The King turned to the Queen : " Let us go ! " he said. It was to the scaffold that the Sovereigns were going. Roederer walked first, followed by the Ministers and the National Guard, then by the King with his family. The Dauphin was amusing himself by kicking up the leaves which the exceptionally hot weather had already scattered on the paths. " They are falling very early this year," said the King : he was never to see the young leaves on the trees of the Tuileries gardens again.

THE FALL OF THE THRONE

In great agitation the Assembly (very few members were present) was awaiting the coming of the King. He seated himself on the left of the President, Vergniaud. A cruel fate destined the Bordelais to sit in the presidential chair of the Convention when the King's death sentence was pronounced : even now he was to preside over the Legislature's reception of the Sovereign it was shortly to abandon to his fate. Little could that have been augured from the tone in which he spoke : " Sire, you may rely on the firmness of the National Assembly ; its members have sworn to die in support of the rights of the People and the constituted authorities ! " The phrase of a tribune ! the man of words was about to act as purveyor to the gaoler—in preparation for the executioner.

There was a difficulty about finding places for the royal intruders : they were crowded, at last—the King, the Queen, their children, Mme. Elisabeth, and some of the attendants —into the box reserved for the " logographer " (the stenographer) of the Assembly. Moore admired the steadfast dignity of the Queen : but the German Bollmann writes that the King seemed " stunned and helpless."

A few minutes previously, a little Corsican officer, watching Louis' unresisting departure from the terrace of the Tuileries, had murmured the words " *Che coglione !* " Pensively, Captain Napoleone di Buonaparte surveyed the downfall of the throne and the populace crowding into the Tuileries.

*   *   *   *   *

The investment of the Palace had begun at eight o'clock in the morning. By the King's order the Swiss troops had retired into the interior of the building, and the defence of the courtyards had been left entirely to the National Guard. The Marseillais called on it to surrender. The actual assault was being delayed pending the arrival of the men of Saint-Antoine, " the glorious Faubourg," who were to be led by Santerre. But Santerre, hearing on his way that he had been appointed Commandant-General of the National Guard, had hurried to the Hôtel-de-Ville, and was issuing his orders thence.

Conflict between the Swiss Guard and the Rioters.

These orders were quite superfluous : the gunners at the

Tuileries had opened the gates, and even the gendarmes had gone over to the people. Very soon the guns were turned on the Palace itself. The Swiss troops were wildly excited. Were they to let this mob get in without making any resistance, and perhaps have their own throats cut as well ? " Surrender to the Nation ! " shouted Westermann to them in German. " We should think ourselves dishonoured ! " was the reply of the brave fellows.

Two of the Swiss, who had detached themselves from their fellows to parley with the insurgents, were fired on, and instantly their comrades fired back : the discharge was almost point-blank, for the rioters were on the steps. The leader of the Marseillais fell, and a hundred dead and wounded men lay on the stones of the courtyard. The terrified assailants fled in every direction (which proves how completely Roederer had misled Louis XVI). Then the Swiss stepped over the corpses, seized the cannon, recovered possession of the royal entrance, crossed the Place du Carrousel, and even carried off the guns drawn up there.

The fugitives ran into the column arriving—at last—from the Faubourg Saint-Antoine. They gathered fresh courage, and the assault began again : it was difficult for the Swiss to repulse it : they had hardly any ammunition left : they were driven back on the Palace at once, leaving a number of wounded men behind them on the flagstones.

The noise of the firing had reached the hall in which the deliberations of the Assembly were dragging their slow length along. Messengers announced "the massacre of the People," and also that an entrance into the Palace was to be forced. Upon this the Assembly made a truly sublime flourish : it passed a decree placing "the security of all persons and all property under the safeguard of the People of Paris ! " It then proceeded to send twenty of its members to the Tuileries, and twelve more to the Hôtel-de-Ville : they were to confer with "all those in whose hands *any authority, legal or illegal, and even the apparent confidence of the People, may at this moment be found.*" Even in all this tragedy there is a touch of humour.

Pressed by the deputies, the King signed a note ordering

the Swiss to cease firing and to proceed to the Manège. They obeyed. In a moment they were pursued, surrounded, and **Massacre of** massacred. This happened everywhere, within **August 10.** the Palace and in the gardens ; others who had gone towards the Hôtel-de-Ville were summarily sentenced by one of the members of the Commune there, cut down, and then torn to pieces. Fires were lighted to consume the heaps of corpses in the courtyards of the Palace. All this fury is not very comprehensible ; hardly 400 persons (376 according to M. Sagnac), had been killed on the assailants' side. Yet the Swiss were by no means the only victims. While some honest fellows were doing their best to prevent the ruffians from sacking the Tuileries, allowing them only to smash the " looking-glasses in which Antoinette had too long been studying the hypocritical air she showed in public," less harmless performances were going on elsewhere : Therwagne de Mericourt was having the journalist Suleau, who had formerly ridiculed her, murdered. But within the Palace the throats of the very cooks were cut : gentlemen, too, Gardes du Corps, the Dauphin's assistant tutor, d'Hallonville, fell, and among many others, the unhappy Clermont-Tonnerre, one of those generous-hearted aristocrats who had been the first defenders of the cause of democracy in the States-General.

It is only the first drops of blood that alarm the shedders : the human beast was loose now. That very evening the horrified Dumas saw " very young boys playing with human heads," and Frénilly heard an honest artisan remark : " Ah, sir ! Providence has been very good to me, I killed three of the Swiss with my own hand ! " August 10 was really the first day of the Terror : M. Sagnac reckons that 800 people were massacred.

* * * * *

While the massacres were going on Louis XVI was spending hours of misery at the Assembly.

The gathering of members, as I have already said, was most incomplete : the deputies of the Centre and the Right, who were greatly alarmed, had not dared to put in an appearance : some members knew nothing of what was going on (Condorcet, who was at Auteuil, did not reach the Manège till the evening): barely 290 deputies out of the 750 were present, and almost all of these were members of the Left **"The Magis-** "under the orders of the galleries," as a letter **trates of the** written the following day puts it, and completely **People."** terrorized. The Assembly, as we know, had dispatched a deputation to the Hôtel-de-Ville, but on its way thither it had passed the delegation proceeding from the Hôtel-de-Ville to the Manège. These "new magistrates of the people," as the intruders called themselves, entered the presence of the trembling legislators to give them their death-sentence : they demanded the convocation of a *Convention.* Towards ten o'clock Guadet had replaced Vergniaud in the presidential chair : he greeted the usurpers with praise, and fancied he would thus get rid of them. "The Assembly," he said, "applauds your zeal . . ." and he invited them to "return to their post." But now the popular orators invaded the rostrum : "Learn," cried one, "that the Tuileries are on fire, and that we shall not hold our hand till the People's vengeance is satisfied ! "

The People's vengeance—that meant the King's deposition ! All the Assembly was able to do was to refuse to *depose* him, **The Assembly** but to vote for his *suspension* until "the National **suspends the** Convention should pronounce its verdict." The **King.** debate had occupied the whole of the day : the Royal Family sat by, in an overpowering atmosphere and watched the fall of the French Monarchy. At ten o'clock that evening they were conducted to the Convent of the Feuillants, where they spent a comfortless night on hastily improvized beds : the next morning they were brought back to their box in the Hall of the Manège. Thence they were to be taken to the Temple. The Assembly had decided first of all that the King should be interned at the Luxembourg, and then (a Section having demonstrated that the Royal Family might easily make its escape from the Luxembourg "through the Cata- **The King** combs,") at the Ministry of Justice in the Place **handed over to** Vendôme. But the Commune made a formal **the Commune.** protest, and declared its sole right to the custody of the King. Once more the Assembly gave in under a hail of abuse from the galleries, and the sovereign who had sought safety

272

in its arms was handed over to the insurgents of the Hôtel-de-Ville. On August 12 Louis XVI and his family were " confided " to the Commune, which shut them up in the Temple. And, while the Assembly thus " confided " the King's person to Chaumette, it was to confide the ruling power to Danton. Louis XVI was not the only beaten man that day : the Girondins, outwitted and abased, had surrendered themselves when they surrendered others.

SOURCES. Works already quoted by Sergent Marceau, Malouet, Carnot, Le Coz, Barère, Dumas, Barbaroux, John Moore, Madame Jullien, Azema, Thiébault, Roederer, Fournier l'Américain, Choudieu, Madame de Tourzel, Pontecoulant, Vaissière ; Aulard (*Jacobins* IV).—Malliaud (deputy), *Lettres* (*Rev. Rev.*, I) ; Roux, *Lettre*, published by Maricout (*Rev. Hebdomadaire*, 1908) ; Martinécourt (deputy) *Lettre* (*Journal des Débats*, March 23, 1905) ; Chaumette, *Papiers* (Braesch ed.), 1900 ; Dejoly, *Relation du 10 août* in Montjoye, *Vie de Marie-Antoinette*, 1897 ; Gibelin, *Documents sur le 10 août par Amiel*, 1866 ; Princesse de Tarente, *Souvenirs*, 1901 ; Peltier, *Dernier Tableau de Paris*, 1794.

WORKS. Those already quoted by Sagnac, Claretie (*Desmoulins*), Mortimer-Terneaux, Robinet, Hamel; Talmeyr, *La Vérité sur le 10 août* (*Gaulois*, August 11, 1908).

CHAPTER XXI

DANTON

INVASION AND THE MASSACRES

The Executive Council. Jacques Danton. His programme.
The Invasion. The forces on each side. The volunteers. The
work of Dumouriez. The taking of Longwy and Verdun. Fear-
ful crisis in Paris. The Commune in conflict with the Assembly.
To strengthen its own power the Commune plans a massacre.
The Days of September. Attitude of the Council and of the
Assembly. Danton and the massacres.

THE real victor on August 10 was Jacques Danton.
Hated though he was by the "Bordelais," they were
forced to accept him. Having decreed the election
of an Executive Council, and added a proviso that the chief
place in this Council was to be given to the first deputy elected
The Executive to it, the Assembly forthwith put Danton in that
Council. place. By 222 votes out of 285 he was promoted to be Minister of Justice. His colleagues were to be
Monge and Le Brun, Ministers respectively for the Navy and
Foreign Affairs, with Roland, Servan, and Clavières, each in
his old place.

The very choice of these men set Danton on the pinnacle
of power. Servan, whom the "Bordelais" considered their
devoted adherent, was to allow himself to be subjugated, and
still more was this to be the case with Monge the mathematician,
whom Condorcet, his colleague at the Academy of Sciences, had
pushed into an office in which that "bear," as La Révellière
calls him, was to behave like "an idiot," writes Barbaroux.
Le Brun was to do exactly as Danton told him. Clavières
had always been a mediocrity. Roland remained, indeed,
but within the last three months the poor man had aged
greatly : domestic troubles were fast unsettling his mind, and

274

he had never been anything but a learned Encyclopædist—there was nothing of the statesman in his composition. His wife, who had been everything in the world to him, was now the object of his suspicion, and this caused him bitter suffering.

To sum it up, this ministry was a gang of bewildered clerks. A single gesture from the " Cyclop," who had been carried into office " by a cannon-ball," as he said himself, sufficed to put them all to silence.

Hitherto this Danton had been considered a rather vulgar agitator of the Clubs and Faubourgs; fierce, dangerous, not very serious compared with the grandiloquent Vergniaud or Robespierre. Yet in our eyes he towers high above them.

He was the son of a procurator in Champagne, and not at all the *parvenu* he has been described as being : a brilliant scholar and student of the greatest authors,

Danton. Dante, Shakespeare, Corneille, Rabelais; then so remarkable a lawyer that before 1789, Barentin, the Keeper of the Seals, would have taken him into his own office : but this, foreseeing the advent of the " avalanche," he refused. He even disposed of his own practice so as to keep his hands freer, and deliberately threw himself into that same " avalanche " from its first movement in 1789. He may have been an agent of the Duc d'Orléans : he certainly tried the Masonic lodges, and then, finding they suited him better, turned to the most advanced of the Clubs where, for the past three years, he had been busily engaged in working revolutionary opinion up to fever pitch. He had been at the bottom of every fresh movement, and had now been carried by the wave into the chair hitherto occupied by d'Aguesseau.

He hardly sat himself down in it : from this chair he " bounded " upwards to the dictatorship. Before he did so, with a gesture at once brutal and childish, he broke off with his thumb the gilded *fleur-de-lys* of the clock in his cabinet which marked the hour of his advent to power. The man's whole impulsive nature is shown in that action : he broke off the hand ! Robespierre would have had it taken off and put away.

Impulsive he was, and violent, passionate, audacious rather than persevering, loving life, wearing it and himself out, boasting more of his vices than of his virtues, ambitious, but not deeply calculating, noisy and powerful as an orator, but nothing of a rhetorician, and always ready to shed tears of blood over the disasters his own speech had let loose.

Everything about him accentuated the excessive violence of his language—most of all his face, the face of a " Mirabeau of the mob," with something in it of the bulldog and something of the lion.

" He was a man," says Sorel. Michelet took him to be " a sublime actor " : what a mistake ! He was horribly sincere : everything came from the depths of his heart—pity, rage, love, ferocity. He had no venom, was easily touched, quick to forget injuries done him by others, often driven to despair by those he wrought himself : rancour and calculation were alike foreign to him. He loved money, but we have no absolute proof that he ever made it dishonestly himself, though he allowed those about him to do so ; for indeed, he never set up to be " incorruptible."

He had a great brain and a warm heart : he adored the Revolution and the Fatherland with the same deep-seated devotion : he was a Frenchman to the very marrow of his bones : when the day came the call of his country in danger stirred the very depths of his soul. This fact makes the man, so repulsive in some particulars, a great man in our eyes. He was a volcano, but above the horrible flood of lava played the purest flame.

One other feature to conclude : he was lazy. He was capable of every kind of audacity, and prone to the extremes of indolence. His action was always violent and spasmodic : he knew nothing of slow labour and patient hatreds. Robespierre would have reprobated the weakness that led him to pardon an enemy before that enemy was dead. Royer-Collard says he was " magnanimous " : this magnanimity may well have been the outcome of his indolence : he tired swiftly of everything, even of his own anger.

He was not overburdened with theories : he would have preferred to see the widest toleration everywhere : he married again in the middle of the Terror, and had his union blessed by a Roman Catholic priest : yet he had allowed a hundred priests to be murdered at the Carmelite

Danton's Programme.

276

Convent, and had shielded the murderers. His dream was to see France united in the face of the threatening German : the Republic, to him, was a government that should mean unity, not division. He found it very hard in 1793 to endure the rancour of the Girondins, and in 1794 to believe in the hatred of Robespierre. In August 1792, he began to dream of a great movement which was to raise the whole nation against the foe. Idle as he was, his patriotism was to keep him absorbed for weeks and weeks in a huge and urgent labour—the total reorganization of a country that had fallen a prey to the most unexampled confusion.

Taking him all in all this Danton was a great power.

* * * * *

The Left had realized the fact : the " Bordelais " might have placed Roland at the head of the Government ; but, though they did not say so to Mme. Roland, they thought him quite unequal to the task, which was tremendous. True, they destroyed themselves when they appointed "the Cyclop " : but they saved France. Nobody was to think of putting the giant aside till the enemy had retreated across the frontier.

His first step was to lay his ideas before the Council : the Girondins were idealists, he was a cynical realist : he did not believe France was Republican : till she rallied to the Republic she must be coerced. For this purpose revolutionary Paris must be the weapon.

The Girondins would have preferred to rely on the provinces against the Paris Commune. But he swept all their objections **Danton and** aside. Mme. Roland was the only one who **the Rolands.** stood out. From the very outset she detested the man who was eclipsing her own friends : she hated his genius, his vices, even his person—" repulsive and atrocious." We find a vivid proof of this woman's hatred in the magnificent, terrible, and to some extent untrue portrait of Danton written by her hand and lately published. He would have been glad to be on friendly terms with her, but when he found husband and wife were doing their best to thwart him covertly, he followed his invariable custom—thrust aside these people, who clung to their old rancours, with a motion of his brawny arm. This brought the part the Rolands had played to an end. Danton had subjugated the remaining members of the Government. He was master now.

And, indeed, everything bowed under the law insurrection had evolved. La Fayette, who had tried to rally his army, had been forced to flee. The provinces, which had protested against the doings of June 20, made no protest when August 10 came. The departments, all except eight, which betrayed some hesitation, gave in their adhesion at once. All this was due to the Brunswick Manifesto.

Paris made merry : it seemed as if some nightmare had been swept away. The letters and articles of the period would lead us to fancy some new era had opened for the human race—a sort of cheerful emotion everywhere, dancing, laughter, congratulations : one might be reading the pages of Wells' novel, "In the Days of the Comet " ; the air seems clearer, the men " carry their heads higher," the women are more chaste : everything appears "in a sublime harmony " : Mme. Jullien's letters are lyrical as the "Song of Songs." Meanwhile the King and his family were shut up in the Temple, and the people would go in the evening and flout " the new Agrippina " ; as early as August 20 some were demanding the head of the " tyrant despot."

For the invasion was beginning. On the 19th the Prussians, with a troop of *émigrés*, had crossed the frontier at Redange. **The Invasion.** The *émigrés*, in spite of all their blindness, had sore hearts (many a letter might be quoted here) : it was a terrible and solemn moment, and one of the invaders, Chateaubriand, has left us an emotional picture of it. But as to the success of the undertaking no doubt was entertained : the Prussian officers, who declared themselves instruments of the Most High, were making appointments to meet at the Palais Royal at the end of August : there they would find good cheer and everything else. " Never," says Chuquet, " was scorn of the adversary carried to a higher pitch."

Condé's tumultuous and fantastic army proposed to march as the vanguard, with the (laudable) object of receiving the repentance of the Nation beneath the folds of the White Flag. But the Powers, who were more concerned with fortresses than with repentance, would not hear of this.

DANTON

Brunswick had 80,000 men—this was the "Army of Lorraine," consisting of 42,000 Prussians, and only 29,000 Austrians;
The Forces of the Coalition. but in the North, the Duke of Saxe-Teschen was threatening Lille with 25,000 Imperial troops and 4000 *émigrés*; and in reserve there were 17,000 Austrians and 5000 of Condé's men ready to invade Alsace; 131,000 Coalition troops in all.

The Prussians especially seemed formidable: they had the benefit of the extraordinary prestige enjoyed by the Great Frederick's armies ever since Rossbach. M. Chuquet has revealed all the unsuspected weakness that lay behind this imposing front; their artillery especially—and on this the success of battles was to depend—was very inferior to ours. The Generalissimo, too, was certainly "the least fitted of all men to lead an invading army." His officers were full of boasts, perhaps, but he was full of doubts. This "Philosopher" Duke of Brunswick disapproved of a war against the Revolution which had brought freedom, and like a good Prussian, he loathed the Austrians his allies. Finally, he was by nature undecided and inclined to pessimism—one of those generals who on the eve of a battle think chiefly of the best means of covering a retreat.

This was not known in Paris: the invasion was considered horribly threatening, but fear, instead of depressing the populace, stirred it to wild excitement. Gouvion-Saint-Cyr says that the Brunswick Manifesto gave a hundred battalions to France.

They were not the best of battalions to begin with, far from it. For years an obstinate legend attributed our first **The French Forces.** successes to these Volunteers of 1792, who, if the truth must be told, went very near to compromising them.

The real heroes of Champagne, of Lorraine, and later of Belgium, were the soldiers of the old army and the volunteers of 1791. "These are Frenchmen and of a good sort," wrote a general; insubordinate fellows, who had yet learnt, after the defeats of May 1792, to submit to discipline of a severer kind. But their coming had not swelled the ranks of the army enough to make its numbers (82,000 men) equal those of the army of the

279

THE FRENCH REVOLUTION

Coalition (131,000). The Legislature had consequently decreed a second levy : and this had been very inferior in quality to that of 1791. None of the generals attempt to conceal the fact in their letters. Still, they do not seem to despair of turning these noisy, hot-headed fellows into soldiers ; to that end Kellermann, from this time forward, recommended what he called " amalgamation."

The Work of Dumouriez. Dumouriez had taken La Fayette's place at the head of the Army of the North, and Lückner, who had been provided with the empty title of Generalissimo, was soon to be banished to the rear, and his position at Metz filled by Kellermann. In reality Dumouriez, who had obtained full forgiveness both from Servan and from Danton, directed all the operations.

His aim was to exploit the enthusiasm of the volunteers without subduing it. The army had become far more republican than the nation in general. It was in the throes of a genuine paroxysm of civic feeling ; such sentiments, properly handled, might develop it into a magnificent force. Our readers must consult the campaign letters and journals of officers published in the course of the last twenty years, from Fricasse to Bricard, from François to Joliclerc, and twenty others whom we leave unmentioned. Never was there such an exhibition of mystic faith : their faith saved them. They put the *Marsellaise* into action.

And Dumouriez, who thought "the dough of 1791 " good, knew how to knead it. His skilful handling turned the fugitives of Mons and Tournai into the heroes of Valmy and Jemmapes. When battle came they stood the ordeal well. " Blue earthenware," the *émigrés* scornfully called these soldiers in their blue uniforms. The earthenware had already been put into the fire for the first time. It had seemed to crack. But "the stuff was good " : the levy of 1791 had brought the best type of Frenchmen to the camp : one of them, that ex-drummer who was to become Marshal Victor, spoke of the movement, in later days, with deep emotion : "Oh, splendid outburst of 1791," he cries, "would that I could extol thee worthily ! " "We lived," writes Marmont, " in an atmosphere of light : I feel its heat and power now, at fifty-five, just as I felt it the first day ! "

280

DANTON

The volunteers were called on to elect the commanding officers of their battalions (a hazardous experiment), and as a rule they chose them well : Bessières, Championnet, Delmas, Haxo, Laharpe, Lecourbe, Suchet, Pérignon, Jourdan, Victor, Oudinot, Marceau, Moreau, Davout—one-fourth of the future Generals of Division under the Republic, seven of the future Marshals of the Empire. In two years these young men were all of them to be general officers ; emulators of those subordinates who were also to rise to superior rank within a year: Lefebvre, Bernadotte, Ney, Murat, Augereau, Soult, Pichegru, Moncey, and Hoche. These two sets of men—to which must be added the young leaders of 1792 : Mortier, Gouvion, Brune, Lasalle, Joubert—were to lead their battalions under fire in admirable fashion, till they were called to the command of armies. For France this was an unspeakable good fortune, and she had further retained a certain proportion of her artillery and engineer officers, less prone to emigrate than those of the infantry and cavalry : these men, grave and resolute, were to wait behind their guns for the onslaught of that magnificent Prussian infantry which, before six weeks were out, was to waver before the bronze barrier they had raised : the steel of the volunteers of 1791, and their fiery courage, were to do the rest.

The Volunteers elect their Officers.

*   *   *   *   *

Six weeks was a brief span in which to evolve a new army out of chaos. There was no possibility of defending Longwy, which capitulated on August 20 : the garrison marched out, but the imperturbability of its civic faith disconcerted émigrés and Prussians alike : not a man (and this disproved the optimistic predictions of the émigrés) consented to join the enemy's ranks. The German officers were greatly impressed by their behaviour.

Capitulation of Longwy.

Kellermann, who reached Metz on August 27, found things in some disorder, but the *moral* of the troops was excellent. There were shouts of " Ça ira ! " at Metz, and more shouts of " Ça ira ! " at the camp at Maulde, where Dumouriez, as much by his good temper as by his firmness, had recovered his hold upon the men.

THE FRENCH REVOLUTION

Brunswick hoped to slip between the two : the King of Prussia, spurred by the *émigrés*, was urging him on towards Paris : the Duke would have preferred to take a few fortresses : from August 24 to 29 he lingered in camp at Praucourt, where the Prussian troops, soaked by the rain, contracted the first germs of dysentery. Yet so great was their prestige that it **Capitulation of** sufficed to bring about the capitulation of Verdun **Verdun.** on September 2. But there again the attitude of the garrison was calculated to impress the conquerors. Commandant Beaurepaire blew out his brains rather than sign the capitulation, and when the French troops evacuated the town they shouted as they marched past the Duke : " To our next meeting on the plains of Champagne ! "

Meanwhile, Kellermann at Metz, and Dumouriez at Sedan, were hastily, but busily, forging the weapons of the coming revenge.

* * * * *

Nevertheless the successive falls of Longwy and Verdun were alarming facts : the enemy had reached one of the crests **The Crisis in** overlooking the plain on which Paris lies. Ex- **Paris.** citement rose higher and higher in the city. The Government was overwhelmed. " Although we have no time for sleep, and we work with a superhuman activity," writes Mme. Roland, " it is not possible to repair the effect of four years of treason in the space of a few hours." And the situation really was terrible. The Assembly, having " suspended " the King, had assumed the reins of government, but it gave but little help to its Executive Council. It was ruled by the Clubs and the Commune : sometimes it would obey them—as when it established universal suffrage in connection with the elections for the Convention, and sometimes it would stand out against them. It was truly a " Rump Parliament " : out of 750 members hardly 258 to 260 attended the sittings : the Right had taken to flight, the Centre had practically disappeared : the Left was oppressed by the Extreme Left.

It had consented to permit the organization of a preliminary Terror : nobles and priests alike were now looked upon as conspirators and treated as suspects. On August 17, in the belief that it would thus forestall massacre, it had set up a regular

282

revolutionary tribunal to try "the crimes of August 10," in other words, the crimes of the aristocrats. The prisons were already full : and, indeed, the Assembly had decreed on the 15th that all fathers, mothers, wives, and children of *émigrés* were to be considered hostages, and imprisoned accordingly ; and on the 26th that all non-deported refractory priests were also to be thrown into prison. On August 28 Danton had secured the passing of a decree authorizing domiciliary visits, which almost invariably led to incarceration of the suspected persons in the Abbaye, La Force, or Les Carmes.

The Commune claimed the right to govern Paris : Vergniaud, in the Assembly, Roland, and even Danton, in the Council, **The Assembly cowed by the Commune.** trembled before it. Its numbers were swelled by the leaders of the Jacobin staff, from Billaud to Chaumette, and it had only left Pétion at the Mairie on condition that he obeyed all its orders ; in vain did Mme. Roland groan over this "mad Commune," which Mme. Jullien herself considered "too haughty," in vain did the Assembly strive to break its power : Danton, though he had but little love for it, saved it. He hoped to bring about a fusion of the two powers : he made an appeal for concord. These two bodies, he declared, must unite their common efforts to overcome the common enemy—threatening Germany. On September 2 the population was to be summoned to the Champ-de-Mars, and a new body of volunteers should be enrolled. " The tocsin that is about to ring is not an alarm-signal : it sounds the charge against the foes of the Fatherland. To over come these, we must dare, and again dare, and without end dare, and so France will be saved."

Danton's apologists affirm that, seeing the populace preparing to descend upon the prisons, he tried to lure it to the Champ-**Danton acquiesces in the proposed Massacres.** de-Mars, there to turn the men who would fain have cut their fellow Frenchmen's throats into soldiers of the Republic. Danton certainly nursed no murderous dreams himself, but he was not blind ; he knew well that murder was being plotted, and that at the first news of any reverse in Lorraine, the massacre would begin ; and, before the news had spread in Paris, he himself had been informed of the capitulation of Verdun.

That neither he, nor Roland, nor Servan, nor Pétion should have had the prisons safely guarded may have been the result in Roland's case, or Servan's, of a most lamentable carelessness : in that of Danton, it can only have been caused by his deliberate complicity. But the elections to the Convention were just coming on : those in Paris were in the hands of the Commune, and Danton was a candidate. The Commune was determined on the massacre as a method of inspiring terror : Danton was determined to be blind. Carnage, indeed, was by no means repugnant to his fierce nature : he would have given orders for the bloodshed, if he had thought it necessary : he allowed it to go forward, believing it to be inevitable : the crime lies heavy on the memory of a man who, in spite of all, was not, as we have seen, an utter monster. Far from preventing the massacres, Danton facilitated the work : he attracted the geniune patriots to the Champ-de-Mars, and left the prisons at the mercy of the dregs of the population. To suppose that he did not see this clearly would be to take him for a fool. There was little of the fool about him.

On the night of September 1 excitement had reached the boiling-point. Our citizeness writes that the populace is waking up : " Well ! Let it have its way ! And *ça ira !* " Danton let it have its way, and *ça alla !*

* * * * *

On the morning of September 2 the surrender of Verdun became known in Paris. The Commune, which had seen the **The Commune** Assembly rise up against it in what had been an **plans the** almost unanimous resistance—for one short hour **Massacres.** —was bent on a " day " which should finally establish its power. And then France was on the brink of an election. Whom would she choose ? *Brissotins*, perhaps, or *Rolandists !* The country must be terrified. Collot confesses : " But for September 2 there would never have been a National Convention "—he meant any Mountain within the Convention.

The popular ferment was great, and legitimate enough. Everything was done to excite it : John Moore heard the orators in the city squares indulging in invectives of the most

284

extraordinary description : according to them there was a traitor hidden beneath every paving-stone in Paris : from Marie-Antoinette, solid as her bonds were, to Mme. Roland, her sworn foe, and little to be suspected of any royalist tendencies, all were hatching treason : the accomplices of "Coblentz" were concealed in every corner. On September 1 a pamphlet was scattered all over the town : *The Great Treason of Louis Capet. Discovery of a plot for assassinating all good citizens during the night between the 2nd and 3rd of this month . . . etc.* The patriots were really beside themselves with terror : they were told that they were to be murdered, so they let murder be done.

In reality the supporters of the Commune were much more anxious to strike at Roland than at the Royalists. Since the Rolands had refused him a grant out of the Secret Service fund Marat had been pouring the vilest abuse upon both husband and wife. He was resolved to strike them down.

For the first time, the odious journalist who had been throwing Paris into a fever for the past three years began to act for himself. On his own authority he installed himself as a member of the "Committee of Surveillance" appointed by the Commune, and from the heights of that Sinaï he spake the law : the men on the Executive Council would let the culprits go free : these culprits must be executed, and, at the same time, such people as the Rolands and Brissot must be suppressed. Marat, whose self-confidence never failed him, signed an order, without the smallest authority for doing so, for the arrest of the Minister of the Interior, Roland.

Meanwhile, the "Sections" were getting under way. La Poissonnière took the initiative : it decreed that "all priests The September or suspected persons in the prisons in Paris, Massacres. Orleans, and elsewhere, were to be put to death." Certain of the other Sections gave in their adhesion, and the Committee of Surveillance promulgated the order for the massacre to begin.

This embodied an "injunction" that the culprits should be tried. On whom did this injunction rest ? On everybody. "Judges" were soon procured : failures in their own lines, such as Dugazon the actor, whose "harsh voice" still rang in

Salamon's ears years and years afterwards : he was the fore·
most of them all, with Maillard, whose reputation had already
been made in connection with the Days of October, and whc
was the principal judge now. He was anything but a
demoniac in appearance. "He arrived wearing a black coat
and with his hair powdered : his face was not repulsive."
These "judges" easily found executioners to carry out their
sentences, Federates from Marseilles, who had no stomach for
the fight on the frontiers. "*Triple nom de D* . . ." shouted
one of them in the presence of Maton de la Varenne. "I've
not come all these 180 leagues to go back without having
stuck 180 heads on the point of my pike !" and the heads
he meant were to be French heads! There were bandits,
too, mixed up among these wretches. Méhée de la Touche
relates real acts of brigandage, theft and pillage ; but
these men swept the humbler part of the populace along with
them. Dr. Cabanès looks on these September days as one
of the most incontestable phenomena of the revolutionary
neurosis, made up of terror, enthusiasm, cruelty, and lust.
The horrible treatment of the Princesse de Lamballe, at
La Force and in the streets, proves the murderers to have been
seized, for a time, with a paroxysm of Sadic fury.

Louis Blanc, who was supposed to have excused the
massacres, repudiated the suggestion that he had tried to
"cover up the blood with sand." We will sprinkle no sand on it
either, but we may say, to the honour of the people of Paris,
that according to the most pessimistic calculation, the actual
murderers did not number more than 150 men. The really
horrible thing is that these 150 wretches—a mere handful—
should have been able to wreak their will for three whole days,
amidst an apparent indifference, born of the terror that had
overwhelmed the Government in the first instance, then the
Assembly, and, finally, the populace.

The "tribunal" proceeded to the Abbaye : the prisoners
were brought before it : some few were liberated, others were
driven out : the murderers were waiting for them, and cut
them down. When all was done, Maillard left the Abbaye.
"There is nothing more here : let us go to Les Carmes." Les
Carmes was full of priests, the Archbishop of Arles among

others. The assassins would have made short work of then
"Wait, wait!" cried Maillard, "don't kill them so fast: w
must try them!" And "try them" he did, in the dark
corridor which still stands. Thus all the prisons were "visited."
There is a list of 1176 murders duly set down: but 438 other
persons likewise disappeared from the prisons at the time, and
may fairly be added to the number of the prisoners "tried"
by Maillard: thus 1614 defenceless beings were put to death:
116 at Les Carmes, 100 at the Conciergerie, 65 at La Force,
73 at the Tower of St. Bernard, 76 at the Seminary of Saint-
Firmin, 223 at the Châtelet, 318 at the Abbaye: and so fierce
was the horrible lust for blood that the monsters even carried
their murders as far as the madhouses of Bicêtre and the
Salpétrière, where scenes of the most abominable description
were enacted. Those which took place in the streets are already
known to our readers: the tearing asunder of the victims'
bodies, the profanation of corpses, the filthy laughter, the
deliberations of the executioners over the writhing bodies
of the dying. The stories told by eye-witnesses must be read:
no summary of such scenes is possible. But here and there
we note a flash or two of human kindness, a proof that among
these bandits there moved some Paris *titis*, ready, as ever, to
put a touch of generous feeling into the drama.

*   *   *   *   *

The Commune had loosed the bloodhounds, or at all events
had let others loose them: Billaud-Varenne had gone to all
The Apologists the prisons, "wading through blood," encourag-
of the ing "the people": "People! you are slaying
Massacres. your enemies! you are doing your duty!" and
taking care that each of Maillard's ruffians should receive
a sum of four-and-twenty *livres*. On the morrow, the Hôtel-
de-Ville was to send out a circular to the Departments, vaunting
the "act of justice which has seemed to it (the People) indispensable for the restraining by terror of the legions of traitors
hidden within its walls, at the very moment when it was about
to march against the enemy," and urging the nation to "adopt
measures so necessary to Public Safety."

Pétion, as usual, played the part of Pontius Pilate. At

an early stage of the massacre, a physician, Dr. Seiffert, came and besought him to save the Princesse de Lamballe, and he replied : "The people of Paris administers its own justice, and I am its prisoner." On the third day the murderers made their appearance at the Mairie. Pétion, who was entertaining Gensonné and Duhem at breakfast, received these blood-stained "workers" : "Monsieur le Maire," they said, "we've despatched those rascals : there are eighty of them left still, what are we to do with them ? " "I am not the person to whom you should apply," he answered in a hollow voice : but he had wine poured out for them to drink.

The terrorized Assembly, too, was *resolved* to be powerless. During the evening of the 2nd, though fully aware that the Attitude of the mob was gathering with the intention of breaking Assembly. open the prison doors, it pretended to know nothing about the matter. It decided to send Commissaries to "speak to the people and restore quiet." Two hours later the Commissaries were back at the Manège acknowledging their impotence. Choudieu reports in his Memoirs that one of the judges at the Abbaye, the comedian Dufraise, said to him, "If you have come to stop the justice of the people it is my duty to tell you your efforts will be vain." Dusaulx, one of the Commissaries, informed the Assembly that "*the darkness did not admit of our seeing what was going on.*"

The Assembly was bent on remaining, if not in this happy state of darkness, at all events in a convenient twilight. Yet the Commune took a cruel delight in keeping it informed of "what was happening," and Tallien added, on his own account, that the prisons contained nothing "but villains." The deputies made up their minds to close the sitting. On the 3rd they did nothing at all. The Mountain had adopted Tallien's theory : it shared the opinion expressed by Mme. Jullien on the 2nd : "I cast . . . a veil over the crimes the people has been driven into committing by all those whose miserable victim it has been for the last two years"; and she further affirmed that, "When one wants a thing one must accept the means that will bring it about : *there must be no barbarous humanity.*" The "Bordelais" were in a state of great emotion : in the course of the evening of the 3rd Gensonné made a request from the rostrum that " the People should be recalled to a sense of its own dignity." A decree was voted calling on the authorities " to ensure respect for individual safety " : the Commissaries deputed to convey this edict to the Sections made the lateness of the hour a pretext for delay (it was ten o'clock), and stayed where they were : the massacre went on all through the night. Even Roland, the virtuous Roland, strove to calm men's scruples. In a letter which, of course, contained a reference to his own " virtues," he went on to say : " Yesterday was a day over the events of which we must perhaps draw a veil. But I know that the People, terrible as its vengeance is, *has yet tempered it with a kind of justice.*" But, indeed, there is something tragic about his affectation at this moment : if the " popular effervescence must be checked," writes the Minister, it is " because *a bad use might be made of it !* " As a matter of fact the Assembly and the Council allowed the bloodshed to continue for five whole days. " The People," writes Couthon coolly on the 6th, " is still exercising its *sovereign justice* in the various prisons in Paris." And indifference seems to have been the general rule. " The assassinations are still going on," writes Morris on the 6th; "the weather is pleasant." "No sign of emotion appears on people's faces," writes an " aristocrat" on the 5th. And yet Fournier l'Américain had put the finishing touch to his illustrious reputation by having fifty-three prisoners, who were being conveyed to Paris from the Orleans prisons, out of which they had been snatched, murdered at Versailles : prisoners of importance, too, for among them two of Louis XVI's former ministers, de Lessart and d'Abancourt, were put to death.

* * * * *

" We lie under the knife of Robespierre and Danton. . . . Danton is the secret leader of the whole horde," writes Mme.

Danton accepts responsibility for the Massacres. Roland on the 5th. Her hatred led her astray. Danton was not the leader. But he was the accomplice. "No power could have stopped them !" he was to say of the massacres. A convenient excuse ! In reality the massacres served his interests tolerably well, and we have already explained how. If any hand could have put a stop to them it would have been his :

but he had no intention of quarrelling with the Commune. The worst of it is that his own "cabinet" compromised him. It was under his signature that Fabre d'Églantine sent round the horrible circular letter which justified the massacres. A certain popular Society (that of Rouen) writes on the 12th that it has received Danton's "official notice": it is quite probable that his signature was surreptitiously obtained. (Mme. Roland herself admits that "he would confide the stamp bearing his signature" to other hands.) And then, not choosing to look as if he had been deceived, he may have preferred to figure as a leader rather than as a dupe, and so have made a cynical boast of having let the murderers loose. "I did it!" he said to the Duc de Chartres. And later, in the Convention, "What do I care if they call me a drinker of blood?" And, indeed, all his party made up their minds, after some hesitation, to extol the business rather than to blame it: Billaud boasted that he had stopped the King o' Prussia: Mme. Jullien asserts, on the 6th, that all that had been done was to prevent a set of wretches from "defiling the earth with the blood of the People." This was the accepted legend: the Federates from Brest wrote home on the 3rd that "circumstances rendered these executions, so to speak, *excusable*"; by the 6th, they thought them *necessary:* "The people has exercised justice in the prisons." One of the most moderate members of the Mountain, Robert Lindet, was to write that all he had perceived was "*an impartial application of the principles of natural law.*"

It is true that this same Lindet, having obtained clearer information on the subject, was to write in the year IX: "*There was no question of a popular movement: everything was ordered beforehand.* . . . I admit that if any one of the three authorities (the Assembly, the Executive Council, the Paris Mayoralty) had *refused* its consent to what was proposed, France would never have been stained by these events." Mature reflection convinces us that this confession on the part of a trustworthy Jacobin legislator of the year 1792 is a very terrible one.

SOURCES. Works already quoted by Beugnot, Barbaroux, Hua, Madame Roland (*Mémoires, Lettres*), Madame Jullien, Dubreuilh, Moore,

DANTON

Couthon, Thiébault, Rabusson-Lamothe, Frénilly, Fournier l'Américain, Morris, Dumas, Choudieu, Salamon, Vaissière, Aulard (*Jacobins*, IV).— Aulard, *Actes du Comité de Salut public* (Conseil Exécutif), I, 1889 ; Barras, *Mémoires*, I, 1895 ; Buzot, *Mémoires*, 1866 ; Marolles, *Lettres d'une Mère*, 1901 ; Barère, *Mémoires*, I, 1842 ; *Lettres des Fédérés brestois* (*Rev. Fr.*, 1897) ; Chardon, *Cahier des procès-verbaux des Jacobins de Rouen*, 1901 ; Chateaubriand, *Mémoires* (Biré ed.), 1898 ; Condorcet, *Œuvres*, I, 1855 ; La Réveillère-Lepeaux, *Mémoires*, I, 1873 ; Garat, *Mémoires*, 1795 ; Miot, *Mémoires*, 1867 ; *Récits des Massacres de Septembre*, re-published by G. Lenôtre, 1910 ; Weber, Marquise de Tourzel, *Souvenirs d'un Vieillard*, Maton de la Varenne, Méhée, Jourgniac de Saint-Méard, the Abbés Berthelet, Vialar, and Sauvin, and the registers of the murderers.

WORKS. Those already quoted by Dard (*Hérault*), Sorel (III), Esmein, Biré, Colfavru, Pingaud, Montier, Charavay, Chuquet (I).—Bougeart, *Danton*, 1861 ; Robinet, *Danton, homme d'état*, 1889 ; Aulard, *Études sur Danton*, Études I, II, IV ; Alméras, *Fabre d'Eglantine*, 1905 ; Madame de Blocqueville, Davoust, 1860 ; Caron, *La Question des Volontaires* (*Rev. Hist. moderne*, 1909) ; Rousset, *Les Volontaires*, 1882 ; Chuquet, II, *Valmy*, 1898 ; Cabanès, *La Névrose révolutionnaire*, 1905 ; A. Dubost, *Danton et les Massacres* (*Rev. Fr.* VII) ; Lenôtre, *Les Massacres de Septembre*, 1909 ; Masson, *Les Massacres de Septembre*, in *Jadis* III, 1909.

CHAPTER XXII

VALMY

The Legislative Body in ruins. The " Thermopylæ " of France.
The knoll at Valmy. The soldiers of the Nation drive back the
" soldiers of Rossbach." " A new era."

THE Assembly lay "crushed beneath the ruins of the
Constitution it had overthrown," writes one of its
members. But it really was crushed beneath the
weight of the massacres it had done nothing to prevent. It
"did hardly any work at all," wrote Couthon on September 8.
The Legislative It lay dying amidst the general scorn. "The
Body in ruins. sight of the Assembly has by no means dazzled
me," said a provincial to the Mayor of Brest. "I could not see
anything majestic about it."

It had scattered ruin all over the face of the fatherland,
and, what made it yet more despicable, perhaps, this ruin was
unintentional. It was the heir of the Constituent Assembly, it
had remained faithful in appearance to the pacific doctrine
of that Assembly, and yet, whether deliberately or not, it had
hurried France into a war for which she was ill-prepared :
on September 19, just before its final dissolution, it was to
learn that the defiles of the Argonne had been forced. A
Constitutional body, it had torn the Constitution to pieces, and,
though it had not desired the Republic, it had permitted the
destruction of the monarchy. The majority of its members
had been moderate men, yet, by its weakness, it had given over
the citizens its decrees had cast into prison, to the hands of
murderers : and Paris, its enemy in spite of all, and eager to
insult it, was about to elect certain of these very murderers
to sit in the new Convention.

Yet the Girondins—as though not content to have thus
destroyed peace, the monarchy, freedom, justice, the Constitu-
292

tion they had sworn to defend, and their own cause, from sheer love of empty phrases or dread of the more violent party—were bent, *in extremis* as they were, on adding yet another ruin to the pile. At its closing sitting on the 20th, the Assembly voted the decree establishing divorce, and in such a form that the home and family, the very corner-stone of France, was, for many a long year, to be cruelly shaken. This we shall realize from 1795 onwards.

And then, amidst the ruin it had wrought, it awaited the advent of that new Assembly which, before many months were out, basing its action on words pronounced from the rostrum of the Legislative Body, was to send the Girondin leaders of the old Assembly to face the Public Prosecutor.

*　　　*　　　*　　　*　　　*

But France, threatened though she was on every side, was not to perish : at the very hour in which, under a gloomy sky The Thermo- (the month of September of that year was ex-pylæ of France. ceedingly rainy) the politicians of the Assembly were declaring the dissolution of their body, young soldiers shod with wooden sabots and clad in blue jackets, soaked to their skins, but with the cheeriest of hearts, were shouting " Long live the Nation ! " while they scaled the western heights of the Argonne which the enemy had held for a short time. It was on September 20 at eleven o'clock that Kellermann, in front of the mill at Valmy, which the Prussian bullets were battering, stuck his hat with its tricolour feather on the point of his sword, and shouted, " Long live France." And France was going to live !

Dumouriez had practically reorganized his army, and this done, had set himself to breathe courage into his men. " Come ! let us be merry ! " he wrote. And with these brisk and vigorous soldiers he had sworn to defend the Argonne, " the Thermopylæ of France." Brunswick might have forced his way through the very day after he took Verdun, but, as always, he was torn between his ideas and his duties, his own plans and those of the King his master. He lost time : and, meanwhile, his army, ravaged by dysentery—that celebrated *courée prussienne*, which was to be the joke of the Meuse country for many a long year—was growing strangely demoralized. The *courée* had a good dea to do with it, but the behaviour of the Lorrainers did its part as well : the Prussian officers, who had expected, on the strength of what the *émigrée* had told them, to enter a country ready to surrender, found all the people they came across strong in their resolve to "keep their Revolution." "The devil take this war !" wrote one Prussian officer, "why on earth have we mixed ourselves up in these quarrels, which are no business of ours ? " This state of feeling embittered the relations between the Germans and the *émigrés*, and, further, the Prussians, who saw that the Austrians were besieging the fortresses in Flanders, were daily becoming more convinced that Vienna, the object of their hearty detestation, was making the King of Prussia pull the chestnuts out of the fire. As dirty " as pigs," soaked with rain, its health disordered, its courage damped, the "formidable infantry of Prussia " was marching with uncertain steps, and the officers of the Staff were grumbling. Brunswick took all this to be a further reason for hastening slowly.

Kellermann seized the opportunity to march, in his turn, on the Argonne : leaving Metz, he moved along the enemy's left flank, by Bar-le-Duc, and on the 18th he reached a spot to the rear of the " Pass of Thermopylæ." It was high time : the Germans had forced their way through at two points, and Dumouriez was reckoning on the Metz army to re-establish his position. He it was who urged Kellermann— recalcitrant at first—to occupy the plateau of Valmy, the spur of the mountain-chain running out into the Champagne country, and so cut the Prussians off from the road to Paris.

On that small plateau, on September 20, Kellermann deployed his little army under a drizzling rain, just opposite **The victory at** the plateau of La Lune on which Massenbach **Valmy.** had established his Prussian batteries. These had been plunged in fog : when it lifted the Germans caught sight for the first time of the tricolour flags waving over troops who presented a steady front to the enemy.

Brunswick felt uneasy : he put off the regular engagement, tried the effect of a discharge from the big guns, which did not seem to stagger the French troops, and, finally, consented to allow his infantry to advance. The French soldiers were singing the *Ça ira* and the *Marseillaise,* waving their hats, shouting "*Long live the Nation.*" And the French gunners now began to send a hail of shot upon the Germans. The Prussians fell into confusion. They were overwhelmed with sheer surprise. These "tailors and cobblers" in blue jackets could aim and fire accurately, and besides, their enthusiasm produced its effect. Suddenly Brunswick turned to the King of Prussia and suggested that the fighting should cease. The rain was coming down in torrents by this time, and he made it his pretext. Frederick William complied. The Prussians had acknowledged themselves beaten—morally at all events.

Thus the Frenchmen had won the day. So great had been the firmness displayed by the troops of the Nation that the last **Disillusionment of the Prussians.** of the Prussian illusions had been swept away. These vagabonds had kept the soldiers of the great Frederick in check. Brunswick, who had always advised against the advance, his officers, most of whom disliked the Austrian alliance, and hated the *émigrés,* the men, who were worn out with sickness, and the King himself, who realized at last that he had made a false step when he had insisted on marching on Paris, felt, every one of them, from the highest to the lowest, that they had suffered a sharp rebuff. The country was not safe, the French troops were steady, the *émigrés* had lied, and while the Prussians had been moving imprudently along the road to Paris, with the chance of being crushed before they got there, Austria was threatening and bombarding the fortresses of the North, and would certainly enlarge her borders in Flanders. Every suspicion, every old rancour lifted up its head once more. Before long Prussia was to beat a hasty retreat. She had reckoned on an easy victory : and as so often happens, she passed from her over-presumptuous mood to one of exaggerated despondency.

But our soldiers, excited by their partial success, made it— like Goethe among the Germans—the point of departure of a **Moral Effect of Valmy.** new era. There was no need for Dumouriez to incite them to a joyous confidence : they were sure of themselves, now : The Great Nation, capable of the conquest of a world, was to leap from the knoll of Valmy.

And the sittings of the Convention were about to begin—

that Convention which, amidst the most frightful tempests, was to create, with the help of these enthusiastic soldiers, soon to become hardened warriors, the splendid nucleus of "the fourteen armies of the Republic."

SOURCES. Works already quoted by Madame Roland (*Mémoires, Lettres*), Buzot, Barbaroux, Dumas, Couthon, the Brest Federates, Aulard (*Jacobins*, IV); Aulard (*Actes*, I); Carnot, *Correspondance*, published by Charavay.

WORKS. Those already quoted by Cahen, Charavay, Chuquet, Albert Sorel, Chassin, and Hennet, *Les Volontaires Nationaux*, 1899-1906; Picard, *Valmy* (*Revue de Paris*, 1908).

PART III
THE NATIONAL CONVENTION

CHAPTER XXIII

THE " GIANT ASSEMBLY "

The elections of 1792. Tendencies and characteristics of the
Assembly. The Girondins. The Mountain. The Marais. " The
political arena."

BETWEEN September 5 and September 20 the Convention issued from the electoral urns. In Paris only was there any passionate interest in the struggle, for only in Paris did two parties stand face to face : " Robespierre's party has sworn the destruction of Brissot "—the words were written on the 5th.

A violent campaign had been carried on against the " Brissotins." Collot had given the watchword to the democrat electors : " men who are too much inclined to think they belong to a superior species must not be elected." This was a direct blow at Brissot and Condorcet, the two outgoing deputies for Paris.

The Elections of 1792.

September 5 itself had brought certainty with it : out of 525 votes, 338 had been cast for Robespierre, whereas Pétion, suspected of " Brissotism "—" pure gold changed into vile lead "—only obtained 136. The next day Danton was elected by 638 out of 700 voters. And each succeeding day had brought fresh triumphs to the Jacobin extremists : Marat was elected, then came the turn of the great men of the Commune, Collot, Billaud, and even the very murderers, Tallien, Panis : the last of all these " Romans " (as Mme. Jullien dubs them with unconscious irony) to obtain election was Citizen Egalité, descendant of Saint-Louis, and one of the candidates of the Commune. " An execrable set of deputies," writes La Révellière, a Girondin. In spite of Mme. Roland's feigned optimism, it was with a pen

Triumph of the Jacobin Extremists.

299

tremulous with fury that she wrote, "The choice made by the departments reassures us ! " Her husband and her friend Buzot had, indeed, both been elected to fill provincial seats, and Condorcet, though defeated in Paris, had been chosen by five country departments.

There was no evidence of struggle in the provinces. How should there have been any struggle ? There was no electoral programme. *The question of the Republic* was brought forward in Paris only : the department of Seine-et-Oise had been the only one which charged its representatives to demand "the deposition." The royalists, terrorized or banished, seemed to have vanished into space : but the real truth was that the provinces, which were still devoted to the monarchy, evaded the question. There was great talk, on the other hand, about "*securing the rights of property.*" Rabaut notes, on September 21, that "most of the departments have made a point of sending up deputies who are land-owners because of the terror inspired by the doctrine of spoliation."

So these new deputies were really conservatives of a kind. But most of them, being compromised by the Revolution, and now dependent on it, were to spend their lives between two terrors, *that of a counter-revolution attended by reprisals, and that of a social revolution that would dispossess them.*

Tendencies and Characteristics of the Assembly.

A great deal of terror and very few ideas. The Constituent Assembly had been over full of these, the Convention seemed to have none at all. These members of the Convention were all opportunists and realists : circumstance alone was to guide their steps. And they were to guide them to self-mutilation : between the expulsion of the Girondins and the fall of Robespierre, the average number of deputies present at the debates was to be something between 220 and 250 out of a total of 750. In 1792 there was no ruling principle whatever. The monarchy was only abolished by confirming "the deposition " : nobody dared to proclaim the Republic. We are inclined to wonder whether there were ten Republicans sitting in the Manège ! If they were anything at all these jurists were Cæsarians. The Constitution of the year VIII was to be their Promised Land. There was to be no fundamental alteration in them when they became functionaries (and often very good functionaries) under Napoleon.

Nor was there any clearer view as to the relations between Church and State : most of the deputies were anti-Catholic : " The moment has come," said Manuel, "*to unnail Jesus Christ !* " This was much like the programme put forward by Voltaire—a vague one. These men hardly dreamt of such a thing as separation between Church and State in 1792, and were only to make it, in the end, for the sake of a few millions of money. Their original idea, most probably, was simply what Fouché wrote to Condorcet : " Treat the parish priests with consideration and keep an eye upon them at the same time ! There was no conception, either, of a foreign policy : the member of the Convention of 1792 had no feeling either in favour of "*the natural frontiers*" or against them. He was to adopt, and reject, and re-adopt that doctrine, according to circumstances.

There was one idea only in 1792, and that was to stand out against all "*levelling*" theories. This explains why Robespierre, who was a tepid Republican, a great advocate of gentle treatment for the priests, and a great defender of the rights of property, but an opportunist on almost every occasion, was to dominate this Assembly so long.

To make up for the lack of ideas there was an assortment of grudges. The great majority arrived full of hostility against the Paris Commune, and, generally speaking, against "the Dictatorship of Paris." The newcomers' letters are very explicit on this head. This state of feeling at first secured a following to the Girondin leaders, who were returning to Paris hot with rage against the city which had cast them out.

The " Gironde "—the word was beginning to be used currently—seemed to have gained strength, but fate drove it **The Girondins.** in its turn to the benches of the Right. Yet these men were not less republican and anti-clerical than Robespierre—far from it. But they hated the revolutionary Commune, and so became the hope of all the elements of order. If they had been content to attack the Commune only ! But Mme. Roland's friends joined her in a chorus of vituperation levelled at "that city nourished on blood and lies " ; their adversaries replied that Paris had made the Revolution, and that therefore any one who fought against Paris was a bad patriot, a bad Republican—before long a Federalist. Further, the dictatorship of Paris was the only thing, so the members of the Mountain were convinced, to ensure the unity of the country : it alone would make it possible to set up that Government of Public Safety which the foreign war then raging, and the civil war that was soon to follow it, would certainly necessitate : the Girondins shrank from this Dictatorship of Public Safety, which was to authorize the establishment of the Terror : there lay the root of the quarrel. But when circumstances made this dictatorship indispensable, those who had always commended the idea triumphed, and any man who had stood out against it, or only resigned himself unwillingly to its existence, was either thrust aside or crushed outright. This was the real story of this terrible rivalry.

How many were there of these Girondins, whom we know already, having seen them on the benches of the last Assembly ? They were never sure of this themselves. They did not form a " group," in the parliamentary sense of the word : they used to gather at social meetings, some of them in Mme. Roland's house, some in Mme. de Condorcet's : a certain enemy of theirs declares that one of his colleagues never voted with the Right except just after he had left one or other of these Egerias. It was a curious flock, kept together solely by these feminine hands. M. Aulard calculates that about 165 deputies may really be called Girondins.

They did not agree on every point. Vergniaud was much inclined to support union between all Republicans : in the course of the King's trial he carried this idea to the length of himself capitulating at the last : on the other hand, the small group known as "Rolandists" detested the Mountain : Buzot, Barbaroux, and Louvet, all of them directly influenced by Mme. Roland, were the bitter enemies of the deputies of the Commune. Condorcet, again, was a follower of Voltaire, and Lanjuinais was an avowed Catholic. Almost all these men— tenors from Marseilles and Bordeaux, philosophers and writers —possessed a certain amount of talent, and thus constituted the very worst staff imaginable for practical purposes—a staff of original personalities.

* * * * *

Over against the Gironde sat the terrible Mountain. We have defined its policy in opposing it to that of the Gironde. An exceedingly empiric policy : a collective dictatorship, the nation placed in a state of siege, all opposition to be crushed, the country to be forced into " regeneration," and pending that, into submission to the law of Public Safety : an inhuman policy, but one which circumstances were to justify. This policy was the one bond of union of a party even more heterogeneous than that of its opponents.

The Mountain.

In the earlier sittings Danton was its most prominent figure : we know him already. Near him sat his " cabinet," Desmoulins and Fabre d'Eglantine, both of them elected by Paris with "the master" : Camille, his face blotched with bilious humours, his eyes flashing under his heavy eyebrows, with his bitter tongue, his merciless pen, his hesitating speech ; Fabre—called " the immortal author of *Philinte* " by the *Vieux Cordelier*—the poet of " *Il pleut, bergère !* " a dubious figure, a disquieting mortal, who was to compromise his whole group by his endeavours to secure the profits his *Philinte* had failed to bring him, by trafficking in army stores. With the Danton triumvirate we see Hérault de Séchelles, " the Alcibiades of the Mountain," a sceptic who was wont to say he belonged to " the party that snapped its fingers at the others," but a good speaker, with a fine manner, a pupil of Demosthenes and of Mlle. Clairon.

Robespierre, too, was to gather a few friends about him : he was coming back, as the chief representative of Paris, to that Hall in which he had been so often flouted between 1789 and 1791. Was it this humiliating memory that kept him so silent and reserved for several weeks, though always correct and well-nigh elegant in his blue coat ? Beside this prophet sat a fanatic, the ex-" Chevalier " de Saint-Just, the Benjamin of the party and of the Assembly, cold as the executioner's steel ; a hateful youth, who knew not how to smile, but who had talent and will, and a confidence in his own powers at which Desmoulins did wrong to jeer, for his jeers cost him his head. The master's other lieutenant was Couthon, a pitiful cripple, afflicted with all sorts of complaints, whom we see in his little carriage, groaning and toiling, and who was to help dig the graves of those two handsome fellows, Hérault and Barbaroux.

On the " crest " of the Mountain, and kept at a prudent distance by his neighbours, we note a Mediterranean half-breed, deliberately sordid and evil-smelling, with olive skin and black locks escaping from the bandanna handkerchief soaked with vinegar, worn to alleviate headaches of the most unendurable description : this was Jean-Paul Marat, the very antithesis of Robespierre, with his neatly powdered head; a man whose violence sometimes verged on insanity, as a rule quarrelsome, cynical, and cunning. For ten whole months he was rarely applauded, save from the galleries—for was he not *the People's Friend ?*

These were the most prominent figures : all about them a strange medley of men : Stanislas Fréron, a King's godson ; the Marquis de Rovère, first a Terrorist, then a reactionary ; the despicable Tallien, whose father had been a lackey ; Collot-d'Herbois and Billaud-Varennes, whom we shall see again later : but scattered among these devotees of violence we find a capable accountant and merchant from the South, Cambon ; Carnot, an austere soldier ; the illustrious David, a great artist and a shallow politician ; Lepelletier, ex-President of the Chamber, a multi-millionaire bent on saving his stakes ; Anacharsis Clootz, a German baron, nicknamed *Canard Six* by the Faubourgs ; Chabot, the ex-Capuchin monk, who was always talking about virtue but never practised it ; and close to Marat, that unworthy Bourbon, soon to be a regicide, " Philip the Red," the " Citizen Egalité."

*　　　*　　　*　　　*　　　*

Between these two parties lay the Centre, amorphous, irresolute, silent: *the Plain*, it was called, or *the Marsh*. It
The Plain or supplied the majorities, floating hither and
Marsh (Centre). thither, driven to and fro by perpetual apprehensions. " Upright deputies," says Durand de Maillane, of his colleagues of the Centre, " *who, like myself, remained motionless*
304

during evil deliberations." Sieyès, Cambacérès, Boissy d'Anglas, and a hundred more, who later became notable, " lived on," as one of them described it. Robespierre, sickened by the dissolute and disorderly ways of his own neighbours, cast a not unfriendly eye on this Plain, whereon so many worthy citizens lived and voted in a silence born of lacerated hearts and terrified minds, "motionless during evil deliberations."

They were to watch their neighbours on either side tear each other to pieces : and after Right and Left alike had been decimated, they were to lay their hands on the Republic at last, after Thermidor the 9th, and provide it with a sensible Constitution, and a franchise based on a reasonable property qualification.

For the moment the Convention, as they saw it, was " an arena "—as Fockedey, one of the members of the Convention The political termed it—and they sat to watch the " gladiators " Arena. cut each other's throats.

An arena indeed ! death was to be the fate of those who entered it : for there were no mere opponents, but avowed enemies : and these enemies were to proclaim each other "factious persons " or " wretches."

One and the same feeling lay at the root of all this fury. Standing on ground that was shaken by a perpetual earthquake, these men, who felt themselves every day in greater jeopardy, lived under the terror of a perpetual menace. A mighty fever devoured them, and was to end by driving them into delirium. So on they marched, without any settled plan to guide them. Thanks to strange labours, of which these *bourgeois* with their somewhat narrow ideas little dreamed when they came to take their seats at the Manège on September 21 they were to bend a rebellious country to their will and vanquish the whole of Europe.

SOURCES. Works already quoted by Madame Roland (*Mémoires, Lettres*), Beugnot, Choudieu, Louvet, Buzot, Morris, Pinet, Barère, Dubreuilh, Grégoire, Madame Jullien, Barbaroux, Barras, Soubrany, John Moore.—Aulard (*Jacobins*, IV–V, 1892, 1895) ; Durand de Maillane, *Histoire*, 1825 ; Baudot, *Notes*, 1893 ; Lanjuinais, *Œuvres*, 1860 ; Dulaure, *Esquisse*, 1823 ; Fockedey, *Souvenirs* (*Rev. Rev.*, III and IV) ; Le Bon, *Lettres* (*Rev. Retr.*, XVIII, 1903) ; Rabaut, *Notes* (*Rev. Fr.*, 1902) ; Levasseur de la Sarthe, *Mémoires*, 1829–81.

THE FRENCH REVOLUTION

WORKS. Those already quoted by Sorel (III), Biré, Sagnac, Esmein, Dard (*Hérault*), Claretie (*Desmoulins*), Cahen, Arnaud, Almeras, Pingaud, Guadet, Robinet, Bonald, Hérissay (*Buzot*).—Aulard, *Les Orateurs de la Convention*, 1886 ; Claretie, *Les derniers Montagnards*, 1868 ; Bougeart, *Marat*, 1765 ; Cabanès, *Maret inconnu*, 1891 ; Turquan, *Madame Tallien*, 1890 ; Louis Madelin, *Fouché*, 1901 ; Frédéric Masson, *Romme* (in *Jadis*, II, 1908) ; Mautouchet, *Le Mouvement électoral de Paris en août et Septembre 1792* (*Rev. Fr.*, 1908).

CHAPTER XXIV

THE ASSAULTS OF THE GIRONDINS

September—December 1792

The proclamation of the Republic. The Gironde against Paris. Successive desultory attacks on Marat, Danton, and Robespierre. Louvet's accusation. The Mountain stands together. The conquests on the frontiers. Dumouriez and the Gironde. The Girondins apparent masters of the situation.

" NOTHING new to-day, *except that the Convention has met and declared that there shall be no more King*," writes Morris on September 21. His tone is flippant, if not ironic.

On the previous evening, in fact, the 871 deputies who had reached Paris had come to the conclusion that their number Proclamation warranted them in taking their places. At that of the Republic. moment the Girondins seemed to be in a majority : Pétion was elected President by 235 votes, Robespierre only obtaining 6. All the elected secretaries were prominent Girondins, from Brissot to Vergniaud. " Our Paris deputies dare not open their mouths," wrote Mme. Jullien on October 7.

On the 21st the Assembly, by a unanimous vote, proclaimed *the sanctity of property*. But it seemed less decided to proclaim the Republic. After a great deal of hesitation the decree for the abolition of royalty was passed. But there was no positive proclamation of the Republic, which " slipped in furtively," as Robespierre was to admit. As, however, the Assembly declared *the Republic one and indivisible* on the 25th, we are forced to the conclusion that it did exist.

The extreme coldness with which the event was received in the provinces proves how little republican feeling there really was in the country. " The Assembly," as M. Aulard

807

wittily writes, "seems to have said, 'There is nothing else to be done.'" The nation was even less categoric.

Meanwhile Danton seemed to be giving the law to the Executive Council : though he had been elected a deputy, The Gironde he still (quite illegally) retained his portfolio : against Paris. Roland, as a protest, had ceased to attend the Council, a course which only gave it over into the "Cyclops'" hands. But husband and wife were making a covert attack on Danton and his friends in the *Sentinelle* through the medium of their semi-official journalist, Louvet. Danton replied, and on the 29th he denounced the interference of Citizeness Roland in public affairs coarsely enough from the rostrum.

Mme. Roland was embittered : her home-life had been miserable since Roland had begun to turn a suspicious eye on the "beloved" Léonard Buzot. "Cato" had never been attractive : he was becoming unendurable : he was gloomy and splenetic : Mme. Roland alone ascribed his jaundiced state to the September massacres. She, too, was beginning to flinch : Marat and Hébert were dragging her through the mud : her one cry was for vengeance on the wretches, "villains," whom she longed to overthrow, from Danton to Marat !

As Paris seemed to support these wretches, she stirred up all the Rolandist deputies against the city and the Commune : Lasource exclaimed that it was time Paris should be reduced to its "eighty-third share of influence," and some departments offered to come up and protect the representatives of the nation against the "monster." This threw the Mountain into a fury. "The Senate," wrote one of its female supporters, "must have two sentinels only—Justice and Love !" No doubt ! But, in face of the attitude of Marat's followers, it was not surprising that the Right should have desired to strengthen the hands of those two estimable divinities by the addition of a few sturdy Girondin Federates.

The misfortune was that the Girondins, burning with zeal though they were, had no regular plan of campaign. Paris filled them with suspicion : the Commune was anathema to them ; Marat sickened them ; Danton terrified them ; Robespierre exasperated them with his hypocrisy. But Paris and the Commune were two separate things : there was no love lost between Danton and Robespierre : and both detested Marat. The Girondins should have made up their minds **Successive** which foe they would attack, and not have **desultory** flown first at one and then at the other, thus **attacks on the** constraining their enemies to join forces. Each **Jacobins.** member of the party acted as his personal antipathies prompted, and obliged the " enemies " to stand shoulder to shoulder.

As Marat was odious to everybody alike, a beginning was made with him. There he sat, alone on his bench, **Marat's** like one plague-stricken; he cared not a whit, **Defence.** called his colleagues " idiots " and " swine," and finally *bourgeois*. Jeering and sordid, he mounted the rostrum : " Down with you ! " shouted his opponents. " I have many personal enemies in this Assembly," he began. " All of us ! " shouted the Right. " I recall them to a sense of decency : I exhort them to refrain from their furious clamour and unseemly threats against a man who has done more service to liberty and to themselves than they think ! " The demagogue's ready and justifiable thrust astonished his audience : he gained a hearing, and his brazen impudence cowed the Assembly and foiled the attack.

The Right seemed to drop him then, and turn upon a still stronger adversary : on October 18 Roland, with an affected care for the minutiæ of business, submitted his accounts to the Chamber, and his friends forthwith asked for those of Danton, clearly hinting their lack of confidence in his honesty. Twelve days later Danton was once more indicted for the September massacres. He showed a brave front, made no excuses, rather accepted the responsibility by way of clearing the ground. " I say that no throne was ever shattered without some worthy citizens being wounded by the fragments ! . . ." So powerful were his eloquence and his brutality that his accusers' mouths were closed.

Then Louvet flew at Robespierre : even to his own friends this *Robespierride* of October 29 came as a surprise. It grew **Louvet accuses** out of the previous debate. When Roland, in **Robespierre.** his report on the massacres, asserted that some persons were even daring to demand " a fresh letting of blood," the Right turned hostile eyes on Robespierre. He changed colour. "Nobody," he exclaimed, "will dare to accuse me to my face!" Quivering with hatred, Louvet sprang to the rostrum: "I! Yes, Robespierre! *I accuse you* of having slandered, for a long time, the purest of the patriots . . . *I accuse you* of having continually put yourself forward as an object of idolatry. . . . *I accuse you* of having evidently aimed at the supreme power. . . . etc."

These accusations were absolutely vague, and Robespierre did not appear by any means formidable to such men as Vergniaud. He gave no support to Louvet's attack. "A huge mistake," writes the latter in his Memoirs, "to spare Robespierre was to invite our own ruin." Robespierre, indeed (who seemed somewhat out of countenance), asked a few days law to prepare his defence, and made a skilful answer, full of humility, about a week later. But he took his revenge at the Jacobin Club, from which he caused Brissot, in the first place, then Louvet, and finally Roland himself, to be expelled.

From that time forward the Mountain thus hastily and unsuccessfully attacked, stood shoulder to shoulder, and began **The Mountain** to prepare its own assault. This seemed a for- **concentrates** midable undertaking, for the Girondins, in spite of **its Forces.** their tactical errors, still preserved an appearance of strength. Danton had been obliged to leave the Council at last: Garat, now Minister of Justice, was to become his adherent, but for a time the Rolands believed he was their friend. Pétion had left the Mairie, and two moderate men, Lefebvre d'Ormesson and Chambon, followed him there successively. The Girondin press, directed by Gorsas, Brissot, Louvet, and Carra, seemed to be leading public opinion. The Assembly somewhat absurdly admitted Mme. Roland, on whom an attack had been made, to the honours of the sitting. The Gironde, which ruled the Committee on the Constitution, had deputed Condorcet to draft a Constitution of the most democratic nature, which, once it was voted, would certainly earn its authors the people's gratitude. Finally the chief leader of the nation's troops, Dumouriez, belonged to the party, and his triumphs seemed destined to increase its strength.

* * * * *

ASSAULTS OF THE GIRONDINS

Now Dumouriez was the hero of the hour. He had just carried out his plan for the conquest of Belgium, and the aureole of glory still shone about his head. "You'll see how those little cocks will strut now," wrote a Prussian the day after the battle of Valmy; "*we have lost more than a battle!*"

Conquests on the Frontier.

And, indeed, the Prussians did seem to have suffered more than a defeat. Brunswick, as we know, had obtained the King's leave to retire. All of a sudden Berlin became aware that a second partition of Poland between Austria and Russia was being arranged behind her back. The Hohenzollern took alarm and beat a hasty retreat.

Dumouriez, all for leaving a " golden bridge to the beaten foe," had no desire to fight a battle in Lorraine : his hatred of Austria inspired him with an almost friendly feeling for the Prussians : he did not wish to humiliate them, he even generously offered them, as the price of an alliance with France, all that part of Silesia still in Austrian hands. The one thing he longed to do was to go and "spend the carnival in Brussels."

The Prussians really seemed panic-stricken. They abandoned Verdun without drawing a sword, Longwy without striking a blow, and were back across the frontier on the 20th.

And already the French troops were occupying not Belgium only, but Mayence, Porrentruy, Geneva, Savoy, and the county of Nice, and overrunning Europe in every direction.

Custine, Biron's lieutenant, had made a bold dash upon the Rhine—that river in which the French warrior of every epoch has longed to water his horse. Enterprising, rough, presumptuous, believing himself as good a diplomatist as he was a strategist, trusted by his men, who were amused by his fierce and hairy countenance, " General Moustache," as they called him, had hoped to strike terror into the hearts of the Princes of the Empire, and of the King of Prussia himself, by carrying the war up to the banks of the Rhine. He declared he had been summoned by the " Rhenish patriots," proclaimed that he was bringing "freedom" with him, occupied Spires, Worms, and on October 24, Mayence, and pushed on to Frankfort, where he levied heavy contributions.

While this was going on, Montesquiou had invaded
Savoy. He entered Chambéry, where the magistrates hailed him
Annexation of as a liberator. Within a very short time the
Savoy and Assembly of the Allobroges was convoked, and
Nice. offered the country to France. The people of
Nice followed this example ; they were conquered by Anselme,
and sued for annexation. Intoxicated with all this success,
the Executive Council already dreamt of proceeding to Turin,
there to consummate the ruin of the " King of the Marmots "
whom Paris was lampooning : pretexts were advanced for
threatening the "Patriciate of Genoa" and the " Pope of
Rome " in their respective cities, and while Geneva accepted
a kind of protectorate at the hands of Montesquiou, Porrentruy
—the first step on the road to Basle—had been occupied by the
troops of the Republic.

*   *   *   *   *

The Convention was embarrassed by the questions arising
out of this rapid series of successes. It had no time to build
up any kind of doctrine. Was it to adhere to that enunciated
by the Constituent Assembly on the May 22, 1790, when, with
a solemnity which my readers will recollect, it "*repudiated
all conquest*" ? Danton himself seemed to oscillate between the
policy of principles and the policy of audacity. Was the country
to enter on those great adventures which seemed to promise it
glory ? Glory has to be bought with a price : was the Republic
just proclaimed to expose itself to the risk of bringing forth a
Cæsar or a Monk ?

Dumouriez, who would have been quite ready to play the
part of either of those personages, was for the moment debarred
Dumouriez from doing so. He was anxious, first, to show
and the some victory other than the tentative campaign in
Girondins. the Argonne. His heart was set on getting leave
to hurry his troops on Brussels. That would be a fine reply to
the siege of Lille. This town, according to the words of the
Commissaries of the Convention (October 5, 1792) had "lived
under a vault of bullets," and had not surrendered : the
" cannibal who was bombarding Lille has retired at last,"
writes Couthon on October 11, and Le Bas assures us " everybody is wild with joy."

ASSAULTS OF THE GIRONDINS

In the midst of these rejoicings Dumouriez arrived in Paris, his head full of plans. It was as a " patriot " that he desired to conquer Brussels ; it was as a disgusted citizen that he proposed to make use of his eventual victory to restore order in France.

Unaware of his secret intentions, the Girondins gave him their support. He coaxed Mme. Roland into forgiving him his " treachery," by casting a bunch of red roses at her feet, with the smile of a *cavaliere servente*. He was the " conqueror of the Prussians," she wrote ; her heart was touched. Sometimes in her house, sometimes in Julie Talma's, he met the members of the group, and accepted their homage. In Julie's house in the Rue Chantereine especially, there were brilliant evening gatherings, at which Madame Candeille, Madame Vestris, and Madame Fusil were the delight of an eager circle, which feverishly discussed the fate of the Republic and the conquest of Europe to the tinkling of a harp in the intervals of dances. The Clubs took alarm : Marat came down to the Rue Chantereine and hunted out the General in the most boorish fashion. It is inevitable to recall in this connection, that in this very house—which was to pass, some three years later, into the possession of Joséphine de Beauharnais—the *coup d'état* of the 18th Brumaire was to be elaborated. In October 1792 Dumouriez was planning conquests that were to enable him to confiscate the power of the Republic in the very rooms where, in the month of Vendémiaire of the Year VIII, regicide deputies and victorious generals were to accept the advent of Cæsar. But in those autumn days of 1792, the time was not yet ripe.

Dumouriez was given full powers to conquer Belgium ; he started, and Belgium was conquered within a month : Conquest of Belgium. Dumouriez moved forward on October 28 with 78,000 men : on November 6 he came upon the white-coated troops of Austria before Mons, and, after a magnificent engagement, carried the heights of Jemmapes. This was the first great victory won by the Republic. On the 14th the General was before Brussels, whence a terrible panic had driven the Austrian government and the French *émigrés* pell-mell a few hours before; on the 15th he entered the town ; on the 28th he was at Liége ; while the gates of Antwerp were opened to admit Miranda, one of his lieutenants. Deputies assembled at Brussels proclaimed the fall of the House of Austria, and sent delegates to Paris to plead for the independence of their country.

* * * * *

The Convention was doubtful. The Savoyards, the men of Nice, the men of Mayence, had all sued for union with France : the Belgians prayed for liberty. Was the policy of aggrandizement to be pursued or not ?

Jemmapes had stirred the country's pride : Vergniaud, indeed, regarded it as " the victory of humanity " : and it was in the midst of great emotion that the following decree, big with consequences, was voted : " *France will grant her help to all peoples who desire to recover their liberty.*" The Assembly was sincere when it thus led the country in the name of freedom to take so vast a step towards domination.

Domination was what the Jacobins wanted : it suited their temperament and served their ends. Parties had suddenly changed places. In the spring of 1792 the Girondins had wished for war : it was sweeping them onwards now, yet they already felt it would be made a pretext for the establishment of the " Public Safety," and this thought filled them with alarm. On the other hand, Robespierre's followers, who had once opposed the war, now looked on its prolongation and extension with a most friendly eye. The annexation of Belgium, of Mayence, and of Savoy would perpetuate the condition of war for many a year, but this state of war would bring about a state of siege, and a state of siege meant the rule of the party of violence. Though Dumouriez was advocating a simple recognition of the independence of Belgium, the Jacobins flooded the country with agents of their own, who had orders to pave the way for annexation.

This did not suffice them : Holland, it was said, " was aspiring after liberty " ; that country, too, must be invaded—
Proposed still in the name of freedom. In reality the
Annexation of Mountain had accepted the theory of the " natural
Belgium and frontiers." When the " Allobroge " deputies came
Holland. to offer the country of Savoy to France, Grégoire,
who was appointed to report on the subject, concluded in favour of the union. Having " *consulted the archives of Nature,*"

he asserted on November 27 that " *France could have no frontiers but the Pyrenees, the Alps, and the Rhine!* " This seemed likely to lead the country into an undertaking of some magnitude !

For the theory, as a matter of fact, involved not only the annexation of Savoy, but that of Belgium too, and the invasion of Holland into the bargain. Now none of these things could be permitted by England. The Cabinet at St. James's was shortly to affect a profound interest in the captive Louis XVI, but not until Antwerp was occupied by the Republic. What would happen when Amsterdam was seen to be in danger ?

The Mountain insisted on having Belgium and Holland. Cambon drew attention to the empty coffers of the Treasury : the wealthy Low Countries would have to pay regular taxes. The Jacobin financier did certainly veil this practical policy of his with very showy pretexts, but the fact remains, that the question of domination was at bottom a question of money. On December 15, the Assembly passed a decree whereby the conquered peoples were placed under the guardianship of France : the guardian was too needy not to have made a careful choice of wealthy wards. Thus the annexation of conquered Belgium was decided, and, in addition, the conquest of Holland.

This fresh invasion was confided to Dumouriez. The Girondins lauded the General to the skies, and on his account The Girondins accepted the policy of conquest. When the seem Masters Assembly decided on January 13 to institute a of the Situation. Committee of Defence, they took possession of it, just as they had taken possession of the Committee on the Constitution.

Thus, in the early days of 1793, they seemed masters of the situation. The Mountain had hoped to give the country a Constitution, but the Gironde had taken possession of " Sinaï." The Mountain had pushed on the war; the Gironde had the direction of it. But the Mountain was waiting its opportunity, and was to hasten it : the trial of the King was to cut the Girondin party into halves and hand it over to its enemies. A war to the knife, the germ of which lay in the decree of December 15, was to do the rest.

ASSAULTS OF THE GIRONDINS

SOURCES. Works already quoted by Aulard (*Jacobins*, IV, and *Actes du Comité de Salut public*, I, II), Schmidt, Vaissière, Couthon, Rahaut, Dubreuilh, Madame Jullien, Morris, Madame Roland (*Mémoires, Lettres*), Fockedey, Buzot, Durand de Maillane, Dulaure, Louvet, Louise Fusil; *Lettres de Le Bas* (in Stéphane Pol's *Autour de Robespierre*, already quoted) ; *Constitution Girondine* (text in *Rev. Fr.*, 1898).

WORKS. Those already quoted by Cahen, Rigaud, Chuquet (II), Sorel (III), Dard, Esmein, Hérissay.—Colin, *La Campagne de 1793*, 1902 ; Bord, *La proclamation de la République* (*Rev. Rev.*, II and III) ; Lenôtre, *Pache*, in *Vieux Papiers*, I, 1907.

CHAPTER XXV

THE DEATH OF THE KING

December 1792—January 1793

The King's trial, and the struggle between the two parties. The trial. The question of an appeal to the People. Pressure. The ballot. The vote of January 17. Louis XVI on the scaffold. The results of January 21.

DID the Girondins desire to save the King? "Yes!" says Guadet; "No!" says Biré. Both are right and both wrong, because each presupposes the Gironde to have been a homogeneous party. Now this very incident of the King's trial shows us how divided the Gironde really was. Out of the thirty-six members proscribed in June 1793—all the chief men of the party—only six voted simply and clearly in favour of the death-sentence: ten others supported it on condition it was suspended, and twelve voted for detention. And these are the figures of the terrible ballot of January 16 and 17. Between November and January the pressure of events must have told on vacillating wills.

The Struggle between the two Parties over the King's trial.

A careful study of the event convinces us that in November 1792, the Girondin leaders did really desire to save the King. But to this battle, as to its predecessor, they marched without discipline, without a single fixed idea, compromised by the previous declarations of certain of their number, and shaken by their fear of being thought not such " good Republicans " as their opponents.

The Mountain, on the other hand, was resolved, less from ferocity than from calculation, that the King should die. Robespierre knew an event of this sort was sure to make divisions among his adversaries: and that in itself would have sufficed

317

to make him press extreme measures on those about him. And, further, the King's death would usher in the rule of the party of violence, by rendering its position "inexpiable." When the death-sentence was voted, on January 20, Le Bas wrote to his father, " *The roads are broken up behind us :* we must go forward now whether we will or not, and at this moment we may truly choose to live in freedom or die!" From the month of November onwards a daring minority had been resolved to " break up the roads." The Girondins were to break their own limbs on them afterwards.

* * * * *

So determined was the Mountain, that from the very first it was opposed to *trial* of any kind: Robespierre and Saint-Just **Arraignment** demanded a decree for the King's *execution.* **of the King.** The Convention was not, and could not be, a Court of Law: " Cæsar," said Saint-Just, "was put to death in the middle of the Senate, with no formalities beyond two-and-twenty dagger thrusts!" A State murder was what these men recommended : this sort of thing was not to be incorporated into the habits of the country till a few months later (the deaths of the Girondins, of Danton, and of Robespierre, were nothing else). The Gironde thought it had won a great victory when the Convention decided that " Louis was to be tried." They fancied themselves humane because they had beaten the would-be assassins, and their horror of *regicide by the State* drove them towards *regicide by the majority.* The one was no more defensible than the other. A section of an Assembly that had no legal right to sentence anyone, a section only outnumbering that which opposed it by a single member, was about to arrogate the right to arm the executioner.

The "judges" too, whose appointment was most illegal, were to preside at a trial which, according to the law, could not be brought in any, not even in a legally constituted court. The Constitution of 1791 had established the irresponsibility of the monarch. On this Louis XVI relied. A final scruple made him shrink from giving the violent party an excuse for fomenting a sanguinary attack upon the Temple and its prisoners, by refusing to appear before his " judges." He lent himself to the judicial comedy, thinking, very possibly, it would not be carried to the length of murder.

On December 11, after Barbaroux had read the " enunciative statement " drawn up by Lindet to the Assembly, the King was summoned to appear and deal with the thirty-three questions it contained. Cambacérès was deputed to conduct him from the Temple. The future Grand Chancellor was not yet an exponent of the complicated protocol with which he was to hedge himself about in later years. (" In public you must call me *Your Highness !* " *Prince* Cambacérès said one day to his intimate friends, " amongst ourselves, *Monseigneur* will be sufficient ! ") " Louis Capet," he began, " I come . . ." His democratic pedantry annoyed Louis XVI : " My name is not Capet," he replied, but he consented to follow Citizen Cambacérès—later "His Highness."

The Trial of Louis XVI.

Barère was presiding in the Assembly. "An affable man," says Choudieu. There was something feline about him, in fact, and his manner deceived the King. Barère recommended correctness of behaviour on the part of the deputies : " Let your attitude be in harmony with your new functions ! "

It is difficult to give an idea of a cross-examination : we should all read that of Louis XVI. The King's demeanour was perfect ; simple, yet full of dignity. Seated in his armchair, he replied to every question with the utmost ease, now defending himself by appealing to the Constitution forced on him in 1791, and now denying that the facts had the bearing actually ascribed to them.

The Assembly was so visibly impressed that Lanjuinais was emboldened to propose that the trial should be abandoned. Then the infuriated Mountain fiercely accused the whole Right of desiring to " save the tyrant." It created a panic : all that the Right dared to ask, and could succeed in securing, was leave for the King to have lawyers to defend him. Louis chose Target and Tronchet ; Target excused himself. Such was the temporary revulsion of feeling that the market-women, as we read in a letter dated the 19th, " carried rods to Target, and flowers to Tronchet." The aged Malesherbes, who had supported freedom of opinion for so many years under the old *régime*, offered his services, undertook to act as the King's counsel, and brought the young and eloquent Desèze to help him.

Desèze was the man who really pleaded the King's cause: he was touching and skilful, extolled the goodness of the
The King's King, whose love of justice and personal virtue
Advocates, had never failed, and invoked the inviolability of
Malesherbes the Sovereign's person, formally secured by the
and Desèze. Constitution. Any man who reads that speech must admit its conclusions: the Convention could not do otherwise than acquit the King. But Robespierre had given the word: " *You are not judges, you are statesmen, and you can be nothing else !* " Yet the grave voice of Desèze comes to us down the century: "I say no more: I pause in the presence of History: remember that it will give its verdict upon yours, and the verdict of History will be the verdict of the ages to come!" Having read that, let us read the verdict passed a hundred years later by Albert Sorel, whom few will accuse of hostility to the Revolution: that honest historian's reply to the lawyer's solemn appeal is a terrible arraignment of the Convention.*

*   *   *   *   *

In the Assembly opinions were divided. Terrible pressure was put on those who were disposed to hesitate. This stirred
The Assembly the indignation of Mme. Roland herself, but a
terrorized. short while since so unfriendly to the Sovereigns : " Almost all our deputies," she writes on December 25, " now go about armed to the teeth : thousands of people warn them never to sleep anywhere except at an hotel. How delightful is the liberty of Paris ! " The Commune, in fact, was using every weapon at its command.

On the 27th, Salle, a member of the Gironde, made a timid complaint about the pressure exerted, taking it as a text for
A Referendum suggesting an appeal to the people. Robespierre,
suggested. greatly alarmed, passionately opposed the idea : he evidently felt no certainty that the provinces would ratify the death-sentence. " Virtue," he declared, " has always

* *L'Europe et la Revolution*, IV, p. 270.

been in a minority on earth." Saint-Just made a still more serious admission : "*An appeal to the people . . . would not that be the recall of the Monarchy ?* " Yet the notion seemed to make way : Vergniaud spoke in favour of it. "It is a toss up !" wrote Mme. Jullien, echoing her husband, now a deputy, on January 8.

It may be imagined how the pressure increased between the 8th and the 15th, when the voting was to begin. One of the regicides, La Revellière, says, "I must acknowledge that it involved *more courage*, at that particular moment, *to absolve than to condemn.*" The Clubs, the Sections, the Commune, were all in full cry. Barère had decided that the members' names were to be called out as they voted at the rostrum, thus the spectators in the galleries would be able to mark the "pure and the impure." Buzot, Gensonné, and Kersaint all made complaints to the Chamber of the manœuvres practised by the Commune. The "assassins of September" were swarming in the Tuileries. A delegate from the department of the Loire-Inférieure, Sotin, writes on the 8th that the Assembly is "about to vote *at the dagger's point.*" He knew the deputies for his own department were inclined to vote against the death-sentence, but saw that they were "extremely uneasy" : and three of them, in fact—among them Fouché, who had been resolved the very night before to save the King's life—voted for the execution.

To this external action a moral pressure was superadded : on January 15 the question of the King's *guilt* was put

The King   forward. All the deputies, without exception, declared guilty. declared him guilty. "Personally, this was a great affliction to me," writes one of them, miserably. But this unanimity produced a great effect. The Right was under the impression that its participation in this verdict would give it a right to insist on an appeal to the people : the question was discussed : "That would mean civil war," said Barère. Yet the Right fully reckoned on success—and what a triumph for the Girondins such a success would have been ! It would have given them a precedent for an appeal to the provinces against Paris. But pressure was already breaking down the resistance of the waverers. Fouché, who had been sitting with the Right only a day previously, voted against his comrades, and many of the more moderate men were overwhelmed by the prevailing terror! In vain did the Girondin leaders cast a solid vote in this one ballot : *the ratification of the sentence by the People was rejected by 424 votes to 283.* This was a serious matter.

* * * * *

The question of punishment remained. The voting began at eight o'clock on the evening of January 16. For four-and-twenty hours the deputies, one after the other, were to mount the rostrum and proclaim their decision aloud. The roll of the Departments opened with the letter G, and this inspired some hope, for at the very beginning the Gironde—twelve deputies, all of them determined, as it was believed, to show mercy—would record their votes. If we may believe Harmand (of the Meuse), Vergniaud had said to him the night before: " If I were the only man so minded, I would not vote for the death-sentence ! " He occupied the presidential chair, and from that chair he voted for it. Eight of the Bordeaux deputies followed his example. And then the waverers gave way. At ten o'clock on the morning of the 17th a deputy of the Mountain wrote, from his seat in the Assembly : " The death-sentence seems likely to carry the day."

The Death-sentence voted.

At eight o'clock that night the ballot closed. It fell to Vergniaud to proclaim the result. His own weakness had led him to share in bringing it about, but it was the death-sentence of his own party as well as the death-sentence of the King. " *Voters* 721 ; *majority* 361 ; *in favour of death,* 387 ; *against it, or in favour of death on certain conditions,* 334.

On the 18th, as a last resource, the Girondins raised the question of reprieve. It was too late. The slaves of the majority were safely bound to the chariot-wheels of the victorious Mountain. With threatening gestures, Robespierre, Couthon, Tallien, Barère, called them to order ; De Bry, who only one day previously had published a tract embodying his opinions in favour of reprieve, now voted against it. Some hopes had been set on Danton's " magnanimity." When he pronounced against the reprieve an " Oh ! " of disappointment rose from the Right : but the

A Reprieve negatived.

THE DEATH OF THE KING

Duc d'Orléans was greeted with cries of a very different type. On the preceding evening he had voted for the King's death : when he advanced, the sweat standing on his brow, and mumbled his " No " to the question of the reprieve, the Right yelled mercilessly at him : " We cannot hear you ! " And Egalité had to repeat his " No." Nothing was lacking in this Shakespearean tragedy, not even this act of fratricide !

* * * * *

Louis XVI had asked for three days to prepare himself for death. These three days, in which he showed such serene courage, raise him immeasurably in the estimation of posterity

He was executed on January 21 in the presence of a city literally stricken dumb. The authorities may have feared Execution of worse things, for the testimony of two Marseillals, Louis XVI. both very hostile to the King, assures us that Paris had practically been placed in a state of siege. A great green coach, with a strong escort round it, conveyed the fallen Monarch to the former Place Louis XV. There, where the statue of the bad King ("After me the Deluge ! ") had once stood, the "good King " of 1789 was now to die. With a firm step he climbed the steps that led to the scaffold : he was greater on it than ever he had been on his throne. Samson was the executioner. We have a curious account of the execution written by him on the following morning : " He himself helped us to take off his coat. He made some difficulties when it came to binding his hands, which he held out himself, when his confessor (the Abbé Edgeworth) told him this would be a final sacrifice. . . . He mounted the scaffold, and tried to advance upon it as if to make a speech. But it was represented to him that this, too, was impossible. He then allowed himself to be led to the spot where he was fastened down, and there called out very loudly, ' People ! I die innocent ! ' Then, turning to me, he said to us, " Sirs, I am innocent of that of which I am accused ! I hope my blood will consolidate the happiness of all Frenchmen.' " There was a struggle at this moment, if we may believe Samson ; the executioner appeared to hesitate, and Santerre, who gave orders for the drums to beat, hurried him on. All that was heard after that was " a terrible scream, which was choked by the knife." The executioner, who was much impressed, adds : " In respect for the truth [it must be said that] he endured all this with a coolness and a firmness that astonished us. I am convinced that he derived this firmness from the principles of his religion." An exceedingly " patriot " inhabitant of the Meuse wrote to his department that " he died bravely." There were a few shouts of " Long live the Nation ! " but generally speaking the populace looked on in dreary silence, which Mme. Jullien describes as " a Roman majesty."

In reality a terrible emotion wrung every heart, and the hearts of those who had voted for the execution most of all.

Consequences They were overwhelmed. " A tiring week," wrote of January 21. one member of the Mountain. That "tiring week," heavy with destiny, was to be the death of some—such as Vergniaud and Robespierre—before two years were spent : and in the rest it was to cause a sort of mental *alienation*—in the true sense of that word—which was to send all their lives astray. For them a change had come over all things ; they never were to look at life again, save across the guillotine of Louis XVI.

And the character of the Revolution, too, was to undergo a change. " The roads were broken up " ; and, as a member of the Convention wrote, they had to " march on, whether they would or no." March on, indeed—but in what a gloomy frenzy ! True, this frenzy, which was to drive them into the Terror, was also to lead them to a mighty victory over " the tyrants " of Europe : for having condemned one king, they had now to subdue all the kings upon the earth. And, feeling death must be their portion if they failed, they were to stand shoulder to shoulder, and constitute that *regicide oligarchy* which was never to know security till another " tyrant," Bonaparte by name, founded a government strong enough to promise them protection against reprisals.

But had the real object of the Revolution that had dawned in 1789 been a never-ending war, a necessary state of terror, the formation of an oligarchy, and the dictatorship of a single man ? It was to these that the vote of January 17 led " the Revolution of Freedom."

THE DEATH OF THE KING

SOURCES. Works already quoted by Aulard (*Actes,* I, *Jacobins,* V), Vaissière (*Lettres d'aristocrates*), Le Bas (in Stefane Pol), Dubreiulh, Madame Jullien, Choudieu, Barère, Fockedey, Couthon, Morris, Garat, Larevellière-Lepeaux.—*Lettres de Minvielle et Ricord aux administrateurs des Bouches du Rhône (Rev. Retr.,* XVI, XVII) ; *Lettre de Migevant au Directoire de la Meuse,* January 24, 1793 (*Société des Lettres, Sciences et Arts de Bar-le-Duc,* 1909) ; Harmand de la Meuse, *Anecdotes,* 1820.

WORKS. Those already quoted by Guadet, Robinet, Biré, Pingaud, Cahen, Meynier, Madelin.—Vaissière, *La Mort du Roi,* 1910 ; *Autour du Procès de Louis XVI (Études religieuses,* 1906); Mellinet, *Histoire de Nantes,* V, 1825.

CHAPTER XXVI

THE TREASON OF DUMOURIEZ

January 21. The political parties and Europe. Europe against France. The Gironde quails before the policy of Public Safety. Danton and the Gironde. Measures for public safety. Discontent of Dumouriez. The insurrection in the West. La Vendée. The treason of Dumouriez. The Mountain aims at Dictatorship. Dumouriez throws off the mask and brings destruction on the Gironde.

JANUARY 21 had been a victory for the Mountain. In vain had Vergniaud and Barbaroux voted for the death penalty : their having suggested an appeal to the people was enough to make the Clubs accuse them of a hypocritical attempt to " save the tyrant." Many of their friends, again, had voted against the death-sentence. All of these were dubbed, more or less open " enemies of the people." Robespierre and his adherents were to turn this poisoned weapon against them.

January 21, the political Parties and Europe.

Further, the European Coalition was evidently about to become a fact, and one general was preparing to betray his country : the old frontiers would consequently be threatened at once : and, to fill up the measure, civil war was to break out in the West. This state of things was to make measures for Public Safety indispensable. The Girondins were to support them, but in so hesitating a fashion, that before long they were to appear quite unfit to apply them. Within a month Robespierre was to drive them out of all their positions, from the Committee of Defence to the Committee on the Constitution. Their fall was caused by their own mistakes in part, but also by a state of things which demands examination.

* * * * *

Two excited Marseillais wrote, on the evening of the day

on which "the tyrant" died: "All kings are dead!" But the kings would not die.

And, further, the " crime " which England was to proclaim the next day "the most odious and atrocious ever known in England   history " (forgetting how the head of Charles I had intervenes.   fallen at Whitehall), gave them a pretext.

England was determined to face anything rather than allow us to take possession of Antwerp. Now Danton, who had hesitated for a time to accept the doctrine of the "*natural frontiers,*" accepted it loudly. "*The limits of France are marked out by Nature. We shall reach them at four points, the Ocean, the banks of the Rhine, the Alps, and the Pyrenees* " : this meant the annexation of Nice, Savoy, Geneva, the Swiss Jura, the Rhenish provinces, Belgium, and part of Holland.

All England rose up in anger and protested. The Convention took no notice of the outcry, and gave Dumouriez orders on January 29 to march on Holland. England, followed by Spain, in which country the " murder of the King " had stirred a sort of religious indignation, was now to enter the lists.

The Alliance between the German princes, momentarily shaken, was at once consolidated. On January 23 Russia and The German   Prussia shared a second remnant of Poland be-Diet declares   tween them, and Austria for a moment seemed War against   to accept the situation : she was promised com-France.   pensation in the shape of Flanders, Alsace and Lorraine, and England was permitted to hope that Antwerp would be left in her hands. The continental armies were to be kept up with British gold : this was duly poured out at Madrid, Turin, Naples, Vienna, and Berlin. Finally, the German Diet declared war. Its sentimental pretext was the death of the King : its real reason, the doctrine of the " natural frontiers," and, still more, the hope of speedily dismembering a country " on the verge of dissolution."

An early realization of this hope seemed probable. Hardly had Dumouriez entered Holland, on February 17, when he was Reverses in   forced to retire. The Austrians had thrown Holland and   themselves on Belgium: on March 3, Miranda Belgium.   who had laid siege to Maestricht, was obliged to raise it hastily and fall back on Liége, in such disorder that

327

within two days the Austrians were able to drive him out again. On March 8, Dumouriez was recalled to defend Brussels. Back he came, more furious with the regicide Convention than with the European Coalition. Though he had not, as yet, won the laurels indispensable to the *coup d'état* he meditated, he was more set on it than ever. On the 12th his fury against the Convention had grown so fierce that he was unable to contain it, and he recklessly despatched a letter of reproach, closely resembling a declaration of hostility, to the Assembly.

    ❀   *   *   *   *

This was a terrible blow for his friends the Girondins. They, too, had been outwitted by Robespierre's skilful manipulation of events.

The Mountain was determined to fight to the death : the more so as the opposition of the Gironde seemed supported by a coalition of all malcontents—and these were legion. It must be added that at this juncture the Right allowed itself to be driven out of all its positions.

In the Council, Garat had joined the Mountain, followed by "good Papa Pache," a former subordinate of Roland, who had been sent to the Ministry of War to take Servan's place, and had immediately turned round on his benefactors and made himself the disciple, not even of Danton, but of Marat. This placed the Rolands in a most difficult position. " Manon " was growing demoralized : "Marat," she wrote on November 25, "never ceased snarling at her for a moment." " I doubt," she goes on, " that more horrors can have been published against Antoinette, to whom I am compared, and whose names are bestowed on me ! '? Re-enacting the scene in the *Princesse de Clèves*, M. Perroud tells us, she had acknowledged her platonic but fervent love for Buzot to Roland : the old man had taken her confidence very ill. Worn out and exasperated, he sent in his resignation, and the majority in the Council at once passed into the hands of the Mountain, for now only two of its members, Lebrun and Clavières, were left to represent (and that very feebly !) the Girondin policy.

Robespierre and Marat were gaining ground—too much ground in Danton's opinion : he would have been glad to be reconciled with the Gironde : his dream, indeed, was a general union of all parties in face of the enemy that threatened the country. He made advances, suggested con-ferences. But Mme. Roland had no talent for forgetting, and her friends took up all her hatreds. " Anything ! " cried Guadet fiercely, " anything ! save im-punity for the murderers *and their accomplices !* " The words were aimed at Danton. He looked fixedly at Guadet. " Guadet," he said, " *you know not how to forgive : you will perish !* "

Danton's Efforts for a Fusion.

Danton had been driven to attempt this reconciliation by the general state of affairs, which was truly terrible. He had travelled to Belgium and had seen the invasion. He desired the Assembly to forget its quarrels and concentrate upon building up armies, finding money, and casting cannon.

But while Danton was content to ask only for soldiers, Robespierre was crying out for fetters for the " accomplices of the foreigner." The Sections were preaching the prime necessity of the institution of a *Revolutionary Tribunal.* It was opposed by many of the Girondins. " An inquisition," cried Vergniaud, " a thousand times more formidable than that of Venice ! " The demand for the crea-tion of a *Committee of Public Safety* was also rejected by them : the *Commission of Defence,* which was in their hands, was quite sufficient, in their opinion.

Measures for Public Safety.

Their opponents resolved to force their hand : and for this a day was appointed—March 10. The attempt failed. But the taking of Liége by Austria stirred public opinion and staggered the Convention. Robespierre taxed the Assembly with " culpable indulgence " : Danton, always ready for strong measures, supported him by his speeches, and carried the decree instituting a *Revolutionary Tribunal.* We know that just a year later, almost to the day, this Tribunal was to send Danton to his death.

Thus the first part of the Terrorist machine was forged. The next step was to set up the *Committee of Public Safety.* The *Commission of Defence* opposed the measure, but just because the Gironde controlled the majority in that Commission, its destruction was important to the

Mountain. Its president, Guadet, was detested by Robespierre. Were he and his friends strong enough to hold the fort ? Suddenly, on the 14th, Dumouriez dealt them a cruel blow. His letter had reached Paris : the Commission suppressed it, and decided to send Danton and Delacroix to bring the General back to a sense of his duty. If his threats were carried out the men of the Gironde, already in sore peril, would be altogether lost.

Dumouriez had no intention of putting his threats into execution till he had won a victory : he was seeking his oppor-**Disaffection of** tunity, and thought he had found it at Neer-**Dumouriez.** winden on March 20. For a moment he seemed to have won the day, but his undisciplined volunteers played him false, his left wing gave way, and he had to beat a retreat.

Then he made up his mind, as he could not carry back laurels to Paris, to return without them. Danton had hard work to get him to address a few words of apology to the Assembly.

However, they came too late. On March 25, the Convention, forced into extreme measures by the defeat at Neer-**The Committee** winden, had instituted the famous *Committee of* **of Public** *Public Safety*, in which, as a matter of transition, **Safety.** the leaders of the Gironde were included—but the majority had passed from them. And before long the Committee was to " purify " its composition, and the Girondin members were to be expelled.

Thus the Gironde had lost all its positions. It is miraculous that it contrived to maintain itself on the benches of the Assembly for another six weeks.

* * * * *

Circumstances which had made the policy of Public Safety a necessity, were becoming more and more unpropitious **The Rising in** to the fallen party. Just at this juncture two **Western** fresh events—the rising in the West and the **France.** final treason of Dumouriez—completed the justification of this policy.

The Convention did not wait till Liége was taken to hurl

fresh troops upon the threatened frontier of the North. But it was hopeless to reckon on more volunteers. On February 25 a decree was passed calling out 800,000 *conscripts, to be chosen by lot.*

This first *forced levy* caused a great deal of excitement in the country. In districts which were favourable to the Revolution the operation was carried out without too much disturbance. But in the discontented parts of France it was the spark that caused the final conflagration.

For many years, the *Bocages*—western cantons, situated in La Vendée, La Manche, and Normandy—had remained untouched by all the great streams of current events. They were peopled by rough peasants; *bourgeoisie* there was none : small country gentlemen lived among the peasants, and led much the same life—and in the parishes there were priests, held in great affection by their flocks. It is not surprising that the *Civil Constitution* should have done more than the Revolution itself to create disturbance here. La Vendée had only been waiting for its chance to rise against the "satanic" *régime*. The Marquis de la Rouerie's attempted rising had revealed the fact that the whole country was undermined and ready to explode.

The decree of February 25 provided the excuse. This monstrous Revolution, not content with proscribing the "good priests," now wanted to tear the *gars* (young men) away from the district, and turn them into the Devil's soldiers. Since fighting there must be, the boys should fight *against* the Devil !

When the gendarmes tried to lay their hands upon the *gars*, blows were exchanged. These peasants constituted a rural democracy : their first leader was Cathelineau, a carrier, a worthy fellow, kind-hearted, rugged, and devout. He stirred up the men of Saint-Florent to begin with, but within a week the train was fired all over the Vendéen Bocage.

The Vendéen leaders.

There was no royalism about it at first; the men fought "for religion," which had been attacked by the "Paris rascals." Besides the leaders of humble birth—Cathelineau, Stoflet and Gaston, some very modest country gentlemen—Bonchamps,

Lescure, Elbée, Larochejaquelein, and Charette, came to the front. The Nation, taken by surprise, had no troops in that part of the country beyond the National Guard of the neighbouring towns, and a few line battalions. These were all routed, and very soon the whole of Anjou was in revolt. Before two weeks had gone by the *gars* were masters of the small towns, such as Chatillon and Bressuire. Meanwhile Bonchamps (a retired officer) and his friends were bringing a certain amount of order into the rebellion : they organized three armies, Bonchamps', on the Loire ; Charette's, in the Marais ; and between these two, the " Great Catholic Army " led by Elbée.

By the first days of March Angers and Nantes were seriously threatened : both Normandy and Brittany were in a ferment. The rising in the West might very well find imitators elsewhere : and the South, where wild passions raged, might break into revolt from Bordeaux to Toulon, and from Marseilles to Lyons. Civil war threatened in every quarter.

* * * * *

And, in addition to all this, Dumouriez was certainly playing the traitor. He had opened communications with Coburg, who commanded the Austrian troops. If Coburg would undertake not to cross the frontier the general would make Belgium over to him. And he actually evacuated that country. On March 26 he fell in with three prominent Jacobins at Tournay ; intoxicated by a success which he considered certain, and carried away by his own anger, he committed the inconceivable folly of revealing his intentions to them ; he meant to march on Paris, shut up their Club, and " deliver " the Assembly from their tyranny. Then he proceeded to write a fresh letter, full of threats, to Beurnonville, the Minister for War.

Thus the Convention received due warning. Between the two terrors—the rising in the West and the treason in the East—
The Terror   its sittings were marked by the most feverish
organized.   excitement. The Girondins—who were sincerely
devoted to the Revolution, and did not wish, in any case, to be taken for the accomplices either of the Catholics of La Vendée

832

or the rebel General—were forced to vote with heavy hearts, all the measures the Mountain demanded : the proscription of the nobles and the priests on March 19 : the establishment of a *Revolutionary Committee* in every Commune on the 21st : the laws of March 28 and April 5, which condemned the *émigrés* to perpetual banishment : and the creation on April 5 likewise, of the *Army of the Revolution* in the interior of the country. Thus, in three weeks, the whole organization of the Terror was complete. Now came the election of the real, the great *Committee of Public Safety*, numbering nine members, to be invested, for the first time, with executive powers. Marat had said : " It is by violence that liberty must be established ; and it is indispensable that a momentary *despotism of liberty should be established to crush the despotism of kings !* " On April 6 this new Committee, with the powers of a dictatorship, was duly installed. Not a single Girondin was elected to it. Danton was its ruler, though Robespierre was shortly to drive him from that position. In any case this gave the death-blow to the Gironde.

Meanwhile Dumouriez was completing and aggravating his crime, and so bringing hopeless ruin on his party. Four **Dumouriez** Commissaries, chosen from among the members **goes over to** of the Assembly and the Minister of War, had **the Enemy.** been despatched to him. Their orders were to bring him back, whether he would or no, and set him at the bar of the Convention. On April 4 he handed them over to the Austrians, tried to induce his army to revolt, failed, and took refuge in the enemy's camp.

The Girondins disavowed him in all sincerity. But they had put him forward and supported him in days gone by. **His Defection** The unspeakable scandal of his treachery over- **the Death-blow** whelmed and ruined them. Now that they had **of the** been driven out of the Committees their civic **Girondins.** loyalty was suspected. The Club proclaimed them " the accomplices of Pitt and Coburg." From that day forth their destruction became a certainty. Robespierre had fixed his little green eyes upon the prey, and Marat, with the vilest insults, was calling on popular vengeance to devour it.

THE FRENCH REVOLUTION

SOURCES. Works already quoted by Vaissière (*Lettres d'aristocrates*), Schmidt, Choudieu, Durand, Buzot, Dubreuilh, Madame Jullien, Garat, Couthon, Barère, Grégoire.—Aulard, *Actes du Comité de Salut Public*, II, 1889 ; Aulard (*Jacobins*, V, 1895) ; *Correspondance de Carnot*, I, II, 1892–94 ; Madame de Larochejaquelein, *Souvenirs*, republished in 1908.

WORKS. Those already quoted by Chuquet (I and III), Meynier, Guadet, Biré, Lenôtre (*Pache*), Levasseur, Hérissay, Esmein.—Chassin, *La Guerre de Vendée*, 1897 ; Blachez, *Bonchamps*, 1902.

CHAPTER XXVII

THE FALL OF THE GIRONDINS

April–June, 1793

The campaign against the Girondins. [The Girondin defence. Marat before the tribunal. The Commune against the Assembly. Marat acquitted. The Commission of Twelve. The insurrection of May 31. June 2. The Assembly captive. The scene on the Carrousel. " Gunners ! to your guns ! " The Assembly gives up the Girondins.

"**B**RISSOT and Gensonné must have a taste of the guillotine : they must dance to it ! " The words were spoken in May 1793 by Carrier, in Garat's presence.

Even now the Girondins were in the way. The Mountain, it must be acknowledged, had a tolerably clear conception of the situation : France was refusing to advance. "Everywhere," writes Jeanbon (a Commissioner), to Barère, on March 26, " *people are weary of the Revolution.*" The conclusion drawn was that this " weary " country must be forced forward by the proclamation and the triumph of the " great law of Public Safety." And though the Girondins were ready to support certain measures, they stood out against this one. Therefore the first step towards Public Safety must be to suppress the Girondins.

The campaign against them was growing fiercer and fiercer. Danton, recklessly attacked by the Right, had made up his mind to join in the onslaught. " To save himself and his friends," writes Garat, "he crossed every Rubicon." He had allowed Desmoulins, his second in command, to publish his infamous *History of the Brissotins*, in which its frantic author (who was eventually to shed bitter tears over his own folly), demanded that the Brissotins should be " vomited forth from

335

the Convention," and in the course of a few days 4000 copies of the pamphlet had been printed.

Marat's blows were naturally increasing in fury, and were now delivered from above : as President of the Jacobin Club he accused the Girondins to the departments, and summoned the " traitors " who would have saved the King by voting for an appeal to the people, to appear at the bar. The *The Girondins defend themselves.* Gironde struck back straight : on April 13 it denounced Marat's address to the departments as an incitement to bloodshed, and carried a motion whereby the *Ami du Peuple* was summoned to appear before the Revolutionary Tribunal.

This unexpected success on their adversaries' part roused the men of the Commune to fury. They were determined to strike terror into the heart of the Assembly, thus " turning again to its vomit." The *bourgeois* must be terrified : the populace was half starved, and the most advanced of the deputies had nothing wherewith to meet its appeals save fine phrases in the antique style of rhetoric : " the hut of Fabricius," quoth Robespierre, " has no reason to envy the palace of Crassus ! " Once more the Commune was to stir up a rising of the famished mob, and so terrify an Assembly of *bourgeois* members. On the 18th, Pache, whose notorious incompetence had forced him out of the Ministry of War, but who had been acclaimed Mayor of Paris, appeared at the bar of the Convention, bearing a petition in favour of the *Maximum;* prices to be reduced to a fixed maximum, a frankly socialistic measure based on communistic arguments : " *Let no man object on the score of the rights of property : the fruits of the earth, like the air, are the property of all men.*"

*   *   *   *   *

Nothing could have terrified the Assembly more completely : it referred the petition to the Committee charged with *The " Maximum " voted.* the duty of dealing with such subjects : the Commune proceeded to proclaim itself " *in a state of revolution* as long as the supply of food was not ensured." Thus threatened, the Convention yielded, and the *Maximum* was voted on May 4. From that day forth the Commune fully realized its own power.

It had put pressure on the Tribunal to induce it to acquit Marat, whose trial the Clubs considered an unendurable scandal.

Marat impeached and acquitted. His acquittal would mean the condemnation of the Girondins. On April 24 the Tribunal acquitted him. The most indescribable scenes ensued. The Friend of the People was snatched from his seat at the bar and borne back to his seat in the Assembly first, and then to his chair in the Jacobin Club, and carried on the shoulders of the populace from the Palace of Justice to the Tuileries in a delirium of popularity. The door of the hall in which the Assembly sat burst open—broken in : the outcast of the preceding day appeared, carried shoulder high, his olive brow wreathed with laurels, a Cæsar draped in rags. A cruel smile curled his lip—for his revenge was at hand. He spoke, and plaudits rained upon him : then, when he had sufficiently humiliated his accusers, he let himself be borne away again towards the Jacobin Club, where his apotheosis culminated.

The Girondins kept a brave heart, but their exasperation, Levasseur (of La Sarthe) tells us, had reached such a pitch that they began to lose their heads. They inveighed helplessly against Paris.

And while they talked the Commune acted. For the stroke it meditated it needed an army, and though the post of Commander-in-chief of the National Guard had been suppressed by law, it appointed one Boulanger, an ex-journeyman tailor, as its general.

The usurpation was flagrant, the intention evident. The Assembly betrayed its uneasiness. The Gironde proposed two measures : to break up the Commune, and to convoke the supplementary deputies at Bourges. This double measure would either ward off the insurrection that was being so openly prepared or nullify its effects. But the Assembly was literally eddying round the Commune, fascinated by its enemy as the **The Commission of Twelve appointed.** bird is fascinated by the snake. It had been struggling " convulsively," writes one member of the Mountain, as early as on May 18. Barère hoped to gain time when he brought in a proposal to nominate *Commission of Inquiry of Twelve Members*, to consider the situation.

This might have buried the matter, but the Gironde was resolved this should not happen. Command of the *Commission of Twelve*, appointed on May 24, was secured by the Right, and it at once decided on the reinforcement of the guard of the Assembly, and the arrest of Hébert, who, under the title of Deputy-Procurator, had become the life and soul of the Commune. When a deputation from the Commune arrived on the 27th, and boldly demanded the release of its representative, Isnard, who was in the presidential chair, poured out the vials of his wrath upon it. In his speech — which really passes all bounds—we recognize the bitterness of a party well-nigh strangled by the cowardice of the Assembly. "Listen to what I am about to tell you. If in one of the insurrections which have recurred perpetually since March 10, and of which the magistrates have never warned the Assembly, any attack were made on the representatives of the Nation, I declare to you, in the name of the whole of France, that *Paris would be destroyed : yes ! the whole of France would avenge the outrage, and men would soon be wondering on which bank of the Seine Paris had stood !* "

Poor tribunes, who fancied their phrases would strike terror to men's hearts ! Yet such was the feverish instability of the Assembly that the President's words were greeted with a wild tumult of applause, and Hébert remained under arrest. The Girondins, believing they had won the battle, left the hall. But Hérault de Séchelles, who replaced Isnard in the presidential chair, was bent on giving the petitioners satisfaction. "*The might of reason and the might of the people are one and the same thing.* You ask us to give you a magistrate, and justice : the representatives of the people will restore them to you." And suddenly the Committee of Public Safety intervened, induced the Assembly, reduced now to a hundred members, to vote the discharge of Hébert, and, what was still more important, the suppression of the Commission of Twelve. In the course of the evening the Girondin deputies, who had departed all too soon, learnt by public rumour that their last weapon had been snatched out of their hands.

* * * * *

THE FALL OF THE GIRONDINS

They recaptured it next day (May 28). They mustered in force, had the decrees of the 27th repealed, and the Commission of Twelve re-established.

What did the Hôtel-de-Ville care ? The Commune was resolved and ready to strike.

The rising began on the evening of May 30. The Paris Sections (as on August 10) appointed Commissaries, who met The Insurrec- at the Archiepiscopal Palace, close to the Hôtel-tion of May 31. de-Ville : they had the gates of the city locked, and the tocsin rung. The Council-General of the Commune waited, in friendly fashion, till the committee of the insurrection was duly constituted. And, as a reward, the Commissaries proceeded to re-invest the Council with the confidence of the " People," on condition it undertook to maintain " holy liberty and holy fraternity." The tocsin was to be sounded, the drums were to beat the alarm, the populace was to be called to arms : every soldier who fought for the insurrection was to get forty *sous* a day : plenty were to be had for the money—and good ones too ! To make all things complete, the armed forces were given a leader, an unknown man, " General " Hanriot.

The tocsin had announced the rising on the evening of the 30th. The Girondins had no desire to have their throats cut in the dark, and honestly believed, so Louvet tells us, that they were to be murdered immediately. They hid themselves : but once day had dawned nothing could keep them in their hiding-places. Early on the morning of the 31st they proceeded to the Tuileries (the Assembly now held its sittings in the old Theatre of the Palace) where they found only three members of the Mountain in the new hall of assembly. Danton was present : he felt no anxiety, he said. " It will be nothing ! " But he was no adept in the wearing of a mask : when the Girondins saw his face they knew they were undone. " Do you see," said Louvet to Guadet, " what a horrible hope shines on that hideous countenance ? This day, no doubt, Clodius is to send Cicero into exile ! " These men were to die with the *De Viris illustribus* on their lips.

The hall began to fill. " Bravely," says Thiers, Guadet, who was secretary, made his way to the bureau (perhaps to become a pillory for him).

The Assembly requested the attendance of the Mayor and the Minister of the Interior. Garat reassured it: this was only a " moral " insurrection. (Between 1789 and 1799 we meet with a series of expressions of this sort which, if they had not cost so many heads would delight the humorist). As for Pache, he vowed everything was quiet, and that as long as he lived nobody " would dare " to set a match to a cannon. Before the words were out of his mouth, the cannon had begun to roar. Hanriot had " dared."

Meanwhile petitioners began to put in an appearance (the scenario of these commotions never varied). In spite of Garat's assurances, their intentions seemed anything but " moral," for they were all armed to the teeth. This did not intimidate Guadet: he denounced the condition of Paris, which had fallen into the hands of " a handful of agitators and factious persons ": there was a cry for the suppression of the Twelve, whose powers ought obviously to have been increased, for the identity of the persons who had ventured to ring the tocsin and fire the guns should have been inquired into. Couthon defended Paris, and made an attack on the Twelve. He was supported by the mob, which had streamed into the hall, flouting " that wretch Isnard " and the Twelve, and demanding the impeachment of the twenty-two deputies. In a scene of extreme confusion Grégoire, who was in the chair, conferred the honours of the sitting on the petitioners.*

The Suppression of the Twelve voted.

Barère, who always appeared on the scene at the decisive moment—from the King's trial to the 9th Thermidor—to deal the last treacherous blow, raised his gentle voice to demand the suppression of the Twelve, in the name of the Committee of Public Safety. This was equivalent to handing over the twenty-two deputies.

The discussion began amidst deafening noise: the day dragged slowly on: at last Robespierre mounted the rostrum.

* The expression has no real equivalent in English. In France " admission to the honours of the sitting " is a pure formality of courtesy. For instance, a speaker in any assembly (Institut, etc.) which had conferred this honour on any particular individual, would address his remarks to him in the first place In the Assemblies of the Revolutionary period the practice was a common one.

He demanded the arrest of the twenty-two, but, as usual, he wrapped up his death-dealing proposal in cumbrous and involved sentences. " Conclude, conclude ! " cried Vergniaud, impatiently. "Yes *!* " said the other, galled to the quick, "*yes! I will conclude, and against you!* " And, without further ceremony, he demanded their heads.

Robespierre demands the Arrest of the Girondins.

The Assembly had no intention of granting his request. But towards ten at night, when, as Durand de Maillane tells us, " all the gangways of the Chamber were obstructed by an armed multitude," it made up its mind to suppress the Twelve.

The populace was assured that it had won the day. Paris was illuminated : but the agitators openly said "that only half the business had been done, that it must be finished, and the people must not be allowed to cool down."

* * * * *

" Citizens, keep on your feet, the dangers of the Fatherland make this your supreme law ! " This proclamation wás posted up on the morning of June. It was a Sunday. Nothing could be done that day, but Hanriot, undisturbed by the authorities, continued to organize his army. Marat, to whom the events of the 31st had been a great disappointment, resolved to act on his own account. When evening fell he slipped alone into the belfry of the Hôtel-de-Ville and set the tocsin tolling. From first to last, the *Ami du Peuple* was to lead the Revolution of June 2.

In the course of the 1st the Commune had secured fresh forces. A body of volunteers, whose minds were in a most inflamed condition, had started for La Vendée : they had been recalled, and were to be employed in chastising the " Paris traitors " till the turn of the " factious persons " of the West should come. By nine o'clock in the evening an armed mob was besieging the Assembly. Grégoire was reading out a fresh petition from the forty-eight Sections demanding the impeachment of " the Twelve, the correspondents of Dumouriez, the men who are stirring up the inhabitants of the provinces against the inhabitants of Paris." The Assembly referred this petition to a Committee. But

The Day of June 2.

towards midnight the clash of arms was heard: Hanriot's battalions were taking up their fighting positions round the Tuileries: at daybreak sixty pieces of artillery were trained on the Palace, the volunteers for the West were in possession of the Carrousel, and more than eighty thousand members of the Sections held all the various exits. The deputies, as they arrived at the Palace in the early light, came like mice into a trap.

Out of the twenty-two deputies threatened with proscription, two, Barbaroux and Lanjuinais, sprang boldly into the gulf. They were followed by Isnard, Lanthenas, the Abbé Fauchet, and Dussaulx, all of them "suspects." Lanjuinais behaved admirably that day. Under a storm of hooting he took the offensive, made an eloquent protest against the oppression that was being exercised, demanded the suppression of the rebellious Parisian authorities, attacked the Commune, and, though insults were hailed upon him, did not leave the rostrum till he had said all he had to say.

Then the petitioners had their turn: " The crimes of the factious members of the Convention are known to you. *We have come to accuse them before you for the last time.*" The Assembly, exasperated at last by the insolence of these people, proceeded to the consideration of current business. Then a wild cry rose up. The semicircle lately filled by the petitioners emptied, so did the galleries; the men of the Sections all rushed to the doors, shouting: " *Let us save the Fatherland! To arms!* "

* * * * *

The Assembly, thrilled with excitement first, and then cast down by fear, looked about for some means of escape. The insidious Barère thought he had found one when he suggested that the accused deputies should hand in their voluntary resignations. Lanjuinais refused: when Chabot hurled some insult at him, he turned on the unfrocked monk: " When the ancients made ready for the sacrifice, they crowned the victim with flowers and fillets, and so led it to the altar: the priest put it to death, Chabot, but he did not insult it ! " And, as he said the words, it seemed, La Rèvellière tells us, as though " an aureole of glory shone around his head."

Barbaroux also refused. His beautiful inspired face ("Antinous," Mme. Roland called him), looked like a martyr's. "I have sworn to die at my post : I will keep my oath." The deputies, writes La Rèvellière, "sat in a stupor." The silent Hérault presided over a dumb Assembly.

Suddenly a knot of indignant deputies made their entry. They had attempted to leave the Tuileries and had been **The Assembly** roughly handled (Boissy d'Anglas showed his **captive.** torn clothes). They had been driven back into the Palace with the butt-ends of muskets.

"*Let us prove that we are free !*" cried Barère, "I propose that the Convention shall proceed to hold its deliberations in the midst of the armed forces which, *no doubt,* will protect it !"

Hérault rose to his feet. No more decorative leader than this handsome magistrate with his commanding presence could have been found. Hat on head he moved towards the door, followed by the deputies bareheaded, as if the Assembly were about to do homage to the Sovereign.

Three hundred members soon appeared in a compact body on the Carrousel. On August 10, it will be remembered, Louis XVI, on the brink of his final fall, had taken that same road.

＊　　　＊　　　＊　　　＊　　　＊

Facing him Hérault perceived the line of guns, and in front of it the staff of the revolutionary army. It was headed by a **The Scene in** figure with which he was unacquainted, a general **the Place du** with great plumes in his hat. This was Hanriot ; **Carrousel.** " a harsh, grimacing countenance," says a police report . . . "irascible, coarse, never opening his lips without vociferating," an adventurer who had been a beadle, a lackey, a brandy-seller. While the deputies walked forward, hat in hand, the little man with the feathers sat in state upon his horse.

When Hérault reached the spot he spoke to him " politely," says Barère. " What does the people want ? " the President inquired, " The Convention only desires its happiness." " Hérault," replied the ex-lackey, " *the people has not risen to listen to empty talk : it demands that twenty-four guilty men shall be handed over to it.*" " Hand us all over ! " shouted the deputies nearest to the speaker.

The " General " vouchsafed no reply : he turned his horse about, and "with a yell that would have reduced a fortress "Gunners ! to to silence," he shouted, " *Gunners ! to your your guns !* " *guns !* "

The Convention retreated : Brutus was their exemplar, not Decius. Then the unhappy band began to wander round and round the prison in which it was shut up : through court-yards and gardens it went, seeking some outlet, under the scornful eyes of the troops, who shouted, " *Long live the Mountain! To the guillotine with the Girondins.*" At the swing bridge they found Marat, at the head of some soldiers. He flew at them, screaming, "I call on you to return to the posts you have abandoned like cowards ! " And back to their posts they went, with Marat snarling at their heels. The troops were all jeering at them : the " Giant Assembly " was a laughing-stock, just as the Cæsars of the decadence were mocked by the Pretorian Guard before they were murdered. The germ of every future *coup d'état* lay in this first one. On June 2 Hanriot shut the doors in the deputies' faces. On the 19th Brumaire, Marat was to throw them out of the windows.

*   *   *   *   *

The real object was to hold them up to derision, and then force them to decimate themselves. For they had hardly regained their benches ere they were compelled to listen to an harangue from Couthon—a piece of sanguinary buffoonery : " Citizens, all the members of the Convention must now *feel reassured as to their liberty.* . . . Now that you *realize that your deliberations are free,* I ask, not for the impeachment of the twenty-two accused members, but for a decree of the Convention whereby they will be placed under arrest in their own houses ! " To put a stop to this humbugging speech a Girondin called out, " *Pray give Couthon his glass of blood : he's thirsty !* "

What were the names of the twenty-two ? Marat set himself to enumerate them, now striking out a name, now inserting The Assembly one, jeering at his prey, playing with it, cat-like. gives up the One by one the names were called out. There Girondins. was not a man of them but had helped the revolution forward notably : Lanjuinais, who had founded the

first revolutionary club in 1789 ; Rabaud, one of the leaders at
the Jeu de Paume ; Vergniaud, Gensonné, Guadet, Isnard, who
had paved the way for August 10 ; Barbaroux, who had
attacked the Tuileries ; Pétion, who had favoured that attack ;
Brissot—the "great Brissot" of 1791 ; Gorsas and Louvet,
the two energetic Jacobin journalists of 1792.

The decree was voted by the Mountain ; " all the rest," says
Durand, "remaining mere spectators." And when amidst
the joyful shouts of the populace the news spread outside the
Tuileries that the Assembly had sacrificed its best members,
Hanriot withdrew his guns, the Carrousel gates were flung
wide, and the deputies were permitted to depart.

They departed under a hail of sarcasms. More than one,
in sacrificing his brother-in-arms, had sacrificed himself. The
withdrawal of Hanriot's guns was to be a very temporary
measure.

SOURCES. Works already quoted by Rabaut, Grégoire, Barère,
Durand de Maillane, La Révellière-Lepeaux, Garat, Schmidt, Madame
Roland.—Aulard, *Actes du Comité de Salut Public*, III, IV, 1890–91 ;
Pétion, *Mémoires*, 1866 ; Riouffe, *Mémoires*, 1795.

WORKS. Those already quoted by Dard, Claretie (*Desmoulins*),
Hérissay, Levasseur.—Walton, *Le Tribunal Révolutionnaire*, 1881 ;
Campardon, *Le Tribunal Révolutionnaire*, 1862 ; Lenôtre, *Le Tribunal
Révolutionnaire*, 1909 ; Lenôtre, *Hanriot* (*Vieux Papiers*, III, 1906).

CHAPTER XXVIII

THE INSURRECTION IN THE PROVINCES

June—July, 1793

Risings in the Departments. The Constitution of 1793—a hoax.
Defeat of the Norman insurgents. *Federalism* suppressed in the
South. Danton and Robespierre face to face. Danton driven
out of the Committee of Public Safety.

"*T*HEY* are supposed to have gone to join *their* army
in La Vendée." Thus did Couthon report the flight
of certain of the Girondin leaders. The venomous
sentence betrays the existence of a plan: the Mountain was
resolved that its adversaries should be taken for royalists,
Triumph of who were casting off the mask at last. This
the Commune. might do something to discourage protests in
the Assembly (seventy-five deputies had already entered one),
and above all, it would give a false idea of the expected
insurrection in the provinces.

In Paris the Commune triumphed: Vergniaud, Brissot,
Gensonné, and several others, had been arrested. Buzot,
Guadet, Isnard, Barbaroux, and Pétion had fled, and the names
of the Rolands and of two ministers, Clavières and Le Brun,
had been added to the list of proscribed persons. Danton
thought all this very extreme: the arrest of the Minister
of Foreign Affairs, his own right hand man, had offended
him greatly. So necessary was Le Brun to him that the
prisoner was to be seen, day after day, managing the business
of his department, holding conferences with the Committee,
and sending out despatches to Europe, with two gendarmes
keeping guard over him. But Danton, tricked by Robespierre,
had been obliged to proclaim May 31 and June 2 " glorious
days," and thus the Commune had won a second victory.

346

INSURRECTION IN PROVINCES

Paris was busy denouncing the vanquished. The town, so skilfully allowed to starve on the 1st, was miraculously well supplied with provisions on the 2nd. Surely it was thanks to the downfall of "those Brissotins" that the Poissy market was full of cattle and that calves were to be had at a reasonable price at the Pont de la Tournelle! Consequently the deputies who made protests must be starvers of the poor, royalists, friends of Pitt and of Coburg! Good General Hanriot must take another walk about the Tuileries for the benefit of the seventy-five who had ventured to protest! So nobody protested any more: the Commune was left to itself, and even Danton had to defer any attempt to keep it within bounds.

❋   ❋   ❋   ❋   ❋

In the provinces things were following a very different course. The Departments were rising in revolt. Louvet asserts **The Revolt in** that sixty-nine departments entered protests: **the Provinces.** Meilhan gives the number as seventy-two. The standard of revolt was formally hoisted in twenty.

Lyons had not waited for June 2. The Commune's reiterated attempts in the course of the month of May to oppress the representatives of the people had appeared sufficient justification for a revolt that had come like a thunder-clap; Chalier, the Jacobin Mayor, an odious despot, had been seized, tried, and executed: and when, on the morrow of June 2, Lindet had been sent down by the Convention, he had been informed that the city would not recognize the authority of the Assembly "till that body was complete, and the decree of June 2, which had placed a portion of its members under arrest, had been rescinded." The great town had then proceeded to organize a *Commission of Public Safety of Rhône and Loire.* Marseilles was rising, and could easily hold out a hand to Lyons by way of Avignon, which seemed favourable. But Bordeaux, above all, seemed bent on making itself the very centre of the movement. On June 8 the constituted bodies called on the Sections to form a *Commission of Public Safety*—this was done on the 9th—which invited the other Departments to take concerted measures. Dauphiné and the Franche-Comté both seemed ready to join. And the Gironde had sympathizers, too, at

Nantes and at Brest. Normandy, inspired by Buzot, who had escaped from Paris, completed a formidable half-circle which seemed destined to draw closer and closer round the author of the events of June 2 and crush them.

Bordeaux ought to have remained the centre of the movement. But Buzot, himself a Norman, persuaded Guadet, a Bordeaux man, and Barbaroux, a Marseillais, to pass into Normandy, and thus hostilities began at Evreux. This involved trying to carry on the fight not from its centre, but from the extremity of the left wing—bad tactics. Yet it was at Caen that the first meeting of the united assemblies of the departments took place, on June 13. The violence of public excitement here is proved by the fact that from this little town Charlotte Corday, great-niece of the poet Corneille, set out with soul on fire to stab Marat, persecutor and executioner of the most virtuous of citizens, in his bath, on July 13.

This was the only—or almost the only—result of Buzot's efforts. He and his friends, from Caen to Lyons, found them- The Girondins selves in a most difficult position. They raised embarrassed by battalions, indeed, but the men they enlisted in royalist Allies. them were royalists—a fact which served the plans of the Mountain most successfully. Brest and Nantes were Girondin cities, but they were republican cities too: they would have no dealings with the royalists of La Vendée. In Normandy we see Puisaye, a royalist, serving under the orders of Wimpfen, a republican: at Lyons, Précy and Virieu, both of them declared royalists, took the head of the army: at Toulon the insurgents called in the English fleet and acclaimed " Louis XVII." With allies so compromising as these the republican revolt was doomed to failure. The very successes of the *Blancs* (Whites) of La Vendée, who had taken Angers and Saumur, and were threatening Nantes, forced the *Bleus* (Blues) to stand shoulder to shoulder in the West. The republican departments began to waver, and look about for some pretext for a reconciliation with the Convention.

The Convention furnished this in the most skilful manner by making all haste to vote, on June 24, the long-expected Constitution. We do not know that any other chapter of the world's history registers so complete and perfect a mystification as this *Constitution of* 1793. Its author, Hérault de Séchelles, had begun by making fools of his colleagues of the The burlesque Constitutional Committee, by sending them—he Constitution of had a genius for solemn practical jokes—to ask for 1793. the Laws of Minos at the National Library. Then he proceeded to pack the Constitution (which he knew could never be applied) with cheap " democratic guarantees " : a legislative assembly to be elected for one year only ; universal suffrage ; a referendum (perfectly illusory) ; and to begin with, a ple-biscite, without the approval of which the provisions of the document were not to be carried out.

Then every deputy lauded this constitution—which, as somebody wrote on the 25th, " would ensure the happiness of the commonwealth "—to his own electors, and proceeded to add, with due emphasis, that once the Constitution was accepted " the Convention would have fulfilled its mission, and a new legislative body would take its place." Thus reassured, the departments, which had been on the brink of insurrection, calmed down. The Constitution was acclaimed—1,801,918 votes were cast in its favour, 11,600 heroes voting against it at the peril of their lives—and the provinces, save some ten depart-ments, seemed content.

But the long-desired result having been attained at last, this Constitution, " far too Spartan in its nature to suit France," was declared too beautiful to be exposed to any risk of destruc-tion by use. But that no man might doubt its existence, the parchment was shut up in a sort of shrine, placed most in-conveniently in the centre of the hall of the Convention. " That cradle was its tomb ! " adds Barère, another imperturb-able augur.

* * * * *

But the end, as we have said, had been attained. Just after July 13 Wimpfen's troops were defeated without much diffi-Defeat of the culty before Vernon. On the pretext that the Norman Constitution had satisfied all their demands, Insurgents. Eure and Calvados abandoned their beaten com-rades to their fate. Buzot, Guadet and Barbaroux escaped arrest, which had been imminent, and succeeded in reaching the coasts of the Gironde by sea, but only to find that Bordeaux had opened its gates, and that Tallien and Isabeau were there busily engaged in organizing the Terror.

In the South, the Jacobin Societies, Constitution in hand, had cut off all communication between Bordeaux and Marseilles, and between Marseilles and Lyons. General Carteaux had found no difficulty in defeating the little army of Marseilles, and had entered the town on August 25. Fréron and Barras were soon to teach its inhabitants "respect for the Convention," by what methods we shall shortly see.

Only Toulon and Lyons seemed disposed to stand out against the victorious Assembly. On the 28th, Toulon, terrified by the "Cordelier's club" wielded by Fréron in Provence, was to open its gates to the English, from whom the town was only to be torn, after a famous siege, on December 19. As for Lyons, insurrection was to reign there till October 8, when fierce representatives of the Nation, armed with a decree for total destruction, were "to crush the dying fragments of a strangled *Federalism*."

* * * * *

Federalism—this was the expression to be applied in future to the revolt of the summer of 1793—was crushed, on the whole, long before the autumn. But it had served a useful purpose, and was to serve it for a long while yet: it constituted the supreme pretext for the definite formation of the government of Public Safety—the reign of "salutary terror"—and, incidentally, for the expulsion from the great Committee, on behalf of Robespierre, of Danton, already considered "too indulgent."

Federalism crushed in the South.

This expulsion proved a very simple matter: the lion allowed the fox to take him in his toils in the most foolish way imaginable.

"*The Republic is nothing but a great besieged city!*" said Barère. Nothing, therefore, could be more legitimate than the proclamation of a national state of siege. This state being all in favour of the Mountain, Robespierre saw no objection whatever to the prolongation of the siege. And this explains how he became a partisan of "war to the knife." Danton, on the contrary, would have been glad to reduce the area of the war, and make overtures of peace abroad, in the hope of achieving peace at home.

This man's curious nature is a perpetual puzzle to the historian. We find no difficulty in following Robespierre, his adversary, along his slow and calculating course, but we are constantly led astray by the impulsive quality of Danton's character. His dream, now, was all of peace and union. But Sorel has ably shown how vulnerable his recent past made him, and also that other source of weakness—the necessity for maintaining his popularity (often a very unwholesome popularity) at a moment of general fever. To achieve this he was forced to " raise loud cries for vengeance, while insinuating measures of compassion." And then, like Mirabeau, he was perpetually carried away by his own temperament—that of the parliamentary orator—now quite in contradiction with his ideas as a statesman. Proofs in hand, Sorel shows him to us striving to reconcile France with a certain section of the European Powers, and then suddenly exclaiming, from the rostrum, " It is with cannon-balls that we must announce our Constitution to our enemies. This is the moment for us to take that great and final oath that we devote ourselves to death or to the destruction of all tyrants ! "

Coldly, Robespierre watched the struggle between temperament and policy. He caused underhand attacks to be made on the Committee of Public Safety, in which Danton—in spite of the entrance of Saint-Just and Couthon still commanded a majority : the Committee was too weak. Mayence, which had been besieged, was to capitulate on July 23, and Valenciennes on the 28th, but their fall was already foreseen : there was some sign of a return to offensive tactics on the part of the Piedmontese : the Spaniards were threatening Perpignan and Bayonne : La Vendée was victorious : Westermann, one of Danton's friends, had been beaten in the West. The opportunity seemed a good one. The General was severely censured : Danton knew the blow was intended for himself : he made no defence. He was better able to make an attack than to undergo a siege : and Robespierre had planned his investment very skilfully. Danton was sick of politics (now and then he would

The Struggle between Danton and Robespierre.

raise a cry of disgust and weariness): he was absorbed, too, in the delights of his recent marriage, which enervated him, for he was sensual. His enemy, who never gave a thought to anything but politics, got rid of him as easily as he might have won some childish game. On July 10 he proposed that the number of members on the Committee should be reduced from sixteen to nine. Danton was not one of the nine.

Danton expelled from the Committee of Public Safety.

. . . And when Robespierre felt quite sure—for he moved cautiously—that he would have a faithful majority behind him in this new Committee, he joined it himself, on the 24th. This was the great Committee of the Year II, which was not to be dissolved till the 9th Thermidor.

Danton consoled himself with the thought that he would have more elbow-room outside the Committee. This is the delusion of the man who allows himself to be driven out of the stronghold.

SOURCES. Works already quoted by Aulard (*Jacobins*), Schmidt, Madame Roland (*Mémoires, Lettres*), Couthon, Le Bon, Barère, Dubreuilh.— Aulard, *Actes du Comité de Salut Public*, IV, X, 1891, 1892.

WORKS. Those already quoted by Montier, Hérissay, Esmein, Guadet, Biré, Dard.—Charlety, *La Journée du 29 mai à Lyon* (*Rev. Fr.*, 1900); Lenôtre, *Madame Boucquey* (*Vieux Papiers*, III, 1906); Gros, *Le Comité de Salut Public*, 1904; Guibal, *Le Mouvement fédéraliste en Provence*, 1908; Wallon, *La Révolution du 31 mai et le Fédéralisme*, 1886.

CHAPTER XXIX

THE GOVERNMENT OF PUBLIC SAFETY

The war the pretext for a Jacobin dictatorship. The Committee of Public Safety. The Convention, a "machine for passing decrees." The Commissaries. A double system : the Popular Societies and the Revolutionary Committees. National Defence. The Amalgam. The "Fourteen Armies of the Republic." The "organization of victory" and Lazare Carnot. The soldiers of the Revolution.

THE crown was set on the *régime* of "Public Safety" when Robespierre joined the Committee.

There would have been no time to organize it if the enemy had pushed straight on to Paris in the summer of Dilatory 1793. "But for the systematic slowness of the methods of Austrians," writes Thiébault, "our cause would the Austrians. have been lost a hundred times over. They alone saved us, by giving us time to form soldiers, officers, and generals."

"Systematic slowness ! " The soldier's view was the true one, as Sorel has demonstrated. Discontent as to the division of Poland, in which Austria had not shared, had not diminished at Vienna. Austria's heart had been set on Cracow : she was offered Strasburg and Lille—if she chose to conquer them. She nursed a grudge against Prussia for this. And Prussia, on her part, was finding unexpected difficulties about taking full possession of her fragment of Poland, and suspected Austria of stirring up trouble. Never had there been less friendly feeling between these two "allies." Their westward march was devoid of any real understanding, and lacked all spirit, so great was their mutual suspicion. Prussia recovered possession of Mayence, and then halted on the frontiers of Alsace : Austria carried the towns of Condé and Valenciennes,

z

and threatened Lille, but laid no real siege to it. England, who was spending money freely, could not contrive to galvanize these china dogs. And, indeed, the greedy claims she had herself put forward had done much to sow division amongst the members of the Coalition.

The *émigrés* did their best to urge them on ; France was on the eve of dissolution now : it would be quite easy to restore the King. In the ears of Europe all this sounded like a ridiculous old song. The European diplomatists lost patience and became cynical : " *Then you really think we are making war to please you !* " said Mercy, in answer to the indignant outcry of the *émigrés* when they saw the Austrian flag flying over Valenciennes, " one of the King's fortresses " ; " *You'll see a good deal more of this sort !* "

The Powers reckon on the partition of France.

His " good deal more " meant the French provinces, the partition of which was already planned between the Allies. But, because the agreement as to this partition was not complete, the Powers were hanging back. Why should they not wait ? France, torn by civil strife, was delivering herself up to her foes : it was only a fortnight's march to Paris : they meant to arrive there with their treaty of partition regularly drawn up. Never was the sale of the live bear's skin undertaken with greater folly and assurance.

* * * * *

Meanwhile the bear himself was bracing his muscles and sharpening his claws. The Convention, out of bits and scraps, had built up its Revolutionary Government and with the Revolutionary Government, the National Defence, destined to a long series of successes, was being organized.

The organization of National Defence.

At the head of it all was *the Committee* : this was really the executive power (the *Executive Council* was to disappear on the 12th Germinal of the Year II). The very Ministers were suppressed : they would only have been in the way of their superiors—the members of the *Grand Committee*.

All business was soon centralized in this Committee ; all the executive machinery directed by it. Beside it only one other independent Committee existed, the *Committee of General Security*, a genuine Ministry of Police, which the Committee The Committee of Public Safety had power to summon to its of Public deliberations, thus ensuring unity ¨ of action. Safety. Except in financial matters the Committee ruled everything. It had received, with enormous secret service funds (the essential principle of all omnipotence), the right to appoint and cashier generals, and thus to direct them as it chose : to instruct the representatives of the Nation sent on missions into the departments : to remove civil functionaries and appoint others in their places, and to conduct the foreign policy of the country without any control whatever. Even the departments of Public Instruction and Civic Festivals were in its charge, and those of Religion and the Fine Arts as well. The Committee had power to open private letters ; it had an office for secret business and it disposed of secret funds. Could there be more convincing proofs of the reconstruction of a government ? How long was it to last ? On October 10, 1793, Saint-Just was to proclaim " *until peace is made !* "

We see a token of the Committee's power in the fact that it set up its headquarters in the very home of the murdered King. That famous " green room " in which the *decemvirs* sat—the entrance to the corridor was flanked by cannon, the sovereign's guard—was on the ground floor of the *Pavillon de Flore*. " The steps of the throne ! " said Baudin to Barère with a smile, as they stood before the stairs leading up to the Pavilion.

The Ten had divided nearly all the various departments of government amongst them. Robespierre, who kept his eye The Decemvirs more or less on everything, was to be primarily of the Com- the organ of the Committee at the rostrum; mittee. Saint-Just, his right hand, was chief manager of all police business : that right hand reached far, even to the frontiers, whither as Commissary to the armies, it carried " the thunderbolt " more than once. He was fond of intervening in military matters, for stripling though he was, he believed himself to be omniscient. Couthon, too, was employed on matters of domestic policy, but Billaud and Collot were soon to be entrusted with the *correspondence with representatives sent on missions*. Hérault was absorbed, for a considerable time, in diplomacy—if the word diplomacy can be applied to the policy of the clenched fist—but Barère disputed his supremacy in this department and ended by supplanting him : he, as M. Gros justly remarks, was the "factotum of the Committee," for he had also obtained the management of Public Instruction and of the Fine Arts : Prieur (of the Marne), the least prominent of the *decemvirs,* was constantly away on missions. Prieur (of the Côte-d'Or) managed the food-supply, in connection with which Lindet, a most hard-working man, showed praiseworthy activity : Jeanbon Saint-André undertook naval matters, and Carnot set himself to reorganize the army.

In reality all of them, at certain moments, took a turn at everything. Carnot exaggerated when he spoke after Thermidor (for special reasons), of two separate groups in the Committee, the "politicians" and the "workers." The politicians were perpetually at work, and the workers turned their attention to politics, on occasion. A study of the "Transactions of the Committee," published by M. Aulard, proves that there were no watertight compartments between these "departments." Never was solidarity more complete than that of this merciless Committee.

And never was the activity of any Ministry so tremendous. "A miracle ! " says Joseph de Maistre : and, if we believed in such things, we should be tempted to say so too. For months these men lived in a sort of voluntary gaol : spending their days and nights digesting documents, and with them *human flesh* ; casting suspects to the guillotine, and troops upon the enemy's guns ; condemning thousands of men, some to prison, some to victory, and almost all to death ; restoring the muscles of a nation, infusing fresh blood into its veins, reconstituting the brain and the heart of an exhausted country. Sometimes, overcome by weariness, they would throw themselves down on some mattress, snatch three hours of sleep, and then rise up and set to work again.

The tireless Activity of the Committee.

This is no idle tale. That "green room," at the end of the dark passage, was first a laboratory, in which a nation was manufactured, and then a forge, where it was hammered on the anvil. From those men's hands it was to emerge disfigured, indeed, but tempered like steel. At the bottom of his heart

Napoleon felt a legitimate gratitude towards those who forged him so tough and flexible a weapon.

Officially, the members of the Committee were merely the Ministers of the Convention. But, as in the case of many **The " Machine** ministers, their sovereign was their ward—their **for passing** voluntary ward. Thibaudeau tells us that the **Decrees."** mind of the Convention was the mind of the Committee ; it recognized itself in these men and supported their authority ; it never cast them off till the peril had gone by. The Committee proposed decrees and the Convention voted them. In three years it passed 11,200 ; at certain of its sittings it voted ten, fifteen, all the *Decemvirs* required to enable them to rule, and kill, and win victories. Carried away by Danton's principle that in times of revolution " *there must be dispatch*," it dispatched, and triumphed. It had suppressed all the guarantees (trifling as they were) provided by the two preceding Assemblies as a protection against their own enthusiasms : there was no more declaration of urgency, no second reading of any decree. " Thus it came about," says M. Aulard, " that the most serious decrees, the Terrorist decrees, were passed in a single sitting." The Convention lived under the eye of the Committee, soon to develop into a tyrant. It rebelled from time to time, but always in secret—as Louis XIII might have rebelled two hundred years earlier against some vigorous measure forced on him by Richelieu : but generally speaking, it voted willingly enough. In any case the " machine for voting decrees " was ever at the service of the terrible mechanics in the Pavillon de Flore.

* * * * *

What instruments did this Government employ throughout the country ? It was the whole country, after all, that had to **The Govern-** be " made to march." The instruments for this **ment agents** purpose were to be the *Commissaries*, the *Repre-* **throughout** *sentatives sent on Missions*, the *Popular Societies*, **the Country.** and the *Revolutionary Committees*.

On March 6, 1793, the Convention had already ordered the dispatch of two of its members into each department to superintend the raising of the great levy decreed on February 24. But to ensure the removal of every obstacle that might have

357

hampered them in their task, power was now given these members to break down every obstacle, political, administrative, financial, economic, or religious. They were thus authorized, nay invited, to transform themselves into *proconsuls*. Once the levy was made, and the army supplied with men, they were to remain in the departments to stifle all " *liberticide plots*."

The Committee laid its hand on these Commissaries : and they thus became the henchmen of this ten-headed Richelieu. On the 9th Nivôse of the Year II, a fresh mission was to be given them : they were to *purify the administrations, which were infected with " Federalism," and watch the suspects*. But how were they, who came as strangers into the localities, to recognize suspects ? Their first care must be to enter into communication with the *Popular Societies*.

The Committee, itself born of the Jacobin Revolution, knew—none better—where the strength of that Revolution The Popular had resided from the earliest months of its Societies. existence : in the " Great Club " and its affiliated clubs. The great Society was now to spread its meshes over even the smallest villages. The Committee knew its power, and having taken possession of the Commissaries, who had been called into existence before its own formation, it now took possession of the Societies, to which it owed its birth. The Society of the Jacobins, carefully cultivated by Robespierre—and flattered in the person of Collot d'Herbois, the great favourite of the year 1794—and its off-shoots, became the Government's official instrument. This masterly organization worked abreast of the Commissaries. The crushing machine had a double movement, and Robespierre handled it with consummate skill. When the Commissaries, towards the end, refused to be driven forward by the Committee, their places were filled by the appointment of the *National Agents*, young ruffians chosen from among the personal followers of the *decemvirs*, of whom " little Jullien," sent by Robespierre to Nantes and Bordeaux and Toulouse, was, as we shall see, a perfect specimen. And when the Popular Societies, puffed up by the decree of 14th Frimaire of the Year II, which gave them the right to elect all functionaries (a right not claimed by the

858

Commissary), seemed disposed to presume, they were driven back into obscurity by a recommendation to confine themselves to their true function, " the provision of saltpetre " (a cant phrase of the day). Their place was taken by a fresh system, concocted by the Government, which was to spread its network all over the unhappy country, lying daily more helpless in its bonds : the *Revolutionary Committees.*

By a decree passed on March 21, 1793, a Committee, charged in the first instance only with the duty of watching strangers, The Revolu- was set up in every Commune. The surveillance tionary Com- exercised by these committees was soon extended mittees. to all suspected persons. On September 17, 1793, they were authorized to draw up lists of these, and on the 14th Frimaire of the Year II, to " apply all the revolutionary laws." The drawstrings of this net, with its close meshes—as M. Aulard calls it—were in the grasp of the Committee of Public Safety. These local committees, formidable from the outset, and soon to become execrable, completed the system of the Government of Public Safety, an organization which must be thoroughly understood if the rest of this history is to be intelligible to our readers.

* * * * *

The first result of this strange reconstitution of the Government was the organization—stringent in its laws, and magnificent in its results—of *National Defence.*

When Barère sketched out the plan of this defence to the Assembly on August 23, he was greeted with thunders of National applause. " From this moment until that in Defence defined which every enemy shall have been driven out of by Barère. the territories of the Republic, every Frenchman is permanently under requisition for service with the armies. The young men will go out and fight : the married men will manufacture weapons, and transport stores : the women will make tents and clothing and nurse in the hospitals ; the children will scrape lint from old linen : the aged will betake themselves to the public squares, there to raise the courage of the warriors, and preach hatred against kings and the unity of the Republic. The levy will be a general levy : unmarried citizens and childless widowers between the ages of eighteen and twenty-five will be the first to march. . . . The battalion to be raised in each district will be gathered round a banner bearing this inscription: ' *The French Nation risen against tyrants !* ' " As Carnot has said, " popular fury was to receive military organization."

A forced levy was indispensable : the great burst of enthusiasm that had marked the years 1791 and 1792 was gone.
The Amalgam. France was weary and, above all, she was disgusted. She clung still, indeed, to the principles of 1789, and the conquests those principles had made, but she realized that she was being used by a party for its own ends. In spite of the momentary intoxication of a vision of unexampled military glory, she asked herself, with good reason, whether this glory was not a fresh snare laid by the fowler so that he might shut her up more closely than ever in his cage. The decree of February 24 had been coldly received in the country. But for the rough methods of the Commissaries it would never have produced a fresh army of 200,000 men. And when, in the following September, the first levy shadowed forth by the decree of August 23 began, the Commissaries were obliged to drive the young men along at the sword's point. Yet these recruits, once they had been forced into heroism, were to become the finest soldiers in the world. " These youths," writes Rivarol, " driven in their thousands towards the frontiers, trembled as they reached them, and then made all Europe tremble."

In spite of which this new levy might very well have been as unsatisfactory, as regards discipline, as that of 1792. But warned by the deplorable incidents of 1792, the Paris government had already decided that the volunteers of that year were not to be left to follow their own fancies, and the levies of 1793 still less. They were to be absorbed, by a process of amalgamation, into the old regiments of the line. Chassin and Camille Rousset have both told us how the process was carried out, and how two battalions of volunteers, merged into a battalion of veterans, formed those famous " half-brigades " which were to cover themselves with glory. These fusions were performed in a ceremonious manner to the sounds of the *Marseillaise,* with speeches from the Commissaries of the Convention, and much exchange of fraternal embraces while

360

tears flowed freely. The ceremonial seems rather puerile to us now, but out of those tears and embraces rose the splendid army before which all Europe was to tremble. They started these peasant lads and young artisans on the road to glory.

The Convention, in its artless love of pompous phrases, had demanded the sudden evolution of "fourteen armies":
The fourteen Armies of the Republic. fourteen armies each of 100,000 men! It was a childish notion. The 752,000 men the Republic was really to have at its disposal were divided by Carnot—a practical man, who put some reality into Barère's phrases—into bodies of unequal strength, of course, according as they were employed in the interior of the country or on its frontiers. The Army of the North and the Meuse numbered 113,000 men, the Army of the Interior had only 4000.

This Lazare Carnot, with his muster-rolls and his maps, became from that day forward the Chief of the Nation's **Lazare Carnot, the Organizer of Victory.** General Staff. A sturdy Burgundian, a model officer of the scientific branch, capable, too, as he did not fail to prove, of rushing like any hussar into a hail of bullets and shot; a born calculator, methodical and clear-sighted; out of his element in politics, which, as we shall see, were always to be a source of embarrassment to him, not easily discouraged, still less easily wearied; a man of destiny, sent by Fate at that special moment to serve France. Amidst the effervescence of the nation he became not "the organizer of victory" only, but thanks to his apparently icy calm, "the organizer of discipline" as well. That blood-stained and bombastic Terror which, as its apologists aver, would have sufficed to secure our victory, would surely have brought us nothing in addition to its hideous hecatombs at home, save hecatombs yet more hideous on the frontier, if this cool-headed engineer officer had not driven the flood of lava upon points where it rendered useful service. We will say it again, as so many others have said it before us: that man, sitting in his office among his green portfolios, saved France from invasion, and, by the victories he gave her, saved the Revolution, too, from unmitigated opprobrium.

* * * * *

But the "fourteen armies" had to be armed and fed and clothed and paid. The money was found by turning the con-
The Soldiers of fiscated property of the *émigrés* into a national
the Revolution. war-chest. Thousands of new *assignats* were issued. The manufacture of gunpowder was begun. The scientists of the Revolution applied their minds to this : Fourcroy, Monge, Berthollet, Guyton-Morveau, demonstrated the Republic's great "need of chemists." Guyton directed and improved the art of military ballooning, which was to astonish the armies at Fleurus ; and Chappe was enlisted and given the rank of telegraphist-lieutenant. As for clothing and food-supplies these were partly kept up by requisitions made by the Commissaries ; at Marseilles, Barras suddenly requisitioned two shirts each from twenty thousand well-to-do citizens ; while at Lyons, Fouché commandeered all the boots of the civil population : and we must not forget that a decree passed on November 10 requisitioned "the eighth of all the pigs of the Republic " for the support of the troops !

When the army had been raised, amalgamated, armed, and clothed, leaders had to be found for it. Here was a serious problem ! If the army should be given over to the "patriots " recommended by the Clubs, it would be lost. Happily, young men were found who were at once ardent patriots and distinguished military chiefs—Hoche, Jourdan, Moreau ; and others too, were to prove themselves splendid soldiers—like that General Chancel who said to his starving men: "Learn that it is by a long course of labour, privation, weariness, and suffering, that we must buy the honour of fighting and dying for our country ! "

These Generals were closely watched by the Commissaries with the armies. But though, in certain cases, valiant and unfortunate leaders fell victims to this system, in others terror seems to have wrought up genius to extraordinary heights. Or rather, perhaps, daring—that daring dear to Danton and preached by the proconsuls—which found an easy way into these young leaders' souls, transforming them into strategists who were to disconcert every plan of campaign conceived by the old and stolid tacticians of the European Powers.

GOVERNMENT OF PUBLIC SAFETY

When in the autumn of 1793 Europe made up her mind to act, she was to find herself confronted both by a government and an army, and was to feel the weight of them, to her cost.

Unhappily France, too, was learning to her cost that she was in an iron grip : before the Government of Public Safety had proved its power in Victory it was to manifest it in Terror.

SOURCES. Works already quoted by Aulard (*Jacobins*, V), Choudieu, Durand de Maillane, Aulard, *Actes du Comité (passim)*.—Thibaudeau, *Mémoires*, I, 1824 ; B. Constant, *Correspondance*, 1895 ; Billaud-Varennes, *Mémoires et Correspondance* (Begis ed.), 1893 ; Carnot, *Correspondance* (II and III, 1892–1897) ; Fricasse, *Journal*, 1892 ; Gouvion-Saint-Cyr, *Mémoires*, 1829 ; Marmont, *Mémoires*, 1857 ; Lannes, *Lettres* (*Rev. Fr.*, 1900).

WORKS. Those already quoted by Gros, Chuquet (I and II), Rousset, Chassin, Schmidt (*Jeanbon*), Hamel (*Robespierre*, II).—Aulard, Introduction to the *Recueil des Actes du Comité de Salut Public*, 1889 ; De Maistre, *Considérations*, 1796 ; Guillaume, *Le Personnel du Comité de Sûreté Générale* (*Rev. Fr.*, 1900) ; Young, *Dubois-Crancé*, 1884 ; Bonnal de Ganges, *Les Répresentants en mission aux Armées*, 1908 ; Lévy-Schneider, *L'Armée et la Convention* (in *Œuvre Sociale de la Révolution*, 1901) ; De Sérignan, *La vie aux armées sous la Révolution* (*Rev. des Questions historiques*, 1908) ; Bliard, *Prieur de la Marne*, 1907.

CHAPTER XXX

THE FIRST TERROR

July—December 1793

The frontiers threatened. The Terror. A permanent guillotine.
" The Red Mass." The Revolutionary Tribunal. Fouquier-
Tinville. The procession of " guilty persons." Charlotte Corday.
Execution of the Queen. A holocaust of Girondins. Manon
Roland on the scaffold. Philippe-Egalité. Soldiers at the
guillotine. The Law of the Suspect. The Terror in the provinces.
Noyades, death by bullets, by grapeshot, by the guillotine. " Put
it on the Convention ! "

IT is impossible to extemporize an army, even if it be
welded on the anvil with the mightiest strokes. The
autumn was marked by some passing successes only,
followed by a few reverses—enough to provide the necessary
pretext for the Terror.

While Europe maintained a stupid inactivity—lost in the
" labyrinth of the Coalition," complicated, happily for France,
The Frontiers by the eternal Polish question—France had
threatened. offered battle. Houchard, spurred on by Carnot,
fell upon the Austrians at *Hondschoote* on September 6, 1793 :
he beat them, but, being old and timid, he took no advantage of
his victory, allowed a fresh fit of panic to distract his troops, and
thus left Coburg to resume the offensive and carry Maubeuge.
He was forced to relinquish his command, and summoned—
according to the custom then established—before the Tribunal.

Jourdan, indeed, avenged these defeats on October 15
and 16 at *Wattignies,* the real "Denain" of the Republic :
Carnot himself helped to lead the troops under the Austrian
fire. But at that very hour Wurmser, who had taken
the offensive in Alsace, turned us out of *Wissembourg,*
and thus both Strasburg and Lille were placed in a most

864

dangerous position. It was fortunate that the Polish business should have become envenomed just as this moment; this sowed suspicion among the members of the Coalition, and paralyzed all its efforts for several weeks. The young and enterprising Hoche on the Moselle, and the wily Pichegru on the Rhine, were thus enabled to prepare a fresh offensive movement. Yet, even so, on the eve of the first two decisive victories won in November and December, at *Kaiserslautern* and at *Landau*, things looked terribly threatening. This winter of 1793–1794, destined to be so glorious, began very ill. What was to become of France if Pitt—declared, by a decree passed in the Convention on the 7th of the preceding August, "the enemy of the human race"—contrived to galvanize the Coalition into life, and if Coburg, now reconciled with Brunswick, determined to take Strasburg?

* * * * *

This alarming state of things served the ruling party's ends. The defeats gave it a pretext for carrying out its horrible The Terror intention: the Terror was to be let loose. The begins. intermittent threats of Europe were to be answered by executions. What executions? Those of patriot generals, such as Custine and Houchard; of patriot deputies, such as Vergniaud and Brissot; of patriot women, such as Mme. Roland. These names force us to recognize the imposture practised by a party which was simply gratifying its own hatreds under pretext of saving the country.

"*It is a falsehood*," says Louis Blanc himself, "*to say that the Terror saved France, but it may be affirmed that it crippled the Revolution.*" However, it established the power of Robespierre's faction.

Let us not exaggerate, and make Robespierre a scapegoat, as is usual. Neither the name nor the system was of his invention. But he took possession of them, and improved upon them, to keep out his rivals and to turn the machine against the very men who had devised it.

As early as September 5 the Sections had come to the Convention to demand that *Terror should be made the order of the day*. It was not till December 25, and after many heads had fallen, that Robespierre, who had left things to ripen, was to formulate the doctrine that "in times of peace the springs of popular government are in virtue, but in times of revolution, they are both in virtue and in *terror*."

"*Men's minds*," writes Barère, "*were in a state of delirium*." Barras acknowledges the real motive. "*We must guillotine others*

Supposed royalist Plots a Pretext. *or expect to be guillotined ourselves*." Robespierre, himself quite calm, found his account in the delirium of those around him.

The methods were never to vary much : "royalist plots," "complicity with Pitt and Coburg"; Marie-Antoinette and Mme. Roland, Mme. Elisabeth, and Camille Desmoulins, Barnave, and Hébert, were all to perish—prodigious paradox —under the same ·accusation : that of a vast plot against Liberty. Many Terrorists ended by believing in this. We think Couthon was sincere on January 18, 1794, when, maddened by a gloomy and terrifying fury, he wrote that "an infamous plot has been discovered, the original object of which was to murder all the deputies of the Mountain, and then proclaim the boy Capet King," that "the number of accomplices is immense, and over 4000 persons have already been arrested." "Patience ! " he adds, " in due time we shall succeed in delivering the Republic from all her enemies ! " Now let us note, with M. Aulard, that no shadow of any royalist plot existed between August 10 and the 9th Thermidor. This "royalist conspiracy" was simply an ingenious method of ruling.

Yes ! of ruling ! The people, as we shall see, were starving. The Government, unable to give "*panem et circenses*," like the ancient Cæsars, confined itself to *circenses* alone. Mme. Roland saw it clearly enough : " The time has come, as it was foretold, when the people would ask for bread, and be given corpses." There was no corn, so the starving multitude was to be made drunk with blood.

And this course was to satisfy and ensure the allegiance of a compact body of supporters : informers, ruffians, petty tyrants. Hearken to the joy of that petty despot Achard, The Commissaries in the Provinces. when Fouché and Collot mowed the men of Lyons down with grape-shot ! " What *a delicious moment* wouldst thou have enjoyed," he writes to a friend, " if thou couldst have seen the justice of the Nation taken on 209 villains the day before yesterday! . . . *What a sight, worthy indeed of Liberty!* . . . *Ça ira!*" His letter ends, "*Good-day to Robespierre!*" These wretches worshipped the great man, for he was perpetually telling them that their "thunderbolts" were, serving the cause of "law and liberty." These informers who, as Lameth said, "would have denounced the Eternal Father," and whose denunciations were accepted, so Mme. Roland tells us, "as a proof of their civic virtue," saw their foul services painted with the most resplendent hues. They were the servants of liberty, of their country, of its laws, and gloried in their work. Albitte protested against the line in which Chénier makes his *Caius Gracchus* plead "for laws, not blood!": "this maxim," he cried to the whole audience in the theatre, "is the last refuge of the Feuillantists!" But the more crafty Robespierre asserts that the blood spilt is spilt in the service of the law.

*　　*　　*　　*　　*

The guillotine, then a recent invention, was to facilitate massacre. Desmoulins jested when he described the exe-
The Red Mass. cutioner, in 1791, as *the representative of the executive power.* But it is certain that Samson might soon have legitimately assumed the title! He might even have considered himself a priest officiating at an altar, for a sort of worship of the guillotine, "the holy guillotine," grew up. "*Let us go to the foot of the great altar,*" quoth Amar in the Convention one day, "*and attend the celebration of the red Mass!*"

It was Fouquier-Tinville who furnished the victims for the sacrifice. He was the "Grand Inquisitor, "the Public Prose-
The Revolu- cutor," the mainspring of the great Revolutionary
tionary　Tribunal.
Tribunal.　　　Rather than tell the hideous story of that Tribunal afresh we would refer our readers to the records of the trial to which judges, jurymen, and "the Prosecutor" himself were all brought, after the days of Thermidor.

The Tribunal, created as we have seen on March 10, had promptly become the "bulwark of the Republic." It held its sittings in the great hall of the Palace—transformed, by a stroke of sanguinary irony, into the "Hall of Liberty"—and on that stage was played a tragedy in a hundred acts, which was to last for fourteen months.

Fouquier-Tinville took the leading part. A financier, soured by poverty, who was to make his new "patrons" pay a bitter price for his past sufferings. "Black-haired, with bushy eyebrows, little round glistening eyes, a low forehead, full cheeks, a sallow skin, a short pock-marked nose, thin clean-shaven lips, a stubborn chin," and invariably dressed in black, there was nothing very tragic about his appearance. He would joke and jeer, wading in blood with a sort of enjoyment, only getting into a fury when any attempt was made to "spoil a job he had in hand."

M. Campardon has given us a study of this Tribunal in an authoritative volume : M. Lenôtre has added many characteristic features. We must refer our readers to their pages. "Men of very mediocre capacity," says M. Campardon of the judges. Herman, the first President appointed by Robespierre's influence, and Dumas, who succeeded him—*Dumas the Red*, as he was called in his native Jura—extracted the quintessence of iniquity from the Tribunal. As for the jurymen, who received eighteen livres a day each, M. Dunoyer has made us acquainted with two, Vilatte and Trinchard, edifying figures both; the majority were "idiots," such as Ganney, to whom that epithet was applied; the intellectual of the band was Brochet, an ex-lackey, who had composed the prayer "Heart of Jesus! Heart of Marat!" To no one of them did it occur that they were there to ensure the triumph of truth and justice; their work was to give heads to the executioner.

By June 1793 Fouquier's "work" had become absorbing : a succession of decrees had made the whole country over to him : he had power to arrest whom he chose, save generals and deputies : he was proclaimed in all seriousness "the Saviour of France."

* * * * *

And then the long procession began. At first death sentences were comparatively rare : between April and November one every two days ; between November and March, 1794,

65 a month; 116 in Ventôse of the Year II; 155 in Germinal; 354 in Floréal; 381 in the first twenty-two days of Prairial; **The Procession** and after the Law of that month, to which we **of guilty** shall refer later, 1366 in forty-seven days. In **Persons.** Paris 2625 victims in all were made over to Samson. (It must be remembered that the "Days of September" had already "emptied the prisons.")

On July 12 the "assassins" of Léonard Bourdon, a member of the Convention—he was alive and well, and most of his "assassins" had never set eyes on him—were condemned to death.

Charlotte Corday, whose "crime" was at least avowed, made her appearance before the Tribunal five days later, so beautiful, so "antique," so full of scorn for life and for man, so serenely content at having suppressed "a monster," that the jury hesitated for a moment and the "job" was very nearly "spoilt" for Fouquier.

The Queen came next. She had been removed on August 1 to the Conciergierie, a horrible place, where she was so closely **Trial and** watched that she did not even dare to change **Execution of** her linen. Yet this proud figure, with its crown **the Queen.** of whitened hair, was still admirable. Girodet painted her in her mourning gown, her white cap with its black crape trimmings, her lawn kerchief crossed upon her breast, her little black shawl over her shoulders ; more queenly than when she had been crowned with gems. But the suppressed anguish of the face wrings our hearts.

She had been sentenced in advance when she was brought before the Tribunal on October 14. Our readers know what filth was poured upon her by Hébert, "the witness," and Fouquier : they declared, with obscene details, that she had corrupted her own son. When they called on her, with coarse words, to answer the accusation, she replied, " If I have given no answer it is because nature itself refuses to accept such an accusation brought against a mother. I appeal to all the mothers here present." So evident was the sympathy evoked by this exclamation that Herman threatened, in a fury, to have the court cleared. In great alarm Fouquier hurried on the pleading : the lawyers were to finish all they had to say within a quarter of an hour. And the Queen, worn out, had only one desire, to see it all ended. "*Will not the people,*" she sighed, "*soon tire of my weariness ?* "

She carried her majesty without arrogance to the very scaffold. "The jade," wrote a hostile witness of the execution, "had the courage to go to the scaffold without flinching ! " The vile Hébert went up to the Capitol, "after having with his own eyes seen the head of the female Veto cut off her harlot's neck ! " Within six months, the pamphleteer, haled to the scaffold himself, was ignoble in his cowardice.

* * * * *

Next came the Girondins. Amar had read a formal accusation (full of lies) to the Assembly on October 3, and the deputies The Downfall implicated had been sent to take their trial. of the On the 7th Fouquier sentenced Gorsas. On Girondins. the 14th the others were brought into his presence. They may have had little hope of saving their heads, but they were resolved to defend them, and did it so well, being lawyers, that the jury's determination to convict them seemed shaken. " Need there be so much ceremony about shortening the bodies of wretches already sentenced by the people ? " wrote Hébert. The Convention, on whom this view had been pressed, decreed that after three days' debate the jury might declare itself sufficiently informed. That very day the jury announced that it had heard enough, stifled all further discussion, suppressed the pleadings, and found the twenty-one deputies guilty. In their indignation the unhappy men rose up and protested against such treatment. Vergniaud alone, with his fine air of " boredom," seemed to scorn this fresh proof of iniquity. As the sentence was being read out he felt a tremor run through Valazé who was standing beside him. " What is the matter ? Are you afraid ? " he asked. " I'm dying ! " was the answer. He had stabbed himself. Dragged away by the gendarmes, his fellows raised a last despairing cry : " Friends, to the rescue ! Long live the Republic ! "

No need of Lamartine's glowing pages to fill our hearts with emotion ! It is enough for us to look at these men, young— four of them under thirty, and eight not yet forty—and full of talent, all of them to die, crushed out of life by the vilest hatred, without for one moment losing faith in freedom and the brotherhood of man. Fauchet, a poor enthusiastic cleric, made his confession to a " refractory " priest, and so, at the end of his life, went back into the bosom of the Catholic Church ; most of them died " philosophers," but without any parade of impiety. Vergniaud was particularly pensive. They may not have sung that *Marseillaise des Girondins* which Lamartine has sent to echo down the ages. They probably met their deaths in a much simpler fashion. Valazé, though dead already, was also laid beneath the knife. That trait shows how hideous the Terror had become. Not a head was to be lost !

"It may be," writes Manon Roland in December 1792, " that pure victims are needed to call forth the reign of justice !" **Execution of** Yet her soul revolted against this sacrifice of the **Mme. Roland.** purest. She herself was condemned : on July 1, 1793 (she had been in prison since the month of June), the Committee of Safety had declared itself satisfied of " the complicity of this sham Lucretia and her hypocritically virtuous husband, in the plan for perverting the public mind." In her prison she wrote those famous Memoirs in which she laid her heart bare, every page of them thrilling with the indignation that filled her heart. Bravely as she kept up in her friends' presence, Riouffe knew she would sit and sob for hours, thinking of her proscribed old husband, and of Buzot " the beloved," tracked and hunted.

She heard of the death of Vergniaud and her other friends, admired the way in which they met it, felt herself detached from this " abominable " world, and on November 8, dressed all in white, passed almost joyfully, into the presence of her judges. She cared less to defend herself than to extol the men who had once followed her lead. The court silenced her—she was " eulogizing crime." The night before she died she finished her Memoirs ; on the last page we read : " Nature, open thine arms ! God of Justice, receive me ! At the age of thirty-nine." She was a true daughter of Rousseau.

One of her women friends saw her pass on her way to execution, serene, " cool, calm, smiling." A statue of Liberty

stood over against the scaffold: "Oh Liberty!" she exclaimed, "what crimes are committed in thy name!" She
had often regretted that she had not been born a Spartan or a
Roman . she was both Spartan and Roman in her death. She
was no saint, but she was a great personality.

A few days later, old Roland, hiding in a Rouen by-street,
heard the news of the death of Citizeness Roland shouted by
Miserable End newsvendors: he went out without a word and
of the Girondin killed himself. On his body a note was found;
Fugitives. it ran: "May my country abhor all these horrors,
and may it return to serious and humane sentiments!" He
had always been fond of lecturing; the habit clung to him to
the last.

Meanwhile at the other end of France there were men who
wandered to and fro, from cavern to barn, cadaverous, unshaven,
ragged: Salles, Guadet, Pétion, Louvet, Barbaroux, Buzot.
Guadet and Salles were taken first of all, haled to Bordeaux,
and guillotined. One evening, Barbaroux, Buzot, and Pétion
believed themselves trapped, and tried to kill themselves.
Barbaroux was found weltering in his blood, half his face blown
away, his beard all stiff with gore. Dying as he was, he was
taken to Bordeaux and executed. A few days after that the
corpses of Buzot and Pétion were discovered, half devoured by
dogs: the "beloved" Buzot, the popular tribune! Pétion,
the whilom "Messiah" of Paris!

Condorcet, too, was to destroy himself, and thus cheat
Fouquier-Tinville of a splendid trial. "So much talent," wrote
Benjamin Constant at the time, "all massacred by the most
stupid and cowardly of men!"

* * * * *

Meanwhile the procession was passing along in Paris. Soon
after the Queen (his enemy) Philippe d'Orléans went to the
Execution of Conciergerie first and then to the scaffold. He,
Philippe who had proved himself so contemptible for
Egalité. three whole years, was haughty and careless
when the end came, and went to his death cheerfully after a
hearty meal. It was not a full year since he had helped to send
Louis XVI to the guillotine. Here and there, amidst this

debauch of judicial murder, we light on some act of immanent justice.

And now the heads began to roll one upon the other into the headsman's basket. Fouquier was "rushing" his men. Men of mark some of them: the whole "Curtius Museum" of 1789. In the absence of La Fayette, imprisoned, luckily for himself, in a German fortress, we see his "crony" Bailly undergo his famous martyrdom. When the mob saw that head, grown white in the service of science and liberty, fall into Samson's basket, it burst into fierce applause. Manuel, another idol of yesterday—not even of the day before—suffered soon after. Then Barnave took his turn, and Duport, a former "Jacobin" minister, and Kersaint, a patriot whose words had been greeted with wild enthusiasm by the Convention but six short months before, and then— Clavières having killed himself in prison—Lebrun, who had spoken to Europe in the proud language of the Revolution, and three of the earliest of the "patriot" soldiers, old Lückner, the bold Custine, the elegant Biron ; close on these followed the valiant General de Flers, the heroic General Chancel, and Houchard, a war-worn veteran who, when he was charged with cowardice before the Tribunal, tore open his clothing to show the marks of his fifty-five wounds.

The action was quickened : a strange mixture—servants and great nobles, nuns and courtesans, soldiers and deputies of the three Assemblies. The Du Barry, poor antiquated beauty, had her turn ; she simpered before the Tribunal and wept upon the scaffold, beseeching "M. le bourreau" to give her "one moment more !" On her heels came eight Carmelite nuns whom Fouquier had dubbed "foolish virgins."

Death of Madame du Barry.

The judges' eyes were growing fiercer : the accuser made his batches larger and larger. The executions became the daily entertainment of the idle element of the population. The Law of the Suspects, "an open warrant put into the hands of the populace," as Sorel calls it, voted on September 17, and finally promulgated on December 16, kept the prisons packed. Dauban has described these prisons to us : a strange and careless life was led within their walls. Executioners and victims

alike grew accustomed to it all. Garat, lately a minister, was
sent to prison : Cambon, who needed his assistance, used to
have him fetched by gendarmes, and brought back by them,
as if the prison had been his hotel. Nobody was astonished
at anything. The Terror perverted some hearts, it fortified
others. Honest artisans cheered Samson to the echo, and
Versailles dolls died like antique heroes. Foreigners "were
aghast," writes Benjamin Constant, "at the resignation of
the victims."

And yet in this winter of 1793–1794, with which we have
not yet finished, Paris had not experienced the "great Terror"
—which was not let loose there till after Germinal.

* * * * *

In the provinces it had begun already. Certain Commissaries who had departed on their errand between the
months of March and July, 1793, had set it in motion: from
Nantes, where Carrier was engaged on the chastisement of La
Vendée, to Lyons, where Collot and Fouché were avenging the
"virtuous Châlier."

And here we pause, for courage fails us. Other writers
have made this dreary journey round France, but they have
Character of   written volumes in their effort to describe it.
the Commis-   Any summary involves an apparent coarsening
saries.   of the lines, though in reality it wipes out many of
them. Let us merely say that many Commissaries confined
themselves to their duties as recruiters and providers of supplies
for the troops : others, full of their mission as "reformers of the
public mind," tyrannized, but did not slay : some even did
their best to disarm the local tyrants. Another chapter of this
book will show them at work on their task as proconsuls. A
certain proportion were butchers, and to these we must make
a brief reference here.

"*We can be humane when we are certain of victory*," wrote
Hérault of the Grand Committee, to Carrier. Such a man as
Carrier needed no such exhortation to "republican severity."
The war in La Vendée had stirred the rage of the Commissaries
in the West to frenzy, from Carrier at Nantes to Lequinio at
Fontenay.

374

Carrier seems to us to have been a madman. To the very end he affirmed that he had saved his country : and this The Terror in seems to prove him a maniac, for he believed the Provinces. it. Was it necessary to the salvation of his country to have 1800 persons shot in the quarries of Gigandet and in the meadows of Mauves : to set the guillotine at Nantes working unceasingly : to choke the Loire with 1800 corpses—thanks to his marvellous invention of boats out of which the plugs were pulled, so as to finish the work more quickly—and only depart after he had sacrificed, in the space of four months (October 19 to February 14) 4000 defenceless beings to the "safety of the country" ? The gloomiest form of mania overcame him at the end, and till his last hour he believed himself to be " Socrates " or " Cato."

This dementia appears to have been general : Lequinio, his neighbour, was likewise affected by it. He insisted on actually tasting blood : lived and took his meals with the executioner, had prisoners guillotined in his own presence, dispatched one with his own hands, and replaced a Tribunal, which seemed to him too slow, by a Commission that pronounced its sentences without hearing the evidence in favour of the accused. At Brest, at Lorient, the same hecatombs were made.

In the South-West, Tallien is the prominent figure. After September 19, on which day the capitulation of Bordeaux took place, he and Ysabeau laid " royalists " and " federalists," —any one, in fact, they took a fancy to destroy—under the same knife. The Military Commission set up by these Commissaries knew nothing of shades of guilt : in the eyes of these judges, the Duc de Vauguyon, and Duranton the Girondin and ex-Minister, were both *liberticides*. And if only 801 persons were guillotined between October 29 and the 9th Thermidor, this was because Tallien had fallen under the influence of the fair Therezia Cabarrus, who saved many a head —not infrequently for a money consideration. The Commission itself was not clean-handed : and Lacombe, its president, was himself to end on the guillotine, after he had been found guilty of " corruption."

A certain number of heads fell in the valley of the Garonne, at Toulouse, at Albi, at Cahors, at Agen. But in that part of the country Jacobinism had been strong ever since 1790, and the hecatombs were smaller in consequence.

Things were far worse along the valley of the Rhone. Since March 1793 Stanislas Fréron had been ruling in Provence— his morals, those of a Turkish Pacha, brought many a frown to the brows of his friends the Cordeliers, men of purer life than he. This man, described by M. Arnaud, his latest biographer, as a person " of weak and easily excited brain," is a forbidding figure. A born journalist, cracking jokes in the midst of carnage and combining the parts of Don Juan and Torquemada. Supported by Barras he wielded " the Cordeliers' club " in the Bouches-du-Rhône and the Var. At Marseilles this club was to crush out 120 lives in ten sittings. At Toulon, which had been retaken from the English by Dugommier—a success due in part to a young artillery officer of the name of " Buonaparte "—the " Cordeliers' club " found plenty of occupation. Fréron himself jokingly assures us that he had 800 of the male inhabitants of the city shot. In reality only 282 were executed—these pro-consuls were fond of boasting of their crimes. But this warning given, our readers must be referred to the letters published by M. Aulard. The population of Toulon, which had become Port-la-Montagne, fell from 29,000 to 7000 souls : yet Fréron and Barras made their triumphal entry into Marseilles and were hailed as the " Saviours of the South." The South was saved after the same fashion at Orange, where, between 1st Messidor and 16th Thermidor, the " Commission " sent 882 " accused persons " to the scaffold in forty-two sittings— gorgeous " red Masses " truly !

Fréron's Work in Provence.

But never were they of so deep a tint as when Collot and Fouché officiated at Lyons.

We have already referred to this Lyons Terror : it was far worse than the Paris Terror : Fouquier was beaten here at his own game. Fouché was to do his best, in later days, to shuffle his own responsibilities on to the broad shoulders of the ex-comedian Collot, who had become a tragedian and a notable drunkard to boot. But there are letters signed by both men describing

Collot and Fouché at Lyons.

"their secret satisfaction," "their real delight." What was it that stirred all this joy ? The volleys on the plain of the Brotteaux, where, on the 14th Frimaire, sixty-four young men, all firmly bound, were mown down by grapeshot and then dispatched with sword-thrusts ; 209 citizens suffered the same fate on the 25th, and a similar "treat" indeed, was daily provided for "patriots"—not to mention the performances of the guillotine so admiringly described by that worthy *sans-culotte* Pilot ! The pro-consuls declared themselves "unmoved in the accomplishment of their mission" ; their object being to ensure "the happiness of posterity by the destruction of certain individuals." It was to ensure the happiness of posterity that Fouché remained in Lyons till he had murdered 2000 persons "whose blood-stained corpses," he writes, "cast into the Rhone . . . inspire a feeling of terror and a picture of the omnipotence of the people on either bank."

The merciless Javogue, who had set up his guillotine at Feurs, a neighbouring town, writes in less pompous fashion. "The butchery has been good," says he. He preferred simpler formulæ !

* * * * *

Everywhere the "butchery had been good !" At Arras— we must not linger over the carnage in each of the terrified **Le Bon at** provinces—Le Bon directed the work. An ex-**Arras.** priest of the Oratory, he was probably suspected at first of a certain tendency to weakness, for the Committee warned him to beware of "false and mistaken humanity." So thorough was his avoidance of it that he soaked two departments in blood. In the town of Cambrai alone 150 citizens were "shortened" within six weeks. But his best efforts were reserved for Arras. There this pale-faced, blue-eyed young man killed like a maniac "in a sort of fever," as his secretary writes, watching all the executions, and, when he went home, imitating the grimaces of the dying to amuse his wife. His subsequent trial revealed such terrible details that he himself was stupefied, and exclaimed : "You ought to have blown my brains out ! "

Most of them six months afterwards were aghast at the

877

thought of what they had done. The intoxication of an un-trammelled despotism had waked the wild beast in them; in a few cases the horrible fear of being taken for "weaklings" had produced a similar effect.

In Paris everything possible was done to hound them on. We have letters from the Committee, written to stimulate the zeal of Carrier, Tallien, Fréron, Fouché, and Le Bon. One of these, recommending "an inexorable severity" on the part of the Lyons Commissaries, is written in Robespierre's own hand. "Strike!" wrote Barère and Collot to Le Bon. "Put it on the Convention!" the miserable wretch cried when the parri-cide's red shirt was forced upon his back before he was taken to the scaffold.

SOURCES. Works already quoted by Aulard (*Jacobins*, V), Vaissière (*Lettres d'Aristocrates*), Madame Roland (*Mémoires, Lettres*), Barère, Couthon, Salamon (*Mémoires*), Louvet (I), Sophie Grandchamps, Pétion, Dubreuilh, Barras, B. Constant (*Correspondance*), Vaublanc, Buzot.— Aulard, *Actes du Comité*, XIV, 1893–7; Carrier, *Correspondance* (*Rev. Retr.*, 2nd series, IV, V); *Procès de Joseph Le Bon*, Amiens, 1795; Robespierre, *Rapport sur les principes du Gouvernement révolutionnaire*, 25 décembre, 1793; Letter of Citizen Lapierre on the execution of Marie-Antoinette (*Rev. Retr.*, XVII).

WORKS. Those already quoted by Lenôtre (*Tribunal*), Wallon (*Tribunal*), Campardon, Claretie (*Desmoulins*), Goncourt, Arnaud, Madelin, Stéfane Pol, Dard, Almeras, Gros.—Perroud, *Préface aux Mémories de Madame Roland*, 1905; Lenôtre, *Madame Boucquey*; *La Fin de Roland* (*Vieux Papiers*, III, 1906); Lallié, *Carrier* (Paris, 1900); *Le Bon*, 1876; Hamel, *Schneider* (*Rev. Fr.*, 1898); Fleischmann, *La Guillotine sous la Révolution*, 1908; Dauban, *Les Prisons de Paris*, 1897; Mortimer-Terneaux, *Histoire de la Terreur*, 1830; Wallon, *Les Représentants en Mission*, 1890; Dunoyer, *Deux Jurés du Tribunal révolutionnaire*, 1909.

CHAPTER XXXI

ROBESPIERRE AND THE " FACTIONS "

January–March 1794

The " factions." Danton's distress of mind. Maximilien Robespierre. Desmoulins in favour of clemency. The *Vieux Cordelier*. Hébert and the *Père Duchesne*. The Hébertist Commune. The " socialist " movement. Chaumette: dechristianization of France. The Worship of Reason. Robespierre condemns the " indulgent," the " extravagant," and the " corrupt."

NOWHERE was the fear inspired by the Terror greater than in the Convention which seemed to direct it. Now that the Girondins had been expelled, and the seventy-five deputies of the Right who had ventured on a protest cast into prison, Robespierre was perpetually denouncing The "factions" on the remaining benches: the "Factions." faction of the " indulgent," the faction of the " extravagant," the " faction of the corrupt." The Assembly, Thibaudeau tells us, felt that " the thunderbolt " was always ready to fall on it.

Marat, now deified by his admirers, no longer stood in Robespierre's way, nor in Danton's : but he had left them face to face. Robespierre was in power, but September 6 had very nearly restored his rival to the highest place. The Convention had requested him to return to his seat on the Committee, and he, knowing the majority of the members to be followers of Robespierre, and preferring, as he said, to " stimulate the action of the Committees " without serving on them himself, had refused. But on the 25th an assault was made on the Committee itself; its composition must be changed, was the cry ; Robespierre bitterly denounced the " perversity " of his antagonists, asserting that he recognized the hand of Pitt

379

in their manœuvre. Danton allowed his adversary to win the day : he shrugged his shoulders in silence, remarking only that Robespierre's comments were " asinine."

Danton was passing through a period of terrible mental distress. The Terror sickened him : the condemnation of the Girondins—his beaten enemies, indeed, but enemies whom in his heart he had admired—had filled him with consternation. In vain did he strive to quiet his own conscience, repeating, in jeering accents, the words he was to use on the eve of his execution : " Brissot would have had me guillotined just as Robespierre is doing : Cains, all of them ! " He had told Garat, during the trial, " with great tears in his eyes, ' I shall not be able to save them ! ' " And when Desmoulins burst into tears, the night they were sentenced, and sobbed, " Ah ! wretch that I am ! It is I who have killed them ! " he wept with him. All this bloodshed was a nightmare to him. " Look ! " said he to Desmoulins, " The Seine is running blood ! *Ah ! There has been too much blood shed !* Come ! take your pen and plead for mercy : I will support you ! " But in the Convention he held his peace, as if exhausted by his mighty efforts in 1792 and 1793 ; he was disgusted, too, by the cowardice of certain of his friends—" *sick of men*," as he said. His apathy was astonishing : but he would come out of it now and then with a start. One night at Sèvres Suberbielle said in his presence : " Ah ! if I were Danton ! " " Danton sleeps," was the sudden answer, " but he will wake up yet ! " In times of revolution the hour of the tribune is brief ; if he falls asleep he always wakes too late.

Danton's Distress of Mind.

* * * * *

Robespierre never slept. And perhaps the time has come for us to look more closely at this man who governed the Convention by means of the Committee. What manner of man was Robespierre? One of his disciples answered the question as follows : " Maximilien is the Man of Virtue."

Maximilien Robespierre.

A virtuous man he was : upright, chaste, moral; he " dreaded money," so said Danton himself, and most of all he dreaded women. He was to pursue them always with a special hatred : he it was who did most to bring Mme. Roland to the scaffold : he, too, who was to cast poor little Lucile Desmoulins, who fancied herself his friend, under the knife, and he would have sent Therezia Cabarrus, the wife of Tallien, to the same fate. Even his own sister Charlotte was coldly thrust out of his existence. And, hating women as he did, he despised any one who loved them. For the first time in history sentimental and laughter-loving France was ruled by a sworn enemy of women and of laughter.

Yet he was not ugly ; the Duplay sisters thought him charming ; no authentic picture of him reveals that " cat-face " of which Buzot spoke so bitterly. Citizeness Jullien thought his features " pleasing " : his portrait by Danloux almost justifies the expression ; it shows us an elegant youth, by no means unprepossessing, his nose and mouth just a trifle too wide : light green eyes, we must admit, glisten behind his blue spectacles. He was the perfection of neatness, his hair curled and powdered, his face clean-shaved, his thin little body buttoned into a blue or chestnut-coloured coat worn over a kerseymere waistcoat and an embroidered shirt : this *sans-culotte*, too proud to sacrifice his appearance to republican disorder, wore silk breeches : and his garments remained spotless till that hideous morning of the 10th Thermidor on which we shall see them spattered with his own blood (" a coat of Silesian cloth covered with bloodstains," says the official record). His business room was always neat, and those who entered it remarked the number of portraits of himself " in every form " collected there—a detail character-istic of the man.

For above all things he was self-occupied. No man ever carried pride in his own identity to a higher pitch. " Virtuous " himself, he believed it his mission to make virtue rule. A hideous misfortune had given France over to the hands of one of those terrible missionaries who, like Cromwell, appear now and again to crush out " the impious " and the " corrupt." These are the worst tyrants of all. Everything is sacrificed to their " mission " and friendship first of all : Robespierre guillotined all the friends of his childhood and his youth. " A hateful being," wrote Mme. Roland, " who lies to his own conscience." No! he obeyed its behests : his conscience, convinced of the sanctity of his mission, was to make him resort to calumny—against the Girondins more especially—and, if necessary, even to forgery (as in the case of Hérault) to destroy his enemy—*because that enemy was the enemy of Virtue.*

As the incarnation of virtue he held the truth, and this imbued him with a sort of grave serenity : that of a priest, which from 1792 onwards struck all who approached him. "*Robespierre is a priest,*" wrote some one at that period. He was an infallible pontiff, almost a prophet. "There was something of Mahomet in the man," writes Thibaudeau, "and something of Cromwell." He had all the pontiff's impassive calm. He was not immovable, for, as M. Sagnac has pointed out, he was "a great opportunist," not immovable in attitude, but the idea that ruled his existence never altered. His belief in it was sincere, and his strength lay in his sincerity. He considered himself the incarnation of Liberty, of the Republic, and the Revolution, and was convinced, in all sincerity, that his own foes were the foes of the Revolution, the Republic, and Liberty. Now being as he was—and this is the most odious feature of his character, "biliously jealous" of all who gave him umbrage, he was constantly adding to the number of his enemies. All of these he dubbed "bad patriots" because they attacked or jeered at him, Virtue and Truth embodied.

Being an infallible pontiff he was naturally exceedingly dogmatic. He had three dogmas: *the support of Virtue by Terror ; the existence of the Supreme Being ;* and *the absolute sanctity of Property.* Every man was expected to accept this threefold doctrine : he who preached indulgence, or practised the methods of the Terror without being virtuous himself, was a bad citizen : so was the man who denied the existence of the Supreme Being : and equally so the man who dared to attack the rights of property. But how few elect and how many reprobate sat in the Convention! Robespierre's daily deepening gloom was born of his horror of these "nonconformists," who must—as his master Jean-Jacques had counselled him—be driven out of the City. Every heretic was an

332

enemy in this pontiff's eyes. As M. Aulard ironically puts it, Robespierre was "the Master of Truth."

* * * * *

Saint-Just.

He had but few friends in the Committees and the Assembly: Couthon, Saint-Just, Le Bas, his brother Augustin, and perhaps David. Couthon's views on spiritual matters attracted him, for he too was a reader of the "*Vicaire Savoyard*"; on the 27th Floréal we shall hear him inveigh against the "philosophers" who would fain empty heaven and deny that virtue is sanctioned by divinity. But the prophet's real disciple and vicar was Saint-Just, who might be called his "acolyte," had he not been more intelligent and gifted than his master. "A mind of fire, a heart of ice"; thus Barère described him, and truly it would seem. This handsome youth, whose charming portrait by Greuze may yet be seen, was a "terrible stripling." "His enthusiasm," writes his friend Levasseur, "was the outcome of a mathematical certainty. To found the republic of his dreams," he goes on to say, "he would have sacrificed his own head, and also the heads of a hundred thousand other men." "He never spoke more than a sentence at a time," says another member of the Convention, one of Robespierre's followers, "and shaped them with an eloquence at once cutting and thrilling." "He regarded all dissidents as criminals," says yet another deputy, and this attitude delighted Robespierre. He was fanatically devoted to the "Master," and served him, but he urged him on as well. Being the bolder of the two he suggested his enterprises, and through his agency they were carried out. A fanatic, too, but after a more touching fashion, was young Le Bas, who devoted his whole life to Robespierre and then died for his sake. Only prophets find such servants, and great egotists such friends.

On the rest of the political world Robespierre cast a suspicious eye—from Collot the drunken boor, and Barère the humbug, to Hérault "the rotten," and Desmoulins "a child" who ventured to speak in favour of indulgence before he had received authority to do so.

During the winter of 1793 this "faction of the indulgent" was really more of an annoyance than a difficulty to Robespierre.

In it he included Danton, Hérault, Desmoulins, and Fabre. Desmoulins had made himself its spokesman. *"That poor Camille!"* Mirabeau had called him: he was still "that poor Camille," the impetuous journalist, without a grain of calculation, an *enfant terrible* whose acrimony had been softened by a happy and well-endowed marriage. He, too, was enduring much agony of mind just at this time: he could not forget the friends who had been present at his marriage—Brissot, whom he had sent to his death; Pétion, who was to kill himself; Robespierre, who was to turn upon him. Remorse and terror assailed him: he would have enlisted, gone to the front and faced death there, "to deliver himself from the sight of so many horrors," but Danton showed him a better work to do—that of fighting the Terror with his pen.

(margin: Desmoulins advocates Mercy.)

Whether by policy or from an illusion, he affected to recognize the enemy not in the Committee, but in the Commune and its chief organ, *Le Père Duchesne,* edited by Hébert. He published his own *Vieux Cordelier,* which flew at the throats of Hébert and the "new Cordeliers," the blood-drinkers, informers, and destroyers. The Jacobins, in alarm, began to utter threats. "Camille," writes Nicolas, one of the jurymen of the Tribunal, "*is brushing against the guillotine.*"

(margin: The "Vieux Cordelier.")

Robespierre left Desmoulins to compromise himself: we may add that the destruction of Hébert and Danton was one of his own dreams; he was not at all sorry to see a friend of Danton's shaking Hébert's position: once the *Père Duchesne* had been destroyed, the *Vieux Cordelier's* neck should be wrung too. When Momoro, Hébert's particular ally, attacked Camille at the Club, on the 19th Nivôse, Robespierre defended him with perfidious arguments. But before long he forsook his cause. When Camille took the seventh number of the *Vieux Cordelier* to the printer, the man, who had been terrified, refused to publish it: Robespierre had thundered out a sudden denunciation of the "indulgent." On the 24th a cry of terror rose from Camille's hearth: Lucile Desmoulins wrote to Fréron: "Come back, Fréron, come back quickly. You have no time to lose. . . . Robespierre has denounced Camille to the Jacobins."

Fréron was to come back, indeed, but slowly, for the " Saviour of the South " had excellent reasons for avoiding a meeting with Robespierre, who was striking just then at Danton's faction and that of Hébert in turn, and looked on Fréron—so great was the confusion—as a member of both, and as " one of the corrupt " into the bargain.

*   *   *   *   *

Yet after some deliberation Robespierre had come to the conclusion that, as Danton had many friends in the Convention, the wisest course would be to begin by striking at Hébert and his " exaggerated " followers.

Taking him altogether this Jacques Hébert represented everything that Robespierre most detested: atheism at open **Hébert and** war with deism, and to a certain extent active **the " Père** communism. And the agent of the Commune **Duchesne. "** was a real power, for Jacques Hébert was the *Père Duchesne.* " This low sheet," as Mme. Roland called it, was more read than any other Paris newspaper, and was also sent, so Barras tells us, " in floods to all the armies." Enlivening his commonplace style by a liberal sprinkling of the coarsest expressions, the pamphleteer delighted the populace of the Faubourgs, who imagined him to be a bold and truculent giant, whereas he was but a noisy little cur with white hands and a puny figure.

He was always putting forward extravagant claims. He and Chaumette, his chief, ruled the Hôtel-de-Ville, and had turned it into a stronghold of " exaggerated " views. His wife was a pious Catholic, but he was bent on the triumph of atheism, and, though he himself lived the most regular of lives in a comfortable home, he spent his time preaching the revolt of greed against " opulence."

The Commune which, since August 10 had believed it might do anything it chose, looked on itself as a government almost **The Hebertist** equal to the Committee. This alone would **Commune.** have sufficed to infuriate Robespierre. But the Commune was powerful, for it controlled the mob.

It used the prevailing hunger for its own ends. The war with England had raised the price of bread higher still. The *maximum* imposed on the persons who sold it had resulted

2 B

in the closing of hundreds of bakers' shops: oppressive decrees, coming fast one upon the other, had only hastened the ruin of trade without lowering the price of food: economic laws regard neither threats nor decrees.

The Commune was not to be checked by such trifles as this —besides it was more concerned with its own unwholesome **The Socialistic** popularity than with the people's welfare. On **Movement.** the 8th Vendémiaire of the Year II (September 30, 1793), it secured a vote for a *general maximum* which completed the work of commercial ruin, and led agriculturists to keep back their corn, or at all events to abstain from growing more. Chaumette's reply was to put forward the first thoroughly socialistic idea: " If the manufacturers abandon their workshops the Republic must take possession of all raw material and of the workshops, for under the popular system everything is done by labour and nothing by gold." And then began the maddest outbidding, which it would be edifying to describe in detail, concluding with that idea of the " bread of equality " which Chaumette had to import from the provinces.

It was Fouché, indeed, Fouché, a future millionaire, who had taken up in the summer of 1793 this singularly demagogic and almost communistic position in the Nivernais and the Bourbonnais. It tended to the triumph of the theory that " *Under the reign of equality wealth and poverty must both disappear.*"

The Commune had sent its congratulations to Fouché: " the Nation must be invited to take possession of all trade and all manufactures, and must have all work performed for its own benefit." It determined to convert Robespierre to the idea of " wiping out," so ran a letter addressed to him, " the mercantile aristocracy." It desired " the revolution in its integrity," in other words social revolution.

Robespierre had not the slightest intention of " wiping out " the mercantile aristocracy: exceedingly conservative as to all social matters, he viewed the efforts of Hébert, Chaumette, Fouché, and their fellows in favour of the communistic revolution with growing irritation, and finally concluded that the moment for putting a stop to them had come.

*   *   *   *   *

And, further, another movement, emanating from the same quarter, was offending and even scandalizing him. These The dechris- people had set out to *dechristianize* the country, tianization and establish the triumph of *Reason*. of France. The Commune was now openly proclaiming its intention of putting down Christianity and organizing a purely civic worship of Reason and Liberty.

The chief instigator of this was Chaumette, an adventurer with morals of a nature that in our days would have brought him into the criminal courts—to be tried *in camera!* Anaxagoras Chaumette would probably in such a case have invoked the names of certain Greek philosophers: like them, he had lost faith in the gods. And he wanted to drive out Christ with the rest. The first step in Paris was to unhang all the church-bells, the " trinkets of the Eternal Father," now to be transformed into cannon and bronze coins: then the belfries, " which by their height above other buildings seemed to contradict the principles of equality," were to be pulled down.

The stage began to cast ridicule on the old religion in such plays as *Le Tombeau des Imposteurs* and *L'Inauguration du Temple de la Vérité*, in the last of which a parody of High Mass was sung.

The Convention showed little inclination to favour this campaign. Yet the Revolutionary Calendar proposed by The Worship Fabre d'Eglantine—a very ingenious arrange-of Reason. ment which abolished Saints and Sundays, and was destined to give a considerable impetus to the de-christianizing movement, had been adopted. Certain members of the Convention, too, had been the first to attempt to replace Christian worship in the provinces by civic cere-monial, in the autumn of 1793. At Abbeville, Dumont, having informed the populace that the priests were " harle-quins and clowns in black garments, who showed off marionettes," had set up the Worship of Reason, and, with a not uncommon inconsistency, organized a " marionette show " of his own of a most imposing description, with dances in the cathedral every *décadi*, and civic festivals on the " observance " of which he greatly insisted. Fouché was the next to abolish Christian worship; speaking from the pulpit of the cathedral at Nevers he formally erased all spiritualism from the republican programme, promulgated the famous order which declared " death an eternal slumber," and thus turned the key on heaven and hell alike. Chaumette had travelled to Nevers and urged Fouché on: his example was followed by other pro-consuls in the Centre and South, notably by Dartigoeyte and Cavaignac in Gers, and by Laignelot, who turned one of the parish churches at Rochefort into a " Temple of Truth."

The movement grew more general: the people began to burn miracle-working images of the Virgin and carry off church plate. The Bishop of the Allier made his abjuration at Fouché's feet: and Gobel, too, trampled his crozier under foot. There were details of the most grotesque description: one convert washed his head in the presence of the whole club to " unbaptize himself ": and at the Gannat Club Béchonnet, an ex-priest, was solemnly divorced from his breviary.

Thus encouraged, the Commune put pressure on the Convention, where Grégoire, who had reckoned on Robespierre, offered most courageous but almost unsupported resistance. But Hébert's party—men of whom Grégoire relates that they would bring their wives to him to confess, and their children to baptize, and yet insult the worship and teachings of the Church in public—raged uncontrollably.

Fouché was sending up cases full of chalices and crucifixes, which were unpacked in the presence of the Assembly. The sight of these went to the members' heads. When, at a carefully prepared sitting on the 17th Brumaire, Year II, poor Bishop Gobel was dragged to the bar of the Convention, where the wretched man publicly cast off his cassock, the Assembly, itself won over, finally gave way. In his congratulatory address to the ex-bishop, the President declared that as *the Supreme Being* " *desired no worship other than the worship of Reason, that should in future be the national religion !* "

Chaumette at once obtained a decision from the Commune to the effect that, " to celebrate the triumph won by Reason

The Festival of Reason in Notre Dame.

at that sitting over the prejudices of eighteen centuries," a civic ceremony should be held on the 20th Brumaire, " before the image of that divinity, in the edifice which was formerly the church of the metropolis."

ROBESPIERRE AND "FACTIONS"

Many descriptions have been written of this famous festival, and of how Liberty (borrowed from the Opera) throned it—gracefully draped in the folds of a tricolour flag—on the altar of Reason! The Assembly having excused itself from attendance on the score of business, a procession (of a very mixed description) attended the goddess to the Tuileries, and in her presence forced the deputies to decree the transformation of Notre Dame into the *Temple of Reason*. This not being deemed sufficient, another goddess of Reason, the wife of Momoro, a member of the Convention, was installed at Saint-Sulpice on the following *décadi*. Before long these *Liberties* and *Reasons* were swarming all over France: wantons, only too often, with here and there a goddess of good family and decent behaviour. If it be true that the brow of one of these Liberties was bound with a fillet bearing the words " *Turn me not into Licence !*" the suggestion, we may say, would hardly have been superfluous in any part of France: for saturnalia of the most repulsive kind were the almost invariable rule: at Lyons, we are told, an ass was given drink out of a chalice.

All these things disgusted Robespierre. When in Frimaire of the Year II, Payan cried out upon " these goddesses, more Protests against degraded than those of fable," Maximilien applauded his remarks. Collot, who had been the " Cult of Reason." lectured by the Committee, stigmatized " this sham Reason which is running about the streets with the conspirators " (the party of Hébert, which was even then threatened) " and concluding their so-called festivals with licentious orgies." At the Festival of Victory Couthon spoke as a deist.

Danton, equally disgusted, made a protest against the hymns to Reason sung in the Assembly, and declared that for the future he desired to " hear nothing but reason in prose at the bar ": Robespierre encouraged this reaction: his settled purpose was to begin with Chaumette and Hébert, and ultimately destroy the whole of this little band of " atheists " who were going up and down the country and driving even the Vicaire Savoyard from his presbytery.

And, further, he looked upon these pro-consuls of the " Revolution in its integrity " as corrupt men, and dreamt, generally

389

speaking, of trying conclusions with the Commissaries who were setting themselves up as satraps, and whose hands were all against the Supreme Being, against property, against virtue. About Frimaire of the Year II his agents, from young Jullien to Augustin Robespierre himself, everywhere began the fight against " corrupt " or " atheistic " deputies. Carrier, Tallien, Barras, Fréron, Javogue, Fouché—Robespierre had them all recalled to Paris by the Committee: a terrible affair for these pro-consuls (" factious persons " in Robespierre's eyes), for when they reached the city they were to find Hébert and Chaumette, Danton and Desmoulins, all laid low.

Robespierre, destroying one faction by another, was to overthrow them both in Germinal of the Year II.

For bibliography *see* that of Chapter XXXII.

CHAPTER XXXII

THE FALL OF THE FACTIONS

Robespierre undermines the "factions." The first performance of *Epicharis et Néron*. Saint-Just at the rostrum. The fall of the "Extravagant." The extinction of *Père Duchesne*. Danton arrested. The trial of the Dantonists. The death of Danton.

"TOO many laws are made and not enough examples: you only punish prominent crimes, *hypocritical crimes go unpunished. . . .* My friend, draw the attention of the Society (the Jacobins) *to maxims that are powerful for the public good : let it turn its mind to great methods for the government of a free State !*"

Robespierre undermines the "Factions." Thus did Saint-Just, then on a mission to Alsace, appeal to Robespierre on the 24th Frimaire. He points his finger at the "hypocrites," Danton and Hébert. Maximilien must strike and strike unceasingly ! Thus must a free State be ruled !

Robespierre, according to his wont, hesitated, only because he was waiting his opportunity. Danton was in his way, Hébert disgusted him. At which of the two should he strike first ? At the man who commanded the least support—Hébert. Danton himself, who abhorred the "extravagant" party, would stand by Robespierre: had not Desmoulins been the first to deal heavy blows at the *Père Duchesne?* Then, when Hébert and Chaumette were overthrown, the *Père Duchesne* broken to pieces, the Hébertist Commune dissolved, and the Robespierrist Commune set up, the attack on Danton should be made, and with the support of Robespierre's henchmen at the Hôtel-de-Ville, the Convention would be forced to submit.

Danton was only too glad to make any move against anarchy. He supported Robespierre on the 16th Frimaire when he carried a decree granting freedom to all forms of worship and

391

thus delivered Catholics from the tyranny of Reason: Reason now trembled on her altars, and Desmoulins continued his **Desmoulins** passionate attacks on Hébert. At the same time **attacks the** he made an assault on the Terrorist dictatorship. **Dictatorship.** To every independent mind the necessity for the existence of this dictatorship now seemed much less pressing. On November 28, 29, and 30 Hoche had shaken Brunswick's position at *Kaiserslautern*, and had marched, in concert with Pichegru, on *Landau*. Then came the Alsatian campaign of December 1794. A series of successes: *Lembach, Reichshoffen, Froeschwiller*, on the 22nd; and, to wind up, the recovery of the lines of *Wissembourg* and, after a fierce battle at Geisberg, the raising of the blockade of *Landau* on the 28th. As Kellermann had likewise driven the 2500 Piedmontese who had threatened to invade the South back over their own mountains, there was good reason to hope great things from the reorganized armies. And, as a matter of fact, the spring was to witness a magnificent return by France to offensive tactics; Belgium was to be reconquered, and the Sambre and Meuse campaign was to lead up to the decisive victory at Fleurus. Danton noted this success: he took it to be a reason for the simultaneous pursuit of an indulgent policy at home and a pacific policy abroad, and thus made himself yet more odious in the eyes of Robespierre, to whom war daily appeared more and more indispensable to the success of his policy of Public Safety.

Robespierre put pressure on the Committee, all the members of which, from Barère to Collot, believed their position threatened by the " Indulgent." Barère asked the Convention to declare its intention of carrying on the war to the bitter end, and gained his point. The fact that " the tyrants are still threatening us ": received a formal recognition, but Robespierre now proceeded to draw the conclusion that the tyrants only threatened because they had accomplices inside the country. The Convention must " *stifle all these enemies, within and without, these factions marching under various banners to the disorganization of popular government !*" His speech was lengthy, and it was much applauded.

*   *   *   *   *

Danton felt that the blow was aimed as much at him as at Hébert. There was nothing tortuous in his nature: he always went straight to the point. He sought an explanation, asked for an interview with Robespierre, thinking it might result in a loyal alliance against the " blood-drinkers." But Robespierre's tone became bitter at once: Danton grew angry, deplored the persistence of the Terror, declared there must be an end of these hecatombs in which " the innocent were confounded with the guilty." " Eh! who told you, pray," cried Robespierre, " that a single innocent person had been put to death ?" Danton, exasperated by this prodigious unconsciousness of guilt, which he regarded as a piece of abominable hypocrisy, turned to the friend who was with him: " What do you say ?" he sneered in his hoarse voice, " not one innocent person has perished !" and he left the room abruptly. This was at the beginning of January.

Though Robespierre meant to strike Hébert before he struck Danton, he plainly saw that the Commune was falling into **Robespierre** discredit, and craftily prepared Danton's ruin **discredits** the while. Before he attacked him openly he **Danton's** proposed to soil his reputation through the **Supporters.** men about him. On January 6 he assailed Fabre d'Eglantine at the Jacobin Club. Fabre really was a thief, and found it difficult to defend himself. Chabot, also one of Danton's supporters, was another rascal. On January 14 Robespierre had this " band " arrested, and Couthon wrote: " The Convention has purged itself !" Then came a larger mouthful, Hérault de Séchelles, Danton's only supporter in the Committee. He was a " corrupt " man, whose scandalous debauches at Chaillot, shared by another rascal, the Abbé d'Espagnac, were offensive to " virtue." Sitting at his work one day in the Pavillon de Flore Hérault looked up and saw Robespierre's eye fixed upon him: from that moment he had no doubt as to what his fate would be.

Danton felt himself threatened: his supporters were being swept away. He knew his own danger: he talked openly of " the unendurable tyranny of Robespierre." At the first performance of Legouvé's *Epicharis et Néron*, the two foes came face to face; Robespierre was in a box, Danton, with a bodyguard of friends, was seated in the orchestra. An actor spoke the words " Death to the tyrant !" There was applause from the floor of the house, and Legouvé relates that Danton, turning towards Robespierre, shook his fist at him. White with rage and fear, his teeth clenched, his hands twitching convulsively, Robespierre sat brooding on his vengeance. Scenes such as these hurried on the crisis.

* * * * *

Robespierre sent for Saint-Just, " the exterminating angel," as M. Claretie calls him. He made the decisive speech which Saint-Just at the Rostrum. set forth the whole programme: " *What constitutes the Republic is the destruction of everything opposed to it. A man is guilty* against the Republic when he takes pity on prisoners: *he is guilty* because he has no desire for virtue: *he is guilty* because he is opposed to the Terror." Every sentence meant the fall of twenty heads in the Convention. A decree was passed whereby " justice and probity " were made the order of the day. Robespierre's immediate followers put on airs of gloom. " *Though Hell may be against us*," wrote Couthon, " *Heaven is on our side, and Heaven is the master of Hell !*" This is in Torquemada's best style.

Hébert—that instrument of " Hell "—was overthrown by a backhanded blow. Collot, who had followed him for a time, went down to the Jacobin Club, demolished him, and deprived him of the Club's support. He might, perhaps, threatened though he was, have raised the mob in his favour, but he was a contemptible fellow; he took fright, wavered, poured forth recriminations, lost a great deal of time. When the Cordeliers did proclaim an insurrection, it hung fire. Hanriot did not even need to draw his sword against these puppets. He took them in their own homes: on the 20th Ventose, Hébert, Ronsin, Clootz, Vincent, and Momoro joined Fabre and Chabot in the prisons of the Republic. Chaumette and Gobel were to follow them ere long. All were arrested as accomplices of Pitt and Coburg, and guilty supporters of a dictatorship which they had intended to bestow—save the mark !—on Pache, " Papa Pache !"

Their trial lasted from the 1st to the 5th Germinal. These men were not interesting figures, it must be acknowledged, but

they certainly were victims, like the Girondins, of judicial
murder. The only accusation brought against the eighteen
prisoners—apart from certain extremely vague
and unjustified political offences—was that their
morals were bad. They were unable to make any
defence. Hébert seemed a " blockhead." He whimpered when
the sentence was read, and was carried out in a faint. His
behaviour on the scaffold was no less sorry. Paris gazed in
astonishment at the dreaded *Père Duchesne*, in the person of the
little white-faced man, shivering at the prospect of death. His
victims, the " Widow Capet " and " the woman Roland " had
died in very different fashion. Clootz, an honest man, shouted
to the people from the tumbril: " My friends, pray don't confuse me with these rascals !"

The Death of " Père Duchesne."

A gloomy joy shone on the faces of Robespierre's, and even
of Danton's friends. Chabot, in his prison, rejoiced, in the
curious will which has come down to us, over the fall of these
wretches, and hoped, indeed, he might soon see it followed by
that of such " Catonists " as Robespierre. But Chabot and
Danton were both to die before the " Catonists " took their turn.

*   *   *   *   *

Hébert's blood was still fresh upon the guillotine when
Danton's downfall was determined.

He had a strong following in the Convention: he might have
resisted, and even sent his enemies to the very scaffold towards
Demoralization which they were striving to hurry him. But his
of Danton. weariness seemed to grow greater every day. " I
would rather be guillotined than guillotine others . . . and
besides, *I am sick of the human race !*" Sometimes he would
break out into fierce talk, incoherent, and, above all, futile.
" He would eat Robespierre's entrails !" he said to Thibaudeau
one day: in the presence of other persons he called down the
" execration " deserved by all tyrants on his head. And then
again he would protest, with tears in his voice, that he was
" a good friend, a good citizen." Such words from a man who
had overturned a throne and held the Continent of Europe at
bay, point to some serious disturbance of the nervous system.
Now and then he said something really sublime. A friend

Fouquier thought that all was lost: he sent an imploring letter to the Committee asking for a decree that would silence the defence. The accused men were dangerous ruffians, he vowed; "*their observations* (note the delightful expression) *disturb the Tribunal.*"

The Committee played its last card: it forced a decree which was to close the prisoners' mouths from the terrified Convention. This was read aloud in court: the public murmured: Danton tried to protest: but Herman closed the proceedings. On the next day (the 13th) Trinchard, foreman of the jury, declared the jury's mind was sufficiently enlightened. A moment afterwards all the accused had been condemned to death. It was a real butchery.

Danton had realized whose hand it was that had first sent him to the Tribunal and was now strangling his defence: " Vile Robespierre !" he cried. " The scaffold claims you too. *You will follow me !*"

Within three months he followed him.

* * * * *

" The spring is very warm: all the trees are in blossom . . . life has not been so pleasant for many a year," wrote a Parisian

Execution of Danton. that day. In the most glorious weather Danton went to his death. " Big game," said the gaoler to Samson, as he handed over the condemned men.

Danton was quite unchanged. He made rough jokes to Desmoulins, who was crying quietly: " Horace ! Lucile ! My beloved !" and to Fabre, the true literary man, who was complaining bitterly because the authorities had seized a manuscript of his, *L'Orange de Naples*, and he was certain that wretch Billaud, whose work had been hissed more than once, would take possession of it: a fine play, in splendid verse ! " *Des vers !*" jeered Danton. " *Avant huit jours tu en feras !*" Till his last moment he was Shakespearean !

Paris saw fifteen condemned men go by that day ! Frénilly has told us how Danton's " huge round head fixed its proud gaze on the dull crowd." Arnault saw Hérault, flushed scarlet, but quite calm. " That epicurean," says M. Dard his biographer, " was only thirty-four, but he fancied he was eighty !"

THE FALL OF THE FACTIONS

The eyes of the terrified mob were fixed on Danton: but the women looked at the handsome Hérault: on the very square where the execution was to take place a woman's hand waved him a farewell from one of the windows of the Garde-Meuble, and a smile flitted across his face. Danton saw David on the terrace of a café coolly sketching him and his fellow-prisoners, and shouted "Lackey!" at his old friend in his rage. In the crowd, we are told, a priest, the Abbé de Kéravenan, who had blessed Danton's marriage a few months previously, followed in the tumbril's wake, pronouncing the absolution as he went.

It had grown very late by the time the procession reached the scaffold: the executioner was in a hurry: when Hérault tried to embrace Danton he interfered: "Fools!" cried Danton, " You won't prevent our heads from kissing each other in the basket !" Hérault was the first to perish, Danton the last. For one moment his heart seemed to fail him. He, too, worshipped his young wife. " My beloved ! Shall I never see thee again ?" Then he pulled himself together: " Come Danton ! No weakness !" he was heard to murmur. And then, to the executioner: " Show my head to the People, it is worth it !" A moment more, and just as darkness fell on Paris, the basket received that formidable head.

SOURCES. Works already quoted by Aulard (*Jacobins*, V), Schmidt, Barère, Choudieu, Baudot, Madame Jullien, Durand de Maillane, Dulaure, Madame Roland (*Mémoires*), Barbaroux, Buzot, Dubreuilh, Frénilly, Couthon, Riouffe, Grégoire, Miot, Thibaudeau, Carnot (*Mémoires*, II), Desmoulins (*Œuvres*, 1871).—Aulard, *Actes du Comité*, X-XII, 1897–8; Saint-Just, *Œuvres* (edited by Villay, 1908; *Correspondance de Le Bas et Saint-Just* (quoted in Stéfane Pol's *Autour de Robespierre*); *Notes oratoires de Robespierre* (*Rev. Fr.*, 1906); *Chroniques de Paris du 9 novembre*, 1792; *Vente des effets*, etc. (*Annales Révolutionnaires*, III); Legouvé, *Soixante ans de Souvenirs*, 1826; *Testament de Chabot Intermédiaire* (February 28, 1903); No. 7 of the *Vieux Cordelier* (*Annales Révolutionnaires*, IV); Roederer, *Œuvres*, III, 1870; Vilate, *Causes secrètes de la Révolution de Thermidor*, 1802; Courtois, *Papiers trouvés chez Robespierre*; Chaumette, *Mémoires* (Braesch ed.), 1903.

WORKS. Those already quoted by Hamel (*Robespierre*), Gros, Dard, Robinet, Montier, Almeras, Claretie (*Desmoulins*), Arnaud, Levasseur, Madelin, Lichtemberger (*Le Socialisme et la Révolution*), Tiersot, Bonald, Lenôtre (*Tribunal*).—d'Hericault, *Thermidor*, 1878; Stéfane Pol, *De Robespierre à Fouché*, 1905; Lacour, *Trois Femmes de la Révolution*, 1905; Aulard, *Le Culte de la Raison et le Culte de l'Être Supreme*, 1892;

Brunemann, *Robespierre*, 1898; Lenôtre, *Saint-Just* (*Vieux Papiers*, I); *Hébert* (II), *Chaumette* (III), *La Mère Duchesne* (IV); Mautouchet, *Philippeaux*, 1900; Mathiez, *Chaumette franc-maçon* (*Rev. Fr.*, 1902); Aulard, *Les Soixante-treize* (*Rev. Fr.*, 1894,; Braesch, *Chaumette et l'Hébertisme* (*Rev. Fr.*, 1908); D'Estrée, *Le Père Duchesne*, 1909; Mathiez, *Les Origines des Cultes révolutionnaires*, 1904; idem, *La Question Sociale pendant la Révolution*, 1903; Louis Madelin, *Le Règne de la Vertu* (*Revue des Deux Mondes*, February 15, 1911); Gautherot, *Gobel*, 1911.

CHAPTER XXXIII

THE REIGN OF VIRTUE

March–July, 1794

The "Dictatorship" of Robespierre. Fleurus. Virtue as the basis of government. A bloodstained "Salentum." The Great Terror. The prisons, the tribunal, and Samson's "little window." The resurrection of the Deity. The Festival of the Supreme Being (20th Prairial). The opponents of Robespierre and Fouché. The Law of Prairial. "Heads are falling like slates ! " Fouché undermines Robespierre's position.

ROBESPIERRE was master now. In Europe a belief arose that a Cromwell had been born who would put an end to the Revolution and found a stable government with which it would be possible to treat.

The Powers seized on this pretext for remaining inactive. In reality they had been demoralized by France's return to offensive tactics. On the day when Hoche drove out the Germans from Wissembourg, and Dugommier dislodged the English from Toulon, the soil of France had been saved. And, in the course of that same autumn of 1793, Kléber and Marceau had won an engagement at Cholet and finally crushed the resistance of La Vendée at Savenay.

Robespierre Dictator.

The defeated Powers were at greater odds amongst themselves than ever. In March 1794, Poland, led by Kosciusko, rose in rebellion, and Carnot, meanwhile, threw the armies of the East into the Low Countries. Pichegru marched his 160,000 men to combine with Jourdan and his troops, and the latter general, now at the head of 230,000 men, made a bold advance. On May 18 the Austrians were beaten at Tourcoing. The King of Prussia having diverted to Warsaw the reinforcements that should have gone to Brussels, the Emperor feared he was to be fooled again in the matter of Poland, and penned a sour note to his Chancellor : " We shall be left out of the partition ! "

Jourdan took advantage of these disagreements. His troops were magnificent, that *Army of the Sambre and Meuse* whose name still resounds like an epic trumpet-call. It had learnt warfare now, it had learnt discipline, but it still preserved that revolutionary frenzy which increased the natural *furia* of the Frenchman tenfold : " We fought one against ten," writes one of these soldiers, " but *La Marseillaise* was fighting beside us ! " On June 26th this army was attacked at *Fleurus,* and crushed its assailants utterly. It was a magnificent victory, and after Wattignies, the greatest military triumph of the Revolution.

The victory of Fleurus.

Its effects soon became evident : on July 6 the Allies evacuated Brussels, and on the 11th Jourdan entered the city. On the 23rd Pichegru, driving the English before him as he went, took possession of Antwerp. From that moment Belgium was ours. And meanwhile the Army of the Alps was threatening Turin. The Coalition, undermined by the Polish business, began to weaken.

The discomfited European statesmen cast a veil of hope over their defeat. What had been their object ? said the Cabinet of Vienna to the Cabinet of England. To put an end to the Revolution ! Well ! Robespierre would soon do that !

* * * * *

He was not dreaming of any such thing. The one and constant thought of that mediocre brain and narrow soul was to protect himself against " his enemies." These he discovered in every quarter : to destroy them he kept the guillotine permanently employed, and bent as he was, too, on restoring his " Supreme Being," and defending the rights of property, he was forced to carry on his policy of blood, for without it would not his enemies cast the terrible reproach of " moderatism " upon him ?

The Terror essential to Robespierre.

Everything was in his hands. When the Convention handed Danton over to him it made itself his slave : the members voted without any preliminary discussion, " and with a contented air," otherwise, says Baudot, " Saint-Just turned his attention

402

THE REIGN OF VIRTUE

to you, just as in the days of Nero." It was unsafe to look sad, or even thoughtful. Barras tells a story of one deputy who fancied Robespierre looked at him when he was in a dreamy mood, and exclaimed in alarm: "*He'll be supposing I was thinking about something!*" Billaud, speaking one day, stopped suddenly short, and then, with an imperious intonation, said: "I think I hear murmurs!" The Committee was a ten-headed Cæsar, and it was absolutely ruled by Robespierre.

For a time at all events all the members of the two "great Committees" seemed under the yoke. In the provinces the The École Commissaries were being recalled and replaced by de Mars. henchmen of the dictator. In Paris, Fleuriot the Mayor and Payan the Agent of the Nation held the Hôtel-de-Ville for Robespierre: through Dumas, Fouquier, and the jurymen, all of them his creatures, he ruled the Tribunal. He fancied the Army was also his tool: the General Staff was fed by the École de Mars, the idea of which, due to Barère, had been "eagerly hailed by Robespierre," M. Chuquet tells us. The pupils, dressed in the style of the ancient Romans, received frequent visits from the Master: one of them, Bangofsky, has left us an account of these, and tells us how great was the influence Robespierre wielded over him and his fellows. In any case the "Army of Paris" was devoted to him, for it was commanded by the scoundrel Hanriot, "Robespierre's donkey" as he was nicknamed at the Halles. Property owners, reassured by his views, put their faith in him, and led by Grégoire, the "constitutional" clergy, to whom the worship of a Supreme Being gave a certain satisfaction, seemed to favour him. And then he was "*the Man of Virtue.*"

That dictatorship of the Year II really was a Dictatorship of Virtue. Robespierre had borrowed the term from the sentimental phraseology of his day, but he had amplified its meaning. "Virtue" became a *sine quâ non :* in an address presented to the Convention on the 5th Floréal, Therezia Cabarrus herself prayed that young girls should be taught "to practise virtue" —Therezia! And we see a popular society—that of Provins—get "a schoolmaster, guilty of having delayed the regularization of his *liaison,*" marched off to prison. Robespierre, who was busy with the purification of the Palais-Royal, himself,

403

as I have already said, set an example of every kind of virtue in his lodging over Duplay the cabinet-maker's shop, and in the bosom of a virtuous family. " We desire," said he to Lindet one day, " to found a Salentum." A Salentum red with blood !

*　　*　　*　　*　　*

" Virtue, apart from which terror is baneful ; terror, apart from which virtue is powerless." That was Robespierre's whole theory. Thus, the greater his longing to estab-lish virtue, the fiercer did the Terror become under his sway.

The Great Terror.

The Tribunal saw to that. Fouquier, after a lecture from the Master, had exhorted Dumas to "tighten the screw for the chatterboxes," and, thanks to this advice, the work of the sittings was swiftly done. *"Heads,"* he wrote joyously, *" are falling like slates !"* But he hoped for better things yet : *" Next week I'll take the tops off three or four hundred ! "*

In April the batches had doubled in size. Who was to be held a " pure " republican now Danton had perished ? A promiscuous crowd ! Chaumette, who had been accused, among other sins (this is in the true Robespierre vein) of having suppressed the midnight masses, and Gobel, who died with the words " Long live Jesus Christ ! " upon his lips, were executed with a bevy of royalists and nuns. The ex-bishop was im-plicated in the *Conspiracy of the Prisons*, for the prisons were asserted to have plotted against Robespierre's life ! In this fantastic plot he caused not Gobel only, but General Dillon, an ex-nobleman, the widowed Mme. Hébert, once a nun, and poor Lucile, " a little Greuze girl," writes M. Claretie, " who died like a Roman," to be implicated. On April 18 seventeen men and women, accused of manœuvres " for starving the people," died together. On the 20th a batch of Parliamentarians—Pasquier, Rosambo, Ormesson, Molé, " twenty-four gentlemen," writes Trinchard proudly, " all of them *si deven* (*ci-devant*) presidents or councillors," were followed by the aged Malesherbes, and by d'Espremesnil, who, having once desired to de-Bourbonize France, had been the idol of Paris for a day (a far-off day, seven years before !). Then came the Duchesse du Châtelet and the Princess Lubomirska,

404

to whom were added a witness who "had not given his testimony well!" then the "virgins of Verdun," twenty-eight farmers-general (Lavoisier among them), and Madame Elisabeth, sent to the scaffold with twenty other victims, priests, soldiers, domestic servants, all condemned on the testimony of *a single witness!*

The prisons, emptied perpetually, were filled again perpetually. The chief charge never varied, the accused had "*depraved public morals*"; this fitted in well with the policy of virtue; when it affected the Sainte-Amaranthe, captured at one swoop with her tribe of fashionable lovers, the accusation, as Beugnot says, admits of some defence, and the same may be said of the arrest of Therezia Cabarrus on her return from Bordeaux; but Malesherbes! and Madame Elisabeth!

The Prisons, the Tribunal, and Samson's "little window."

Yet all these "wretches," these "depravers of morals," were crowded in endless succession into the Abbaye, Sainte-Pélagie, La Force, Les Carmes, the Luxembourg, to be drafted thence into the Conciergerie, whence they were passed on to Fouquier and so to Samson.

It was like an epidemic. People "contracted imprisonment," a less disagreeable complaint than the cholera, because while you waited for death you might spend delightful days in a charming and picturesque society full of unexpected features.

The whole country seemed doomed to the scaffold. Just before Thermidor every one seemed to be in prison. André Chénier was there at the feet of Aimée de Coigny; General Hoche at those of Joséphine de Beauharnais; pontiffs of the worship of Reason rubbed shoulders with prelates of the Roman Church; "heroes" of August 10 were mingled with Marquises from Versailles; Garat the minister, Suvée and Robert the painters, Kellermann the victor of Valmy, the mistress of Tallien, members of the three revolutionary Assemblies, and men and women of the best blood in France, all destined to lie in that cemetery of the Madeleine which had already received the ashes of Danton and the Queen, of Hébert and Charlotte Corday, of Chaumette and Louis XVI.

Massacre did not cease in the provinces when the Terrorist Commissaries were withdrawn, and imprisonment showed even less sign of abating : on the 7th Thermidor, 1000 persons were shut up in the prisons of Arras, 3000 in those of Strasburg, 1500 at Toulouse, and something like 7000 in Paris itself : all doomed to death to ensure the triumph of " Virtue."

* * * * *

Some " consecration " of this " Virtue " seemed essential. This was the theory of the " virtuous Couthon," who inspired Robespierre in this domain. On the 11th Thermidor, Tallien was heard to say with a sneer that Robespierre would have " turned the Eternal out of His place to take it for himself." For the present he was about to restore the Deity.

The Restoration of the Divinity.

"*If there had been no God,*" he proclaimed on the 1st Frimaire, "*we should have been obliged to invent Him.*" "*The idea of a great Being who watches over oppressed innocence, and punishes triumphant crime, is a thoroughly popular one.*" On the 17th Germinal, the " impious " members having been cleared out of the way, Couthon announced that the Committee was preparing to hold a Festival of the Supreme Being. " Pure souls," he wrote, " felt recognition and adoration of a superior Intelligence to be a real need." Whoever did not feel this need was a " wretch."

On Floréal the 18th Robespierre made his celebrated speech on " *the relation between religious and moral ideas and republican principles*," which was conceived in a similar spirit, and wound up by proclaiming the necessity for the institution of a deistic religion. A decree in this sense was duly voted, and everybody accepted the idea. Lescot, the Mayor, expressed a strange and mystic faith : God would reward France for passing this decree by granting her "abundant harvests." God surely owed His prophet Maximilien some mark of favour !

So the *Festival of the Supreme Being* was organized. It was to be the apotheosis of the new Vicar of the Faithful. He might be King, if only somebody would make an attempt upon his life ! And this, too, happened very opportunely; a little girl was caught in Duplay's yard with two small knives upon her person. Here

The Festival of the Supreme Being.

406

was "a Corday!" The Incorruptible was to have been murdered! Little Cécile Renaud was sent to the scaffold with fifty-three "accomplices," whom she had never seen, the black veil of the "parricide" cast over her head. For was not Robespierre the Father of his Country?

On Prairial the 16th, to enable him to preside officially at the festival on the 20th, he was appointed to the Presidency of the Convention. Some perfidious enemies of his voted in his favour: they hoped to make the evidence of this dictatorship more tangible, and so be better able to incriminate him.

David, now official decorator to the Republic, was making the arrangements for the Festival: Marie-Joseph Chénier had been commissioned to write the hymn, for which Gossec was to provide the orchestral accompaniment; but Robespierre, who hated Marie-Joseph, considered him unworthy of the honour, and refused to accept his hymn: a true pontiff, he now pronounced excommunications, major or minor. Mehul and Gossec, duly provided with an "orthodox" hymn, proceeded evening after evening to superintend the practice of the sacred strains in every Section, and for a week Paris, in obedience to a mandamus, followed by an official order, was busily engaged in rehearsing a canticle addressed to the Most High. It sounds like a dream!

There have been many descriptions of this Festival. Robespierre, in his blue coat, which had already attained something like celebrity, and with tricolour plumes waving in his hat, presided over the proceedings first at the Tuileries, and then on the Champ-de-Mars. From the platform—pulpit or throne—he spoke a lengthy rhapsody, the composition of which, in his desire to strike the correct note, he had confided to a worthy priest, the aged Abbé Porquet. This done, a hundred thousand voices chanted the praises of the Lord. Incense was burnt the while on the summit of the symbolic Mountain on which Maximilien stood, and concealed him in its clouds. For one moment this most prudent of men forgot his caution; his face, usually grave, was brightened by a smile of triumph. For a moment the Vicar of God fancied he was himself God!

*   *   *   *   *

He did not hear the muttering of the storm about him.
Amongst the members of the Convention standing behind him
Signs of
Opposition to
Robespierre. murmurs had arisen, and even "inprecations,"
says Baudot. That very evening the *Decade*
contained jeering allusions to the new State
religion : and when Robespierre, still giddy with triumph,
entered the Jacobin Club, he encountered the gloomy face of
Joseph Fouché.

This " dechristianizer " happened to be president of the Club.
He made a feint of sharing in the general delight, but added,
after a few commonplace remarks : " Brutus rendered worthy
homage to the Supreme Being when he buried a dagger in a
tyrant's heart : learn to follow his example ! "

Robespierre understood : and proved it within a few days,
when he charged Fouché with being at the head of the conspiracy against himself. But the president's bold words had
been applauded : and Robespierre had evidently made his
first mistake.

There were none left for him to make now. All eyes were
watching him closely. If the " tyrant " himself did not fall,
a whole group of men knew their time was come : he had received the " missionaries " just back from the departments,—
" Hébert's and Danton's tail," as he would have called them—
with most significant harshness : Fréron, Barras, Tallien,
Fouché, had all been terrified by that face of his, " as hard as
the cold marble of a statue." The first three were " corrupt
members " to be offered a sacrifice to " virtue " : the fourth
was an " atheist," and deserved the severest chastisement.
On Floréal the 18th it was said Robespierre had addressed
him by name from his own desk. " Come, tell us, Fouché,
who deputed you to assure the people that the Divinity does
not exist ? "

Fouché was no Danton : he never used violent impreca-
tions : manœuvres were his *forte*. Here were terrified men,
all trembling for their own heads : he fused these fears and
hates together, joined Hébert's " tail " to Danton's, ran about
from one to another, and stirred up unwonted opposition from
the Jacobin Club to the Convention itself : for Carnot, Billaud,
Collot, and even Barère felt themselves in danger, and were

already looking about for allies. Thus Robespierre was not mistaken; he had judged Fouché for the past three months to be his worst enemy. What was his rage then, when he beheld the " enemy " seated in the presidential chair of the great Club, *his* Club ! And what his fury when, on the very evening of his great apotheosis, this " wretch " shot from that very chair the poisoned arrow that was to rankle in the pontiff's wound !

* * * * *

His answer was swift. Three days later (22nd Prairial) Couthon brought forward a proposal intended to deliver the last of Robespierre's enemies into his hands.

The Decree of the 22nd Prairial.

" *Every delay is a crime, every formality is a public danger : the only delay necessary in punishing the enemies of the country is the time it takes to recognize them.*" The accused were to have no more lawyers to defend them, and the juries were to sentence them in batches. There were to be no more " cases "; one general accusation : " all those who attempt to destroy liberty, whether by force or by deceit," were to be declared " enemies of the people." This meant the handing over of the dictator-ship to the Public Prosecutor : but everybody knew that the Public Prosecutor was ruled by Robespierre. Nor was this all— and here the true object of the plan revealed itself; hitherto no representative of the people—from Brissot to Danton— could be haled before the Tribunal without the authorization of the Convention : *in future it was to be done on the mere order of the Committees.* This was a blow aimed at Lecointre, Legendre, Fréron, Tallien, Barras, and Fouché. And many others, too, felt they were threatened. " If this law passes," cried Ruamps, " I may as well blow my brains out at once ! I ask for an adjournment." Everybody agreed with him, and supported his motion.

Then Robespierre rose to his feet : he would have his law, he would have his heads : " For a long time the Convention had been debating and voting decrees, because for a long time it has been ruled entirely by the power of factions. I propose that the Convention shall not notice the motion for adjournment

and shall continue, if necessary, to discuss the proposal submitted to it till eight o'clock to-night ! "

What was this man's strange hypnotic power? His
trembling opponents held their peace, and within half an hour
the death-dealing law was passed.

He departed, believing his vengeance was assured. But
the very next day the Assembly revolted. Bourdon (of the
The Decree rescinded and reinstated. Oise) and Merlin secured the passage of a resolution whereby the clause affecting members of
the Convention was struck out. These miserable
men were ready to sacrifice France, but they would not sacrifice
themselves.

To Robespierre this clause was the most important of the
whole law : he ventured to demand the heads that would
have escaped him. " Intriguers," he said, " were striving to
carry the Mountain away with them, and make themselves
the heads of a party." " Name them ! " came the cry from
terrified throats. He ought to have named them : in the state
of wild alarm then reigning in the Assembly he would have been
granted the heads thus specified. But he committed the mistake of leaving the terror to hang over them all without saying
anything to reassure the majority. " I will name them when
necessary." But he had spoken, the others bowed their heads.
The clause was reinstated.

*   *   *   *   *

Armed with his new law Robespierre began his operations
that very night. Fouché's presence at the Jacobins was a
scandal which had lasted only too long. On the evening of
the 23rd Prairial Robespierre proceeded to attack him there :
Fouché was no orator : he made a poor defence, closed the
sitting, and came back no more : but in the shadow he began
to lay his snares.

Those six weeks between the 23rd Prairial and the 9th
Thermidor were horrible. Under the tremendous power of
" Heads falling like slates." the weapon placed in the hands of the Committee
and the Tribunal by the passing of the new law,
the country learnt what the extreme of terror meant. All the
" weaklings "—those who did not frequent Duplay's house—
had been eliminated from the jury. " No more witnesses ! "

Fouquier had said. It was a massacre, neither more nor less : 40, 50, 60, heads in a day. In the course of those forty-nine days 1367 heads fell in Paris. " Butchery," says M. Aulard, and it is the right word.

Paris was packed with Robespierre's "unofficial" emissaries, and everybody lived under the watchful eye of a merciless police. Fear was on every side, in the creak of a door, an exclamation, a breath. Drawing-rooms were empty, wine-shops deserted : the very courtesans ceased to go to the Palais-Royal, where, (extraordinary sight !) virtue now reigned supreme. The dreary city waited on, under the burning summer sun. What was it waiting for ? From the sacristy to the house of ill-fame the same fear brooded everywhere and over everyone. Suspicion was on every head : the exccutioners of yesterday were in worse case than their own victims. When a Fouché, who had mowed the men of Lyons down with grapeshot, was accused of failure in civic duty all might well tremble ! The Convention was well-nigh deserted : none but members of the Committees now sat in the presidential chair : Prieur was elected to that position by 94 out of 117 votes (the normal number of the Assembly was 750) : the deputies had given up sleeping at home. Among those who still attended, says Thibaudeau, " the timid ones wandered from seat to seat, some did not dare to sit down anywhere, and slipped away when the necessity for voting arose." Suspicion hovered over every bench.

Opposition was crushed : the Master's immediate circle grovelled : Barras found General Brune, later to become a Marshal of France, in Robespierre's lodgings, helping Mme. Duplay and Eléonore, the cabinet-maker's daughter— said to have been Robespierre's *fiancée*—to peel potatoes. Another constant attendant there was Curée, a member of the Convention on whose motion the Empire was ultimately to be proclaimed, and who was already taking lessons in the art of servitude. But except for Le Bas, Couthon, and Saint-Just, his three favourite henchmen, and his agents, Fleuriot the Mayor, Herman the Minister of the Interior, Payan the National Agent, Dumas the President, Fouquier the Public Prosecutor, the faithful jurymen who, with Duplay, habitually escorted Robespierre when he went out of doors, and Hanriot, his tool, not a man was considered really reliable. Maximilien had revived the "whosoever is not with me is against me," of all religions.

There was no excuse whatever for the tyranny so brutally applied by the official underlings, and none, consequently, for the Terror which attended it. The danger to the country from without had passed away; Fleurus had reassured the mind of France ; a plan for the invasion of Italy was in course of preparation; Europe was retiring at every point. "*Victories,*" writes Barère, "*pursued Robespierre* !" He was well aware of it : Saint-Just warned Barère there must be no more "working them up." Barère refused to comply with the order. He enjoyed the business, and once Saint-Just's injunction revealed Robespierre's plan, he took a perfidious delight in inflating his own lungs and the importance of the successes achieved.

In his mouth even disasters were turned into victories : this is what happened when our naval squadron was defeated; The Legend of Barère transformed the *Vengeur* which, as M. the "Vengeur." Lévy-Schneider has unfortunately proved, sank just as she surrendered, into a magnificent wreck whose crew went down with her rather than strike their colours to the enemy. But more genuine victories than this furnished legitimate texts for his patriotic oratory. It was applauded by the Assembly and cursed by Robespierre ; for every fresh victory cast more odium on a dictatorship which was now without excuse.

Yet the Convention continued to submit to the Committee. And then at last Robespierre's enemies perceived the point on which their action must be directed. They must break up the Committee itself and attack the dictatorship within its bosom. Once disunion prevailed in the Committees, they would hand the tyrant over to the Assembly. The intrigue which began in Messidor, and was to reach a successful issue on the 9th Thermidor, was hatched in the Pavillon de Flore.

For there was no hope of any help from the country in its terror, or from the Assembly, in its bondage.

412

THE REIGN OF VIRTUE

SOURCES. Works already quoted by Aulard (*Jacobins*, V), Fricasse, Malouet (II), Couthon, Baudot, Barras, Barère, Durand de Maillane, Frénilly, Louise Fusil (II), Miot, Beugnot (II).—Aulard, *Actes du Comité*, XIII–XV, 1900–3; Mrs. Williams, *Letters*, 1793–94; Charlotte Robespierre, *Mémoires*, 1830; Bangofsky, *Souvenirs*, 1908; Philarète Chasle, *Mémoires*, 1867; Duchesse de Brissac, *Pages sombres*, 1903.

WORKS. Those already quoted by Aulard (*Le Culte*, etc.), Gros, Lenôtre (*Tribunal*), Dunoyer, Esmein, Claretie (*Desmoulins*), Stéfane Pol (*Autour de Robespierre, De Robespierre à Fouché*), Tiersot, Montier, Turquan (*Madame Tallien*), Arnaud, Madelin (*Fouché, Le Règne de la Vertu*), d'Héricault, Hamel, Cabanès (*Névrose*), Dauban (*Prisons*), Goncourt, Pingaud, Gautherot.—A. Chuquet, *L'École de Mars*, 1899; Lévy-Schneider, *Les Démêlés dans le Comité de Salut Public* (*Rev. Fr.*, 1900); Du Bled, *La Société dans les Prisons* (*Revue des Deux Mondes*, 1890); Frédéric Masson, *Joséphine de Beauharnais*, 1907; Bellanger, *La Société populaire de Provins*, 1908; Liéby, *Marie-Joseph Chénier et la Fête de l'Etre Suprême* (*Rev. Fr.* 1902); Frédéric Masson, *La Religion de Robespierre* (*Jadis*, I); *Le Déisme sous la Révolution* (ibidem); Etienne Lamy, *Introduction aux Mémoires d'Aimée de Coigny*, 1906; Lenôtre, *Héron* (*Vieux Papiers*, I); *Hanriot* (ibidem, III); Mathiez, *L'Affaire Catherine Théot* (*Contributions à l'Histoire religieuse de la Révolution*, 1907).

CHAPTER XXXIV

THERMIDOR

Dissensions in the Great Committee. The last tumbrils. The two plots. The sitting of the 8th Thermidor. The evening of the 8th at the Jacobin Club. The night of the 8th Thermidor at the Pavillon de Flore. The sitting of the 9th, the fray, Tallien's dagger, Robespierre's party proscribed. The Hôtel-de-Ville against the Convention. The misadventures of Hanriot. Robespierre at the Hôtel-de-Ville. The fall of " Catiline." The execution of Robespierre. The events of Thermidor misinterpreted by the people.

THE Committee had long been attacked as a " block," and as a " block " it had resisted. A few cracks in its fabric had appeared in Ventôse, but these had been plastered up after Danton's execution. Others more formidable had made their appearance in Prairial. Collot and Billaud—extreme Terrorists both of them, and Hébertists at bottom—objected to the punishment of the Commissaries who had carried the Terror, and with it the principles of Chaumette, into the provinces. On the 23rd Prairial a violent quarrel broke out between Billaud and Robespierre. Another evening, Collot, always brutal in his manners, had threatened to throw Robespierre out of the window, Saint-Just and Carnot were on bad terms. In Floréal the former had done his best to get the latter expelled from the Committee : " You'll go out before me, Saint-Just ! " said Carnot : but since that moment he had been upon his guard, and Prieur stood by him. Lindet could not forgive Robespierre for Danton's death. Barère, as always, was a trimmer. But his reports to the Convention of the opinions rife in Europe were a somewhat perfidious demonstration of the prestige the Dictator was acquiring at the expense of the republican idea.

Dissensions in the Great Committee.

414

THERMIDOR

The *Committee of Public Safety* was now quite definitely hostile to Robespierre. Save Le Bas, a faithful adherent, and David, who was not to be relied on, all its members, led and influenced by old Vadier, loathed "the tyrant." Vouland and Amar did not hesitate to say that somebody ought to catch him near an open window and "throw him out upon the pavement." This Committee of Police was seeking out a joint in the dictator's harness. A mad woman of the name of Catherine Théot had been going about foretelling the advent of the Son of God, and Vadier, in his report to the Convention, exaggerated the importance of the business and even insinuated that this Messiah, according to Catherine was the pontiff of the 20th Prairial. Now this old buffoon from the South, who, as Philarète Chasle tells us, was like Voltaire, had a knack of grimacing that made people laugh. He raised a laugh at the expense of Robespierre, who was exceedingly annoyed by the incident, and hushed the business up—a blunder which gave the Gascon's insinuations a certain air of probability.

Catherine Théot's "prophecies."

In reality Robespierre's nerve was failing him : he realized the increasing hostility of the Committees. On the 10th Messidor he recalled Saint-Just, then with the armies, and reassured by his "sword-bearer's" presence, sulkily turned his own back on the insubordinate Committee, and ceased to attend its sittings. On the 13th he made a bitter complaint of the cabals in the Committee to the Jacobin Club.

He had originally issued from the Club : he wished now to go back to it, seek fresh strength within it, and drive his enemies out of it. He had the name of Fouché, "the leader of the conspiracy which must be foiled," and several others struck off its list. But Fouché carried on his underhand campaign more vigorously than ever. He put lists of the persons likely to be proscribed into circulation, and would go and see one or other of them, and remark, "If he does not perish you will perish most assuredly yourself !" Busily, with his nervous fingers, he was knotting the strands in which Robespierre was suddenly to find himself entangled.

* * * * *

415

By the beginning of Thermidor the work was done, but how frail was the whole net ! The slightest tug would have been enough to break it ! Couthon tried his best at the Jacobin Club, where, on the 5th, he ventured to accuse Carnot. Barère spoke in his defence. Meanwhile Fouché had brought about a reconciliation between Collot and Billaud who had quarrelled. The Mountain was preparing a move against Robespierre, but for this the support of the Centre was indispensable, and the Centre, which had less esteem for Collot, Tallien, Fouché and the rest than for Robespierre— Durand de Maillane reveals this feeling to us—hesitated to favour these survivors of Hébertism at the expense of a man who treated the moderate party with consideration. Robespierre went to Cambacérès and begged him to beware of Fouché : but Tallien and Legendre had already sounded this " toad of the Marsh " and shaken his allegiance. Yet Boissy d'Anglais openly expressed his esteem for Robespierre, and Durand de Maillane had offered him most lively congratulations on his spirituality. Without the Centre—the great mass of members—nothing could be done : the scale into which its support was cast must inevitably be the heaviest. The thing that troubled Durand was " those sixty or eighty heads a day." In vain did Augustin Robespierre declare himself a " moderate " at the Club. On the 7th Thermidor André Chénier was guillotined, and twenty-three others with him : on the 8th, fifty-five condemned persons, among them nineteen women, were to go to their deaths. Such proofs of " moderation " gave little satisfaction to Durand, Boissy, and Cambacérès. But still they held back.

The last Tumbrils.

Intrigue was rife in every corner : and heads were at stake everywhere. There was no time to lose ; both parties were meditating a sudden blow. If the dictator's enemies were resolved to strike, so too was he. A study of certain documents shows us that an outbreak in support of Robespierre was being prepared for the 10th Thermidor. Hanriot, Fleuriot, Payan, and Dumas were the instigators. The festival of the two youthful heroes, Bara and Viala,* to attend which the École de Mars

Plots and Counterplots in the Convention.

* Joseph Bara, a heroic boy soldier of the Republican army killed in

had been summoned to Paris, was to be the pretext for a gathering during which the " thunderbolt " was to fall. Robespierre, who had spent the past three weeks shut up in Duplay's house, consented, under pressure from Saint-Just, to prepare the way by the delivery of a great speech in the Convention on the 8th.

Meanwhile Fouché was working harder than ever, and Tallien had made up his mind to the most extreme measures. According to a legend accepted by a serious biographer of the Talliens, Therezia Cabarrus, who was worshipped by the former pro-consul, had sent him word from her prison that she was about to die, "thanks to his arrant cowardice." This may be true.

On the 8th Thermidor (July 27) the sun rose fiercely upon a world that had already reached the boiling-point.

* * * * *

The emotion was intense in the Convention when Robespierre was seen slowly ascending the steps to the rostrum.

The Sitting of the 8th Thermidor.
" This was the beginning of a great trial," writes Crevelier, one of the members.

From the very first, he adds, this " Catiline " took an arrogant line, " that despotic tone which was beginning to weary us."

The speech, which has been preserved to us, had been carefully polished during the period of the speaker's seclusion. It

Robespierre's Speech.
indicated a decided change in Robespierre's policy: he appealed from the Committees to the Assembly " which they had oppressed "; he was attacked by these Committees only because he did not belong to any faction, but to the Convention itself. " For the last six weeks, at least, my powerlessness to do good or check evil has forced me absolutely to forsake my functions. Has patriotism been better protected? faction more timid? the country happier?" The yoke of the Committee, now in a state of anarchy, must be

La Vendée in 1793, aged 13. He refused to save his life by crying "Long live the King," and fell shouting " Long live the Republic ! "

Joseph Agricole Viala, a boy soldier celebrated for his courage, born at Avignon in 1780. He was killed on the banks of the river Durance while trying to cut the cables of some pontoons laden with royalists who were endeavouring to get across the river.

shaken off. " You were not appointed to be ruled, but yourselves to rule the persons on whom you have bestowed your confidence ! " Then, turning towards the Centre, and the benches, now very empty, of the Right, he recalled the fact that in spite of the hatred of the Mountain he had saved the seventy-five supporters of the Girondins from the guillotine. Thinking himself sure of the Centre, which had listened to him in silence, he began a bitter criticism of the financial system (a hit at Cambon), the "prevaricating agents " (the pro-consuls), the management of the war (Carnot), and, with a boldness passing all belief, the Terror itself. "Let us admit the existence of a plot against public liberty ; that it owes its strength to a criminal coalition which carries on its intrigues in the very bosom of the Convention; that members of the Committee are sharing in this plot ; that the coalition thus formed is seeking the ruin of patriots and country too. What is the remedy for this disease ? *To punish the traitors,* renew the composition of the Committee of General Security, *purify that Committee,* and subordinate it to the Committee of Public Safety, *purify the Committee of Public Safety itself :* constitute a united government under the supreme authority of the Convention : *thus crush all factions* by the weight of the national authority, and raise *the power of justice and liberty* on their ruins."

The Convention, which had listened in dead silence, sat in a stupor. Vague as the speech had been, the attacks on Cambon and his finance, on Carnot and his armies, Vadier and his police, the two Committees, and the ex-Commissaries, had filled its hearers with bewilderment and alarm. A tremendous crisis seemed about to open, " a gulf," says a witness of the sitting (Mrs. Williams), and nobody knew " what part of the city was to be swallowed up, or whether the whole of it would disappear." The very tendencies of the Revolution had been arraigned : " *We do not even possess the merit of having undertaken great things from motives of virtue.*" What did all this mean ? Must the whole thing be done over again ? Was this a prosecuting counsel's charge or a last testament ? Should leave be given to print this dangerous speech ? Couthon contrived to carry a motion in favour of " printing."

But the persons at whom the attack was aimed did not

intend to let themselves be strangled without protest. Vadier made an attempt to repeat his tale about old Catherine Théot. But Cambon did not give him time : he flew to the rostrum : " Before I am dishonoured I will speak to France ! " he cried. And speak he did, fiercely : *" One man alone paralyzes the will of the Convention : that man is Robespierre ! "*

The words were a signal for a rush to the rostrum. First came Billaud : before Robespierre's speech was printed it ought to be submitted to the Committee for consideration. " We must tear off the mask ; *I would rather my corpse should serve as the throne of an ambitious man than that by my silence I should become the accomplice of his crimes ! "* The excitement rose higher. Panis asserted that a list of proscribed persons had already been made : it must be communicated to the Convention : Robespierre protested against this, but refused to " whitewash this man or that." He did not realize how wise he would have been to mention ten men and to reassure three hundred. " When a man boasts of having the courage of virtue," cried Charlier, " he ought to possess the courage of truth ! Give the names of the men you accuse ! " " Yes ! Yes ! The names ! " clamoured the members. " I adhere to what I have said," he replied.

Hostile Replies to Robespierre.

Amar stigmatized the " wounded vanity which had made a disturbance in the Assembly." Fréron pressed for the withdrawal of the Committee's right to imprison members of the Convention. Some sought weapons, some shields. Barère made as though he would have quieted everybody with wheedling phrases : but Bréard made a fresh onslaught, and the decree ordering the printing of the speech was annulled.

At five o'clock the sitting closed. Robespierre had lost the first game of the rubber.

He reckoned on winning the second that very evening : his plan was to go to the Jacobin Club, where the plaudits of its members would sow terror at the morrow's sitting of the Convention.

He felt no anxiety. The night was beautiful after a sweltering day ; he went for a walk in the Champs Elysées, and said to Eléonore Duplay, who accompanied him : " Fine weather for to-morrow ! " Then he betook himself to the Club.

There he was given an ovation. He made his speech over again, and, inflamed by the general enthusiasm, attacked *The 8th Thermidor at the Jacobin Club.* Collot and Billaud, who were both present. There were shouts of "To the guillotine!" and the two suspects hastened to the Tuileries where the Committee was still at work. Hot as the summer night was, they must have felt the chill of the knife upon their necks!

As for Robespierre, so high were his spirits when he got home, that his optimism astonished Duplay. Before midnight struck the light was out behind the blue curtains of his famous chamber.

* * * * *

Prieur, Barère, and Lindet have all described the scene presented meanwhile by the Committee in its disorder and dismay. *The 8th and 9th Thermidor at the Pavillon de Flore.* The members were gathered round the celebrated "green table" when, at eleven o'clock, Collot, in wild excitement, hurried in from the Jacobin Club. Through the open door Saint-Just was to be seen writing busily in the adjoining room. Beside himself, Collot addressed him: "You are drawing up our accusation?" It was true. Saint-Just answered boldly, "Well, yes, you are not mistaken. . . ." and then to Carnot, spitefully: "I shall not forget you in it, and you will find I have dealt with you in masterly fashion!" Carnot shrugged his shoulders. But now Billaud arrived, blazing with fury. He poured out the vials of his wrath upon the phlegmatic young man, who began to feel he had said too much; he begged he might be allowed to finish his work; his speech was so far from being of the nature they supposed, that he intended to read it to the Committee next morning, before he made it in the Assembly. He wrote all night long, while his fellows, who had gone back into the green room, talked and wrangled. At five o'clock in the morning he rose to his feet, coolly took his leave, and as full of confidence as his leader, he departed to cool his blood in the Bois de Boulogne, through which he was seen galloping half an hour later.

The day seemed likely to be thundery. By noon the temperature had risen to forty degrees; thunder muttered in a sky like lead. The members of the Committee, in a state of

420

feverish anxiety, awaited Saint-Just's return. At half-past ten a note from him was brought in. "You have blighted my heart: I am going to open it to the Convention." Overwhelmed with emotion they all hurried thither.

They found the corridors seething with excitement. All night negotiations had been going on between the various **The Sitting** parties. The surviving members of the Right **of the 9th** were besieged with threats and flattery. "Oh, **Thermidor.** that Right!" cried Bourdon inanely, "what worthy fellows, to be sure!" When the members of the Committee made their appearance, Tallien and Rovère rushed to meet them and raise their courage.

They needed it. Above the Assembly, "a volcano with a boiling crater," the galleries, full of Robespierre's adherents, were raging furiously. They had greeted the arrival of Robespierre—in the blue coat he had worn on the 20th Prairial, his head as neatly powdered as ever—with wild plaudits; he walked as one on the verge of apotheosis. Saint-Just had joined him, wearing the chamois-coloured coat, white waistcoat, and pale-grey breeches—in which, all blood-stained rags by that time, he was to stand at the bar of the Tribunal before forty-eight hours had passed.

The younger man mounted the rostrum. Collot was presiding over the sitting: the presence of their accomplice in the presidential chair was to be the strongest trump in the hand of Robespierre's antagonists. The setting of the scene presented its usual appearance: the hall had been the old theatre of the Palace; the narrow rostrum faced the wide writing-table; on either side of the President hung the two canvases representing the murdered deputies, Marat and Lepelletier, and in the centre was the ark in which the still-born Constitution lay enshrined. The benches of the Right were partially depleted; the Mountain showed a gap made by the execution of Danton and Hébert, and their followers; the Centre sat all together, compact, mute, awaiting the event. Robespierre had seated himself in front of the Centre, so as to face the rostrum.

Saint-Just was only allowed time to pronounce two sentences of the accusation he had so laboriously prepared on the preceding night : Tallien broke in upon him rudely. Scaling the steps of the rostrum he pushed the other from his place, **The Uproar in** crying: "*I ask that the curtain may be torn away!*" **the Convention.** "It must ! It must !" came the answer from a hundred throats. That was the signal for the attack : it was led by Billaud, who had taken possession of the rostrum almost before Tallien had left it. He denounced the scene at the Jacobin Club on the preceding night, at which "*the intention to murder the Convention had been clearly expressed,*" declared he saw the author of the proposal in one of the galleries, had him expelled, and so struck terror into the general public. "*The Convention will perish if it is weak!*" "No ! No !" cried the Mountain, with much waving of hats.

Le Bas tried to speak : he failed. Robespierre's enemies had sworn to stifle the voices of all his friends. The tumult was very great ; Collot rang his bell unceasingly ; the Centre alone sat motionless in the midst of the tempest. Billaud never ceased his attacks on Robespierre : the President of the Tribunal had publicly proposed at the Jacobin Club that all the men it desired to sacrifice should be driven out of the Convention, "but the people is there, and patriots will know how to die !"

Robespierre made a rush to the rostrum : a mighty shout drove him back to his seat in the centre of the hall. "Down **"Down with** with the tyrant !" was the cry ; and, indeed, **the Tyrant !"** Tallien was in possession of the rostrum once more. He was set on delivering the final blow himself: Therezia was to say one day : "This little hand did something to overthrow the guillotine." Tallien, in fact, must have realized that all would be over with her, and himself too, indeed, if Robespierre's ruin were not accomplished within the next ten minutes. He raised his voice louder yet : "*I saw the meeting at the Jacobins' Club yesterday : I trembled for my country : I watched the formation of the new Cromwell's army, and I have armed myself with a dagger which shall pierce his breast if the Convention has not the courage to decree his accusation !*" And amidst huge emotion he did actually wave a dagger in the air. The arrest of the " Generals "—Boulanger and Hanriot —and of Dumas was decreed. The Assembly was not brave enough, so far, to strike at Robespierre himself, but his arms, his soldiers and his judge, were taken from him. Once more he tried to speak, and once more he was howled down. Collot, Hébert's former friend, had left the chair. It was Danton's old follower, Thuriot, whose inexorable gestures refused the wretched man's appeal for leave to speak. And all the time the President's bell rang on, like that of a ship in distress.

Above all things the rostrum had to be held so as to keep Robespierre out of it. Barère went to it first, and then Vadier, who tried again to tell his tale about the prophetess, till Tallien, not choosing that the drama should deteriorate into comedy, silenced the old dotard by pouring out a fresh denunciation of Robespierre, his cowardice on August 10, the hypocrisy of his civism and his " virtue."

For the third time Robespierre rose to his feet, and moved, with a congested countenance, towards the rostrum. He spoke **Robespierre's** as he went, but nobody could hear a word, for **Arrest** Thuriot kept ringing his bell unceasingly. It **demanded.** sounded the condemned man's knell. An obscure deputy, Louchet, reached the rostrum, and demanded his "*arrest.*" The word had been spoken at last! and the Mountain rang with applause. Then the younger Robespierre did a chivalrous thing : " I am as guilty as my brother : I share his virtues. I ask that my arrest may be decreed with his."

Finally, with a desperate effort, Robespierre made himself heard. "*For the last time, will you give me leave to speak, President of assassins!*" Here was the pretext : the tyrant had insulted the Assembly. "President," shouted Charles Duval, "is this man to be the master of the Convention ? " " Let us put the arrest of the two brothers to the vote ! " clamoured his hearers.

At bay, Robespierre turned to the Centre, which had hitherto sat " on the watch," as Barère tells us : " *Men of purity! men of virtue! I appeal to you! Give me the leave to speak which these murderers refuse me!* " Durand and his friends, no doubt, had been counting up the hands raised on the Left against the unhappy man : they saw that he was lost They rose up against him too, and Durand goes so far as to record his own lofty words of indignation on the occasion.

Thus repulsed, Robespierre wandered to and fro between the Centre and the Right : he tried to speak, but his rage choked him. "The blood of Danton chokes thee !" cried Garnier of Saintes. He tried to clamber up the benches of the Right. "Keep back !" screamed Fréron, "that is where Condorcet and Vergniaud used to sit !" Truly he was stumbling over corpses ! At last he dropped exhausted on a seat, while Billaud poured fresh abuse upon him.

Then things began to hurry on swiftly : a clamour rose up for the "monster's" arrest. Le Bas, ever noble-hearted and generous, claimed his right to share the fate of his unhappy friend. Billaud named Couthon, on whose head, as on that of Saint-Just, Fréron, eager to avenge Desmoulins, cast a hail of insults : "Couthon is a tiger, thirsting for the blood of the representatives of the nation (*Yes ! Yes !*) . . . *He hoped to have made our corpses so many steps by which he would have climbed to the throne !*" The cripple, sitting in his little carriage, cast a bitter glance upon his legs : "Yes !" he sneered, "I would have climbed to the throne !" And Fréron concluded his speech : "*I ask for a decree of arrest against Saint-Just, Le Bas, and Couthon !*"

Robespierre and his Lieutenants arrested.

The decree was voted, and a moment afterwards the gendarmes were in the hall, and the five men were prisoners.

It was now half-past five o'clock : the heat was extraordinary. The exhausted Assembly suspended its sitting until seven o'clock. It believed it had won the battle.

* * * * *

It was mistaken. By seven o'clock things had gone wrong and the game had been very nearly lost. Robespierre, favoured by a last turn of Fortune's wheel, was throning it at the Hôtel-de-Ville, and threatening his own proscribers with proscription. This is what had happened.

The Hôtel-de-Ville opposes the Convention.

All that day the Mayor and his friends had waited on, hoping for good news, persuaded that "virtue" would surely triumph. When Fleuriot heard it had suffered defeat, he had the gates of the city closed and the tocsin rung, summoned the

424

Council-General of the Commune, and forbade any gaoler to accept the custody of the "victims." The Jacobins, to whom he also sent a message, were requested to despatch a posse of brawny arms—"including women "—to the Hôtel-de-Ville, and they hastened to obey. Meanwhile, the mob, attracted by the tocsin, was gathering on the Place de Grève.

A military leader there must be. Hanriot would have been the man : he knew how to bring an Assembly to reason. Unfortunately he had been breakfasting freely in the Faubourg Saint-Antoine, and was quite drunk. On his return to his own home he had found men waiting to arrest him, gave instant orders that they should be killed, and then began to yell: "To-day must be another 31st of May, and 800 wretches sitting in the Convention shall be exterminated ! " Out he went, got on his horse, and galloped off hatless in the blazing sun. He reached the Place du Palais-Royal, where he harangued the astonished passers-by, was pulled off his horse by gendarmes from the Convention, safely bound, and shut up in the offices of the Committee. This incident was calculated to disorganize the revenge Robespierre's party had planned. Payan, too, had been arrested, and Dumas plucked from his judge's bench and put in safe ward.

But, meanwhile, the gaolers, having absolutely refused to receive the dangerous prisoners dispatched by the Assembly to their care, the Mayor had sent for the "martyrs," whose presence he desired at the Hôtel-de-Ville.

In the first instance Robespierre refused to go : this " dictator " was, at bottom, a somewhat timorous legalist : he took refuge at the Mairie on the Quai des Orfèvres, preferring to leave all the responsibility of what might happen at the Hôtel-de-Ville to Fleuriot. This was not Fleuriot's view by any means. He had Robespierre carried off from the Mairie, thus forcing him to cross the Rubicon : a moment later Maximilien was making his triumphal entry into the apartments of the Hôtel-de-Ville, where Saint-Just, Le Bas, his brother Augustin, and later, Couthon, joined him. The provisional Government was ready. It had now to be imposed on the Assembly by cannon.

The Misadventures of Hanriot.

Coffinhal, vice-president of the Tribunal, started forth to the Tuileries boldly with 200 gunners, found his way to Hanriot, set the General at liberty, and urgently besought him to open a cannonade on the Palace forthwith. But for the moment the General's misfortunes had broken his spirit. He refused to do anything of the sort, and made his way to the Hôtel-de-Ville. For the moment the Assembly was saved.

* * * * *

The terror there had been inconceivable. The Committees of Public Safety and of General Security, which had been sitting in a state of feverish anxiety the whole evening (we have a full report of these events in the collected Proceedings of these Committees), had only just escaped capture, and white with terror, had sought refuge with the Convention. Every one of the members acknowledged afterwards that they believed themselves lost. However, Hanriot was declared an outlaw.

This would not have availed them much; but Hanriot, still very unsteady, had departed. The Assembly, delivered from him, pulled itself together, declared the " rebels "— the insurgent deputies and their adherents—outlaws, too, and decided that they should be arrested at the Hôtel-de-Ville.

Who would be brave enough to go ? No military leader was at hand. The Assembly appealed to Barras, who had served in the army, and whose selection Fréron recommended : under his leadership, a delegation consisting of Fréron, Rovère, Legendre, the two Bourdons, and Féraud, was directed to signify the decree of the Convention to the Hôtel-de-Ville. They set forth boldly on their errand, and the rebels, meanwhile, were proclaimed outlaws in all the Western quarters of the town.

At the same hour, and with the same ceremony, fourteen members of the Convention were duly declared outlaws in the East of Paris : this was the rejoinder of the Hôtel-de-Ville.

* * * * *

Hanriot had reappeared there at ten o'clock at night. But he seemed afflicted with acute mania : he again began to gallop to and fro through the terrified crowd, shouting " Kill ! Kill ! Rip up the gendarmes ! " The sight of this leader, evidently mad, greatly diminished the confidence of the already hesitating mob.

And, further, Robespierre was hampering his own defence. He dared not adopt any definite course. The weak point of his brain—or of his heart—became patent at this crisis. He was no man of action; there was nothing of Danton—nor even of Barras—about him. " When he could make no more speeches," says this last, "' the orator spent his time splitting hairs about small details of diction." It was proposed, in fact, to draw up a call to insurrection : " an appeal to the armies," Couthon called it. " But in whose name ? " objected the formalist.

The Mayor made up his mind to act himself : he signed the decree outlawing fourteen deputies, including Collot, Bourdon, Fréron, Tallien, Carnot, and Fouché, "enemies of the people," " who have been more daring than Louis XVI, for they have placed the best of patriots under arrest ! "

But meanwhile the emissaries of the Convention were hurrying from one Section to another, and rallying them all Barras leads to its cause. The Sections sent their bat-Troops to the talions to the Tuileries, while a disorganized Hôtel-de-Ville. mob buzzed helplessly round the Hôtel-de-Ville. The Assembly had a little army of its own now. Of this Barras took command, and led it along the quays to the Place de Grève.

Anarchy still reigned within and uncertainty without the Hôtel-de-Ville. Towards midnight the mob heard that the Sections were going over to the Convention, and was much shaken by the news. Suddenly the rain, which had been threatening ever since midday, began to fall in torrents. The crowd made this an excuse for taking its departure. By one in the morning the Place was well-nigh deserted ; even Hanriot's gunners had gone home.

Robespierre made up his mind at last to sign the appeal to arms. It was too late. The paper still exists. At the foot The Fall of we see the beginning of a signature, the first two " Catiline." letters, Ro. . . . For many years it was asserted that he had cast his pen away, overcome by fresh fears or fresh scruples. But the bloodstained paper—nothing more thrilling than those brown stains can be conceived—tells its own tale.

427

The gendarmes from the Convention broke into the room : one of them—a man of the name of Méda claimed the honour of the exploit—fired : the bullet struck Robespierre, passed through his cheek, and shattered his jaw. He must have dropped face downward on the paper on which, for the first time, the cautious revolutionary was venturing to sign a call to insurrection.

A regular stampede followed the gendarmes' appearance with the Commissaries on their heels. Le Bas blew his brains out : Augustin tried to escape by crawling along a cornice, fell off, and was picked up shattered in every limb : Saint-Just let himself be arrested quietly : Coffinhal, in his fury, had taken Hanriot by the shoulders and thrown the drunkard into a court-yard, where he was discovered, bathed in blood, the following afternoon. As for Couthon, he was found hiding under a table : cruelly enough, the cripple was thrown out on to the staircase ; he rolled down it and into a corner, whence he, too, was dislodged on the morrow, feigning death. It was a mere rag of humanity, blood-stained and muddy, that was cast into the headsman's tumbril the next day.

In the cool darkness, Paris grew calmer : in many quarters men knew nothing of the bloody drama : the Opera had given *Armide ;* at the Opéra-Comique, *Paul et Virginie* had been played. Only at the *Théâtre des Sans-Culottes* the words " No performance " had been posted up.

The incident was to assume a symbolic meaning.

* * * * *

Robespierre was taken to the Assembly : it refused to admit him to its presence. " The Convention, by a unanimous im-
Execution of Robespierre and his Satellites. pulse," says the official report, " refuses to allow him to enter the sanctuary of the laws, which his presence has long polluted." Covered with blood, he was thrown on the table of the room set apart for the use of the Committee of Public Safety : a box of munitions was thrust under his tortured head. That green room, which had always seen him so neat and so haughty, saw him now disfigured, shoeless, his bloodstained shirt hanging open on his breast, his coat torn, his white stockings soiled and dropping

423

about his ankles. Blood was oozing from his cheeks; without
a word (he seemed to be in a dream) he gathered up a few squares
of the paper that had been left lying on the table and staunched
the flow. Some cowardly wretches taunted him ignobly: "Sire,"
quoth one, "Your Majesty seems to be suffering!" "What!
you have lost the power of speech? You do not push on
your motion?" He made no answer, and, indeed, his mouth
was full of the fragments of his shattered jaw. His wound
was dressed: and a few hours later all the prisoners were
conveyed to the Conciergerie.

As outlaws they were brought before the Tribunal for
identification only—but this gave Robespierre time to see the
spot from which Danton had thundered: "Vile Robespierre!
You will follow me!" Fouquier was present, hideously livid;
the "executor of justice" knew his own fate was sealed. On
the previous night he had refused to suspend the sittings and
the executions. "Go on with your work!" he had sent word
to the executioner, and forty-two heads, the last, had fallen,
humble people, nearly all shopkeepers, and one poor woman, a
widow. Dully the crowd had watched the tumbrils pass, tired
of it all at last.

     *   *   *   *   *

Its interest was to be quickened on the following day.
While the inmates of the various prisons sat in astonishment
at hearing no names called (Beugnot and others have described
the horrible anxiety they endured), Fouquier was sending his
own friends to the scaffold.

At four o'clock in the afternoon twenty-two "accomplices"
climbed into the four tumbrils. Leaving the Conciergerie
they took the usual slow way through the crowded Rue
Saint-Honoré. The procession passed Duplay's house, towards
which, but three short months before, Desmoulins had pointed
an avenging finger as the cart in which he was being conveyed
rolled by. In that house Robespierre's life had been centred.
The tumbril halted, a boy went to fetch blood from a neighbouring butcher's shop, and the closed door was sprinkled with
it. Robespierre, who had been laid in the cart and bound to
the rails, opened his eyes, and shuddered. The mob applauded:
it was in the highest spirits. The sky had cleared after the

storm, there was a sort of intoxication in the air. The populace felt the era of hecatombs was almost over, already a storm of wild delight was brewing. But there were women in the crowd, widows and mothers in mourning, who called down curses on the tyrant.

At seven o'clock the scaffold was reached. Couthon, pale as death, was carried like a corpse on to the platform; his crippled body was awkward to deal with; under the rough handling given it by Samson's men he groaned aloud. Then came Augustin Robespierre, also crippled by his fall. Saint-Just was the only one who stood up, straight, cool, and elegant, even in the presence of death. Hanriot, a hideous object with a gaping wound on his forehead, and his right eye hanging down upon his cheek, still seemed half drunk, and stupefied. Robespierre was the twentieth prisoner to mount the scaffold (Fleuriot, the Mayor, came last of all). " The executioner," writes an eye-witness, " after he had fastened him to the plank, before he swung it over, roughly tore off the bandage on his face. He uttered a roar like that of a dying tiger which was heard all over the square." To stifle our own pity we must remind ourselves that since this man had snatched the Law of Prairial from the Assembly, the blood of 1376 victims, some of them old men, women, and even children, had flowed like a river over the stones of our public squares.

Three heads were held up to the mob: Robespierre's, Dumas', and Hanriot's—the "dictator," "his judge," and his " soldier,"—as though to say: " It really is finished ! "

And, straightway, a mighty cry of joy went up from a hundred thousand human throats. " We are all throwing ourselves into each other's arms," we read in one newspaper. " We are free at last . . . the tyrant is no more ! " and in another : " All true patriots breathe more freely."

To such men as Billaud, Collot, or Barère, the death of Robespierre and his " accomplices " was a political incident, like that of Hébert or of Danton—that, and no more. The man had planned their deaths: they had killed him : it was a Palace revolution. But the people looked at the matter very differently. To some Robespierre had been the incarnation

The Events of Thermidor misinterpreted by the People.

THERMIDOR

of the Terror, to the rest he had been the incarnation of the Revolution itself. Therefore the overthrow and execution of Robespierre must undoubtedly mean the end of the Terror, and, perhaps, the end of the Revolution too. Thus the incident became a tremendous event. Robespierre had insisted on the passing of the Law of Prairial, therefore this was the close of the Terror ; Robespierre had been the personification of the Government of Public Safety, therefore the Government of Public Safety would now be abolished ; Robespierre had been bent on the continuation of the war, therefore the end of the war was now to come.

And, suddenly, the Revolution, thus checked at an unexpected corner, turned on its own tracks. To the astonishment of the very men who had brought about the events of the 9th Thermidor, the 9th Thermidor was to work a reaction in the country, because the country was longing for freedom and peace.

One phase of history had been accomplished.

Sources. Works already quoted by Aulard (*Actes*, XV), Barère (II), Barras, Grégoire, Carnot (*Mémoires*), Couthon, Beugnot, Vaublanc, Phil. Chasles, Durand de Maillane, Courtois.—Aulard, *Société des Jacobins*, VI, 1897 ; *Discours de Robespierre du 8 Thermidor*, Imprimerie Nationale, Year II (*Bibliothèque Nationale*, Lc. 38–1869) ; Aulard, *Paris sous la Réaction Thermidorienne* (Documents), I, 1898 ; Crevelier, *Lettre* (*Revue de Paris*, 1908) ; Sénart, *Révélations*, 1824 ; Duval, *Souvenirs thermidoriens*, 1860 ; Prieur (of the Marne), in *Mémoires* of Carnot ; Charles de Constant, *Lettre du 4 juin*, 1796 (on Madame Tallien) (*Nouv. Rev. Retr.*, I, II) ; Miot de Melito, *Mémoires*, 1856.

Works. Those already quoted by Héricault, Gros, Stéphane Pol, Louis Madelin, Mathiez (*Catherine Théot*), Arnaud, Lenôtre (*Hanriot*, *Héron*), Hamel (*Robespierre*), Montier, Lévy-Schneider (*Jeanbon* and *Les Démêlés dans le Comité*, etc.), Chuquet (*École de Mars*), Bliard, Turquand (*Madame Tallien*).—Savine, *Le 9 Thermidor*, 1909 ; Vialles, *Cambacérès*, 1908 ; Nauroy, *Révolutionnaires*, 1891 ; Aulard, *Robespierre et Méda* (*Etudes*, I).

CHAPTER XXXV

THE FALL OF THE JACOBINS

July—September 1794

The Centre takes possession of the movement. Tallien against the Terrorists. The reaction after Thermidor. The " Gilded Youth " of Paris and the *Réveil du Peuple*. Fréron and Therezia Tallien. Therezia goes in person to close the Jacobin Club. Will the " Revolution be annulled ? "

WHEN the Convention issued from the Tuileries on the morning of the 10th Thermidor, its members were astonished by the acclamations with which they were hailed : but when Tallien, Barras, and Fréron appeared, the excitement became delirious, flowers were strewn before The Centre and them, and young men kissed the tails of their the Reaction. coats. These men, so lately butchers of their brethren, and quite prepared to be the same on the morrow, learnt, to their stupefaction, that they had put an end to the Terror !

When they struck down their enemy, this had by no means been their intention, but, finding themselves thus acclaimed, they allowed themselves to be borne along by the reflux of popular opinion. And, indeed, on the 9th Thermidor they had surrendered themselves, in the bosom of the Convention itself, to a group of politicians ten times as numerous as the Mountain ; the " Belly," which had hitherto been content to " exist," was now to break into sudden activity, and a desire to rule. " The men of the Centre," writes Choudieu, " welcomed Fréron and his former accomplices as liberators." But these liberators were soon to be put in their places. " The Mountain," writes a member of the Centre, " which had ruled all too long, became a servant, in its turn." It was the Centre that had taken decisive action when the hour came : it was the Centre that

432

had overthrown the tyrant. Men, who had been trembling the day before, were proud of themselves now. "I, too," said each to himself, " am a thunderbolt of war ! "

And public opinion upheld this reactionary Centre.

Since the 10th the prisoners who had awaited death with bowed heads, were lifting them up in joyous hope ; the daily
Joy of the reprieved Prisoners of Thermidor. roll-call had ceased, it was never to be heard again. The Tribunal, now thoroughly purged, was busy with the trial of Terrorists only, and of these some—Dumas and Fouquier to begin with—had but lately throned it in the *Salle de la Liberté*. And while sixteen tumbrils conveyed seventy-two members of the Commune, the judges and jurymen of the Tribunal, and finally Fouquier himself, soon to be followed by Le Bon and Carrier, to the scaffold, each day saw their former captives set free, one by one to begin with, and then in little batches.

Meanwhile some hundred thousand suspects were issuing from their hiding-places. They were secure enough : the Revolutionary Committees were occupied in saving their own heads. Thibaudeau has described the joy, at first uncertain, then outspoken, and finally delirious, of these proscribed beings who had just escaped annihilation. " It was as if they had risen from the tomb, or been born into life again."

Life—that was all these ghosts asked for to begin with : so sweet it seemed to them, so passionately thankful were they to those who had restored it—even to such men as Tallien and Fréron. And these, who had dreaded their vengeance, were well pleased with this unexpected magnanimity. " They congratulate themselves," writes M. Thureau-Dangin shrewdly, " on having been on the side of the judges when the balance was struck in the Convention, whereas they might have been so deservedly numbered with the accused ! " They raised a cry for " oblivion." " A people which has consummated a revolution should never look back," said Legendre. Astounded, they realized the sense the Nation attributed to their victory : it forced them to welcome the triumph of humanity in their own seraglio-revolution. At once they perceived where their chance of safety lay ; as the apparent dispensers of clemency, they hoped to establish their own claim to it, and escape imminent justice.

*   *   *   *   *

Some members of the Mountain, less compliant, or more sincere, did not fall in so easily with this process of mystification. **Tallien** These, who had been turned out of the Committees **against the** since the beginning of Fructidor, did their best to **Mountain.** make a stand against the mighty reflux of opinion which threatened to overcome and perhaps destroy them.

Tallien was now conducting a campaign against these belated members of the Mountain. This wretch was in great haste to suggest scapegoats, seeing more of these were wanted, and so to avoid the part himself.

Scapegoats were essential. Its hour of joy that knew no hate once over, the mob was beginning to turn on the " blood-drinkers." We have just read the police-reports published by M. Aulard : they contain proof of the unanimity and spontaneity of the movement. The popular reaction really spurred on the Convention.

Other writers have already described the extraordinary condition of Paris just after Thermidor—the whole city in-**The post-** toxicated with delight and vengeance. When **The midorian** congratulations on having cheated death had been **Reaction.** exchanged, each sufferer reckoned up his or her corpses. Not much time was lost in mourning them—festivities went on over the very graves, as we shall show our readers—but it seemed expedient to avenge them.

Every day brought fresh and terrible testimony from the provinces : every day the pile of records destined to fill even a Le Bon with stupefaction grew higher. The first page of each invariably showed a letter from the Committee of Public Safety urging the local pro-consuls to fresh efforts : these letters bore the signatures not only of Robespierre, Couthon, and Saint-Just, but also of Collot, Billaud, and Barère. In Paris itself each quarter was compiling its retrospective chronicle, and demanding an account. For a long time the belief prevailed that none but " aristocrats " had been brought before Fouquier, and handed over to Samson, in the course of 1793 and 1794 : and on this account, wonder was expressed that the reaction after Thermidor should have found the bulk of its supporters among shopkeepers and working men : but two-thirds of the " customers " of Fouquier and Samson were small tradesmen, artisans, and domestic servants. The fathers, brothers, and sons of these humble victims clamoured—and far more loudly than the *ci-devants* themselves—for the chief executioners' heads. Hence the reaction in Paris after Thermidor : a thoroughly popular movement, it carried the Jacobins away, and swept them from its path. Paris, where they believed themselves all-powerful, turned her back upon them, to their intense astonishment, and went over to the camp of the most violent opponents of the Revolution.

* * * * *

Paris would not have been Paris if this movement had not started in the theatres. Immediately after Thermidor anti-Jacobin plays were acted and applauded : first came the *Journée du 9 Thermidor*, at which citizens hissed Robespierre at the *Variétés* every two or three evenings. Soon after that *L'Intérieur des Comités Révolutionnaires* held up the various " accomplices," great and little, to public scorn and insults. Even plays in the classical style were turned against the beaten tyrants : as, for instance, Chénier's *Timoléon*, the astonishing success of which is reported on the 25th Fructidor. Every apt allusion, whether in vaudeville or tragedy, was hailed with applause.

The Reaction in the Theatres.

> " *Exterminez, grand Dieu, de la terre où nous sommes,*
> *Quiconque, avec plaisir, répand le sang des hommes !* " *

These lines made *Mahomet* popular. It was played by request, and loudly acclaimed at the *Théâtre de la République*.

The younger generation was on the warpath, and fashion did her part. The "Gilded Youth " of the day would pour, its blood still on fire, out of the playhouses, and raise riot on a small scale against the "blood-drinkers "; in the streets they formed a staff to begin with, an army before very long : they had a uniform of their own, the square-skirted coat of the *muscadin*, on

The " Jeunesse Dorée " and the " Réveil du Peuple."

---

* Exterminate from our Earth, great God,
  Any who delight to shed the blood of man.

which the green cape of the Chouans of Brittany was soon to
appear : the remaining features of the dress are well known
to our readers;' ' *oreilles de chiens, cadenettes, cravate à écrouelles*,'*
short waistcoats, tight-fitting trousers, low boots—strange
attire for " soldiers." Yet these soldiers were soon to rule the
roost. "A dictatorship," writes one of them, "which nobody
opposed, for it fulfilled everyone's wish ! " Every army needs
a war-song, and in this case the war-song was the *Réveil du
Peuple*, the words by Souriguière, the music by Gaveaux :

> " *Le jour tardif de la vengeance*
> *Fait enfin pâlir vos bourreaux !* " †

The *Réveil* was soon to be sung everywhere, from the
theatres, where it was chanted at the beginning and after the
close of each play, to the galleries of the Convention, where
it brought a frown to more than one brow.

The journalists urged on the young men : " Liberty for the
Press or death ! " Tallien had cried on the 2nd Fructidor.
The press, which had suffered proscription at the tyrant's
hands, was taking its revenge now. Many new publications
appeared, the great majority of them supporting the Thermidor
movement, and, besides the newspapers, there was a rain of
pamphlets, all of which fastened their teeth in " Robespierre's
Tail." The Goncourt brothers and other writers have left us a
formidable list of these publications, and the National Library
contains a collection of them which soon becomes wearisome,
so close is the resemblance between them all.

Words were followed by deeds : the red caps of liberty,
forced by a despotic hand on every head, were banished :
the sticks of the " Gilded Youth " sent them back into
their owners' cupboards. By Fructidor, the *Journal des
Hommes Libres*, one of the few Jacobin newspapers remain-

* *Oreilles de chien.* Locks of hair longer than the rest, which hung in
front of the ears.
Cadenettes. Similar locks of hair, plaited at the back of the head,
worn by the Hussars of the Armies of the Republic. and preserved for
a long period as a distinguishing mark of the dress of these regiments.
Ecrouelles, scrofula. So-called because the cravat hid all the neck.
† The tardy day of vengeance
At last makes your assassins pale.

ing, was to exclaim: " Listen to the complaints of the patriots oppressed by the aristocracy, which has been so imprudently set free ! "

The unfortunate thing for the Jacobins was that the " aristocracy " had nothing at all to do with it. These young *bourgeois* had two leaders—we should rather say one leader and one idol —and no greater paradox could well have existed, for these two men bore the names of Fréron and Tallien !

Stanislas Fréron, elegant, sceptical, corrupt, had cast in his lot with the reaction. He it was who invented the terrible ex-
Fréron. pression "Robespierre's Tail," and nobody struck more vigorous blows than he at the tail in question. He was further a first-rate journalist, clever and unsparing in his methods; the *Orateur du Peuple* was the most popular of all the public prints. "Have you read Fréron?" was a question asked every morning. For every morning he bit off a fresh piece ; now from Collot and now from Billaud. And then again he would lay down his pen, take up his cudgel, and lead his readers, turned into his troops, on a "Jacobin-hunt." The man who had wielded the "Cordeliers' club" all over the country from Toulon to Marseilles, now wielded the cane of the first *muscadin* in Paris.

Tallien hovered on a higher plane. As a matter of fact he had not wit enough to write newspaper articles, and was
Therezia far too cowardly to brandish a stick. But events
Cabarrus. and a woman had exalted the ruffian—for this base politician, ever ready to recant, lay in the hollow of Therezia Cabarrus' little hand. This creature of beauty and grace was already, though covertly, the mistress of the city in which she was to reign supreme. Firmly established, at last, in a recognized position, the former Marquise de Fontenoy, one day to become Princesse de Chimay, was for the moment keenly enjoying her existence as the Citoyenne Tallien. Her captivity had set an aureole about her head, and she possessed that quality of easy good-nature which stops short of sacrifice. She was beautiful, and seductive we are told, beyond all expression. It would seem as though it were only right—after the reign of Robespierre the woman-hater, after the dictatorship of the Terror and of Virtue—that the new *régime* should find its

437

incarnation in the person of a fascinating and smiling woman of easy morals! Tallien was proud of her, though she was generally believed to be common property. When a member of the Terrorist party questioned him coarsely about " la Cabarrus," in the month of Nivôse, he sounded her praises from the very rostrum : " In the presence of our colleagues, in the presence of the people, I declare this woman to be my wife ! " And Therezia, sitting in the gallery, was hailed with plaudits long drawn out, " *Our Lady of Thermidor !* " " *Our Lady of Succour !* "

So this strange Madonna reigned. She stirred up Tallien against Collot and Billaud and their fellows : for this Lady of Succour was, as M. Claretie has told us, " an Herodias of clemency." She it was who urged on Fréron and Legendre. Collot was not deceived : " Certain wretches have promised our heads to their concubines. . . . *We shall die because new Fulvias, loved by new Antonies, wait with their bodkins ready to pierce our tongues !* " And she was, in fact, if Lacretelle is to be believed, directing the anti-Jacobin campaign in the press, rewarding the writer of a brilliant article with a kiss. She it was again who completed the disruption of the old Mountain, sent Collot to the galleys, and brought Tallien, the " September murderer," to the benches of the Right.

* * * * *

The campaign grew hotter. On the 7th Fructidor the Revolutionary Committees were abolished, and though the The Jacobin foes of the Club did not dare, as yet, to strike Club closed. at it openly, they maimed it cruelly by severing it from its off-shoots : on the 26th Vendémiaire of the Year IV all federation of Popular Societies was forbidden. The tentacles of the octopus were lopped off.

The Jacobins felt this to be a deadly blow. For several weeks exasperation had been growing more and more bitter in the Club ; the reports of proceedings bring us echoes of the violent language used. On the 13th Brumaire, Billaud in a speech to his fellow members, made a fierce attack on the policy of reaction. " *The sleeping lion is not dead, and when he wakes he will exterminate his foes !* " Poor lion ! The gay young men of the town were to make him a laughing-stock **before** they destroyed him. They marched upon the Club, defended chiefly by the *Tricoteuses*, forced the " haunt of the Jacobins " to capitulate, drove out the men, spitting upon them as they went, and fustigated the women. And these were the proud Jacobins before whom all France had trembled but three short months before ! The Committees of the Convention, now entirely ruled by the Centre, realized, on this, that " the lion's " teeth and claws had disappeared, and made up their minds to dispatch it altogether. A decree for the closing of the Club was passed. Fréron resolved to keep the execution of the order in his own hands ; he proceeded, accompanied by Merlin (of Thionville) to lock the doors, and brought back the keys to the Convention. Mme. Tallien was to relate, in a letter written at a later date, that she had formed one of the party ; the presence of this light-hearted woman of loose life indicates the depth of the ignominy into which the dead Club had fallen ; the very corpse was scoffed at. For, indeed, the strength of this " lion " had always lain in his victims' cowardice.

From that moment the battle was in the hands of the supporters of Thermidor. "The infernal Society," as was written shortly after this date, now only numbered some fifty deputies, " a minority doomed to the silence and humiliations it had once, sword in hand, imposed on its opponents ! " The remnants of the old Right, the " Seventy-three " to begin with, and then the sixteen survivors of the Girondins, were recalled : Louvet and Isnard came back full of bitter hostility to the Revolution. There was now a possibility of making the Convention " *retrace its steps.*" This was effected by degrees. On the 5th Nivôse, in spite of all the discontent in the Faubourgs, the reasons of which we shall shortly set forth, the law of the *Maximum* was repealed. A skilfully planned amnesty was offered to La Vendée, already half subdued, and the Assembly, though it took no formal decision on the subject, permitted the return both of refractory priests and of *émigrés*, who began to show themselves " almost in the galleries " of the Convention. Finally, the separation of Church and State, which had established freedom of worship, and seemed to show equal favour to every form of belief,

The surviving Girondins recalled.

suddenly brought about a resurrection of Catholic feeling which exceeded all expectation.

In vain did the Thermidorian party in the Convention do its best to save its face by holding a solemn celebration on January 21, a proceeding which, according to one deputy, was to shut the mouths of Billaud's friends, who were raising a cry against " counter-revolution." The proposal was condemned by the populace itself, which declared—so the police reported—that " it would be better to give it bread than to arrange festivals."

During the closing months of the winter of 1795 (Year III of the Republic) the French people was in fact, in the throes of a crisis not so much political, as economic, social, and we will even say moral. To understand the consequences of this crisis, we must now pause and consider it seriously. The purely artificial system of the Year II had crumbled away, and behind its shattered façade was a country strewn with ruins, where a dislocated society in a bewildered nation struggled amidst the most tremendous anarchy ever seen.

SOURCES. Works already quoted by Aulard (*Jacobins*, IV, and *Paris sous la réaction*, I), Duval, Choudieu, Levasseur (of the Sarthe), Barras, Lacretelle, Frénilly, Thibaudeau, Durand de Maillane, Mallet du Pan, Miot, Soubrany, La Revellière, Marmont, Madame du Chastenay.—Aulard, *Actes du Comité*, XV–XVII, 1903–1906 ; *Réponse de Barère, Billaud*, etc. (*Rev. Fr.*, 1898) ; D'Andigné, *Souvenirs*, I, 1900 ; Hyde de Neuville, *Souvenirs*, 1900 ; Roederer, *Œuvres*, VII.

WORKS. Those already quoted by Pingaud, Chuquet (*École de Mars*), Arnaud, Vialles, Claretie (*Derniers Montagnards*), Turquan, Lallié, Lenôtre (*Tribunal*) ; Thureau-Dangin, *Royalistes et Republicains* ; *La Question de la Monarchie ou de la République du 9 Thermidor au 18 Brumaire*, 1888 ; Welschinger, *La Théâtre de la Révolution*, 1897

CHAPTER XXXVI

FRANCE IN THE YEAR III

France a " sick person." Famine and the Faubourgs. Poverty and the "newly enriched." The "empty bellies" and the " rotten bellies." The peasant, free and well-to-do, longs for a settled government. The sale of " national property." " Fears and hopes." The uncompromising attitude of the claimant to the throne estranges friendly feeling. The enriched Jacobins bent on forcing themselves on the Nation. The necessity for war. The " Generals must be given something to do." The doctrine of the " natural frontiers." The way prepared for a resolute man.

FRANCE lay sick : the fever of 1789, the superhuman effort of 1792, the blood-letting of 1793 and 1794, the never-ceasing starvation of all those years, had brought on a kind of anæmia complicated by neurasthenia. The royalist, Mallet du Pan and the Republican, La Revellière-Lepeaux both use the same imagery in this connection. "The Nation," says one, "seems worn out, just as a madman is worn out when his reason returns, by bleedings and baths and severe dieting." "A burning fever," says the other, "was followed by a complete prostration of strength." France lay exhausted but for a spasm now and again. Her one longing was to seek cure in perfect rest. No remedy for her state would be found in fresh revolution or in counter-revolution : so with a weary gesture, she waved both aside. Because, *though her passions were almost, if not quite burnt out, she still had interests :* she clung to the conquests she had bought so dearly : sick and anæmic she was indeed, but she had laid herself down upon a treasure she was resolved to guard.

*　　*　　*　　*　　*

441

These interests are what we must study now. In them we shall find the explanation of everything, from Germinal of the Year III to Brumaire of the Year VIII : the interest of the artisan in the resumption of industry, of the proletarian in the lowering of the price of bread, of the man who had grown rich in the preservation of his gains, of the peasant in the safe possession of his land, of the successful politician in his maintenance in office, of the soldier in the defence of his conquests. Each of these assertions we must now justify.

Various Interests safeguard the Republic.

There was a great deal of poverty. The gold had all gone out of the country. It had been replaced by piles of paper-money: the *assignats*. To the origin of the *assignats* we have already referred : we should have been glad to relate their full history here, but space forbids it. There had been great abuses in connection with them : compromised from the first by a somewhat dubious origin—a confiscation never accepted by the former owners of the confiscated property—they had suffered further from the outrageous manner in which the issue had been handled. Too many had been printed : the speculator seized on them in the first place and the forger followed on his heels : thus the *assignat* fell lower and lower in the public estimation. At the period we have just reached—January 1795, Nivôse of the Year III—the gold louis was worth 130 *livres* in *assignats* : in March it was to be worth 227 ; in June, 750 ; in September, 1200 ; and 2500 when the Convention ceased to exist ! Yet these figures are quite modest compared with those we shall have to record under the Directory. All salaries and incomes were paid in *assignats,* and our readers will realize how this affected government officials and owners of small investments, more especially as shopkeepers would only accept *assignats* at all at the current rate of the day on which they were offered.

Poverty and financial Disorganization.

Added to this the cost of living had become exorbitant. The war with England, resulting in the blockade of French ports, increased the state of famine which, growing steadily worse ever since 1789, had raised the price of provisions to an extraordinary height. The *Maximum* had been abolished on the 5th Nivôse, but this had brought **no**

Famines in the Faubourgs.

FRANCE IN THE YEAR III

relief; the peasants had ceased to send out corn. " There was no bread in Lyons for five whole days," in January 1795.

In Paris, where intense cold prevailed, long files of people waited outside the bakers' shops. We may refer to the police reports for the months of Frimaire, Nivôse, and Pluviôse. Everybody hungry. A bushel of flour cost 225 *livres*; a bushel of haricot beans cost 120 ; a cartload of wood, 500 ; a bushel of charcoal, 10 ; a pound of brown sugar, 41 ; twenty-five eggs, 25 ; and the time was not far distant when a pound of bread was to be sold for 45 *livres*, a pound of bacon for 560, and a leg of mutton for 1248 *livres* !

When a man of the lower middle class was paying 10 *livres* for a cup of coffee, our readers may image what hunger

The " empty Bellies " and the " rotten Bellies."

the really poor were enduring. When the sentinels challenge rang out : " *Qui vive !* " the people would answer back : " *Empty bellies !* " And we shall see these " empty bellies " rushing upon the Convention in their despair : a despair that wrung their bowels. For there was no employment to be had : all the workshops were closed. The workmen were the chief victims of the Revolution. We shall see what the middle-class and the peasant got out of it : it cost the artisan his occupation, and refused him every right, the right of coalition, the right to strike, the right to vote. The artisan class, therefore, had an interest of its own, negative though it might be : a settled system of government must make it possible for the workshops to re-open their doors and the price of food to go down, or else a democratic form of government must at least give that class a right to share in the making of the country's laws. Under the Convention they had neither security of labour nor political power. " If the rich had to eat food like ours," they grumbled, " the Convention would have ceased to exist long ago ! " The man who would avenge the populace on the Assemblies— those " rotten bellies "—which had fooled the working class, the man, above all, who would give it work, and cheap food, would be welcomed, to begin with, and beloved ere long.

*   *   *   *   *

There were rich men, but they were evil men, the " newly rich."

443

THE FRENCH REVOLUTION

The Revolution, too long regarded as a mere transposition of power, was above all a tremendous transfer of wealth from **The newly** one set of persons to another; a transfer of **enriched.** property in favour of " buyers " and of capital for the benefit of " speculators."

Within the space of five years the old *régime* had been liquidated. It is a very uncommon thing for liquidators to come out of an operation involving the handling of huge sums with perfectly clean hands. When a government is so short of money that on certain days there are not more than 100,000 *livres* in its coffers, and the population it governs is dying of hunger, it may be taken as a certainty that the money which should have passed out of the hands of its former owners into those of the government and the people has been misappropriated, somehow and somewhere. The professional speculator pounced on France. A huge black band—from the sacristy to the palace—having turned the Revolution into money within the country, was preparing, as it followed in the track of our victorious armies, to perform the same process outside its borders.

In 1795 the process within the country was complete. The aristocracy had been driven out and a plutocracy had come into existence. This was a logical development : but because no such subversion had ever been seen either in Greece or Rome—of so rapid a nature, at all events—no substitution was ever so prompt or so brutal. Guglielmo Ferrero has lately told us the story of the fall of an aristocracy, that of the Roman patricians. But it had taken the " Gilded Bellies " (Knights) a century to supplant the patricians of Ancient Rome.

France had been a battlefield, and on that battlefield the strippers of corpses had been at work.

Wealth that has been hastily and wrongfully acquired is sure to be swiftly and foolishly spent. The luxury of the **Luxury and** year 1795 was insensate. When we turn to the **Frivolity of** study of the Directory we shall examine the social **1795.** world in which the owners of these newly acquired fortunes took their pleasure. Their merrymaking began in the Year III.

444

FRANCE IN THE YEAR III

Extraordinary it was, and general! While the theatres, thanks to numbers of discreet retiring-rooms, became, as the police reports assure us, " perfect sewers of debauchery and vice," no less than 644 public ballrooms opened their doors. This new-born society shivered with a fever of delight; it was the reaction of life against death. The owners of the new fortunes led the dance : the ruined nobles followed whither wealth beckoned them, and mingled with the *parvenus* ; Mme. Angot entertained the former duchess ; Mme. Tallien, in her " cottage at Chaillot," led the great ball—" a ball over graves," wrote one who took part in it.

This kingdom which Therezia ruled has been most thoroughly described. The thousands of documents collected by M. Aulard " Bals des in his *Paris Thermidorien,* have only deepened, Victimes." whatever he himself may say to the contrary, the colours of the picture we already possessed. There was a sort of Sadism in all this enjoyment : the *bal des Victimes,* at which one of the favourite figures danced simulated the incidents of an execution by guillotine, would suffice in itself to enlighten us as to this. Dancing went on in every quarter, from **Les Carmes,** where the blood of 116 priests still bespattered the walls, to the Cemetery of Saint-Sulpice, on the gate of which the inscription *Bal des Zéphyrs* had been hung.

There was gambling too. Schmidt has written on the gambling prevalent in 1795, and supplied us with most curious details. A passion for play seized everybody : there were a hundred gambling hells in the Palais-Royal, and every table was heaped with gold. There was an immense amount of eating, and dainty eating, too : the waiters of the restaurant La Maison Egalité (the Palais-Royal) declared that more money was being spent than they had ever seen spent before. This report is dated 14th Pluviôse, Year III. The Directory, under which feasting, gambling, and merrymaking were to reach a pitch that bordered on insanity, was still five months ahead.

The populace was starving, the rich were flaunting their luxury. Under the date of January 15, 1795, we read : " The brazen way in which luxury is now displayed in Paris, especially in the toilette, exceeds the most immoral exhibitions

445

of that nature ever seen in the days of the Monarchy. The wife of a deputy of the name of Tallien lately paid 12,000 Madame *livres* for a gown in the Greek style." A good Tallien's deal of money, indeed, for the dress of a goddess Expenditure. whose charms were usually so slightly veiled! Fréron had never ceased to pay great attention to his dress. Just after Thermidor he demanded the release of a citizen named Vilkers, who had always, he gravely asserted, "supplied him with braces of the most elegant description." Paris took the lead, but in Lyons where, we are told, "the stones are stained with the blood of 7000 citizens, there are two theatres, and a number of public balls, all of them constantly full."

Naturally this strange society was convinced everything was going well. Nothing is less surprising than that Mme. Tallien should write, in Fructidor of the Year II : "*Paris is happy !* " And yet these merrymakers were not so demented that they did not hear the grumbling of the angry mob as it reviled the "rotten bellies." A dread of popular clamour existed. Yet nobody could desire a counter-revolution, since that might involve disgorging the spoils. Those who had become royalists professed a royalism of strictly limited liability—or rather of non-liability. Louis XVIII had refused to clean the slate, and the plutocracy, which had small confidence in such protection as a Republican government would give it, was to incline naturally to a Cæsarian solution.

* * * * *

The peasants, curiously enough, were in an exactly similar state of mind.

"The peasant is the only contented man . . . he is the only man who is making money : he has bought up almost The Sales of all the meadows, fields, and vineyards belonging "national to the *émigrés.* . . ." The words are quoted Property." from a letter written by young Mallet during a journey through France in 1796. But in 1795 the condition of things had been just the same. Thibaudeau notes it at that period : "Agriculture was prospering. This was the result of the suppression of feudal rights and the sale of national property."

The moment has come for us to state, in the space of a

few lines, the result of an operation which had transformed a political revolution into a social revolution of the most tremendous kind.*

The value of national property, which had its origin in two sources (the property of the Clergy, finally alienated on March 17, 1790, and the property of the *émigrés*, offered by sale in obedience to a decree passed on August 30, 1792), amounted altogether to a sum approaching six billions of *livres* (£240,000,000). In the year 1795 the greater part of it had been already sold. A certain amount, most undoubtedly, had been acquired by proprietors, men who already owned land in 1789, and were delighted to enlarge their boundaries cheaply, very cheaply, seeing that as a result of the general depreciation of values, land that had been bought for 152,625 francs, and was probably worth twice that, was sold in the end for 5652 francs. No doubt, again, many of the purchasers were *bourgeois*, and some of them even nobles. But, and this is the point a certain school of opinion—in opposition to that other school which took an exaggerated view of the transactions—has thought it necessary to deny, *numbers of very small peasants, workmen, modest shopkeepers, and*

* We need hardly say that we can do no more than just touch on the question. It is both delicate and complex, and though a most interesting light has been cast upon it by recent writers, and more particularly by M. Marion in his fine study of the subject, it is one that cannot be safely handled in a summary fashion. To arrive at any categorical conclusion we must await the results of many other investigations giving us the exact conditions under which the sales were carried out in all the various departments. Thanks, however, to the help afforded us by certain excellent labourers in this particular field, we are beginning to see light. The sale of the property of the Nation was neither an event which, as the fanatical supporters of the Revolution hold, was the sole creator of the small holding system of France, nor one, as the opponents of the Revolution believe, which exercised no influence at all on the evolution of that system; and the notion, so dear to Michelet ("The Jacobins became purchasers") that the humbler folks among the devoted adherents of the Revolution and they alone then acquired land must be dropped : but we must also refuse to believe, with M. Jaurès (whose clever pages we nevertheless recommend to our readers' attention), that the whole operation was carried out by the middle classes for their sole benefit.

In an article in the *République Française* (October 26, 1910) we have made a study of the question which, short as it is, supplies details want of space prevents us from inserting here.

others just below the middle class were enabled through these sales to become landowners. When the first sales took place (1791–1793) the large buyers, as M. Marion's researches in the Archives of the Gironde and the Cher have shown us, were in the majority, though the smaller ones were not entirely shouldered out ; but when the second series of sales took place (1793–1794)—the properties were purposely cut up into small lots this time—modest buyers had their chance. M. Lecarpentier has given us the results of a calculation based on the sales in eighteen different districts, and acknowledges the existence of 220,000 peasant buyers, as against 140,000 *bourgeois* ; and M. Vialay's study of the Burgundian cantons proves that out of 556 purchasers in ten Communes, 399 had not paid the tax known as the *vingtième* previously to 1789, and, consequently, had owned no land at that period.

The land sold in large areas in 1791 and 1792 was soon cut up and resold, so a letter dated Prairial of the Year VI informs us, "in an infinite number of lots." The inquiry ordered by Bonaparte, in the Year VIII, and that of his Prefects in the Year IX, were to certify a considerable increase of small landowners, and therefore of small peasant proprietors, on the number existing in 1789. In the Year X a newspaper reckoned at two millions the number of families that had acquired property. Even if we take the number of these to have been smaller by one half in the Year III, and grant the existence of as many former landowners who had added to their domains,' as new owners among them, the fact, an important one, that the millions of money put into circulation in 1790 and 1792 had changed hands, still remains. The principal result of the sale of national property had been to transform numerous small landholders into men of many acres, but it had also turned a goodly number of men, who had not owned a rood in 1789, into possessors of a certain area of soil. And even the peasant who had bought no land at all had not forgotten the days when he had been forced to submit to endless annoyances and pay many dues. The Revolution had brought him freedom, and, as a rule, it had enriched him as well. He clung to it, but in his own fiercely conservative way.

448

He had never, at any moment, been a republican, nor even a liberal. And further, he was well aware that the " levellers " in Paris were preaching the necessity for an agrarian law. In 1795 Babeuf and his *"Equals"* were to make an attack on property : and the Government was to appear unable to put proper restraint upon them. Finally, the peasant was still profoundly Catholic : this is proved by the fact that the villagers habitually gathered in their churches, though there was no priest to serve them, and chanted the office. The peasant wanted to see his " good priests " given back to him : but on condition that the priests did not claim the restitution of "property," nor ask him to pay tithe again.

Conservative Instincts of the Peasantry.

The enduring popularity of Napoleon in rural France is explained by his realization of this complex desire.

Thus, for various reasons, artisans, *bourgeois*, peasants, were all awaiting the advent of "the man." "*The mass of the people,*" writes Mallet in December 1794, "*cares as little for the Republic as for Royalty, and simply clings to the advantages, local and civil, the Revolution has conferred upon it.*" Clear-sighted, as ever, he adds, "*It will accept the law from any master who knows how to bind it by its hopes and fears.*"

"Hopes and fears " reigned likewise among the constitutional priests who, weary enough of the revolutionary system, since the harsh persecution meted out to them in 1794, had every reason, nevertheless, to dread a counter-revolution, and among the soldiers of the Revolution, who had won advancement within two years, which the old *régime* would never have granted them at all, but whose hearts overflowed with scorn for the politicians who ruled the country. All these classes, workmen, peasants, *bourgeois*, soldiers and priests, formed "*a solid mass of anti-royalist strength,*" as Malouet has called it. And, beside them, we see another mass of patriots who, though they viewed the Terrorists with horror, had no intention of relinquishing the conquests won, and yet another, composed of those "renovated brains " in whose minds " the government of the old days is as completely wiped out as that of Clovis."

"Hopes and Fears."

All these men—nine-tenths of the inhabitants of France,

who cared little for the Republic, indeed, but very much for the Revolution—would assuredly have recoiled in alarm from any thought of monarchical restoration, unless the monarchical idea was to be utterly sundered from that of the despotism lately abolished, of the hated system of the old *régime* and, above all, from any thought of claims and reprisals. And the representatives of the Royal House, moved as though by a sort of madness, were doing their utmost to strengthen France in this attitude.

*   *   *   *   *

"The Bourbon Princes," says Sorel, "were much more inclined to found a State Inquisition than to grant a civil Edict of Nantes."

Uncompromis-ing Attitude of the Bourbons. We know the princes in question: Provence, Artois, Condé. For three years they had been enduring a miserable fate : enduring it—the future Louis XVIII more especially—with a courage which checks any inclination to scoff at these "kings in exile."

We have elsewhere related, on the authority of a singularly well-informed historian, the story of their Odyssey, wanderings shared by the unhappy *émigrés* who had followed their fortunes, and, like them, were driven hither and thither, mocked and persecuted, by an inhospitable Europe. But, whereas most of these poor people, the great majority of whom had joined the emigration more from necessity than as a matter of choice, only longed, as one of them put it, to get back to France, "no matter what the cost and the conditions imposed might be," the princes and their immediate circle had raised their pretensions higher and higher as their misfortune increased. The "Regent," ultimately to become Louis XVIII, continued to preserve his absolute faith, not only in his kingly rights, but in the duty laid upon him to restore everything exactly to its former condition. The people about him, who so perpetually inveighed against the state of things in France, knew nothing at all of the new France that had come into existence. They suffered from that "*sickness of exile*" which, as Tocqueville writes, "teaches men nothing, and brings the intelligence to a standstill." Not only was the old order to be restored, but examples were to be made, nay, executions on a large scale !

FRANCE IN THE YEAR III

In a very remarkable study of the days following on Thermidor, M. Thureau-Dangin has accumulated proofs of the existence of this spirit of vengeance : the Terrorists, the regicides were to perish, and the men of 1789 too, the moderates. "We will sweep away all the filth of the Constitutional Assembly ! " This was the constant cry, the general watchword. Constant sat beside a young *émigré* at a dinner who said to him (in March 1794): "Ah ! If I were Provost-General of France I would have 800,000 persons executed ! "

So these royalists, while they waited to crush the Revolution, were killing royalty itself. It was not quite dead in The Royalists 1795; a whole group of politicians was ready to bent on recall it to life, and the whole of society, it may be, Reprisals. would have welcomed it, had it been a moderate and constitutional monarchy, ready to respect newly conquered liberties, newly acquired rights, and recent conquests, and above all, opposed to reprisals and reaction of any kind. When the unhappy little Louis XVII met his miserable end within the walls of the Temple, a reassuring word from Louis XVIII was eagerly expected. At last the answer to the question set by the neo-royalists of the country was sent forth from Verona, embodied in that famous proclamation which announced that everything must be unreservedly restored, absolute monarchy re-constituted, the new liberties suppressed, the new proprietary system abolished, and every man concerned in the Revolution punished. And the commentary came in the attempt forthwith made to raise revolt in La Vendée, and that mad Quiberon expedition, which carried *émigrés* and Englishmen together on to the Breton coast, and once more emphasized that which Frenchmen most abhorred in the royalist policy, its alliance with the foreigner. This was suddenly to turn the whole Convention into one solid block. It would have mattered less, if it had not finally cut at the root of the royalist sympathies of the liberal and moderate party, large-minded men of solid sense, who had lost all their illusions as to the Revolution, and were now driven to seek a solution elsewhere.

Thus, from Verona, Louis XVIII did his part to help on the accession of Napoleon.

* * * * *

And, meanwhile, he was ensuring the safety of the "regicides." We must now consider these "revolutionaries in possession." Though they too had risen from the ranks, they were far from popular with the people, and yet they contrived to force their rule upon the country, maintain it by sheer violence, and, to justify their action, keep up the never-ending war; alter the country's destiny in a word, against that country's will, till at last the man appeared who was to shelter them, and associate them with himself in a strong system of government which delivered them from all fear of restitution and reprisals.

The enriched Jacobins cling to Power.

Albert Vandal's merciless phrase " revolutionaries in possession " has been universally accepted. " Well-to-do Jacobins " he calls them, too.

They were not all equally well-to-do, and yet we note the realization of Dumouriez' prophecy, which declared, even in 1792, that "Chabot would be at Chantilly, Bazire at Rambouillet, Merlin at Chanteloup." Sieyès had not as yet settled at Crosne, nor was Fouché at Ferrières (far from it), but Barras owned Grosbois, Boursault had Brunoy, Merlin had the Mont Valérien, " with two or three millions of ecclesiastical property," as we read under the date of November 15, 1795. Tallien was leading a brilliant existence in his " cottage " at Chaillot : Barère had been entertaining Vadier and his followers at the Château de Clichy. They were a hungry race ! The Committee of the Year III alone, M. Sorel tells us (this body contained all the leading men of the party that came into power in Thermidor) contained a future Prince (Cambacérès) thirteen future Counts, five future Barons, seven future Senators of the Empire, six future Councillors of State; and, besides these, a good fifty " democrats," the future Duc d'Otrante and the future Comte Merlin among them, who were to own titles, arms, plumed hats, coaches, fortunes, entailed estates, town-houses and country residences before fifteen years were out, were then actually sitting in the Convention. Fouché was to die worth fifteen millions of francs.

But all that was nothing. The thing to which they clung was power, because that alone, it seemed to them, could save their necks. On the eve of the elections, Mallet reports an unexpected agreement among the regicides, who had been quarrelling among themselves, "*The 21st of January is before them,*" he says, and his words were true.

Three hundred and eighty-seven deputies had voted for the King's death, and six hundred and ninety-one had previously declared him guilty. Out of these voters sixty had followed the monarch to the scaffold, and ten more were to go the same way in Prairial. Three hundred regicides remained, and these were to form a solid party. We have followed the career of one of these men from 1793 to 1815 : he was to be Minister under the Directory, under the Consulate, under the Empire, and under Louis XVIII; all through these various phases of his life the same thought haunted him. M. Faguet tells us, in his final summing up of Fouché's life, that he looked at every event "through the little window of Louis XVI's scaffold." This grim yet true pronouncement may be applied to all the regicides of January 1793.

The Regicides haunted by fear of Reprisals.

Never before or since has history shown us so considerable a body of men thus set between the scaffold and power. If once they fell they must fall into the abyss.

In 1795 they were between two perils. On their left they had the "anarchists" as they called them, the Jacobins, who had obtained nothing and were longing to dislodge those who had provided for themselves ; these last were to crush their tormentors without mercy. On their right was Louis XVIII, who had just published his resolve to send them to the scaffold the moment he himself returned to power : our readers will readily understand that even the least compromised among them looked coldly on any idea of restoration, and did their utmost to prevent it. They were convinced the counter-revolution would begin the moment they were turned out. So they clung desperately to power. They were a hateful crew, indeed ! The fact cannot be disputed, and we shall lay yet greater stress upon it when we see them, on the very brink of their departure, force themselves on the electors of 1795 by a sudden parliamentary manœuvre. They were hated because of their share in the Terror, and because they were suspected, in many cases, of having found their dishonest profit in it.

In **Vendémiaire** of the Year IV, Lindet himself accused his colleagues of having speculated in *assignats*, and the fact that many pro-consuls had returned from their missions to the provinces with hands that were anything but clean was a matter of public knowledge. They were eager enough, now, to make themselves acceptable : " *Let us make the Republic lovable* " . . . cried Fréron. The working class was soon to make acquaintance with the " lovable " Republic in the person of Mme. Tallien, who would spend a hundred louis a day on dress in the midst of a starving population.

So these men, knowing themselves hated, strove to force themselves on the Nation primarily by the continuance of the war.

* * * * *

From 1791 to 1794 this war question had influenced our home policy : it may be fairly asserted that after 1794 the question of home politics influenced that of war. The Terrorist party had used the war to force the Government of Public Safety on the country : the members of the Convention had fallen into the habit of this method of procedure. And, besides, a new peril had grown up, a peril that war was to increase in the future, but which for the moment it was averting—the military peril. The hour had come when the troops had to be sent out to fight so as to keep their leaders busy. For these two reasons the continuation of the war was soon to be one of the fundamental items of the programme.

Continuance of the war a political Necessity.

Europe was tired out already. " We shall get back across the Rhine, little by little, and say ' *So be it !* ' " wrote a Prussian the day after the defeat at Kaiserslautern. The Prussians went back in October. On the 6th the French occupied Cologne ; on the 12th they were in Coblentz. So bitter were the quarrels about the Polish business that Prussia was threatening to go to war with her Austrian ally, and sent word to Barthélemy, our minister in Switzerland, that she was ready to come to terms.

The Thermidorian Committee despatched a haughty reply. This agreed with the policy of the party, but it agreed likewise with the natures of these legists, worthy successors, as we have already pointed out, of those of the Capetian kings : Prussia and Austria proposed peace, and the Committee refused to accept it, save on Draconian conditions. This was altogether against the wish of the country. The wish of the country was not only for peace but for peace both within and without its borders. In spite of this the Committee caused Holland to be invaded on October 10. " *The Republic,*" declared Merlin (of Thionville), " *after she has advanced her frontiers to the Rhine, will dictate the laws of Europe !* " Though Barthélemy was allowed to treat with Goltz, the Prussian envoy at Basle, in January and February 1795, he was instructed to impose conditions of the severest kind. Even if Prussia and Spain came to terms with France, the Committee knew well that it would be years before Austria consented to acknowledge the Rhine as the frontier-line of France, and England accepted the presence of the French in Antwerp. Thus the army was sure to have plenty of work to do.

And this was indispensable. The moment was perhaps the most splendid the French army ever knew. We have seen " The Generals how its courage had been tempered under the must be given fire of the enemy's guns : it was now superb : something its valour was unchanged, and it had been further to do." strengthened by a discipline of occasionally merciless severity. It was splendidly led by young commanders who were at once valiant warriors and bold tacticians. All of them—Hoche, Marceau, Moreau, Kléber, Masséna, Jourdan, Augereau, Lannes, found matchless strength in the confidence of their men. " It was the period of war," writes Soult, " in which the level of virtue was at its highest in our camps."

But these men, so lately raw volunteers, had developed into soldiers. Though they did not always take much interest in politics, they had conceived the most insulting scorn for the Paris politicians : their letters prove the fact. And, further, they were rough and active men, full of ardour. If peace were made how could anyone hope that they would go back quietly to the homes they had forsaken in 1791, 1792, and 1793 ? A score of witnesses authorize the assertion that fear of the troops had haunted and harassed every Government since 1791.

Roland put the thought into words in 1792, Billaud again, with more violence, in 1793, and Reubell, with far greater reason, in 1795.

The military leaders were especially feared. The Committee of the Year II had laid an iron yoke upon them, but after Thermidor this pressure had relaxed. Very soon it was perceived that the character of these leaders was altering, because the character of their troops was altering too. Before a year had gone by men were speaking of "the soldiers of Hoche," and "the soldiers of Bonaparte." Generals were now as used to command as to action. Once back in France, was it likely that these officers, already talking with open scorn of the "lawyers," would be ready to obey? The Convention saw clearly enough on the whole. The troops, in future, would refuse obedience to anyone but a soldier, the soldier who would impose his rule upon them. Thus the wisest course was to keep them busily employed.

But the more victories they won, the more was the spirit of domination to fill their souls ; and the greater their successes, the more dearly was the country to love them. The war thus continued to keep them busy was to raise them higher and higher. And, with the most singular imprudence, the ruling party was first to call them to membership of the body politic, by the Constitution of the Year III, and summon them next into the very precincts of the Convention, to defend it against the insurrectionary movements of the spring and autumn of that year ; finally—a far graver matter—to invite them to violate those sacred precincts for the benefit of a faction, in Fructidor of the Year V. So that the "revolutionaries in possession" did their best to put the soldier into possession.

For the moment their sole thought was how to impose themselves on the country to the exclusion of all other competitors, anarchist or royalist, military or civilian.
The Patriciate. They were to constitute what one of them, La Revellière, calls a sort of *patriciate*. It was this *patriciate* which, in Vendémiaire of the Year III and Fructidor of the Year V was to violate the liberties of the Nation, and then destroy them, so as to keep itself in power. But, when it appealed to the troops to carry out this purpose, it helped to

install an authority far more popular than its own. Augereau may have gone away fuming, after Fructidor, but he had shown Bonaparte the way into the Councils of the Nation.

The truth is that everybody and everything, from 1795 onwards, concurred to hand over the French Nation to the dictatorship of a single man: the artisans, who were soured, and accused the Republic of having fed them with false hopes; the middle class, which had grown rich, and felt the refuge offered it was anything but safe; the peasants, whose great desire was that the Revolution should be consolidated. A thousand interests opposed the restoration of a king who was deaf to every plea for compromise, but all were agreed in their readiness to welcome a personal ruler who would protect the work the Revolution had accomplished. And in the camps of the army this government was being prepared, with the complicity, not always conscious, of the " well-to-do Jacobins."

The Way prepared for Napoleon.

Only a year previously Catherine II had written as follows : " If France emerges from all this . . . she will be as obedient as any lamb : *but what she needs is a man of superior intellect, skilful, courageous, above all his contemporaries, and perhaps even his century. Has that man been born into the world ? "*

He had been born into the world, and every force was working in his favour.

SOURCES. Works already quoted by Schmidt, Aulard (*Paris, I*), La Revellière, Mallet du Pan, Lacretelle, Thibaudeau, Vaudreuil, Morris, Malouet, B. Constant (*Correspondance*), Baron de Staël-Holstein, Barras (III), d'Andigné, Madame de Chastenay, Fricasse.—Rovère, *Correspondance*, 1909 ; *Lettres* (in Bailleu, *Preussen und Frankreich*, 1881, I, 393-418) ; *Correspondance de Grimm avec Catherine II*, 1829 ; Babeuf, Notes (*Rev. Fr.*, 1905) ; Lindet, *Essai sur le crédit public, An IV, Tableaux de la dépréciation du papier* (re-published by Caron, 1909) ; Charlety, *Vente des Bien Nationaux*, 1906.

WORKS. Those already quoted by Levasseur, Stourm, Thureau-Dangin, Goncourt, Sorel (IV and V), Lichtenberger (*Le Socialisme et la Révolution*), Chassin, Lanzac de Laborie (*Mounier*), Arnaud, Nauroy, Ernest Daudet (*Emigration*).—Brette, *La Vie économique de la Révolution* (*Rev. Fr.*, 1905) ; Gabriel Deville, *L'Histoire Socialiste*, vol. v, 1906 ; Caudriller, *La Trahison de Pichegru*, 1908 ; Beauchesne, *Louis XVII*, 1866 ; Lacour, *Le Grand Monde après la Terreur*, 1892 ; Marion, *Les Biens Nationaux*, 1908 ; Lecarpentier, *Les Biens Nationaux*, 1908 ; Vialay, *Les Biens Nationaux*, 1908 ; Roger Peyre, *Napoléon et son Temps*, 1890.

CHAPTER XXXVII

THE " EMPTY BELLIES " *VERSUS* THE " ROTTEN BELLIES "

September 1794—*September* 1795

The ranks of the Right filled up. The " Crest " turns the " empty bellies " to account. The Germinal insurrection. The Terrorists proscribed. Famine increases. The 1st of Prairial. The Assembly invaded. The " last of the Mountaineers." Repression in the Faubourgs. The reaction of Prairial. Quiberon. The Committee of the Year III. The *decree of the two-thirds.* Anger of the country. The regicides' fate apparently sealed.

FROM the day when seventy-five proscribed deputies resumed their seats on the benches of the Right (18th Frimaire), from the day when—it almost amounted to a scandal!—non-regicide deputies entered the Committee of Public Safety, the men of the old Committee were lost. Even Carnot, Lindet, and Jeanbon **The Right** were attacked; and worse dangers threatened **reconstituted.** Collot, Vadier, Barère, and " Billaud the rectilinear." On the 12th Ventôse they fell: a decree for their impeachment was passed in the Assembly, and their trial fixed for the 3rd Thermidor.

The citizens of Paris said that if these men perished their fate " would bring more than 80,000 persons to the guillotine." Carrier had already suffered on the 26th Frimaire. Our readers will imagine how many anxious hearts there were, both on the benches of the Assembly and in the wineshops of the Faubourg Saint-Antoine. The " pure " Republicans took alarm. Since these hypocrites in the Convention pretended they were striking at " anarchy " simply because it was " a royalist method," they must be forcibly unmasked by a demand for the application of the Constitution of 1793, which was all the more

458

attractive because, as Tallien put it, it was still shut up in " its box."

These men in jeopardy, these belated and nostalgic Terrorists had an army ready to their hand: the famine-stricken populace.

" Not bayonets ! Bread ! " the Faubourgs howled. The cry for bread resounded everywhere ; mingled, adds a horrified police official, with "indecent outbursts against the Convention." Starving women shrieked : " Take a gun and shoot us rather than leave us to die of hunger ! " Suddenly, one day, the Faubourgs " came down." This first rising of the " empty bellies " took place on the 12th Germinal.

The Assembly had been listening that morning to a speech from Boissy d'Anglas—*Boissy-Famine* they called him in the Faubourgs, for he was responsible for the food-supply, and quite unable to ensure it. The mob had been gathering for an hour when, just as Boissy said the words " *We have re-established liberty*," it broke in the doors with a shout for " Bread ! " This was not the last occasion on which the two words were to be placed in opposition.

The Convention, greatly astonished, rose to its feet shouting " Long live the Republic ! " But for several days already The Insurrec- the police had been sending in reports to the effect tion of the that the Republic, or rather its executive, was " Crest." being very roughly handled by the starving people. Merlin (of Thionville) fancied he had done a great deal when he proceeded to kiss the hungry women. They surged hither and thither, not very sure, indeed, what they wanted. Some of the deputies of the Mountain—the *Crest men*, as members of the Extreme Left, the *Crest of the Mountain*, were called—were both disconcerted and surprised. " My friends ! " shouted one of them, Gaston, " you want bread and you want freedom for patriots, you shall have both, but get out of this, for we are being suffocated by the heat ! " Mingled with the women were alarming-looking men, " with bare arms and uncovered breasts," as an eye-witness informs us.

Legendre, who retained the vigour of his former exploits in the service of the Revolution in his present support of the reaction, had gone out in search of defenders. The ex-butcher was hand and glove with the *Muscadins* : he called them together, and they made a sudden irruption into the Convention, armed with whips and cudgels, and followed by a handful of gendarmes. A rigorous hunt ensued, the wretched petitioners " tumbled down " the tiers of the seats, or took refuge on the benches of the Mountain : in a moment the coast was clear. The *Gilded Battalion* had won the day. General Pichegru, too, appeared upon the scene, as though by pure accident, and was invested with the command of the troops in Paris. The Assembly was saved.

Naturally, having been terrorized, it was resolved to punish somebody. To begin with, Collot and the other accused deputies were deported without trial or sentence : eight members of the " Crest " who seemed to have had an understanding with the rioters, were sent out of Paris. And, as the crowd began to stop their carriages, Pichegru was obliged to interfere. His bayonets cleared the way for the convoy that conducted the last remnants of the " Great Committee " to the galleys ; on the 13th the General announced to the Assembly : " Representatives ! your decrees have been performed ! " and the honours of the sitting were straightway conferred upon the soldier. This was the first step on a dangerous path.

* * * * *

But to strike is not to answer. The deportation of Collot and Billaud to Cayenne had not given bread to the populace of Paris.

A perusal of the police reports of Germinal and Floréal of this year is worth all the descriptions writers can give : these reports demonstrate the existence of a state of distress that was driving the Faubourgs to despair ; sometimes they openly regretted Robespierre, who killed, indeed, but never stole. Sometimes a cry would rise : " Are they trying to force us to ask for a king ? " On the 19th Floréal the murmurs against " the Government and the Convention " had reached their height. The "empty bellies" were really rising in revolt against those who were known everywhere as the " rotten bellies."

The " last of the Mountaineers " could not but rejoice at the sight of the difficulties against which the Thermidorian reactionaries were struggling. These "members of the Crest" had seen their friends deported ; their own position was full of danger ; they did not bring about the riot (M. Claretie has feelingly narrated the tragic fate of these "last Romans," and absolves them from complicity): nevertheless they were reckoning on the exasperation of the populace to bring about the restoration of the Constitution of 1793, and "the reign of virtue." And the event was to compass their own ruin and their death.

On the 1st Prairial the populace, drunk with the madness The Revolt of of hunger, more terrible, perhaps, than that of Germinal. wine, rushed wildly upon the Tuileries, feeling death would be better than further suffering, and ready to face every risk.

This time the Convention had been warned : and on the 28th Germinal the decree forbidding troops of the line to come within ten leagues of Paris had been repealed. Large bodies of cavalry were poured in from all the neighbouring garrisons. And the " gilded youths," too, were determined to defend the once abhorred Convention, and not with mere whips this time. "I laugh, and I blush too, when I think of it, even now," one of these *Muscadins* was to write later.

But, in spite of all this, the attack, like that of Germinal, was so sudden, that for several hours the Assembly was helpless, and barely escaped.

At five o'clock in the morning the tocsin began to ring (the whole movement was directed by an insurrectionary committee, the composition of which is wrapped in mystery) and the rioters rushed upon the Tuileries. " *This*," they cried, " *is the struggle of the black hands against the white !* " (the note of social warfare begins to appear in these convulsions). " *These rascals must be blown up.*" Before the clock had struck ten the Palace was surrounded : before noon the Hall of the Convention was invaded. The women stalked like hungry wolves through the bays crying out " Bread ! " Dumont, who had acted as pro-consul in the Somme, took the presidential chair and tried to feed them with fine sentences. " No talk ! " they yelled, " Bread ! " Even through the dryness of the *Moniteur's* report we get an idea of the confusion in the Assembly : it must certainly have been extreme, for some of

461

the deputies called out: "Is the Convention afraid?" Creuzé-Latouche was to acknowledge, in a letter written afterwards, that he and his colleagues were all convinced their last hour had come.

The troops, which had been duly summoned, did not appear: and, meanwhile, the Faubourgs were pouring down their thousands: a few *Muscadins*, armed with cudgels, had just succeeded in clearing part of the precincts, when a door on the President's left gave way under pressure, and a fresh avalanche of human beings rushed in, sweeping everyone before it.

Dumont had surrendered the President's chair to Boissy d'Anglas. It was a proof of high courage on his part to take it, for few men were so unpopular as "*Boissy-Famine.*" He was greeted by a hail of invectives, but at last he beheld a few battalions drawing near: fortunately, so Lacretelle writes, "the attack was as irresolute as the defence." The troops had not yet got into the habit of charging the populace. Meanwhile fresh hordes of rioters kept pouring in through every entrance: one of the deputies, Féraud, made a brave attempt to stem the torrent at one point: he was knocked down, kicked by wooden sabots, dragged out of the hall, and killed by a tavern-keeper who, with a return to the good old traditions, "sliced off his head like a turnip," seized it by the hair, and threw it to the crowd, which carried it into the presence of the Assembly on the end of a pike, a moment afterwards. It was held up in front of Boissy: pale as death, he bowed reverently to his murdered colleague. His gesture has become historic.

At nine o'clock that night the "Crest" made up its mind to take action. In the midst of the tumult Soubrany was acclaimed President; Romme carried a motion decreeing the baking of "only one sort of bread": Goujon and Bourbotte secured measures against the reactionary press, Duquesnoy one for breaking up the Committees, "and also the creation of a provisional commission," chosen entirely, of course, among the members of the Mountain, which announced its intention of retiring to deliberate in private forthwith.

On its way out, it fell in with the "good citizens" (so says the *Moniteur*) led by Legendre.

"EMPTY" v. "ROTTEN BELLIES"

The Committees, writes Lacretelle, had contrived to arm a small body of men with swords and muskets. They marched right upon the crowd with bayonets fixed, and drove everybody, the deputies of the " Crest " and their escort as well, before them. The mob tried to resist, but was soon expelled. " I still cannot understand how they contrived to disappear so instantaneously," writes La Revellière.

And then, as Commines said of Louis XI, the thought of vengeance followed. The scapegoats were ready to hand : **The Terrorists** the deputies of the Crest, who had compromised **proscribed.** themselves. The Assembly, which had learnt what terror meant, turned upon them savagely. " Vengeance ! Swift vengeance ! " cried Tallien. Denunciation was the breath of this man's nostrils : " *Down with the assassins !* " he cried—himself one of the September murderers. Goujon, Duquesnoy, Romme, Soubrany, and others were proscribed. Tallien would fain have had many other heads : those of men who desired to re-establish " the infamous Commune " (he forgot he had belonged to it himself) : he even went so far as to demand the arrest of Lindet and Carnot.

Outside in the streets the storm still raged. In the course of the night the insurrection seemed to gain strength. The Assembly would have to substitute offensive for defensive measures. It faced the necessity : on the 2nd Prairial General Dubois (who has left us a very interesting letter on the subject) opened fire upon the Faubourgs. But it was not till the 4th that Generals Kilmaine and Montchoisi invested the " glorious Faubourg." The mob tried to parley, but Montchoisi's dragoons would not listen : " When we are on duty," they shouted, " we only talk with our swords." The Faubourg Saint-Antoine capitulated to the troops just six years after the neighbouring Bastille had been destroyed. And Paris, already shivering with hunger, began to shiver with fear.

The reaction—on the morrow of the insurrection of Prairial —was fierce. The terrified Faubourgs obediently handed in their arms. " There is no difficulty," says a writer on the 7th Prairial, " about getting in the pikes." Three thousand cavalry occupied the approaches to the Tuileries : Tallien, Fréron and Barras, if they could have had their way, would have burnt the " glorious

Faubourg " to the ground—even in the midst of reaction the thought of fierce measures haunted these Terrorists. They might have fancied themselves back in the good old days when they had inspired terror in the name of " liberty." Only this time it was in the name of "order." Five thousand Jacobins lay in prison, sixty-two deputies of the Mountain had been impeached, and six condemned to death; this was good indeed. Tallien would fain have swelled the list by the addition of a few more of his colleagues : Carnot was only snatched from death by the cry of some friend (his identity has never been revealed) from his seat in the Assembly : " *Carnot ! but it was he who organized our victories !* "

The last of the Mountaineers stabbed themselves when they heard their death sentence read aloud : Goujon passed on the dagger to Duquesnoy with the words " Here, Petus ! "— even then they talked Plutarch ! Those who did not succeed in killing themselves were guillotined. " The courage of those six ruffians astonished everybody," says a newspaper of the day. Such a man as Tallien might well feel astonishment ! Was it worth while to bring about a revolution, and be guillotined just when the time for enjoying it had come ?

" *Rotten bellies,*" the " *hungry bellies* " of the Faubourgs called the deputies. After those two days of the 1st and Famine increasing. 2nd of Prairial, the unpopularity of the Convention was unparalleled. Poverty was increasing everywhere (we should have liked to quote the police reports for the spring and summer of 1795) ; it was estranging the populace from the Republic, and almost from the Revolution. When the Faubourgs were informed that there was to be a solemn celebration of the Festival of August 10, a man called out to a deputy : " Give us bread, not music ! " and the following phrase, which deserves special attention, was constantly heard : " The representatives rejoice : *the Revolution profits nobody but them !* " Still not a finger was raised : the reorganization of the National Guard had placed it entirely in the hands of the new oligarchy. " It will be entirely composed in future," writes Benjamin Constant, gleefully, on the 10th Prairial, " *of reliable men, who would lose something*

*in any disturbance, whereas hitherto a certain proportion of its
members had everything to gain by insurrection."*

* * * * *

The genuine reactionaries seemed masters of the situation.
In Paris the " gilded youths " were taking payment for the help
they had rendered by indulging in a great deal of licence : they
carried it far : when the Guard of the Convention tried to play
the *Marseillaise,* they shouted " Not the *Marseillaise !* " and the
Guard obediently played the *Réveil !*

In the provinces, again, especially in the South, the counter-
revolution in all its integrity seemed to be under way. We
The White   have heard the expression *the White Terror.*
Terror.   The words are not correct if they are taken to
assimilate certain risings, sanguinary indeed, but local and
intermittent, to the *Red Terror,* which a government, backed
by troops, judges, committees, and official executioners, had
lately spread abroad over the whole country. Nevertheless
the *companies of Jehu* did spread terror in the South : that
fierce South, which had been so cruelly oppressed from Toulon
to Lyons, took its revenge, hunted the Jacobins first, then the
Republicans, and then the purchasers of national property ;
and as Albigeois and anti-Albigeois still nursed their old resentments, religious hatred soon envenomed political strife.
From Tarascon, where the Jacobins and their " accomplices "
were cast headlong from a tower, to Lyons, where the "matavons"
(accomplices of the Jacobins again) were murdered in the fort of
Saint-Jean, we are forced to recognize the existence of a violent
reaction, swiftly to be tinctured in this country of extreme views
with royalism. The Commissaries of the Convention themselves were drawn into a most bitter reaction. Isnard, once
Vergniaud's right-hand man, swept away by his resentment
against the Jacobins, exclaimed to the young men about him :
" If you have no arms, dig up your fathers' bones, and use
them to exterminate the wretches ! "

At the other extremity of France, though La Vendée was
apparently subdued, the Chouannerie, a guerilla war, had
sprung up in Brittany and part of Normandy.
The Chouans.   This might well have favoured a general uprising
which would have facilitated that descent of the *émigrés* and

the English on the French coasts so long discussed in the circle of the Comte d'Artois.

Even in the Convention a certain number of the deputies of the Centre, apart from the blind supporters of reaction—several witnesses agree as to this—were inclined to favour the idea of a restoration, provided it were of a moderate, liberal and constitutional nature. " The little fellow," as Louis XVII was called in the Faubourgs, might be brought out of the Temple, and a Regency appointed, composed of members of the Convention. Then, when the " little fellow " died, on the 20th Prairial, a message from Louis XVIII was anxiously awaited. We have already described this message : it took the form of the Verona proclamation, of which a certain intelligent royalist said that the men who had recommended it were " criminals."

" The royalists in the interior of the country are in despair," writes Mallet du Pan, soon after its arrival. But joy reigned in the hearts of the Thermidorian coterie. The thought of any, even the most moderate restoration, filled them with alarm, for the regicides felt they would always remain " unpardonable." Tallien, who had been accused in the Faubourgs of having sold himself to the claimant to the throne (whereas he was really convinced he would certainly be hanged if the King ever came back to France) was even trying to shake off any compromising acquaintances he had.

Great was the joy then, when news reached Paris that a descent—premature in any case—had been effected by the *émigrés* at Quiberon on the 7th Messidor (June 26). The disembarkation had been carried out with the help of an English fleet—a co-operation so odious in the eyes of the Breton royalists themselves, all of them hereditary enemies of Britain, that it had chilled their ardour. Thus the support of the Chouans had been half-hearted, and the English, once they had landed the *émigrés* on the beach, had done nothing at all. Betrayed by those who had summoned them and those who had conveyed them to the spot, the royalists were overcome and forced to capitulate. Within a day of their landing Hoche, who was conducting operations in the West, had cut off six thousand

The
" Émigrés "
at Quiberon.

prisoners, one thousand of whom were *émigrés*, in the peninsula, and the Convention was called on to decide their fate.

Tallien saw in the royalists' providential imprudence a means of reassuring the ruined Jacobins, and recalling the moderate party, now inclining to the royal cause, to its allegiance to the Republic of Thermidor. As on every future occasion the supporters of the Revolution closed up their ranks in response to all the mad "Quiberonnades" (the word is Mallet's) of the uncompromising royalist party. Tallien was sent to Quiberon, and had all the *émigré* prisoners shot down —a hideously memorable hecatomb. He flattered himself that the aristocratic blood of Quiberon would wipe out the blood of the Paris Faubourgs shed in Prairial. However that may have been, the royalist movement certainly was destroyed, alike in the Assembly and in the small southern towns. When the 9th of Thermidor, the anniversary of the ever memorable day saw Lanjuinais — lately suspected of royalism — and the triumphant Tallien seated at the same festive board, the union between the two factions which had overthrown Robespierre, "in their *common hatred of all tyrants*" was apparently complete. The Convention materialized the fact by singing first the *Marseillaise* and then the *Réveil*. "Anarchy" had been put down in the Faubourg Saint-Antoine, royalism had been scotched at Quiberon, and the men of Thermidor believed themselves close on their haven of safety—the Constitution of the Year III, republican, but anti-democratic.

* * * * *

There had been some idea of asking Sieyès to draw it up. We have already told our readers how the oracle had mounted Constitution of the tripod in 1789; there he had remained, the Year III. veiled in clouds which under the Convention he deliberately thickened, to avoid being drawn into any dangerous enterprise. He had thus left Condorcet, and Hérault after him, to build their fragile edifices without him.

This strange Sieyès, considered the "first of political architects," never revealed his plans to anyone. Just as Albert Vandal depicts him to us in 1799 (we refer our readers to those lively pages), so he already was in 1795 : mysterious, haughty,

dogmatic, vague. It was being said, indeed, that if two Constitutions had already expired, one from premature wear and
tear, and one from congenital weakness, it was because the
oracle had not been consulted. In 1795, the hour in his opinion
being not yet come, he once more refused to come down from
his Sinaï, and take the seat to which he had been appointed
on the Commission. This refusal, as the course of subsequent
events will prove, was an incident of some importance.

Deprived though it was of the oracle's help, the Commission
of Eleven applied itself to its task. It was full of members
of the Right and the Centre : Daunou, Lanjuinais, La Revellière,
Louvet, Durand de Maillane, Thibaudeau, Boissy d'Anglas,
bourgeois all of them, to whom horror of the Constitution of
1793, "that Constitution of the Faubourg Saint-Antoine,"
as Durand called it, was the beginning of wisdom. Daunou,
the real author of the new Constitution, made a final attempt
to secure Sieyès' help : "I have made a profound study of
these matters," said the sage, "but you would not understand
me."

It would be interesting to follow the discussions of the
Eleven through the memoirs and letters of the members of the
Commission. We must be content to record the fact, that
when they rejected the idea of an executive government to be
elected by the people, it was, as Louvet cynically affirms,
"because the people might possibly have elected a Bourbon."
The Government, therefore, was to be elected by the Chambers,
and to consist of five members : this was the Directory of the
Republic.

There were to be two of these Chambers. Galiani, considered
a thinker in those days, had said to Barras : "The more natural
petulance there is in the race with which you have to deal,
the more, if you propose to endow it with a system of national
representation, you must cut that up into Chambers." And,
he added, with more wit than politeness, that if you would give
a nation of monkeys twelve, you must give "at least four to
the French race." Carnot, too, set forth a whole plan for
separate Chambers.

It was finally decided that there were to be two : "one,"
said Baudin, "which would include all the younger men, would

468

be *Imagination,* the other, the Senate, would be *Reason !*
Carnot was already dreaming of a Conservative Senate which
should interpret the Constitution. Sieyès, who had been
coaxed into joining the Commission at the very end of its
labours, made up his mind to propose something of the same
sort, a Constitutional Jury, in addition to the two Chambers :
but his suggestion came too late, and he could not get it
accepted : this inspired him with a bitter hatred for the
Constitution of the Year III.

In spite of all this the Constitution, after debates which
lasted from the 16th Messidor to the 30th Thermidor, was
adopted on the 5th Fructidor of the Year III : it was to be
submitted to a plebiscite, and many citizens being suspected of
reactionary tendencies, it was settled that the troops, supposed
to be far more republican as a whole, should be allowed to
vote.

* * * * *

The distinguishing mark of this Constitution is *its return
to the system of a restricted electorate, based on the payment of*
Return to the   *taxes.* From the outset it takes property to be
property   the sign and basis of political competency. " A
Qualification.   country governed by owners of property is a
country of social order," said Boissy. Electors in the first or
second degree were simply to be electors who paid more or
less in taxes. This system was to produce a Legislative Body
divided into two Councils, both of them elected by a system
of list voting in every department, one third of the members
of which were to be re-elected every year : the *Five Hundred*
(*Imagination*) were to have the *sole right of proposing legislation :*
but they might only convert their proposals into *resolutions,*
which the *Ancients* (*Reason*) could transform into *laws.*

The executive Directory, composed of five members, was
to be elected by the Legislative Body : the Five Hundred were
to select fifty names. and out of thçse the Ancients were to
choose the five chief magistrates. One member of this
Directory was to present himself for re-election every year.
There had been an idea, for a moment, of giving the Directory
the power of appointing official functionaries, refused to
Louis XVI in 1791 : but the compilers of the Constitution

lacked the necessary courage, and the Government was thus
to find itself obliged either to usurp this prerogative (which
it did) or to sit helpless at the head of an undisciplined
administration. And, further, the Government was deprived
(as Barras and La Revellière were bitterly to complain) of the
management of the National Treasury, which was handed over
to Commissaries elected by the deputies—a financial system
which paralyzed the executive power. To conclude, there
was to be no *Veto*. La Revellière, who had been one of
those who would have refused it to the King in 1791, was to
think the institution a very good one when he found he was not
to have it under the Directory. To add lustre to the prestige
of the Directors, thus stripped of their arms, they were given
very fine clothes ; even in their own homes they were to wear a
magnificent costume, " as a protest," Boissy d'Anglas tells
us, " against *sans-culottism*."

Mignet expresses great admiration for this Constitution.
We confess we do not understand this admiration. The Constitution of the Year III skilfully organized conflict between
the two powers : if the Directors stood out against the deputies
elected by the Nation they could not be overthrown, as our
present Chambers can overthrow a ministry : the Legislative
Body would have to wait three years before the majority of the
Directory could be made in its image. And, on the other hand,
if the Councils seemed to be moving in direct opposition to the
fundamental principles of the Republic, the Directory had no
power to appeal to the country by dissolving them, nor could
it delay the passing of a law it considered unconstitutional
by applying its veto until the country had pronounced its
verdict. The Councils ought to have been given the right to
absorb Directors who opposed the will of the people, or the
Directors should have been allowed to *dissolve* Chambers which
seemed to misuse their power.

But, as every student will perceive, this clumsy organization
was the result of the terror that haunted the Convention of the
Year III. 1789 had filled them with fear of a strong executive ;
1794 had inspired them with a most lively apprehension of the
abuse of strength in which a single and omnipotent Chamber
might indulge. So they left the two powers face to face this
470

time, and both of them unarmed, as though no disagreement between them was likely to ensue. But he who does not foresee conflict provokes it : to withhold means of preventing it is to doom it to greater bitterness. Four *coups d'état* were to be born of this Constitution. Can anyone maintain that it was a good one ?

There was one man, at all events, even in 1795, who thought it abominably bad. Mortified because, as Mallet says, "his metaphysical oracles had lost their prestige," Sieyès went about declaring : " this is not the right thing yet ! " And, as we have already said, his hostility to the labours of "the Eleven" was no light thing.

       *   )   *   *   *

" The Constitution will be accepted : we should accept the Izurveidan itself," wrote the *Courrier Français* on the 21st Fructidor : and after a hit or two at the *offspring of eleven fathers*, the "reactionary" newspaper went on to say : "*the French Nation will take this virgin to wife, even though it be exposed to the risk of an ultimate divorce.*" This was the general feeling. The Convention proposed to guard "the virgin daughter of eleven fathers " from any danger of "divorce" by setting a jealous watch over the newly married couple : and where were more jealous guardians than its own members to be found ? Conscious of its own growing unpopularity, and bent on perpetuating its existence in the next Legislative Body, it had shamelessly set about forcing itself on the electors, who were longing to be rid of it. This was the aim of that tremendous stroke of parliamentary compulsion known as the *Decree of the Two-Thirds.*

On the 3rd Fructidor of the Year III, a police inspector had reported that the " empty bellies " were " beating the call to arms and ringing the tocsin of the Convention."

The Decree of the Two-Thirds. There was a universal feeling that " those rogues must not be re-elected " ; not one of them ! for " the old members would spoil the new ones." The members of the Convention were aware of this ; save for about fifty of their number—such as Boissy, Daunou, and Lanjuinais—they were all to be swept away, and above all, the regicides, the September murderers, and the pro-consuls of the Year II—" rotten bellies " everyone of them.

Such a man as Tallien, who was all these things, was certain to find himself cast out after his brief moment of exaltation. The couple—" Her most Serene Highness Madame Cabarrus " and " her august spouse "—were already the objects of fierce attacks. At this juncture Tallien perceived that he had not a moment to lose. He began to express the most serious alarm as to the fate of the Republic : this was the regular rule of the game. If the electors were left to do as they pleased, the " *counter-revolution* " (a singular admission) " *would be a constitutional fact before three months were out.*" And we are bound to admit that his cynical assertion was justified by facts. Now, from 1795 onwards, Tallien and his fellows, as Mallet tells us, knew that they must either " reign or perish."

Straightway they proved themselves adepts in the art of gaining their ends by strong and sudden blows. On the 5th Fructidor Tallien proposed a decree to be embodied in the Constitution *whereby two-thirds of the deputies of the new Legislative Body, five hundred in all, must be chosen amongst the outgoing members of the Assembly.* One deputy only, Saladin, uttered a word of protest. The decree was passed the very day it was proposed.

Accustomed though the public was to usurpation, there was a stir this time. In Paris, especially, the indignation was Indignation of extreme : the press of every party denounced the Public. these " perpetual members." Well, there was one very simple solution : the electors would not obey the decree ; they would not re-elect men who had sat in the last Convention. Then, on the 13th, the Assembly passed a new and additional decree : *If the electors failed to re-elect the Five Hundred, " the number was to be made up by deputies re-elected by the Convention* "; in other words, the Convention was to dispense with the formality of an election, and itself select these extraordinary " representatives of the people." The boldness of this proceeding stupefied the Nation. As Malouet truly wrote, " At this moment the Convention is at war with the manifest wishes of the majority in France." Tallien would have granted that, with his usual cynicism, but he was bound to " reign or perish ! "

The Convention had indeed decided that these two decrees

were to be submitted, with the Constitution, to a plebiscite. But it was also making preparations for applying pressure, and even for fraud should occasion arise. The Verona proclamation was to be placarded; this was quite fair, in an electoral campaign; the threats of the Comte de Provence would rally the uncertain provinces, and especially the purchasers of national property, to the standard of the republican Constitution: as for the decrees, their meaning was not properly understood in country places, but they were declared an inseparable concomitant of the Constitution. For Paris a more brutal weapon was to be employed. Troops were poured into the city : a newspaper published on the 12th Fructidor draws its readers' attention to the " formidable preparations displayed under the walls of Paris and in its neighbourhood." The Sections had already entered their protest against these on the 11th.

The acceptance of the decrees was announced: the figures given were absurd, 263,000 votes for the whole of France : 95,000 were graciously accorded to the opposition. "An evident fraud," writes Mallet, " Paris and its environs alone must have made up more than 95,000 votes." "*A feat of strength and sleight of hand,*" writes one of the Foreign Ministers, an almost amused witness of this thimble-rigging performance. In certain departments not a single vote was cast in favour of the decrees. In the department of Paris (where the authorities did not dare to tamper too much with figures) there were 21,734 votes against them and only 1156 in their favour. What strikes the historian most is the enormous number of abstentions —amounting to millions. There can be no clearer proof that the country was really losing its interest ; the general sense of fear, and still more of scorn and disgust, was doing more to prepare the way for Cæsar than the most violent opponents of the Government.

The proof of the fraud became evident when the elections took place, and the country, in spite of all the pressure put upon it, only chose 376 out of the required 500 members, thus forcing the choice of the remaining 124 deputies on the Convention itself. For the elections were proceeding—one long disaster for the Jacobins.

The newly elected deputies were former members of the Constituent Assembly, of very moderate opinions, old Feuillants, **The new Assembly of Moderates.** or else new men, all hostile to the present crumbling *régime*, many of whom had been prisoners under the Terror. And the members of the Convention who had obtained re-election were Lanjuinais, who was chosen in seventy-three Departments, Boissy, who was elected in seventy-two, and various members of the Right, elected all over the country by eight, ten, and twenty constituencies at once : a cruel mortification for the Mountain.

In spite of the desperate efforts they had made to maintain their position for the past two years, the Terrorists were doomed to be driven out, or at all events, reduced to impotence : it was already clear that the new Directory would be composed of moderate men: Lanjuinais, it was said, and Boissy, Pontécoulant and Daunou, and Cambacérès, who was already beginning to deny that he had " voted for death." With terrified eyes the regicides gazed into the hideous abyss that gaped to receive them.

But once again, on the 13th Vendémiaire, the impatient members of the royalist party were to be their salvation.

For sources and bibliography, see those of Chapter XXXVIII.

CHAPTER XXXVIII

THE THIRTEENTH VENDÉMIAIRE

The royalists save the regicides. The Sections of Paris oppose
the decrees. The royalist insurrection. Barras appointed
Generalissimo. " Buona-Parte " at the Tuileries. The defeat
of the Sections. Bonaparte makes his entry. The dying Convention. The last sitting. The work of the " Giant Assembly."

IN that summer of 1795 the royalists were what they had
always been, and always were to be throughout the Revolution, the Jacobins' most precious allies and their final
refuge. These last were hated and rejected by the country. Some
unconscious longing for a liberal monarchy it may have had :
The Royalists the choice of deputies in certain departments
save the —old friends of La Fayette and Barnave, and
Regicides. even of Mounier—strengthen this supposition,
and it is quite possible that France, by the way of a moderate
republic, might have come to the peaceful restoration of a
constitutional Bourbon monarch.

But among the genuine royalists this idea found no favour.
We know they abhorred the moderates as heartily as they
abhorred the Jacobins. They firmly believed that the one wish
of the country was to return to its allegiance under the sceptre
of Louis XVIII : their enemies were preventing this : they
would raise a revolt. Yet Madame de Staël, now back in Paris,
gave them fair warning that they were mistaken : the excesses
of 1793 had filled her with horror, but she was all for a reaction
within the law : any insurrection would be a failure. The army
would be delighted to march against the royalists, who had
been the allies of the foreigner for so long : the Faubourgs,
whatever the royalists might deceive themselves into thinking,
hated them as much as they hated the Convention, though for
different reasons : and the Jacobins, between the devil and the

475

deep sea, would defend themselves to the death. Further (as Mallet acknowledges), the material preparations for insurrection were lacking : the royalists had a bare three thousand muskets and some twenty tons of powder.

The reaction had certainly won over most of the Sections, yet they contained many prudent men who were wisely waiting for the resistless trend of public opinion. But for two months Paris had been swarming with Chouans and *émigrés*, " madmen come in from outside," writes the prudent Mallet, " who were always spurring on the hotheads."

The Sections regarded the decrees as an abuse of privilege : they refused to accept them : they organized a central committee which sent up address after address in opposition to these " decrees destined to perpetuate the power of men who are either gorged with pillage, or the instigators of massacre." Thirty Sections out of forty-eight adhered to this manifesto. The Convention replied by proclaiming the acceptance of the Constitution by 914,853 votes to 95,373, and declaring the decrees " which the country had approved " (under what conditions we have already related), to be the law of the State.

The Sections oppose the Decrees.

There was a regular uproar (as the police reports prove) ; the figures had been tampered with ! And the excitement, far from calming down, rose higher and higher. So great had it become on the 3rd Vendémiaire, that the Convention threatened to leave Paris. The Sections scoffed at this curious threat. Troops were poured into the town ; but "the men with the epaulets and feathers " were openly defied ; in the Palais-Royal the mob hooted the soldiers till it drove them to draw their swords.

On the 11th the Convention announced the dissolution of the primary Assemblies, which had finished their work, " on pain of being prosecuted as guilty of an attempt against the *sovereignty of the Nation.*" Such words, from the lips of the authors of the decrees, sounded like a sinister joke : and the heralds dispatched to publish the decree on the squares and open spaces of the City found their task impossible—their voices were drowned by the hooting of the mob. Meanwhile the electors assembled at the Théâtre Français : here opinions were so divided that they could not come to any decision. But the Lepelletier Section (Boulevard des Italiens) was the centre of a far larger gathering, stirred by a most dangerous agitation. The Committees of the Convention were well aware that all Paris was quivering with excitement. The members of the Committees were too numerous to organize any effectual resistance : an Executive Commission of five members was chosen; Barras, who had worn a great sword ever since Thermidor, and was considered an Achilles, was associated with them. This staff looked about for reliable troops. " No better plan could be discovered," writes Barras, " for fighting adversaries such as these, than to set their natural enemies upon them, the patriots cast into prison in consequence of the reaction of Thermidor." Hideous figures hurried up, in response to the Commissions' summons, remnants of the Revolutionary Committees, and murderers of the Days of September, "guillotine-lickers," rioters of the Prairial insurrection, just let out of prison, 1500 ruffians in all. " We called them," says Barras, " the sacred battalion. . . ."

The measure was ill-advised : it infuriated all honest folks, and delighted the royalist ring-leaders. On the morning of the 12th, the Lepelletier Section announced, to **The royalist Insurrection.** the rolling of a drum, that weapons had just been served out to the " blood-drinkers," and that to prevent massacre all good citizens must arm themselves at once and hurry to their various Sections. The Section of the Corn Market had the Terrorists of that quarter seized and imprisoned at once : the other Sections flew to arms, so as to be ready to succour whichever of its fellows was attacked.

This was the Lepelletier Section. The Five had made up their minds to stifle the budding insurrection, and had deputed General Menou to perform this duty. Menou was a moderate man : his soul revolted at the sight of the " pack of wretches and murderers masquerading as *patriots of '89* " the authorities wished to associate with him. The columns sent to attack the Lepelletier Section did it feebly, and receiving an exceedingly vague promise of dissolution from the electors, they retired.

By the time Menou had been deprived of his command, and General Verdière had been ordered by the Five to march once

THE FRENCH REVOLUTION

more on the Section, things had grown much worse. Paris, seeing Menou retire, had burst into a flame. The Sections, which had organized a little army, had occupied the Pont-Neuf, under the direction of General Danican, a former " patriot." A Committee of Insurrection had been formed, and was composed, of course, of royalists. On the morning of the 13th the position of the Convention appeared most serious.

* * * * *

Barras was now definitely given the supreme command : from that day forward he called himself " General Barras," but he was a poor strategist. So he appealed for help to the Jacobin officers, who had been in disgrace for some months past. In the midst of this " Robespierrist " staff now gathered, strange as it may seem, round the " victor " of the 9th Thermidor, he soon perceived an old acquaintance : the little Corsican officer who had served under Dugommier's command at the siege of Toulon, had organized *the battery of men who feared nothing*, and more than any other living man had helped Fréron and Barras to snatch back the town from the hands of the English and the royalists. Suspected, since Thermidor, of being an impenitent follower of Robespierre, dismissed on the 29th of the preceding Fructidor because he had refused the command of a brigade of infantry in the West—he was an artilleryman heart and soul—this little " Buona-Parte " (thus is his name written in all the reports of the period), had hesitated somewhat when he had been asked to join these men of the " rotten " party. But there he was after all, his pale face looking out under his tangled mop of hair, in his shabby brigadier-general's uniform—his appearance not much in his favour.

Now Barras wanted an artilleryman : he did not give the Corsican the rank historians have attributed to him, relying on a *galéjade** in the *Mémorial:* but he did keep him close to his own person : he was to command the batteries " General Barras " was about to organize. The

Side-notes: Barras appointed Generalissimo. Buonaparte.

* A *patois* expression used in the South of France, and applied to the exaggerated tales of their prowess ascribed to the inhabitants of that part of the country. *See*, for instance, Daudet's " Tartarin."

478

thing most lacking to these batteries were guns. There were forty of them at the camp of Les Sablons, and all in great danger of being carried off by the Sections, if the troops did not seize them first. Bonaparte was consulted about the matter, and suggested the employment of Murat, a man who would face all risks, and one of the keenest Jacobins among the officers of the French army. Joachim Murat, with a squadron of the 21st Chasseurs, rode at full gallop to Les Sablons, found a column sent by the Sections there already, drove it off, seized the guns, and at six o'clock in the morning had brought them back, still at full gallop, to the Tuileries. Neither the young general nor the dashing horseman dreamt that when they helped Barras to these guns, to be used against royalists, each of them had secured a crown for his own head.

Reinforcements were now reaching Barras from the outskirts of Paris, but the guns, above all, enabled him to turn the Tuileries into an impregnable fortress. Two hours earlier a small body of men might have invested the Palace with the greatest ease. But it was a rainy morning, and when " worthy folk " set about an insurrection they do it after the fashion of " worthy folk," very ready to be killed, but with an insuperable objection to getting wet.

For this reason Danican had never stirred from the Pont Neuf. When the rain stopped he led his " army " against the Tuileries. Soon the Rue Saint-Honoré was crowded with the men of the Sections : they had taken up a strong position round the church of Saint-Roch, and seemed to be preparing to surround the Palace. Danican dispatched emissaries bearing a flag of truce, who were to confine themselves to a demand that the dangerous ruffians who had been given arms on the preceding day should be deprived of their weapons.

These messengers did not obtain a hearing : yet the Assembly believed it was about to be stormed, for cartridges and muskets were distributed to all the members. Suddenly, at half-past four o'clock, the deputies heard a loud discharge of artillery. Bonaparte was making his entrance into history.

❦   *   *   *   *

The struggle had begun—its immediate cause, probably,
being a shot fired at the men of the Sections from some window.
Enter General They had replied with a volley : the troops,
Bonaparte. writes Creuzé-Latouche, had sprung joyfully
to arms, " as if they had been going to a wedding."

If we are to believe the *Mémorial*, Bonaparte then decided
the fate of the day by turning his famous guns upon Saint-
Roch. This, no doubt, was an important incident in the proceedings, but not so important as our manuals generally make it :
the reports to the Convention lay no particular stress on this
cannonade, and the nature of the position would have made it
difficult for Bonaparte to sweep Saint-Roch with grape-shot.
But it would also seem that recent historians, in their desire
to disparage the part played by the future Emperor, have made
too little of what he did. His guns did not " sweep Saint-
Roch," but they did greatly terrify people whose courage,
indeed, it was not very difficult to shake. They retreated.
Danican and his supporters abandoned their position at Saint-
Roch, and betook themselves to the Lepelletier Section, there
to deliberate as to the expediency of a second attempt.

This, made from the left bank of the river, was equally
unsuccessful. The column, which endeavoured to attack the
Palais-Royal by way of the Quai Voltaire, was repulsed by
Verdière, who turned his heavy guns upon it, and before his
third volley it fled along the Rue de Beaune. Then Barras
charged and cleared the Rue de Richelieu. And by ten o'clock
in the evening it was all over.

All that now remained to be done was to subdue the Sections :
at nine o'clock on the 14th, the defenders of the Lepelletier
Section, threatened by General Berruyer, departed to their
homes, and Barras took possession unopposed. By noon on
the 14th the troops had occupied Paris. The insurrection had
been put down.

* * * * *

The Convention was moderate in its triumph. Knowing
how frail was the foundation of its rights, it was more afraid
Last Hours of of its allies of the preceding day, the famous
the Convention. " patriots," than of the royalists it had just
crushed. It was resolved that the repression of the Sections

should not be made the starting-point for a Terrorist reaction. Three courts-martial, summoned on the 15th, punished a few of the ringleaders : a great many were allowed to leave Paris, and among them Castellane, who replied to the " *Qui vive !* " of the sentinel who challenged with him a smiling " *Castellane, contumax !* ". There were only two executions, those of the president of the Théâtre-Français Section, and one of the leaders of the army of the Sections, Lafond, a returned *émigré*. The " patriots of '89 " were quietly dismissed.

One man only rose suddenly to the surface. On the 17th Barras presented the officers who had come to his assistance on the 14th to the Assembly, and called on it to receive their names with the applause they merited : Fréron, then high in the good graces of the lovely Paulette Bonaparte, was anxious to put forward the man he regarded as his future brother-in-law. He vaunted the part Bonaparte had played, declaring he had " crushed the hydra of royalism." Barras, who saw in this modest-mannered little general a future henchman of his own, made no attempt to contradict these praises. He appointed the Corsican, or had him appointed, second in command of the Army of the Interior, the chief command of which he had kept for himself : but this he resigned a few days later in favour of his young *protégé*, who had taken important military measures, and was protecting the dying Convention.

" Bonaparte—who the devil is he ? " people were saying.

The cannon of the Italian campaign was to answer them before long.

* * * * *

Tallien and his friends would fain have taken advantage of the " victory " to annul the reactionary elections, and perpetuate the whole Chamber without further form or ceremony. But this the Assembly, thinking the extreme reactionary party sufficiently paralyzed by the suppression of the royalists, refused to do. For the moment, the members who had seemed rather too favourably inclined towards the Sections, Lanjuinais, Boissy, and some others, had apparently lost all power. The regicide oligarchy, supported by the troops, would now be able to force itself on the new Councils : five of its members were to form the Directory. This seemed enough.

The fact was that the Assembly was thoroughly exhausted. " Four years spent under the assassin's blade have worn out our faculties, physical and mental," writes Dubreuilh of the Mountain. " It is high time we cleared out," added the indefatigable Merlin (of Thionville), who was weary too. If such a man as he was failing, what must the condition of the weaker men have been ! Morris, noting their exhaustion, wrote on August 23 : " *I still feel persuaded they will fall under the yoke of a single despot.*" It is a curious fact that the last act of this Convention, which had sent Louis XVI, Danton, and Robespierre to the scaffold, was to set the foot of Napoleon Bonaparte, destined to be that "single despot," in the stirrup.

That was its dying act. It was execrated by everybody. So great was the misery in the Faubourgs that on the 2nd Brumaire, two days before the final dissolution, Roux proposed the re-establishment of the *Maximum*. On the 3rd, at the last sitting but one, there was a final debate upon this question, and so many home-truths were bandied that Vallée exclaimed : " Are we setting up a counter-revolution here ? " The Assembly would have none of that : it proclaimed a general amnesty at its closing sitting on the 4th Brumaire, but only to exclude the accomplices of the Vendémiaire rising, the refractory priests, and the *émigrés*. Nevertheless it decreed that the Place de la Révolution, so lately drenched with blood, should henceforth be called the *Place de la Concorde !* The scaffold had disappeared, indeed; that plaster statue of Liberty which Manon Roland had once addressed in tragic accents stood alone in the centre, but the newspapers, without drawing any particular conclusion from the fact, were pointing out that Liberty was cracking visibly, and crumbling away.

❖　　✱　　✱　　✱　　✱

An obscure deputy of the name of Genissieu presided over this last sitting. The decree just mentioned was the last item The final in the order of the day, and he rose to dismiss the Session. Chamber.

A certain solemnity was imparted to the moment by the thought of the tremendous career of the expiring Assembly.
482

THE THIRTEENTH VENDEMIAIRE

In the space of three years it had lived a hundred, amidst unheard of perils: it had proclaimed the Republic in the France of Louis XIV, and it had organized, in the name of Liberty the most formidable tyranny any country had ever known; it had sent a king to the scaffold, and raised armies that had driven back the Powers of Europe; by its decrees it had shielded the Terror which had ploughed bloody furrows even through its own ranks; it had put down civil war, and in spite of tragic vicissitudes, it had carried France towards her natural frontiers; it had voted two Constitutions, driven God out of the Temple, and then recalled the Deity, the God of *Sans-culottes,* under a new name; it had separated Church from State, it had proposed every kind of problem, and till its very last moment it had crushed out "factions." It would be unjust not to remind our readers that by the law of the 3rd Brumaire—its political last will and testament—it finally set before its successors the great problem of Public Instruction, remembering the words of the most remarkable of its members and the most illustrious of its victims, that "next to bread, the most urgent need of the people is education." So convinced was the Assembly of the truth of these words, that in spite of the innumerable dangers that hemmed it in, it founded (on the 7th Ventôse of the Year III) the *lycées* of the future, the *Écoles Centrales*; on the 7th Vendémiaire of the same year the *École Polytechnique*; and on October 30, 1793, the *École Normale*; it reorganized the Natural History Museum and the Collège de France, it organized the Conservatoire des Arts et Métiers, and, finally, proceeded to that "great and majestic creation," as Daunou called it, the Institute of France. Thus it had destroyed and built up, it had terrorized and it had pacified, it had touched the nadir of crime in some men's eyes, and the zenith of virtue in those of others.

Yet so discredited was it at last, that it seemed as if the president did not dare to enumerate its services.

"I declare the session closed. Union, friendship, concord between all Frenchmen : these are the true means of *saving the Republic !* " Astonished, Thibaudeau called out : " But declare that the Convention has fulfilled its mission ! " Once more Genissieu rose to his feet : " *The National Convention declares its mission fulfilled and its session closed."* Shouts of "*Long live the Republic*" rose on every side.

This was on the 4th Brumaire of the Year IV, at half-past two o'clock. "What o'clock is it?" inquired a deputy who had a weakness for detail. A voice was heard: "The hour of justice!" The assertion was a little premature. I wonder whether that hour has struck even now!

SOURCES. Works already quoted by Aulard (*Jacobins, VI*), Schmidt (III), Barras (I and II), Duval (II), Lacretelle, Mallet du Pan (II), Frénilly, Malouet (II), Thibaudeau (I), La Revellière-Lepeaux (I, II), Dubreuilh, Morris, d'Andigné, Durand de Maillane, Carnot (*Mémoires*, II), B. Constant (*Correspondance*), Thiébault (I).—Aulard, *Actes du Comité, XVI–XVIII*, 1903–9; *Paris sous la Réaction*, I, II, 1898–9; *Lettre du Général Dubois sur les Journées de Prairial* (*Rev. Fr.*, 1904); Roederer, *Du Gouvernement*, 1795 (*Œuvres, XII*); *Les Journées de Prairial, Documents* (*Rev. Rev.*, V); Creuzé-Latouche, *Lettre* (*Nouv. Rev. Retr.* XVIII).

WORKS. Those already quoted by Thureau-Dangin, Claretie (*Derniers Montagnards*), Arnaud, Turquan, Caudrillier, Reynaud (*Merlin*; Dieudonné, *Les Préliminaires des Journées de Prairial* (Rev. Fr., 1902); Zivy, *Le 13 Vendémiaire* (*Bibliothèque de la Faculté des Lettres*, 1898); Masson, *Napoléon et sa Famille*, I, 1897; Champion, *La Séparation en 1794, 1903.*

PART IV
THE EXECUTIVE DIRECTORY

CHAPTER XXXIX

THE DIRECTORY AND THE COUNTRY

Inauguration of the Directory. The Councils. The "Five Majesties." Barras. Carnot. Reubell. La Revellière-Lépeaux. The parties face to face. The Babouvists, a "radical socialist" party. The Royalists. The "National" party. The policy of the Directory. The Military Peril. The Clerical Peril. The empty Treasury. France demoralized, hatred the only feeling left. "General indolence."

ON the 13th Brumaire of the Year IV (November 3, 1795) a strange procession took its way through the streets of Paris, from the Tuileries to the Luxembourg : two hackney carriages, a hundred infantry-men, and a hundred and fifty dragoons, so ill-found that most of them rode without boots : in the vehicles, four men, three of them quite unknown to the crowd, the one celebrity amongst them, Barras, attracting general attention by the great sword he held upright between his knees, the sword of Vendémiaire. The "Five Majesties," as they had already been derisively dubbed, were short of their number by one. Sieyès had refused to serve, and the new Government was embarrassed in consequence : for this little band was the new Government of France.

Inauguration of the Directory.

The Directors reached the Luxembourg, wnich the Constitution had assigned to them. The only person present to receive them was the porter. Since the Comte de Provence had departed, the palace, left to fall into ruin, had been mysteriously stripped of all its furniture. The great gilded saloons—very cold they were—had become absolute deserts. Hither and thither the four Directors wandered, and stopped, at last, in the first small room in which they found a table and a fireplace. The table—one of its feet, rotten with damp, had fallen off—

was as lopsided as the Government. The porter lent them four straw-bottomed chairs and brought in a few logs of wood. One of the quartette had brought a quire of letter paper with him from the Pavillon de Flore. And sitting round the shaky table, the Directory, incomplete as it was, proceeded to inscribe the report of its own installation on cheap notepaper.

Its members had been elected on the previous day by the two Councils which had assumed their duties on the 5th.

The newly elected representatives of the Nation—the third Third—were liberals of a somewhat timid type. General Mathieu

The Councils. Dumas; Tronson-Ducoudray, the advocate; Dupont of Nemours, the economist; the learned Royer-Collard; Barbé-Marbois, the ex-diplomat; Portalis and Siméon, both Provençal lawyers; and Pastoret, a former legislator, were thoroughly cured of the eager enthusiams of the year 1789; they were all prudent men, very much averse to adventurous undertakings. There was "nothing about them," so Thibaudeau says, "to alarm the Republic." Marbois styles them "the national party."

But this very fact exposed them to the suspicions, almost to the hatred, of most of the former members of the Convention. These, accustomed as they were to reign, regarded the newcomers, not compromised by any former action, as—here Marbois speaks again—"usurpers." True it is that if these new deputies desired a republic at all, they desired one from which sectarians, corrupt men, and criminals should be expelled. Tallien and his like had good reason to tremble.

The "regicide" faction had succeeded in procuring the election of five of its members to the Directory: Barras,

The "Five Majesties." Reubell, Sieyès, Letourneur, and La Revellière: thus the name of regicide was still the hallmark of the "good republican." A germ of conflict lay in these elections, which really were something akin to a *coup d'état* against the electors, who in seventy-three departments had acclaimed Daunou and a policy of moderate reaction.

Sieyès, noting the approach of this conflict, had retired: he had no liking (as somebody said) for bearing the brunt. His place was taken within a few days by Carnot, a regicide again, but considered by the newly elected Third to be a zealot who had *cooled down*. A perusal of the official report of his installation makes us feel that his colleagues already considered him an intruder.

* * * * *

Save in the case of its most recently elected member, the new government was not likely to raise the prestige of the Republic. These *Pentarchs* were neither very reputable nor very lovable. The best known among them was Barras ; and his celebrity was of an unfortunate kind. The Vicomte Paul de Barras, a rake in the days of the monarchy, who had borne a sword in the King's service, was related to all the noble houses of Provence, from the Castellanes to the Brancas. Elegant, luxurious, wildly extravagant, a refined debauchee who imported a certain amount of cruelty and a great deal of baseness into his excesses, he avows himself with a sly smile somewhere in his memoirs the cousin of the Marquis de Sade. A sensualist, the plaything of his own passions now and then, but well able, as a rule, to find his account in those he inspired, we shall see him throw his own mistresses with cynical impudence into the arms of men he desired to watch, allotting Josephine to Bonaparte, Therezia to Ouvrard. As devoid of moral feeling as man could be, he carried his inherent depravity into everything—politics, business, and love. He devoured money, and desired power for mercenary reasons. His contemporaries paint him in the vilest colours, but his own Memoirs are his strongest indictment. "A filibuster" he was called, even in 1795.

He had no political principles. "He would throw the Republic out of window to-morrow," wrote one of the foreign Ministers, "if it did not pay for his dogs, his horses, his mistresses, his table, and his cards ! " More than this : in place of principles he had one ruling terror—the fear of being hanged. So long as he did not hold a letter of pardon from the brother of Louis XVI—which he meant to solicit, and probably obtained —he was resolved to keep in close touch with his comrades in regicide. This discredited noble took a sort of pride in receiving anarchists and Terrorists at his *petit lever* (for he "played the prince," says Fouché); red heels and red caps met under his roof.

The irony of fate had associated Carnot, the austere, with this "*most dissolute of rakes.*" His sturdy figure is in curious contrast to Barras' supple elegance. And morally the difference was more extraordinary still. This conscientious family man and scientific officer, "*who belonged to the corps of engineers in politics as well as in war,*" as Albert Sorel acutely says, was serious, proud, moral, a trifle hard, exceedingly irascible, thoroughly consistent. He, too, loved power, but because he desired to direct and bring order out of chaos; he was, as Napoleon was to say of him, "easily deceived." Barras soon found this out, and spun his web about the man who threatened to give him trouble.

Carnot.

As "the organizer of victory" he had escaped from the reaction after Thermidor and the unpopularity into which his colleagues had fallen. Fourteen departments had elected him to the Assembly. His passage from the Convention to the Directory was his road to Damascus. A sincere republican, convinced, so we are assured, that the act of regicide was "irremissible," his upright character, to which anarchy of any sort was repugnant, made him as antipathetic to the belated champions of Terrorism as to the dissolute masters of the Luxembourg.

Reubell, on the other hand, was the least repentant of Jacobins. This Alsatian lawyer, whose self-confidence had never once failed him—a full-faced, high-coloured, broad-shouldered figure—was one of those merciless special pleaders who looked on the Revolution as a lawsuit to be won against, and in spite of everyone. From his place in the Committee of Public Safety he had been accustomed, for a year or more, to treat all Europe with a certain scorn, and thus his natural arrogance had increased. Two of his colleagues, La Revellière and Barras, were both offended and intimidated by it. He favoured violent measures, and was heard to exclaim, in Prairial of the Year IV, that "*the deputies who opposed the Revolution ought to be put in sacks and cast into the river!*" One of his disadvantages was that he had the reputation of being corrupt. "*Reubell,*" said Sieyès spitefully, "*is obliged to take something for his health every day of his life!*"

Reubell.

Letourneur, another engineer officer, and a man of very mediocre powers, simply followed Carnot—" whom he considered infallible "—and as Reubell and Barras were pretty well agreed as to the necessity of governing, temporarily at all events, with the help of the Jacobins, La Révellière was supposed to hold the casting vote. He was one of the old Girondins, and had barely escaped the Revolutionary Tribunal, saved only by the scorn of some deputy of the Mountain : " Why should time be wasted on such a paltry fellow as that ? " Yet, as the Terror had proscribed him, it had been fully expected that once he reached the Luxembourg he would declare himself the open enemy of the men who had done their best to hand him over to Samson. This argued little knowledge of politics : here precedents carry no weight.

La Revellière-Lépeaux.

The truth is that the strongest feature of his character was an irrepressible hatred of priests. His mind was really a religious mind, but there was something of the anti-pope about him. An upright man, as far as appearance went at any rate, this Puritan, sickened by the looseness of Barras' life, would have treated the " debauchee " as an enemy, if his mind had not been *alienated* in the true sense of the word by an obsession. Absorbed in his dream—the foundation of a *natural religion*—and the hatreds on which it fed, he became an easy prey. If Carnot had been living for months hypnotized by a blood-red spectre, and Reubell by a white one, the spectre that haunted La Révellière was black. Carnot and Barras both make mocking reference to this attitude. We may add that the man was particularly ill-favoured, hump-backed, with a dishevelled head far too large for his body, and legs too thin to carry it. He looked, says a contemporary " like a cork set on two pins." His judgment was as crooked as his back ; he became the tool of his colleagues, who used him for the purposes of their shady transaction in Fructidor of the Year V—whereby he believed himself to have struck at Pius VI rather than at Louis XVIII—and got rid of him in the most unceremonious manner in Prairial of the Year VI.

When these five men made their first appearance in their gala dress of satin, with capes *à la François Ier*, red hats

and feathers, laces and scarves and swords, silk stockings and
rosetted shoes, the mirth of the public was extreme. The
crimes of this Government were sometimes overlooked in amusement at its absurdity. "The Luxembourg Masquerade" it
was called from its earliest days.

* * * * *

The worst of it all was that to cope properly with the situation a really superior genius was needed. Our readers should
read the lamentable picture of France in Brumaire of the Year
IV, drawn by La Revellière himself : everything, he practically
tells us, lay in ruins, from roads, all cut up, to desolated hearths,
from deserted hospitals to cracked brains, from an empty Treasury
to corrupt hearts. Every foreigner who ventured into French
territory told the same tale. The most terrible verdict that
could have been pronounced on this Government is embodied in
the fact that in the course of the four years of its existence
it failed to restore one ruin and wrought many more.

The parties prepared forthwith to tear each other to pieces.
On the left the Terrorists had lifted up their heads again
The Parties   since the events of Vendémiaire. This faction,
face to face.   which hatred of the party of Thermidor had
driven for the past year into a close alliance with Babeuf
and his followers, had thus, as M. Aulard expresses it, formed
a sort of *radical-socialist party*, whose efforts were all directed,
of course, to the accession of the " socialists " to power. Though
the *Pantheon Club*, the meeting-place of the party, was liberally
supplied with money by Félix Lepelletier, a wealthy Jacobin,
Babeuf constantly preached the social revolution within its
walls. A regular plan of upheaval, which was to ensure " the
common happiness," was formulated, and its champions were
already numerous. " The party is swelling considerably," runs
a police note dated 2nd Nivôse, " the artisans, especially, are
joining it eagerly." Now for a considerable time, in spite of
Carnot's objurgations, Reubell and Barras refused to strike a
blow at these dangerous " *anarchists*."

This was because the two " Jacobin " Directors perceived,
so they declared, that the royalists were coming to the front
again. Yet no trace of any well-organized royalist party was

to be seen. The " heaters " and " brigands " infesting the West, the Centre, and the South of the country, certainly declared themselves adherents of the King, but this was only to give some cloak of respectability to their hideous exploits.

The Comte d'Artois had made a sudden appearance on the Ile d'Yeu, with a view to some fresh *quiberonnade,* but he had **Hoche in La** sailed away again to England, and finally given **Vendée.** up all attempts upon the West, where Hoche was engaged on the work of pacification. The General, who had been despatched to " cure this colic of the Republic, which nobody has known how to treat," had begun by cutting into the live flesh : Stoflet and Charette fell in February and March 1795 : and then, the war being ended, the General signed the " Edict of Nantes for La Vendée," allowed public worship to be resumed, and poured oil into the worst wounds. The great majority of the royalists, whether in Paris or in the provinces, put away their hopes for the time being : many forswore them altogether. Some, " whose numbers are great, sigh for peace," we read, " *and will accept it whatever may be the quarter whence it comes* " (these were the men who were to rally to Bonaparte); others went so far as to " grow accustomed to living under the Directory, and to have no hope save in new elections."

But all these remnants went to strengthen a party called the " reactive " party, though the title of " restorative " would have been juster : this, without contemplating any sacrifice of the essential benefits won in 1789, was bent on reconstructing the ruins scattered all over the country since that date ; on gradually destroying the " revolutionary code " ; on re-establishing the old form of worship ; on tempering, to some extent, the laws against the *émigrés ;* on restoring order in financial matters ; and eliminating the Jacobin element from the Government. This party had resolutely declared its constitutional and liberal principles. And it was a party that was hated and feared both by the " Left " in the Directory and by a large proportion of the regicide oligarchy, for they knew it was determined to drive them out.

* * * * *

Had the Directory any party of its own to support it against all these others, the Extreme Left, the Right, the Centre ? It never succeeded in forming a party; even in the field of politics it had no constructive ability. What was known as the " *party of the Directory* " was never more than a coterie—a syndicate in possession shall we say ? Constant was to formulate the doctrine : " *Repose should be every man's portion, but enjoyment and pleasure must belong exclusively to the Republic.*" We come back, at the end of it all, to this handful of regicide leaders at the head of their little army of compromised men. Listen to Treilhard when he tells Mathieu Dumas the conditions on which he will be granted his certificate as a "good republican " : " *Go to the rostrum and declare that if you had been a member of the Convention you would have voted for the death of Louis XVI !* " The words reveal the single idea of the party. It started on its way without a chief, without a programme, it lived, and broke up, and came together again, just as events and its own terrors drove it. It was quite unable to impart any great strength to the Government now looking to it for support, and itself exposed to the daily attacks of three score and ten newspapers, representing every shade of opinion.

Like this party, the Directory had no programme : it made no attempt to rally the citizens, whether of the Right or Left, to its own banner ; its only thought was to intimidate by rough usage. The Nation, in Barras' eyes, was " *divided into two armies.*" An abominable conception of government ! From it all the rest proceeded. The Government believed itself to be " besieged " : it made sorties, sometimes against one army, sometimes against the other, from its dismantled fortress. Never was any Government so persuaded of the fact that, being in a minority, it must " set the country in motion." When the elections came on commissaries were sent down " *to guide the electors* "; the secret service funds, concerning the disposal of which Barras makes such barefaced revelations, were used for this purpose. When one tribunal, as we shall see, treated "the enemy" in too indulgent a fashion, the accused person was sent on to another. Merlin (of Douai) who, first as Minister, and then as Director, was long a moving spirit in the

The Policy of the Directory.

494

Government, said some terrifying things : " *Jurisprudence is dictated by reasons of State,*" he artlessly asserted one day,.

If the country, in spite of pressure and corruption, in spite of arbitrary interference with the normal course of justice, refused to submit to the yoke, the elections were to be annulled : if the Legislative Body gave cause of offence it was to be forcibly decimated. And because, as Sieyès acknowledged, " *we shall all be destroyed if peace is made,*" the war was to be carried on. Such was the plan evolved within the walls of the Luxembourg for governing an already ruined country !

And, unhappily, the Legislative Body was unable either to put a stop to disorder or stand out against tyranny, because its members, as a body, had fallen into the most extreme discredit. The country, noting the incoherence or the uselessness of their labours, either made a jest of them, or groaned over them. These deputies, in spite of the famine that prevailed towards the close of the last Convention, had increased their own remuneration from eighteen to thirty-six *livres:* this, as Levasseur of the Sarthe had foretold, had brought their legislative functions into disrepute. Shortly afterward, when a fresh fall in the value of *assignats* occurred, they were to find means of protecting their own official incomes. Meanwhile preparations for " lodging the Five Hundred in the Palais-Bourbon, which is to be made very magnificent," were going on. The passers-by broke into murmurs as they gazed on the sculptured stones. " A starving man," says one police report, " exclaimed in a sorrowful voice : *Dic ut lapides istæ panes fiant !* "

This state of things, as we shall see, was to fill the public with a contempt that was big with consequences. Government and Parliament alike seemed incapable of building up the ruins and saving the country.

And on the other hand the popularity of the troops was daily increasing ; every military leader was beginning to have his plans, his party, and his own Constitution in his pocket—from Pichegru, who was selling his influence to Louis XVIII, to the loyal Hoche, who was pouring out his theories for the reorganization of the Republic in curious letters to General Chenin. The army swarmed with parturient

The military Peril.

495

Moncks and Cæsars. The rank and file seemed ready to follow in their train: their talk scandalized the police: " *The deputies ought to be in a wood, and the wood set on fire !*" they said— most alarmingly.

*   *   *   *   *

But the Directory did not realize the full measure of this danger. The clerical peril, on the other hand, inspired it with supreme terror.

" *Our Revolution has been a failure as regards religion,*" Clarke was to say to Bonaparte a few months later. " People
The clerical   have gone back to the Roman Catholic faith, and
Peril.   we are perhaps on the point of being obliged to appeal to the Pope himself to support the Revolution in the country, through the priests, and consequently through the rural districts, the government of which they have succeeded in getting back into their hands." Hoche, remembering what he had seen in La Vendée, was of the same mind.

There was an evident " *revival of Catholicism* ": a *revival* it hardly was, an explosion rather of the faith that had been too long suppressed. In the country districts the desire and demand for the return of the " good priests " had never ceased. The *Constitutional Church*, which after 1791 had represented a mere minority, only lived on while the State upheld it. Not even the lofty virtue and obstinate tenacity of a Grégoire could save it. The Convention destroyed that church when it separated it from the State on the 3rd Ventôse of the Year III. The Catholic revival was all in favour of the Roman Catholic Church. In his well-informed and authoritative work M. Aulard quotes innumerable characteristic instances of this spontaneous restoration. A sort of religious intoxication seized, not only the peasants, apparently so indifferent but a short while since, but the upper classes, once so deeply tinctured with infidelity. From the humblest hamlets, where the priest, armed with the *Decree of the 3rd Ventôse*, took possession of his altar once more, to the Lycée where La Harpe preached, " *persecution,*" as the Protestant Mallet writes, " *had resuscitated religion.*"

This " resurrection " disturbed the Directors extremely, and La Revellière most of all. He took it to be the triumph of the " Popery " he hated; his fellows regarded it as an advance on the road towards that restoration they dreaded. Thus at the Luxembourg it was resolved to suppress "*sacerdotal prejudices*" and destroy, as a police official of the Year IV described it, "*the infernal ascendancy of the priesthood.*"

The result was an intermittent persecution, sometimes violent, sometimes underhand, now and then absurd : a priest imprisoned here, a church-bell unhung there. "*The Directory really desired to destroy the Roman faith,*" writes M. Aulard. La Revellière aspired to replace it by another. He favoured, even to the extent of levies on the secret funds, that strange and idyllic religion known as *Theophilanthropy*, which was shortly to parade its puerilities in various churches. Then came the proclamation of the "*Culte décadaire*" (worship celebrated on *décadi*) more especially preached by François de Neufchâteau, ultimately one of the Directors, who, when necessity arose, would himself (though he was not the best of authorities on the subject, being a bad husband) celebrate civic and republican marriages within the churches.

These "*civic buffooneries*" as Grégoire calls them, might cause the Catholics discomfort, but they made no converts.

* * * * *

But anxieties of another sort were in store for the Directory. The coffers of the State were empty : the Nation had ceased to pay the taxes. So there must be a fresh issue of *assignats* : 36 billion, 603 million *livres* in the Year IV. The result was a state of discredit that soon became fabulous. On the day the Directors assumed their functions the gold louis (24 *livres*) was worth 8400 *livres* in paper money : on the 15th Brumaire it was worth 4000 *livres*. Six months later Charles de Constant found it was worth 12,000 livres. The peasants, when they refused this paper money, would say, "*We would take it if the horses would eat it.*" Benjamin Constant writes : "*The assignats are going completely to the devil.*" The Government cast the blame on the Bourse, and sent dragoons to close it, "Did anybody ever see credit upheld by cavalry before ? " asked a foreigner. For four years we shall watch this Government struggling in the most hopeless financial difficulties.

The Treasury empty.

The public had to suffer for it. Nobody had any money. In a year the general misery, which had seemed to reach the highest possible point in the Year III, had grown still worse. The fabulous prices paid for food, which amuse us now, when we turn over the leaves of the old account-books (bread at 60 *livres* a pound and haricot beans at 1400 *livres* a pint), did not amuse our forefathers at all. We could quote fifty distracted letters to prove our assertion. " In the streets," one report tells us, " numbers of poor wretches are to be seen, shoeless and unclothed, picking up earth and other *filth* out of the rubbish heaps to satisfy their hunger ! "

And in the face of all this suffering society felt no pity ! " Events," says the *Gazette* of the 25th Brumaire of the Year IV, " *have dried up men's hearts.*" " Legislative Body ! Directory ! " cries the same newspaper. " On you are turned the eyes of the unhappy wretch whose half-naked feet tread the wet ground ! Alleviate our sufferings, first of all, but give us morals too ! "

We shall see the quality of the " morals " the Directory was to give to the society of which the Luxembourg was to be the centre.*

France was demoralized, and she was broken-spirited too. This feature was the last to be developed by the unhappy country. *No public opinion existed in it,* or rather the only opinion that did exist was compact of hatreds : hatred of the Directors, hatred of the deputies, hatred of the Terrorists, hatred of the Chouans, hatred of the rich, and hatred of the anarchists, hatred of the Revolution, and hatred of the Counter-Revolution.

Directors and deputies alike—we could quote a hundred instances to prove it—were decried, despised, derided, and detested.

But hatred reached its most violent paroxysm in connection with the owners of the *new fortunes.* " *What is the use of having destroyed kings, nobles, and aristocrats, since their place has now been taken by deputies, farmers, and shopkeepers !* " Yells of hatred, indeed ! But they were empty yells. The moment Babeuf suggested a social revolution, or the " king's " agents

---

* Cf. " The Society under the Directory," chap. xliv.

enlarged on the benefits of a Restoration, the noisy shouters shrank out of sight.

For, above and beyond all things, the country was weary. Nothing roused it now, not even victories. Numbers of men **General** were deserting from the army. " Why should **Indolence.** we go and get ourselves killed for the rascals who are robbing us and leaving us to die of hunger ? " they said. Everybody sighed for peace. Bonaparte won more popularity by concluding the Peace of Campo Formio than by making its conclusion possible at Rivoli. The Nation, in fact, had turned its back on everything, on glory and on liberty alike.

"*A general indolence, a general indifference,*" these are expressed in every letter, every police report, every newspaper. There was no strength left to resist the tyranny of the Directory, or break it : so the country waited for its liberator. " Let a man of genius come to the front," wrote a foreign diplomatist, " and all will bow before him."

Amidst all the ruin the Directory had found and increased —ruins of parties, of power, of the representation of the Nation, of churches, finance, homes, consciences, and reason—none was so pitiful as this last, the ruin of the national character.

SOURCES. Works already quoted by Barras (I, II) , La Revellière-Lépeaux (II), Thibaudeau (II), Mallet du Pan (II), Mathieu Dumas (III), Lacretelle, Carnot (II), Mallet junior (in *Malouet, II*), Frénilly, Levasseur of La Sarthe (IV), Morellet Vaublanc.—Debidour, *Procès-verbaux du Directoire*, I, 1911 ; Aulard, *Paris sous le Directoire*, II, 1899 ; Bailleul, *Preussen und Frankreich* (Correspondence of Sandoz Rollin, Gervinus, and Peter Roin), I, 1881 ; *Lettres* of Brinkmann (in the *Correspondance du Baron de Staël* already quoted ; *Letter* from Madame de Staël to Roederer (in Roderer, *Œuvres*, VIII) ; Madame de Staël, *Considérations*, 1818 ; Bailleul, *Examen des Considérations de Madame de Staël*, 1818 ; Carnot, *Réponse à Bailleul*, 1797 ; Réal, *Essai dans les Journées de Vendémiaire*, 1795 ; Charles de Constant, *Lettres* (*Nouv. Rev. Retr.*, I and II) ; Barbé Marbois, *Journal*, 1884 ; Fouché, *Mémoires*, I, 1824 ; Hoche, *Correspondance* (Rousselin ed., 1877).

WORKS. Those already quoted by Thureau-Dangin, Daudet (*Emigration*, I–III), Sorel (IV–V), Meynier, Deville, Sciout (*Constitution Civile*), Stourm (II), Levasseur, Turquan.—Sciout, *Histoire du Directoire*, I, II, 1895 ; Goncourt, *La Société sous le Directoire* (ed. of 1909) ; Espinas, *Babeuf*, 1899 ; Robiquet, *Buonarotti*, 1910 ; Ch. Bonnet, *Le Babouvisme*, 1907 ; Mathiez, *Les Théophilanthropes*, 1904.

CHAPTER XL

BARRAS, BABEUF, AND BONAPARTE

September 1795—May 1796

Financial penury. The forced loan of the Year IV. The territorial drafts. The Panthéon Club. Bonaparte sent to close it.
Babeuf arrested. The "constitutional frontiers." Bonaparte
and the Directory. His marriage. Bonaparte sent to Italy.

THE Directory appointed its Ministers—the most remarkable among them was Merlin of Douai, sent,
by some strange paradox, to the Ministry of Justice
—and straightway found great difficulty in supplying them
with funds. The Constitution, as our readers will recol-
Forced Loan of lect, had taken the key of the Treasury out
the Year IV. of its hands. The Directors made known their
necessitous condition at the Tuileries, and the Councils,
after certain formalities had been observed, granted a sum
of 20,000,000 *livres*, not to the Directors—a proof of considerable lack of confidence—but directly to the various Ministers.

This dip into the Treasury revealed the fact that it was
empty. And 600,000,000 *livres* had to be found ! But where ?
The country was exhausted. An appeal was made to the owners
of large fortunes in the shape of a *forced loan—of a frankly progressive nature*. One-fifth of the tax-paying community was to
be affected. To palliate this financial operation some concessions were made, apparently to democratic doctrine, but in
reality to the outcry of the demagogues. In his defence of
this impost Vernier dropped an assertion that it was "*directed
against the rich*." The words were spoken six years after the
men of 1789 had proclaimed the equality of all citizens in
the matter of taxation to be the primordial law of the new
system. But when Dupont of Nemours recalled this prin-
500

ciple, Vernier branded him as a "bad republican." One of the Ministers, Faypoult, who was always to have a great leaning towards extortion, lauded this " act of justice." The populace was delighted to see " the millionaires of recent date " bled. But Constant deplored the " *creation of a privileged caste in this country.*" We should have been glad to quote his letter in full ; it is interesting, and proves his foresight to have been remarkable.

Aware of their own unpopularity, the Councils did not venture to reject the proposal. The law was passed by the Five Hundred on the 17th Frimaire, and on the 19th by the Ancients. Nobody remembered Buzot's saying : " *The misfortune is, that when we kill the rich we kill the poor as well ! *"

Within a few weeks the terrible eloquence of facts had demonstrated the truth of his words. " We will pay the loan," the tradesmen had said, " but we shall sell everything accordingly." Merchandise accumulated and workshops were closed. Very soon the population of the Faubourg Saint-Antoine, finding wealthy men had ceased to order furniture, were wishing the so-called " democratic " tax to the devil. The rural proprietors, hitherto devoted adherents of the Revolution, lost their tempers. " *This exaction,*" wrote one, " *brings more hatred on the Directory than was ever felt for Robespierre's government.*"

And in addition to all this the tax failed to bring in the hoped-for sum. The Government had reckoned on 600,000,000 *livres.* On the 1st Germinal the Treasury had received 12,000,000 in specie and valuables : the 293,000,000 millions of paper money also paid in were of no very great value. At the end of the whole business 20,000,000 *livres* were collected, and almost universal ruin had been the result. This was the Directory's first false step.

But pecuniary resources had to be discovered somehow. In the course of the operation just concluded the value of the assignat had fallen to zero. So the Government created a *territorial draft,* " a new security, representing a fixed and special value, which would place a guarantee, a mortgage *which could never suffer any loss of credit,* in the hands of the creditors of the Republic." But the *assignat,*

The territorial Draft.

501

after all, had been guaranteed on the same basis. These drafts were nothing but *privileged assignats*, and their very issue— a recognition of the fact that the *assignat* was affected by a sort of bankruptcy—shook the credit so indispensable to the draft. What guarantee was there that the draft would not end by sharing the fate of the *assignat?* The public received it in a most distrustful spirit. Within a few days of the issue it had lost 74 per cent. of its original official value, and before very long several more million *livres* of paper money were thrown into circulation, a fresh cause of discontent.

This twofold financial adventure augured ill for the future.

* * * * *

At the sight of all the difficulties in which the Directory was floundering the opposition, somewhat timorous at first, grew bolder.

Secretly encouraged by Carnot, it entered the lists. On the 19th Nivôse, Pons (of Verdun) presented a report to the Five Hundred, suggesting a return to the old methods of vigour and rigour in the application of the law touching the *émigrés*; whereupon Dumolard (this was considered most audacious) made some sharp comments on a measure in which" all ideas of justice had been upset and overthrown." His interference was declared scandalous. Tallien and Chénier called it an insult to " *republican morality.*" But Boissy d'Anglas supported Dumolard, and the measure proposed by Pons was only passed by a very small majority, while the Ancients threw it out altogether, by 101 votes to 86. This, however, was the sum total of the Right's successes. It made an attempt to secure the proclamation of religious liberty, but met with defeat here. A small majority ensured the passage of the law of the 22nd Germinal, which was frankly aimed at the Catholics, and forbade all ringing of church bells. The bells, which had begun to make themselves heard again, timidly enough, were silenced, and the liberal party deferred further action in the matter till the lapse of a few months should permit it to lay this singular case before the electors.

Meanwhile another case was to be decided: the voting

at the last few sittings of the Councils having somewhat allayed the fears of the Government as to the influence likely **The Panthéon** to be wielded by the " counter-revolutionary **Club suppressed.** party," following that see-saw policy to which it was always to adhere, it resolved on striking a blow at " the anarchists."

The *Panthéon Club*, which had been the offspring of the coalition between the Terrorists and the adherents of Babeuf, constantly rang with appeals for a social revolution, which was to ensure " the common happiness," and lachrymose expressions of regret, roused by the august memory of Robespierre. On both these heads the men of Thermidor, now occupying the Luxembourg, felt that the Club was showing a great want of tact.

Carnot, whose desire to see the anarchists suppressed grew stronger every day, drew attention to these excesses, and, what was far more serious, pointed out that the Babouvist element was getting a hold on the Legion of Police.

On the 13th Nivôse of the Year IV (January 3, 1796), the Directory, not daring to strike an open blow at the Left, had created—for the purpose of dealing with the Chouans, it had said—a *Ministry of General Police*, and advised by Carnot, had appointed Cochon, a most repentant member of the Convention, to direct it. He had forthwith stiffened every muscle of the new Ministry into resistance to the anarchists. His reports ended by producing an impression at the Luxembourg. On the 8th Ventôse, Bonaparte, who was still in command of the army in Paris, proceeded, by order of the Directors, to close the Panthéon Club. It must be added that on the same day—out of respect for the see-saw system—the Théâtre Feydeau, where a piece that glorified the Chouans had been given, was likewise closed, and also the Church of Saint-André-des-Arts, where vespers had been sung, a most scandalous proceeding.

Babeuf, to whom Barras had dispatched encouraging messages under the rose, did not appear to feel the matter very keenly : every day his agents were obtaining a greater hold on the police legion, the soldiers of which would reassure the workmen of the Babeuf party, saying : " Fear nothing, the soldiers will not be against you ! "

Strong in the assurance of such protection, the propaganda spread in all directions : the *Tribun du Peuple* and the *Égalitaire* carried on a lively campaign against both Directors and deputies, those " Tartufes " of whom France ought to be rid by a " good massacre in the September style." The *Analyse de la doctrine de Babeuf*, and still more the *Manifeste des Égaux*, set forth a complete plan of social revolution, and promised the land, " which belongs to nobody," to all and sundry. The *Analyse*, which was posted up, was " applauded," so one police agent reported, " by the majority of its readers, and notably by the working men."

Meanwhile the purely Jacobin wing of the party, which was much less anxious to ensure *" the common happiness "* **Arrest of** than to secure its own return to power, was **Babeuf.** preparing a movement on its own account. It wanted armed men : the leaders applied to Adjutant-General Grisel, who had the reputation of a " pure " republican : he denounced their proceedings to Carnot, who obtained a decision (in the absence of Barras, whom his colleagues regarded with suspicion) for the arrest of the whole body, Babouvists and Terrorists. On the 21st Floréal they were all under lock and key, and a proclamation informed the population that it had been saved.

The Directory seemed to be inclining to the Right. Was it going to make an end of the new " hive of Jacobins ? "

Bonaparte was not there to do the work. When the Directory crushed the " Terrorist plot " it did so with all the greater confidence because its favourite general was covering it with glory. On the 21st Floréal, Bonaparte, after a series of unprecedented victories, was preparing to make his entry into Milan, and his name, but yesterday unknown, was passing from mouth to mouth, borne first, over all France and then across Europe on the wings of Fame.

* * * * *

There had been sore need of his intervention to retrieve the military position of the Republic, which, prosperous as it had been in the spring and summer of 1795, had become extremely uncertain during the winter of that year.

BARRAS, BABEUF, BONAPARTE

On the 16th Germinal of the Year III, Prussia had signed at Basle a peace which recognized the left bank of the Rhine as French territory. The Empire had manifested an inclination to separate its own quarrel from that of its Austrian chief, and also come to some separate arrangement at Basle. On the 21st Floréal the "Batavian Republic" had passed under the Caudine Forks, relinquished the left bank of the Dutch Rhine, surrendered the town of Flushing, and formally acknowledged the suzerainty of France. And in the course of the summer (4th Thermidor) the Spaniards had retired from the lists, leaving their colony of San Domingo in the victor's hands.

Military Operations.

Europe meted out severe treatment indeed—as far as words went—to the secessionist princes : " A king without ruth or truth," Catherine II called the Prussian monarch. She immediately pressed Austria to constitute herself the champion of monarchy on the Rhine, and this Power marched fresh troops upon the river. But the hostility of England appeared as inveterate as ever. The French Government (the Committee was still in power), hoped to bring her to reason by closing all the European, and more particularly the Mediterranean ports to her shipping : to this end, having absorbed Holland, and received the Swedish envoy, Baron de Staël, with great civility, it sought to ally itself with Spain, and make sure of Italy.

Success was reckoned on to raise the courage of the troops. Jourdan, who had crossed the Rhine at Düsseldorf on September 7 (20th Fructidor of the Year III), had driven Clerfayt's Austrians back to the Main : and Pichegru, who had also crossed the river (which his men, in splendid braggadocio called " the big brook ") at Huninguen, was marching onward unopposed.

On the 9th Vendémiaire of the Year IV the Convention, before it finally broke up, had solemnly voted the absolute annexation of Belgium, and formally proclaimed the principle of the natural frontiers, to which it gave the title of " *constitutional frontiers.*" This proclamation was tantamount to a declaration of perpetual war, for it was evidently destined to result in at least twenty years of struggle.

For various reasons, as we know, the Directory—the lineal descendant of the Convention—saw no objection to this pro-

Projects against Austria and England. longation of the war. It was dazzled by dreams of greatness. As Austria was held to be the chief foe, the idea—it had been a tradition for two centuries past in the minds of the rulers of France —of striking a blow at the Hapsburgs in Italy, came to the front once more. In the Year IV this idea was put into action. A military expedition which would force peace on the Piedmontese, make Genoa the vassal of France, and ensure the neutrality of the two Sicilies, might also snatch the valley of the Po from the hands of Austria, and close the whole Italian Peninsula to English ships. La Revellière further believed that it would force the Pope of Rome to surrender at discretion. Finally, the possession of the Pactolus to be found in the rich plains of Northern Italy, would do away with any necessity for a recurrence to the ill-starred attempt at a forced loan : all the letters of the time reveal the practical considerations that underlay this plan.

There were other projects, too : to injure perfidious Albion along all the coasts from Genoa to Naples would be good ; but better still would it be to attack her in Ireland—and the preparations for this attempt had been confided to General Hoche.

* * * * *

But who was to be chosen to lead the expedition into Italy ? Schérer, a very second-rate soldier, then at the head of the Army of Italy, had halted at the Alps : but the necessity for a strong attack on the Austrian flank was becoming urgent ; without it any attack on its front was doomed to certain failure.

Pichegru, why nobody could understand at the time, had been seized apparently with some sort of paralysis immediately

Pichegru's Defection. after his capture of Mannheim. Jourdan was endeavouring to effect a junction with him, after which they might have carried out a combined movement on the Danube, and threatened Vienna. But Pichegru, after a most damaging pause in his own operations, wantonly left two divisions of his army to be crushed by Clerfayt at Heidelberg, and allowed Clerfayt's troops to effect a junction with Wurmser's.

Charges of incapacity were brought against the general; he ought to have been accused of treason. Won over by royalist promises, the conqueror of Holland had followed the example of Dumouriez. This melancholy story has been fully told by M. Caudrillier, after M. Ernest Daudet and M. Albert Sorel, and M. Albert Vandal, in the course of an admirably written article, has briefly stigmatized the general's dereliction from the path of duty.

Courting defeat, he had retired, had allowed himself to be forced back on Wissembourg, and on the 10th Nivôse of the Year IV (December 31, 1796), had signed an armistice, which to the Directory appeared utterly inexplicable. Jourdan, whose position had been exposed by Pichegru's retreat, was obliged to follow in his footsteps, and himself make a retrograde movement across the " big brook."

Pichegru was simply replaced by another general (the authorities still believed him to be suffering from some temporary aberration). Moreau was promoted to the command of the Army of the Rhine. This was to be the pivot of a gigantic military operation, now deferred till the spring of 1796, which was to bring the army to the banks of the Danube, there to be joined by the troops known as the Army of the Sambre and Meuse, of which Jourdan still held the command: the two were to march upon Vienna, while the army of Italy threatened the city from the other side, by the valleys of the Po and the Adige. " A gigantic plan," in the words of Carnot, who, for the second time, was " organizing victory."

With Schérer at the head of the Army of Italy there could be no reliance on the success of this undertaking; Hoche, **Bonaparte to** Jourdan, and Moreau were already holding im- **command the** portant commands. The Directors were anxious **Army of Italy.** to send a daring and vigorous general to command the troops beyond the Alps. Their minds were set on a raid that would furnish millions, and they wanted a man who, while personally honest, would have no scruples as to the means employed to fill the empty coffers of the State. He must hold his own against princes and priests, therefore he must be chosen out of the ranks of the " good Jacobins." And, finally, lest he should emancipate himself once the victories had been won, he must be selected from the ranks of the Government's own creatures. Carnot wanted a fiery war-chief; Reubell a bold man of action; La Revellière an enemy of all "shaveling priests "; Barras, a man of compliant character. Each one of them suggested Bonaparte: and each one of them, within a year, vowed that he it was who had discovered him.

All of them, indeed, were acquainted with the soldier who had stood by them in Paris : but not one knew him. His intimacy with the Vicomtesse de Beauharnais had brought him into still closer connection with Barras. His passionate love for the seductive Creole amused those who knew all about the escapades of this lady, a good-natured creature, of easy virtue, thoughtless, non-moral, and exceedingly fascinating. In the elegant and frivolous society of which Joséphine was the centre this little man, with his tanned face shaded by tangled hair, careless in dress, abrupt in manner, clean in life and pure of heart, was a strange anomaly. Barras, whose intelligence sometimes played him false, did not take him quite seriously, regarding him as a convinced Spartan, and, consequently, a simpleton. It has been asserted that the young Corsican, to make sure of the command of the Army of Italy, married the cast-off mistress Barras disinterestedly handed over to him. This is a calumny. Bonaparte married a woman with whom he was madly in love, and who, to a certain extent, had dazzled his imagination. Save in the dubious remarks of the ex-Director himself, we find no trace of this well-nigh infamous bargain. Further, it would seem that it was Carnot who proposed the man to his colleagues, and La Revellière tells us that their acceptance of him was unanimous. He was appointed on the 8th Ventôse. The very next day, Dupont of Nemours wrote to Reubell: "*I can hardly believe you have made such a mistake. . . . Do you not know he is one of those Corsicans? . . . All of them have their fortunes to make.*"

Certainly this particular Corsican was by no means the man Barras took him to be. We shall speak, at a later stage, of the labour and the studies by which he had prepared himself for the career now opening before him, and of the fashion in which the powers of the wonderful actor now entering on the scene had been nourished and fortified.* But our readers already know something of the genius hidden behind that forehead veiled by tangled locks, of the fire that raged within that slight frame, and of the strange mistake made by Barras, who thought himself so crafty !

Bonaparte's marriage took place on the 17th Ventôse. He spent two days of delirious happiness, though even in his

Bonaparte's Marriage. mistress' arms he never forgot himself, mingling the raptures of his love with his dreams of greatness and glory. On the 22nd he departed, Barras looking at him almost sneeringly as he went, so pallid beneath his tangled hair, so worn, that those who saw him thought he had one foot in the grave, " shabby " they said, almost contemptible, silent, with closed lips and dull eyes.

The Directory, completely deceived, expected victory indeed, but of a moderate and unimportant kind.

For sources and bibliography see the end of Chapter XLI.

---

* In the volume dealing with " The Consulate and the Empire," which will follow the present work.

CHAPTER XLI

BONAPARTE APPEARS UPON THE SCENE

May 1796—March 1797

The triumphant campaign in Piedmont. Lombardy conquered.
The Directory expects Bonaparte to send money. Paris thunderstruck. The country against the Directory. The Grenelle
affair strengthens the reaction. The royalist conspiracy. The
great Italian victories. The German campaign of 1796. The
evening of the Battle of Rivoli. Bonaparte desires peace. The
Directory terrified. Tolentino. Leoben.

"SOLDIERS ! In the space of a fortnight, you have
won six victories, taken twenty-one standards, fifty-five
pieces of ordnance, several fortified towns, and conquered
the richest part of Piedmont : you have made 15,000 prisoners,
and killed or wounded 10,000 men. . . . But, soldiers, you have
Campaign in done nothing, for you still have work to do ! . . ."
Piedmont. Thus Bonaparte, on the 6th Floréal (April 26),
scattered laurels on his troops.

He had come, and seen, and conquered. Our readers will
not expect us to retrace the features of that memorable campaign : that little general, that " slight mathematician "
imposing his will with a gesture on his rough lieutenants,
and, as Masséna acknowledges, " almost frightening " them ;
his call to the 36,000 men he was to cast, without a tremor,
upon full 70,000 Austrians and Piedmontese, pointing to Italy
as to a rich and certain prey : the swift passage of the Apennines,
then Augereau thrown upon the Austrians at *Montenotte* on
April 12, Masséna and Laharpe again at *Dego* on the 15th,
Augereau, meanwhile, at *Millesimo* on the 14th, all communication between the enemy's two camps cut off and
their centre driven in. Then the Austrian retreat, the
Piedmontese surrounded at *Ceva* and beaten at *Mondovi* on

510

the 28rd, and the road to Turin thus opened to the victors; the King forced, within ten days of the hero's first dazzling appearance, to sign at *Cherasco* an armistice that surrendered his fortresses, made over his country to the victor, opened the gates of Lombardy, and when it was transformed into a peace, left France in definitive possession of two provinces. Such was the meaning of that famous proclamation of April 26, the eloquence of which magnificently cloaks realities more magnificent still.

Bonaparte had begun to soar. Nothing was to arrest that great flight. " You have done nothing, for you still have work to do ! " To himself, before all others, the stirring summons was addressed.

The Po must be crossed : by a successful ruse he drew the enemy to Valenza, crossed the river at Piacenza meanwhile, and drove Marshal Beaulieu behind the Adda, spanned by the *Bridge of Lodi.* And here was fought a battle the memory of which will live for ever in the annals of the Army and the Nation. The cold-blooded tactician proved himself a fearless soldier. On the Bridge of Lodi, under a hail of grapeshot, we see him leading on his wavering men and falling upon the enemy, breaking their ranks first, and then driving them, in hideous rout, back to Mincio. This was on May 7 (27th Floréal), 1796.

In four days Lombardy was conquered : Pavia and Cremona opened their gates, and on May 15 the victors made their entry Lombardy   into Milan, the delirious triumph of which readers conquered.   of Albert Sorel's unforgettable description may for a moment share. And then we hear the hero's words, prouder far than those of April 26, addressed not to his own soldiers this time, but to the nations : " People of Italy ! the army of France has broken your chains : the People of France is the friend of all other Peoples : come to greet it ! . . ." Dazzling visions of the future, Cæsar already an Augustus, a liberator, a restorer—all this do we see in the proclamation of May 15.

Europe beheld the sudden rise of a star that was to change the face of the whole world, and stood astounded.

*   *   *   *   *

Nobody was more astounded than the Directors. They had fancied they were flying a hawk that would bring them game : they discovered they had let loose an eagle that soared far above their heads. But so great was the glory shed on the Government by these events that its members were torn between alarm and joy. And, further, all the General's letters announced that he was sending millions home.

Now the Directory, reduced to absolute penury, wanted money, and more money, as much as it could get. While The Coffers of Bonaparte at Milan was proclaiming civil liberty, the Directory and religious tolerance, and orderly freedom to filled. the Italian populations, the Directors were writing from the Luxembourg : " Would it not be possible to seize the Casa Santa (of Loretto) and the immense treasures heaped up there by fifteen centuries of superstition ? they are valued at 10,000,000 *livres* sterling. *This would be a financial operation of the most admirable nature, and would harm nobody except a few monks.*" As a matter of fact money came pouring in : Bonaparte's letters read like those of some *conquistador* let loose in the empire of Montezuma. Delighted, the Directors wrote to him : " *You are the hero of the whole of France !* "

The hero of France he was, not because of the money, but because of the glory he had won. All over the country his April campaign had excited unspeakable admiration. The episode at Lodi, which soon became known, transported the populace with delight. The astonished police officials saw the weary nation suddenly lift its head. Bonaparte had stirred the pride of the nation which hoped further for peace, after victory, from his hand. Every party sought to draw him to it. Joséphine was assailed with homage from all quarters : she was hailed as *Notre Dame des Victoires*. A passionate, an almost tender curiosity surrounded this soldier, now exalted to the rank of demiurge—almost of demigod. Paris, especially, turned to him, as Paris will turn to any man who dares to fly on brilliant and impetuous wings, and the love the great city so suddenly bestowed was never to fail him till the end.

*   *   *   *   *

Before long the Directory was forced to follow the stream of public opinion. There was no means of stopping the man, so it heaped adulation upon him. " You possess the confidence of the Directory ; the services you render it day after day Discredit of entitle you to this ; *the considerable sums* the the Directory. Republic owes to your victories prove that your attention is devoted at once to the glory and the interests of your country." Some dozen letters in the same vein have come down to us. When the *Festival of Victory* took place, in Prairial of the Year IV, the Directors had the audacity to deck themselves with the eagle's plumes.

This was necessary : it was expedient to dazzle a country which was becoming exasperated. The elections threatened to be very disastrous to the Luxembourg.

The Babeuf plot had provoked a recrudescence of reactionary feeling. Thus the excitement, when it became known that the friends of this Gracchus had made an attempt, in the course of the night of the 23rd Fructidor, to stir up a rising against the government at the camp of Grenelle, may be easily imagined. At eleven o'clock that evening, finding the Luxembourg too well guarded to permit of their attacking it, a band of six or seven hundred men proceeded to Grenelle, where Malo, the commandant, greeted them with a volley of musketry fire. He had the rioters surrounded, and one hundred and thirty-three of them were arrested.

There was a general outcry. " Let anyone dare after this to preach forgetfulness of past crimes and amnesty for these ruffians who never cease their plotting ! As long as the creature lives the poison lives too, and the reptile must be crushed ! " Military courts were opened, and between the 27th Fructidor and the 6th Brumaire, eighty-eight rioters were sentenced, thirty-one to death, among them three ex-members of the Convention. Meanwhile the imprisonment of Babeuf and his accomplices at Vendôme grew still more severe, until Prairial of the Year V, when their trial ended in further death sentences.

The Government felt itself overwhelmed; it was divided against itself : moreover, Reubell, in the fresh alarm the reaction had caused him, had drawn nearer to Barras : La Revellière leant first to one side and then to the other. A most chaotic policy was the result. " The authorities," writes Mallet, on December 5, 1796, "dismiss a Jacobin from his office one day and employ a far worse one the next." And, meanwhile, the people, so the police reports inform us, "continue to pour forth curses on the Government."

The discredit into which the executive had fallen inspired the Councils with a certain boldness. Here the reactionary feeling was fast gaining strength. In the Council of the Ancients, Portalis, in the course of his opposition to the motion of the 17th Floréal to revive the laws of persecution directed against the Catholic priests, had made a ringing speech on religious liberty, and finally succeeded in getting the resolution thrown out. "*There can be no further question of destruction,*" he exclaimed, "*it is time for us to think about governing.*" The words, significant under their apparent triteness, were evidently in agreement with the general feeling, for a report dated the 10th asserts that the public, "setting aside party feeling . . . had showered encomiums" on Portalis.

The Right, indeed, had some hope of winning over the Directory. Dumas, Pastoret, and Dumolard were frequently Plots and at the Luxembourg. Not that the Directors were Counterplots. in the least inclined to submit. But they were in despair. The Government, in its dread of "bad elections," began to look about it for a plot, that chosen refuge of rulers standing on the dreaded brink of an appeal to the electorate. And again the irreconcilable section of the royalists was its refuge in the hour of need.

On the 11th Pluviôse three of Louis XVIII's agents were taken in the act of plotting against the Republic. They were men of no importance, but none the less perfectly genuine "powers," signed by Louis XVIII, were found on the persons of the Abbé Brottier, Duverne de Presle and La Villeheurnois. These agents had artlessly solicited the help of two important military officers, Malo and Ramel; to seduce them they had actually exhibited the "authority" they had received from the King, and a list (highly imaginary) of the various deputies in both Councils, who, so they declared, had entered into an agreement with them. Without a moment's hesitation Malo ordered the arrest of the conspirators.

This counterblast to Babeuf's plot filled the Government

514

with joy. The position of Barras, which had become very insecure, was at once immeasurably strengthened. The discovery was noised abroad in all directions. Yet the plot seemed to hang fire. One party thought it an odious invention on the part of the Government, the other declared it an unimportant demonstration on that of unauthorized agents. Public opinion still ran high in favour of reaction : the Babouvists and the royalists, all of whom were threatened, combined against the Government, and in the spring of 1797, during which the elections were to take place, the Directory found itself face to face with an unpopularity even greater than that which had been its portion just before the first Italian campaign.

* * * * *

Meanwhile the troops were still covering themselves with glory. In Italy Bonaparte reigned supreme. Everything went down before him. Having crushed the rising at Pavia on May 25, he marched against Field-Marshal Beaulieu, forced his way across the Mincio at *Borghetto,* drove the routed Austrians back into the Tyrol, and after he had secured possession of the three Venetian fortresses of Legnano, Peschiera, and Verona (the neutrality of the Republic of Venice notwithstanding), he proceeded to lay siege to Mantua, the only town in Italy still held by the Emperor.

The great Victories in Italy.

He had become the arbiter of the whole country. He received its homage and took ransom from it as well. By this means he gave unfailing satisfaction to the Directory : he thought of everything, even despatching magnificent horses to the "Five Majesties," to replace "the indifferent horses that drew their carriages." He had risen so high by this time, that he cast his alms to the negligible Government with a scornful hand. He plundered Italy : the Dukes of Parma and Piacenza purchased peace with payments, one of 2,000,000 the other of 10,000,000 *livres.* Murat, ever bold, made a descent on Leghorn and carried off English goods worth more than 12,000,000 *livres.* When the General forced the rule of the Republic on Naples his prestige rose in proportion to the depth of the humiliated Bourbon's fall : but what a height it had reached when, from Bologna, he imposed the ransom of Rome itself upon the Pope! All Italy lay at the victor's feet, and he, in his turn, laid it at the feet of France.

Jourdan, meanwhile, after a pause necessitated by the reorganization of his army, had crossed the Rhine at Neuwied, The German with Kléber and Marceau as his subordinate Campaign commanders. The ground was cleared by of 1796. successful engagements at *Uckerath* and *Altenkirchen:* at both of these Kléber was the victor, while Marceau blockaded Mayence. Thus Jourdan found it possible to reach the Main, and then, driving the enemy before him, to enter the valley of the Raab, and so seize Amberg, a few days' march from Vienna.

And Moreau, at the head of "Rhine and Moselle," had straightway moved on the right bank at Kehl, had beaten the enemy at *Renchen, Rastadt, Malch,* and *Neresheim,* and detached Baden, Würtemberg, and Saxony from the Coalition. Thus, while Italy humbled herself, Germany seemed on the brink of submission.

But though nothing was to check Bonaparte's own flight, his emulators on the path of glory were not to be so fortunate. A young prince of six-and-twenty, the Archduke Charles, the only military leader who was ever to prove himself capable of coping with the Republican generals, was just entering on his career. His first stroke was the stroke of a master. For on August 16 at *Neumarkt* he beat Bernadotte's division, which was to have formed the connecting-link between the armies, separated the two, fell upon Jourdan, forcing him to retire on *Amberg,* met him again at *Wurzburg* where, on September 3, 30,000 Frenchmen fought all day long against 60,000 of their enemies, drove him back to the Rhine, made a fresh breach in his force at *Altenkirchen,* where the noble Marceau fell at the age of seven-and-twenty years, and ended by forcing his adversary to withdraw, sorely discomfited, into Alsace. Meanwhile Moreau, whose position had became dangerous, was constrained to undertake what a foreign observer has called that "superb retreat," which, interspersed as it was with brilliant successes, enabled him to pass back into France at Brisach, covered with glory.

BONAPARTE UPON THE SCENE

Everything, even the checks experienced by his rivals, combined to increase the greatness of Bonaparte. And in his own career he was advancing by leaps and bounds. For him the period between August and November 1796 was one blaze of glory. Wurmser, coming down with 70,000 men to raise the blockade of Mantua, was surprised on the way, the leaders under his command were beaten at *Lonato*, he himself was defeated at *Castiglione*, and driven back with the remnants of his army into the country of the Upper Adige. Then Davidovitch was defeated at *Roveredo* and *Caliano*, Trent was taken, Wurmser, returning to offensive tactics, was beaten at *Primolano*, on September 7, completely routed at *Bassano*, and obliged to shut himself up in Mantua after the glorious engagement of *San Giorgio* on September 15 : thus, with ten mighty strokes, a whole army had been brought to nought. Thereupon Alvinzi made his appearance with 50,000 men set free by the French retreat in Germany and strove to dislodge Bonaparte from the country he had conquered. For three days the struggle went on in the marshes of *Arcola* where, as at Lodi, the hero rushed to the post of danger and succeeded, on the third day, in forcing the Austrians to retreat (November 17). In January 1797, Alvinzi was back again with 70,000 men behind him. What matter ? By this time Bonaparte, in the eyes of his troops, was invincible. Their belief in victory and in his star had become fanaticism. For one moment, at *Rivoli* on January 12, Joubert's men wavered : but Bonaparte flew to the spot, gave battle again on the 14th, and swept away the foe, who soon lay broken in the neighbouring ravines. On February 20 the gates of Mantua opened. In the course of a few months the victor of Arcola and Rivoli had surpassed the soldier who had seemed the greatest of all warriors at Lodi.

Led by that incomparable chief the army had been superb. On the evening of the Battle of Rivoli, Lasalle, who had been slashing and thrusting and charging for four mortal hours, was standing, white with weariness, beside the colours which were being carried in from every corner of the field and cast at Bonaparte's feet. The great chief turned to the young leader, not more than twenty at that time, pointed to the heap of

517

trophies, and said : "*Lie down on them, Lasalle, you have deserved it.*" The whole army of Italy, after that year's campaign, might, like Lasalle, have lain down upon a bed of trophies.

* * * * *

In spite of the attacks made on it within the frontiers of France, the Directory, strong in its victories, and indifferent, apparently, to its defeats, was carrying on the most arrogant of foreign policies. The treaties concluded with Prussia at Berlin on August 5, and with Spain at Sant Ildefonso on the 19th, encouraged it in this course. By her alliance with the Bourbon at Madrid, who constituted himself "the Grand Admiral of the Republic," France had become a formidable enemy for England. Pitt made as though he would come to terms : his suggestions were received with arrogance. For three months he beat about the bush, and then withdrew. The manœuvre served his purpose. When Hoche attempted to effect a landing in Ireland, in January 1797, he failed ; the hour had gone by. Everything, as we have already said, conspired to set all the hopes, and pride, and love of the country on the fortunate general in command of the army of Italy.

He had resolved to make peace. The moment was propitious : Catherine II had died on November 17, 1796, just as she and her Cossacks were preparing to enter the European lists. The Czar Paul, who loved Prussia, and whose brain was disordered, wrote to Vienna : "the alliance is falling to pieces." Thugut wrote from Vienna, when he heard the old Czarina was dying : "*Our misfortunes must surely have reached their highest pitch!*" They did, indeed, after Rivoli. When Mantua capitulated, and even England seemed inclined to give in, Austria realized that the day of her overweening pride was over. Bonaparte foresaw this state of exhaustion more clearly than the Directory. He was determined to conclude a peace which should be *his* peace.

For a year past he had been treating, between one battle and the next, with various princes, just as a Roman pro-consul once treated with the Prusias. At Tolentino, he had recently come into contact with the most diplomatic, possibly, of all the Powers, the Roman Curia. In
513

his dealings with it he had displayed all the resources of the most extraordinarily versatile genius ; he had been terrifying, insinuating, full of fascination, and as full of cunning. He was resolved that the Pontiff's throne should not be sacrificed, yet by threatening to overthrow it he completely forced the hand of the Roman plenipotentiaries. At Tolentino Pius VI surrendered the Legations, Avignon, the Comtat, to France, with 15,000,000 *livres* worth of treasure, ranging from statutes taken from the Vatican, to plate taken from the churches. And so cunningly had Bonaparte played his part, now the raging *tragediante*, and now the caressing *comediante*, that the Pope's envoys had departed stripped, indeed, but full of gratitude ! Another stake had been set up to mark the future road.

But on February 3 the Directors had *advised* their General, in a now celebrated letter, to proceed to Rome, and there extinguish " the torch of fanaticism." " Such," they added, " is the *wish* of the Directory."

This was what they had come to ! They watched his rise with terror. They had tried, in a somewhat underhand fashion, to thwart it, endeavouring to divide the command between him and Kellermann after the taking of Milan, and to send Clarke to share it with him just before Tolentino. He had always coolly offered to resign his command, thus forcing the Directors to give way, and doing as he chose in spite of them.

He was now preparing to carry out an operation which, in his eyes, was absolutely essential. The Viennese Cabinet must be forced to make the peace on which the heart of all France was set. But, broken as Austria was, she would never consent to relinquish her hold on Belgium, Lombardy, and the left bank of the Rhine at one fell swoop, and acknowledge, on the very morrow of the German victories of the Archduke Charles, the omnipotence, nor even the existence, of a Republic which had sent a Hapsburg to the scaffold, unless she received a compensation satisfactory to her greed, and still more to her pride.

Bonaparte's profoundly practical mind had realized all this. He had no intention of giving back a rood of the conquered **Negotiations** territories, but, being no more troubled with **with Austria.** scruples than the European statesmen themselves, it occurred to him that Austria might be appeased by a gift of something belonging to a third party. For the past six months he had had his eye on Venice : if he brought that State into subjection he might hand it over to Austria and so console her feelings. And until he found himself in a position to do this he would carry on negotiations with Vienna, even though he could not hope they would succeed.

While he waited to acquire possession of the pledge, he would do something to alarm the house of Hapsburg ; leaving Tolentino, he made his way to the north, where the Archduke Charles was waiting for him. Before he drew the sword he sent him offers of peace.

Austria was between two fires : Hoche had taken Jourdan's place on the banks of the Rhine. In April 1797 he crossed the river, once more proved himself a mighty leader in a series of successful battles at *Neuwied*, *Uckerath* and *Altenkirchen*, killed 8000 of the enemy, and took seven standards, and sixty pieces of ordnance. Meanwhile, Moreau, after winning a battle at *Dursheim*, was advancing towards the Upper Danube, through the Black Forest.

The Archduke had left the Danube : he had been sent to meet Bonaparte. But who could stop Bonaparte ? Bonaparte, not caring to let Hoche and Moreau reach Vienna before he was there himself, marched on with his little army of 53,000 men, forced the lines of the *Piave*, the *Tagliamento*, and the *Isonzo*, and—Masséna and Joubert having occupied the passes of *Tarvis* and *Tolbach*—passed right into Austria by the valley of the Drave. At *Leoben*, forty leagues from Vienna, he called a halt.

Forthwith he sent proposals of peace Austria accepted the idea. On April 18 the Austrian plenipotentiaries reached *Leoben*. On the 18th Bonaparte suggested Venice as the basis of an arrangement : the suggestion was accepted.

The Directory was no more troubled with scruples than the European cabinets : it would have made no difficulty about Venice handed sacrificing Venice, but it had to reckon with over to the Councils : here the liberals were gaining the Austria. upper hand, as we shall see : they were hostile to Bonaparte : they put pressure on Carnot, who shrank from the signal injustice involved in this "attempt on Venice."

520

BONAPARTE UPON THE SCENE

The Government refused to countenance the General's suggestion. He had recourse to his usual weapon : he offered to retire from the army. "My civil career," he wrote, "will be as simple and uniform as my military career has been !" *My civil career!* The words sent a shudder through the Luxembourg. The General was given a free hand. Venice, already doomed, hastened her own fate. On April 17 the French troops left in Verona, a Venetian town, were basely massacred by the populace ; the "Great Nation" could not have submitted to this treachery in any case ; Bonaparte pounced on the incident, which served his ends. On March 12 the French troops were in Venice. And Bonaparte, once armed with his pledge, pushed on the negotiations sharply. For a month already he had been alternately flattering and terrifying the Austrian envoys. On the 11th Prairial (May 31) he wrote to Paris that "Venice would pay for the Rhine." Peace seemed assured.

But, at that very hour, this certainty was compromised by a crisis of the gravest kind, an internal crisis which was the most important event in the history of the Directory. And, on this account, we too must turn for a moment from Leoben to Paris, where the Directory and the Councils, renewed in the month of Germinal, were preparing for battle.

SOURCES. Works already quoted by Aulard (*Paris* . . . III, IV, 1899–1900), Débidour (*Procès-verbaux*), Mallet du Pan, Creuzé-Latouche, Barras, Barbé-Marbois, La Revellière-Lépeaux, Carnot (II), Charles de Constant, Sandoz Rollin (in Bailleu), B. Constant (*Correspondance*), Thiébault (II), d'Andigné (I).—*Analyse de la Doctrine de Babeuf*, 1795 ; *Manifeste des Egaux*, 1795 ; *Lettre de Dupont de Nemours à Reubell* (*Rev. Fr.*, 1898) ; Pache, *Sur les Factions et les Partis*, 1795 (*Rev. Fr.*, 1891).

WORKS. Those already quoted by Sciout (*Directoire*), Sorel (V), Thureau-Dangin, Goncourt, Caudrillier, Stourm.—Robiquet, *Babeuf et Barras* (*Revue de Paris*, 1896) ; Félix Bouvier, *Bonaparte en Italie*, 1899 ; Frédéric Masson, *Napoléon et sa Famille*, I, 1897 ; Sorel, *Hoche et Bonaparte*, 1897 ; Roger Peyre, *Napoléon et son Temps*, 1891.

CHAPTER XLII

THE COUNCILS *VERSUS* THE DIRECTORY

March—August 1797

The elections of Germinal, Year V. The electors determine to be free. The new majority. Barthélemy elected a Director. The religious question the chief subject of conflict. "The worship of our fathers." The Jordan report. Disgrace of the "reactionary" ministers. Talleyrand in the ministry. The Constitutional Club *versus* the Clichy Club.

BY Ventôse it had become clear that the Germinal elections would go against the Government. The trial of the Babouvists, far from satisfying the reactionary party, had justified its fears, and thus increased its strength. And this increase of strength had not been checked by the Elections of trial of the royalist conspirators.
Germinal,   In vain had the Directory striven, by a series
Year V.   of measures (thwarted, indeed, by the Councils) to put down the movement and stop the mouths of the "royalist" electors.

The electors were not royalists : what they sighed for was liberty, and for religious liberty above all things. There is something singularly symbolic and touching, too, in the fact that, in the country villages, these elections turned on the question : *"Shall the bells ring?"* The meaning of that cry was that the people wished to be free *to practise their religion as well as to believe in it.* The electors of the Year V did not inquire whether a candidate was republican or royalist : they voted for the man who promised them the bells should ring again and the priests come back. That a few royalists obtained election as "honest men" is a certain fact : but the contention that the country elected, or intended to elect a royalist body of representatives cannot be upheld. The general object was

522

to drive out the old Jacobin coterie : almost all the former members of the Convention who constituted the out-going Third lost their seats—205 out of 216. The constitutional party itself had pressed for this expulsion of the " wretches," so Mme. de Staël had written to Roederer a few months previously : " Let us have honest men ! " was her cry too.

As a matter of fact the electors' choice far exceeded any expectations, and " even exceeded anybody's interests," wrote Constant, sorely disconcerted, in Germinal of the Year V. In Paris, where the " honest men " on whom the electors' choice had fallen were supposed to be royalists, one, Fleurieu, had actually served as a minister in the time of Louis XVI. Other cases quoted were those of Imbert Colomès, elected at Lyons, a recognized agent of the claimant to the throne, and General Willot, chosen in Provence, who had been connected with the " White Terror." But these royalists, as we have already said, were exceptional. (We leave Pichegru, of whose relations with the claimant friends and enemies alike were ignorant, out of the question.) The great mass of the 205 newly elected legislators were—if we may be excused these neologisms—liberal and conservative *bourgeois*. Camille Jordan was a fair type of them all, and he was elected at Bordeaux to carry out a programme involving the restoration of religion on the basis of a liberal *Separation*. All these men supported the Constitution. This was a recognized fact : the police-reports affirm that " the intentions of the lately elected Third had been found to be pure and in conformity with the aspirations of all the friends of the Constitution."

And, further, there was a party within this new majority which would have been able to paralyze any action on the part of the royalists : this was composed of such men as Thibaudeau and Boissy, who simply sought to ensure "*more virtue in the Government*"—at once a modest and an excessive demand.

In reality the new majority included various groups swayed by various tendencies—a whole gamut of shades from con-
The new stitutional royalism to constitutional republi-
Majority. canism—and each of these groups contained partisans of violence and partisans of more prudent courses; hence the constant jars which were to prevent the Right from

ever forming itself into a resolute party, bent on the realization of a fixed programme, and expose the majority to the encroachments of a daring minority. One Larue confesses that the prudent men " hampered the majority," but Dumas and Barbé-Marbois complain that only too often the "active party " gave a " cold reception " to their suggestions. Pichegru adds, in his Journal, that he noticed " *more jealous competition than sincere co-operation.*" Perfect union was never attained till the Government had dispatched royalists and republicans, " prudent " and " active " politicians, shut up in iron cages, to the Sinnamari hulks.

For the truth was that the Government loathed them all. What did the Directors care whether Siméon, Portalis, Barbé-Marbois, or Boissy d'Anglas longed to destroy the Republic or not, so long as they knew them to be bent on their own destruction ? They had been elected to oppose the Directory, and they would surely destroy it. The Government, powerless to dissolve the Councils, had no resources but proscription and deportation. "*The Directory,*" writes a correspondent in Messidor, " *cannot govern with the Councils, and must therefore either conspire, or obey, or perish.*" But clear-sighted men were already beginning to realize that the coming struggle between the majority, " entangled in the bonds of that unfortunate Constitution," and the Directory, " which would contrive to shake it off," was neither equal, nor uncertain. " You are making a great deal of dust ! " said Mme. de Staël jeeringly to Dumas. She had rallied to the standard of the Directory. To the glory of this honest and loyal majority the General's retort to Barras' new ally was : " That is better, surely, than making mud ! "

* * * * *

The Councils met on the 1st Prairial (May 21, 1797) and the general feeling was forthwith manifested by the election of Barbé-Marbois as President of the Ancients, and that of Pichegru as President of the Five Hundred. Then Letourneur having lost his seat on the Directory (there was some suspicion that Barras, a most skilful trickster, had contributed to this), the Councils, no doubt to affirm their desire for peace, sent the Marquis de Barthélemy.

Barthélemy elected a Director.

524

THE COUNCILS *v.* DIRECTORY

who had negotiated the Basle treaties, to take his place. Carnot would have been glad, in the ungrateful struggle he was just about to face, to have had the company and support of his friend Cochon, a regicide, but a most repentant regicide, and a strong man too. His refusal by the Right damped Carnot's ardour, and it was generally acknowledged, on the other hand, by those who had seen him at work, that Barthélemy would probably be anything but a tower of strength for the policy of the newly elected Third. In any case the new majority had only a minority with it inside the Luxembourg; and, further, the support given it by Carnot, a sincere republican, was likely to be uncertain, and that of Barthélemy, an insignificant personality, would surely be timid.

Meanwhile the Councils had opened their campaign. On the 7th Prairial one of the newly elected members, Gilbert Desmolières, asked for a statement of accounts. For months, as everybody knew, Bonaparte had been sending home millions of money: how had those millions been spent? The Commission of Finance ordered Desmolières to present a report on the subject, and he proceeded to bring a more direct charge of malversation against the Government. On the 30th Prairial a resolution, which placed a strong curb on the Directors, was voted, and the Ancients, though they softened it to some extent, transformed it into a law most irksome to the Luxembourg. Reubell and Barras, who disliked this check upon their expenditure, were furious.

La Revellière was far more exasperated by the " clerical " movement. On the 4th Prairial Dumolard had applied for the nomination of a Commission to revise *the laws affecting the government of religious worship.* This was duly appointed: Camille Jordan was elected chairman, and the Council, while waiting for his report, sent a message to the Directors demanding the immediate release of all incarcerated priests.

On the 29th Jordan presented his report: its substance was contained in four proposals which to us, at the present day,

Camille Jordan's Report.
seem innocent enough;

1. *That every believer should be allowed to choose whatever priest suited him.*

2. *That every priest should be free to perform his office without taking an oath of any sort.*

525

3. *That the church bells might be rung.*

4. *That every form of worship should be allowed its own cemetery.*

This, after all, simply amounted to a strict application of the system of separation ; but such was the condition of things at that moment that friends and enemies of Catholicism alike realized it meant the early and complete restoration of the proscribed religion.

A wild outcry rose from the Jacobin press. All the old anti-religious leaven began to work again. The *Ami du Peuple* lifted up its voice : there would be a recrudescence of " *the vile policy of the Medici.*" Every article it published teemed with Inquisitions and Saint-Bartholomews and revocations of the Edict of Nantes—less disturbing, truly, to their readers' minds than the constant allusions to Church property, the present possessors of which would, it was declared, be most certainly threatened by this offensive return of the " fanatics."

But, in spite of all this, the pressure in favour of Catholicism grew stronger. In the Year IV the number of churches given back to the Catholics in Paris alone had risen from fifteen to forty. In vain had the Directory commanded its agents to "hamper the movement " by "trying the patience of the priests." The priests would not be discouraged. On the 6th Thermidor of the Year V the *Annales de la Religion* announced that public worship had been restored in 31,214 parish churches, and that 4511 more had applied for leave to follow their example. The movement was general, spontaneous, and unceasing. The Prussian Minister wrote home that " *never had the thirst for religion been so deeply felt.*" The bells were quivering in the village steeples.

On the 20th Messidor, amidst the deepest emotion, the debate of the Five Hundred on Jordan's report began. How could the deputies have failed to feel it ? The moment had come when the real problem of the time was to be decided. Was the Church of tradition, the Church they had believed for ever banished, to recover her power ? For how could any man doubt, so said the anti-Catholic philosophers and politicians, that the restored freedom of the Church would lead to the re-establishment of her sovereignty ?

526

Yet the first shot was fired, not by a philosopher, but by a soldier. General Jourdan delivered a speech embodying the point **"The Worship** of view of the military section, in which the hatred **of our Fathers."** of "cant" was stronger than in any other class of the nation. He denounced the priests, who had opposed the soldiers of the Republic in every corner of La Vendée; but Lemerer, a member of the Extreme Right, extolled "*the ancient worship of our fathers.*" His words infuriated Eschassériaux. "*Never! no, never! with all your perpetual talk of the religion of our fathers will you bring us back to their absurd beliefs, and foolish prejudices, and frenzied superstitions!*" His insults roused the majority to fury. But Boulay de la Meurthe, a new-comer, who was to become one of the leaders of the Left, spoke more violently still: the priests, he vowed, once they were rid of the oath, "would re-establish the old parishes and dioceses, make fresh converts, and use all the means their moral power would give them to recover their property and overthrow the Republic which had sold it." And, as a crowning argument, he pointed to a reconstituted Church in the hands of a foreign potentate—the Pope—whose destruction the Republic had sought.

In eloquent language Royer-Collard, Boissy d'Anglas, and Pastoret supported Jordan's conclusions. Royer-Collard claimed "*justice, and again justice, and justice, ever and always!*" Yet such was the feeling among political men on the religious question—there were many *philosophers* in the ranks of the conservative *bourgeois*—that the Council maintained the enforcement of the oath by 210 votes to 204. But, on the other hand, the laws of proscription were repealed. The Council of the Ancients transformed the resolution of the Five Hundred into a law on the 7th Fructidor: the declaration on oath was now to be no more than a simple "*undertaking*" not to disturb the public peace: this the most royalist of priests might conscientiously give.

*   *   *   *   *

The decision was one of capital importance. We are convinced it had a decisive effect on subsequent events. La Revellière would have hesitated (as we know from the testimony of various witnesses) to join Reubell and Barras to the extent of consenting to proscribe (as he himself had been proscribed) the elected representatives of the nation. He was always to deplore **Dismissal of the "reaction- ary" Ministers.** the events of the 18th Fructidor, though, as he himself acknowledged, they "would not have taken place" without him. It was when he saw how resolved the majority was to "*establish the Roman superstition,*" or allow itself to be led into doing so, that he consented to form one of the *triumvirate* which was now to enter the lists. Compare the dates : the Five Hundred voted their resolution on the 27th, on the 28th—as a preface to the *coup d'état*—the dismissal of the "reactionary" Ministers, whereby La Revellière desired to strike at Jordan and Pius VI, took place.

Barras' mind had long been set on the destruction of the Councils. The Councils were less resolved on his, or rather he had a clear conception of the path to be followed—the appeal to the troops : his opponents overlooked this. The two powers began to try each other's strength : the struggle became acute over the question of the Ministers. Four of these, Schérer, Delacroix, Merlin, and Faypoult, were "Jacobins"; two others, Cochon and Bénezech, were imbued with the new spirit. The Councils were bent on inducing the Directors to dismiss the four "Jacobins." Carnot supported the opposition in the Luxembourg. Reubell regarded this proposal on the part of the Legislative Body as "a violation of the Constitution": the *triumvirs* refused compliance and, passing from defensive to offensive tactics, forced Bézenech and Cochon to resign. **Hoche and Talleyrand elected Directors.** They then sacrificed Schérer and Delacroix, insignificant allies, and replaced them by Hoche, whom Barras destined to be the instrument of his projected *coup d'état,* and Talleyrand, whose accession to the ministry brought a whole group of deputies to Barras' aid.

This group, which had gathered round the Baronne de Staël and Benjamin Constant, seemed determined to fight "the reaction," and had founded the Constitutional Club to counterbalance the influence of that known as the Clichy Club, to which all the members of the Right belonged, "a perfect den of aristocrats."

528

This Constitutional Club was resolved that one, at least, of the men in power should be its representative. The office fell to Talleyrand.

He had reappeared upon the scene a short time previously, and had naturally turned to his old friend of 1789, Germaine de Staël. Looking about for stepping-stones to help him on his upward path his eye fell on the good-natured Baroness, who had declared he " had all the vices both of the old and the new *régime*," but who always allowed herself to be swayed by persons she despised. Barras hesitated long before he would allow this dangerous adherent to " set his lame foot in the Luxembourg." The Baroness fairly forced him on the Director. He was accepted at last. Intriguers are a terrible race : Barras' violent measures had no more persevering instigator than this mild-mannered diplomat.

Encouraged, on one hand, by this representative of the " moderate " members of the Directory, Barras was assailed, on the other, by the distracted Jacobins. Did he not see that his hesitation was bringing about the ruin of the Republic ? Sieyès, secretive as ever, was urging on the attack, and keeping himself out of it. During the closing days of Messidor Barras, strengthened by the help thus coming to him from various quarters, made his arrangements to " restore concord between the powers," even by the sword if necessary. The *coup d'état* was imminent.

Same sources and works as for preceding chapter, and in addition :
SOURCES. Works already quoted by Malouet (II), Mathieu Dumas (III).—Le Coz, *Correspondance*, II, 1900 ; La Rue, *Le 18 Fructidor* (*Mémoires*), 1895 ; V. Pierre, *Lettres des Déportés de Fructidor*, 1895 ; *Lettres de Madame de Staël* in Roéderer, *Œuvres*, VIII ; Pierre, *Le 18 Fructidor* (Documents), 1903.
WORKS. Those already quoted by Sciout (*Constitution Civile*), Pingaud (*De Bry*) ; *Un agent secret* , *Le Comte d'Antraigues* (ed. of 1894) ; Lady Blennerhassett, *Madame de Staël*, 1860 ; Sorel, *Madame de Staël*, 1898 ; Méric, *L'Abbé Emery*, 1895 ; Pisani, *L'Episcopat Constitutionnel*, 1909 ; Asse, *B. Constant et le Directoire* (Rev. Rev., III) ; G. Pallain, *Le Ministère de Talleyrand sous le Directoire*, 1895.

CHAPTER XLIII

THE *COUP D'ÉTAT* OF FRUCTIDOR

August—September 1797

" The Army shall pronounce its decision." An inspection of swords. Barras and Hoche. Failure of the first attempt. Bonaparte and the majority. The Venetian question. Bonaparte *versus* " Clichy." Addresses to the armies. Augereau in Paris. " You were a fool ! " The evening of the 17th. Flight of Carnot. Barthélemy arrested. Augereau at the Tuileries. The deputies at the Temple. The sittings of the 18th and 19th Fructidor. Proscriptive decrees. The consequences of Fructidor. " The sword is the law."

A N appeal to the sword had become inevitable. The Councils, in fact, infuriated by the dismissal of the " reactionary " ministers, appeared resolved, for a moment, to impeach the Directors. Dumas complained bitterly to Moreau of " the insult." Pichegru threatened to " mount his horse." And so great was the tension that, to the evident astonishment of the police, " circumstances seemed to have swallowed up all amusements."

The Army invoked.

Barras inspected the swords at his command : Moreau, " a political nonentity " (what better praise can a soldier desire ?) ; Bonaparte, dangerous, and too far away : Hoche was the only man ! The Director summoned him to Paris on pretext of his appointment to the Ministry of War (in reality Hoche had not reached the age required for ministerial office). When Barras convinced him that the men sitting at the Tuileries were about to restore the throne, Hoche undertook the unpleasant task. " We have settled with the General," writes Barras, " *that his army shall pronounce its will.*" The word was out : the era of the *pronunciamiento* had begun. Four regiments were to be detached from the army of Sambre-et-Meuse, and marched, nominally, on Brest. Once they reached Corbeil they were to cross the "constitutional boundary" boldly and proceed, on the 14th or 15th Thermidor, to place themselves at the disposal of the authorities in the Luxembourg.

The plan was discovered : on the 4th Thermidor Aubry warned the Five Hundred that the troops had started : the **Hoche** deputies appealed to Carnot, who naturally replied **disavowed** that he knew nothing of this suspicious move- **by Barras.** ment of troops ; but he questioned Barras, who took fright and denied everything. Carnot, who was President of the Directory, determined to clear the matter up, and sent for Hoche, who was in Paris awaiting the arrival of his four regiments. A painful scene ensued : Hoche, in the noblest way, shielded Barras, who had disavowed him like a coward. But he left Paris that very evening, full of scorn and regret and so sorely stricken, that the mysterious malady which had been sapping his strength for some time past carried him off a few days later. Carnot seemed reassured : he contented himself with requesting that posts might be erected all round Paris to mark out the "constitutional boundaries." Barras must have laughed heartily in his sleeve at this precaution. His fears allayed, he looked about him for another sword, and so fell back on Bonaparte.

Bonaparte had been keeping a watchful eye on all that was happening in Paris. He was strongly opposed to any **Bonaparte and** royalist restoration, and knew he had many per- **the Five** sonal enemies in the "reactionary" majority. **Hundred.** The new deputies, indeed, were hostile to him : to them he was the Jacobin soldier, the "Man of Vendémiaire." And, further, led by Barthélemy and Carnot, they were raising an opposition to his Italian policy. Then the other side grew louder and louder in acclamation, and the Jacobin press extolled him to the skies : Bonaparte was dubbed "the buckler of the Republic."

This was a fresh reason for disliking him as far as the Councils were concerned. A whole party detested the "little shrimp with his tangled hair, a bastard son of Mandrin," fated before long to "expiate his mountebank notoriety."

Their hostility declared itself when Dumolard made a violent attack at the Clichy Club on Bonaparte's plan for the destruction of the Venetian Republic. Dumas and Vaublanc (though they represented two distinct shades of the opposition) both agree in describing their colleague's speech as an exhibition of the most imprudent folly. His denunciations, in fact, filled up the measure of the General's rage : " the Clichy party wanted his head ! " he would defend it—and the Republic at the same time ! Adulation and incitement were poured out upon him from Paris by the whole of the Constitutional Club, by Mme. de Staël, by Talleyrand. And the protest of the army was only delayed till its great leader should give the sign.

The army loathed the new deputies. " Our well-known opinions," says Marbois, " had rendered us odious to the army." These lovers of " cant," these " protectors of Chouans and *émigrés*," who were " adversaries of the natural frontiers " into the bargain, were so much filth which must be swept away. " Woe to Clichy ! " cries Joubert, one of the most moderate of the party, in his letters to his father. From Messidor onwards, the troops, from the Rhine to the Po, were all for throwing the " King's deputies " out of window !

The anniversary of July 14 (25th Messidor) appeared a favourable occasion for a demonstration. Marmont was Manifestoes of dispatched by Bonaparte to pass the watchword the Army. round to all the generals. The various divisions were instructed to pronounce their decision, in the form of *Addresses*. Augereau's division distinguished itself : " Men who are covered with ignominy, and saturated with vice, are rising and plotting in the midst of Paris, while we have been triumphing at the gates of Vienna : they would fain drench the country with blood and tears, offer a fresh sacrifice to the demon of civil war, and march by the funereal light of the torch of fanaticism and discord across heaps of ashes and of corpses, upon the liberty they desire to immolate. We have restrained our indignation : *we reckoned on the laws : the laws hold their peace !* Who will speak now if we do not break the silence ? . . ." The conspirators must be made to tremble. . . . " The tale of your iniquities is complete, and *the price of it lies on the points of our bayonets !* " The other divisions followed this lead. That of Joubert

532

exclaimed : " The armies must purify France ! " Bonaparte
swelled the concert at last. In a proclamation addressed to the
troops, he cried : " *The men who secured the country's triumph
over the European Coalition are still here. . . . The royalists, if
they show their faces for a moment, will have ceased to live !* "
And then, sending the Addresses and his proclamation to the
Luxembourg, he added, " *The necessity for a decision on your
part is imminent. . . . I perceive the Clichy Club desires to
trample on my corpse, and so succeed in compassing the destruction
of the Republic. Are there no more Republicans in France ? . . .
If you need force, call on the armies !* "

His letter reached Paris just at the moment when Barras
had abandoned Hoche. He was forced to accept Bonaparte,
who seemed to be offering his services. The Directors fancied
he would come in person and drive the deputies out. They did
not know him, as yet. He was not at all inclined to compromise
himself personally in this " chamber-warfare." His plan was to
set things in motion, and keep his own hands clean : he
read Plutarch in his tent at Mombello, but he certainly read
Machiavelli also. For the moment he was content to supply
the Directors with certain most unexpected and most precious
weapons. At Verona, he had seized the Comte d'Antraigues
and his private papers : these last furnished the most incon-
trovertible proof of Pichegru's guilt.

Pichegru was to be the ruin of the members of the Clichy
Club : they were all to be involved in a web of which they knew
Pichegru's nothing. This piece of good fortune exceeded
Intrigues every hope ! The very first president these men
detected. had elected in the Council of the Five Hundred
was a general who had sold himself to the King and betrayed
the Republic ! The discovery, as Mallet admits, was the most
terrible blow the opposition could have received : it was publicly
placarded on the morrow of the *coup d'état,* and for a short
time appeared to justify it.

* * * * *

Meanwhile the arrival of the Addresses had caused the
liveliest excitement. Carnot attacked them at the Luxembourg : Willot did the same in the Five Hundred. Yet the
Councils contented themselves with addressing a very stiff

request for explanations to the Directory, both as to the movements of the troops, and as to the Addresses.

But the Triumvirate was now in a much stronger position. On the 20th Thermidor Augereau had reached Paris. Bona-

Augereau in Paris. parte, who thought him "an ignoramus," considered him well fitted to carry out the proposed police operations on a large scale. The future Duc de Castiglione, a fierce Jacobin, and, as La Revellière writes, "an uneducated person," made no secret of his intentions : "I have come here," he said, "to kill the royalists." These military men are apt to simplify formulæ. To Bonaparte he wrote in still more emphatic fashion : "Our purity and our courage will save the Republic from the hideous precipice into which the agents of the throne and the altar have plunged it." This huge fellow, rapping out oaths, astounded the Directors. "A splendid brigand !" Reubell exclaimed after he had seen him for the first time. But he reassured them. Their answer to the message from the Five Hundred demonstrates this ; it was presented to the Legislative Body on the 23rd. The explanation of the Addresses was to be found, said the Directors, somewhat haughtily, "in the legitimate anxiety into which a large number of good citizens had been thrown by certain attempts to plunge France into the horrors of a fresh Revolution, and reverse the present order of things by treason or by force."

No very great effort was needed to intimidate the Right ; this was sufficient. Dumas' letters to Moreau do not conceal the uneasiness—and the indignation—caused him by Augereau's arrival, and by the language and behaviour of "some 5000 or 6000 officers discharged from the service," who had appeared in Paris, were making attacks on the priests, and "encouraging the soldiers to commit the worst excesses." They were talking about "drawing and quartering" Pichegru. There is something astonishing about the indulgence with which Pichegru now accepted a movement that was a personal menace to himself. But M. Caudrillier has recently shown us how certain signs had convinced the unhappy man his treachery had been discovered. He knew his crime must destroy his whole party, and the thought had paralyzed his energy.

However this may have been, the Councils could only discover one appropriate reply to all these threats—the reorganization of the National Guard. This was a failure. The Triumvirs raised a cry of *coup d'état*; the National Guard was only called out for the purpose of "setting up the throne again" (said La Revellière to the Prussian Minister), and the Paris *bourgeoisie*, grown weak and cowardly, refused to enlist. The Directors had made up their minds to act : the way was being prepared. Rumours were put about : the deputies were going to "dispossess the purchasers" (of national property), nay, more, they were going to "make a fresh Saint-Bartholomew," revise the trial of Louis XVI, and send every soul who had had a hand in the Revolution to the galleys. The police, not content with listening to these stories, helped to propagate them. When, after Fructidor, the deputies were conveyed to Rochefort, they were to hear the populace that crowded round their iron cages say : "*Those are the men who wanted to reestablish the subsidies and the salt-tax !* "

At the Luxembourg there were bitter quarrels every day. When Carnot refused (if we may believe Talleyrand's con-**Dissensions** fidences to Sandoz) to sign a message which **among the** was calculated to impede the reorganization of **Directors.** the National Guard, Reubell called him "a criminal," and accused him of having tried to send them all to the scaffold in Robespierre's time. Barras broke into coarse abuse : Carnot was a wretch, he declared. "There is not a louse on your body but has the right to spit in your face." Carnot flew at him. They were separated. The air was thick with portents of the coming storm.

Augereau had just been appointed to command the Army in Paris. It seems incredible that even in the face of such a warning as this all the Legislative Body did was to groan. " If we had been a genuine party . . ." writes Vaublanc— those words explain all ! More than ever they were divided, and, consequently, paralyzed. When on the 3rd Fructidor Tronson-Ducoudray brought back the reply to the "incendiary" message sent by the Directors, so moderate was it in tone, so completely did it "reveal the depths of our weakness," a supporter of stronger measures tells us, that it encouraged

Barras to be bold. And the vote of the Ancients on the 7th Fructidor, which revoked the laws against refractory priests, had so exasperated La Revellière that he had finally bound himself to his " fellow conspirators."

That very day the " philosopher " assumed the presidency resigned by Carnot. On the 10th the ex-Girondin made an exceedingly threatening speech " in the name of the Government." " A new May 31 " seemed imminent.

If the Councils had struck the first blow they might have parried the danger. On the evening of the 15th a certain colonel went to Dumas and offered to have Reubell and Barras seized and put out of the way. The " ideologist " turned with horror from the suggestion. On a later day he told the story to Napoleon : " *You were a fool !* " said the Emperor, " *You understand nothing about revolutions !* " The reader will share the Emperor's opinion—to the honour of the deputies who were proscribed in the Year V.

*   *   *   *   *

On the 17th Fructidor all five Directors were present at the daily sitting. No interesting business was transacted. 17th Fructidor, At four o'clock La Revellière closed the sitting, 1797.   smiling as he rose. " All my life," writes Carnot, " I shall see that cannibal smile."

Early in the day the Prince de Carency—one of those wanderers who spent their lives during that troublous period passing to and fro between the secret meetings of the opposition and the back-offices of the police—had warned Barras that he was to be impeached. The Director was resolved to be beforehand with his enemies.

At eight o'clock that evening the Three met again. " In consequence of the reception of warnings as to the danger to which the Republic is exposed, and of the attack the *royal conspirators* are preparing to attempt for the purpose of *cutting the throats of the Directory* and overthrowing the Constitution . . . the executive Directory, consisting of the Citizens Reubell, Revellière, and Barras, has decided to sit permanently." To preserve these precious Directors to the Constitution the Constitution itself was to be destroyed. Ugolino's policy ! Monsieur V. Pierre has published the full reports of this sitting, which lasted forty-eight hours, and opened with the piece of hypocrisy just quoted. Every line of these reports contains some order for investing buildings, for expulsions, or incarcerations. The work of "*saving the Constitution*" went on all night, but by dawn nothing was left of it save ruins.

Carnot was the first to hear he was to be arrested and sent to the hulks. Barras would probably have felt no regret if a **Flight of** bayonet-thrust had chanced to rid him of this **Carnot.** troublesome fellow. "If *Carnot had been killed*," he wrote, "*it would have been a very legitimate thing, for it is better to kill the devil yourself, than to let him kill you* "—a self-evident proposition. So Carnot, warned in time, did a wise thing when he took to flight. He slipped out of a postern gate in the Luxembourg to Reubell's extreme fury. Barthélemy was less cautious. At three o'clock in the morning an officer came in and arrested him as he lay in bed. " By whose order ? " " By the order of the Directory." " I am one of the Directors ! " " You are a traitor and my prisoner ! " He was kept under close guard till nine o'clock, when his resignation was demanded : he refused to give it, and was conducted to the Temple, whence he was to be taken to the galleys.

Carnot had found means of warning Pichegru, who, as " Inspector of the Council-Chamber," slept at the Tuileries. When Carnot's message reached him there was a hedge of fixed bayonets all round the Palace. Augereau had received orders to surround the Legislative Body. As the deputies came in he was either to arrest them or send them, if they belonged to the Five Hundred, to the Odéon ; if they were "Ancients," to the College of Surgeons, where the " good deputies " were to meet, while the factious persons were despatched to the Temple. Orders had been sent out that morning, and regiments from the towns lying round Paris were pouring in, crossing the " constitutional boundaries," and joining Augereau's command.

Pichegru and Willot, meanwhile, had sent hasty appeals to the two Presidents, Siméon and Laffon-Ladebat ; and Ramel, who commanded the grenadiers of the Legislative Body, had issued a call to arms. These eight hundred men occupied the gates into the gardens, which were besieged by Augereau's twelve thousand men, with forty guns—a regular

" *hanriotade.*" Ramel was called on to withdraw his grenadiers. He refused, and went to consult with Pichegru and Willot. It was then three o'clock in the morning. At half-past three a gun was fired at the Pont-Neuf, and at the signal, the soldiers threw themselves upon the gates. The grenadiers of the Legislative Body at once went over to the enemy. "We are not the Swiss Guard," they said, "we are not going to fight for Louis XVIII ": and they allowed their ordnance to be turned upon the Tuileries.

Then Augereau appeared : this valiant soldier was followed by a vile escort : Fournier, the man of the days of September, Augereau at Santerre the ex-General, Pache, Rossignol, ghosts, the Tuileries. all of them, of the days of massacre. Now we understand why Bonaparte had preferred to stay in Italy ! Augereau himself was more like a brigand than a soldier : he took Ramel by the throat, tore off his epaulets, and struck him in the face with them. "He had drunk a certain quantity of champagne," says Barras, "to prepare himself."

While this " operation " was going on the deputies began to arrive : they were allowed to enter. but within an hour General Verdières had sent them to the Temple. Yet Siméon and Laffon-Ladebat assumed their presidential chairs, and refused to allow themselves to be taken away. When they appealed to the Constitution the soldiers sneered at them : with great oaths they seized the deputies by their collars. When they came to Pichegru they faltered; this man had conquered Holland. His journal gives us the story of the disgraceful scene. A soldier threatened him with his bayonet : Pichegru pushed him aside : there was a rush, and a dozen men threw themselves on the General. Pichegru, we must acknowledge, was not a very interesting person : he, too, was a soldier who had strayed from the path of duty. None the less is it a fact that on this occasion the blows that fell on him were showered on the electors of the country.

Siméon was torn from his chair, but he had time to dictate one final sentence to his secretaries : "The Council is dissolved by force of arms." "These," so Marbois says, "were *the last words uttered under the rule of the Constitution of the Year III, which ceased from that moment to be the law of the*
538

French Nation." In an hour's time both the presidents were in the Temple.

At eight o'clock that morning various deputies, who had gathered from one quarter or another, made an attempt to get into the Tuileries : they were driven back, dispersed by dragoons, seized by gendarmes. Some of them protested "in the name of the law." " *The sword is the law !* " shouted an officer. The simple words sum up the situation.

All through that day the deputies were being carried off. By four o'clock in the afternoon the prison of the Temple was The Deputies full of them. La Rue, the royalist deputy, in the Temple found himself side by side with Rovère and Prison. Bourdon, regicides both of them, cast, under an accusation of *royalism,* into the very cell in which Louis XVI had been confined.

And, meanwhile, the grenadiers of the Legislative Body who had betrayed them were conducted to the Luxembourg, congratulated by the Directory in the first place, and then by the rumps of the two Councils. On the 19th Brumaire, these very grenadiers, logically enough, were to hand over both Directory and Councils to Bonaparte.

*   *   *   *   *

The Councils, or what was left of them, had gathered, one at the Odéon, the other in the College of Surgeons. The Directors meant these miserable men to become the proscribers of their colleagues. Their own action was confined to the publication and placarding of a proclamation denouncing "the conspiracy." This contained a lying assertion to the effect that "the Chouans had attacked the sentries round the Directory "; the Directors thus attacked by the Chouans must be avenged !

The Five Hundred, who met at nine o'clock in the morning at the Odéon, appointed a Commission charged with the duty of ensuring the " preservation of the Constitution " (our readers will observe how lie was piled on lie), but which was really to be employed in drawing up the list of proscribed persons. It waited for its masters' orders. They came, couched in the form of a message denouncing the plot and supporting its assertions by revelations forced from Duverne de Presle, the royalist agent, and more especially by the documents Bonaparte had seized at Verona. D'Antraigues' papers were certainly overwhelming in their testimony against Pichegru: but did that imply that both Pichegru himself and fifty-two other deputies ought to be deported without a hearing? This was the proceeding for which Boulay de la Meurthe had asked, and on which the Council had decided the previous evening. There must be no recourse to the ordinary methods of justice. A far-sighted man had said, in the course of this preliminary deliberation: "The public spirit is *too bad* to permit of our running so dangerous a risk. We have strength on our side for the moment. Let us take advantage of it!" Boulay spoke in much the same sense from the rostrum: "*You must feel that slow and purely judicial formalities cannot be used at this moment. . . . You are victors to-day; if you do not make use of your victory the battle will begin again to-morrow, but it will be terrible and bloody.*" Viller, an ex-member of the Convention and an expert in Jacobin policy, then proposed that the elections in forty-nine departments should be annulled, that certain members should be deported, and that the severity of the laws against the priests should be increased. Some of the deputies, like Marat on June 7, 1793, began to hand in names, and vied with each other in accusing their fellows—many of them for fear they should be thought lukewarm. Yet, mutilated though the Assembly was, it hesitated, and the laws of proscription were only voted after prolonged opposition. The members were allowed to depart at midnight (18th–19th Fructidor). As young Barante left the gallery he noticed on a playbill outside the theatre the name of the play to be performed that night—*Le Consentement Forcé*—and realized how witty chance may occasionally be!

The Ancients' consent was given yet more unwillingly. All through the 18th they hesitated. At five o'clock on the **Decrees of Proscription.** morning of the 19th, a Commission appointed during the preceding night, begged for fuller information and more convincing proofs. General Marbot, a very brutal Jacobin, replied that "*there was no necessity for proofs against royalist conspirators.*" This was the pure doctrine of Fouquier-Tinville, whose death had decidedly been untimely.

540

COUP D'ÉTAT OF FRUCTIDOR

All that day the discussion went on, while the soldiers, who had crowded into the galleries, shouted, "Come! sound the charge!" The Directors sent a fresh message to spur on the timorous legislators: "*People will talk to you about principles, and seek for established rules, and ask for delay. . . . What a fatal idea!*" Then, at last, the list of proscribed names was put to the vote. The immense majority of the Assembly, "purified" though it had been, kept their seats, and did not vote at all: out of a gathering nominally consisting of two hundred and fifty members, fifteen voted for proscription and seven against it!

* * * * *

Though the elected deputies had been sitting in the Assembly and making laws for four whole months, these decrees of the 19th Fructidor invalidated the Germinal elections in forty-nine departments. Thus one hundred and fifty-four deputies were turned out: and the elected officials and magistrates of these departments shared their fate. Further, the electorate, to prevent it from taking its revenge, was mutilated by the deprivation of the right to vote inflicted on all *relations of persons who had emigrated*, and by the exaction of an "oath of hatred to royalty." Clause thirteen of the law further condemned one hundred and sixty-five citizens, two of whom were Directors, and fifty-three deputies, to deportation without trial. The laws against *émigrés* who had returned to France were revived: their backs to a wall, and twelve bullets fired point-blank at them; and the refractory priests were once more condemned to the hulks. Finally—and this definitely established a dictatorship—the Directory was invested with the right to issue individual decrees for the arrest of priests who "disturbed the public peace," and all priests who refused to take the oath of hatred to royalty were to be considered as belonging to this category. Meanwhile the newspaper offices, like the presbyteries, were to be laid waste: the hated press was to be handed over to the will of its opponents, and all troublesome journalists, from the redoubtable Richer-Serizy to the gay street-singer Ange Pitou, who has told us the story of his "Day of Fructidor," were to be deported. Thus was Barras to be avenged on all his enemies.

This proscription-list, whereon perfidious hands had written the names of royalist conspirators next to those of good republicans, reads to us in the main like a roll of honour : Jordan, Siméon, Marbois, Mathieu Dumas (who, only the night before, had refused even for the sake of warding off the blow to violate the law), Laffont-Ladeval, an austere, but liberal-minded Protestant, Tronson-Ducoudray, who, even under the Terror, had been allowed to defend so many proscribed persons, Portalis, Suard, a former Permanent Secretary to the Academy, and with them, Barthélemy, who had signed the glorious Treaties of Basle, and Carnot, who had organized the victories of France : all that represented the worth, the virtue, and the honour of the country was there— and was to be deported : Barras was left to France !

Seventeen of these illustrious prisoners, shut into iron cages, and safely guarded by General Dutertre—himself condemned **Deputies sent** to the galleys on a former occasion for theft, **to Guiana.** arson, and murder—were to be conveyed to Rochefort (Victor Pierre has told us the well-attested story of their martyrdom) and thence sent to Guiana. Some of them were to die of the climate—a service their proscribers had expected from it. One of these victims of the "dry guillotine"—more odious, in some respects, than the other— Tronson-Ducoudray, protested to the very end that he had never desired anything but "an honest republic."

That was just what made him so dangerous a conspirator : for his aspirations would have led to the ruin of the reigning faction. Was not a deputy who had supported the Fructidor business heard to exclaim—somewhat too frankly—from the rostrum : "*We were walking betwixt the hangman's rope and the guillotine !*"

Military Commissions, set up in all directions, reassured the friends of Barras in the completest fashion. They sentenced (here again our readers should turn to the work of Victor Pierre) 160 persons to death, and sent 329 to Guiana, where 167 perished. But, as La Revellière writes, the glorious day of Fructidor passed "*without the spilling of a single drop of blood !*"

The population betrayed no sign of interest. La Revellière goes so far as to assert that he heard shouts of "*Long live La*

Revellière-Lépeaux ! " This puts a touch of burlesque into the tragedy. " A stupid indifference," we read, " such as used to be seen at Constantinople, when, every three months or so, some emperor was murdered or dethroned."

* * * * *

And this was one of the dangers to which the policy of the Directory was exposing the country. It was beginning to look
Consequences on violations of the Constitution, the Laws, and
of Fructidor. the Sovereignty of the People, as quite a natural thing. That soldiers should hold political deliberations in their camps, that generals should be invited to pronounce their decisions, that the most illustrious of them all should scornfully depute one of the men under his command to close the Chamber in which the representatives of the Nation were holding their debates, that grenadiers should be congratulated because they had betrayed the Legislative Body, that deputies should be deported without trial, and justice and liberty be suppressed—these were the things over which the Government expected the people to rejoice. It did not rejoice, but it grew accustomed to the sight of them. " *A fatal example !* " wrote La Revellière, later, when he himself had become the victim of another *coup d'état:* and Barras tells us, cynically: " *This violation really brought the compact of the Year III into dishonour and disrepute.*"

Even if the decimated Councils had been labouring to restore the throne, they should still have been sacred. But with very few exceptions, the members were not doing anything of the sort. We began our study of this point in the preconceived conviction that they had desired to restore the monarchy : our researches have convinced us that the dream of the majority was a loyal trial of a liberal republic.

"A fatal example," and consequences no less fatal : *the Government which had just triumphed had no legal status at all.*
The No undertaking against it could be regarded as
Constitution an act of conspiracy, if it took shape ; nor as an
ceases to exist. act of usurpation if it succeeded (as on the 19th Brumaire). The Councils had amnestied, approved, and supported violence, and, as a consequence, *the Directory was to be led into attempting fresh violence at the expense of those who had approved its first blow; the Councils were to do the same thing*

with regard to the Directory; and, finally, the promoters of the coup d'état of the 19th Brumaire were to strike at the whole régime. How could any man be accused of upsetting a Constitution which (as Siméon had declared just before he was dragged from his presidential chair) had ceased to exist ?

From that day forward the people's scorn for their deputies, for the folly of those who had succumbed, for the cowardice of those who had proscribed them, increased twofold. The representation of the Nation had become a Rump Parliament waiting for the coming of its Cromwell.

The suppression of the press—which " contributes to the suppression of public spirit," as M. Aulard says—and the ill-treatment of Parliament, both accustomed the public mind to the idea of a dictatorship. This dictatorship really existed already, since the Directory—in direct contravention of the Constitution—was about to assume the right of doing away with the election of functionaries. The germs of all this lay in the events of Fructidor. Cæsar's couch was prepared for him.

And that same Fructidor was bringing Cæsar himself. The army had pronounced itself at a sign from the *Imperator.* This *Imperator's* tremendous career of victory and conquest might have been checked if the day of Fructidor had not, as Sorel has so clearly proved, re-opened the way before him. The " faction " Fructidor overthrew was bent on a reasonable peace, the " faction " *that triumphed was in favour of eternal warfare.* That warfare was to be successful, thanks to the presence of the *Imperator,* and unsuccessful in his absence. Whether as victor or saviour Bonaparte was predestined to be borne in triumph.

The 18th Fructidor, on which day " the law became the sword," may have deferred the coming of Louis XVIII—but it created Napoleon I.

Same sources and works as for preceding chapter, and in addition :
SOURCES. Fauche-Borel, *Mémoires,* II, 1824 ; *Journal de Pichegru* (in Caudrillier, *op. cit.*) ; *Procès-verbal de la Séance du* 17–18 *Fructidor* (in Pierre, *op. cit.*) ; *Dossiers de Commissions Militaires* (idem, 185–449) ; Gohier, *Mémoires,* I, 1830 ; *Journal d'Ange Pitou* (in Savine, *Les Déportés de Fructidor,* 1910) ; Ballot, *Le Coup d'État de Fructidor, Documents,* 1906 ; Miot de Melito, *Mémoires,* 1856.
WORKS. Chevrier, *Joubert,* 1884.

CHAPTER XLIV

SOCIETY UNDER THE DIRECTORY

"Pleasure is the order of the day." The reign of Therezia.
The society entertained by Barras. Fashions. After the
sans-culottes, the *sans-chemises*. Pleasure resorts. Balls. The
"Gizzard" of Paris. Gambling. The theatres. "The soup-
pot upset." Home life destroyed. The ravages of divorce.
Vice. Morals and politics.

MEANWHILE pleasure reigned supreme. Stress must
be laid on this : for if the course of politics was
leading Cæsar to the place of power, the love of
pleasure, by enervating the whole of society, was giving it
over into his hands as surely as his victories in Italy, and
the violent measures of the Luxembourg.

There was a wild rush for pleasure. "Pleasure is the order
of the day," wrote Ch. de Constant, on the 27th Floréal of the
"Pleasure the   Year II : and his entertaining letters prove it.
Order of the   Ever since the 9th Thermidor pleasure had been
Day."   the order of the day, and it was to remain so until
the 19th Brumaire.

Of such things as politics and war, literature and the higher
forms of art, society thought but little.*

On the 21st Floréal of the Year IV an anarchist plot
whereby, so it was said, the whole of Paris was to have been

* We have not thought it well in this place to dwell more than
incidentally on literature and art under the Revolution. This study
will be taken up in our next volume dealing with the Consulate and
the Empire. A successful study of David and Girodet, Marie-Joseph
Chénier and Le Brun, Mme. de Staël and Geoffroy, Andrieux and
Legouvé, Talma and his rivals, first under the Revolution and then
under the Empire, would not be possible. From 1789 to 1815 letters,
arts, and sciences, were all evolved from the same spirit, and they
will find a more appropriate place in our consideration of the classicism
of the Empire.

handed over to the plunderers, was discovered. What did the newspapers say ? "An event : the alteration of the style of hairdressing affected by Mmes. Tallien and Bonaparte, For a considerable time they had been remarkable for the splendour of their black tresses, but these have had to give way, at last, before the mania for fair wigs."

In Pluviôse of the Year V we note royalist conspiracies to bring back the old form of government, the victory of Rivoli, the capitulation of Mantua. "There is a whisper that the fair wig is shortly to disappear. A Greek style of hairdressing, with double or triple rows of curls, is now in favour."

In Germinal there were elections, the outcome of which was certain to be a terrible conflict, even according to some opinions a restoration of the monarchy, and according to others the triumph of anarchy. Meanwhile the peace of Europe was being debated at Leoben. An important event is recorded : "the delicious Sophie" had appeared at Bagatelle wearing a "spencer."

In Messidor of the Year V, when the imminence of a *coup d'état* directed by the Councils against the Directory, or of a similar blow dealt by the Directory against the Councils, is evident ; "what occupies everybody" is "the great duel between the spencer hat and the turban hat." "A fan in the form of a canary bird's tail, embroidered with spangles," has been brought out : will it be a success ? The red buskin must make way for the green morocco slipper, but to show this off, "the right arm must be thrust, to one-third of its length, under the folds of the gown, so as to hold it up to the calf of the leg !"

On the 19th Fructidor the proscribed deputies were to be conducted to their convict prison : priests were to be snatched in their hundreds from the steps of the altar : the Nation had been gagged : but all this was of little moment, since the doors of three hundred ballrooms and thirty theatres still stood open !

* * * * *

"Not a soul thinks of anything now but eating and drinking, and enjoyment," thus writes Mallet du Pan in 1796.

Two years later he makes the same remark. In Messidor of the Year VII we read in one newspaper: "The thirst for pleasure, the stream of fashion, a succession of dinners, the luxury of their splendid furniture, and their mistresses, are the objects that chiefly employ the thoughts of the youth of Paris." What mattered it that Babeuf, or Louis XVIII, threatened to step into Barras' place? It was "Therezia I," "Her Most Serene Highness," who really held the sceptre.

The Reign of Mme. Tallien.

Her sceptre was a fool's bauble, her court a saraband. Barras, who had proclaimed her "dictator of beauty," had taken her from her "cottage at Chaillot"—she was about to divorce Tallien—and installed her queen of the Luxembourg. And, indeed, the fascinating jade was far less immoral than the profligate rake with whom she now consorted.

She must have been a really enchanting woman. Let our readers turn to the exquisite portrait Ch. de Constant—more inclined, generally, to severity than to enthusiasm—drew of her on June 4, 1796: let them even consult Barras himself, who rarely shows much mercy to his former loves, and Lacretelle, who was proscribed by the Luxembourg, and Norvins, so often harsh, and Frénilly, who talks so unceremoniously about "la Beauharnais," and Marmont, the young soldier, and Mme. de Chastenay, another pretty woman: they all use the same word, fascination.

Not beautiful, but charming, with an instinctive desire to fascinate. And she succeeded. All through four years of the blackest misery her famous "red coach" passed up and down, the only one in Paris that escaped insult. And, indeed, she bestowed royal alms upon the populace: she never shut herself up in the Luxembourg; she showed herself, half-naked, in the public places of the city: she was a Phryne who did not keep her charms for the Areopagus alone, but revealed them to the whole Agora. The populace which had hooted "that demirep," the Citoyenne Hamelin, when she walked, stripped to the waist, from the Luxembourg to the Champs Elysées, never hooted Therezia Tallien. Her soft eyes held government, society, and populace in captivity.

She it was who set the fashions. She desired to do honour

to the Sultan's envoy : at once turbans leapt into vogue ; and then cashmere shawls, because Barras, one fine day, had seized a bale of Indian merchandise. Black hair was popular, and no other tint, as long as she showed her own raven tresses : but when the fancy took her to be golden-haired, fair wigs reigned from that day forth.

She did the honours of the Luxembourg. Barras was the only Director who received company. That company was mixed : a huge demi-monde. Therezia shone there, and General Bonaparte, and Juliette Récamier too; Delescluze saw "that Raphael Madonna," as Thibaudeau called her, sitting on Barras' left, while Therezia throned it on his right. This looks as if the " ermine" enjoyed picking her way in the mud. Now and then Mme. de Staël would dine at the Luxembourg : but before long her entertainers found their vehement friend a little in their way. All the rest were small fry, which had followed Mme. Tallien from the " cottage " to the palace : Mmes. de Mailly-Château-Renaud, Regnault (de Saint-Jean-d'Angély), Hainguerlot, Hamelin, de Krudner, de Navailles, Rovère, Jouberthon, a whole band of *merveilleuses*, the wives of *émigrés* and regicides, generals and deputies and contractors, Creoles brought in by Joséphine, foreigners uprooted from their own countries, such as Mme. Visconti from Italy, and Mme. Grant from Hindustan. Mme. Grant, " *la belle et la bête* in one," who owed her introduction to Talleyrand, actresses, such as Guimard and Arnould, and a Marquise de Noailles too, and a hundred more, from every corner of the horizon, Faubourg Saint-Germain, Théâtre-Français, the upper world of Finance, the Indies—Cosmopolis, in short : all these were to be met in Barras' rooms. But Mme. Barras, the only woman in whom Barras roused no interest at all, was never seen in Paris.

Military men were few and far between ; they were all busy elsewhere. The greater number of the men were either *parvenus* of the financial world or men who were making their fortunes there. " The young men who have taken the places of the Marquises and the pages of old days," we read on June 25, 1796, " are contractors and speculators." The taste for speculation having become general (to such a point, we are

(margin note: Society round Barras.)

assured, that all the ladies trafficked in sugar, and coffee, and land, and *assignats*), the great speculators were naturally the princes of the situation : Vanderberghe, Séguin, Hainguerlot (who had supplied the stores for the " fourteen armies " and had made more than fourteen millions out of the transaction), Perregaux, a sort of official banker to the Government, Delessert, Hottinguer, the Michel brothers, the Enfantin brothers, and, soaring above them all, the " Bonaparte of finance," Ouvrard (owner of Raincy, Marly, Luciennes, and other properties), the Marquis of Carabas of the Directory.

Into this dubious assemblage of " goddesses " and " Turcarets " came a sprinkling of nobles hungering for amusement. How often were the sons of the guillotined seen dancing with the daughters of the men who had guillotined their parents ! Thus a sort of feverish excitement reigned in this chaotic, ill-composed society, consisting as to the great majority of its members, of persons risen to sudden fortune ; without tact, without taste, bent on a swift enjoyment of wealth that had been swiftly won. Can our readers wonder that the sovereign of this kingdom should have been Therezia Cabarrus, daughter of a foreign banker, to be known, at different epochs, as Marquise de Fontenoy, Citizeness Tallien, Princesse de Chimay—herself the very incarnation of the society she ruled ?

*   *   *   *   *

Fashions were most eccentric. Our readers should turn over Bosio's drawings, and the leaves of the *Almanach de Gottingue :* the modes changed every three months ; scarves and turbans were soon cast aside, buskin and slippers too. Louise Fusil describes one moment of these fluctuating styles : " Frontlets, diadems, bracelets ' *à la Cléopâtre*,' belts with an antique clasp, Cashmere shawls draped as cloaks, or gold embroidered cloth mantles thrown over one shoulder ; sandals with diamond fastenings " ; this is the dress worn by " reasonable women." The " unreasonable " women hardly wear any clothes at all : they are the celebrated " *sans-chemises* " : " the arms and bosom bare, with a gauze skirt and flesh-coloured drawers beneath it "—this was the costume called " *à la sauvage* "—" circlets set with diamonds

Fashions : the " Sans-chemises."

549

round the legs and thighs." The antique was all the fashion. David, now back in his studio, and his pupils, were filling this new society with Greeks and Romans. Here were goddesses, indeed, in flesh and blood! Gowns " à la Flore," and tunics " à la Cérès," which came, in the end, to their wearers being very nearly naked. " You would only have had to take very little off them to make them just like the Venus de' Medici." And yet the dressmakers were kings ; they were expected to combine the maximum of elegance with the minimum of material. The shoemakers were kings too, and so were the hairdressers, who spoke of themselves as "artists in hairdressing." And they were kept busy, these " Michael Angelos ! " Mme. Tallien had five-and-twenty wigs of golden hair, and all the other ladies followed suit. The reign of the *sans-culottes* had been followed by the reign of the *sans-chemises.*

The belles made their way down from the Luxembourg to the public gardens. All Paris was bent on amusement. Bagatelle, Pleasure Tivoli, Frascati, the Elysée-Bourbon, the hamlet of Resorts. Chantilly, were so many battlefields of fashion and gaiety. And there were other resorts, the gardens of Marbœuf, Paphos, Idalia and Mousseaux. Tivoli was particularly in favour on account of Ruggieri's fireworks : " for a crown, you can see the most brilliant entertainment in all Europe twice a week." " The number of persons present at the re-opening of the Tivoli entertainments is reckoned at 12,000, and the value of the receipts at 29,000 *livres*," writes the *Publiciste* on the 24th Prairial of the Year VI. But then the Pavillon de Hanovre began to send up rockets : and Franconi opened his circus in the garden of the Capucines, Franconi, the gold-laced equestrian, just the man to please this society of Byzantine tastes, who soon pulled down the receipts of Ruggieri, " that pyrotechnist of genius." And how many other attractions, too ! At the Richelieu Ball, " an ark of transparent gowns," " we behold," writes Mercier in 1797, " a hundred perfumed goddesses crowned with roses." And they were not courtesans, but the wives of deputies—legitimate or irregular—of Ministers, of Directors. These ladies appeared at Ranelagh, too, where Victor de Broglie had his first sight of Mme. Tallien, in her tunic of rose-coloured gauze, split up on one side, her bare feet blazing with jewelled rings : and at Frascati's they were to be seen in the pale yellow room relieved with bronze-green, painted by Debucourt. When the public taste, jaded by so many delights, began to flag, the ingenious Piconet revived it, at the Jardins d'Idalie, by *tableaux vivants* which beggar description.

All these things were passionately enjoyed, but dancing above all. It went on everywhere ; there were 300 public balls : it became a mania : there was dancing on the Place de Grève, where the guillotine had so lately stood : the nights were given to dance, the days to excursions in the woods. The drive to Longchamp had come back into fashion : amidst 2000 carriages," writes one enthusiastic journalist, " Mmes. Tallien and Récamier may be seen shining in the crowd, like gentle beams that fall upon the night."

There was a great deal of eating, too—we mean among people who could afford to pay 1248 *livres* for a leg of mutton. It The "Gizzard" was in 1795 that the restaurant-keeper, who of Paris. serves up good food and good wine to his customers, in rooms blazing with looking-glasses and gilding, made his first appearance : " the *pot-au-feu* has been upset," writes a contemporary : home-life had been forsaken, everybody dined at the Palais-Royal now : the men who had been cooks in the old families had become eating-house keepers : Vatel's name was Véry now, or Beauvilliers, or Méot, " the great Méot," as one of his clients calls him, with a touch of emotion. Good eating was studied. These were the days when Brillat-Savarin meditated and Grimod de la Reynière wrote. One greeted the reappearance of the truffle, " the diamond of the table," the other joyously hailed the close of a boorish Revolution, in the course of which " even the recipe for making a fricassee of chicken had been very nearly lost." And Grimod's heart was filled with the sincerest admiration for the splendid restoration of the Years IV and V. " The hearts of most wealthy Parisians," he writes, " have turned into gizzards ! " This was touching praise !

At the Palais-Royal there was play, too, and high play, for " the Citoyenne Bentabole, wife of a deputy, lost two millions on a single card," which leads one to the reflection that her

husband cannot always have contented himself with his parliamentary salary.

We need hardly say that all the thirty-two theatres were
crowded. "Everything in them," says a police-report,
"breathes ease and gaiety, pleasure and delight."
The Theatres. There was a passionate love of the actor's art:
for, besides the public theatres, there were two hundred others
in which private theatricals were given. And what models
there were for the amateur to copy !

Never did such a company exist: Comtat, Raucourt,
Duchesnois, Julie Talma, Lange, Mars, Montansiei ! Talma,
who had dabbled in Jacobinism, was not left long in disgrace,
and "Molé enchants" all. Vestris, too, was carrying off
hearts on the tips of his toes. Though "women are noticing,
with sorrow, that Michu (of the Opéra-Comique) is ageing
visibly," the "incomparable Lays," "the god of song," was
still causing even his enemies to gape with wonder. But the
greatest mania of all was for Garat, who had brought ballads
into fashion, and sang them "adorably." These theatres,
whose performers, whether they declaimed, or sang, or danced,
were every one of them "beloved beings," put the finishing
touch to a town so delightful that no foreigner, as we read
under the date of Brumaire of the Year V, "can help confessing
Paris to be the first city in Europe ! "

*   *   *   *   *

What astonished the foreigner most of all (we have his
letters) was the prevailing looseness of manners. The family
Ravages of the had been destroyed. Under the old *régime* it
Divorce Law. had been the very foundation of society. The
abolition of the law of primogeniture, and still more the
triumph of the spirit of criticism, had emancipated sons and
daughters alike. "When the Revolution cut off Louis XVI's
head," says Balzac's Duc de Chaulieu, "it cut off the
head of every father of a family in France." Yet Napoleon
had restored order in the family when the words were put into
Chaulieu's mouth. Under the Directory parents and children
were living in a sort of familiar comradeship which stupefied
the returned *émigrés* more than any other social change.
But, indeed, fathers and sons saw little of each other. Home

552

life had gone to pieces. The decree of September 20, 1792 which established divorce, and was carried still further by the Convention in 1794, had borne fruits within four years of which the Legislature itself had never dreamt : an immediate divorce could be pronounced on the score of incompatibility of temper, to come into force within a year at farthest, if either of the couple should refuse to separate before that period had elapsed. On the 28th Floréal of the Year II, authority was given to any husband or wife to break the bond and re-marry, if his or her partner had been absent for six months, so that "no exception having been made in the case of the de-fenders of the country" any soldier might come back from Italy, covered with glory, and find a new husband installed in his home.

There had been a rush for divorce : by the end of 1793—fifteen months after the passing of the decree—5994 divorces had been granted in Paris. We refer our readers to Sagnac for an explanation of the law, and to Goncourt, for its con-sequences. Under the Directory we see women passed from hand to hand by a legal process. What was the fate of the children born of these successive unions ? Some people got rid of them : the number of foundlings in the Year V rose to 4000 in Paris and to 44,000 in the other departments. When the parents kept the children a tragi-comical confusion was the result. A man would marry several sisters, one after the other : one citizen presented a petition to the Five Hundred for leave to marry the mother of the two wives he had already possessed. So great was the abuse, and so demoralizing the consequences, that the Five Hundred were roused to inquiry : in Nivôse of the Year V a report was read from the rostrum of such a nature that one knows not whether to laugh or cry over it : but they failed to discover any remedy. The family was dissolved. Yet there was a pompous celebration on the 10th Floréal of the *Festival of Marriage* and another of the *Festival of Filial Piety* on 16th Pluviôse. A real farce !

At that moment of unparalleled perversion death itself was regarded with indifference, to say the least of it. Ch. de Constant was astonished by the furtive way in which the dead were buried. In France, where our strongest reverence has always been our reverence for our dead, death seemed to have lost all claim to respect and even to attention.

We must cast a glance, now, at the lower deeps of these depths. Mallet du Pan, a declared enemy of the Revolution, **Vice and** may be suspect when he talks of " Sodom and **Perversity.** Gomorrah," and Ch. de Constant, bred on the Lake of Geneva, may perhaps be charged with over-sensitive Puritanism. But Picquenard, the Police Commissary, is an authority of a very different kind, and he makes a comment covering ten pages on the following statement: " Nobody can form any idea of the public depravation ": he proceeds on the 5th Prairial, to give Merlin of Douai a picture of the condition of morals of such a nature that we are quite unable to echo it even in milder terms. The newspapers of the time (which can hardly be taxed with Puritanism) complained that obscene books, " the favourite reading of our young girls," were spreading strange vices abroad. One report, dated Prairial of the Year VII, states the nature of these vices in terms so brutal that it would be impossible even to translate them. All came to the same conclusion. " There are no longer any morals."

    *   *   *   *   *

" The royalists smile on this depravation : they feel how much the spirit of dissolution that is entering into every class **Morals and** of society is doing to degrade the republican **Politics.** spirit. . . . Catholics are filled with sorrow for the fate of religion, which, persecuted as it is, can no longer impose a healthy check on all these misdeeds." In these words the police official underlines a feature which brings us back from morals to politics.

This worn-out society itself realized that it was hurrying towards the abyss. And the fierceness with which it threw itself into its amusements inevitably doomed it to occasional days of the most cruel weariness. There was a vague longing for the reconstitution of the fast disappearing family. Those (in the upper classes) who had been votaries of " philosophy " were beginning to ask themselves whether this banishment of the Deity from society had not been too swiftly done. Some of them called out for strong legislation. " *Do we need a God for this great work ? "* inquires Commissary Picquenard, *" No ! we only need wise republican institutions."*

But nobody believed now in wise republican institutions, seeing that Barras, seated on the ruins of the Constitution, still held sway at the Luxembourg.

So the cure had to be sought elsewhere, outside these republican institutions.

SOURCES. Works already quoted by Frénilly, Norvins (II), Ch. de Constant, Aulard (*Paris* . . . passim), Madame de Chastenay, Louise Fusil, Mallet junior in Malouet (II), Miot de Melito.—Madame de Rémusat, *Mémoires*, 1873 ; Duchesse d'Abrantès, *Mémoires*, I, 1834, and *Les Salons de Paris* ; *Almanach de Gottingue* ; Mercier, *Almanach des Gens de Bien*, 1798 ; Grimod de la Reynière, *Manuel des Amphitrions*, 1808 ; Mercier, *Tableaux de Paris* ; Piquenard, *Rapport* (Rev. Retr., VIII) ; Brazier, *Chronique des petits Théâtres*, 1799.

WORKS. Those already quoted by Nauroy, Turquan, Cabanès (*Névrose*), Goncourt, Lacour (*Le Grand Monde*), Welschinger (*Théâtres*).— David, *David*, 1879 ; Delécluze, *David*, 1855, Henriot, *Madame Récamier*, 1904 ; Sorel, *Madame de Staël*, 1898 ; Lacroix (*Le Bibliophile Jacob*), *Le Directoire*, 1884 ; Comte Fleury, *Grandes Dames de la Révolution*, 1900 ; *La Mode pendant la Révolution* (Rev. Retr., IV) ; Auteville, *Le Divorce pendant la Révolution (Rev. Retr.*, II) ; Renouvier, *Histoire de l'Art pendant la Révolution*, 1883.

CHAPTER XLV

BONAPARTE AND THE DIRECTORY

September 1797—May 1798

" Power by escalade." The new Directors, Merlin and François
The rush for place. The Terror after Fructidor. The bankruptcy of the *Two-Thirds*. The rupture between the victors of
Fructidor. Bonaparte at Udine. Campo-Formio (25th Vendémiaire, Year VI). Bonaparte's enormous popularity. Mombello,
words of peace. Bonaparte reaches Paris. His reception at
the Luxembourg. Bonaparte at the Institute. He desires to
go abroad. The Directory revolutionizes Italy. Bonaparte
leaves for Egypt.

"**L**ET *us banish these absurd theories of pretended principles
and stupid appeals to the Constitution !* " Thus, like the
bear in La Fontaine's fable, did Bailleul, in the name of
the Fructidor Directory, crush the fly on the head of the system
he championed with a paving stone ! Words such as these
Merlin and clearly prophesied the fact that everything, as
François Mme. de Chastenay put it, was about to "take
Directors. on a character of violence and conquest."

The advanced guard of the Jacobins having, as the same
lady says, " *seized power by escalade,*" began by exacting
payment for services rendered. On the day, not far distant,
when the Directory was to grow weary of their demands, and
refuse to satisfy them, the struggle between the victors of
Fructidor was to begin, a duel in two acts, that of Floréal,
Year VI, and that of Prairial, Year VII.

"Hitherto," writes one of their number, Joseph Fouché,
"the *patriots* had always walked on thorns : it was high time
for the tree of liberty to bear sweeter fruit for those who were
to gather and enjoy it." One never knows whether this Fouché
is serious or not.

556

BONAPARTE AND THE DIRECTORY

The finest fruits were forthwith gathered by Merlin and François of Neufchâteau. To the mortal vexation of Talleyrand, who had offered himself and had been rejected (" notwithstanding the intrigues of both sexes," says Barras) they were appointed Directors.

François was an intellectual, the author of a certain " *Paméla ou la Vertu*," which had procured his admission to the Institute : his morals were lamentable ; he preached virtue on the boards, but practised it very little behind the scenes : he was a libertine, but with philosophic leanings, for which he was welcomed by La Revellière : his colleagues soon found him so dull that their one desire was to get rid of him as quickly as they might, perhaps by hastening fate.

Merlin was more remarkable, too remarkable. La Revellière and Barras both agree in giving us a hideous picture of him : his powers were above the average, but there was " something savage " in his eyes and his voice : he was a lawyer, and so well versed in laws that he always had one ready wherewith to stifle equity. The 18th Fructidor had created the exceptional state of government that suited this Cæsarian jurist (who was to serve as Attorney-General under Napoleon I), and he stood out for a moment "the most powerful (writes one of his enemies), as he was the most hated and hateful of men."

The Directors once appointed (we might tell an amusing tale of this rush for place, drawn from the various documents in our hands), they dealt out posts and favours to their friends and accomplices. " A kindly dew," writes one who profited by it, "of under-secretaryships, portfolios, commissariats, legations, and embassies."

* * * * *

Though Paris had remained indifferent, some of the departments had betrayed an inclination to rebel against the proscription of their elected representatives : this occurred in the Allier for instance. " It will feel the lash," wrote Bernadotte to Bonaparte on the 24th, " eight thousand men are marching into that neighbourhood from all over France." The departments thought the Terror was to be let loose on them again : they held their peace. In Paris the only symptoms of opposition were a

The post-Fructidorian Terror.

few demonstrations in the theatres and the medical and other professional schools. All the administrative bodies and tribunals had undergone a weeding process, and the dread of the new " judges " was great.

The theatre (the press had already been muzzled) was carefully censored in its turn : nothing but " the oracles of morality, the sacred maxims of philosophy, and the great examples of virtue " were to be permitted on the stage—this was the style of François of Neufchâteau: *Pamela, ou la Vertu,* and *Le Dixhuit Fructidor,* which showed Augereau leading the assault on a pasteboard Tuileries, were soon to be the only plays the authorities would tolerate.

Finally, a real Terror was organized against the nobles and the priests. Any *émigrés* on whom the Government laid its hands were shot without mercy. Every now and then a volley rang out over the plain of Grenelle : " *Nature groans, but the law speaks !* " as the semi-official communications in the press put it. And a curious campaign was opened to procure the proscription of any *former noble* ; the man who was to become Comte Boulay de la Meurthe, and Régnier, the future Duc de Massa, were both particularly violent in their attacks on the bearers of any title of nobility. No *former noble* was to enjoy the rights of citizenship.

But, above and beyond all, the Catholics suffered cruel treatment : this was inevitable, since that one so-called attempt at a " Roman " restoration had driven La Revellière-Lépeaux, the great protector of Theophilanthropy, and the Abbé Grégoire, intent on the resurrection of schism, and Germaine de Staël, who believed Protestantism to be the only " means of destroying the Catholic religion," into the arms of the sceptic Barras.

Disappointment was in store for every one of them. Germaine de Staël and Grégoire were to find out to their sorrow that the present crusade was directed against Christianity of every sort. And La Revellière-Lépeaux was to endure the bitterest mortifications. The *Theophilanthropists* were everywhere greeted with contumely. By Brumaire of the Year VI this quasi-State religion (the State supplied it with churches and with funds), had become bankrupt. It was the laughing-stock of the Halles, so one report tells us : " In everything the people say against it," this report goes on, "*we notice a scarcely natural interest in the Catholic religion.*" On the 1st Vendémiaire of the Year VI, when La Revellière offered up a "prayer to the Author of Nature " in the presence of "an immense assemblage " on the Champ-de-Mars, the sight of the tall hump-backed priest cast final ridicule upon his adherents : Robespierre had at least known how to look the pontiff.

"*A scarcely natural interest in Catholicism!*" This had to be stifled forthwith ! Clause 24 of the Law of Fructidor **Deportation** had invested the Directors with the power of **of Priests.** arbitrary arrest, for very often the warrant that sent a priest to the galleys simply bore the words " a man of abominable morals." In the course of the first three months of the Year VI, 464 priests were deported in this fashion, 431 in the next three, 185 in the next, and 386 in the last : 1448 *in a single year, without counting the 8235 priests seized in the Belgian departments.* And even then the authorities complained that they were prevented from laying their hands on more by the devotion of "blind agriculturists." Everywhere, indeed, the peasants hid their clergy : in Messidor of the Year VI the Directory expressed its indignation at the way in which the inhabitants of the country sheltered the priests, " though they are a more formidable scourge than any robbers or murderers."

Those who were not shot were sent to the convict prisons, and there they died, almost all of them : out of one hundred and ninety-three ecclesiastics, conveyed to Guiana on board the *Decade,* only thirty-nine had escaped the fever of the country twenty-one months later.

And this crusade, as we have already said, was frankly anti-Christian. François of Neufchâteau ordered the school-masters to teach their pupils "rationalism," and noted the failure of the Constitutional Church with a considerable amount of satisfaction. " Grégoire the First of Paris " was as roughly handled by the Jacobin journalists as " Pius the Last of Rome." Priests who had taken the oath were insulted as constantly as those who had refused to take it, and so were the " former nuns," out of whose hands the education of the " young citizenesses," whom they would have turned into " bigots," had to be taken at once !

THE FRENCH REVOLUTION

To sum it up, the 18th Fructidor had borne all the fruits expected of it : deputies had been proscribed, the nobles stripped of their rights, the press reduced to servitude, the theatre muzzled by the censor, the departments terrorized, the priests deported, the *émigrés* shot down : it was neither more nor less than a hypocritical Terror, decked out with formulas in the manner of François of Neufchâteau.

*   *   *   *   *

The *coup d'état* had also borne fruit for its supporters, as we have seen ; but their agreement as to the disposal of the spoils "Bankruptcy did not last two months. The Directory, how-of the ever, took advantage of the temporary lull to Two-thirds." snatch from the " regenerated " Legislative Body that which the Councils had refused just before Fructidor to grant : *the bankruptcy of the Two-thirds.*

The financial situation was growing terrible : nobody was paid, neither troops nor officials, and annuitants and holders of State securities only very irregularly. But, irregular as these payments were, the debt pressed heavily upon the impoverished State. As revolutionary methods were now the order of the day, the hour had apparently arrived for reducing the amount of this debt by a very simple process. In future the Government's creditors were to receive interest on one-third of their capital : the other two-thirds were to be paid off. All this was regular enough. But the two-thirds were to be paid off in Treasury bonds, representing *territorial drafts.* Now the value of these drafts had dropped to zero. This simply amounted to hypocritical bankruptcy. Ramel would never have dared to suggest such a thing to the deputies of the Assembly of the Year V : yet the proposal had been drawn up beforehand, for it was on the 19th Fructidor that the " purified " Councils were invited (the expression has a special flavour of its own) " to regenerate the finances."

The Councils agreed to everything : the proposal, which was passed by the Five Hundred on the next complementary day,* was transformed into law by the Ancients on the 9th

* Days inserted here and there in the Republican Calendar, which reckoned the days by tens (*Décadi*, &c.), to complete the necessary number of days in the year.

Vendémiaire. On the very morrow bankruptcy had become an evident fact : the drafts had fallen to one per cent. of their face value ; the man who owned enough to bring him in 300 *livres* a year could only get 110 *livres*. The Legislative Body must have been singularly cowed before it thus betrayed the interests of a whole body of its electors.

But people were beginning to say—and Floréal, following on the heels of Fructidor, was soon to prove it true—that in France, now there was in the last resort, but one elector, *the great elector, the Government.*

* * * * *

Meanwhile a whole group of the Left was breaking into revolt. Once the financial law was voted the Directory **Rupture** seemed less inclined to satisfy the demands of **between the** those who had stood by it in the Fructidor **Fructidorians.** business : the Directors, and Reubell more especially, were accused of keeping all the good things for their own relations ; they were charged with " reaction," nay more, with " corruption."

This new campaign, inaugurated in Brumaire of the Year VI, was moral in its tendency. The Jacobin opposition began to take on puritanic airs. The picture of current morals which we have purposely laid before our readers will convince us the game was a promising one, and enable us to guess why they chose to play it. Though the winter promised to be gay enough at the Tivoli, at Ranelagh, and at the Luxembourg, it threatened to be cruel in the Faubourgs. No work to be had, and poverty on the increase everywhere. The owners of small incomes, ruined by the law just passed, were to swell the ranks of the starving population. From that time forward the unpopularity of the "newly rich," all of them held to be "swindlers" and "rotten fellows," increased rapidly. But who were the protectors of these men ? The Luxembourg : Barras was another corrupt man, Reubell was a thorough thief, Merlin had made millions out of the Revolution. Naturally enough the demagogues began their secret operations. The Directory, too, was to be " *regenerated !* "

On the 14th Brumaire General Marbot opened hostilities : from the rostrum he painted an alarming picture of existing morals, public and governmental: if the Councils did not raise themselves above the level of "this ocean of corruption" the Nation would certainly smite them with the "*moral proscription*" it was applying to the Luxembourg! The Constitutional Club, which was now ruled by the partisans of extreme measures, followed Marbot's lead. It attacked the Directors. They (quite wrongly, as we shall see) fancied it would be easy to stifle the dangerous movement in its birth. They closed the Club: the rupture became more obvious. But the Government faced the struggle with a light heart: for a moment the peace of Campo Formio had won it the indulgence of the public, a pale reflection of Bonaparte's transcendent popularity.

*　　*　　*　　*　　*

Yet "the General" (was there any other general?) had concluded that peace in spite of the Directors. They would have been quite content to go on making perpetual war; we know why. At this moment they feared the troops more than ever. What would the soldiers do once peace was restored? "Plant their cabbages? But they must have cabbages to plant!" said Barras. This was the reason why Leoben, in the Directors' eyes, was no more than an armistice; though they had treated with the English at Lille, and with the Czar Paul (who had seemed inclined to attack us) at Berlin, they had put very little heart into their negotiations.

The Directory opposed to Peace.

The *coup d'état* which had overthrown Barthélemy, had ensured the triumph of the party in favour of "the natural frontiers," a popular and grandiloquent expression beneath which lay an imperialism that scorned all limits and a most warlike policy. And it had likewise puffed up the Directors, as though it had been the Continent of Europe that Augereau had defeated round the fountain of the Tuileries.

They broke off the negotiations at Lille and Berlin, and they had meant to put an end to those Bonaparte was carrying on with Austria.

But Bonaparte was resolved on peace, because what he was now aiming at was power. The man who should give peace, a glorious peace, of course, to France would be the most

562

popular of men. He had no intention of returning, to use the phraseology of his time, till he could bring back the laurel-branch of peace bound up with the palms of victory. When the order to break off the negotiations reached him, he pretended to believe the Directory " doubted his virtue," and informed them he was coming back to " *recruit his strength amidst the mass of his fellow citizens.*" In their fright the Directors gave him a free hand. The letter they dispatched to him from the Luxembourg on 8th Vendémiaire breathed such terrified submission that its base humility must have given him the measure of his own power.

He pushed on his negotiations. They opened formally at Udine, where Cobenzl arrived on September 27 (5th Vendé-miaire), armed with full powers from the Austrian Government. And after the now celebrated discussion, which proved Bonaparte's genius to be as great in diplomacy as in battle, had lasted a fortnight, the famous treaty of October 17, 1797 (25th Vendémiaire of the Year VI), was signed at midnight, in the little village of Campo Formio, hard by Udine, and the peace of the Continent temporarily insured.

The Peace of Campo Formio.

This treaty set the seal of Europe on the unprecedented greatness of the power of France. Austria relinquished Belgium (long since annexed to France), and Lombardy, which, with the addition of the Valteline, snatched from the Grisons, and the territories taken from the Pope, the Duke of Modena, and the Venetian Republic, was to be formed into a *Cisalpine Republic*, under the close protectorate of France. Unhappy Venice, and the Venetian territories bounded by the Adige, were handed over to Austria. In consideration of certain indemnities, to be decided by a Congress to assemble at *Rastadt*, the greater part of the left bank of the Rhine was to remain in French hands.

This last clause, indeed, was heavy with threatened storm and mental reservations. Would the Holy Empire consent to be cut in pieces ? Austria reckoned on a conflict arising out of this question. It was her full intention to use this semblance of peace for the purpose of restoring the strength of her armies. England, in the same expectation, was filling up her war-chests at that very moment by every sacrifice she could devise. This peace could only be a temporary peace. It may have been with this mental reservation that the Directors agreed to countersign it, which they did on October 26 (4th Brumaire).

* * * * *

Great joy reigned all over France. A score of police reports, a hundred newspaper articles, numerous contemporary letters, show us a nation " *drunk with happiness.*" In vain did the inspired press attribute the merit of this peace to the Fructidor Directors. " *On every side,*" we read, " *the praises of General Bonaparte resound.*" It was a tremendous explosion of enthusiasm and affection. From the remotest country places (we have some rough notes written by peasants) to the Paris Faubourgs, watched by the attentive eye of the police, it ran like a lighted train of gunpowder. The French nation was in a pitiful strait : a generous-hearted people, it loves to love, and for seven whole years it had been cut off from love, and had known naught but fear and hatred. It loved Bonaparte for being, very literally " *amiable* "—lovable. And, as in the case of all great affections, it made itself an ideal picture of the hero who had brought it peace, which certain of his very genuine characteristics seemed really to justify and strengthen. The affection of the country crowned him with an aureole of all the virtues, valour, wisdom, magnanimity.

Astounding Popularity of Bonaparte.

At Mombello, where for three months " the General " had held a real court, he had received many Frenchmen, and talked a great deal in their presence. His remarks had gained currency. The things he said were very different from those France had been hearing for years : *peace for men's consciences ;* let every man follow the form of religion he prefers without trying to render it oppressive ; *peace for their interests :* let every man enjoy what he owns, free from disturbance, taxation, and vexation. *Union for the common good, forgetfulness of quarrels, vigour in government, but moderation in laws, liberty, and order.* And on November 11 (20th Brumaire) fearing, perhaps, he had not made himself heard enough, he condensed his doctrines into a fraternal proclamation addressed to the sister Republics

564

of Italy, the Ligurian and the Cisalpine, but really intended for France.

Further, he was not to be considered an advocate of *militarism*. " It is a great misfortune," he wrote, " that a nation numbering thirty millions of inhabitants, and in the eighteenth century, should be forced to have recourse to bayonets to save the country." The fact that this student of Machiavelli had himself sent out the bayonets on the eve of Fructidor had slipped everybody's memory. Quivering with fond emotion his hearers listened to his wise and moderate words.

The Directory alone was uneasy. It tried to keep the troublesome fellow away by appointing him plenipotentiary at Rastadt. But Paris was set on beholding its god. The Directors were forced to send for him. Perhaps, indeed, if they " *officialized* " him, they might contrive to compromise him as well. And Barras had a vague hope that he might find, unchanged, his " creature " of Vendémiaire Year IV. Vendémiaire of the Year IV ?—That was a century ago !

*　　*　　*　　*　　*

He came.

Under a shower of adulation and regret he had left Italy, Bonaparte made his triumphant way through Switzerland, arrives in and kept the German envoys at Rastadt, for Paris. several weeks, in alternate throes of alarm and admiration.

Suddenly the news spread that he had reached Paris and gone to " his wife's house." In a fever of eager curiosity Paris hurried to gaze upon him in the Rue de la Victoire. But he, who had no intention of wearing out the sympathy of the public, was determined not to gratify its curiosity.

Had he any definite plan ? Perhaps he hoped, as all men believed he did, to enter the Directory, though he had not reached the legal age (which was forty, and he was only twenty-eight). Once there he would soon bring his colleagues to heel. He mentioned the project to a few confidential friends. Barras slily put obstacles in the way. On the whole the General concluded that " the pear was not yet ripe." That fact being clear, it became difficult for him to stay in Paris : he might

compromise himself. " The ground seemed to burn his feet,"
writes La Revellière : his words exactly describe the situation.
He sought a means of escape, the splendour of his position
made it all the more difficult. " If I cannot be master I will
leave France," he said again. Meanwhile, as he could not rise
and was determined not to fall, he held carefully aloof.

He shut himself up, and by so doing raised public curiosity
to fever pitch. The populace, ever ready to look tenderly on
the object of its fondness, admired his attitude as a proof of
his engaging modesty.

On the 10th Frimaire he was solemnly received by the
Directors. Paris came in its thousands to the Rue de Tournon
to see his entry into the Luxembourg, and " society " crowded
the courtyards and hailed him with loud acclamations. " Crazy
enthusiasm," a foreign witness called it.

" Here he comes ! " In his plain uniform, " pale under his
long black hair," he was the Bonaparte Pierre Guérin painted
in 1797 : the searching eye, imperious nose,
and compressed lips, free as yet from the sulky
expression of later years, the chin strong and
obstinate, the forehead high beneath the " dishevelled " locks. Hardly any embroideries about him : in the
face of all those Directors, Ministers, and deputies, decked with
feathers, gold lace, silks, and satins, his scorn of show stood out,
deliberately expressed ; his bearing was stiff and even awkward :
but every gesture and every look betrayed a formidable
strength of will.

Bonaparte received at the Luxembourg.

So keen was the impression he produced that a " religious
silence," a kind of stupefaction, reigned for an instant. It
was soon broken by a roar of enthusiastic plaudits.

Barras was in the chair : he boasts of the cleverness displayed
in his harangue : to us it seems a tissue of platitudes mingled
with hypocritical irony. Some day, perhaps, said the Director,
they might have to appeal to the hero and " snatch him from his
studious retirement." Bonaparte replied without apparent
dexterity in a " rough and jerky " voice. One sentence only
attracted notice : " *When the happiness of the people shall have
been ensured by better organic laws. . . .*" With a pensive look
Talleyrand turned to Barras : " *There is a future in that,*" he

said. The ex-bishop was already preparing his own place in that future : for when he gave an entertainment in the General's honour, to which " two hundred of the prettiest and most richly attired women " of Paris crowded, the only one to whom the host paid gallant compliments was the " General's wife."

But that gay evening was, and remained, an exception : Bonaparte refused all invitations ; yet the " hero " was seen **Bonaparte at** in the house of François of Neufchâteau, where **the Institute.** he won the hearts of all the members of the Institute, flattering and dazzling Lagrange, Laplace, Sieyès, Chénier, Daunou, and David. He desired to be a member himself. " A great honour for the Institute," writes the *Ami des Lois* on the 10th Nivôse. He read some memoranda before the *Section of Mechanics, in the Science Class.* On the 15th Germinal he was present at the " meeting of the five classes " : he was welcomed by Andrieux, and " three times over he was applauded with transports of enthusiasm." These " intellectuals " were almost the only people with whom the General consorted— and we shall note the consequences of the incident at a later date.

To all the rest of humanity he continued invisible. Noticed one evening in a box at the Théâtre des Arts, and applauded by the audience, he at once retired. Everybody was taken in by this " modesty." The letters of a former member of the Constituent Assembly, Rabaut-Pomier, show how completely he was deceived : the hero, " whose favourite book was said to be Plutarch's *Lives of Illustrious Men,* was no Cæsar, but a Cincinnatus : he never went abroad save " to walk in his modest garden." The few who wished him ill concluded " he was rapidly declining." And the fears of certain men were calmed.

That was just what Bonaparte wanted : he could not act, so he had lulled his foes to sleep. But he was determined to depart. The expedition against England had been confided to his charge. In his opinion, and certainly in that of the Directory, it was doomed to failure : this was a trap, and he scented it. He asked the Government to put him in command of an expedition to Egypt. The Directory, which would gladly have sent him to the devil, sent him to the Mamelukes . In the month of Germinal, the General secured the acceptance of his plan for an expedition to the East : a huge turning movement, which was to take England in the rear, snatch the Mediterranean from her grasp, seize Malta and Alexandria, complete the old plan for the occupation of Corfu and Ancona, and threaten the enemy's hold on India.

Preparations for the crusade began.

* * * * *

The plan, excessive as it appeared, was defensible. From one point of view it was most serious, and marked with the dazzling The qualities of far-sighted genius. Bonaparte's idea Egyptian was that France should hold the Mediterranean, Expedition. " *our sea*," as his Latin ancestors had called it. There, for a whole century, the key of the situation was sure to lie : the English proved they knew it, by adding Malta, Cyprus, and Alexandria to Gibraltar, as the years rolled on. Nevertheless, the General's wish to make himself regretted, and the Directory's desire to see him depart, must have been strong indeed, or he would never have secured the triumph of his plan. For there could be hardly any doubt, in those spring days of the Year VI, that Europe was making ready for a fresh assault on France.

Thanks to Austrian intrigues the negotiations at Rastadt were being deliberately prolonged. It was not till March 9 that the German powers finally consented to the cession of the left bank of the Rhine, and then only with the proviso that the Emperor's consent must be obtained. And the Emperor was seeking some pretext for stirring up Europe.

He found more than one to his hand. Funds were wanted for the " expedition against England " (which was to mask Extortions the expedition to the East). Where were these in Italy. funds to be had save in Italy, Switzerland, and Holland ? The expedition to Rome was only decided on (after the Trasteverine populace had murdered General Duphot) for the sake of " filling up the chest," and when Berthier went to Rome he went as " treasurer of the expedition to England." He entered Rome on March 15 evoking " the manes of Cato and Brutus," though the sole object of his coming was to plunder the tomb of Crassus. When Pius VI had been overthrown, he proceeded, as a matter of form, to establish a *Roman Republic*, March 20 (29th Ventôse), the strange history of which, as recounted to us in most instructive fashion by Albert Dufourcq, is simply a tale of inordinate extortion.

Switzerland was to be invaded for the same reason. The pretext was the defence of the " Vaudois patriots " against the " *tyrants of Berne.*" These were overthrown on March 4 (13th Ventôse) by Brune, who did not forget to lay hands on the millions found in the coffers of the conquered State, and give orders that the booty was to be increased to fifteen millions by means of imposts levied on the country. The result of all this was the setting up of a unitarian and democratic republic, held in tight bondage by the conquerors.

Meanwhile, the Republic of Mülhausen had offered itself— of its own free will—to France, and had been annexed forthwith.

In Holland (still far too independent) the Government was so completely *fructidorized*—the word was in current use—by Joubert that, thanks to a treaty signed on April 12 (22nd Germinal), he was able to lay "ships and treasure " at his country's feet.

As Cisalpine Italy had likewise been " bound with chains of iron " on February 22 (5th Ventôse), as the King of Sardinia had been forced to abandon Piedmont to the French, as Garat had been sent to Naples to pave the way for a similar arrangement, and Sotin had been despatched to Genoa for the sole purpose of putting further pressure in the Fructidor style on a republic that had not yet learnt complete docility, France seemed to be offering Europe every pretext she could desire.

Happily, Austria was not quite ready, so she beat about the bush at Rastadt : but everybody knew Russia was " waking up," and felt that Europe was on the eve of a great war.

Meanwhile, on May 19 (29th Floréal) Bonaparte had set sail with ten thousand sailors, thirty-five thousand soldiers, a **Bonaparte** brilliant staff, Berthier, Kléber, Davout, Lannes, **sails for** Desaix, Murat, Bessières, Duroc, Marmont, Menou, **Egypt.** Brueys, and Villeneuve, and—a most interesting fact—with a body of delegates from the world of letters, of science, and of art, which imparted a quality of scientific exploration to this epic crusade.

THE FRENCH REVOLUTION

A few days later news reached Paris that Malta had been seized without a blow. On June 30 (11th Messidor of the Year VI) the expedition landed at Alexandria. *"Gone at last!"* sighed Barras. The heartfelt exclamation betrays a strange policy, dominated by the perpetual fear of death.

SOURCES. Works already quoted by Aulard (*Paris* . . . IV, V, 1900–1902), Barras (III), La Revellière-Lepeaux (II), Grégoire, Mallet du Pan, Thibaudeau (II), Sandoz Rollin (in *Bailleu*), Fouché (I), Madame de Chastenay, Thiébault (II), Miot, Lacretelle, B. Constant, Baron Brinkmann (in the *Correspondance du Baron de Staël*).

WORKS. Those already quoted by Lady Blennerhassett, Sciout (*Directoire*), G. Pallain, Roger Peyre, V. Pierre (18 *Fructidor*), Daudet (II), Sorel (V), Pinguad (*Debry, d'Antraigues*).—Masson, *Napoléon et sa Famille*, I ; Gautier, *Madame de Staël et la République de 1798 (Revue des Deux Mondes*), 1899 ; Bourgeois, *Le Général Bonaparte et la Presse de son temps*, 1907 ; Dufourcq, *Le Régime Jacobin en Italie*, 1903.

CHAPTER XLVI

FLORÉAL. THE DIRECTORY *VERSUS* THE ANARCHISTS

May 1798—*May* 1799

The elections of Germinal, Year VI. " Anarchist " elections. The *coup d'état* of the 22nd Floréal, Year VI. Fury of the Jacobins. The struggle for " virtue." The elections of the Year VII. All parties coalesce against the Directory. The Catholics support the " anarchists." The Second Coalition. The Egyptian Expedition. Reverses in Germany and Italy. Suwaroff and his Cossacks. Italy lost.

BEFORE he took ship Bonaparte heard that the struggle between the Jacobins and the Directory, begun in the month of Brumaire, had ended, apparently, in a fresh *coup d'état*—that of the 22nd Floréal.

" The matter is decided," the Prussian minister had written
The Elections on the 7th Frimaire, " *they* [the Directory] *have*
of Germinal, *resolved to curb the Jacobins' upward flight . . .*
Year VI. before they have time to strengthen themselves
by new recruits."

This was all the more urgent because the Germinal elections were to be particularly important. The deputies invalidated in Fructidor had never been replaced, and this time more than half the whole body of members—437 out of 750—were to be renewed. All parties now threatened, in their exasperation, to coalesce, even if the result was to be the election of " anarchists."

To overcome this coalition the Directory resorted to its usual methods. First of all the Government selected its own official candidates : the list of these, Barras tells us, was handed to the ministers. This done, it was decided, as a "support to the electoral operations," to " send fresh agents

571

into the provinces." All these were provided with money, thanks to a "corrupting decision," adds the Director, pirouetting on his heels. Then, on the 1st Germinal, the Festival of the Sovereignty of the People was celebrated with great pomp : in this performance, six months after Fructidor, and only two before Floréal, burlesque may be said to have reached its apogee.

But as the Government, in spite of this mixture of pressure, corruption, and bribery, feared the population would "vote badly," it was settled that *the powers of the newly elected members were to be verified, not by themselves, but by the retiring . . . or retired . . . deputies.* Thus the elections of the members of the new legislature were to be declared valid or invalid by the very men they had beaten. The resolution, loudly applauded, of course, was converted into law on the 12th Pluviôse.

And, finally, the *Publiciste* of the 12th Germinal—the very eve of the elections—published a semi-official note to the effect that if " Terrorists " were elected " *they would not be accepted, and the departments which had chosen them would be left without deputies.*" On the 22nd the two newspapers of the " anarchist " opposition, the *Hommes Libres* and the *Ami des Lois*, which had made severe references to this note, were suppressed.

Such were the preparations for the elections held in Year VI of the Republic and Year IX of Liberty !

* * * * *

In spite of them all the elections were to be disastrous for the Government.

Disheartened by the events of Fructidor the " honest men " stayed at home. And thus the violent party swept the board : " Anarchists " almost everywhere the Terrorist party had a clear elected. majority in the primary assemblies. So, at an order from Paris (enforced in Paris in the first instance), the minorities in favour of the Directory *seceded*, formed separate assemblies, and, with imperturbable gravity, elected minority deputies in the faces of the deputies elected by the majority.

When these operations were concluded—on the 30th

Germinal—it became evident that out of the 437 vacancies filled, over 800 deputies, duly chosen by the majority, would be hostile to the Directory. Taken with the deputies who had not been obliged to retire, and who had been acting for the last two months with the " anarchist " opposition, these would constitute a most formidable majority against the Directors. The Legislative Body would have to elect a fresh Director at once (François was retiring) and would certainly introduce an enemy of the Government, an " anarchist," into the fold : the idea was most alarming.

The Directors took their measures. They had a free hand till the 1st Prairial when the Councils, in their renewed form, were to meet. In the first place they decided to make François retire a month before his time and have his successor elected (illegally) by the outgoing members of the Councils. They sent Sieyès, " whose buzzing," and still more his relations with the " Jacobins," alarmed his fellow Directors, to Berlin ; they secured the election of Treilhard (20th Floréal), a *bourgeois* (Mme. de Chastenay is the person who applies the term to him), whose soul—the soul of a Cæsarian legist—battened on his hatred of the " anarchists."

Measures had already been taken to get the men elected by the opposition out of the way. The leaders of the beaten majority, Régnier, Chénier, Bailleul, and Crassous, had been going to the Luxembourg every evening to " arrange the purification."

It was in the Council of the Ancients that the shell burst on the 8th Floréal. Régnier, who was to be the Emperor's Chief Justice (all these men were going through a course of training in strong measures) demanded a purification of the new deputies. He declared (and this was the watchword) the elected " anarchists " to be " royalists in disguise." This " initiative " was supported, on the 13th, by a pressing message from the Directory : the blow delivered at the royalists in Fructidor had been a good thing : but it was necessary to take " measures as efficacious as those of Fructidor against the former partisans of Robespierre," and " no more make compromises with Babeuf than with the partisans of a phantom king ! " " *Off with their heads !* " says Barras himself.

THE FRENCH REVOLUTION

On the 14th Floréal a Commission was appointed to inquire into the elections. Bailleul, its chairman, proposed that

every election considered dangerous to the Directory should be quashed once for all. De Bry expressed his strong approval of this measure : had not the Government striven to secure republican and conservative nominations ? (The word conservative is a new one for that time, and proves the existence of a new attitude of mind.) And, since it had failed, in spite of the serious warnings addressed to the majority of the electors, these electors (admirable theory !) must be considered blind, and deaf, and unfit to pronounce any opinion. The Five Hundred passed the measure : the Ancients accepted it, and transformed it into the *Law of the 22nd Floréal*—the second great blow delivered by the Directory.

In seven departments the elections were annulled, and twenty-two deputies who, to make assurance doubly sure, were not to be replaced, were thus unseated. Thirty other individual elections were declared invalid : that of General Fion, because he was a "Babouvist," that of Lindet because he was "too violent," that of Lequinio, because "he had terrorized." "Terrorized !"—and Barras was installed in the Luxembourg ! Finally, and above all—this was the great idea—the Councils assumed the right, as to the twenty-one departments in which a split had occurred, to choose between the elect of the two primary assemblies, and in nine cases out of ten, declared the minority candidate duly elected : we may point out that in the department of the Ardèche, for instance, the electoral assembly had numbered 280 voters, and the minority that had made the split, only fifty-seven. *To sum it all up, fifty-two elected members were refused and a hundred more put aside, and their minority competitors selected in their place.*

In equity this was too much, but it was not enough to secure the safety of the Directory. A considerable group of the Jacobins of the opposition still continued to exist : the Government may have hoped it had frightened them into silence ; their violence was soon to sweep the majority along with them. The *coup d'état*, cynical and underhand as it had been, did not even yield the hoped for result : in the eyes of every party the Directory had exposed itself to all the odium of a fresh attempt on liberty, and garnered none of its expected fruits : a *coup d'état* that has failed is one of the worst of political catastrophes.

* * * * *

The Jacobins who had been spared reached their places in the Councils in a state of fury. Our readers already know **Fury of the** the line of their intended attack. " *Down with* **Jacobins.** *corruption !* " was the cry : at last the "rotten bellies " were to be destroyed ! Merlin kept mistresses, Barras was a mass of corruption, Reubell surrounded himself with cheats and rascals, Treilhard was a brute, and La Revellière a bigot who had strayed from the ordinary path, indeed, but a bigot all the same : We give the summary of twenty accusations. As for the ministers, Ramel represented the interests of the newly-made fortunes, and Talleyrand was "a vile creature." The drawing-rooms in which society was wont to gather were simply public haunts of vice : perversity, imported from the Luxembourg, reigned openly in them all. These "stables of Barras must be cleansed."

The line of attack had been skilfully chosen. It is a curious fact that in France, which is by no means a Puritan country, a campaign in favour of virtue almost invariably commands a certain amount of success. And, further, this platform (which can hardly be called a strictly political platform) was spacious enough to permit all the enemies of the Directory, from Catholics to Terrorists, to join forces upon it, during the elections of the coming year. And this, as we shall see, is what came to pass.

Yet the " moralizing " party did not venture to open its campaign at once. But in Thermidor it began. A Commission **The Champions** deputed to inquire into " the demoralization " **of Virtue.** existing in the country brought in a report, somewhat vague, but really alarming: " There is not a department of the public administration into which corruption and immorality have not found their way. . . . Any continuance of indulgent treatment would make us the accomplices of the persons who have fallen under the censure of the public. These men, whose huge fortunes are a proof of the infamous means they have employed to acquire them, will be *struck down from the heights of their sumptuous chariots and hurled into the abyss of public scorn.*"

During the reading of the report two names passed from lip to lip, Barras, Reubell.

Barras betrayed no surprise : " an old umbrella," he would have said, like Thiers in later days, " on which too much rain had already fallen " : but Reubell was very much alarmed, and even fell ill. Barras may have spoken truly when he said, that though the man was surrounded by knaves, his own hands were clean. He wanted to resign : "but," writes an impartial witness on the 9th Thermidor, "his relations, in their greed for money and place, strongly object to his doing so."

The Directory was all the less able to stand against the attack because it was divided within itself. Treilhard considered Reubell a most compromising colleague : " Ill ! " he said, " It's his bile ! " Merlin would have been quite ready to turn out Barras and Reubell : and Barras, for the sake of peace, would have been just as ready to sacrifice his former " accomplice " of the days of Fructidor. The enemy, informed of these divisions, increased the fury of its onslaught. It was encouraged by a young and newly elected orator, an active, dangerous fellow, whose name was Lucien Bonaparte.

*　　*　　*　　*　　*

Now the elections of the Year VII were drawing near. They threatened to be even more unfavourable to the Directory Elections of　than those of the Year VI.
the Year VII.　　The winter was exceptionally severe : " such bitter cold," we read in a newspaper of the month of Pluviôse, " that the eagles of the Alps seem to have found the temperature of Paris as low as that of the high mountains. One has been killed near Chaillot." The Romans would have taken this eagle, hovering over Paris just nine months before Brumaire, for a portent !

Food was growing dearer and dearer : hunger was tearing at every poor man's vitals : the denunciations of the orgies of the Directors and their friends hit the mark. Workless workmen

(the Seine had been frozen over for the past two months) began
to say " outrageous things " against the Government, and
besides this, an evident though tacit alliance was growing
up between the opposition on the Left and all the Christian
feeling in the country.

For, in spite of everything, religion was on the increase ;
though oppressed, it gave strength to its votaries. In vain had
the authorities deported the priests and shot them down ; in
vain, as Vandal so forcibly puts it, had they "torn the tongues
out of the church bells." The faith they had thus driven out of
the churches was all the stronger in the hearts of those who clung
to it : when, for instance, the Government closed all the oratories
(14th Floréal, Year VI), the eight churches left to the Catholics
in Paris were " frequented with a sort of fury."

Notwithstanding all this the Theophilanthropists, fallen
though they were into the lowest depths of public scorn, were
given fifteen churches, the name of every one being changed
(Notre-Dame became the *Temple of the Supreme Being*, Saint-
Sulpice the *Temple of Victory*, Saint-Roch *the Temple of Genius*,
and so forth).   Then the worship on *décadi* was set up, and an
attempt made to force citizens to frequent its sanctuaries
(where nobody would go because the ceremonies were so tiresome) : officials who did not make their families attend these
places were threatened with dismissal : the authorities tried
to stop work on the *décadi* and force people to work on
Sundays : but *décadi* was fairly beaten in this " quarrel
between M. Dimanche and Citizen Décadi " : then the shopkeepers were sentenced for shutting up their shops on Sundays.
" An unceasing struggle," says M. Aulard.   The lowest forms
of vexatious treatment were practised : the sale of fish on
Fridays was forbidden.   Funeral processions headed by a cross
bearer were stopped, and the few crucifixes left in the schools
were unhung, for " a wall must be built up between public
instruction and worship " ; and so far was all this carried
that, as a police official triumphantly writes two months before
the elections—in Pluviôse of the Year VII—*the Catholic religion
is gnawing its curb.*"

That was the truth : the Catholics were *gnawing the
curb*. But one means of vengeance they had. They were

debarred from electing " honest men " who shared their opinions, because in the Year VI and the Year VII the Government threatened to annul any election of a "reactionary" kind : well ! since, on the whole, they could not expect worse treatment even from the "*anarchists*," they would vote for the "*anarchists*." And this time the pressure would be so strong that there would be no chance of a repetition of the story of Floréal; the persecuting Government would be killed outright.

Coalition against the Directory.

A tacit alliance was made. The police reports of the last weeks before the elections point to a movement that was growing more and more general. A coalition was taking place between the two extreme parties. " In one place," we read, " the Vendémiairists (the Right) have chosen a fierce anarchist ; in another, the anarchists have elected a fierce Vendémiairist."

The result soon became known : the " Jacobin " officials who had been dismissed by the Directors, and almost all the deputies turned out by the *coup d'état* in Floréal, had been returned. " Genuine reprisals for the 22nd Floréal," writes Barras. Never indeed did effect follow more logically on cause, for never did any Government so skilfully prepare the coalition of all the parties it had disgusted, and its own ruin. All these deputies arrived, as Barras tells us, " full of passion and fury."

* * * * *

The difficulty of the governmental position was accentuated by the fact that peace had been broken, and the affairs of France were in a bad state.

Second European Coalition.

" At last ! " Barras had cried, when he saw Bonaparte depart, and Europe had followed his example. Austria, once her conqueror was out of sight, had persuaded Paul I to enter the lists.

Openings for invasion had been prepared, as if deliberately all along the newly conquered marches : the Swiss Republic, forced into submission on 22nd Fructidor of the Year VI; the Dutch Republic brought into servitude on 14th Prairial of the same year; the Cisalpine Republic, crushed under our generals' heels, and choked by our ministers; the Roman Republic, ruined by our financial agents; were all quivering with fury under the yoke. From Naples, Marie-Caroline, knowing her danger, called on her nephew of Austria for help. The conferences at Selz, with which Austria had been amusing France, were broken off on July 6 (17th Messidor of the Year VI).

Frederick William II, who had been won over to a policy of almost benevolent neutrality, had been succeeded by young Frederick William III, a monarch so hostile to the revolutionary idea that he was inclined to regard even an attitude of unfriendly expectancy to France as a treason to crowned heads. And once he was on the throne all the negotiations at Rastadt, where Prussia had hitherto supported us to a certain extent, were to fall to the ground.

A general dissolution it was, in fact, and war was breaking out, a most formidable war, for Austria and England were to be joined by Russia. The huge extent of frontier we had seized, the marches we now had to hold, from the Zuyder Zee to Corfu, made a fresh difficulty over and above those of 1792. Further, the Government had no money, and could not hope for a renewal of the splendid outburst of enthusiasm of those bygone days.

From Egypt only good news was coming in. This is not the place in which to tell the story of that dazzling series of
Bonaparte exploits which led our soldiers in the footsteps of
in Egypt. the mighty ancestors who had carried the Crusade, six centuries before, from Damietta to Damascus. What a realization of a gorgeous dream was there ! nothing but the details lack of space forbids me to cite can give any idea of the real nature of this strange chapter in our national history. Bonaparte commenting on the Koran before the muftis between two battles with the Mamelukes ; Lasalle astounding the horsemen of Ibrahim and Murad by his feats of strength ; Murat, with a handful of men, carrying off the astounded emirs out of their very tents in the hostile camp ; pilgrimages, punctuated with battles, from the Pyramids, with their memories of the Pharaohs, to Bethlehem, the birthplace of the Christ ; the *Institut d'Egypte* and its excavations—and the adventures of honest Captain François, "the Egyptian dromedary," who passed from prisons where he was threatened with impalement to the

arms of Eastern houris—a story out of the *Arabian Nights* that lasted four hundred days, an episode of the *Gesta Dei* in the lives of " the sons of liberty ! "

Bonaparte had landed on June 30 (11th Messidor of the Year VI), opened his way to Cairo by victories at *Ramanieh* and *Chebreïss*, forced his entrance into the city by his successful *Battle of the Pyramids*, on July 21, and having driven the owners of Egypt out, established his own residence in the heart of the country. Though Nelson destroyed the French fleet and hemmed in the army by his victory at Aboukir on August 1, this, in Bonaparte's eyes, was only an incentive to vaster daring yet, for he was resolved " to issue thence as great as the whole world." After he had crushed a revolt at Cairo, and brought all Upper Egypt into subjection, he made himself ready, in the springtime of 1799, to deliver an attack on Syria, and before long the battles of *Tiberias*, *Nazareth*, and *Mount Tabor* seemed to foreshadow the fall of Saint-Jean d'Acre. In his magnificent audacity Bonaparte dreamt of a return to Paris by Damascus, Constantinople, and Vienna.

＊　　＊　　＊　　＊　　＊

But in Europe French affairs were going less smoothly. Joubert had occupied Piedmont, indeed, and Championnet had hurried from Rome and seized on Naples, where the fantastic *Parthenopeian Republic*, which was to live for 113 days, had been set up under a French protectorate. But all this was fragile in texture, and not likely to withstand the first onset of the European troops.

Reverses in Germany and Italy.

By December 17, 1798, the Coalition was an accomplished fact, threatening the whole line of the French defences from Naples to Amsterdam.

Schérer was sent to Italy, Brune and Bernadotte to Holland ; between the two countries, Jourdan, with 40,000 troops in Germany, and Masséna with 30,000 in Switzerland, were to be the poor defence of the ancient borders of France : far away to the right, at Naples, was Macdonald with 30,000 men : 170,000 men in all were sent out to oppose the formidable massed armies about to descend from all quarters on the Republic.

FLOREAL

On February 28 (9th Ventôse of the Year VII) Jourdan crossed the Rhine. Within a few hours the Congress of Rastadt (there was no object in keeping up the farce) broke up, but, in shameless violation of international law, the French plenipotentiaries, De Bry, Roberjot, and Bonnier, were attacked at the gates of the town by Hungarian hussars, and the last two were murdered. This hideous feature presaged the inexpiable nature of the approaching war.

Jourdan had only penetrated a short way into Germany. He was defeated by the Archduke Charles at *Stokach*, and retired on Strasburg. Just at the same time Schérer was defeated at *Magnano*, April 5 (15th Germinal), beat a hasty retreat behind the Adda, very nearly lost his whole army, and was obliged to hand over the chief command to Moreau. Greater misfortunes yet were drawing near. Russia intervened, and for the first time Europe was to behold those barbarians of the North, destined to make the first real impression on the " *Grand Armée* " some thirteen years later, and who, even in 1799 were momentarily to shake the courage of the French troops. At their head rode a leader whose portrait I will not attempt to draw ; too many other writers have described Suwaroff, a barbarian and devotee, a warrior with the mind of a mystic, brutal and scornful, a kidnapper of men, a destroyer of cities, a formidable foe : " his blade in his adversary's bowels," this was his motto. This terrible tactician, with the qualities of an Attila to boot, was a very different opponent from the dilatory Brunswick of 1792.

(Marginal note: Suwaroff and his Cossacks.)

If Vienna had left this barbarian of genius a free hand for a single year France would have been ruined—till Bonaparte came back. Happily he had to reckon with Austria. And Austria, which had supplied the bulk of the army of the Coalition (the Russians only numbered 30,000) was determined to keep the military operations in her own hands ; though she gave the " savage " full liberty at first, she soon began to put spokes in his wheels. In spite of all this France had good reason to regard her own state as desperate : there were 26,000 Austrians in the Grisons and 46,000 in the Tyrol, 86,000 more in the Venetian territory, and Suwaroff with his 30,000 Russians on the Po, while 40,000 Anglo-Russian troops were disembarking in Holland : 320,000 men against 170,000 Frenchmen, and these already shaken and depressed.

On April 27 Suwaroff came into violent contact with the French army. Throwing his troops, by a surprise movement, across the Adda, he drove in Moreau's centre, and forced him back to the other side of the Po, and into Piedmont : Moreau still hoped to effect a junction with Macdonald, who hurried up from Naples, fighting his way across Italy (our readers should consult Thiébault as to this march), three parts of which were in revolt. But Suwaroff, applying Bonaparte's own tactics against the French, threw himself between the two armies. He made himself master of Milan and drove out the " Jacobin Government " installed there, fell on Turin next and then rushed on Macdonald : for three days, June 17–19 (28th–30th Prairial) the fight raged on the banks of the Trebbia : the French were outnumbered and defeated, though Macdonald, thanks to a superhuman energy, succeeded in joining Moreau with the remnants of his army.

But Italy was lost : at Naples, at Rome, at Milan, the " Jacobin " governments had fallen with a crash. Within Italy lost two months, the Cossacks had cleared the to France. " impious Frenchmen," as their leader, a great worshipper of icons, called them, out of the valley of the Po. The ancient frontiers of France were threatened : Masséna, who had been placed at the head of the " Army of Germany," found it impossible to re-establish order there now Jourdan had failed him; Switzerland had risen in revolt, Bavaria and Prussia both seemed likely to abandon their neutral position and turn against France. England was scattering money broadcast. Was France, torn by internal dissensions, ill-governed, penniless, outnumbered, about to succumb ?

On April 12 Bonaparte had offered to return. So great was the alarm with which he inspired the Luxembourg that, even in the presence of such perils as these, the Government brushed aside his offer. The misfortune was to grow deeper yet before the Directory, in its distress, ended by calling back " the saviour."

For sources and bibliography, see those of Chapter XLIX.

CHAPTER XLVII

PRAIRIAL. LAST EFFORT OF THE JACOBINS

May 1798—July 1799

The Councils of the Year VII and the Directory. Sieyès is elected. Barras betrays Reubell. The *coup d'état* of Prairial against the Directory. The Mountain again. The new Directors. Sieyès rules the Directory. Three Jacobin laws. The Conscription of the Year VII, the Forced Loan of the Year VII, the failure of the progressive tax. The law of hostages. A general upheaval.

EVEN before disaster had reached its height the foes of the Government had begun to use it as a weapon of offence. The Councils, due to retire in Prairial, had confirmed all the Germinal elections, " regardless," writes a foreigner, " of the displeasure of the Directors," who conse-The Councils of quently found themselves face to face with a the Year VII. most powerful opposition.

This was composed of two groups : a very noisy Extreme Left, clamouring for nothing less than the revival of the Committee of Public Safety and all the Terrorist laws, and another party consisting of a large body of politicians animated by the most bitter feeling against the Government. These, whose aim was simply to "regenerate" the Directory once more, were led by Boulay, Chénier, Baudin, and Berlier.

At first they attacked Barras more especially ; then they began to spare him. By what mysterious means did he make his peace with them ? Whatever these may have been it became quite evident, in a few weeks, that all future blows were to be rained on Reubell and Treilhard, and that the " perpetual Director " was to escape scot free. He had simply betrayed his friends, as was his wont. Though, as he tells us himself, he regarded Reubell as " the soul of the Directory," he had made up his mind that the body, sick as it was already, must dispense with its soul. Some external impulse—Barras gives us to understand that no difficulty was made as to the transaction—was imparted to the wheels of fate, and Reubell took his leave. To soften the pain of parting, the Directory—if we may believe Barras and La Revellière—allotted the retiring Director a sum of 100,000 *livres* out of the secret service funds, and allowed him to take away "his carriage and horses." Sieyès —but his testimony is not altogether reliable—declares that Reubell also carried off all the furniture, and even the very candles, from his apartments in the Luxembourg.

Sieyès had refused to become a Director over and over again, because he would not serve with Reubell, whom he abhorred. Sieyès elected Now one was gone the other could come in. a Director. It is difficult to conceive the prestige enjoyed by the ex-Vicar-General of Chartres. It was no mitre, it was a tiara this unfrocked priest had won by the Revolution. "His partisans," wrote a diplomat of those days, "extol him as if he were a god, and his detractors abuse him as if he were a devil "—a twofold glory.

We have already made the man's acquaintance. "*Deeply imbued with the pride of philosophy*," as the Prussian Gervinus wrote, he believed the hour to have struck, at last, when, with the Tables of the Law in his hand, he might come down from Sinaï. If anyone inquired as to what was written on the stones he kept a scornful silence ; our own belief is that he really knew very little about it. If he hid things it was because his brain was more cloudy than others dreamt : his own perception was not invariably clear.

He was a scornful being : that was a strength. Above all things he despised the "band" that had held sway for the last four years and more. He divided it into two groups : the rascals and the energumens. His plan was to drive "the merchants out of the Temple" with the help of the latter first of all, and then to drive out "the hangman's varlets themselves." That done he would alter the Constitution.

He was elected, and—"at last," as one deputy says— sent word from Berlin that he would accept the seat. "A measure of public safety !" cried his friends. "*There are few sovereigns*," wrote the Swedish agent on June 13, "*whose*
584

*accession to the throne in circumstances of difficulty has caused
a deeper sensation. . . . If* he is not successful his example will
be a brilliant proof of the fact that genius most deeply versed
in abstract speculation is' not always fitted to hold the helm
of the State. . . ." This was in fact demonstrated: *the
appeal to the philosopher* was to be the fore-runner of *an
appeal to the soldier,* and the philosopher himself, realizing his
own inadequacy, was to call on the soldier for his help.

The Directors hated Sieyès: they were thunderstruck.
" A calamity," was La Revellière's comment on the event.
From that day forth Barras gave up any thought of rule;
his one idea was to stay where he was : " I shall always agree
with him," he sneered; " he'll think me nearly as clever as
himself, and we shall get on together perfectly."

❋   ❋   ❋   ❋   ❋

While the opposition waited for the " philosopher's " coming
it kept up a lively war. The military reverses, as Fouché cyni-
Dismissal of   cally puts it, " served it splendidly." It sent
Treilhard.   a rough message to the Directors, demanding
their explanation of the disasters. " Tremble, inept and imprudent triumvirs ! " cried Bertrand tragically from the rostrum.

And, indeed, Barras had blenched : yet he continued to
negotiate. He had already sacrificed Reubell : he now sacrificed
Treilhard. He was hated by the deputies, for, unlike Barras,
he treated them with gross contumely. " Churl," they shouted
to him one day, " you shall pay for this ! " They were
waiting Sieyès' arrival now to punish both the " churl " and
his fellows.

The ex-Abbé arrived on the night of the 17th Prairial;
but he did not appear at the Palace till the 20th, and then with
an affected air of sedateness which he maintained for ten days.

The Five Hundred were still waiting for the Directors'
reply to their message. None came : they lost patience, and
proceeded to wreak punishment—on that " churl " Treilhard
in the first place.

This was a very simple matter : legally, Treilhard had never
belonged to the Government, for he had been elected, contrary
to the rules of the Constitution, by the outgoing Councils;

the " Constitution must be re-established" (there never had
been so much talk about re-establishing the Constitution as now
that it had been violated every three months); so Treilhard was
invited to resign. The Directors met, and he read his colleagues'
determination to sacrifice him on their gloomy faces. He was
a simple sort of man : rising to his feet, he took his umbrella—
his habits were not those of Reubell—and went home to his
bed in his own house in the Rue des Maçons.

The Five Hundred forthwith elected Gohier to fill his place ;
he had been Minister of Justice, and Mme. Roland had aptly
described him by the one word " mediocrity." The description
still fitted him exactly. He was the creature of the Councils :
combining with Sieyès, and the " traitor " Barras, he was to
drive out Merlin and La Revellière.

These two saw the blow coming : in a tortuous speech
delivered to the assembled Directors on the 29th Prairial,
Sieyès demonstrated that in their own interests the two condemned Directors ought to retire. La Revellière, in great
indignation, refused to comply.

So it became necessary to resort to strong measures. Boulay
undertook to carry these out : this man, destined to become
The " Coup   one of the Emperor's ministers, was a doughty
d'état " of   champion, always to the fore in violent crises
Prairial, 1799. —Fructidor, Floréal, Prairial now, Brumaire to-
morrow. He went to the rostrum and poured forth a diatribe.
" A great blow " must be struck, he said, at certain undesirable
members of the Government : not a single fact was adduced.
A Commission was at once nominated, and Boulay appeared
again (as its reporter this time) and denounced—in his mouth
the words had a comic sound—" arbitrary acts and illegal
detentions " of which La Revellière and Merlin (why Barras
was immune nobody knew) had, he averred, been guilty : the
Council adopted his conclusions.

At eleven o'clock a deputation proceeded to the Luxembourg
and announced that if Merlin and La Revellière did not resign
with a good grace, they would be forthwith arrested. The two
Directors made a few more difficulties. Barras pressed them ;
he was first insinuating and then violent : he reproached Merlin
with the vileness of his life, and added, " Make haste to clear

out ! " La Revellière made an emotional speech—given *in extenso* in his Memoirs, which depicts him, in his own eyes at least, as the last of the Romans, save in the matter of conciseness : for this " Cato's " eloquence was heavy. But his colleagues frightened him : he " shed tears," and then, with Merlin, he " cleared out," on the evening of the 30th Prairial.

Two new " Majesties " were appointed : Roger Ducos, a magistrate, and Moulin, a " general of barricades," quite unknown to fame. Universal stupor was the result. " The wise energy of the Legislative Body," wrote a semi-official newspaper, " has saved the body politic . . . the People may now believe in liberty since it beholds the destruction of *the directorial Colossus !* " Poor Colossus !

But the People's belief in liberty was gone : never, if various witnesses are to be credited, did it betray such utter indifference. " Discontent," writes Lindet, " is tempered by apathy." It may interest our readers more to listen to the summary of the business contained in a peasant's journal, which enables us to gauge the feeling of the humbler classes. Laviron, a vine-grower in the Doubs, writes thus : " In the early days of June 1799 the Convention (*sic*) decided that the *Jacobin elections* were valid. The members of the Directory, *whose sole desire was to make large fortunes*, as they have been publicly reproached with doing, handed in their resignations. They retired, each of them with a treasure too large to be packed into a single vehicle. . . . The authorities at Besançon were at once changed *and replaced by men of blood.*"

Men of blood, men of prey ! France was fated to fall out of the hands of one into the hands of the other. Such during the summer of 1799 was the opinion of humble folks in village and Faubourg alike.

* * * * *

Were the " *men of blood* " to come back ? It seemed more than probable. The " new Mountain " was there already—
Resurrection the Mountain of the old days, in other words,
of the which had renewed its strength, and " broken
" Mountain." down " the " corrupt Directory." This Mountain was resolved to be worthy of its predecessor. From the 1st Messidor onwards it poured forth the most extravagant

proposals. The enemy was at the gate, therefore the Committee of Public Safety must be set up again, and the guillotine, of course, as well. "Shall we not see a few heads cut off?" was the cry in the Jacobin cafés, "*will there be no guillotine?*"

Meanwhile the Clubs were re-opening their doors. The Jacobin newspapers were revived. A powerful party in the Councils was talking of a fresh law for a levy of conscripts, of a forced loan to be imposed on the wealthy classes, of a law of hostages. The dangerous position of the country must be proclaimed at once and the Terror restored.

Respectable people were very much alarmed. They were glad, indeed, " to see the fall of the vile wretches who had proved themselves so unworthy of the positions they had occupied," writes a foreign Minister, but the party which had overthrown these men was "far more dangerous to the public peace." The diplomat's language is much the same as the vine-grower's.

The alarm caused by this agitation was strongest of all amongst a certain section of the " victors " of Prairial: the adherents of Sieyès, Boulay, Baudin, and the rest. They thought it most dangerous to set up the guillotine again, and (out of consideration for themselves) " to accustom the populace, once more, to the sight of the scaffold." These men were willing, as a temporary measure, to oblige their allies by passing a few measures specially adapted to the occasion—a Levy of Recruits, a Forced Loan, a Law of Hostages : they would even consent to the re-opening of the Clubs—but they were firmly resolved to close them again as soon as they themselves should have grown a little stronger.

This was the attitude of the new Directory. The " nullity " (we find the same term used by innumerable pens) of the Sieyès Master new " team " made it a tool in the hands of of the Sieyès. That " poor fellow Gohier " had quite Directory. lost his head " when he saw the purple mantle on his own back " : " he called all the people who came to congratulate him " *Citoyen Directeur*," wrote a witness on the following day ; " he saw nothing but Directors everywhere." And, indeed, since he had been chosen, anybody might have been a Director. Certain indications convince us that Sieyès considered him an idiot. General Moulin, on the other hand, looked more like the result of some odious joke: he was said to have been "one of the Du Barry's footmen, to have sold tallow-candles after he left her service, to have acted as adjutant under General Santerre, and then to have become a general himself." At a moment when the roll of the soldiers of France bore such names as Masséna, Moreau, Jourdan, Joubert, Bonaparte, the selection of this "general of the barricades" smacked of comic opera. "When one saw such a man holding one of the highest positions in the State," writes one of his female contemporaries, "one's thoughts flew back to the days when barbarian warriors became Emperors." Sieyès soon judged this "general of the days of Robespierre" to be "a worthless fellow." Ducos he valued for his flexibility. Indeed, Ducos, between his vote for the King's death and his vote in the Senate of 1814, which summoned Louis XVIII to the throne, took a hand in every successive game. Louis-Philippe would assuredly have ended by giving him a peerage if he had not killed himself, in 1816, by jumping out of his own carriage—the only occasion, we may be sure, on which this prudent individual was ever known not to have profited by a change of position. "A slave ruled by Sieyès," he was called in Prairial of the Year VII. "*That cripple Ducos !*" Bonaparte was to exclaim, "*that blackguard Moulin !*"

Barras made no overt sign. He had come to the end of his tether. His heart had long been rotten; the taint was creeping into his brain. Yet he still had wit enough to embark on a final intrigue : he carried on negotiations with Mittau, where the Czar was entertaining the Comte de Lille. M. Ernest Daudet has proved that the former Vicomte had been bought by the future King Louis XVIII. He was merely waiting for the propitious moment. Perhaps, indeed, he was fooling the man who had bought him—he has asserted this to be the case. Be that as it may, he had "gone back to his pleasures," as we read in a document dated 10th Fructidor, Year VII, and had ceased to discuss business with his brother Directors. The "filth" had been swept out, but he had escaped as by a miracle ; he kept out of sight.

So Sieyès was master. He did not give a thought to "Louis XVIII" : for a moment he had dreamt of Orléans— a "Louis-Philippe I," but now his plan was to come to an arrangement with an accommodating soldier. We shall see him at his work. From the outset he startled Gohier by disclosures (which are a surprise to us, coming as they did from so secretive a man) : " . . . When the ice breaks up skilful pilots know how to escape the consequences of the thaw ! " While he waited to find the soldier, his first anxiety, now he had " driven the merchants out of the temple," was to drive out the brawlers too. The neo-Jacobin movement cast a gloom over him; it was soon to fill him with disgust.

* * * * *

The Mountain, indeed, was beginning to rage. And this outbreak demands attention : all authorities agree that it finally drove the citizens into the arms of Cæsar.

The three Jacobin Measures. The Jacobins had begun by demanding and obtaining place—that was the usual custom " The Jacobin gang has got places," we read. They succeeded in turning Talleyrand out : with a quiet smile on his lips he departed (people had not yet learnt that the downfall of the ex-Bishop of Autun was apt to mean the ruin of the Government which had dispensed with his services) : but his place was filled by Reinhardt, too moderate a man to please the Jacobins : and they held the same opinion as to the new Minister of Justice, Cambacérès. They demanded that the Finances should be confided to a " pure " republican, such as Robert Lindet : and ended by forcing his appointment on their opponents. Even this did not suffice them : they began to think they had not been sufficiently paid, and in their eyes Sieyès was already " a traitor."

Fortune was kinder to them in the Councils : they carried *the Law of Conscription, the Law to impose a Forced Loan, the Law of Hostages.* But these were to work a series of ruins, followed by a series of disappointments.

The first disappointment came from the conscripts. This might have been foreseen : Joubert's letters to his father (published by Chevrier) are most distressing : after 1795 all eagerness to enlist had died down, and the men who had been enlisted were deserting. Thus the levy of the Year VII naturally encountered invincible difficulties : a traveller passing through the Southern provinces

The Conscription of the Year VII.

590

saw the conscripts in all parts "in open revolt against the delegates of the Government." One Commissary laid this at the priests' door. But there was no need of the priests to inform the country that the Government had no money, and was sending out troops to be butchered : confidence was dead, and that explains everything. When the news of Bonaparte's landing was noised abroad these rebellious conscripts suddenly gave in and joined the colours. But in the Year VII the whole of the South, like La Vendée at a previous date, rose in rebellion against this new levy " *à la* '93," to which the spirit of '92 and the grip of '93, were both lacking.

The financial disappointment was worse still. We would fain linger over this edifying tale. A certain proportion of the " Prairialists " had issued from the Babeuf clubs : thus this " radical-socialist " party, as M. Aulard calls it, was imbued with the absolutely false notion that taxation should not be the proportional contribution of each citizen to the common expenditure, but a bleeding process applied to the purses of the rich, and we may even say *a penalty* inflicted on acquired fortunes.

These men had learnt nothing from the failure of the forced and progressive loan of the Year IV : it had been a lamentable **Forced Loan of** failure, but that they declared was because the **the Year VII.** " pure " republicans had not been in power : this time the finances of the country were to be entrusted to Lindet. One hundred millions of *livres* had to be immediately raised : the rich men should be ordered to find the money : the tax was to be levied at the rate of three-tenths of any income from real estate that exceeded 300 *livres* a year, and was to rise progressively, in the case of taxpayers whose income (as calculated by a " taxation jury ") was reckoned at 4000 *livres* and more, to a sum representing three-fourths of that income. Such, in general terms, was the new law forced on the Councils by the Jacobins, passed on the 10th Messidor, and rendered still more oppressive on the 19th Thermidor.

It was an exorbitant tax : some tax-payers were rated at 50,000 *livres*, others had to pay 300,000 *livres*, and some even 400,000 *livres*. Yet it was not the rich who really suffered but, as always, the poor.

THE FRENCH REVOLUTION

From the outset, when the triumph of the principle of a progressive income-tax was secured by the vote of the 10th Messidor of the Year VII in the Palais-Bourbon (where the Five Hundred had just installed themselves) the effect produced was tremendous. On the 12th the newspapers contained references to the " sudden stagnation in all business transactions " ; luxury was cut down in all directions ; servants were discharged, and orders for furniture and dress were countermanded. As it became more and more evident that the Ancients were about to yield to the pressure of the Jacobin party, the general alarm increased : merchants began asking for their passports for Hamburg, Switzerland and Spain : some of them, to gain time, declared spurious bankruptcies. Luxury was suppressed, and work ceased.

The *taxation juries* made themselves hated : they served the ends of the meanest vengeances, political and private ; once more the informer flourished, and brought his victims, not to the scaffold this time, but to financial ruin.

And to crown all the big fortunes escaped : the financiers were not all of them landowners, and the wealth which consisted of bills and securities slipped through the tax-collector's fingers. A foreigner relates that one of these financiers, Collot, desiring to avoid an inquiry into his means, offered a sum of 100,000 *livres*. It was refused. " You won't take it ? " said he, insolently ; " You shall have nothing at all ! " The real sufferers, consequently, were the landowners, the much talked-of " purchasers of National property," the Paris merchants, and, finally, and incidentally, the working class. The workshops began to close. " Incivism on the part of the workshop owners," said the Minister of Police, who tried to force the masters to open them again : in reality, as the *Ami des Lois* tells us on 22nd Thermidor, " all the rich people are leaving Paris, people are flying from the *Juries* as they fled from the Committees ; the workmen have no work to do." A cabinet-maker in the Faubourg Saint-Antoine says : " They have spared me six *livres* of forced loan, but they have cost me sixty by frightening away my customers ! " The very coffers of the State suffered from the methods employed to fill them. " Since this loan began the registration and stamp departments " (all business trans-

592

actions having ceased) " have brought in nothing at all. . . . *This may be called killing the laying hen !* "

Meanwhile, at the cost of widespread ruin, forty millions, instead of the expected hundred, had been squeezed into the Treasury. Before three months were out the Councils were fain to admit the failure of their enterprise : and a deputy went to the rostrum and proposed the re-establishment of a proportional tax. It was voted on the 16th Brumaire, just two days before Bonaparte's *coup d'état*, too late to prevent the financiers Collot and Ouvrard from backing the avenger, the proprietors whose possessions had been threatened from welcoming his advent, and the workmen who had been forced into idleness by the imposition of this " democratic tax " from raining blessings on him.

The Law of Hostages was a peculiarly atrocious measure. It was passed on the 24th Messidor. The Terror had smitten The Law of the aristocrats : it had never conceived the idea, Hostages. more monstrous still, of striking down persons it knew to be innocent to punish those it considered " guilty." This was the last great conception of the system. The recrudescence of Jacobinism, far from terrifying the country, had apparently set it on fire : in quite three-quarters of the provinces a genuine guerilla warfare had arisen or revived ; the whole country was in a state of sedition, active or latent. Highway robbers and conscripts in revolt had joined hands. The Government pretended to regard them all as soldiers in the service of Louis XVIII : on the 24th Messidor the extremists of the Mountain forced their last law on the Councils : a list of *hostages* was to be drawn up by every Commune (the " revolutionary committees " restored to life and being) : on these lists the names of all relations of aristocrats were to be inscribed. Every time a " patriot " was murdered, four of these " hostages " were to be deported ; every time a robbery was committed the hostages were to pay the fine.

The law was greeted with a cry of horror. The country refused to allow itself to be further imposed upon ; the provinces, Insurrection in hitherto merely in a state of effervescence, rebelled the Provinces. outright. In one day six departments in the South-West—the whole valley of the Garonne, hitherto so faithful to the Revolution—broke into most formidable revolt. In the course of the night of the 18th-19th Thermidor, 20,000 men all rose at once, spontaneously, without summons, without leaders, driven by their own despair. They were scattered on the 3rd Fructidor, but the remnants of that army were to be transformed into dangerous bands of outlaws.

The West, of course, burst into flame once more, and for a moment the success of the work performed by Hoche seemed compromised. Napoleon agrees with Andigné in attributing this final insurrection in Anjou, Brittany, and Normandy to the Law of Hostages, and to nothing else. By the close of Fructidor 50,000 men had banded themselves together : the leaders were mediocre and vacillating, but the rank and file were valiant fellows, who carried towns that neither Cathelineau nor Charette had been able to reduce : yet none of these people really knew what they wanted—they were moved by a paroxysm of hatred and despair. In the autumn of 1799 fourteen out of the eighty-six departments of France were in open revolt, and forty-six more were mined and ready to explode. That was the sole outcome of this recrudescence of Terrorism. " The unfortunate results of the two laws of the Loan and the Hostages," writes a foreign observer, " are beyond calculation. The first has destroyed business of every kind and is ruining the State, the second threatens the whole of society with imminent destruction."

For the sources and works of this chapter, see those of Chapter XLIX.

CHAPTER XLVIII

THE APPEAL TO THE SOLDIER

July—September 1799

The Directory and Sieyès *versus* the neo-Jacobins. Sieyès decides to appeal to the soldier. A general movement in the direction of this solution. A state of mind favourable to government by Cæsar. General Joubert. Fouché at the Ministry of Police. The Club closed. Death of Joubert at Novi. Suwaroff in Switzerland. The victories of Zurich and Bergen. The exhausted people longs for the advent of a strong man. " Ah ! if Bonaparte were only here ! " Bonaparte and the various parties. " He has landed ! "

THE " regenerated " Directory had done its utmost to put down the recrudescence of the Terror without waiting for any demonstration of its disastrous results. A struggle soon broke out among the " victors of Prairial." The Jacobins were doomed to defeat, but the bitter conflict **The** was to show Sieyès and his friends the extent **neo-Jacobins.** of their own weakness. By the time it was over the existing system had been condemned by both factions, and both turned their eyes towards a soldier, the one hoping for strength, the other for vengeance.

The Clubs, which had reopened their doors after the events of Prairial, were causing special exasperation and alarm. The old Jacobins had reformed their ranks on the 18th Messidor : but the posthumous influence of Babeuf had inspired the new Friends of Liberty with views of a still more demagogic nature. Their programme, indeed, contained (besides the Constitution of 1793) a plan for " integral, equal, and common education," and for the organization of national workshops ; and Babeuf and his accomplices were hailed by the orators of the group as so many " virtuous martyrs." This party soon began

595

to clamour for heads : those of the Directors who had been turned out in Prairial, and of the bloated financiers to begin with. Three thousand adherents joined its banner, and the Society took up its quarters in the *Salle du Manège*, on the very benches, consequently, formerly occupied by the Legis‹ lative Body, as though it had been a sort of official assembly. Other clubs, all tending towards the reconstitution of the famous network of the year 1793, were founded at Bordeaux, Lille, Lorient, Amiens, and Rouen. For two months they rang with speeches that constantly increased in violence.

*   *   *   *   *

Nothing could have been more thoroughly alarming to the real Directorial party, those *Conservatives* whose policy had been defined by De Bry, following in the wake of Benjamin Constant. These were the moderate men of the moment : strange pretenders to such a title, former presidents of clubs, and regicide members of the Convention who had proscribed their fellows in June 1793, in Thermidor of the Year II, in Fructidor of the Year V, in Floréal of the Year VI, in Prairial of the Year VII, and now desired to set up "the State on an unshakable foundation " ; unique moderates for, thanks to their Jacobin temperament, their " moderation " was of the most vigorous description.

The " Moderates " of 1799.

Nearly all of them were already unconscious Cæsarians. They knew the Constitution of the Year III had been reduced to a rag. There must be another Constitution, one which would ensure peace to both *bourgeois* and people, by placing the good things the Revolution had won them under the permanent ægis of a powerful Government. For though these men were " Conservatives," it was the Revolution they desired to preserve. But already they were contemplating the inevitable advent of the man " who, to preserve all things, must hold them all in his hand."

In the Councils, Boulay of La Meurthe was the type of these neo-moderates, sprung from the Jacobin party : a whole bevy of others followed on his heels, members of the Councils and members of the Institute, statesmen and writers, all rallying, day by day, to the opinions he voiced : Bailleul, De Bry,

Baudin, Camus, Riouffe, Réal, Cambacérès, Arnault, Regnault of Saint-Jean-d'Angély, Cabanis. The monster's awakening was driving them further and further along the road of resistance to this new Revolution.

But the man who stood for resistance above all his fellows at this moment was Sieyès. He had fancied, to begin with, Sieyès resigned he might be able to come to some arrangement to Cæsarism. with the Assemblies : " *The deputies,*" he said at that juncture, " *are all of them good or bad, according to the manner in which they are used.*" Then, on a closer acquaintance, he had condemned the system, root and branch, and had approached certain deputies (so one of them relates) with reference to the "necessity for a revision of the Constitution." " It was in consequence of these confidences that Lucien Bonaparte began to cultivate his acquaintance," says Delbrel.

But the Director was not dreaming at that moment of the conqueror of Egypt, far from it. He wanted a general, but one who would be easy to manage : " *We must have two things,*" said he to Fouché, " *a head and an arm !* " He had the head : it was on his own shoulders, the shoulders of Joseph Sieyès, one of the great statesmen of Europe. *But he still had to find, or rather choose, his sword.*

For, indeed, there were plenty of them. But Joubert seemed the only man who realized the ideal type. He was young (just General thirty), handsome, high-spirited, and yet cir-Joubert. cumspect : " He has the courage of a grenadier," Bonaparte had written, " and the coolness of a general." He had deposed a king at Turin and had purified a republic at the Hague, thus he owned a practised arm. Though the Jacobins (to whom he had lately spoken harshly enough in the Manège) disliked him, he was patronized by certain members of the party, such as Fouché. In "conservative" and even aristocratic quarters he was made most welcome. Semonville, who always had a sharp eye on the successful man of the future, actually accepted him as the betrothed husband of his step-daughter, Mlle. de Montholon. Fouché mentioned him to Sieyès. " Very good," said the other, and nothing more ; but Joubert was appointed to the command of the Paris troops, that in which

Bonaparte had made his first appearance. Almost without being told, this new general of the Paris army understood what was expected of him : " *Whenever you choose I'll settle the whole business with twenty grenadiers.*"

*   *   *   *   *

So, his man in reserve, Sieyès opened the campaign against his " enemies." On the 7th Thermidor he made the Ancients

Sieyès attacks the neo-Jacobins. (it was in their Council that his influence was strongest) give the Club formal notice to quit the Manège where it had taken up its quarters. On the 9th the angry members sought refuge in the *Temple de la Paix* (Church of Saint-Thomas d'Aquin). That very day Sieyès who, as President of the Directory, was presiding over the anniversary festival of the 9th Thermidor, seized his opportunity, and spoke less severely of Robespierre than of the men who were dreaming of reviving his methods.

The Jacobin Club replied by a most violent attack upon him. He decided to close the Club. But who would dare to carry out the Director's programme ? The Minister of War, Bernadotte, could not be relied on : he was in the habit of frequenting the Club, and holding forth there. Bourguignon, the Minister of Police, was a "nonentity." Where was the man in the ranks of the "reactionary" party who would undertake to close a Club to which 300 deputies belonged ? Talleyrand, who, though unseen, was still advising his party, judged the case accurately (the psychology of politics was making evident progress, and the cynicism of politicians as well) : " *Nobody,*" *he* said " *but a Jacobin can fight the Jacobins, attack them and overthrow them.*" Puzzled, the Directors turned questioning eyes upon him : " *Fouché,*" he said. Barras supported the motion : he looked on Fouché as a creature of his own.

His creature ! Here we perceive a certain artlessness in Barras, profligate though he was. Fouché was never to be any man's creature. He was, and was always to be, everybody's man, or rather nobody's man. On this, as on every other occasion, he was to scent the coming wind with his usual perspicacity. Other people thought it was blowing from the left ; Fouché felt it coming from the right : reaction, to begin with, and then Cæsar ! The future Duc d'Otrante foresaw it all;

those eyes of his, with their terrifying lack-lustre pupils, could pierce the darkest clouds. The task of overcoming Jacobinism by the Jacobin methods he knew so well suited him better than any other. His brain was wary, his conscience knew no scruple, and both were served by a most muscular hand.

On the 2nd Thermidor he was appointed Minister of General Police. He started from the Hague, where he was Minister, half killed his horses by the rate which he travelled, and reached Paris on the 11th. On the 17th a message, inspired by him, requested the Councils to order the closing of all the popular societies which had " degenerated " from their original purpose.

Fouché Minister of Police.

The Jacobins, once strong enough to force the Five Hundred into voting Terrorist laws, were now beginning to lose ground; but they still had confidence in their power, and rebelled fiercely against the proposed measure. The reading of the message was received with shouts of " Lies ! " The " traitor Fouché " must be the friend of the royalists, that was certain ! That evening the Club rang with furious protests against Fouché's " calumnies." In spite of the tempest he held on unmoved.

On the 27th, just when Lepelletier was holding forth against him, he made his appearance in the Rue du Bac. He walked in under a storm of abuse, declared the society dissolved, had the gathering dispersed, locked up the *Temple*, left a picket of cavalry outside it, and laid the keys on the table in front of his brother Directors, who were astounded by the swiftness of his victory. The political world was petrified with amazement: when Briot tried to raise a protest, at the sitting of the Five Hundred, he discovered his colleagues had no ears for him, and when the *Journal des Hommes libres* made an attack on Fouché and his supporters, it was simply suppressed, by an order issued on the 1st Fructidor.

* * * * *

The beaten party, horrible to relate, now set its last hopes on the country's reverses. One of its supporters, General Jourdan, was all in favour of proclaiming France in danger, a course which would probably have resulted in a fresh Terror. If he hoped for defeat he had reason to be satisfied.

should be made. Bitter words were spoken on both sides: Vienna was determined to get the Russians out of Lombardy whatever the cost might be (the *Hofkriegsrath* was the ruling authority over all the armies of the Coalition), so the Archduke Charles was ordered to leave Switzerland and proceed to Mayence, and Suwaroff was sent to crush Masséna in Switzerland.

This step was Suwaroff's ruin. Furious with the Austrians, his plans all upset, and tired out, it may be—for he was seventy—he was no longer the man he had been at Magnano and Novi.

The crossing of the Alps indeed was an arduous undertaking: his troops were already exhausted when they came into collision with Lecourbe, in the first place, who on this occasion directed one of the finest mountain campaigns on record, and then with the intrepid Masséna. The "Battle of Zurich" is the name given to these operations (August and September, 1799); as a matter of fact they covered the whole of the Swiss tableland. Korsakoff, who had marched in advance of Suwaroff with 30,000 men, was finally defeated at Zurich, which town was only abandoned by the Russians on the 8th Fructidor (August 26) after a splendid struggle, which cost them 8000 killed, 6000 prisoners, and 100 guns. Suwaroff, who had forced his way over the Saint-Gothard with the greatest difficulty, came up, fell in with Korsakoff's routed troups, despaired of retrieving his fortunes, broke away into the Grisons, and so made his way into Bavaria.

French Victories in Switzerland and Holland.

At the other end of the line of operations Brune likewise was covering himself with glory: on September 19 he attacked two separate bodies of English and Russian troops between Bergen and Alkmaar; and the Duke of York, who had been defeated at Castricum, signed the Convention of Alkmaar, which bound the allies to evacuate Holland between September 19 and October 18. Thus victory was "returning to our colours." France might have been expected to break out into loud expressions of joy and relief. France did nothing of the sort. There was an end of all that; even victory roused no enthusiasm in the country, any more than the overthrow of the Jacobins had relieved its anxiety. *Both these benefits appeared uncertain, or temporary, at all events.* And, indeed, the Jacobins, moved by party spirit, were accusing the Directory of having forged the good tidings. The truth was that the population was utterly worn out.

This last crisis had put the final touch to its exhaustion. Belief in liberty and victory were both dead. Only a strong hand could defend liberty against the Jacobins; only an unerring hand could make the victory final.

There was but one man in the world who would be able to work the miracle; but he was far away.

Bonaparte, too, had been tasting failure : in April 1799 the Turks had stopped his progress at Saint-Jean d'Acre : his **"If Bonaparte** gigantic plan for returning to France by Constanti-**were here !"** nople had come to nought : he had been driven back into Egypt, his magnificent and burning prison. He had avenged himself by driving the Turks into the sea at *Aboukir*, 6th Thermidor (July 25). But he was a captive still. His failure at Saint-Jean d'Acre had passed unnoticed by public opinion, indeed, and the victory of Aboukir, which had become known towards the beginning of Vendémiaire, had shed fresh glory on the victor. The public was also aware that the manner in which he was ruling the conquered country was making the name of France at once loved and feared. As ever, his power of establishing order had been as great as his power of conquest.

"*Ah ! If Bonaparte were only here !*" The phrase passed from mouth to mouth. But what chance was there of his coming back ?

*   *   *   *   *

The words, as we have said, were heard on all sides, in the drawing-rooms of the Directory, in the corridors of the Councils, in the "societies" of Paris, in the Faubourgs of the great city, and, as many testimonies still prove, in the most remote corners of the country. One peasant of the Loiret misspells the name, in his rough journal, but all his hopes are set upon its owner's head.

We have repeatedly directed our readers' attention to the various causes which had led up to the coming of this Cæsar, whose name, so long withheld, was now openly pronounced. In some 200 brilliant and convincing pages a great historian, Albert Vandal, has given us a masterly picture of the situation which was to result in the events of Brumaire.

Every class, every party, every section of society, every coterie, every group, the whole of France, if we look beneath the surface, was longing for the appearance of the man who would restore order ; the avenger, the arbiter, the protector— the dictator.

"*It appears evident that France must soon be governed by a single despot . . . a dictator produced by the Revolution, or a Republican General.*" Thus Morris had written to Washington even in 1793. But the event had been foreseen even before that date. In 1790 Rivarol wrote : " Either the king will have an army, *or the army will have a king.* . . . Revolutions always end with the sword." And Pellenc in 1791 repeats : " As the present dynasty will have inspired nothing but suspicion, *the rule of some fortunate soldier will be preferred.*" We have already referred to the words of the great Catherine, who was watching even in 1794 for the advent of " *the superior man, above all his contemporaries, and perhaps above his century,*" who was to take possession of France.

From the time of the Peace of Campo Formio in 1797, the name of Bonaparte had been whispered. He, thinking " the pear was not yet ripe," had slipped out of sight, and to do so more thoroughly, had left the country. His brothers, indeed, were " keeping his communications open " for him. But others, too, were thinking of his return. Réal had mentioned it to Fouché : and in April 1799 Barras proposed the recall of Bonaparte. " The General is very well where he is," said his colleagues. The Jacobin party, indeed, still looked on him as one of its allies : Jourdan offered him a Jacobin dictatorship ; Briot, the " anarchist " leader, was to make a speech at the rostrum hailing his return with joy. Meanwhile many royalists considered him a possible " Monck," and they were to cling to this opinion until 1802. The philosophers of the Institute extolled him and put him forward, but the Catholics remembered his words at Milan, his salutation to the Archbishop, and the consideration with which he had

Bonaparte the Hope of all Parties.

treated Cardinal Chiaramonti (afterwards Pope Pius VII) at Imola. The prominent military men were perhaps the least ardent of his partisans : but these warriors were all jealous of each other : Bernadotte would never have submitted to the triumph of Moreau or Jourdan, nor is it likely that Augereau would have accepted Brune. If the ruler was to be a soldier, Bonaparte was the inevitable choice.

And, above all, the Nation, which cared little for the tastes and opinions of politicians, learned men, or generals, still loved him, and mourned his absence. "It is since he has been in Egypt that our disasters have come upon us ! " writes Thiébault, a soldier who was not his friend : "It seemed to the people that every battle that had been lost would have been won if he had fought it, and that all the evacuated territory would have been held, so deep was the faith of France not only in the genius of the man, but in the magic influence of his name. Not one of the other generals had succeeded in wiping out or lessening the regret and hope with which the country regarded him, and though success, thanks to Masséna, seemed about to return to our ranks, *Bonaparte alone was looked on as the guarantee of our victory.*"

At last the Directors made up their minds to recall him, but their secret thought was that he would not be able to get back. Even if the dispatch reached his hands, how was he to slip past the enemy's fleets ? No ! it would be impossible for him to come ! "Would he fall from the clouds ? " as Fouché, the fatalist, foresaw that he would : they did not believe it. France would not behold the return of her "saviour."

But on the 19th Vendémiaire the strangely-attired "messengers" of the Directory made their appearance at the Palais-Bourbon. What was their news ? A fresh disaster ? Some new financial proposal, despotic and ruinous ? No ! "Citizens ! the Directory informs you with great pleasure that it has received news from Egypt. General Berthier, who landed at Fréjus on the 17th of this month *with General Bonaparte* . . ." Nobody listened to the rest. The deputies, whatever their party, were on their feet, shouting and cheering, the galleries rang with

Bonaparte returns from Egypt.

THE FRENCH REVOLUTION

acclamations. There was a moment of wild delight. "Long live the Republic !" Was it true ? Was it a dream ? In a moment Paris, which had been so listless, Paris, which cared for nothing, not even for victories, Paris, which had been lying senseless and almost dead, was to spring to her feet, quivering with delight, laughing, weeping; men were seen exchanging frantic embraces, rushing hither and thither for news. One name was heard in every direction: Bonaparte ! Bonaparte ! Bonaparte had landed !

Yes, he was there ! Seven weeks before, hearing of the disasters, and hurrying to meet the call, he had left Egypt. For those six weeks the *Muiron*, bearing Cæsar and his fortunes, had been sailing from Alexandria to Marseilles. English ships had come in sight, there had been much tacking, and a most fortunate escape. And so, on the 17th Vendémiaire, the frigate had quietly dropped anchor off the beach of Saint-Raphael. A wonderful voyage ! In its course, before the Nation could speak its will, Destiny had sealed the traveller's fate !

For the sources and bibliography of this chapter, see those of Chapter XLIX.

CHAPTER XLIX

THE ADVENT OF BONAPARTE

Paris wild with Joy. Bonaparte's journey through France. The " Brumaire " party. Sieyès and Bonaparte. The political world, the Institute, the Staff and Bonaparte. The plan for Brumaire. The 18th Brumaire. The sitting of the Ancients. The Generals with Bonaparte. The collapse of the Directory. Bonaparte at the Tuileries. The 19th Brumaire. Paris at Saint-Cloud. Bonaparte and the Five Hundred. " Daggers." Lucien intervenes. The grenadiers in the Orangerie. The Consuls elected. The return to Paris. *Ça ira!*

O**N the 21st Vendémiaire, the man who afterwards became General Thiébault, happened to turn into the Palais-Royal, and there beheld a most extraordinary sight.** Men were clustering about a passer-by, who shouted and gesticulated as he hurried along ; then the groups broke up, and each individual ran off like lightning, as though to deliver some miraculous piece of news. One of these, as he ran, knocked against our chronicler, and shouted to him, as he fled : "*General Bonaparte has landed at Fréjus !* " Within an hour all Paris was making holiday, and military bands were crashing out triumphal marches in the streets. On every side congratulations and embraces were exchanged. In every theatre that night an actor came upon the stage and announced " the news " amidst the wild plaudits of the audience. And in every tavern, meanwhile, glasses were emptied in honour of " the return."

The Directors might have read their own condemnation in the general enthusiasm : in the Legislative Body, the Mountain, which was at open war with the Government, had affected a joy of the most threatening kind.

For some hours the Government continued in a state of great perplexity. Gohier and Moulin distrusted the General, who had escaped Barras, and was overwhelming Sieyès. On the evening of the 20th, when the news was as yet unknown beyond the walls of the Luxembourg, Sieyès had sent for Moreau and Baudin, this last one of the most ardent supporters of the " appeal to the soldier." He told them the General had landed in France : " There's your man ! " cried Moreau (himself a better hand at retreats); " He'll carry out your *coup d'état* far better than I ! " As for Baudin, he seemed perfectly drunk with delight : the very next day he died of apoplexy—died of joy, the Parisians declared. The idea that this former member of the Convention and ex-regicide died of such joy as this is worthy of note. Seeing the universal outburst of delight, the Directory realized that if it failed to chime in it would be swept out of existence. It decided to put a good face on the matter : it could only check the lion with cobwebs.

*　　*　　*　　*　　*

Meanwhile Bonaparte was moving on towards Paris. All through Provence he was hailed with acclamations. The peasants of the Alps attended him, on his night journeys, with lighted torches. Lyons, which had been ground down ever since 1790, seemed like a town in revolution when he reached it.

Bonaparte travels across France.

He passed on, anxious, grave, smiling absently at times. His mind was fixed on a great adventure. When he had informed his comrades in Egypt that he was about to embark for France, he had told them: " I am going to drive out the lawyers." It was the kind of thing Bernadotte might have said, but in Bernadotte's case the business would have ended there ; in Bonaparte's it was the first hint of a gigantic enterprise—*the reconstitution of France.* And, in his desire to achieve this reconstitution peacefully, he dreamt less of a violent blow struck with the help of soldiers and in agreement with a " faction," than of a revolution accepted by all parties, which should carry himself into power as the arbiter of the quarrels of France ; that accomplished, he would found " *a national government.*" This conception embodied the general desire : Bonaparte's arrival was impatiently awaited, writes

603

a newspaper on the 24th Vendémiaire, because men would learn from him "that all parties may be taught to love the Republic."

The country had guessed that the General meant to deal generously and resolutely with it, and it extolled him to the skies ; a thrill like that which had stirred it in 1789 ran through the nation : one of the local administrations writes that "the news has so electrified the Republicans that *several of them have been unwell, others have shed tears, and none of them are sure it is not all a dream.*"

But Bonaparte himself was devoured by personal anxiety : he had heard of Joséphine's infidelities ; all the way from Fréjus to Paris he had carried a bleeding heart in his breast, and it was thanks to his intention of taking his unfaithful partner by surprise, and putting an end to his dishonour by divorce, that his arrival in Paris had been so sudden as to appear miraculous.

On the evening of the 24th he slipped into his house in the Rue de la Victoire, and found it deserted : Joséphine, in her terror, had hurried to meet and pacify him, taken the wrong road, and so missed him altogether. So while Paris was full of wild rejoicing he spent four-and-twenty lonely hours beside his deserted hearth tormented by painful thoughts. Such contrasts as these emphasize the vanity of human greatness.

Bonaparte arrives in Paris.

On the 26th he took his way to the Luxembourg. Anxious not to cause alarm he went in civilian dress, a round-brimmed hat, and olive-green coat : thus attired he was a strange-looking figure, all the more so because during his stay in Egypt he had cut off his long black hair. But the soldiers on guard at the Petit Luxembourg flew to their arms : they knew him by the flash of his eyes, though he strove to veil it, even then. Gohier, who was in the chair, gave him a fraternal welcome, and embraced him. With some nervousness he faltered his thanks. The crowd outside the building cheered him as he departed.

When he got home Joséphine had returned. With tears and supplications she knelt before him, and, like the great actress she was, made her children cast themselves at the hero's feet. He had thought things over : he had come to build France up again : would it be well to begin by destroying h.s own home ? He forgave her, and from that moment his whole mind was given to his great work.

*　　*　　*　　*　　*

Shoals of politicians crowded to the Rue de la Victoire from every corner of the political horizon : Roederer, Réal, Talleyrand, Régnault of Saint-Jean-d'Angély : " You think *the thing* possible ? " the General had inquired. " *It is three parts done,*" they had replied. When Réal had brought Fouché with him, as he did one day, the thing was considered quite done. Yet the prudent Minister did but little himself, he let things take their course. He simply administered an anæsthetic to the Directory, and then handed it over defenceless to the operator.

The " Brumairians."

Sieyès, meanwhile, was expecting the General's advent with a mixture of dignity and anxiety : he had but little liking for him, and Bonaparte, on his part, detested the "ideologist " most heartily. The Institute made them better friends : in the eyes of that body this duumvirate—a mitred philosopher and a philosopher in military boots—was the very ideal of a good form of government. Now the Institute fancied it was directing the whole movement : Bonaparte had never relaxed his attentions to the members ; the first note he wrote after his return was to thank Laplace for having sent him his *Mécanique céleste.* He heaped praises upon Volney the archæologist and David the painter. Monge and Berthollet, who had come back from Egypt in his company, lauded the protector of the *Institut d'Egypte* to all their friends. They were all enthusiastic about him, from Chénier to Lagrange : here was a man who never would have sent Lavoisier and Condorcet to their deaths, nor hounded the chemists out of the Republic ! With his help, if Berthollet was to be believed, the chemists—and the whole Institute in their train—would rule the Republic ! The General had not yet begun to banter " ideology." He paid a visit to old Madame Helvétius, who received him on the threshold of the house at Auteuil in which she had once made her curtsey to " King Voltaire." Sieyès was a member of the Institute, and it was the Institute that brought the former Abbé and the General together.

Once Bonaparte had made up his mind to take this " crafty priest " (thus he had described him in Gohier's presence) into Bonaparte partnership, he deliberately besieged him with and Sieyès. flattery. " We have no government, because we have no Constitution, or at least not the Constitution we need : your genius must give us one."

A conversation begun in this way could only lead up to the predestined conclusion. The Constitution must be altered, the number of chief magistrates must be reduced from five to three, and this must be done, as far as possible, with the support of the Legislative Body. But there was reason to fear opposition from the " Crest " of the Mountain in the Five Hundred. For a moment this section had fancied it had found its avenger in the person of " General Vendémiaire." On the 10th Brumaire Jourdan paid a visit to Bonaparte and offered to help him to overthrow the Directors; but that would have meant to identify himself with a party, and the most unpopular party of all. Bonaparte had no intention of being a " Robespierre on horseback : " he put the unwelcome proposal aside, but courteously, for he was most desirous that when the blow was delivered it should appear to have the support of every party. This was all the more necessary because the army was following the general's lead much less completely than was generally supposed. Hardly any event has been so little understood as this of the 18th Brumaire, until Albert Vandal reconstructed the whole story for us. This " *coup d'état* carried out by Pretorian guards," as it was called only twenty years ago, was prepared by two Directors and two Ministers in their studies ; in the corridors of the two Assemblies ; and in the rooms of the Institute ; everywhere, in fact, save in the offices of the General Staff. Moreau and Macdonald could not make up their minds, Bernadotte was all cunning and caution, Augereau and Jourdan—after his own suggestion had failed —were absolutely hostile : the one Minister the General and his friends feared was Dubois-Crancé, the Minister of War, and they were obliged to take pains to win over the Governor of Paris (Lefebvre), for much as he loathed the " lawyers," he by no means loved the General. The young officers Bonaparte had brought back with him from Egypt were the only military men who exalted him to the skies. The famous "grenadiers" of the popular prints, which have helped to give substance to the idea of a military *coup d'état*, were not the soldiers of the armies of Italy or Germany, but the rough gendarmes of the Legislative Body, who did police duty within the precincts of the two Councils, and whose appearance at the crucial moment imparted a sort of military colour to the *coup d'état* in the Council of the Ancients, a purely parliamentary affair.

Not a Pretorian was there in the whole business save these Pretorians of Jacobinism.

* * * *

But though the soldiers stood aloof the politicians continued their deliberations: "all parties," writes Fouché, **Bonaparte and** "seemed to be waiting motionless in the presence **the political** of Bonaparte." But the "Brumairians" were **World.** not motionless: they were meeting constantly, sometimes in the General's house, sometimes at Rose's restaurant, where they dined together. The police pretended not to see anything. When "poor Gohier" made some inquiry as to the current reports of conspiracy, Fouché boldly replied, "If there was a plot there would be proof of it on the Place de la Révolution [where the guillotine had worked], or on the Plain of Grenelle" [where prisoners were shot]. The worthy Gohier occupied, at that moment, in making assiduous love to Joséphine, paid perpetual visits to the hornet's nest in the Rue de la Victoire: he fancied there was only honey there—and was very cleverly limed.

On the 15th Brumaire everything was ready. The politicians had completely won over the majority of the Ancients and the "Inspectors of the Chamber:" in the Government itself the adhesion of Fouché, Cambacérès, Sieyès and Roger-Ducos had been secured, and Barras, it was thought, would be neutralized at all events. Joséphine had undertaken to dazzle her admirer Gohier; Dubois-Crancé was being deceived by his colleague, the Minister of Police: Murat and Leclerc had very nearly persuaded Lefebvre to join them. Roederer, who, helped by Regnault and Maret, was, as Barras says, Bonaparte's

" canvasser," was everywhere at once : his son had actually entered a printing office so as to be able to print proclamations without anybody's knowledge. Collot, the financier, had advanced millions of money.

This, then, was the plan : the Ancients were to take steps to be suddenly informed that certain partisans of disorder were engaged in a plot against the Republic : they were then to transfer the seat of government to Saint-Cloud and appoint Bonaparte to command the armed forces. Sieyès and Ducos were to resign, Barras and Gohier were to be induced to follow their example. The Government having thus fallen to pieces, the Legislative Body was to constitute another ; but considering the peril in which the Republic stood, it must be made stronger than the last : Bonaparte was to enter it, with Sieyès, the greatest of legislators, and while Sieyès—at last !—was bestowing the ideal Constitution on the country, the General was to crush the " conspirators." The Five Hundred would raise no difficulties, and to make assurance doubly sure, a few reliable regiments were to be marched to Saint-Cloud.

The Plan of the " Coup d'état."

On the evening of the 17th the batteries were drawn up in order and the gunners all ready at their posts. Sebastiani and Murat knew they were to be at the Tuileries at dawn next day, one with his dragoons, the other with his light cavalry. Young Roederer sat himself down to his printing press and Bonaparte went to dine with the Minister of Justice : to put Barras off the scent he had asked himself to breakfast with him the next morning, and Gohier had been invited for the same hour by the fascinating Joséphine. In short, all those who were not accomplices were dupes.

At daybreak on the 18th, the Ancients, who had been summoned in the course of the night by their "Inspectors," had gathered at the Tuileries. One of these inspectors, Cornet, read them a confused, and for that reason all the more terrifying report. ". . . Alarming symptoms . . . gloomy reports. . . . The conflagration will soon become general. . . . *The Republic will have ceased to exist, and its skeleton will be in the hands of the vultures !* " Not a single fact : how indeed was it possible to say anything

18th Brumaire.

613

definite without accusing every one, concerning the things which really threatened the ruin of both Republic and country? Thus the indictment, tragic in its vagueness, bore a close resemblance to the shadowy accusations which had sent Brissot, Danton, and Robespierre to the scaffold. The Assembly did not ask for any further explanation : the country must be saved from the "vultures " : who could do it better than Bonaparte? A decree in five clauses was forthwith carried by acclamation : the Legislative Body was to proceed to Saint-Cloud (on the plea of the risk of a Terrorist outbreak in Paris) ; Bonaparte was appointed to command the 1st Division and hastily summoned to the Tuileries to take the oath. The inspectors went to fetch him from his own house for the purpose.

There they found a numerous (and noisy) company. On the preceding evening Bonaparte had personally invited a number of generals to be at his house by daybreak next morning. They met, they talked, they grew excited. Important men appeared : Moreau, Macdonald, Beurnonville, all very much astonished to find such a gathering, then Lefebvre, then Bernadotte. These had believed themselves summoned to a private talk: they found themselves in the middle of a military club-meeting. They were all induced to remain, even Lefebvre, who refused at first, but ended by allowing himself to be coaxed and carried with the tide ; Bernadotte was the only one who slipped out, and even he went without breaking with his comrades : Sieyès gave Barras a true picture of the Béarnais with his fine gestures : *Feez et cortez* (false and courteous) they called him in his native Béarn ; he reserved his decision and retired, with a noble air, to await events in the house of his brother-in-law, Joseph Bonaparte—an alibi équivalent to partial adhesion.

More than sixty generals were present when the "Inspectors " of the Council of the Ancients made their entry. The newcomers preferred their request. Bonaparte granted it. And suddenly the gate of the garden, full of the buzz and hum of the assembled generals, was seen to open. The conqueror of Rivoli appeared, pale as death, under the now famous black hat, and clad in his embroidered uniform. There was a storm

614

of applause; he addressed his "brave comrades in arms": they would help him to save the Republic! Hands flew to sword-hilts. What need for that? Law and glory were ready to march hand in hand: together they would take the oath in the Council of the Ancients. Then, escorted by Murat's dragoons, that extraordinary procession which was to pass— how symbolic are the words—from the Rue de la *Victoire* to the Place de la *Concorde,* set forth upon its way.

Cheers hailed it all along the road! Eight years—nay! eight centuries!—of glorious deeds moved in that great company of heroes, from the cool Moreau to the fiery Murat. When Ouvrard, the king of the Bourse, looking out of his windows in the Boulevard des Capucines, saw it pass along, he wrote one word to his brokers: "*Buy!*" And that again was an acclamation to which every historian should lend his ear.

The procession reached the gate of the Tuileries: it opened, not forced, as it had been in Fructidor, but with the majestic sweep that welcomes an expected guest. Amidst the plaudits of the whole Assembly, that guest passed into the "Senate." As he entered the crowd raised a great shout: "*Long live the Liberator!*"

* * * * *

The news of the Ancients' unexpected decree reached the Luxembourg at seven o'clock in the morning. It was a surprise The Sitting of to Barras. "I was mistaken by forty-eight hours the Ancients. as to the time of the explosion," he says. But he still believed himself the General's "old friend": he thought it wise to gain time, and, to create an alibi for himself, too, he got into his bath, and shot all the bolts. This would be a defence against any call from his brother Directors.

Sieyès was not to be found: he was in the garden, where he had been practising horsemanship at daybreak for the last few days: for this ex-Vicar-General had set his heart on cutting a good figure at the General's side, even if the *coup d'état* were carried out in boots and spurs. Hearing what had happened, he took his way to the Tuileries, still on horseback, and attended by two officers.

Gohier, the President of the Directory, tried to call the Directors together. But Ducos, too, was in retirement. No valid decision could be arrived at, unless three members were present, and Barras had sent word that he was at his toilet and could not come for another hour : all he did was to send Bottot, his secretary, to the Tuileries. Gohier and Moulin were sitting together, pouring forth streams of lamentation, when Fouché made his appearance with a sham air of melancholy astonishment : taking him to be either a traitor or a fool, they received him very ill. This unfriendly treatment straightway convinced the Minister of the urgent necessity of getting rid of both men before they were twenty-four hours older. Yet he probably found time to insinuate that the only thing to be done was to get rid of Barras (*débarrasser le Directoire*). And Gohier and Moulin, nursing this last hope, betook themselves to the Tuileries to find out what was happening. On the Tuileries everybody was now converging, as happens at a certain point in all well constructed dramas.

The great scene had just been played. It must be admitted that the chief actor had not shone : Bonaparte was always **Bonaparte** nervous and hesitating at the rostrum. He **denounces** stammered forth his vows of fidelity ; he took the **the Directory.** oath, and the sitting broke up. The Five Hundred on the other side of the river were bound by the Constitution to do the same thing, without discussion of any kind. At eleven o'clock Bonaparte rode out of the Tuileries very much put out because he had spoken so badly, and thinking, as generally happens, of what he ought to have said. Suddenly he caught sight of Bottot, Barras' favourite henchman, trying to get speech of him. The General decided that this Bottot should be the incarnation of the Directory : riding down upon him, he poured forth a fierce diatribe against the whole system, in the person of this subordinate : "The Army has joined forces with me," he cried in a loud voice, "and I have joined forces with the Legislative Body." Applause rang out from the crowd. "What have you done with this France, so brilliant when I left her to your care ? I left you in peace, I come back and find war ! I left you victorious, I come back to reverses ! I left you the millions of Italy, I find laws of spoliation and misery everywhere. . . . What have you done with the 100,000 Frenchmen who were my friends, my comrades

616

in glory ? *They are dead!* This state of things cannot go on : *before three years were out it would have brought us to despotism!* But we are determined to have a Republic founded on a basis of equality and morality, of civil liberty and political tolerance. *Under a good government every individual man will forget the faction of which he has been made a member, and will be free to be a Frenchman. . . .* To hear some factious fellows talk one would think that we, who have strengthened the Republic by our labours and our courage, are soon to be accounted its enemies ; we want no more patriotic men than the brave fellows who have been maimed in the service of the Republic ! " The cheers of the bystanders punctuated every sentence. Then Bonaparte turned from the miserable Bottot, dashed across the square on his black charger, rode along the front of the troops, dropping a wildly applauded sentence here and there as he went, and so back to the Rue de la Victoire, believing the battle won.

Won it was, up to a certain point : the Directory was sinking out of sight. The spontaneous resignations of Sieyès **Downfall of** and Ducos would not have sufficed for this. **the Directory.** Barras must make up his mind to go as well. Talleyrand arrived, bearing the draft of a dignified letter to the effect that Barras wished to resign on the score of his need of rest ; only the signature was lacking : the unlucky Director, we are told, cast one glance on the crowd cheering the troops in the Rue de Tournon, and wrote his name. Mme. Tallien, coming in just then, earnestly besought him to be " worthy of himself " (the expression provokes a smile) ; but he had given in utterly : resistance would have been both useless and absurd. So these two parted : they had been the very incarnation of a system that had rotted away, as mouldy things will. She went back to her " cottage": whence she was shortly to issue forth again, Princesse de Chimay, indeed, but severed for ever from public life. He, a few minutes later, left the Luxembourg for Grosbois with a hundred dragoons riding round his carriage. Thus the Vicomte Paul de Barras, the man of Thermidor, of Vendémiaire, of Fructidor," slipped stealthily out of history."

Gohier and Moulin refused to resign : their power was gone

indeed : but it was thought as well to give them a distinguished gaoler at the Luxembourg; the position, a strange fact this, was accepted by Moreau.

With whom did the power lie now ? In the hands of Bonaparte, who commanded the armed forces. The *coup d'état* then was considered an accomplished fact : there was an immediate rise in the price of government stocks. The General's mind was easy. Sieyès, clinging to the traditions of the Directory, would have liked to see forty unruly deputies placed under arrest : the General refused to do it, and sent Salicetti to calm them. But they refused to be calmed; they held a consultation, and prepared to set up Bernadotte against Bonaparte, if necessary. The rain poured down on Paris, and there was a certain amount of agitation.

* * * * *

On the morning of the 19th the weather had cleared, and everybody departed to Saint-Cloud. What was to be done there ? Curiously enough there was no agreement as to this. To the very last the French Revolution was driven forward by a kind of *Fatum*. Bonaparte no more knew what he was going to do on the 19th Brumaire than the men who took the Bastille knew on the morning of July 14, the deputies who upset the throne on the morning of August 10, or those who set up the Republic on September 21.

19th Brumaire

The two Assemblies ought to have been brought under the same roof, their debates should have taken place before noon, and they should have been induced to hail the triumvirate— in which Bonaparte and Sieyès were to play the parts of Cæsar and Pompey, while Ducos undertook the ungrateful rôle of Crassus—with plaudits. The whole thing would have ended, then, in a storm of cheering. But the Ancients had taken possession of the splendid Gallery of Apollo, and the only apartment left for the Five Hundred was the Orangerie, reached by a narrow staircase, and raised but a very little above the level of the ground (the windows opened a few feet above the flower-beds). This room had to be prepared, and thus time was lost. The Ancients and the Five Hundred mingled on the Terrace and talked : the story of the " conspiracy " announced on the preceding day did not come over well out of this exchange of views : it began to look like a myth. By one o'clock, when the rooms were ready, and the deputies poured in, there was confusion among the Ancients, and in the Five Hundred, a whole party was bent on resistance.

Everybody who had any connexion with politics had crowded into Saint-Cloud. Bonaparte had ridden down via Auteuil. He joined Ducos and Sieyès in the reception rooms on the first floor : shivering with the fever of his excitement, he strove to warm himself before the wood-fire which had been hastily lighted.

All Paris at Saint-Cloud.

Meanwhile the deputies, draped in their red togas, were discussing matters. Lucien Bonaparte, who had been President of the Five Hundred for a week past, had taken the chair, and Gaudin had moved for the appointment of a Commission of Inquiry into the dangers threatening the Republic. Sneers came from the Extreme Left : "Down with dictators ! " shouted somebody. The "Brumairians" were disconcerted. To gain time (but why ?) the two parties agreed to an absurd proposal : each deputy was to go to the rostrum and there renew his oath of fidelity to the Constitution.

The Ancients had begun to shuffle too ; they dispatched a message to the Directory ; Lagarde, the secretary, replied that the Directory had ceased to exist. Then Bonaparte appeared, made a poor speech, clumsy and almost incoherent. He defended himself, somewhat awkwardly, against the accusation of being a "Cromwell," and left the presence of this lethargic Senate, wrought up himself to the highest pitch of nervous excitement.

*   *   *   *   *

He realized that these old men would do nothing more. He must force fortune's hand, and make a dash for success. He did just what he had done at Arcola : he sent for a few of the grenadiers of the Legislative Body, and led them into the Orangerie.

On the threshold he halted, overwhelmed by the unexpected tempest his appearance had evoked. Wild shouts rose about him : "Down with the dictator ! Down with the tyrant ! Outlaw him ! " and in an instant the men of the

619

Mountain were upon him. He was a small man, his strength more nervous than muscular; he was almost smothered; one **Bonaparte and** gigantic fellow of the name of Destrem hit him **the Five** with his fist. Hemmed in by the red togas, **Hundred.** shamefully knocked about and struck, he almost lost consciousness. The grenadiers rescued him, and carried him off, while a score of deputies shouted " *Outlaw !* " as they went.

Lucien had lost all power over the members; he was attacked in his presidential chair, made his way down to the rostrum, and held on to it, in spite of every effort to tear him away, so that he might defend his brother. But his voice was drowned. Already the timid members, spurred by their own fears, were joining in the cry of their violent comrades: the shouts of " *Outlaw !* " seemed to grow stronger. That had been the cry in Thermidor, and it had brought Robespierre to the scaffold.

Bonaparte, at first convulsed with agitation, had recovered a little in the saloon, where counsels of vigour were being exchanged on every side. As though by instinct, the troops in the courtyards had massed themselves together; but the Army of Paris was in the second line, and the grenadiers of the Legislative Body, the real arbiters of the situation, stood between it and the Orangerie.

" My horse ! " cried the General. He was terrible to look upon; his pallid face was streaked with red; these streaks were blood. For several days he had been suffering from fever; his face that morning had been covered with a fever rash, and, in his frenzy of impatience, he had torn the pimples with his finger nails. The blood gave colour to the story that the deputies had attacked and wounded him " with daggers ": the troops were infuriated by the thought that these lawyers had dared to lift their hands against the victor of Arcola.

" Soldiers ! Can I rely on you ? . . . " Yes ! Yes ! " and rough curses on the deputies broke from the ranks. " I will bring them to their senses," shouted the General. The dragoons were quivering with impatience, but the grenadiers of the Legislative Body hesitated. They had been told, indeed, that the Assembly was oppressed by a band of murderers, and only longed to be delivered; but what proof had they that this was true ?

620

Suddenly a great shout went up : Lucien Bonaparte, President of the Five Hundred, had just appeared upon the scene.

Intervention of Lucien Bonaparte. By sheer resolution (he was the one *man* of that day) he had contrived to escape, with the help of a few soldiers, and now brought victory with him.

He looked the incarnation of the Assembly over which he presided, and it was in the name of that Assembly that he seemed to speak, when, sitting on horseback at his brother's side, he called on the grenadiers of the Councils for their help : "The President of the Council of the Five Hundred assures you that the immense majority of that Council is living in terror, for the moment, of a few members armed with daggers, who are besieging the rostrum, threatening their colleagues with death, and forcing them into decisions of the most terrible kind. I declare to you that *these audacious ruffians, paid, no doubt, by England* (this was quite after the style of Robespierre) *have rebelled against the Council of the Ancients* and have dared to talk of outlawing the General charged with the execution of its decree. I declare to you that these few factious men, by their attacks on the liberty of the Council, have put themselves beyond the pale of the law. . . . I confide the *duty of restoring the majority of their representatives to freedom* to our warriors ! Generals, soldiers, citizens all, you will only acknowledge as legislators in France the men who shall now gather about me. As for those who persist in remaining in the Orangerie, *let them be expelled by force !* These ruffians do not represent the people, *they represent the dagger !* " And as though he would have swept away the last doubt harboured by the republican soldiers whose action his very presence seemed to authorize, he drew the General's sword out of its scabbard, turned its point against his brother's breast, and with a gesture worthy of a character in one of Marie-Joseph Chénier's plays, swore to pierce that breast if ever the heart of a tyrant should beat within it !

There was one great shout. The grenadiers' minds were made up : they must " deliver the good representatives from the ruffians who were oppressing them." The officers drew their swords : and then, over the tumultuous shouts, another sound rose, dull, rhythmic: the drums had begun to beat the charge. The troops formed into column with bayonets fixed; at their head marched the daring Joachim Murat : he moved straight on the staircase that led up to the Orangerie. The crowd cheered wildly: "Bravo! Down with the Jacobins! The Rubicon! Down with '93! Down with '93!" The words spoke all the hatred, too long suppressed, that had been seething for six whole years. Bonaparte was to benefit by that : the populace would gladly have struck Robespierre down once more.

The Grenadiers
invest the
Orangery.

Within the Orangerie confusion reigned supreme : the deputies were eddying to and fro. The rolling of the drums, faint to begin with, grew desperately loud. Onlookers, first of all, and then deputies, began to drop out of the low windows. The door flew open : Murat and his men advanced to the rostrum and took possession of it. The grenadiers passed down the long room: "Citizens!" they shouted, "you are dissolved!" The cry was echoed by an officer from the presidential chair. Murat shouted that "they must be thrown out." The bayonets gleamed in the dim twilight. Then more windows were broken open : and the red togas fled away into the November darkness : next day their cast-off purple garments were discovered hanging in the thickets of the Forest of Saint-Germain and the Meudon woods. Some of the deputies ran as far as the gates of Paris, which had been closed by Fouché's orders.

An empty precaution this, if it was intended to prevent an insurrection. Two months before that date the workmen of the "Faubourg of Glory," the old soldiers who had served under Desmoulins, Danton, Santerre, and Hanriot, had said: "Let them do as they choose, the Faubourgs will have nothing more to say to it!" This was rather less than ten years and four months since the day on which the Faubourg, hearing Necker had been dismissed at Versailles, had hurled itself upon the Bastille. On the 19th Brumaire of the Year VIII of the Republic that same Faubourg, hearing the recalcitrant deputies had been thrown out of window, was to applaud the action: "Muddlers who have tumbled down like the Cascades at Saint-Cloud!" they said in the wineshops.

＊　　＊　　＊　　＊　　＊

At nightfall, on that same 19th, a new government was being set up. The Ancients had appointed a Commission of Five, **Election of a Consulate.** and this had proposed and carried a vote in favour of the promotion of Bonaparte, Sieyès, and Roger-Ducos to a "Temporary Consulate," the adjournment of both Councils till the 1st Nivôse, and "in consideration of the retirement of the Five Hundred" (the expression was comic) the creation of two Legislative Commissions. Then, while the victors were dining together merrily, an attempt was made to reconstitute the Councils so that they might impart some appearance of legal confirmation to these decisions. Various deputies, with togas or without them, were picked up in taverns, and hackney carriages, and in the park of Saint-Cloud: they were brought back into the dimly lighted rooms. Speeches were delivered by Cabanis and Boulay. Boulay made one happy remark: "We desire to *nationalize* the Republic."

At two o'clock in the morning the three Consuls were requested to take the oath—to whom, or what, nobody seemed very sure. The rooms were crowded with people who had hurried out from Paris: the assembly cheered and shouted when the drums beat the salute and the three Consuls made their appearance. They took the oath, and departed amidst more shouts of "Long live the Republic!"

By six o'clock everybody was back in Paris. The grenadiers of the Legislative Body marched home to their quarters in the **"Ça ira!"** Capucine Barracks singing the "*Ça ira.*" In all good faith they believed they had saved the Republic and the Revolution.

Same sources and works as for Chapter XLV, and in addition:
SOURCES. Works already quoted by Aulard (*Paris . . .* V), Laviron, Gervinus and Peter Roux (in *Bailleu*), Barras (IV), Hyde de Neuville (I), Gohier (I), Morris.—Rocquain, *État de la France au 18 Brumaire (Documents)*, ‚897; Delbrel, *Lettre sur le 18 Brumaire (Rev. Fr.,* 1893); *Lettre de Robert Lindet* (in *Montier, op. cit.*); Chaptal, *Souvenirs,* 1899; Fabre de l'Aude, *Directoire,* 1832; Arnault, *Mémoires,* 1825; Ph. de Ségur, *Souvenirs*;

THE FRENCH REVOLUTION

Destrem, *Quelques Documents sur le 18 Brumaire (Rev. Fr.,* 1910) ; Coignet, *Cahiers,* 1892.

WORKS. Albert Vandal, *L'Avènement de Bonaparte,* 1902 ; Chuquet, *Lecture sur le Retour de Bonaparte faite à l'Académie des Sciences Morales,* 1910 ; Guillois, *Le Salon de Madame Helvétius,* 1889 ; Babeau, *La France et Paris sous le Directoire,* 1887 ; Cadoudal, *Georges Cadoudal* ; Madelin, *Fouché,* I, 1903 ; Néton, *Sieyès,* 1900 ; Berger, *Volney,* 1885 ; Libois, *Les Emprunts forcés de l'An IV et de l'an VII dans le Jura,* 1895.

THE EPILOGUE

*T*HEY *had saved the Revolution.* In the light of the many works on the History of the Revolution published within the last thirty years the words are a truism. According to the historians of the preceding age, the History of the Revolution ended on the evening of the 19th Brumaire. But not one historian of our times would admit the truth of such a conception. The Revolution, on that evening of the 19th Brumaire, simply entered on a fresh phase. Such men as Sorel, and Aulard, and Vandal tell us that in the opinion of the French people only one change supervened between the twilight of the 19th Brumaire and the dawn of the 20th: the Revolution, its principles, its conquests, hitherto so ill-defended, were strengthened, and permanently acquired. In the eyes of France the event was neither a retrogression nor even a halt. And to some extent the view of the country was a true view.

The Republic itself did not appear threatened, it rather seemed renewed. As a fact it was doomed. Cæsar, the inevitable product (we have explained how and why) of past excesses, mistakes, and crimes, was shortly to lay hands upon the State, and do away with the Republic altogether. But the Republic, as we know, had never at any time, nor to any degree, been desired by the great majority of the men, on every rung of the social ladder, who had brought about the Revolution.

The Revolution of 1789 had been the work of the Nation. The " progress of knowledge " had opened the eyes of the upper classes to the abuses of inequality. The excess of the public suffering had driven the popular classes into rebellion. Their firm resolve to abolish the feudal system had stirred the peasants to revolt. The evident anarchy existing in the King's government had roused a general desire for a *Constitution.*

but by the word Constitution nine-tenths of the French nation understood nothing more than a charter which should reorganize the State. *Equality in matters of justice and taxation—the abolition of the feudal system—a methodical and orderly system of government*—these were what the Frenchmen of January 1789 sought to obtain.

By August of that year almost all these things had been secured, and on the 5th of that month the supporters of the Revolution, with many demonstrations of mutual affection, had declared it at an end. For the mass of the rural population especially this was the case.

But no revolution can take place without stirring up eddies thick with turbid elements. These exist in every nation and at every epoch. Above, we have the ambitious politicians, below, the great company of outlaws, social and moral, and between these two categories, all those who fish in troubled waters. From the outset these had been busy. On July 14, 1789, a young journalist had hurled a mob drawn from the Faubourg Saint-Antoine, and containing a strong admixture of thieves and robbers, on the Bastille : the fortress was taken, its defenders, faithful soldiers of the King, were murdered, and Flesselle, the Provost, was murdered too. These crimes seemed to be universally approved. From that moment insurrection was an accepted thing, and before long it became a chronic complaint.

A whole party found its advantage here : the ambitious men and the orators of the Assembly, who set forth the noblest ideas, with intentions occasionally much less noble. The social and political Revolution of 1789 had been carried through so swiftly that time had not permitted them to climb into power with it, so they set their minds on a more far-reaching Revolution which would ensure them leisure to attain their ends. There must be a general renovation, the past must be entirely wiped out, a new and immortal commonwealth must be built up. Many were the Frenchmen, well content with the results already acquired, who endured these politicians though they did not follow them.

They endured them *because they considered them the defenders of the conquests made in the course of the summer of* 1789, *and believed those conquests to be in peril.* The restless men, the men who were pushing their own fortunes, the tribunes, the ringleaders of the Assembly and the mob, found their most valuable allies in the Court of Versailles, and the whilom privileged classes. There was a split in these last, and in the Court itself. They might have done one of two things, organized an open resistance, or put themselves at the head of the movement. Sometimes they seemed to take up one line, and then, again, to follow the other. In their desire to prove their sympathy with the new ideas, priests, nobles, and some of the King's ministers, would sometimes go even further than the democrats. But there were others who did not grasp the fact that a time had come when voluntary sacrifices must be made. And, as a result of this division, the resistance of these classes, according as one view or the other prevailed, was intermittent, impolitic, and occasionally underhand.

This resistance alarmed those Frenchmen who had desired nothing beyond certain reforms in 1789, but were resolved not to lose what they had then gained ; the behaviour of certain princes, spurred on by certain nobles, seemed to justify the assertions made by the leaders of the movement for a total Revolution, to the effect that "the Court" was only waiting its opportunity to take back all it had given, and that before long feudal rights, the tithe, and salt-tax, and the *taille*, and all the lately abolished evils would be upon the people again.

What the Nation needed was a very great king at its head. The Revolution found the throne occupied by a generous, pious, liberal-minded man, not by any means the fool he has been commonly supposed to be, but certainly quite unequal to the task of coping with circumstances of the most crushing difficulty. Between his wife, his brothers, his ministers, his courtiers, the Assembly, and the people, on all of whom he turned a kindly eye, he never could make up his mind to any decision. Sincerely determined to be a "constitutional monarch," he believed "a good-natured king" to be the same thing, and this left the opponents of the Revolution the hope of a sudden change of front.

When, at last, the struggling monarch would fain have resisted his assailants, he felt that one weapon which must ever be the *ultima ratio* of kings, and even of republics, crumble in

627

his grasp: *the army. This, the dissolution of the army, was one of the most important events of the epoch.* Once that had come about what could the King do ? He seemed to resign himself to his fate.

Meanwhile the ringleaders of integral Revolution were sweeping the Assembly, drunk as it was with idealism, into reforms of the most formidable kind. With the utmost rashness everything was overthrown: a strange Constitution—a monument of Utopian fancy without an element of durability about it—was set up, and a splendid Declaration promised everything the Constitution did not contain, and thus condemned the Revolution to go on for ever. Even this, perhaps, the King might have accepted, if the deputies, carried away by their mania for reform, urged on, too, by hatreds far older than themselves, and spurred by financial necessity, had not turned their attention to the ancient church of the country—more ancient even than the throne—and, with the object, in the first place, of squeezing money out of it, set themselves to reform it too. The goods of the Church were declared the property of the Nation, they were offered for sale, and made the basis of a paper currency. When the Church protested against this injustice, an attempt was made to regenerate it by means of the Civil Constitution of the Clergy. This was an immense blunder on the Assembly's part. When it endeavoured, in its simplicity, to reorganize the ecclesiastical hierarchy to suit its own convenience, the Clergy defended itself, and religious dissension, ten times as inextinguishable as civil quarrels, at once broke out.

The King was a most pious Catholic : he had forgiven the Revolution everything, even the humiliation of the throne : *he never forgave it for having forced him to sanction the Civil Constitution of the Clergy.* That drove him into the arms of the counter-revolutionary party, which persuaded him to take flight. He was caught, and brought back, amidst the indignation of his people, and from that day forth the monarchy, which had hitherto escaped attack, began to tremble.

Meanwhile a two-fold movement was going on in the country. The Revolution had wounded, because it had ignored, a thousand interests and feelings. In the opinion of many it had been far too rapid ; commerce having suffered, and consequently industry, numerous small trades had been injured too. The poverty of the lower classes was growing terrible. By 1791 the Revolution had overshot its mark, and fallen under the displeasure of all who had been affected by it, and quite half of those who had brought it about. On the other hand a certain section of adherents had joined its banner—the purchasers of national properties. In 1790–1791 a new class of proprietors had come into existence : in 1792 this class had a recognized being. And now, whenever the Revolution was attacked, a whole army of landowners felt their position threatened. These men had no revolutionary feeling, but they, too, joined the leaders in their assaults upon the Court, because the Court, so they were told, by working against the Revolution, was working to destroy their new proprietorship.

By this time the Court was striving not merely to check, but to drive back the tide of Revolution. And, finding it had no supporters within the country—for the nobles had emigrated, instead of forming themselves into a solid party of resistance— the Court appealed to the interests common to all monarchies, and asked for help from the foreigner.

The foreigner turned a willing ear to the request, not because Europe had any feeling for the solidarity of monarchs, but because she hoped to take advantage of the difficulties of the kingdom, to invade it, and cut it into pieces. Neither Louis XVI nor the absent princes would have admitted this for an instant; they would have let themselves be killed sooner than give up a single fortified town ; but the *émigrés* appeared in the ranks of the foreign armies, and the solid good sense of the Nation detected the intention of Europe, so evident now, to bring about the ruin of France. Connivance of this nature *compromised the King hopelessly in his people's eyes.* His fate was sealed from the time when the German armies began to mass themselves on the frontier ; and he fell on the very day they crossed it.

At the same moment a violent movement convulsed the country. Its independence was in danger, and those who attacked the Revolution were attacking the country too. Thenceforth it became evident that *patriotism was synonymous with civism, and civism with Jacobinism.* The persons who had legitimate reason to dislike the Revolution no longer dared to let their discontent be known, for they would have been taken for agents of the foreigner. A wild excitement spread in all directions, and a fresh, fierce and most horrible fit of revolutionary fever was the result.

The ringleaders seized this opportunity to effect a final perversion of the nature of the Revolution, and so appropriate it for their own purposes. It had been carried out in 1789 to the cry of " *Long live liberty !* " and " *Long live the King !* " These men dethroned the King, and then, to cut off all chance of retreat, they sent him to the scaffold. Next, they used the idea of Public Safety, and the danger of the country, as a plea for setting up a Jacobin dictatorship, and France, which for three years past had been slowly enveloped in a network of Jacobin societies, was cast helpless at the feet of a Committee of Public Safety which, like the Convention, was always to be ruled by whoever appeared the " most patriotic " man of that particular moment. Finally, the Revolution, which declared itself a lover of peace, was seized with a warlike intoxication. It had already driven back the enemy's attack, but now it dreamt of marching into foreign countries and imposing its own theories on them by force of arms. France being what she was, and is, the passions which have always been so hot within her people were maddened by such doings. The idea that, as victory had crowned her arms, *France must take advantage of it to build up a greater France by conquering the natural frontiers,* was accepted. This would entail a lengthy war, and the Terrorist party was well pleased, for it thus found a pretext for remaining in power, and proceeded *to issue a solemn declaration whereby the doctrine of the natural frontiers was formally bound up with the principles of the Revolution.*

In 1793 a comparatively small knot of men had taken possession of France, of the Revolution, and the Republic. Now three-fourths of the Nation longed to see the Revolution ended, or rid at all events of the men who were exploiting it so shamefully : but these last held the unhappy country by a variety of means. Every time it tried to rise it was crushed down again. And these dishonest men, it must be said, were industrious and energetic, and had hardy soldiers at their beck and call.

THE EPILOGUE

As the Terror was indispensable to them if their domination was to endure, they struck down any man who seemed inclined, at any moment, to withstand the Terror, even if he had been one of the most faithful of the Revolution's servants. In this fashion the ranks of the men who first started the idea of reforms in 1789, from Barnave to Danton, were decimated, and after them, the ranks of those who founded the Republic in 1792.

All this destroyed the very nature of the Revolution. It had gone quite astray, and imposed itself by sheer force in its perverted form, on all who were not prepared to recognize in this bloodstained Republic, the smiling Liberty the men of 1789 had thought they were bringing in. Then, in every class of society, a hatred of the new tyrants grew up. The love of the original ideas of the Revolution still endured ; nothing on earth would have induced its admirers to abandon it ; and, beside these intangible principles, interests had grown up which their possessors had no intention of sacrificing : the old *régime* was regarded with detestation, the desire for the maintenance of Liberty and Equality was there still, but it was a desire for *civil Liberty and Equality*: for the organization of the State on this basis. There was a rooted horror of assemblies of orators, and political clubs, and parliaments packed with professional politicians, because their words had all been written in blood. There was a desire, too, that the interests created by the Revolution should be secured, but this was felt to be impossible so long as the Government lived in a frenzy, perpetually endangered by its own excesses, and thoroughly fragile and unstable, as every one recognized this Government to be. Finally, the country desired to maintain the national independence, and even retain certain of the conquests made in Europe ; but it was sick of the ruinous expense of a never-ending state of war. *To sum it up, it wanted, from 1794 onwards, what it had wanted in 1789, and what it was still to want in 1799 : to see France organized on a firm basis, in consonance with the desires expressed in the Memorials.* *

But an oligarchy had come into existence ; it had grown accustomed to power, and declined to relinquish it. *These well-provided Jacobins were not seeking to secure the triumph of a*

* See Chap. V.

single fresh principle, but they had strong interests to defend: their power, their wealth, and above all, their own heads, which they believed would be in sore danger if any counter-revolution were carried through. For this reason, having brought a king, a queen, and thousands of citizens to their deaths, in the name of the sovereignty of he people, they brutally ignored this sovereignty when France, after the Terrorist yoke had been cast off, on the 9th Thermidor, essayed to raise her voice and make it heard. The country, it may be, would have recalled a king who was ready to accept the ideas of 1789, in as far as they were just and fair, sanction the new proprietary system, and avoid civil strife by promising to forget the past. *The Bourbons, in their irreconcilable blindness, made this experiment impossible :* the Nation—the monarchy of 1789, to which it had remained attached all through the struggle, having failed it—concluded its best course was to set up a liberal Republic, and more especially a system of government under which liberty of conscience, now so odiously oppressed, would be restored.

But the very first outcome of such an event would have been the fall of the *revolutionary oligarchy.* It refused to allow itself to be eliminated. *In 1795 it forced itself on the country,* did its utmost to stifle its voice, and failing, closed its mouth by sheer brutality, in Fructidor of the Year V. *From that time forward the whole system was simply a hypocritical fiction.* The country turned from it. It would fain have rid itself of the tyrants : *it fell in love in advance with the man who was to deliver it from them.* It was weary of phrases, and lies, and political orators, and blunderers, and petty tyrants. All belief in liberty was dead, and serious men were terrified to see the Nation drifting along, its strength exhausted by so many successive crises. There was nothing more to be done : *all hopes were centred on the advent of a man.*

The man appeared : *he belonged to the army, and that, too, was inevitable.*

This army, which Louis XVI had not been able to use, because it was on the brink of dissolution, had built itself up again under the enemy's fire. It had fought thirty campaigns, won a hundred victories, conquered provinces and whole countries.

682

THE EPILOGUE

It was the darling of the Nation which it had gorged with glory while the tribunes were deceiving it with talk. Being the Nation's darling it was dangerous ; but, most of all, because it was full of generals of thirty, or thereabouts, conscious of the services they had done their country, and resolved that they would not take orders from a set of rhetoricians.

Amongst these men one had appeared who seemed to have been raised up by fate, just as the ancient tragedians used to set up a god at the close of their plays. He was the outcome, in reality, of a hundred events, both great and small. He dazzled the Nation's eyes, he fascinated it, he subjugated it. The first thing it hoped to receive at his hand was a glorious peace : if, having given it that, this soldier, the Revolution's true son, kept faith with it, established civil liberty and equality on a solid basis, and so secured the ruin of the feudal system once and for ever ; if he endowed the country with that rational and methodical administrative organization which the old *régime* had failed to bestow, but which none of the Assemblies of the Revolution had given it either in any degree, *the hopes of 1789 would be fulfilled.* If he ensured the existence of the new proprietary system by inducing the original proprietors—and the Church more especially—to recognize the accomplished fact, he would be the saviour of important interests, and would lay a salve on many a conscience. If he governed without any party in particular, refused to surround himself exclusively with members of the revolutionary oligarchy, and refrained from proscribing any of the men who had been working since 1789 to complete the Revolution, he would save France from fresh mishaps and fulfil her third desire. And, finally, if he forced Europe to bow her head and accept the new frontiers, *far from destroying the Revolution, he would have perfected and fortified all that portion of its work which the Nation held most dear.* Provided he did all these things the country would cheerfully look its last on public galleries, and assemblies of tribunes, and Popular Societies, and political newspapers, and even on the Republic itself. These were not the things for which it had longed in 1789 ; they were only the parasitic growths which had twined themselves about the tree, and, seeming to adorn it, had sucked its sap, and stifled it.

633

Inevitably, excess in one direction led to excess in another : the Nation now thought too lightly of the political liberty safeguarded by its parliamentary institutions. But this parliamentary system had never really received a proper organization, and *Liberty,* though its name was inscribed on every public building, had never found a place in the Nation's laws, nor in its customs.

Napoleon Bonaparte was to give France all that she expected of him. And for that reason the Revolution did not come to an end on that evening of the 19th Brumaire, for it was to be written now in Codes, and Concordats, and Treaties.

The volcano had cast up its lava. Laden with precious metals and hideous scoria this had rolled down the mountain sides, and, slowly, it had cooled. But a short while since it had been laying all things waste : now, transformed into a granite of the most splendid kind, it was to serve as material for the construction of a new commonwealth. The French Empire (and the modern *régime* for a hundred years after it) was built with that mighty stone formed out of the lava Mirabeau let loose in the winter of 1789, the lava which Bonaparte subjugated in the autumn of 1799.

INDEX

635

INDEX

INDEX

INDEX

INDEX

King mooted, 196; ringing the tocsin, 265; work of the, 376
Cordier, tribune, 197
Corneille, 348
Cornet, report read by, 613-614
Corsica, protests from, 133
Councils, the, 488; money grant to the Directory, 500; the forced loan, 500-501; Barbé-Marbois, president, 524; Barras' designs on, 528; reception of the addresses, 533-534; the proscriptions, 539-541
Courbevoie, 266
Courrier Français, 471
Coutances, Bishop of, 61
Couthon, on the " Right," 214; on Isnard, 216; suggests the dethronement, 220; and the war, 228; on Clavières, 235; on Luckner, 239; on La Fayette, 252; on Pétion, 255; on the massacres, 289, 292; and the Mountain, 304; on Lille, 312; and the King's death, 322; attack on the Twelve, 340; speech on June 2nd, 344-345; reports flight of the Girondins, 346; on the Committee of Public Safety, 351, 355; report of a plot, 366; and Robespierre, 383, 411, 418; and the cult of Reason, 389; purging the Convention, 393-394; the restoration of the Divinity, 406; decree of the 22nd Prairial, 409; accuses Carnot, 416; the 8th and 9th Thermidor, 424; at the Hôtel-de-Ville, 425; death, 428, 430; signature to lists, 434
Coz, Bishop Le, 174, 221, 228, 245; on the Ministry, 248; the Lamourette kiss, 257
Cracow, 353
Crassous, 573
Cremona, 511
" Crest," insurrection of the, 459-460
Creuzé-Latouche, 462, 480
Crevelier on the 8th Thermidor, 417
Crinière, 97
" Cromwell," name applied to La Fayette, 108
Crussol, Baron de, 141
Culte décadaire, the, 497
Curée, 411
Custine, General, 311, 365, 373
Cyprus, 568

DAMAS, COMTE DE, 188-190
Danican, General, 478, 479, 480
Danon, 471, 474
Danton, 14, 23, 199, 202; on the Republic *cited*, 16; and the Cordeliers, 196-197; July 17th, 199-200; and Brissot, 235; and Mme. Roland, 236; machinations of, 258, 260-261; *coup d'état* at the Hôtel-de-Ville, 265-267; Minister of Justice, 274; sketch of, 275-276, 309; his programme, 276-277; decree authorizing domiciliary visits, 283; and the massacres, 283-284; responsibility for the massacres accepted by, 289-290; votes for, 299; and the Mountain, 303; attacks of the Rolands, 308; and the Girondins, 308-309, 335; leaves the Council, 310; policy, 312, 357; the death of the King, 318, 322; the doctrine of natural frontiers, 327; establishment of the Revolutionary Tribunal, 329; efforts for a fusion, 329; and Dumouriez, 330; and the Committee of Public Safety, 333; the rising of May 31st, 339; and Le Brun, 346; and Robespierre, 350-352, 380, 384-385, 391-394; distress of mind, 379-380; and Desmoulins, 384; and the cult of Reason, 389-390; trial and death, 395-399, 405
Danloux, picture of Robespierre, 381
Dard on the elections, 40
Dartigoeyte, 388
Dauban, on the prisons, 373-374
Daudet, Ernest, *quoted*, 507, 589
Daunow, 468, 567
Dauphiné, federation, 148; revolt, 347
David, 304, 383, 397, 399; picture of the sitting in the Tennis Court, 63; and Robespierre, 383, 415; official decorator, 407, 550; and Napoleon, 567, 610
Davidovitch, 517
Davout, 145-146, 281, 569
Debucourt, painter, 551
Decade, the, 559
Décadi, worship on, 577
Decemvirs, the, 355
Defence, Commission of, 329
Defermon, 41, 117
Dego, 510
Delacroix, 396, 528
Delescluze, 548
Delessert, 549
Delmas, 281
Desaix, 569
Desèze, defence of the King, 320
Desîles, Captain, 145; death, 152
Desmolières, Gilbert, 525
Desmoulins, Camille, 14, 23, 28, 202, 390; speech in the gardens of the Palais Royal, 70; the call to arms, 72, 101; relations with Mirabeau, 105; disturbances fomented by, 163-164; on the flight, 193; on La Fayette, 252; conspirator, 261; and the Mountain, 303-304; publication of the *History of*

INDEX

648

INDEX

Fleurus, 162, 362, 392, 402, 412
Floreal, 22nd, of the Year VI, 574–575
Flushing in French hands, 505
Fockedey, 305
Fontaine de Grenelle, 261
Fontenay, Lequinio at, 374
Fontenoy, Marquise de, *see* Cabarrus Thérezia
Force, La, prison of, 75, 283, 287, 405
Forez, demand of, 146
Forced loan of year VII, 590–592
Fouché, on the priests, 301 ; the King's trial, 321–322 ; at Lyons, 362, 366, 374, 376–377, 378 ; the Communistic revolution, 386 ; and Christian worship, 387–388, 390 ; and Robespierre, 408–409, 415–417 ; outlawed, 427 ; property of, 452–453 ; on Barras, 489 ; on the patriots, *quoted*, 556 ; and Joubert, 597 ; Minister of Police, 598–599, 601 ; and Napoleon, 605, 610, 612
Fougeret, 209
Foulon, saying attributed to, 68 ; murder of, 87
Fouquier-Tinville, " No proofs," 224 ; account of, 367–370 ; accusation of the Queen, 369 ; sentence on the Girondins, 370–373 ; work of, 397–398, 404–406 ; and Robespierre, 403 ; " no more witnesses," 410–411 ; at Duplay's house, 411 ; execution of Robespierre, 429 ; victims of, 433–435 ; principles, 540–541
Fourcroy, 362
Fournier, the American, and Lambesc, 73 ; on the march to Versailles, 105 ; on Les Feuillants, 198 ; and Mme. Roland, 248 ; and the Federates, 258 ; conspirator, 261 ; on the massacres, 289 ; and Augereau, 538
Franche-Comté, the bandits in, 89 ; revolt, 347
Francis II succeeds Leopold, 231 ; war declared, 241–243
François, Captain, 579–580
François of Neufchâteau, 231, 497, 556, 558, 559, 560, 567, 573
Franconi, 550
Frankfort, 311
Frascati, 550, 551
Frederick II, 155
Frederick William II, relations with the Assembly, 159–160 ; alliance with Leopold, 231 ; Valmy, 294, 295 ; policy, 579
Frederick William III, 579
Freemasonry introduced into France, 27–28
Frénilly on the *émigrés*, 178 ; on the Legislative Assembly, 214 ; on Pétion, 251 ; on the Brunswick manifesto, 263 ; on

August 10th, 268, 271 ; on Mme. Tallien, 547
Fréron, conspirator, 261 ; at Marseilles, 350 ; warning to, 384–385, 390 ; on Danton's arrest, 396–397 ; Robespierre and, 409 ; the 8th Thermidor, 419 ; and the arrest of Robespierre, 424 ; recommends selection of Barras, 426 ; outlawed, 427 ; hailed by the people, 432–433 ; and Thérezia Cabarrus, 438 ; closing the Jacobin Club, 439 ; dress of, 446 ; saying of, *quoted*, 454 ; and the revolt of Germinal, 463 ; at Toulon, 478 ; and Bonaparte, 481 ; and the Mountain, 304 ; work in Provence, 376, 378 ; and the popular reaction, 437
Fricasse, 280
" Friends of Liberty," 595
Frivolities, dealers in, 132
Froeschwiller, 392
Fronde, the, 132, 176
Fructidor, 1796, 536–544
Fusil, Louise, 313, 548

Gabelle, the, 10
Galiani, on the separate chambers, 468
Gallican Church, the, 170–172
Gambling, prevalence of, 445
Gannat Club, the, 388
Ganney, on the Revolutionary Tribunal, 368
Garat, actor, 552
Garat, Minister of Justice, and Danton, 310, 380 ; joins the Mountain, 328 ; and the Girondins, 335 ; the insurrection of May 31st, 340 ; in prison, 374, 405 ; in Naples, 569
Garde-Meuble, the, 399 ; sack of, 75–76
Gardes Françaises, and the National Assembly, 64–65 ; mutiny, 1789, 20, 71–76 ; at the Bastille, 78–79 ; the proposed " pardon," 82 ; at Versailles, 109
Garnier of Saintes, 424
Garonne Valley, deaths, 375–376
Gaston, rising of, 331 ; and the women, 459
Gaudin, 619
Gaveaux, music of the *Réveil*, 436
Geisberg, 392
General Security, Committee of, 355
Geneva, 311, 312
Genissieu, the final sitting of the Convention, 482–483
Genoa, 600 ; Patriciate of, 312
Gensonné of the Left, 215–216 ; report of, 223 ; and the *émigrés*, 223 ; and Brissot, 234 ; and Mme. Roland, 237 ; and the Constitutional Guard, 246 ; ultimatum

645

INDEX

INDEX

INDEX

649

INDEX

INDEX

Mounier, on the reason for the Revolution, 22; in Dauphiné, 27; on M. Necker, 36; and the memorials, 39; election, 42; his mission to the dissidents, 56–57; motion at Vizille, 62 *note*; the Tennis Court sitting, 62–63; description of events, 86; on the general anarchy, 92; and the Declaration of Rights, 98; on the Constitution, 99–100; president of the Assembly, 100, 101, 105, 114–115; and the women, 106; at the Palace, 107–108; meeting of October 5th, 110; emigration of, 113; on the veto, 120

Mouraille, Mayor of Marseilles, 261

Mousseaux, 550

" Muddy Bishops," the, 8

Muiron, the, 606

Mulhausen, annexation of, 569

Murad, in Egypt, 579

Murat, General, 27, 30, 183, 281, 479, 515, 569, 579, 612–613, 615, 622

Muscadins, the, 459–460; defence of the Assembly, 461–462

Musketeers, freemasonry among the, 27

Nancy, mutiny of garrison in 1790, 20, 151–152; statue of Stanislas, 31; riots, 90; protests from, 133

Nantes, revolt, 348, 358; Carrier at, 374, 375; the "Edict of Nantes" for La Vendée, 493

Naples, 162, 515; the *Parthenopeian Republic*, 580

Narbonne, Comte de, 229–230, 232

National agents, 358

National Assembly, the title adopted by the Third Estate, 60; refusal to withdraw after the royal sitting of June 24th, 64–65; request for withdrawal of troops from Versailles, 68; *see* Assembly

National Defence, organization of, 354; Barère's plan, 359–363

National Guard, the, formation of, 71–72; absence of organization, 76; under La Fayette, 87; in favour of revolution, 91; march to Versailles, 105; at Versailles, 108, 132; oriflamme of the, 149; at the Tuileries, 185, 250–251; arms reversed on King's return, 194; fire on the mob, July 17th, 198–200; terror of the, 246; review countermanded, 253; defence of the Tuileries, 266–267; August 10th, 268–270

National Library, publications in the, 436

National Treasury handed to commissaries, 470

Natural frontiers, doctrine of, 505

Navailles, Mme. de, 548

Nazareth, 579, 580

Necker, M. de, Convocation of the States-General, 3, 42; danger to, 16; bestowal of Ministerial functions under, 26; on the disaffection of the troops, 27; and pensions of Monsieur, 35; character, 36–37; reception of his report, 38; and Mirabeau, 42; alarm at the Assembly at Versailles, 47; speech in the Menus Plaisirs, 54; absence from the Royal Sitting of June 24th, 63; retirement, 65; dismissal, 68–69, 72, 79, 92, 142, 183; France's bankruptcy, 134; and the Church question, 137; on the Legislative Assembly, 213, 219

Nector, on the Legislative Assembly, 214

Neerwinden, 330

Nelson, 580

Neo-Jacobins, the, 595, 598, 601

Neresheim, 516

Nervi of Marseilles rebellion, 142 *and note*

Neubrisach, 239

Neumarkt, 516

Neuweid, 516, 520

Nevers, Fouché at, 387–388

Ney, 30, 281

Nice, 311–312

Nicolas, juryman, 384

Nîmes, mutiny, 146

Nivernais, 37

Noailles, the Vicomte de, *Jean Sans Terre*, 94, 96

Nobles, the, state of, before the Revolution, 18–19; fear of the National Assembly, 60–61; the deputation to Marly, 61; the anti-historic alliance, 63–64; amalgamation of the Three Estates, 65–66; apathy of, 130

Nogaret, Bishop, 222

Normandy, revolt in, 331, 348

Norvins, on Mme. Tallien, 547

Notre Dame, Cathedral of, the Te Deum sung, 82; *Taking of the Bastille* played, 150; the festival of Reason, 388–389; Temple of the Supreme Being, 577

Noue, De la, Commandant at Nancy, 151

Novi, Joubert, killed at, 600

Oath of the priests, 527

Odéon, the, 261; the Council at the, 539

Onou on the elections, *quoted*, 40

Opéra, the, *Armide*, 428

Opéra-Comique, the, 207; *Paul et Virginie*, 428

Orange, the Terror at, 376

Oratory, Church of the, 174

Orléans, prisoners from, murdered, 289

Orléans, Duc d', 299, 304, 372–373; the *Instructions*, 40; a deputy at Versailles,

INDEX

INDEX

INDEX

Rennes, *Introduction aux Cahiers de Rennes*, 40 ; assembly of the bailiwicks, 41 ; parlement of, 132 ; mutiny at, 146, 152
" Republic," meaning of word, 16
Republic, proclamation of the, 307–308
Result of the Council, distribution of the, 3
Reubell, account of the resignations, 96 ; policy, 456, 513 ; the Directory, 488, 490, 491 ; and the Pantheon Club, 492 ; and Bonaparte, 508 ; and the Commission of Finance, 525 ; and the Jacobin ministers, 528 ; on Augereau, 534 ; on the reorganization of the National Guard, 535 ; Dumas and, 536 ; the executive Directory, 536–537 ; corruption, 561 ; attack on, 575, 576 ; leaves the Directory, 583–584
Réveil du Peuple, 436, 465
Revellière, La, the death of the King, 321
Revellière, Meynier de la, on the bourgeois, *quoted*, 23
Revellière-Lepeaux, La, on Monge, 274 ; on the Convention, 299 ; on June 2nd, 342–343 ; on France in year III, 441 ; on the patriciate, 456 ; the revolt of Germinal, 463 ; the Commission of Eleven, 468 ; and the veto, 470 ; the Directory, 488, 491, 496, 497 ; and Reubell, 490 ; a picture of France, 492 ; and Bonaparte, 508 ; policy, 513 ; and the Commission of Finance, 525 ; and the religious question, 528, 557–559 ; on Augereau, 534 ; on the reorganization of the National Guard, 535 ; and the repeal of the anti-clerical laws, 536 ; the executive Directory, 536–537 ; on the proscriptions, 542–543 ; and Barras, 558 ; election, 575 ; on Reubell, 584 ; on Sieyés, 585 ; dismissal, 586–587
Revolutionary Committees, 333, 359–360, 438
Revolutionary Government, set up by the Convention, 354
Revolutionary Tribunal, the, institution, 329 ; Marat summoned, 336–337 ; Fouquier-Tinville, 367–368 ; execution of the Queen, 369–370 ; the great Terror, 404–406
Reynière, Grimod de la, 551
Rhone Valley, the Terror in, 376
Richelieu Ball, the, 550
Richelieu, house of, 14 ; policy, 18
Richer-Serizy, 541
Rights, the Declaration of, 96–99
Rions, Albert de, 142
Riouffe, 371, 597

Rivarol, on the Revolution, 23 ; sayings of, *quoted*, 26, 202 ; reply to Louis XVI, 34 ; on La Fayette, 109 ; on the King's power, 122 ; on the Coblentz manifesto, 206 ; on Condorcet, 217–218 ; on the levies, 360
Rivoli, 162, 499, 517, 546
Roberjot, death, 581
Robert, Belgian journalist, 182
Robert-Keralio, 182
Robert, painter, 405
Robespierre, " the candle of Arras," 116–117 ; at the Breton Club, 117 ; and the mutinies, 147, 151 ; and France's foreign policy, 161 ; on the occupation of Avignon, 163 ; speech at the Cordeliers, 182 ; circumspection of, 196 ; July 17th, 199 ; public accuser, 200 ; a deist, 215, 216 ; and Brissot, 217, 254 ; and Condorcet, 217 ; the *émigrés* and, 221 ; attitude towards the war, 228–229, 245–246 ; and Narbonne, 230 ; and Mme. Roland, 236 ; and La Fayette, 240, 252 ; and the Federates, 258 ; demands the King's suspension, 261 ; Danton compared with, 275, 276, 277 ; votes for, 299 ; policy, 301 ; and the Mountain, 303 ; personality, 304, 380–381 ; and the Plain, 305 ; on the proclamation of the republic, 307 ; and the Girondins, 308–309, 326, 328, 329, 333, 340–341 ; attacked by Louvet, 309–310 ; and the death of the King, 317, 318, 320, 321, 324 ; and the Revolutionary Tribunal, 329 ; and Danton, 346, 350–352 ; joins the Committee of Public Safety, 353, 355, 358 ; power of, 365–366, 367, 368 ; letter to the Commissaries, 378 ; and the factions, 379, 391–396 ; and Desmoulins, 384–385 ; and the mercantile aristocracy, 386 ; and the Cult of Reason, 389–390 ; dictatorship of, 401–403 ; the Great Terror, 404–406 ; restoration of the Divinity, 406–407 ; and Fouché, 408–409 ; the law of the 22nd Prairial, 409–410 ; dissensions in the Committee, 414–416 ; speech of the 8th Thermidor, 417–419 ; the 8th and 9th Thermidor, 421–423 ; arrest, 423–424 ; at the Hôtel-de-Ville, 425–428 ; attempt to sign the appeal, 427–428 ; execution, 428–431 ; signature to lists, 434 ; hissed at the theatres, 435
Robespierre, Augustin, 383, 390, 416 ; arrest, 423 ; at the Hôtel-de-Ville, 425 ; death, 428, 430
Robespierre, Charlotte, 381

656

INDEX

INDEX

Saint-Germain, Forest of, 622
Saint-Huruge, 248
Saint-James's, Court of, 315
Saint-Jean, Fort of, massacres in the, 465
Saint-Jean-d'Acre, 580, 603
Saint-Jean-d'Angély, 597
Saint-Just, on the Revolution, *quoted*, 30 ; and the Mountain, 303–304 ; and the death of the King, 318, 321 ; and the Committee of Public Safety, 351, 355 ; and Robespierre, 383, 411, 414–415, 417 ; attack on Danton and Hébert, 391, 394, 397 ; accusation of Hérault, 396 ; work of, 402–403 ; warning to Barère, 412 ; the 8th and 9th Thermidor, 420–422 ; arrest, 424, 428 ; at the Hôtel-de-Ville, 425 ; death, 430 ; signature to lists, 434
Saint-Louis, Cathedral of, 52 ; meeting of the National Assembly in, 63
Saint-Louis, Chevaliers of, 221
Saint-Priest, 37, 173
Saint-Raphael, 606
Saint-Roch, Church of, 479–480, 577
Saint-Sulpice, 389, 577
Saint-Thomas-d'Aquin, 598
Saint-Waast-d'Arras, Abbey of, 8
Saladin, protest of, 472
Salamon, Papal agent, 170, 286 ; and Barnave, 204
Salicetti, 618
Salle, suggests a referendum, 320 ; death, 372
Salm, Prince, 195
Salm-Salm, demand of, 146
Salpétrière, 287
Salt monopoly, the, 10
Sambre and Meuse, Army of the, 507
Samson, executioner, 323–324, 367, 369, 373–374, 398, 405–406, 434–435
San Domingo, 505
San Giorgio, 517
Sandoz, 535
" Sans-chemises," the, 549–550
Santerre, 28, 248, 258, 264, 269, 323–324, 538
Sardinia, King of, and Napoleon, 569
Sarre Regiment, the, 27
Sauce, Father, 189, 190, 192
Saumur, 348
Savine takes the oath, 173
Savoy, annexation, 311–312 ; proposal to join France, 314–315
Saxe-Teschen, Duke of, 279
Saxony, 516
Schérer, 528 ; in Italy, 506, 507, 580
Schmidt, on gambling, 445
Sebastiani, 613
Séchelles, Hérault de, leaves the Right, 214, 219; and the war, 228 ; proclamation

of, 259 : and the Mountain, 303, 304 ; release of Hébert, 338 ; June 2nd, 343 ; the Constitution of 1793, 349 ; and the Committee of Public Safety, 355–356 ; message to Carrier, 374 ; Robespierre and, 382–384 ; Robespierre's attack on, 393 ; arrest of, 396 ; death, 399
Sedan, 282
Sée, M., 40
Séguin, 549
Ségur, Pierre de, *The Sunset of the Monarchy*, 31
Seiffert, Dr., 288
Seine-et-Oise, department of the, 300
Selz, 579
Sémonville, 597
Seneffe, 132
Sentinelle, the, attacks on Danton, 308
September massacres, the, 285
Sergent and Clavières, 248
Servan, Colonel, Minister of War, 235, 238, 328 ; the Federates enrolled, 246–247 ; dismissal, 247 ; recall demanded, 259 ; on the Executive Council, 274 ; and the massacres, 284
Sévres Bridge, the, 108
Shérer, 581
Shuvalof, Voltaire and, 169
Sicard, Abbé, work of, 20, 21
Sieyès, Abbé Joseph, on the nobles, 23 ; election, 42 ; arrival at the States-General, 58–59 ; the sitting in the Tennis Court, 62 ; speech on June 24th, 65 ; and the Breton Club, 101, 105, 117 ; personality, 116, 305 ; and the Church question, 136 ; on the proposed republic, 197 ; leaves the Jacobins, 198 ; and Condorcet, 217 ; at Crosne, 452 ; Constitution of the year III, 467–468, 469, 471 ; refuses to join the Directory, 487, 488, 495 ; on Reubell, 490 ; on the Directory, 529 ; and Napoleon, 567, 608, 610, 611 ; sent to Berlin, 573 ; elected Director, 584–585, 588–590, 595–597 ; and the neo-Jacobins, 598, 601 ; the 18th Brumaire, 612–619 ; consul, 623
Silesia, 311
Sillery, on Necker's dismissal, 68–69
Siméon, of the Council, 488 ; the 17th Fructidor, 537, 538 ; proscribed, 542, 544
Simiane, Mme. de, 131–132
Sinnamari hulks, the, 524
Societies, the Popular, 358–359
" Society of the Friends of the Constitution," 118
Sommo-Sierra, 162

658

INDEX

INDEX

INDEX

Notes to

The French Revolution

By Louis Madelin

Prepared by

F. Stringfellow Barr, M.A. (Oxon.)

Associate Professor of History in the
University of Virginia

NOTES

3-6—The three estates were the First (clergy), Second (nobility), Third (commonalty). Each of these social groups sent representatives to the Estates (or States) General, the closest French equivalent to the English Parliament. The States-General did not meet between 1614 and 1789.

4-25—In 1762 Jean-Jacques Rousseau published his famous treatise on the state, "The Social Contract," in which he maintained that every true state was based on a contract between the ruler and his subjects, implying mutual obligations. If the ruler no longer fulfilled his portion of this contract, the association became morally dissolved.

9-14—The tithe (*dîme*) was historically the "tenth" part of a crop, required by ancient Hebrew law, for the maintenance of the temple. In France just before the Revolution the tithe was a far smaller portion, an eighteenth on the average, and varied greatly in different provinces. The products on which the tithe was levied, varied greatly also.

10-19—Colbert, Louis XIV's great minister of finance, reformed the system of taxation.

13-28—Voltaire's "royalty" at Ferney in an allusion to the fact that the famous controversialist built a château at Ferney, near the Swiss frontier, over-looking the Lake of Geneva, where he "kept court" for his admirers throughout Europe. D'Alembert, co-founder with Diderot of the *Encyclopédie*, attacked continually with Voltaire and others, "the infamous one"—superstitions. Voltaire commonly terminated his letters to D'Alembert and others of the Encyclopædists with the phrase *Ecrasons l'infâme* (Let us crush the infamous one).

3

13-30—Duclos, writer and moralist, served as permanent secretary of the French Academy, here called the "house of Richelieu" because Richelieu was its official founder. D'Alembert succeeded Duclos as permanent secretary.

14-7—Malesherbes, member of the *parlement* and government official, became director of publications and as such favored permitting the publication of the *Encyclopédie*.

14-18—Citizeness (*Citoyenne*) is the Republican title which replaced *Madame* for some time during the French Revolution. It was of course an ostentatious manner of affirming equality.

21-31—The vicaire Savoyard, or Vicar of Savoy, is a famous character in Rousseau's book, "Emile." The Vicar of Savoy professed an undogmatic "natural" religion, founded rather on feeling and personal intuition than on reason. Even some of the French clergy were admiring this unecclesiastical servant of Christ, and would have welcomed his like as their assistant.

23-24—Cartouche (1693–1721) was a famous Parisian robber, hero of popular legend, finally captured and broken on the wheel at Paris.

25-6—Faubourg, literally suburb, is generally used in this book to indicate the workmen's suburbs, outskirts, or slums of Paris. The Faubourg Saint-Antoine, a workmen's district, often called the "glorious Faubourg," supplied many mobs; but the Faubourg Saint-Germain (see p. 131, 1.16) was, and still is, an aristocratic quarter.

25-7—Mandrin, famous French bandit, born 1724, burned alive 1755. In 1750 he organized a band of fifty-odd men, and carried on a perfect war against the tax-"farmers" (collectors).

25-28—The Parliaments (*parlements*) of France, thirteen in number, were high courts of justice, not legislative bodies. By insisting on the registration of decrees as one of their rights, they attempted somewhat unsuccessfully to exercise a check on the royal power.

27-2, 3—Allusion to the Vizille incident described in the footnote, p. 62.

4

NOTES

27-27—The Comte de Saint-Germain (1707–78), famous general, was appointed by Louis XVI minister of war (1775). The "rod" spoken of here is the Prussian military discipline and corporal punishment which Saint-Germain introduced into the French army, and which earned him his dismissal in 1777.

31-24—*Vert-Galant* was a surname frequently applied to Henri IV, first of the Bourbon dynasty. It means "ardent in love," the *vert* (green) being used in the sense of young and vigorous.

31-25—Maria-Leczinska, daughter of Stanislas I of Poland, wife of Louis XV, grandmother of Louis XVI, was noted for her piety in the midst of an impious family. Stanislas renounced the Polish crown and ruled over Lorraine and Bar from Nancy as capital, where his statue stands.

32-6—Gouverneur Morris, who helped draw up the American constitution, went to France in 1788. In 1792 Washington appointed him U. S. Minister to France. Arrested as a suspect in 1793, he was restored in 1794 to his functions. His journal is of great value, and is frequently cited in this book.

32-26—*Resurrexit*, "He has risen."
Henri IV, whose statue still stands on the Pont Neuf (New Bridge) in Paris, was called "good King Henry" and has remained extremely popular. He was the "vert-galant" here contrasted with Stanislas. It was hoped at the death of Louis XV (1774), that his grandson and heir Louis XVI would be a second Henri IV.

33-20—Salon de l'Œuil-de-Bœuf (lit., Bull's-Eye Parlor) was so called from an oval window known in France as the "Bull's-Eye." This Salon was the ante-room of Louis XIV's bed-chamber in the Palace of Versailles. It was here that the courtiers waited for the ceremonies attending the king's rising in the morning; and here, naturally, that much gossip and rumor could be heard.

35-10—The Comte de Provence ruled France, after the fall of Napoleon (1815 to 1824), as Louis XVIII, dating his reign from the death of the Dauphin, "Louis XVII," in 1795, and thereby ignoring both Republic and Empire. He was succeeded by the Comte d'Artois as Charles X.

35–27—At Ivry Henri IV won a famous victory in 1590. He directed his troops to rally around his white plume.

38–21—*Lettre de cachet* (sealed letter) was the term given to letters bearing the royal seal, particularly those containing an arbitrary order of arrest or imprisonment. Such letters were procured from the king by influential persons for use against their enemies. The *lettre de cachet* is an excellent example of the sort of royal absolutism that existed.

38–21—Freedom of the press, to be created by the States-General; and permanent provincial Estates (or "States") to be instituted.

39–17—Rousseau's sentimental philosophy posited man's fundamental virtue as a first premise. It is here suggested that the government at Versailles leant more to such ideas than to the craftiness of Machiavelli.

40–35—The Duc d'Orléans, known as Philippe Egalité (1743–93), Louis XVI's cousin, was given the Palais-Royal by his father. Throughout this history the term "Palais-Royal" is often used to mean the Orleanists, the group who desired to dethrone Louis and put the Duc d'Orléans in his place. The crowd that overthrew the Bastille formed in his gardens. He was accused of fomenting the march of the women on Versailles in October, 1789 (see Ch. V). He petitioned the Paris Commune to give him a family name, thus displaying his republicanism. The Commune named him Philippe Egalité (Philip Equality). A Member of the Convention, he voted for Louis' beheadal; but was himself beheaded in November, 1793. One of his sons became Louis Philippe, King of the French (1830 to 1848).

42–8—Mirabeau was refused, on a technicality, the electoral rights of a noble. He therefore became a candidate for election by the Third Estate.

42–18—Unlike American elections, the French elections of 1789 permitted localities to elect non-resident candidates. A candidate elected by more than one constituency, could take his choice. Mirabeau chose Aix.

NOTES

44–24—The Concordat (or agreement between Pope and King) of 1516, concluded by Francis I of France with Pope Leo X, providing that the bishops should be appointed by the king, not elected by the French clergy; that the Pope should then invest them; and that certain financial abuses of the Papacy should be restored. This Concordat had always been extremely unpopular with the French clergy.

47–19—Machault (1701–94) was a famous minister of finance (1745–54). In 1749 he had attempted unsuccessfully to remove the nobility's tax exemptions and to limit the increase of church (and therefore untaxable) property.

58–34—The complete title of Sieyès' famous pamphlet was: "What is the Third Estate? Everything. What has it been thus far, in the political scheme? Nothing. What does it ask? To become something." This flattering title naturally pleased the Third Estate.

59–39—"From the presbyteries," or priests' rectories.

63–26—A "bed of justice" (*lit de justice*) was the name given the ceremony of a king's visit to his *parlement*. In cases where the *parlement* declined to register a decree, the king often paid them a formal visit, generally in his "bed" or litter, and ordered them peremptorily to register the decree under his very eyes. The Royal Session of June 24, 1789, was, then, called a "bed of justice" because the king was expected to force his will on an assembly, not this time of the *parlement* but of the Estates General.

69–36—The Ile-de-France is the ancient province lying around Paris, which formed the original nucleus of the French kingdom. But the robbers were over-running many provinces during these months.

70–25—The Committee of Electors were of course the men elected by the people of Paris for the purpose of themselves electing the deputies from Paris, such as Bailly and Sieyès, to the Third Estate at Versailles. Their moral power lay in the fact that they had been recently chosen—though not to govern Paris—by the people, and consequently had their confidence. They had no legal mandate to govern, nor had Bailly, whom they elected Mayor.

73–8—Fournier, an active revolutionary, was called "the American" because he had spent some time in Santo-Domingo, in the distilling business. His nickname is given in its French form, p. 248, 1.33.

73–10—The Pont de la Concorde (Concord Bridge) had been begun in 1787 and was not finished till 1793. It was known as the Louis XVI Bridge (Pont Louis XVI), but was renamed Pont de la Concorde in 1795.

73–13—The Tuileries was a palace extending from the Palace of the Louvre to the Place de la Concorde. Begun in 1564, it was added to by Henri IV and his successors. It derives its name from the fact that part of its site was previously occupied by a *tuilerie* or tile-factory. It was here that Louis XVI came after October, 1789; here that his Swiss guard was massacred on August 10, 1792. In 1793 the National Convention sat here. It became successively the royal palace of Emperor Napoleon I, Louis XVIII, Charles X, Louis-Philippe, and Emperor Napoleon III. In 1871, the soldiers of the Paris Commune burned it. Its site is now a public garden.

75–10—The Garde-Meuble (storehouse for furniture) here alluded to, was built 1760–70. Rare armor, tapestries, gold-plate, and crown jewels were kept here. Crown jewels were stolen from the Garde-Meuble in September, 1792, a crime of which Danton was accused. The building has been occupied, since the reign of Napoleon I, by the ministry of the marine.

76–32—The Fronde (1648–1653) was an insurrectionary movement of the French *parlements* allied with certain powerful nobles against the centralized government of Anne of Austria (widow of Louis XIII) and Cardinal Mazarin, her chief minister. It is so called from the name of a child's game, "sling," played by Paris urchins. When the police appeared, the urchins would scatter, only to reassemble when the police had departed. This, it is suggested by the metaphor, was exactly the behavior of the conspiring nobles.

78–30—"Civic rights" is purely figurative, a translation of "*droit de cité—et déja droit de domination.*"

NOTES

81–25—Duquesnoy (1759–1808), an ardent royalist, was mayor of Nancy and was arrested after the fall of the throne for possessing compromising papers. In the "Year II" (September 21, 1793–September 21, 1794) he was in prison but was released at the close of the Terror.

82–15—*Te Deum laudamus* ("We praise Thee, O Lord"), a church hymn much used in Catholic countries to celebrate military victories, good news, etc.

83–14—A red and blue cockade was being worn by the Paris crowds on July 14. Red and blue were the official city colors. July 17, when Louis visited the Hôtel-de-Ville (Town Hall), white (the Bourbon and therefore royalist color) was slipped in, thus giving the famous tricolored flag of modern France.

87–18—Foulon—or "Foullon"—(1717–1789), famous French administrator, was hated for his hardness and avarice. July 15, 1789, he retired to his country place, and pretended death by having one of his servants buried under his name. After La Fayette had failed to save him, he was hung from a lamp-post and decapitated. His heart was presented to *Monsieur le Maire*, i.e. to Mayor Bailly, on a pike. Foulon was doubly unpopular as having been one of the new ministers that in a sense had ousted Necker, himself an idol of the people, and as having made the remark quoted on page 68. Hence the mouthful of hay.

93–13—"*Canaille*": the mob, the crowd, the lower classes (usually though not invariably applied in a spirit of disdain), meant in its original Italian form, "pack of dogs."

96–30—A verse in the *Te Deum*, rendered in the English service: "The noble army of martyrs praise Thee." Madelin ironically quotes this verse, because many of the nobles and clergy were indeed to be "martyrs" of the Revolution.

103–18—Lilies were the Bourbon or royal insignia; white, the Bourbon color.

103–20—The *Gardes du Corps* were the Royal Guards or members of the "Body-Guard."

105–17—Extreme Left. In most European assemblies of any sort, the members sit according to their political ideas, conservatives to the Speaker's right, radicals to his left. The Extreme Left means, then, not only those sitting furthest to the president's left in the National Constituent Assembly, but those of the most advanced revolutionary opinions. Throughout this book (which was written for French, and translated for English, readers) "the Left" means the party of violence; "the Right," the conservative wing. The "Center" of course means the moderates. The Extreme Left (on p. 105) disliked Mounier because he was considered too conservative (see p. 100).

106–36—The Abbé Maury was the principal orator of the "Right." He was to argue violently against both the Nationalization of Church Property and the Civil Constitution of the Clergy. In October he was already sufficiently identified with conservatism and privilege to incur the anger of the Paris mob at Versailles.

114–36—"Mirabeau the Barrel" (1754–92), brother of the great Comte de Mirabeau, was five years his junior. He was a violent conservative, and represented the nobility; whereas his brother (see p. 116) had been elected by the Third Estate and sat on the Left. "Barrel" Mirabeau earned his nickname from corpulency produced by drunkenness. He emigrated in 1790.

115–20—Lally-Tollendal (1751–1830) was the legitimized son of a famous French general, Dupleix's successor against Clive in India, whose "woe" was to have been imprisoned and executed for treason. His eloquent son with Voltaire's aid had attempted vainly to clear his father's name.

115–28—The Abbé Grégoire was a Jansenist. Jansenism was a doctrine derived by the Bishop of Ypres, Jansenius (1585–1638), from the writings of Saint Augustine, and denying the Catholic doctrine of free will. Jansenism was repeatedly condemned by the Papacy. The Jansenist center at Port-Royal was suppressed by a papal bull, in 1704, and even its buildings were in 1710 demolished. Hence the allusion of p. 165, 1.5. The pope attacked Jansenism again in 1713 by his bull, Unigenitus, alluded to, p. 165, 1.9.

138–15—Two great French bishops under Louis XIV, famous as writers and orators, who enjoyed a power which the Church had now long since lost.

142-27—The Commune or Municipality of Paris was divided into sixty Districts or wards, which were frequently insubordinate. In 1790, they were abolished and Paris was divided into the forty-eight Sections so often mentioned further in the text.

145-1—The officers in the royal army were regarded as "Pretorians," in the sense of being able to subject the state to military control, by the frightened members of the Constituent.

159-23 ff.—Mercy was Austrian ambassador at Paris and therefore represents here the Austrian point of view, as the Tsarina Catherine II does that of Russia. King Frederick William considered the fall of the Bastille, a royal fortress, as an attack on royal authority and therefore on Marie-Antoinette, commonly called by her enemies "the Austrian." Choiseul (1719–85), a famous French diplomat, had fostered an alliance between Austria and France, naturally distasteful to Prussia.

161-25—The "Family Compact," concluded in 1761 between the Bourbon rulers of France, Spain, and Italy to curb England's naval power, included a mutual territorial guarantee. Therefore, when England contested Spain's rights in Nootka Sound in 1789–1790, the Spanish king called on his cousin, Louis XVI of France, for aid.

163-10—The Comtat Venaissin was the "county" or territory around Avignon and had been since the fourteenth century (when the popes lived at Avignon), a papal possession. It was annexed by France in 1791 (see p. 204).

170-6—According to the "Declaration of the Assembly of French Clergy" in 1682, the king was temporally independent; general church councils were superior to the pope; the pope must conform to church canons; his decisions on dogma were not indisputable unless ratified by the clergy. The point of view herein expressed is "Gallican," or favorable to the liberties of the Church "in Gaul."

171-19—Bernis was French ambassador at the court of Pope Pius VI.

173-10—December 26th, the date on which Louis XVI sanctioned the decree imposing on the clergy an oath of loyalty to the

11

THE FRENCH REVOLUTION

Civil Constitution, is Saint Stephen's day in the church calendar.
The "octave" is the eight days: December 26–January 2 inclusive.
During the week or octave following a saint's day festivities are
often prolonged. Lindet, who "cast off the cassock" or priest's
robes after having served as a constitutional bishop, predicts playfully that as stones rained on Saint Stephen, the first martyr of
the Christian faith, stoned for his belief, so the Civil Constitution
would bring a shower of misfortunes.

174–4—The "List of Benefices" was the list of names recommended by the king to the pope for church appointments. These
appointments, often involving handsome incomes, were used for
political gifts.

174–7—*In partibus infidelium:* "in heathen lands." Lydda is
in Palestine and therefore like Babylon Mohammedan. The titles
were honorary. Gobel actually assisted the Bishop of Basle (Switzerland); though Miroudot did get as far as Syria, where he converted large numbers to the Christian faith.

174–20—"The century" is a French idiom to express the idea
of "secular" or non-religious life.

178–3—In one of La Fontaine's fables, a fly on a coach-wheel
believes it is his weight which makes the wheel go round. Sim-
ilarly, the French *émigrés* (nobles, priests, and others who had
"emigrated" from France) imagined it was their activity that was
leading to foreign intervention in France, whereas this activity
was merely incidental. The allusion occurs again, p. 263, l. 7.

186–38—The Prince de Condé was general of the *émigré* army.
The *émigrés* and aristocrats generally were often called "red heels"
because they affected red-heeled shoes.

191–2—"Titi" is a colloquialism for "Paris street-urchin."

198–8—There were two petitions to the Constituent Assembly,
one from the Jacobins and one from the Cordeliers. The Jacobin
petition, which caused a group of members to secede and form a
"constitutionalist" club at the Feuillants' Convent, was sent to
the Champ-de-Mars for signatures on July 16 but was not en-
thusiastically received. It demanded that Louis be replaced "by
constitutional means." The Cordelier petition urged the Con-

12

stituent to declare that Louis' flight was equivalent to abdication, and to call a national convention to draw up a new constitution. The Cordelier petition was carried to the Champ-de-Mars July 17 and is said to have gained many signatures from the crowd the National Guard dispersed that day.

207–37—"O Louis, O my king,
    Thy friends surround thee,
      Our love envelops thee!"

208–6—Free translation:

"Our good King
  Did everything
And our good Queen—
  What times she's seen!
But now they're past
  Their troubles at last!"

215–1—Bordeaux is the chief city in the "Department of the Gironde"—hence the term, "Bordeaux men" (or "Bordelais") and "Girondins" loosely overlap. But many members of the "Gironde" came from Normandy, Provence, and other French provinces remote from Bordeaux. The Girondins are also alluded to as "Brissotins," because Brissot was one of their chief spokesmen.

218–11—Charenton is the seat of a famous insane asylum; hence "bound for Charenton" means "going mad." A similar allusion occurs on p. 262.

222–34—The Legislative Assembly, and later the National Convention, punished emigration by confiscation of property. Louis XIV had used this method against the Huguenots. The Convention actually modelled its legislation on the subject by a close study of what Louis XIV had done.

227–18—Popilius Laenas, Roman Consul, was sent by the Roman Senate to the King of Syria to order him to renounce certain conquests. The Syrian promised to take up the question with his Senate. Whereupon Popilius drew a circle in the sand, all about the king, and ordered him to answer before stepping out of that circle. The king gave way. Metaphorically, to "draw

13

Popilius' circle" about a man is to corner him and forestall an evasive answer.

233–1—The term "Mountain," designating the "Left" in the National Convention, was seldom used during the Constituent Assembly, more used under the Legislative, and became truly current under the Convention. A small group of "Mountaineers" (*Montagnards*) sat on the extreme left of the Legislative, and were already more radical than the Gironde, the "Left" of the Legislative and the "Right" of the Convention. The Mountain derived its name from the fact that its seats in the Assembly were high up.

237–28—Barbaroux was nicknamed "Antinoüs" after a young slave of that name, a favorite of the Roman Emperor Hadrian, and renowned for his great beauty. The Cannebièrre is a celebrated street in Barbaroux's native city, Marseilles.

237–33—Saint-Preux is the hero in Rousseau's novel, "Julia, or the New Heloïse."

245–25—Le Coz was a "constitutional" bishop and member of the Legislative Assembly. But he was very moderate and even defended the non-juror priests before the Legislative. Madelin implies that such a man should have known better than to believe the story that non-juror priests were now fighting on the Austrian side.

245–29—"Hulks" is a translation of *bagne*. See note to p. 524, l. 11, for a description of the *bagnes*, sometimes translated also "galleys."

249–5—The *Salle du Jeu de Paume* ("the Tennis-Court Hall") was the building in which the meeting described on p. 62 took place, June 20, 1789, three years earlier. It was therefore the "fourth" anniversary, counting (as the French count) the original incident.

253–4—"Monkeries" is an allusion to General Monk, who restored the Stuart dynasty in England and hence, from the Jacobin point of view, betrayed the nation.

14

NOTES

254-24—Literal translation:

"We'll treat fat Louis, biribi,
The way they do in Barbary,
   My friend—
Fat Louis, biribi."

255-17—The "infamous Directory" is the Directory or administration of the Department of the Seine, containing Paris. Being relatively conservative, it suspended Pétion and Manuel for permitting the riot of June 20.

255-33—In English, Petion Aristides Pike. The pike was the favorite weapon of the revolutionary mobs. The middle name is typical of the revolutionary hobby for heroes of Greek and Roman antiquity.

262-12—Scaevola was a legendary Roman hero, who volunteered to assassinate Lars Porsena, an Etrurian monarch, when he was besieging Rome. Barbaroux therefore implies that the Federates have come to rescue Paris from royal tyranny.

267-16—The *Maison Commune* and *Hôtel-de-Ville* are here identical terms.

269-23—Napoleon Bonaparte's scornful phrase in Italian, his native Corsican tongue, is roughly translatable: "What a cullion!"

272-35—There are numerous catacombs beneath the city of Paris, which were once quarries.

275-29—D'Aguesseau was a famous chancellor under the French monarchy. Danton, as Minister of Justice, had essentially the same duties.

278-21—The Queen was called the new Agrippina after the Emperor Nero's mother, notorious for intrigue and perfidy.

281-34—*Ça ira* (lit., "That will go") means roughly: "That will do!" or "That's the stuff!" On p. 284, l. 23, the populace cries "It will go!" and Madelin adds sarcastically, thinking of the massacres, "*Ça alla*" ("It went!").

286-9—*Triple nom de D——* ("Triple name of God!") is a French oath of unspeakable violence.

15

302–25—It is implied that as the Roman king, Numa, sought political advice from the nymph Egeria, so the Girondins sought it from Madame Roland and Madame Condorcet. The title of "Egeria" is commonly given women of their type.

303–19—Fabre d'Eglantine wrote "Philinte or 'the Misanthrope' Continued"—a sequel to Molière's play. The *Vieux Cordelier* (Old Cordelier) was the name of Desmoulins' newspaper, which was in 1794 to criticize severely the "new" Cordeliers, a socialist group under Hébert.

303–24—Both Alcibiades, the Athenian, and Hérault, the revolutionary, were handsome rakes of noble birth, elegant and sceptical.

303–35—Saint-Just was the Benjamin in that he was the youngest. He was twenty-two when the Revolution broke out. He really was the son of a "Chevalier of Saint Louis." The Order of Saint Louis was an order of military merit.

304–16—Marat's newspaper was called the "People's Friend" (*l'Ami du Peuple*). For that reason he himself was often called by the same title.

304–27—Lepelletier de Saint-Fargeau was president of the Parlement of Paris at the outbreak of the Revolution. He represented the nobility in the Constituent. On January 20, 1793, eve of the King's execution, he was assassinated in a restaurant in the Palais-Royal by a former member of Louis' bodyguard for having, as a member of the Convention, voted for the King's death. He was, with Marat, the Convention's most famous martyr.

304–28—*Canard Six:* "Duck Six." But *canard* also means a newspaper yarn or bit of gossip.

312–4—The Savoy Assembly took the name, Allobroges, from the tribe allied with the Roman Empire, that formerly inhabited that section of Gaul.

312–9—Victor-Amadeus III, of the House of Savoy, was ruler over the decadent state of Piedmont—the "Kingdom of Sardinia" —which the French were invading. The Piedmontese capital, Turin, was a hotbed of royalist *émigrés*. Piedmont was a decadent state of "marmots"—animals proverbial among the French for their sleepy stupidity. Also the Piedmontese were famous for training marmots as pets and therefore suggested to the contemporary French mind an idea like that which the typical Italian organ-grinder and his monkey suggest to the American.

319–13—Cambacérès was simply applying to Louis the decree of the Constituent, requiring all nobles to abandon their titles and assume the original surname of their family. Louis was a descendant of the Capets, early kings of France. For the same reason the Marquis de La Fayette was called Mottié and the Comte de Mirabeau, Riqueti.

336–19—Fabricius was a Roman consul famous for his scorn of wealth, and his devoted patriotism; Crassus was a Roman triumvir, famous for his great wealth.

339–34 ff.—Clodius was a tribune of the people, who really did send Cicero into exile. It is perhaps insinuated here that Danton derived his power from the same source as Clodius, the mob—of which neither was by birth a member.

"*De Viris illustribus*" is the Latin title of Plutarch's "Lives," favorite reading of the Girondins, and indeed of the Revolutionaries generally.

339–38—The "bureau" of the Convention consisted of the president and six secretaries, elected for a period of two weeks. They sat on a platform facing the deputies' benches.

347–8—William Pitt, British prime minister, was the Revolution's most noted opponent. The Prince of Coburg commanded the Austrian army.

350–20—Note that "Federalism" connoted in France the opposite of what it meant in contemporary America. The Girondins were Federalists in the sense that they wanted France less centralized, with more local self-government than the Mountain desired. They were charged with regarding France as a Federation of departments, instead of a centralized state divided into administrative districts.

354–3—England demanded Dunkirk and the French colonies.

362–8—"The Republic has no need of chemists," remarked the president of the Revolutionary Tribunal, when petitioned for the release of the great chemist, Lavoisier. He had been arrested along with all other ex-farmers-general, or members of the companies to whom the government used to "farm out" for a fixed sum the collection of taxes. The remark is very famous and much quoted.

364–17—The battle of Denain (1712) was a decisive victory for the French troops, against the Allies in the War of the Spanish Succession.

365–21—The Comte de Custine achieved brilliant successes in September and October, 1792, as general-in-chief of the Army of the Vosges; but later he met with reverses and, convicted by the Revolutionary Tribunal of having intrigued with the enemies of the republic, was guillotined August 28, 1793. Houchard commanded the Army of the Moselle. In spite of repeated victories, he repeatedly showed indecision. He was accused of leniency to the enemy and guillotined.

365–22—Vergniaud, Brissot, and Madame Roland were undoubtedly patriotic, but they were also Girondins. Many persons thought that the centralization they fought, could alone save France.

374–18—Lyons royalists, during the Girondin insurrection, had secured the arrest of the revolutionary Châlier. He had been tried and guillotined.

376–23—The Convention planned to rase Toulon to the ground, leaving only barracks for troops, as punishment for the city's siding with the royalists and English. Its name was changed to Port-la-Montagne.

377–9—*Sans-culotte* (lit., "without breeches") means an ardent democrat. Democratic enthusiasts often affected trousers, originally the costume of the working man, instead of the knee-breeches of the upper classes. Revolutionary ardor was often termed *sans-culottisme*. When, under the Directory (1795–1799), society women appeared in public, naked to the waist, punsters christened them *sans-chemises* ("without shirts").

18

NOTES

395-19—Chabot likens Robespierre to the Roman, Cato the Censor, because of his austere "virtue."

397-26—In his oration *Pro Domo Sua*, Cicero, as his own lawyer, plead "for his house," confiscated by Clodius, the tribune. To plead *pro domo* means to be one's own lawyer, as Danton was before the Revolutionary Tribunal.

398-31—"Vers" means both "verses" and "worms." Danton puns on the word: "Verses! In a week now, you'll be making them!" (i.e., worms, in his grave.)

403-17—The *Ecole de Mars* (School of Mars) was founded in 1793, as a national military academy for all classes, unlike the academies for nobles which it replaced.

404-4—Salentum was the mythical city celebrated by Fénelon in his book, *Télémaque*, a Utopia of virtuous citizenship and good government.

404-27—Lucile Desmoulins, Camille's young widow, did indeed look like a painting by Greuze.

404-33—*Ci-devant*, which Trinchard misspells, meant "former." A *ci-devant* marquis was a man who, before the Revolution abolished titles, had been a marquis. Ex-nobles were frequently called simply *ci-devants*.

435-35—The *muscadins* were originally royalists who in 1793 dressed elegantly (and perfumed themselves with "musk") as a protest against the affected roughness of the democrat *sans-culottes*. The *Chouans* were Breton royalists and participated in the insurrection in the Vendée.

436-9—*Réveil du Peuple:* "The People's Awakening" (by inference, from the nightmare of Terror).

438-22—Collot was sent to Cayenne, in French Guiana. See note to p. 524, l. 11 for the "galleys."

438-23—Besides taking part in the massacres of September, 1792, Tallien had been later prominent in defending them.

439-3—The *Tricoteuses*, or Knitters, are the women who during the Terror sat knitting while they watched the guillotining.

439-26—The "seventy-three" conservative deputies alluded to protested against the proscription of the Girondin leaders in June, 1793. They were themselves arrested in October.

465-17—The "companies of Jehu," or "of Jesus," were royalist bands organized for vengeance on the Terrorists, and were not completely broken up for years.

465-21—The Albigensian Crusade (1209–1229), launched against the *Albigeois* or Albigensians of Southern France at the request of the Pope, had the double purpose of stamping out a religious heresy and securing a province to the French crown. It is suggested here that over 500 years later the Southern French still remembered the brutalities of the Northerners. Note that from a Southern point of view the Jacobin tyranny was a tyranny of the *North* (Paris).

483-18—Madelin considers Danton the Convention's most remarkable member; he is the author of an excellent Danton biography.

487-17—The Comte de Provence owned the Luxembourg Palace. After his emigration, it had been used as a prison.

489-36—The *petit lever* was a ceremony of the French kings. It was a sort of reception by the king, of his intimates,—great lords and royal ministers—held as soon as the king arose from bed in the morning, during which the chief personages helped him dress. Admission was a great honor. Barras admitted to his morning reception both the red-heeled aristocrat and the red-capped son of liberty.

490-17—As Saint Paul found conversion to Christianity on the road to Damascus, so Carnot in this period was converted to an anti-Terrorist, conservative policy. Believing the execution of Louis unpardonable, he naturally turned against the regicides.

491-27—Revolutionary Terror was often called the red specter or red peril; conservative reaction, the white peril; and the power of the black-robed priesthood, the black peril.

491-39—*A la François Ier:* in the fashion of Francis I, king of France (1515–47).

NOTES

493-1—The *chauffeurs* or "heaters" were so called because they burned the feet of their victims to make them reveal where they had hidden their money. The bands of chauffeurs disappeared during the strong government of the consulate.

495-27—The starving but somewhat learned man was quoting the Vulgate Bible, Matthew IV-3: "Command that these stones be made bread."

497-34—The Bourse, or Paris Stock Exchange, was most active during the Revolution.

504-4—Molière's character, Tartufe, in the drama of that name, is the perfect hypocrite. So, suggest the two newspapers, the "People's Tribune" and the "Equalitarian," were the Directors and deputies.

505-6—Holland became the Batavian Republic, under French control, thus completely surrendering as the Romans did to the Samnites at the Caudine Forks.

505-19—Madelin speaks figuratively. The blockade against England had been the policy of the Committee of Public Safety (of the National Convention). Of course no such committee existed in 1795-96. Its policy "was still in power."

506-15—The Pactolus is a river in Lydia, in which according to legend King Midas bathed, to cure himself of turning all he touched to gold. The river was said to have inherited the gift from him. Figuratively, a source of wealth.

506-20—The Greeks christened England Albion on account of her white cliffs. The National Convention first nicknamed her "perfidious Albion" on account of her supposedly treacherous and self-seeking foreign policy. The term gained wide currency.

515-37—A branch of the Bourbon family had ruled the kingdom of Naples and another branch, Spain, since 1700. Naturally the French Republicans were pleased when Napoleon defeated Louis XVI's cousin.

519-33—Marie-Antoinette, daughter of Empress Maria-Theresa of Austria, is of course the Hapsburg in question. She was scornfully nicknamed "the Austrian."

524-11—Sinnamari is a village in French Guiana, so unwholesome that it was called the "dry guillotine." *Bagne* is derived from the Italian for "bath," because public bathhouses were often converted into prison camps. Such prisons existed at Toulon, Brest, Rochefort; they replaced the State galleys as places for forced labor, since by 1748 sailing had eliminated oars from State ships.

531-2—According to the Constitution of the Year III (Constitution of 1795), the Executive Directory, which disposed of the armed forces, could not bring or maintain troops within 6,000 metres (about 36 miles) of where the Councils, or "Legislative Body," were meeting, unless it had the Councils' permission. This constitutional boundary was intended to prevent just the kind of thing that happened in Fructidor (Sept. 3, 1797).

536-37—Ugolino della Gherardesca, to whom Madelin compares the three Directors, was one of the most ruthless tyrants in Italian history.

538-1—An *"hanriotade"* is of course an action worthy of "General" Hanriot, the author of the *coup d'etat* of June 2, 1793, against the Gironde.

547-32—The famous Greek courtesan, Phryne, accused of impiety before the Areopagus tribunal, won her case by baring her body. But Therezia displayed her charms in the Agora or marketplace, i.e. the Paris streets.

548-21—The *merveilleuses*, or "wondrous women," included Creoles brought in by Josephine de Beauharnais, later Napoleon's wife and empress, herself a Creole of Martinique. Note that "Creole" does *not* mean a person having negro blood.

548-25—"The beauty and the beast in one." But as *bête* also means "stupid," there is a pun. *Belle et bête*, "beautiful and stupid," is a frequent epithet in French.

549-8—Ouvrard (like the original Carabas in "Puss and Boots," a man of wealth and many mansions), advanced considerable loans to the Directory.

549-12—Turcaret: "newly-rich." The original Turcaret was the vulgar but wealthy hero of Le Sage's comedy by the same name.

NOTES

549-37—The *sans-chemises* (see 377-9: note) dressed *à la sauvage*, "in the fashion of a savage"; the more modest, "in the fashion of Cleopatra," just described. Those of more classical taste followed Flora, Roman goddess of flowers, and Ceres, goddess of harvests.

551-21—*Pot-au-feu* (beef-stew) here means metaphorically eating at home.

551-24—"Vatel" is used figuratively for "noted cook." The original Vatel stabbed himself in 1671 because the supper he had served his master the Prince of Condé, and Condé's guest, Louis XIV, left something to be desired.

562-25—Barthélemy, deported in Fructidor (see p. 537), had negotiated the treaties of 1795 with Prussia and Spain and stood for a policy of foreign peace.

565-1—The Republic of Genoa became in 1797 the "Ligurian Republic," a French protectorate. Its name was derived from the ancient Ligurians who inhabited the territory in Roman times. Bonaparte also organized the Cisalpine Republic, with Milan for capital. In Roman times this territory had been called *cisalpine* because it was—to them—"on this side of the Alps."

567-10—The "Institute of France," organized by the Constitution of 1795 from the old learned Academies (suppressed in 1793), included five "classes" or Academies, of which the Science Class was one.

568-33—General Duphot had accompanied the French ambassador, Joseph Bonaparte, to Rome in 1797. He was killed in a clash between the papal troops and the Trasteverine (i. e. "other side of the Tiber": a quarter in Rome) populace.

569-6—The Swiss canton, Vaud, had been occupied in the 16th century and very harshly governed since, by the aristocratic canton of Berne. It appealed from this tyranny to the French.

573-20—Treilhard occupied important judicial posts under Napoleon and was largely responsible for constructing the various Codes (civil, criminal, procedure, commerce). In this sense he was a legist under "Cæsar."

577–27—*Monsieur Dimanche* ("Mister Sunday") is playfully given the old title of respect, which the democratic revolutionaries had abolished in favor of "Citizen."

580–2—The name *Gesta Dei* (Deeds of God) is often given the Crusades. As the French Crusaders once worked God's deeds in Egypt, so now their descendants, the "sons of liberty," fought there in a new Crusade—this time against English power in the East. Napoleon mounted one of his infantry regiments on dromedaries in this campaign.

594–14—Cathelineau was generalissimo of the "Catholic Royal Army" in the Vendean Insurrection of 1793 (see Chap. XXVIII). He was killed at Nantes in July of that year. Charette, a lesser Vendean chief, fought on against the Republican army till captured and shot in 1796.

598–38—Fouché, after serving as Emperor Napoleon's Minister of Police, was created by him "Duke of Otranto."